Collective Reparations

Tensions and Dilemmas Between Collective Reparations and the Individual Right to Receive Reparations

HUMAN RIGHTS RESEARCH SERIES, Volume 84.

The titles published in this series are listed at the end of this volume.

Collective Reparations

Tensions and Dilemmas Between Collective Reparations and the Individual Right to Receive Reparations

Diana Itza Odier-Contreras Garduño

intersentia

Cambridge – Antwerp – Portland

Intersentia Ltd
Sheraton House | Castle Park
Cambridge | CB3 0AX | United Kingdom
Tel.: +44 1223 370 170 | Fax: +44 1223 370 169
Email: mail@intersentia.co.uk
www.intersentia.com | www.intersentia.co.uk

Distribution for the UK and Ireland:
NBN International
Airport Business Centre, 10 Thornbury Road
Plymouth, PL6 7 PP
United Kingdom
Tel.: +44 1752 202 301 | Fax: +44 1752 202 331
Email: orders@nbninternational.com

Distribution for Europe and all other countries:
Intersentia Publishing nv
Groenstraat 31
2640 Mortsel
Belgium
Tel.: +32 3 680 15 50 | Fax: +32 3 658 71 21
Email: mail@intersentia.be

Distribution for the USA and Canada:
Independent Publishers Group
Order Department
814 North Franklin Street
Chicago, IL 60610
USA
Tel.: +1 800 888 4741 (toll free) | Fax: + 1312 337 5985
Email: orders@ipgbook.com

Collective Reparations: Tensions and Dilemmas Between Collective Reparations and the Individual Right to Receive Reparations

Cover artwork: Pablo Palazuelo, *Monroy II (Yantra)* © Fundación Pablo Palazuelo.

Typesetting: Editing Department, School of Law, Utrecht University

ISBN 978-1-78068-705-6 (paperback)
ISBN 978-1-78068-746-9 (PDF)
D/2018/7849/86
NUR 828

British Library Cataloguing in Publication Data. A catalogue record for this book is available from the British Library.

ACKNOWLEDGMENTS

"The good life is one inspired by love and guided by knowledge"
Bertrand Russel

I would like to express my gratitude to CONACyT whose financial support helped me to conduct this doctoral research. Likewise, my gratitude to my supervisors: Prof. Dr. Jenny Goldschmidt and Prof. Dr. Rianne Letschert for their valuable support and understanding, especially when my other commitments kept me away from my research. Jenny, thanks for your guidance throughout this journey. Rianne, thank you for staying on board despite your busy schedule.

I would also like to acknowledge my reading committee – Prof. Dr. Antoine Buyse, Dr. Mcgonigle, Prof. Dr. John Vervaele, Prof. Dr. Titia Loenen and Prof. Dr. Stephan Parmentier. I would also like to convey my gratitude to Judge Cançado Trindade whose work and commitment to human rights has been a constant source of inspiration. I am truly grateful for our discussions. I would also like to thank Rodrigo Uprimny whose idea on transformative reparations soon spiked my interest about the complexities of collective awards. In addition, I would like to thank Prof. Dr. Héctor Olásolo – thanks for your encouragement to do a PhD (and for your countless invitations to join several projects), and to Enrique Carnero for our discussions on victims' rights.

I would also like to thank and acknowledge several people and institutions where I had the privilege to work throughout my PhD. I would like to thank Dr. Pablo Saavedra and my colleagues at the IACtHR for making my time as a Visiting Professional an inspiring experience. This work has also benefited from my time at INTERVICT as a Visiting Researcher and at International Institute of Social Studies where I worked as a Teaching Assistant. I would like to thank Alphonse, Lorena, Prof. Dr. Karin Arts, and Dr. Jeff Handmaker. Thank you also Peter, Klaartje and Titia for your great editorial work.

I would also like to express my gratitude to my colleagues at SIM where I found a stimulating academic environment. Thanks for your collegiality: Alice, Alexandra, Anja, Hye-Min, Ingrid, Judith, Julie, Machiko, Marie Elske, Marjolein, Paulien, Penny and Tom. And a special thank you to Antoine Buyse. I would also like to express my deepest gratitude to my colleagues of UCU where I have been lucky to find an amazing group of scholars and teachers. Thanks to Agnes, Annemieke,

Anton, Bald, Bas, Bettina, Carla, Christel, Elsa, Filippe, Floris, Gaetano, Gerda, James, Jocelyn, Kim, Mark, Lilian, Patrick, Tijana and Sabine: your passion and collegiality has enriched me greatly not only as a scholar but more importantly as a human being. I wish to specially thanks Dr. Patricia Post and Prof. Dr. Wil Pansters for their constant support.

This journey has been a remarkable period of my life in many ways. I will treasure good memories and great friendships. I realize how lucky I am to be surrounded with invaluable people. Special thanks goes to Angelica, Andreanne, Annick Audrey, Benedetta, Bettina, Boudewijn, Carlos, Caroline, Diana, Eugene, Filippo, Gwen, Irina, Isabelle, James, Jurian, Laura, Marguerita, Mariana, Michael, Nancy, Nora, Terry, Tutty, Sanne, Yadhira, Yayoi, Yenuen Wing and for bearing and beering with me ☺ Alastair, Karina, Nacho and Lalo – thanks for all our precious and crazy memories. Melanie – thanks for your invaluable friendship and constant optimism even during your last days. A heartfelt thank you to my *paranymphs*: Leo and Lidija. Thank you for standing beside me throughout all these years. Your friendship, unwavering support and fun memories have made you one of the best parts of my family. If I ever decide to conquer the moon, I will invite you all to come with me!

It is virtually impossible to give justice to all the people who have contributed in one form or another to make this book come true. My apologies to everyone who I may have forgotten to mention in the rush of finalizing the book.

I would also like to thank my family who has always encouraged me to aim higher while keeping my feet on earth. Ambre, Claire, Colette, Jean Francois, Luc and Peggy – merci d'avoir ouvert la porte de votre famille et de vos cœurs. To Anna, Irma, July, Michel, Trini, and especially to my mum – les agradezco infinitamente su amor y apoyo. A pesar de la distancia, siempre los llevo en mi corazón! Finally, I would like to thank my husband, who is the most important person in my life. David – tu es le plus beau cadeau que la vie ne m'a jamais offert. Thanks for always being there, for making my life a constant and intense adventure, for being the most caring husband, and above all, for sharing your parenting journey with me.

Table of Contents

Chapter III
Collective Reparations at the Inter-American Court of Human Rights

Chapter IV
Collective Reparations in International Criminal Law

Chapter V
Collective Reparations & Non-Judicial Bodies

Chapter VI
Conclusions

Abbreviations

AC	Appeals Chamber
ACHR	American Convention on Human Rights
ACmHPR	African Commission on Human and People's Rights
ACtHPR	African Court on Human and People's Rights
ACHPR	African Charter on Human and People's Rights
Algiers Agreement	2000 Agreement between the Government of the State of Eritrea and the Government of the Federal Democratic Republic of Ethiopia
ANR	Assurances of Non-Repetition
APRODEH	Asociación Pro Derechos Humanos (Association for Human Rights in Peru)
ASP	Assembly of States Parties
CAR	Central African Republic
CCDH	Conseil Consultatif des Droits de l'Homme (National Human Rights Council)
CHRAC	Cambodian Human Rights Action Committee
CMAN	Comisión Multisectorial de Alto Nivel (High Level Multisectoral Commission)
CNDH	Conseil National des Droits de l'Homme (National Council on Human Rights)
CoE	Council of Europe
CR	Collective Reparations
CVR	Comisión de la Verdad y Reconciliación (Truth and Reconciliation Commission)
DIP	Draft Implementation Plan
DRC	Democratic Republic of Congo

ECCC	Extraordinary Chambers in the Courts of Cambodia
EECC	Eritrea-Ethiopia Claims Commission
ECHR	European Convention on Human Rights and Fundamental Freedoms
ECtHR	European Court of Human Rights
ESCR	Economic, Social and Cultural Rights
FEDADOI	Fondo Especial de Administración de Dineros Obtenidos Ilícitamente (Special Fund for the Administration of Money Illicitly Obtained in Prejudice to the State)
FCDG	Fondation Caisse de Dépot et de Gestion (Foundation of the Deposit and Management Fund)
GA	General Assembly
GNR	Guarantees of Non-Repetition
GVHR	Gross Violations of Human Rights
HRC	Human Rights Council
HRL	Human Rights Law
IAC	Independent Arbitration Commission
IACommHR	Inter-American Commission on Human Rights
IACtHR	Inter-American Court of Human Rights
IASHR	Inter-American System of Human Rights
ICC	International Criminal Court
ICC's RoPE	ICC's Rules of Procedure and Evidence
ICCPR	International Covenant on Civil and Political Rights
ICESCR	International Covenant on Economic, Social and Cultural Rights
ICJ	International Court of Justice
ICL	International Criminal Law
ICTJ	International Center for Transitional Justice
ICTY	International Criminal Tribunal for the former Yugoslavia
IER	Instance Equité et Réconciliation (Equity and Reconciliation Commission)

ILA Declaration	2010 ILA Draft Declaration on Reparations for Victims of Armed Conflict
ILC	International Law Commission
Articles on State Responsibility	ILC Draft Articles on Responsibility of States for Internationally Wrongful Acts
IP	Indigenous Peoples
I&TP	Indigenous and Tribal Peoples
JCE	Joint Criminal Enterprise
LRV	Legal Representatives of the Victims
MCR	Mass Claims Reparations programmes
MoA	Margin of Appreciation
NCR	Consejo Nacional de Reparaciones (National Reparations Council)
NGO	Non-Governmental Organization
OAS	Organization of American States
OHCHR	Office of the United Nations High Commissioner for Human Rights
PCIJ	Permanent Court of International Justice
PIR	Plan Integral de Reparaciones (Comprehensive Reparations Plan)
PIR's Law	Ley No. 28592
Principles against Impunity	Set of Principles for the Protection and Promotion of Human Rights through Action to Combat Impunity
Principles on Reparations	UN Basic Principles and Guidelines on the Right to a Remedy and Reparation for Victims of Gross Violations of International Human Rights Law and Serious Violations of International Humanitarian Law
Regulations of PIR's Law	Supreme Decree Ds 015-2006-Jus: Reglamento de la Ley No. 28592
RoPE	Rules of Procedure and Evidence
RUV	Registro Único de Víctimas (National Victims Registry)
SC	Security Council

SCC	Supreme Court Chamber
SCSL	Special Court for Sierra Leone
SCU	Special Crimes Unit of the SPSC
SGBV	Sexual Gender-Based Violence
SPSC	Special Panel for Serious Crimes in East Timor
TC	Trial Chamber
TFV	Trust Fund for Victims
TJ	Transitional Justice
TJM	Transitional Justice Mechanisms
TJP	Transitional Justice Processes
TRCs	Truth and Reconciliation Commissions
UDHR	Universal Declaration of Human Rights
UN	United Nations
UNCC	United Nations Compensation Commission
UNCC Rules	UNCC Provisional Rules for Claims Procedure
UNCHR	United Nations Commission on Human Rights
UNPO	Unrepresented Nations and Peoples Organization
UNMIK	United Nations Interim Administration Mission in Kosovo
UNSC	UN Security Council
VCCR	Vienna Convention on Consular Relations
VCLT	Vienna Convention on the Law of the Treaties
Victims' Declaration	1985 Declaration of Basic Principles of Justice for Victims of Crime and Abuse of Power
VSS	Victims Support Section
WWII	World War II

Chapter I
Introduction

So many roads, so much at stake
So many dead ends, I'm at the edge of the lake
Sometimes I wonder what it's gonna take
To find [and repair] dignity[1]

1 Introduction

It is undeniable that 'human beings are capable of treating other human beings with unspeakable cruelty'.[2] History details the numerous ways in which humans engage in acts of gross violations of the rights of individuals or collectives on the basis of their political affiliation, ethnicity, race, religion or beliefs, amongst others.[3] These actions convey a message of inferiority to targeted groups, because these groups do not enjoy the same rights and protection that are afforded to other groups in a society.[4] Gross violations of human rights are commonly committed within the context of authoritarian regimes or civil conflicts. They form part of both our past and our present. And to a great extent, they continue to occur with impunity. Situations of mass violence in countries such as Rwanda, the former Yugoslavia, Guatemala, Sudan, Darfur, and more recently, Syria, remind us that mass killings, and extreme violence in general, have not decreased since the 'never again' promise pledged at the

---

1 Dylan, B., "Dignity" (song) in *Bob Dylan's Greatest Hits Volume 3.*

2 Peté, S. and du Plessis, M., "Reparations for Gross Violations of Human Rights in Context", in M. du Plessis and S. Peté (eds.), *Repairing the Past? International Perspectives on Reparations for Human Rights Abuses* (Antwerp/Oxford, Intersentia 2007), p. 3.

3 Rubio-Marin, R., Sandoval, C. and Díaz, C., "Repairing Family Members: Gross Human Rights Violations and Communities of Harm", in R. Rubio-Marin (ed.), *The Gender of Reparations: Unsettling Sexual Hierarchies while Redressing Human Rights Violations* (Cambridge, CUP 2009), p. 215.

4 Wolfe, S., *The Politics of Reparations and Apologies* (New York, Springer 2014), p. 2-4; Watson, J.S., *Theory & Reality in the International Protection of Human Rights* (New York, Transnational Publishers 1999); Preface ix; Commission on Human Rights, *Report of the United Nations High Commissioner for Human Rights and Follow-up to the World Conference on Human Rights,* 26 February 2003, UN Doc. E/CN.4/2003/14, para. 7-8.

end of the Second World War. When confronted with the reality of 'again and again', such a promise is reduced to wishful thinking.[5]

The persistence and recurrence of gross violations of human rights have resulted in an enormous number of victims across the world. Those who have not been killed have been deeply affected by the killing of their loved ones, and grave infringements of their rights through abuses such as prolonged detention and torture, mutilation, rape, or the destruction of their properties and their means of livelihood. The physical, psychological, and economic consequences at both the individual and societal levels are to some extent immeasurable[6] and irreparable.[7] Gross violations of human rights deeply affect individuals and they damage the social fabric of a given society[8] as they result in multiple and severe harm.[9] Consequently, such gross violations destroy individual lives and breach the trust fostered between people and invested in political institutions.[10]

Despite the consequences of these infringements, for many years the plight of victims of gross violations of human rights was ignored not only at the national level, but also at the international level.[11] Moreover, history demonstrates that victims consistently face major challenges in their pursuit of justice.[12] Most instances of gross violations of human rights occur in the midst of political instability, when state institutions are barely functioning and the rule of law is absent. In this context, ensuring justice during the aftermath of a conflict is a very complex procedure.[13] In addition, states transitioning to a more democratic form of governance face several hurdles when addressing past abuses. These hurdles may be political and legal in nature, as well as material. A number of factors might prevent victims from being

---

5 Peté and du Plessis, *supra* n. 2, p. 3-10. Despite the fact that ongoing violence has contributed to the recurrence of gross violations of human rights, scholars have suggested that such violence has been declining, albeit unevenly, for millennia. The adoption of international legal instruments by states after WWII to empower individuals has contributed, to some extent, to this decline in violence. See: Simon Fraser University, *Human Security Report 2013: The Decline in Global Violence: Evidence, Explanation and Contestation* (Vancouver, Human Security Press 2014), p. 19, 46-47.

6 Peté and du Plessis, *supra* n. 2, p. 4-10; Tomuschat, C., "Darfur: Compensation for the Victims", 3 *Journal of International Criminal Justice* (2005), p. 580.

7 Sub-Commission on the Promotion and Protection of Human Rights, *Study Concerning the Right to Restitution, Compensation and Rehabilitation for Victims of Gross Violations of Human Rights and Fundamental Freedoms: Final Report*, 2 July 1993, UN Doc. E/CN.4/Sub.2/1993/8, <www1.umn.edu/humanrts/demo/van%20Boven_1993.pdf>.

8 Letschert, R. and van Boven, T., "Providing Reparation in Situations of Mass Victimization: Key Challenges Involved", in R. Letschert et al. (eds.), *Victimological Approaches to International Crimes: Africa* (Cambridge, Intersentia 2011), p. 153.

9 Rubio-Marin, Sandoval and Díaz, *supra* n. 3, p. 216.

10 Hamber, B., *Transforming Societies after Political Violence* (New York, Springer 2009), p. 23-25.

11 Bottigliero, I. *Redress for Victims of Crimes under International Law* (Leiden, Martinus Nijhoff 2004), p. 2.

12 Ibid., p. 13.

13 Ibid., p. 2.

able to seek and obtain justice, such as the large number of victims, a difficulty in determining who is a victim and/or a perpetrator, in particular when it concerns long-term conflicts and the lack of capacity and limited resources of the state in question.[14] These circumstances also limit the ability of states to offer reparations, or prevent them from doing so altogether. Since state authorities are often directly or indirectly involved in the perpetration of gross violations of human rights,[15] a culture of impunity starts to develop from the inability or unwillingness to hold such authorities responsible.[16] The international community has repeatedly witnessed the failure of states to address these crimes. It is often the case that bringing justice and providing reparations to victims therefore only amounts to a mere hope in many corners of the globe.

Until the adoption of international human rights instruments, the question of how a state treated its own citizens was mostly a domestic matter.[17] Initially, international law was not victim-oriented, as only states were considered to be the primary subjects of this legal framework. Monitoring domestic affairs, such as the treatment of citizens, amounted to an infringement of national sovereignty.[18] For many years victims relied upon the willingness and capacity of states to provide any sort of justice, because victims could not resort to international justice mechanisms to bring their claims when national avenues to justice proved unavailable or ineffective.

However, this situation has gradually changed. The suffering of victims, especially those who have been the victims of gross violations of human rights, has become increasingly visible at both the domestic and international levels, and more attention has been afforded to them, in particular during the last two decades.[19] Victims' movements that demanded justice and reparations, efforts to strengthen the protection of fundamental rights, and an increasing emphasis on the need to fight impunity were key elements in bringing the recognition of victims' rights, including the right to a remedy, to the forefront of international law.[20] Against this background, several states started to implement a broad range of measures to provide remedies to victims, including truth commissions; criminal trials; and reparations, including

14 Letschert and van Boven, *supra* n. 8, p. 154; McKay, F., "What Outcome for Victims?", in D. Shelton (ed.), *The Oxford Handbook of International Human Rights Law* (Oxford, OUP 2013), p. 945.

15 Schmid, A.P. , *Research on Gross Human Rights Violations* (Leiden, COMT 1989, 2nd ed.), p. 106-107.

16 Almeida, I., "Compensation and Reparation for Gross Violations of Human Rights: Advancing the International Discourse and Action", in C.C. Joyner (ed.) *Reining in Impunity for International Crimes and Serious Violations of Fundamental Human Rights: Proceedings of the Siracusa Conference, 14-21 September 1998* (Toulouse, Erès1998), p. 401.

17 Scott, S.V., *International Law in World Politics* (London, Lynne Rienner Publishers 2004), p. 29-30.

18 Letschert and van Boven, *supra* n. 8, p. 154.

19 Ochoa, J.C., *The Rights of Victims in Criminal Proceedings for Serious Human Rights Violations* (Leiden/Boston, Martinus Nijhoff 2013), p. 3; García-Godos, J., "Victim Reparations in Transitional Justice: What is at Stake and Why", 26 *Nordisk Tidsskrift for Menneskerettigheter,* (2008), p. 113.

20 Doak, J., *Victims' Rights, Human Rights and Criminal Justice: Reconceiving the Role of Third Parties* (Portland, Hart Publishing 2008), p. 20-36.

official apologies.[21] These measures, *inter alia*, are often part of what is referred to as transitional justice processes.[22]

Redressing, or 'righting', the wrongs suffered by victims, especially when the harm suffered is particularly serious, is nowadays both a moral and a legal imperative for states.[23] International venues that aim to facilitate the redress of gross violations of human rights, including those that amount to international crimes, are now available to victims. In addition, the widespread recognition of a victim's right to a remedy and reparation led to the adoption of the Basic Principles and Guidelines on the Right to a Remedy and Reparation for Victims of Gross Violations of International Human Rights Law and Serious Violations of International Humanitarian Law (2005 Basic Principles, or Principles on Reparations). These Principles act as a comprehensive instrument that outlines the many forms that reparations may take in order to bring relief to victims and highlights the importance of providing reparation in the promotion of justice as a means to prevent further crimes.[24] In addition, the Principles on Reparations are the most authoritative document regarding reparations and are considered to be a codification of the existing rules.

According to these Principles, reparation for victims can take the form of restitution, compensation, rehabilitation, satisfaction, or guarantees of non-repetition.[25] Yet a trend can be identified amongst both judicial and non-judicial bodies regarding reparations awarded to victims of gross violations of human rights. Namely, that when dealing with a large number of victims, predominantly collective awards are granted, as this form of reparation is deemed to be the most appropriate.[26] Furthermore, it is not only governments that are inclined to create programmes that are accessible to a large number of beneficiaries; truth commissions have also

---

21 Wolfe, *supra* n. 4, p. 63.

22 Letschert and van Boven, *supra* n. 8, p. 156; quoting Fletcher, L.E. and Weinstein, H.M., "Violence and Social Repair: Rethinking the Contribution of Justice to Reconciliation" 24 *Human Rights Quarterly* (2002).

23 Nathan, C., "Introductory Remarks" in C. Ferstman, M. Goetz and A. Stephens (eds.), *Reparations for Victims of Genocide, War Crimes and Crimes Against Humanity: Systems in Place and Systems in the Making* (Leiden, Martinus Nijhoff 2009), p. 8; The REDRESS Trust, *Report: Reparations for victims of genocide, crimes against humanity and war crimes: Systems in place and systems in the making, The Hague, 1-2 March 2007* (The Hague, The REDRESS Trust 2007), p. 6. Available at: <http://www.redress.org/downloads/publications/ReparationsVictimsGenocideSept07.pdf>.

24 UN General Assembly, *Basic Principles and Guidelines on the Right to a Remedy and Reparation for Victims of Gross Violations of International Human Rights Law and Serious Violations of International Humanitarian Law*, 21 March 2006, UN Doc. A/RES/60/147.

25 Principle 18, Principles on Reparations. A detailed explanation of what each measure entails is provided in Chapter II.

26 de Greiff, P. , "Justice and Reparations", in P. de Greiff (ed.), *The Handbook of Reparations* (Oxford, OUP 2006); Roht-Arriaza, N., "Reparations Decisions and Dilemmas", 27 *Hastings International and Comparative Law Review* (2004), p. 157-219.

repeatedly recommended collective reparations.[27] In addition, the Inter-American Court of Human Rights (IACtHR), a court that has provided the most wide-reaching forms of reparation among all human rights bodies,[28] has also granted collective reparations to victims of mass crimes.[29] The Extraordinary Chambers in the Courts of Cambodia (ECCC) and the International Criminal Court (ICC) have mirrored this practice.[30] The collective awards granted include housing and health programmes, as well as community development programmes.[31] Notably, these collective reparations are rarely granted in conjunction with individual reparations.[32]

Despite the common practice of governments, truth commissions, and courts in only granting collective reparations to large groups of victims, a reading of the Principles on Reparations reveals the clear need to provide victims of gross violations of human rights with both collective *and* individual reparations. It can therefore be questioned whether awarding *only* collective reparations also fulfils the individual right to reparation. Taking this reading of the Principles as a starting point, this study questions, from a legal perspective, the validity of the normative international framework in granting *only* collective reparations to victims of gross violations of human rights. In addition, this study discusses the ambiguity of the content and scope of reparations, and the problematic aspects that collective reparations present in the fields of international human rights law and international criminal law. The following sections will explain in detail the central dilemma that gave rise to this study.

27 Some examples include the truth commissions established in Morocco, Liberia, Peru, and Sierra Leone. See: Guillerot, J. and Carranza, R. *The Rabat Report: The Concept and Challenges of Collective Reparations* (New York, ICTJ 2009).

28 Huneeus, A., "Courts Resisting Courts: Lessons from the Inter-American Court's Struggle to Enforce Human Rights", 44 *Cornell International Law Journal* (2011), p. 494; Antkowiak, T., "An Emerging Mandate for International Courts: Victim-Centered Remedies and Restorative Justice", 47 *Stanford Journal of International Law* (2011), p. 288; Nash Rojas, C., *Las Reparaciones ante la Corte Inter-Americana de Derechos Humanos: 1987-2007* (Santiago, Centro de Derechos Humanos/ Universidad de Chile 2009, 2nd ed.) p. 32, 42; Antkowiak, T., "Remedial Approaches to Human Rights Violations: The Inter-American Court of Human Rights and Beyond", 46 *Columbia Journal of Transnational Law* (2008), p. 418-419.

29 Rombouts, H., Sardaro, P. and Vandeginste, S., "The Right to Reparations for Victims of Gross and Sytematic Violations of Human Rights" in K. de Feyter et al. (ed.), *Out of the Ashes: Reparations for Gross Violations of Human Rights* (Antwerp/Oxford, Intersentia 2006), p. 408-410.

30 Sperfeldt, C., "Collective Reparations at the Extraordinary Chambers in the Courts of Cambodia", 12 *International Criminal Law Review* (2012), p. 457-489; Contreras-Garduño, D., "Passing the buck: the ICC Trial Chamber's approach in Lubanga Reparations decision", 15 August 2015, blog post, <armedgroups-internationallaw.org/2012/08/15/guest-post-by-diana-contreras-garduno-passing-the-buck-the-icc-trial-chambers-approach-in-lubanga-reparations-decision/>.

31 IACtHR (Judgment) 15 June 2005, *Moiwana Community* v. *Suriname*, para. 215; Judgment) 17 June 2005, *Yakye Axa Indigenous Community* v. *Paraguay*), para. 205; (Judgment) 29 March 2006, *Sawhoyamaxa Indigenous Commmunity* v. *Paraguay*, para. 224. See also: Guillerot and Carranza, *supra* n. 27, p. 9-10, 59; United States Institute of Peace, *Report of the Chilean National Commission on Truth and Reconciliation* (Indiana, University of Notre Dame Press 1993), p. 1057-1074.

32 Chapters IV, V, and VI will provide further information on this matter.

1.1 Reparations Commonly Awarded for Gross Violations of Human Rights

Remedies amount to, on the one hand, access to justice – the possibility to bring a complaint before a competent body – and, on the other, reparations – the means used in order to repair a damage or injury.[33] While the former refers to the procedural element of remedies, the latter concerns the substantive element.[34]

The ideal of reparations is to provide a full remedy (*restitutio integrum*) – the restoration of the *status quo ante*.[35] Accordingly, reparations 'must, as far as possible, wipe out all the consequences of the illegal act and re-establish the situation which would, in all probability, have existed if that act had not been committed'.[36] This rule is considered to be one of the most fundamental principles of international law.[37] However, this is an unrealistic expectation when it comes to serious breaches of human rights.[38] In addition, some measures of reparation may also address societal harm,[39] and thereby contribute, to some extent, to the promotion of peace and reconciliation.[40] In this light most responses to gross violations of human rights include providing reparation to the victims.[41]

Bearing in mind that gross violations of human rights 'cause mass-scale suffering' to individuals and society,[42] it is unsurprising that the consequences of these crimes overwhelm the concept of reparations.[43] Providing reparation for gross violations face several challenges, including, *inter alia*, the irreparable nature of the violation, the large number of victims, the limited resources which are available, and the difficulties in identifying and locating each individual victim,[44] as well as the

33 Remedies are composed of two aspects: the procedural aspect, which refers to the venues available to bring a claim; and the substantive aspect, which refers to the aim to redress the harm inflicted by a wrongful act. For a detailed discussion on remedies and their distinction compared to reparations see: Shelton, D., *Remedies in International Human Rights Law* (Oxford, OUP 2015, 3rd ed.).

34 Tomuschat, C., "Reparations for Victims of Grave Human Rights Violations", 10 *Tulane Journal of International and Comparative Law* (2002), p. 167-168.

35 Starr, S.B., "Rethinking 'Effective Remedies': Remedial Deterrence in International Courts", 83 *New York University Law Review* (2008), p. 699; de Greiff, *supra* n. 26, p. 455.

36 PCIJ (Judgment) 13 September 1928, *The Factory at Chorzów* (*Germany* v. *Poland*), p. 47.

37 PCIJ (Judgment) 26 July 1927, *The Factory at Chorzów* (*Germany* v. *Poland*), p. 21.

38 Freeman, M., "Back to the Future: The Historical Dimension of Liberal Justice", in M. du Plessis and S. Peté (eds.), *Repairing the Past? International Perspectives on Reparations for Human Rights Abuses* (Antwerp/Oxford, Intersentia 2007), p. 37.

39 van Boven, T., "Reparations: a Requirement of Justice", in IACtHR (ed.), *Memoria del Seminario: El Sistema Interamericano de Protección de los Derechos Humanos en el Umbral del Siglo* (Costa Rica, IACtHR 1999), p. 668.

40 Tutu, D., *Geen Toekomst zonder Verzoening* (Amsterdam, De Bezige Bij 1999), p. 60-61.

41 Teitel, R., *Transitional Justice* (Oxford, OUP 2000), p. 127.

42 Letschert and van Boven, *supra* n. 8, p. 153.

43 Freeman, *supra* n. 38, p. 30.

44 de Feyter, K. et al. (ed.), *Out of the Ashes: Reparations for Gross Violations of Human Rights* (Antwerp/Oxford, Intersentia 2006).

sometimes difficult task of distinguishing between who is the victim and who is the perpetrator.[45]

When designing reparations for victims of gross violations of human rights, states usually opt for those that aim to restore the communities or collectives which have been directly affected.[46] Such programmes are based on a wide and inclusive beneficiary approach and aim to provide direct benefits to the victimized populations. Those benefits, however, may not have reparative effects.[47] Such programmes prioritise meeting the basic needs of the victims[48] and communities or groups.[49] Prioritising the basic needs of victims and providing direct benefits can be linked to distributive justice, and has the potential to contribute – albeit modestly – to poverty reduction.[50] These reparation programmes, also referred to as collective reparations, are therefore usually political projects with a potentially enormous scope. They often take place in the context of a transitional justice process,[51] and their main purposes are the following: to promote civic trust, recognition, and social solidarity,[52] as well as 'to re-establish security and respect for human rights'.[53] In line with this, collective reparations aim to rebuild a political community. They do not therefore share the goal of reparations as understood by public international law and international human rights law, i.e. *restitutio in integrum.* However, this does not mean that collective

45 In situations of mass violence, victims and perpetrators do not always belong to two separate groups. This can lead to a so-called 'victim-perpetrator dichotomy'. See: Borer, T.A., "A Taxonomy of Victims and Perpetrators: Human Rights and Reconciliation in South Africa", 25 *Human Rights Quarterly* (2003); Derluyn, I. et al., "Victims and/or perpetrators? Towards an interdisciplinary dialogue on child soldiers", 15 *BMC International Health and Human Rights* (2015); Moffet, L., "Reparations for 'Guilty Victims': Navigating Complex Identities of Victim-Perpetrators in Reparation Mechanisms" 10 *International Journal of Transitional Justice,* (2016).

46 Rosenfeld, F., "Collective Reparations for Victims of Armed Conflict" 92 *International Review of the Red Cross* (2010), p. 731, Contreras-Garduño, D., 'Defining Beneficiaries of Collective Reparations: The experience of the IACtHR,' 4 *Amsterdam Law Forum* (2012), p. 41; de Greiff, *supra* n. 26, p. 466.

47 de Greiff, *supra* n. 26, p. 453.

48 Hamber, *supra* n. 10, p. 196.

49 Magarrell, L., "Reparations in Theory and Practice", *ICTJ* (2007), p. 5. <www.ictj.org/sites/default/files/ICTJ-Global-Reparations-Practice-2007-English.pdf>.

50 Although they might have positive effects in achieving poverty reduction and the levelling of inequalities, these should not be the goals of collective reparations. In fact, these objectives are better served by development programmes. See: de Greiff, *supra* n. 26, p. 470-471.

51 Ibid., p. 459; Firchow, P. , "Must our Communities Bleed to Receive Social Services? Development Projects and Collective Schemes in Colombia", 8 *Journal of Peacebuilding and Development* 2013, p. 52.

52 de Greiff, *supra* n. 26, p. 451.

53 de Greiff, *supra* n. 26, p. 453-456; Tomuschat, *supra* n. 6, p. 587.

reparations are grounded on unfairness.[54] While they often do not uphold a legal approach, collective reparations aim to provide a form of justice to victims.

The benefits obtained through collective reparations are usually in the form of social services: they are symbolic offerings of solidarity with an affected community or collective, or symbolic measures that acknowledge the suffering of victims.[55] For instance, when Norway formulated a national policy to compensate victims for war damages resulting from the Second World War (regressive compensation for damage to means of livelihood), the underlying principle was to assist victims for the purpose of reconstructing the country.[56] Addressing the fact that the whole country had suffered prevailed over addressing individual harms. Some scholars have also stated that reparation programmes 'must at the very least ensure that they do not derogate from [human rights]'.[57]

It could therefore be argued that collective reparations have been designed under different guidance and principles compared to the reparations that are recognised by the current international legal framework, which in fact focuses on individual reparations.[58] Taking this into consideration, de Greiff states that collective reparations 'can hardly include all forms in which reparations may take place as established by international law'.[59] In addition, de Greiff states that the current juridical approach to reparations is founded on the aim to redress violations of human rights in isolated cases. He claims that the understanding of what is 'fair, proper and

---

54 de Greiff, *supra* n. 26, p. 451-455; See also: 'in the process of transition to democracy, in which massive and systematic human rights violations needed to be addressed, [the reparation criteria laid down by international law] had to be redefined' IACmmHR (Report) 23 March 2011, *Garcia Lucero et al.* v. *Chile*, Case No. 12.519, para. 28. Shannon affirms that States often use reparations as tools for diplomacy. Accordingly, reparations are designed on the basis of their benefits in terms of restoring diplomatic relations rather than doing justice for victims as mandated by international human rights law. Thus, States might refuse reparations if they do not bring sufficient political benefits, regardless of their international obligations towards victims. Jones, S., *Apology Diplomacy: Justice for All?*, Discussion papers in diplomacy, Issue 122, Netherlands Institute of International Relations 'Clingendael', 2011, p. 1, 10-13 and 16, <www.clingendael.nl/sites/default/files/20110900_cdsp_discussionpapersindiplomacy_122_jones.pdf>.

55 Mayeux, B. and Mirabal, J., "Collective and Moral Reparations in the Inter-American Court of Human Rights", *Human Rights Clinic, The University of Texas School of Law* (2009), p. 29-33; International Bank for Reconstruction and Development, "Colombia: Collective Reparation for Victims through Social Reconstruction Project", 29 January 2015, <documents.worldbank.org/curated/en/2015/01/23953705/colombia-collective-reparation-victims-through-social-reconstruction-project>.

56 Elster, J., *Transitional Justice in Historical Perspective* (Cambridge, CUP 2004), p. 170; Elster, J., "Land, Justice and Peace", in M. Bergsmo et al. (eds.) *Distributive Justice in Transitions*, (Oslo, Torkel Opsahl Academic EPublisher 2010), p. 22.

57 The REDRESS Trust, *supra* n. 23, p. 26.

58 de Greiff, *supra* n. 26, p. 453. This statement will be further explained in the next section.

59 Ibid., p. 453.

efficient' in the context of isolated cases cannot be the same when addressing mass human rights violations.[60]

2 The Problem in a Nutshell

2.1 Complex Reparations for Complex Harm

Gross violations of human rights usually target groups of persons on the basis of their religion, ethnicity,[61] or political affiliation, and structural circumstances such as, *inter alia*, discrimination, economic exclusion, or social marginalisation may facilitate the commission of such violations.[62] These structural problems not only increase an individual or group's vulnerability to violations, but they have been proven to be the root causes of violent conflicts and, subsequently, gross violations of human rights.[63] These violations cause both individual and collective harm.[64] It therefore seems logical that reparations for victims of gross violations of human rights should address not only individual and collective suffering, but also structural problems that may have been the root causes of such crimes.[65] If this is facilitated, reparations could also help to reduce both vulnerability to similar crimes in the future (a *de facto* guarantee of non-repetition),[66] and the possibility of further outbreaks due to deep-seated inequalities.[67]

---

60 Ibid., p. 451.

61 This list is by no means exhaustive. Factors such as religion and ethnicity might also form grounds for targeting people.

62 UN Human Rights Council, *Report of the Secretary-General: Question of the Realization in All Countries of Economic, Social and Cultural Rights*, 13 February 2007, UN Doc. A/HRC/4/62, <www.unhcr.org/refworld/pdfid/461f794c2.pdf>, para. 31; Hamber, *supra* n. 10, p. 196. According to Rama Mani, structural and systemic inequalities also contribute to conflict. Mani, R., *Beyond Retribution: Seeking Justice in the Shadows of War*, 2002, p. 127-133.

63 Hayner, P. B., "Reconsidering the Peace-and-Justice Debate: International Justice in Africa and Latin America", in K. Hite and M. Ungar (eds.), *Sustaining Human Rights in the Twenty-First Century* (Washington, Woodrow Wilson Center Press 2013), p. 219; Violence condemns 1.5 billion people to poverty, and along with a lack of justice and negligible adherence to the rule of law this generates cycles of violence. See: The 2011 World Development's Report: Conflict, Security and Development. Available at: <http://siteresources.worldbank.org/INTWDRS/Resources/WDR2011_Full_Text.pdf> [Accessed 17th August, 2011].

64 Letschert and van Boven, *supra* n. 8, p. 165.

65 Hamber, *supra* n. 10, p. 150.

66 Mayeux and Mirabal, *supra* n. 55, p. 29-33.

67 Reparations might provide an opportunity for victims to diminish their anger resulting from their victimisation and could therefore be seen as a source of possible reconciliation between victims and perpetrators. This becomes especially important when talking about mass crimes and mass perpetrators who are supposed to rebuild one common society in a given territory. See: Muttukumary, C., "Reparations to Victims", in R.S. Lee (ed.), *The International Criminal Court: The Making of the Rome Statute. Issues, Negotiation, Results* (The Hague, Kluwer Law International 1999), p. 264.

In this context, the Principles on Reparations outline that individual victims' rights to reparations include both individual and collective measures. Restitution, compensation, and rehabilitation are individual measures; whereas measures of satisfaction and non-repetition represent more of a community or collective approach.[68] While some critics have affirmed that the five different modalities of reparations can be granted individually or collectively,[69] others emphasise the need to find a balance between these forms of reparation.[70]

2.2 Legal Foundations of Collective Reparations under Human Rights Law

Under international human rights law there are no legal foundations that justify the granting of solely collective reparations to victims of gross violations of human rights. The current legal framework relating to remedies (including reparations) focuses largely on individual victims and the vindication of individual rights.[71] As collective measures are recognised under international human rights law, they should therefore complement individual awards.[72] The first UN document that referred to collective awards is the 1997 Report prepared by Mr. Joinet: 'Question of the impunity of perpetrators of human rights violations (civil and political)' (the Joinet Report or Principles against Impunity).[73] The report states that the right to reparation can take the form of restitution, compensation, or satisfaction, 'but may also include measures of rehabilitation of victims and guarantees of non-repetition'.[74] Following

68 Letschert and van Boven, *supra* n. 8, p. 173 and 182-183.

69 Bassiouni, C., "International Recognition of Victims' Rights", 6 *Human Rights Law Review* (2006), p. 274.

70 Letschert and van Boven, *supra* n. 8, p. 182.

71 Ibid., p. 155-56. In fact, human rights law in general focuses primarily on the protection of individual rights. See: Westra, L., *Human Rights: The Commons and the Collective* (Vancouver, UBC Press 2012); Bantekas, I. and Oette, L., *International Human Rights: Law and Practice* (Cambridge, CUP 2013), p. 409-412. The literature on minority rights also supports the primacy of the protection of individual rights over collective rights within the international human rights instruments. See: Duchêne, A., *Ideologies across Nations: The Construction of Linguistic Minorities at the United Nations* (Berlin/New York, De Gruyter Mouton 2008); Tavani, C., *Collective Rights and the Cultural Identity of the Roma: A Case Study of Italy* (Leiden/Boston, Martinus Nijhoff 2012).

72 Christine Evans has also submitted that reparations should in principle be 'individualised awards', which can be complemented but not replaced by collective awards. See: Evans, C., *The Right to Reparation in International Law for Victims of Armed Conflict* (Cambridge, CUP 2012), p. 84; Tavani, *supra* n. 71; UN WOMEN Press release, *Turning the tide on sexual violence in conflict, new UN guidance on reparations launched*, 11 June 2014. Available at: <http://www.unwomen.org/en/news/stories/2014/6/new-un-guidance-on-reparations-launched>.

73 The Principles against Impunity have received affirmation by several international tribunals and treaty bodies. Nonetheless they have not been adopted by the UN General Assembly. See: ICJT, "Transitional Justice in the United Nations Human Rights Council", ICTJ 2011, p. 1.

74 Human Rights Council, *Human Rights in Palestine and Other Occupied Arab Territories: Report of the United Nations Fact Finding Mission on the Gaza Conflict*, 25 September 2009, UN Doc. A/HRC/12/48, para. 1866.

this, the right to reparation 'entails both individual measures and general, collective measures'.[75] The report further explains that individual measures are those of restitution, compensation and rehabilitation, while collective measures are symbolic measures of satisfaction and guarantees of non-repetition.[76]

Similarly, the Principles on Reparations state that: '[i]n addition to individual access to justice, states should endeavour to develop procedures to allow groups of victims to present claims for reparation and to receive reparation, as appropriate.'[77] From this wording, it is evident that the Principles only foresee the *possibility* of a group's legal standing to submit claims for reparations and only suggest the *possibility* for them to obtain collective reparations.[78]

However, it is interesting to note that the first draft of the Principles on Reparations recognises that gross violations of human rights affect individuals and collectives, as well as their respective rights. For instance, cases involving indigenous people provide a useful example of when individual and collective aspects of a violation are closely related.[79] Principle 7 initially proposed that:

> [i]n addition to providing reparation to individuals, States shall make adequate provision for groups of victims to bring collective claims and to obtain collective reparation. Special measures should be taken for the purpose of affording opportunities for self-development and advancement to groups who, as a result of human rights violations, were denied such opportunities.[80]

However, this provision had been erased in the draft that was adopted in 2005. Within the meaning of the former Principle 7, collective reparations complement the individual right to reparations. Dinah Shelton notes that states did not welcome the provisions referring to collective reparations, resulting in the omission of any reference to them.[81]

---

75 UNHCR, *Question of the Impunity of Perpetrators of Human Rights Violations (Civil and Political): Revised Final Report Prepared by Mr. Joinet Pursuant to Sub-Commission Decision 1996/119*, 2 October 1997, UN Doc. E/CN.4/Sub.2/1997/20/Rev. 1, para. 40 and Principle 36.

76 Ibid., para. 42.

77 Principle 13, Principles on Reparations [emphasis added]. This principle was the result of a compromise between states when discussing collective and individual reparations and whether they implied the vindication of an individual or collective right. See: Echeverria, G., "Codifying the Rights of the Victims in International Law: Remedies and Reparation" in Permanent Court of Arbitration, *Redressing Injustices through Mass Claims Processes: Innovative Responses to Unique Challenges* (Oxford, OUP 2006), p. 295.

78 The difference between individual and group legal standing to bring claims of reparation falls outside the scope of this research.

79 Sub-Commission on the Promotion and Protection of Human Rights, *supra* n. 7, p. 8.

80 Ibid., p. 56.

81 Shelton, D., "The UN Principles and Guidelines on Reparations: Context and Contents", in K. de Feyter et al. (ed.), *Out of the Ashes: Reparations for Gross Violations of Human Rights* (Antwerp/Oxford, Intersentia 2006), p. 21.

The 2010 ILA Draft Declaration on Reparations for Victims of Armed Conflict (2010 ILA Declaration)[82] establishes that '[r]eparation shall take the form of restitution, compensation, satisfaction and guarantees and assurances of non-repetition, either singly or in combination.'[83] Article 11 stipulates that states 'shall establish programmes and maintain institutions to facilitate access to reparation, including possible programmes addressed to persons affected by armed conflicts other than the victims.' The commentary pertaining to this Article explains that '[t]aking account of the dissociation of rights and enforcement mechanisms in international law, this provision represents a necessary complement to the victims' right to reparation'.[84] Since most reparation programmes established during the aftermath of violent conflicts focus predominantly on granting collective reparations,[85] the content of Article 11 could be understood as supporting the idea that collective reparations complement the individual right to receive reparations. This conclusion is also supported by the reference made in the commentary to Article 11 regarding the need to address both individuals and communities: 'Reparations may also be provided through programmes, based upon legislative or administrative measures, funded by national or international sources, addressed to individuals and communities'.[86]

2.3 Legal Issues Arising from Awarding Only Collective Reparations

Some scholars assert that collective remedies are only available in cases of violations of group rights.[87] This raises the question of whether *all* victims of gross violations of human rights are recognised as a group under international human rights law. If so, it is necessary to question which rights have been conferred upon them.[88] In addition, Koen de Feyter affirms that non-judicial reparation programmes (collective

---

82 Although this Declaration has not been adopted by the UN, it is an initiative that scholars have embraced due to the fact that it clarifies rules of international humanitarian law. See: Bothe, M., *The Handbook of International Humanitarian Law* (Oxford, OUP 2013), p. 685.

83 International Law Association, *Draft Declaration of International Law Principles on Reparation for Victims of Armed Conflict (Substantive Issues)*, Conference Report, 74th ILA Conference (15-20 August 2010), Article 1(2).

84 Ibid.

85 de Greiff, *supra* n. 26, p. 459; Firchow, *supra* n. 51, p. 52; Guillerot and Carranza, *supra* n. 27, p. 9-10. See also: A Measure of Dignity: The Beginning of Reparations in Post-Revolution Tunisia. Available at: <https://www.ictj.org/news/measure-dignity-reparations-tunisia>.

86 The commentary refers to Principle 32 of the Updated Set of Principles for the Protection and Promotion of Human Rights through Action to Combat Impunity: Human Rights Commission, *Updated Set of Principles for the Protection and Promotion of Human Rights through Action to Combat Impunity*, 8 February 2005, UN Doc. E/CN.4/2005/102/Add.1. (Hereinafter, Principles to Combat Impunity). See: International Law Association, *supra* n. 83, Commentary on Article 11. See also: de Greiff, *supra* n. 26, p. 459.

87 Bantekas and Oette, *supra* n. 71, p. 525; Rombouts, Sardaro and Vandeginste, *supra* n. 29, p. 407.

88 Chapter III and Conclusions will provide further information on this matter.

reparations) that benefit large numbers of victims affected by gross violations of human rights should 'interact in a complementary fashion for the reparation and other assistance of victims.'[89] The IACtHR has also stated that collective reparations complement individual reparations: 'the individual reparations to be awarded must be supplemented by communal measures; said reparations will be granted to the community as a whole'.[90]

In recent years, the compatibility as well as the content and scope of collective reparations have been the subject of debate in international human rights and international criminal law. Although international law establishes the individual right to receive reparation, providing reparation on a case-by-case basis seems unrealistic when one is confronted with a lack of resources and a vast number of victims.[91] Collective reparations may be justified as the best or most feasible form of reparations for victims of gross violations of human rights, but as mentioned above, at present this form of reparation does not enjoy a clear legal basis under international law.[92] Collective reparations also challenge the ideal of merely repairing the harm. For instance, Malarino submits: '[o]nly with great effort could it be argued that the construction of a sewage system, a potable water system, or the improvement of highways, [...] "repair" the victims of a massacre.'[93]

Despite being framed as political projects, collective reparations were transferred to the field of international law in particular by the jurisprudence of the IACtHR. The Court has granted collective awards in cases involving both gross violations of human rights and indigenous peoples – scenarios that concern a large number of victims. The IACtHR has nether explained the concept of collective reparations, nor the differences between collective reparations awarded within a

89 de Feyter et al. (ed.), *supra* n. 44 p. vii.
90 IACtHR (Judgment) 15 June 2005, *Moiwana Community* v. *Suriname*, para. 194.
91 de Greiff, *supra* n. 26, p. 454.
92 This is further explained in the next section, which concerns the central question of this research.
93 Solo con mucho esfuerzo podría sostenerse que la construcción de una red de alcantarillado, de un sistema de agua potable o la mejora de carreteras, [...] "reparan" a las víctimas de una masacre (translated by the author). See: Malarino, E., "Activismo Judicial, Punitivización y Nacionalización: Las Tendencias Antidemocráticas y Antiliberales de la CIDH", in Grupo Latinoamericano de Estudios Sobre Derecho Penal Internacional (ed.) *Sistema Interamericano de Protección de los Derechos Humanos y Derecho Penal Internacional* (Berlin/Montevideo/Mexico, Konrad Adenauer Stiftung 2011), p. 25-62.

transitional justice context and those awarded within a *human rights law* context.[94] Moreover, while the jurisprudence of the IACtHR shows that collective reparations usually complement individual awards, the Court has nevertheless sometimes only awarded collective reparations to victims. This raises several questions: does the American Convention on Human Rights,[95] the founding document of the IACtHR, allow for the possibility to award collective reparations? If so, in which cases? Does this imply that the intention behind granting collective reparations is to recognise groups such as indigenous people? If so, would all victims of gross violations of human rights be recognised as a group? Furthermore, and central to this issue, what exactly is the relationship between the individual right to receive reparation and the right to collective awards?

It is important to note that under international criminal law, both the ECCC and the ICC have followed the IACtHR's practice of granting collective reparations. However, the difference between the IACtHR, on the one hand, and the ECCC and the ICC, on the other, is that the respective legal frameworks of the latter two courts explicitly allow for collective reparations.[96] It can therefore be reasonably assumed that regardless of whether collective reparations are consistent with international human rights law, these courts are bestowed with the authority to grant them. Despite this, collective reparations still pose tremendous challenges to international criminal law generally. Although this study is conducted from a human rights perspective, understanding the challenges that collective reparations pose for international criminal law will help to explain the ways in which the right to receive reparation through collective reparations is realised. Chapter VI provides a detailed discussion of these challenges.[97]

---

94 For the purposes of this study, the definition of transitional justice has been borrowed from Roht-Arriaza, who defines this field as a 'set of practices, mechanisms and concerns that arise following a period of conflict, civil strife or repression, and that are aimed directly at confronting and dealing with past violations of human rights and humanitarian law.' See: Roht-Arriaza, N. and Mariezcurrena, J., (eds.), *Transitional Justice in the Twenty-First Century: Beyond Truth Versus Justice* (Cambridge CUP 2006), p. 2. While transitional justice processes and human rights law sometimes share goals – for instance, a victim's right to justice or reparation – there is a difference between these two fields. Transitional justice mechanisms mainly allow for some trade-off between, *inter alia*, justice, accountability, and reconciliation. On the other hand, human rights law does not allow for a trade-off and seeks to bring accountability for past crimes and remedies for victims. Yet, under human rights law some limitation inherent in this field may not allow such justice to be rendered. For instance, jurisdictional limitations and the resources that victims need to bring a case before the courts.

95 American Convention on Human Rights, 22 November 1969, entered into force 18 July 1978.

96 Article 75, Rome Statute of the International Criminal Court, 17 July 1998, entered into force 1 July 2002 (ICC's Rome Statute); Rules 97-98, Rules of Procedure and Evidence of the International Criminal Court, 9 September 2002, UN Doc. ICC-ASP/1/3 (ICC's RoPE).

97 Although this study is conducted from a human rights perspective, understanding the challenges that collective reparations pose to international criminal law will help to explain the ways in which the right to receive reparation through collective reparations are realised. Chapter VI provides a detailed discussion of these challenges.

2.4 Central Research Question

Both the recognition and promotion of the right to reparation for victims and their relatives have acquired unprecedented importance in recent years. The adoption of the Principles on Reparations by the General Assembly in 2005 and the creation of a special rapporteur on the promotion of truth, justice, *reparation,* and guarantees of non-recurrence in situations in which gross violations of human rights occurred[98] represent developments that evidence this growing importance.

It is clear that the Principles on Reparations embrace the idea that victims of gross violations of human rights are entitled to reparations, and that these reparations include both individual and collective measures. While it is clear that both types of measures must form part of reparations, it remains unclear how these measures should be balanced. Moreover, it is questionable whether collective reparations *per se* can fulfil the state obligation to provide full reparation to individual victims.

At present, Mr. Pablo de Greiff, the first Rapporteur on the promotion of truth, justice, *reparation,* and guarantees of non-recurrence in situations in which gross violations of human rights have occurred,[99] has produced six reports. However, while these reports identify reparations as key elements when addressing gross violations, they provide no further clarification of what constitutes adequate reparation for these victims (an individual award, collective awards, or a combination of both) other than the need to take into account the contextual elements where the violations have taken place.[100]

The issue of reparations for victims of gross violations of human rights has been the subject of considerable academic study. The scholarship available has

98 [Emphasis added]. OHCHR, *Human Rights Council Establishes New Mandates on Promoting an Equitable International Order and on Truth, Justice and Reparation*, 29 September 2011, <www.ohchr.org/en/NewsEvents/Pages/DisplayNews.aspx?NewsID=11449&LangID=E>. Among his tasks, the Rapporteur is to undertake a study on the ways and means to implement measures of reparation, taking a victim-centred approach throughout the work.

99 See: OHCHR, *Special Rapporteur on the Promotion of Truth, Justice, Reparation and Guarantees of Non-recurrence*, <www.ohchr.org/EN/Issues/TruthJusticeReparation/Pages/Index.aspx>.

100 UNGA, *Report of the Special Rapporteur on the Promotion of Truth, Justice, Reparation and Guarantees of Non-recurrence, Pablo de Greiff*, 9 August 2012, UN Doc. A/HRC/21/46; UNGA, *Report of the Special Rapporteur on the Promotion of Truth, Justice, Reparation and Guarantees of Non-recurrence, Pablo de Greiff*, 28 August 2013, UN Doc. A/HRC/24/42; UNGA, *Report of the Special Rapporteur on the Promotion of Truth, Justice, Reparation and Guarantees of Non-recurrence (Mission to Spain), Pablo de Greiff*, 22 July 2014, UN Doc. A/HRC/27/56/Add.1; UNGA, *Report of the Special Rapporteur on the Promotion of Truth, Justice, Reparation and Guarantees of Non-recurrence, Pablo de Greiff*, 7 September 2015, UN Doc. A/HRC/30/42; UNGA, *Report of the Special Rapporteur on the Promotion of Truth, Justice, Reparation and Guarantees of Non-recurrence (Mission to the United Kingdom of Great Britain and Northern Ireland, Pablo de Greiff*, 17 November 2016, UN Doc. A/HRC/34/62/Add.1; UNGA, *Report of the Special Rapporteur on the promotion of truth, justice, reparation and guarantees of non-recurrence on his global study on transitional justice, Pablo de Greiff*, 7 August 2017, UN Doc. A/HRC/36/50/Add.1.

focused primarily on individual reparations and on highlighting the importance of the right of every victim to receive '*full reparation*', 'adequate reparation' or 'integral reparation'.[101] Similarly, scholars have contributed tremendously to the analysis of and a comparison between the different approaches of human rights supervisory bodies to reparations and national reparation programmes that address past legacies.[102] As such, these scholars have highlighted that collective reparations are a common response to those violations.[103] Academics have also discussed whether an individual right to reparation exists,[104] with some authors contesting the existence of this right,[105] whereas others support it.[106] In general, the use of reparations as a response to gross violations of human rights has been quite popular.[107]

---

101 Rose, C., "An Emerging Norm: The Duty of States to Provide Reparations for Human Rights Violations by Non-State Actors", 33 *Hastings International and Comparative Law Review* (2010); Rousset Siri, A.J., "El Concepto de Reparación Integral en la Jurisprudencia de la Corte Interamericana de Derechos Humanos", 1 *Revista Internacional de Derechos Humanos* (2011); Sikkink, K. et al. "Reparaciones Integrales en Colombia: Logros y Desafíos. Evaluación comparativa y global" *Harvard Kennedy School and Carr Center for Human Rights Policy* (2014).

102 Cassel, D., "The Expanding Scope and Impact of Reparations Awarded by the Inter-American Court of Human Rights" in K. de Feyter et al. (ed.), *Out of the Ashes: Reparations for Gross Violations of Human Rights* (Antwerp/Oxford, Intersentia 2006), p. 191-223; Rombouts, H. and Vandeginste, S., "Reparation for Victims in Rwanda: Caught between Theory and Practice" in K. de Feyter et al. (ed.), *Out of the Ashes: Reparations for Gross Violations of Human Rights* (Antwerp/Oxford, Intersentia 2006), p. 309-344; Rombouts, Sardaro and Vandeginste, *supra* n. 29, p. 354-455; Antkowiak, *supra* n. 28; Neuman, G., "Bi-Level Remedies for Human Rights Violations" 55 *Harvard International Law Journal*, (2014); de Greiff, P, (ed)., *The Handbook of Reparations* (Oxford, OUP, 2006); Evans, *supra* n. 72.

103 Contreras-Garduño, *supra* n. 46, p. 41.

104 Rosenfeld, *supra* n. 46, p. 731.

105 Letschert and van Boven, *supra* n. 8, p. 167, citing International Law Association, *Draft Declaration of International Law Principles on Reparation for Victims of Armed Conflict (Substantive Issues)*, Conference Report, 74th ILA Conference (15-20 August 2010), p. 2; Tomuschat, C., *Human Rights: Between Idealism and Realism* (Oxford, OUP 2008, 2nd ed.) p. 358-372; Tomuschat, *supra* n. 6, p. 579-589; Evans, *supra* n. 72, p. 40-41. Similarly Seibert-Fohr contests the existence of the right to reparations, See: Seibert-Fohr, A., *Prosecuting Serious Human Rights Violations* (Oxford, OUP 2009), p. 244.

106 Van Boven, T. "Victims' Rights to a Remedy and Reparation: The New United Nations Principles and Guidelines", in C. Ferstman, M. Goetz and A. Stephens (eds.), *Reparations for Victims of Genocide, War Crimes and Crimes Against Humanity: Systems in Place and Systems in the Making* (Leiden, Martinus Nijhoff 2009), p. 21; Zegveld, L., "Victims's Reparations Claims and International Criminal Courts: Incompatible Values?", 8 *Journal of International Criminal Justice*, (2010), p. 85; Buyse, A., "Lost and Regained? Restitution as a Remedy for Human Rights Violations in the Content of International Law", 68 *Heidelberg Journal of International Law* (2008), p. 134, citing M. Kamminga, "'Legal Consequences of an Internationally Wrongful Act of a State against an Individual'", in: M.L. van Emmerik, P. Hein van Kempen and T. Barkhuysen (eds.), *The Execution of Strasbourg and Geneva Human Rights Decisions in the National Legal Order* (The Hague: Martinus Publishers 1999), p. 65-74.

107 de Greiff, P. *supra* n. 102; Roht-Arriaza, *supra* n. 26, p. 157-219; Rombouts, Sardaro and Vandeginste, *supra* n. 29, p. 354-455.

Despite these valuable contributions, 'there is a lack of research on [...] how to deal with the challenges of providing reparation in cases of mass victimisation',[108] as the understanding of reparations for victims of large-scale crimes is still unclear. To date, the study of collective reparations has received little attention within legal scholarship.[109] In fact, the issue of collective reparations is more commonly addressed as a component within studies that address reparation issues in general.[110]

Almost no light has been shed on the legal framework, content, or scope of collective reparations; nor on the relationship between collective reparations and the individual right to reparations. In fact, to date it has only once been challenged whether collective awards can form part of a juridical approach.[111]

Legal research on how the individual right to reparation relates to and is compatible with collective reparations is absent in the current literature on reparations. Bearing in mind the existing legal framework on international human rights, are collective reparations in accordance with the individual and well-established right of every victim to receive reparation?

As noted above, awarding collective reparations has become a common response when providing justice to victims of violations on a large scale. Truth commissions, national reparation programmes, the IACtHR, the ECCC, and now the ICC, have all embraced this approach. Therefore, filling the gap between understanding the legal foundations, scope, and content that underline collective reparations and their use becomes a pressing issue in contemporary legal debate. If the international community could gain a better understanding of these reparations, this may pave the way for the development of guidelines on how to issue them. This research therefore seeks to answer the following question:

What are the tensions between the individual right to receive reparation, and awarding collective reparations for victims of gross violations of human rights?

---

108 Letschert, R., *Inaugural address: Tussen recht en realiteit: Duurzaam herstel na massavictimisatie* (Tilburg, Tilburg University Press 2012).

109 Rosenfeld, *supra* n. 46, p. 732.

110 Roht-Arriaza, *supra* n. 26, p. 181-198; UN Office of the High Commissioner for Human Rights (OHCHR), Rule of Law Tools for Post-Conflict States: Reparations Programmes (HR/PUB/08/1,2008), p. 25; Tomuschat, *supra* n. 6, p. 579-589; Rosenfeld, *supra* n. 46, p. 731; Mégret, F., 'The case for Collective Reparations before the International Criminal court' in J.A.M. Wemmers (ed.), *Reparations for Victims of Crimes Against Humanity: the Healing Role of Reparations* (New York, Routledge 2014); Aubry, S. and Henao-Trip, I. M., "Collective Reparations and the International Criminal Court", *Briefing Paper No.2, Reparations Unit, Essex University* (2011).

111 In *García Lucero et al.* v. *Chile*, the victims' representatives challenged the compatibility of the collective reparation programmes with the individual right to reparation. The Court, however, decided that it had no jurisdiction to analyse this argument in relation to the acts that gave rise to the reparation of the victims. See: IACtHR (Judgment) 28 August 2013, *García Lucero et al.* v. *Chile*, para. 165 and 190.

Answering this question may contribute to the field of international human rights law by enabling a better understanding of: i) reparations in international human rights law and their possible limitations; ii) the definition, content, and scope of collective reparations and their legal foundations under international human rights law; and iii) the tensions that collective reparations may present in light of the individual right to receive reparation.

2.5 Aims and Structure

The aims of this study are threefold. First, it seeks to describe and analyse the concept, content, and scope of collective reparations within the framework of international human rights law as developed by judicial and non-judicial bodies. Second, it compares the concept of collective reparations under human rights law with the concept, content, and scope of collective reparations as created by developments in international criminal law and transitional justice processes. Third, it attempts to evaluate the relationship and possible tensions between collective reparations and the individual human right to receive reparation.

Chapter I presents the central research question of this study and explains the rationale behind comparing collective reparations in three fields. It outlines that victims of gross violations of human rights have the possibility to obtain justice through: i) claims submitted before either of the international human rights tribunals; ii) claims submitted before international criminal tribunals; or iii) mechanisms of transitional justice. Studying collective reparations in these three different fields will therefore enable a more comprehensive understanding of the similarities and differences between such reparations, from the point of their establishment to their actual implementation.

Chapter II provides the reader with the background on the principal developments concerning the state duty to provide reparation under public international law and concerning the general developments behind the right to receive reparation under international human rights law. It also provides the background on how collective reparations were first granted.

Chapters III, IV, and V describe and analyse the elements of collective reparations in the three fields in which they have been awarded: international human rights law, international criminal law, and transitional justice. The three chapters also address the possible tensions between collective reparations and the individual right to receive reparation. This analysis is conducted using a victim-based approach; i.e. by bearing in mind a victim's human right to receive reparation.

Finally, Chapter VI outlines the principal findings of this study and concludes with observations on the concept of collective reparations, with consideration being given to the framework of international human rights law.

3 Key Concepts

While terms such as 'victims', 'gross violations of human rights', and 'reparations' have for a long time been part of the lexicon of lawyers, scholars, and practitioners, it is important to provide definitions of these terms as they are key elements of this research. This section provides such definitions, and highlights the lack of uniformity in the way in which the terminology is used in the available 'black-letter law' and the practice of diverse branches of public international law. This section therefore provides the necessary structure for an analysis of collective reparations, which the following chapters will undertake.

3.1 Victim

The legal definition of a victim is not 'entirely clear',[112] as at the international level there is no consensus on one single definition of this concept.[113] Instead, it is often acknowledged that this term is constantly evolving.[114] In fact, there are only a few documents that define the concept of a 'victim of crime'.[115] The first UN instrument that included a definition of a victim is the 1985 Declaration of Basic Principles of Justice for Victims of Crime and Abuse of Power (Victims' Declaration).[116] Principles 1, 2 and 18 of the Annex to the Declaration establish that victims are persons who either individually or collectively have suffered harm, including physical or mental injury, emotional suffering, economic loss or substantial impairment of their fundamental rights through acts or omissions that are in violation of national or international laws. It also includes 'the immediate family or dependants of the direct victim and persons who have suffered harm in intervening to assist victims in

---

112 Contreras-Garduño, D. and Fraser, J., "The Identification of Victims before the Inter-American Court of Human Rights and the International Criminal Court and its Impact on Participation and Reparation: a Domino Effect?", 7 *Inter-American and European Human Rights Journal* (2015), p. 174.

113 Ochoa, *supra* n. 19, p. 25.

114 IACtHR (Judgment) 1 July 2006, *Ituango Massacre* v. *Colombia*, Separate Opinion of Judge Cançado Trindade, para. 50.

115 Principles 1, 2 and 18 of the Annex to the Declaration, UNGA, *Declaration of Basic Principles of Justice for Victims of Crime and Abuse of Power*, 29 November 1985, UN Doc. A/RES/40/34, (Victims' Declaration); Principle 8, Principles on Reparations; Rule 85, ICC's RoPE; Rule 2 (A), Rules of Procedure and Evidence of the International Criminal Tribunal for the former Yugoslavia, UN Doc. IT/32/Rev.7 (1996); Article 2(25) and (33), Rules of Procedure of the Inter-American Court of Human Rights as approved by the Court during its LXXXV Regular Period of Sessions, held from November 16 to 28, 2009; Article 24, International Convention for the Protection of all Persons from Enforced Disappearance, 20 December 2006, entered into force 23 December 2010; Article 13, Convention Against Torture and Other Cruel, Inhuman or Degrading Treatment or Punishment, 10 December 1984, entered into force 26 June 1987.

116 Principles 1, 2 and 18 of the Annex to the Victims' Declaration.

distress or to prevent discrimination'.[117] Thus, the definition includes both direct and indirect victims, and makes clear that the status of a victim exists regardless of the identification, apprehension, prosecution, or conviction of the perpetrator.

This definition has been widely accepted. It was embraced by the 2005 Basic Principles, which mirrors it *verbatim* and does not add any other element to the definition.[118] In this context, the only difference between the Victims' Declaration and the Principles on Reparations is the substantive scope of each document: while the former focuses on victims of crime and abuse of power, the latter focuses on victims of gross violations of international human rights and serious violations of humanitarian law. Rule 85 of the Rules of Procedure and Evidence of the ICC (the ICC's RoPE) also mirrors this definition.[119] Rule 85 in fact extended the definition of a victim beyond natural persons. It dictates that legal persons, such as organisations or institutions dedicated to religion, education, art, science, charitable purposes, historic monuments, hospitals, and other places and objects for humanitarian purposes may also be considered as victims.[120]

For the purposes of this study, the definition of a victim is the one provided by the 1985 Victims' Declaration, and thus excludes legal persons. The rationale for this is that, at present, the collective reparations recommended and implemented for victims of gross violations of human rights in the context of transitional justice, international human rights law, and international criminal law do not include legal persons. In addition, the core query of this research lies in the relationship between collective reparations and the individual right of each victim to receive reparation. This right pertains to the field of international law, which up to the present has recognised this as a right of only natural persons.

Therefore, the definition of a victim that this study will utilise is the following: 'any natural person who, individually or collectively and directly or indirectly, has suffered harm, including physical or mental injury, emotional suffering, economic loss or substantial impairment of their fundamental rights, through acts or omissions that are considered violations of international law'.

3.2 Gross Violations of Human Rights

Within the UN lexicon, both states and international human rights bodies have made a distinction between human rights violations based on the gravity of a violation.

117 Principles 1, 2 and 18 of the Annex to the Victims' Declaration.
118 Principles 8 and 9, Principles on Reparations.
119 Rule 85, ICC's RoPE.
120 Rule 85(b), ICC's RoPE.

This distinction characterises some human rights violations as 'serious',[121] 'gross',[122] 'flagrant',[123] 'egregious',[124] 'systematic',[125] 'grave',[126] or 'widespread'.[127] Despite the numerous references to this distinction, to date there is no unanimous agreement on the content of these violations.[128] The adjectives are used interchangeably, seemingly as synonyms.[129] This research will refer to 'gross' and 'grave' violations of human rights (GVHR) indistinctively, because this was the first adjective used by a human rights body to distinguish certain human rights violations from others.[130]

GVHR have been defined by Shelton as human rights violations that are particularly serious because of their cruelty (qualitative) and their widespread pattern (quantitative).[131] Some international human rights bodies and scholars have recognised certain crimes as those that amount to gross violations of human rights. For instance, the Human Rights Committee has been prominent in stressing that unlawful disappearances and unlawful detentions amount to GVHR.[132] Within this list Karimova also includes the excessive use of force by police forces; forced displacement; indiscriminate attacks in situations of armed conflict; rape and other sexual violence; torture and other cruel, inhuman, or degrading treatment; indiscriminate attacks in situations of armed conflict; extrajudicial executions and massacres; apartheid; and property rights violations, as acts that many human rights

121 UN General Assembly, *Towards an Arms Trade Treaty: Establishing Common International Standards for the Import, Export and Transfer of Conventional Arms: Report of the Secretary-General*, 17 August 2007, UN Doc. A/62/278, p. 24.

122 United States Foreign Assistance Act of 1961, s. 116; UN General Assembly, *supra* n. 24.

123 UN Security Council, *Resolution 171: The Palestine Question*, 9 April 1962, UN Doc. S/RES/171 (1962).

124 UN Office of the High Commissioner, *Born Free and Equal: Sexual Orientation and Gender Identity in International Human Rights Law* (New York/Geneva, UN 2012).

125 UN General Assembly, *Human Rights Council: Resolution*, 3 April 2006, UN Doc. A/RES/60/251.

126 Human Rights Council, *Situation of Human Rights in the Democratic People's Republic of Korea*, 9 April 2013, UN Doc. A/HRC/RES/22/13.

127 Ibid.

128 Rubio-Marin, Sandoval and Díaz, *supra* n. 3, p. 218.

129 Murray, R., "Serious or Massive Violations under the African Charter on Human and People's Rights: A Comparison with the Inter-American and European Mechanisms", 17 *Netherlands Quarterly of Human Rights* (1999), p. 110-111; Karimova, T., "What Amounts to 'a Serious Violation of International Human Rights Law'? An Analysis of Practice and Expert Opinion for the Purpose of the 2013 Arms Trade Treaty", *Geneva Academy of International Humanitarian Law and Human Rights, Briefing No. 6* (2014), p. 5-6.

130 The document explicitly refers 'to gross violations of human rights and fundamental freedoms', See: Economic and Social Council, *Resolution 1235 (XLII)*, UN Doc. E/4393 (1967), 6 June 1967.

131 Shelton, *supra* n. 33, p. 120-121.

132 Human Rights Committee, *Comments on Argentina*, UN Doc. CCPR/C/79/Add.46 (1995), para. 10.

bodies characterise as gross.[133] Theo van Boven, the former Special Rapporteur on the Right to Reparation for Victims of Gross Violations of Human Rights, also stated that genocide, slavery, slavery-like practices, and systematic discrimination, in particular based on race or gender, can also amount to GVHR.[134] Similarly Ochoa submits that gross violations of human rights include 'summary or arbitrary executions; torture and cruel, inhuman or degrading treatment or punishment; slavery and forced labour; enforced disappearance; and arbitrary and prolonged detention'.[135]

In addition, the Draft Declaration on the Recognition of Gross and Massive Violations of Human Rights states that gross violations of human rights principally include:

> (a) Murder, including extrajudicial, arbitrary and summary executions; (b) Torture; (c) Genocide; (d) Apartheid; (e) Discrimination on racial, national, ethnic, linguistic or religious grounds; (f) Establishing or maintaining over persons the status of slavery, servitude or forced labour; (g) Enforced or involuntary disappearances; (h) Arbitrary and prolonged detention; (i) Deportation or the forcible transfer of a population.[136]

Interestingly, most of the crimes that amount to gross violations (as identified by several international human rights bodies) also amount to an international crime, namely a crime against humanity as defined by the Rome Statute of the International Criminal Court (Rome Statute).[137] It is important to highlight that gross violations of human rights and crimes against humanity also share some key elements, namely that they are committed either systematically or are widespread.[138] Therefore, for the purposes of this study gross violations of human rights are those that fall under the definition of crimes against humanity, as defined by the Rome Statute:

> For the purpose of this Statute, 'crime against humanity' means any of the following acts *when committed as part of a widespread or systematic attack* directed against any civilian population, with knowledge of the attack: (a) Murder; (b) Extermination; (c) Enslavement; (d) Deportation or forcible transfer of population; (e) [unlawful deprivation of liberty];

---

133 Karimova refers to serious instead of gross violations of human rights law. See: Karimova, *supra* n. 129, p. 5; Cherchernichenco, S., Recognition *of Gross and Massive Violations of Human Rights Perpetrated on the Orders of Governments or Sanctioned by them as an International Crime*, 28 May 1997, Expanded Working Paper, UN Doc. E/CN.4/Sub.2/1997/29, p. 32.

134 Sub-Commission on the Promotion and Protection of Human Rights, *supra* n. 7, para. 137(1).

135 Ochoa, *supra* n. 19, p. 23.

136 Article 1 of the Draft Declaration on the Recognition of Gross and Massive Violations of Human Rights Perpetrated on the Orders of Governments or Sanctioned by them as an International Crime, Annex to Cherchernichenco, *supra* n. 133.

137 Cherchernichenco, *supra* n. 133, p. 32.

138 Medina Quiroga, C., *The Battle of Human Rights: Gross, Systematic Violations and the Inter-American System* (Dordrecht, Martinus Nijhoff 1998), p. 7-16. See: definition of Crimes against humanity in Article 7, ICC's Rome Statute.

> (f) Torture; (g) Rape, sexual slavery, enforced prostitution, forced pregnancy, enforced sterilization, or any other form of sexual violence of comparable gravity; (h) Persecution against any identifiable group or collectivity on political, racial, national, ethnic, cultural, religious, gender [...]; (i) Enforced disappearance of persons; (j) The crime of apartheid; (k) Other inhumane acts of a similar [gravity causing great mental or physical harm].[139]

Finally, it should be noted that the content of GVHR is not restricted to violations of civil and political rights as it can also cover socio-economic and cultural rights violations.[140] As such, the 1993 Vienna Declaration and Programme of Action includes in its definition of GVHR 'poverty, hunger and other denials of economic, social and cultural rights'.[141] Further, a few international judicial and non-judicial bodies have also accepted the inclusion of violations of socio-economic and cultural rights in the concept of GVHR.[142] However, such violations are excluded from the scope of this present study.

3.3 Collective Reparations

Despite the repetitive use of the term 'collective reparations' by national and international judicial and non-judicial bodies,[143] there is no single agreement on the meaning of this term. Within legal scholarship, only a few works have attempted to describe or define criteria for this term.[144] For instance, Friedrich Rosenfeld defines collective reparations as the following:

> [c]ollective reparations [are] the benefits conferred on collectives in order to [alleviate] the collective harm that has been caused as a consequence of a violation of international law.[145]

139 Article 7(1)(k), ICC's Rome Statute [emphasis added].

140 Liwanga, R.C., "The Meaning of "Gross Violation" of Human Rights: A Focus on International Tribunals' Decisions over the DRC Conflicts", 44 *Denver Journal of International Law & Policy* (2015), p. 71.

141 U.N. World Conference on Human Rights, Vienna Declaration and Programme of Action, U.N. Doc. A/CONF.157/23, 25 June 1993, para. 30

142 The ICJ referred to the destruction of civilian houses as a massive violation of human rights. See: ICJ, *Armed Activities in the Territory of the Congo (DRC* v. *Uganda)*, para. 208. Likewise, the African Commission on Human and Peoples' Rights (ACmHPR or African Commission) has contended that the destruction of property may amount to GVHR. See: Sudan ACmHPR (Decision) 27 May 2009, *Human Rights Organization and Centre on Housing Rights and Evictions* v. *Sudan,* Communication 279/03-296/05, para. 102. The African Commission has also found violations of the right to education, health, and safe drinking water to amount to GVHR. See: ACmHPR (Decision) 26 March-4 April 1996, *World Organization against Torture, Lawyers' Committee for Human Rights, Jehovah Witnesses, Inter-African Union for Human Rights* v. *Zaire*, Communication 25/89, 47/90, 56/91, 100/93, para. 47-48.

143 Bassiouni, *supra* n. 69, p. 203.

144 Rosenfeld, *supra* n. 46; Aubry and Henao-Trip, *supra* n. 110.

145 Rosenfeld, *supra* n. 46, p. 732. Rosenfeld talks about undoing harm; I have changed this into alleviating harm since it has been argued that human rights violations cannot be undone.

Other scholars have classified three categories of collective reparation measures. The first category is defined according to the right that is violated, the second category is defined according to the beneficiary, and the third category is defined according to the type of award afforded. Therefore, according to this tripartite classification scheme, collective reparations have the following characteristics: i) they are awarded for a violation of collective rights or a violation of rights that impact communities, ii) the beneficiary is a group, and iii) they are awarded when the type of benefit cannot be divided amongst individuals (for example, an apology or the construction of a school).[146]

Thus, for the purposes of this research, collective reparations are primarily defined by taking into account both of the scholarly definitions elaborated above. Collective reparations are: i) measures or benefits that are indivisible and diverse; ii) which are awarded to collectives or groups of people,[147] iii) in order to alleviate the collective harm that has been caused as a consequence of a violation of international law, iv) of either individual or collective rights. These benefits are commonly framed as political projects (social programmes) and have the potential to transform the social conditions of victims as well as to prevent further victimisation through collective violence or conflict.

3.4 Transitional Justice

TJ refers to a temporary and exceptional form of material and symbolic justice, targeted at responding to past GVHR and helping societies to come to terms with the legacies of past abuses, and to move towards a more democratic society.[148]

4 Research Methodology and Limitations

This section addresses the methodology utilised in this work, which is explained in relation to each of the six chapters. It also addresses some important limitations which have been applied in conducting this research.

---

146 Aubry and Henao-Trip, *supra* n. 110, p. 2-3.

147 For the purposes of this research, the terms 'collectives' and 'groups' of people are used as synonyms. However, when referring to indigenous peoples, I will explicitly refer to a group of people but not to collectives. The reason for this is that indigenous peoples are specifically recognized as a group of people under international law.

148 Wolfe, *supra* n. 4, p. 39; García-Godos, *supra* n. 19, p. 111; R. Teitel, *supra* n. 41, p. 4-5.

4.1 Defining the Methodology

First of all, a solely legal methodology has been applied to this research, which was conducted from an outside perspective.[149] The reason for this is twofold: i) the present research seeks to answer a normative query, and ii) a legal approach is necessary in order to answer such a query.[150] Consequently, this research is restricted to a traditional legal approach that relies predominantly on the argumentation techniques and interpretation of existing legal sources,[151] as well as on descriptive and analytical techniques; two common methods of social sciences, including legal scholarship.[152]

The research also takes the form of both pure and applied doctrinal legal research. It focuses on the nature of collective reparations as well as the study of diverse sources of law, or 'black-letter law' (conventional treatises, doctrine, and jurisprudence). This is coupled with the main objective to produce findings that could be useful for the current legal professional needs of practitioners and society as a whole, with a focus on victims.[153] From a doctrinal stance, the findings of this research aim to contribute to a better understanding of collective reparations, which in turn has a practical benefit in that the possible use of those findings could clarify what victims of international crimes and GVHR can expect to obtain from reparations. The findings could also help clarify the way in which claims for collective reparations are framed, and their subsequent implementation within international criminal and human rights law.

This pure and applied doctrinal legal research will apply deductive and analytical methods as well as analogical reasoning when interpreting diverse sources of law. The legal sources under scrutiny correspond to those enumerated in Article 38 of the Statute of the International Court of Justice, and the same hierarchy is applied.[154] The research has examined primarily binding documents ('hard law') such as international treaties, court judgments, and the rules of procedure and evidence of courts. In addition, non-binding documents ('soft law') such as declarations, reports from commissions, international customs, general principles of law, and academic writings have also been examined and scrutinised. The analysis of 'hard' and 'soft' law documents is conducted in strict compliance with the rules of treaty

149 Curry-Sumner, I. et al., *Research Skills: Instruction for Lawyers* (Nijmegen, Ars Aequi Libri 2010), p. 4.

150 Smits, J.M., "Redefining Normative Legal Science: Towards an Argumentative Discipline" in F. Coomans, F. Grunfeld and M. Kamminga (eds.), *Methods of Human Rights Research* (Antwerp/Oxford, Intersentia 2009), p. 46-47.

151 Ibid.

152 Rubin, E.L., "The Practice and Discourse of Legal Scholarship", 86 *Michigan Law Review* (1988), p. 1848.

153 Chynoweth, P. , "Chapter Three: Legal Research", in A. Knight and L. Ruddock (eds.), *Advanced Research Methods in the Built Environment, Technology & Engineering* (Oxford, Wiley-Blackwell 2009), p. 29.

154 Article 38, ICJ's Statute.

interpretation stipulated in Articles 31 and 32 of the Vienna Convention on the Law of the Treaties.[155]

Having established the normative nature and general characteristics of this research, the following sections will outline how these methods are applied in each of the six chapters. Chapter I sets the stage for the central normative query through the description of a legal problem: the potential conflict between an existing right and its realisation. Namely, this is the possible tension that arises between the individual right to receive reparation and the relationship between this individual right and collective reparations. Chapter II describes and analyses the general elements of reparations and charts their development into both an individual right and a state obligation that arises from the commission of an internationally wrongful act. It also briefly introduces the position of collective measures of reparation within the fields of public international law and international human rights law.

Chapters III, IV, and V form the core of the research, each analysing collective reparations within three fields: international human rights law, international criminal law, and transitional justice, respectively. The three chapters employ descriptive, comparative, and analytical methods. They aim to describe the elements of collective reparations, analyse the possible tensions between collective reparations and the individual right to receive reparation, and assess the challenges encountered in the implementation of collective reparations. All three chapters analyse the issue of collective reparations from a human rights perspective, as the individual right to receive reparation is a well-recognised human right.

Chapter VI represents the final chapter. It collects and analyses the conclusions of the main substantive chapters (III, IV, and V) and provides general conclusions and recommendations. It addresses the central research question and proposes a definition of the scope and content of collective reparations.

4.2 Delimiting the Scope of the Research

The scope of this study has been necessarily limited. Namely, it covers only the right to reparations of one category of victims of human rights violations: victims of gross violations of human rights. The rationale of this choice lies in the fact that gross violations of human rights can be addressed in three distinct, yet overlapping fields: international human rights law, international criminal law, and transitional justice. Thus, a victim's right to reparation could in principle be realised in each of these three fields. The entire study is conducted through a human rights lens. However, it also takes into consideration international criminal law and transitional justice, insofar as these two fields deal with collective reparations. Despite there being three fields, each

155 Articles 31 and 32, Vienna Convention on the Law of Treaties.

with a different scope, international human rights law, international criminal law and transitional justice mechanisms still overlap.[156]

Reparation can be granted on an individual or collective basis, and may take different forms: restitution, compensation, satisfaction, rehabilitation, and guarantees of non-repetition. This study will only focus on cases related to gross violations of human rights. It will therefore compare and analyse the cases in which *only* collective reparations have been awarded with cases in which *both* collective *and* individual reparations have been awarded. The main reason underlying this choice is to fill the gap between the lack of literature on collective reparations, and the increasing use of collective reparations by judicial and non-judicial bodies in the context of gross violations of human rights.

According to some scholars, for instance Uprimny and Freeman, awarding reparation on an individual basis for victims of gross violations of human rights – a term that usually implies a large number of victims – presents problems of distributive and social justice in society. Uprimmy and Freeman advocate collective awards on the grounds of, among others, their compatibility with fair wealth distribution and social justice.[157] However, this research does not include a study of collective reparations and their relationship with distributive justice, nor does it offer a study on the position of these awards in different theories of justice. The rationale behind this omission is to limit the length of this study, also considering the time frame within which PhD trajectories are conducted. However, it is also important to note that this research does not aim to analyse whether collective reparations fit within a particular theory of justice. Instead, this study aims to discuss a legal definition of collective

156 The three different fields address gross violations of human rights. In fact, ICL protects human rights violations, but only those considered gross and that amount international crimes. In this light, international human rights law and international criminal law overlap. See: Margueritte, T., "International criminal law and human rights", in W. Schabas and N. Bernaz, *Routledge Handbook of International Criminal Law* (Abingdon, Routledge 2011), p. 436-437. Finally, mechanisms of transitional justice have not only sought to address gross violations of human rights, and reparations have become a crucial feature of transitional justice in addressing past violations. See: Dudai, R., "Closing the gap: symbolic reparations and armed groups", 93 *International Review of the Red Cross* (2011), p. 5-7.

157 Freeman, *supra* n. 38, p. 29-52; Uprimny in particular points out that collective reparations that are composed of social services allow societies in transition (that is societies facing limited resources and institutional capacity) to maximise their resources in a fair manner. In addition, he points out that the legal approach to reparations – achieving *restitutio in integrum* – might allow for secondary victimisation. For a victim who was already poor and marginalised before a violation took place, a legal approach to reparation means that the purpose would be to erase the violation while putting him/her back in the same conditions of poverty and marginalisation. Instead, Uprimny offers a forward-looking approach: transformative reparations that are collective reparations grounded on providing direct benefits to the victims through social services. Uprimny, M.R., "Between Corrective and Distributive Justice: Reparations of Gross Human Rights Violations in Times of Transition", 25 *Netherlands Quarterly of Human Rights* (2009).

reparations based on how these reparations have evolved and been framed within the three chosen fields.

This research adopts a legal approach. Accordingly, and without dismissing the importance of interdisciplinary approaches to victims' rights, it does not include an empirical analysis of the relationship between collective reparations and the needs of victims of gross violations of human rights. Nor does the research attempt to analyse whether victims' hopes, expectations, and satisfaction are obtained through such reparations.

Chapter I is the introductory chapter. Not only does it provide the background of the core research question of this study, but it also sets out the key concepts that underline the entire research. These key concepts provide definitions of the relevant terminology, such as a 'victim', 'gross violations of human rights', and 'collective reparations'. Chapter I also justifies the rationale for comparing collective reparations in three fields of scholarship without looking at the particular nature of each field. It therefore analyses collective reparations only through the lens of international human rights law. As such, it does not explore whether collective reparations are more or less appropriate depending on whether it is the state or individual that is held responsible.

Chapter II provides the reader with the necessary background to understand the principal developments in providing reparation as a state duty and as a human right. The content of Chapter II is therefore limited to the law of state responsibility and the landmark jurisprudence of the International Court of Justice (ICJ) regarding reparations, as well as the landmark case law of the main regional human rights courts: the Inter-American Court of Human Rights (IACtHR) and the European Court of Human Rights (ECtHR). Some references to the jurisprudence of the African Court of Human and Peoples' Rights (ACtHPR) and to the recommendations and concluding observations of treaty bodies are also made. It is important to highlight that the Chapter does not intend to provide an exhaustive analysis of all of the case law of the ICJ, the IACtHR and the ECtHR but rather to provide a general background. In light of this, the case law mentioned has been found through secondary sources (e.g. academic books and articles). Further, this Chapter in relation to the developments in public international law only focuses on the ICJ's jurisprudence. Hence, contrary to other academic works, it does not explore the jurisprudential developments of the international arbitration courts.[158] The reason for this omission lies in the fact that both the European and Inter-American human rights courts have, in several cases, referred to the rulings of the International Court of Justice when awarding measures of reparation.

The focus of Chapter III rests on collective reparations within the context of international human rights law, and it centres its study on the Inter-American Court

158 For instance, the Permanent Court of Arbitration, the London Court of International Arbitration, or the International Chamber of Commerce.

of Human Rights. The reason for this is that this Court was, and still remains, the only court that has allowed the concept of collective reparations to migrate from a transitional justice process to a legal approach. Therefore, Chapter III will study the jurisprudence of the IACtHR related to collective reparations granted to victims of gross violations of human rights. To this end, 39 cases have been selected from the entire IACtHR case law (from its first judgment in 1988 up until December 2017). Neither the ECtHR nor the ACtHPR has ever granted collective reparations when addressing gross violations of human rights. In addition, the ICC and the ECCC when awarding reparations, including collective measures, have extensively cited the IACtHR's jurisprudence.[159] Thus, a critical assessment of the IACtHR's understanding of collective reparations is essential. Although both the Inter-American Commission on Human Rights (IACommHR) and the African Commission on Human and Peoples' Rights (ACmHPR) have previously granted collective reparations, these cases will not be analysed in detail due to time constraints. However, when relevant, the study may refer to such jurisprudence.

Chapter IV studies collective reparations in the context of international criminal law. Among the different existing international(ised) criminal tribunals, only two are bestowed with the mandate to award reparations to the victims at the expense of the person convicted of the crime, namely the ICC and ECCC. In addition, both of these courts may grant collective reparations. While both of these courts are allowed to grant collective reparations to the victims of crimes under their respective jurisdictions, the ICC is the only court that provides for a subsidiary/complementary venue for victims to seek reparations: the Trust Fund.[160] In this light, the Chapter focuses specifically on the case law of the International Criminal Court, in particular the cases of *Lubanga*[161] and *Katanga*,[162] which at present constitute two of the three cases in which this Court has reached a judgment on reparations (while the former is final, the latter is pending an appeal), and in which the ICC activated its reparation mandate. The reason for not including the third case (*Al Mahdi* case) in which the ICC has made an order for reparations is because this case deals with crimes against

---

159 McKay, *supra* n. 14, p. 937; ICC (Judgment) *Prosecutor* v. *Lubanga*, Judgment on the appeals against the "Decision establishing the principles and procedures to be applied to reparations" of 7 August 2012, ICC-01/04-01/06-3129, 3 March 2015, para. 166; ICC (Order) *Prosecutor* v. *Katanga*, Ordonnance de réparation en vertu de l'article 75 du Statut, ICC-01/04-01/07-3728, 24 March 2017, para. 57; ECCC (Judgment) *Prosecutor* v. *Kaing Guek Eav* alias '*Duch*', (Case 001), No. 001/18-07-2007-ECCC/SC, 3 February 2012, para. 683, 700-703, 1323.

160 Articles 75(2), 79, ICC's Rome Statute; Rule 79, ICC's RoPE.

161 ICC (Decision) *Prosecutor* v. *Lubanga*, Decision establishing the principles and procedures to be applied to reparations, ICC-01/04-01/06-2904, 7 August 2012, para.177; ICC (Judgment) *Prosecutor* v. *Lubanga*, Judgment on the appeals against the "Decision establishing the principles and procedures to be applied to reparations" of 7 August 2012, ICC-01/04-01/06-3129, 3 March 2015.

162 ICC (Trial Chamber II Order) *Prosecutor* v. *Katanga*, Ordonnance de réparation en vertu de l'article 75 du Statut, ICC-01/04-01/07-3728, 24 March 2017.

cultural properties in Timbuktu, a crime that does not fall within the concept of GVHR.[163] The Chapter also focuses on the case law of the Extraordinary Chambers in the Courts of Cambodia (ECCC), in particular the *Duch* case and the *Nuon Chea and Khieu Samphan* case, which at present also constitute the two cases in which the ECCC has reached a judgment on reparations.

In its two first judgments on reparations, the ICC ordered collective reparations. Unlike the *Lubanga* case, in the *Katanga* case the ICC also ordered individual reparations along with collective measures. Unlike the ICC, the ECCC's remedial power is limited to moral and collective reparations. Interestingly, the ECCC's interpretation of collective reparations in the *Duch* case was very restrictive so as to exclude any service-based collective measure as part of its mandate.[164] Yet its approached was more open in the *Nuon Chea and Khieu Samphan* case and it did include social services, especially regarding the physical and psychological rehabilitation of victims.[165]

Chapter V focuses on collective reparations granted by non-judicial bodies, mechanisms other than those that fall under international human rights and international criminal law: it explores collective reparations awarded or recommended by transitional justice mechanisms. Under the auspices of transitional justice, collective reparations have been established as national programmes based upon either: i) an agreement borne out of both political will and civil society demands for a responsive justice to victims of gross human rights abuses; or ii) the recommendations of truth commissions. Due to time constraints, this Chapter will mainly explore the collective reparations recommended by two truth commissions – the Moroccan and the Peruvian. The reason for this choice is that of all the collective reparations that have been recommended by truth commissions, only a few have been implemented

163 ICC (Decision) *The Prosecutor v. Ahmad Al Faqi Al Mahdi*, Reparations Order, ICC-01/12-01/15, 17 August 2017, para. 1.

164 Initially, Rule 23 *quinquies* of the ECCC's International Rules as adopted on 7 June 2007 listed examples of collective and moral reparations: 'a) An order to publish the judgment in any appropriate news or other media at the convicted person's expense; b) An order to fund any non-profit activity or service that is intended for the benefit of Victims; or c) Other appropriate and comparable forms of reparation.' However, the ECCC's first judgment on reparations in the *Duch* case dismissed the claims of the civil parties related to different services and only granted: i) including the names of all civil parties and their relatives in the judgment, and ii) the dissemination of the statements of apology made by the defendant throughout the trial. ECCC (Judgment) *Prosecutor* v. *Kaing Guek Eav* alias '*Duch*' (Case 001), No. 001/18-07-2007-ECCC/TC, 26 July 2010; and ECCC (Judgment) *Prosecutor* v. *Kaing Guek Eav* alias '*Duch*', (Case 001), No. 001/18-07-2007-ECCC/SC, 13 February 2012.

165 Yet the reparation programmes awarded in these cases were not ordered to be borne by the persons convicted. See: ECCC (Judgment) *Prosecutor* v. *Nuon Chea and Khieu Samphan* (Case 002/01), No.002/19-09-2007-ECCC/TC, 7 August 2014.

by their governments. The reparations recommended by the Moroccan and Peruvian TRCs are the most developed in their implementation at the time of writing.[166]

In addition, this Chapter will briefly refer to two mass claims processes, namely the United Nations Compensation Commission (UNCC) and the Eritrea-Ethiopia Claims Commission (EECC). Although these commissions firstly deal with victims of humanitarian law violations and the use of force, their inclusion is justified by the similarities in the methodologies used also by TRCs regarding the procedural aspects of mass awards.[167] Secondly, despite the fact that mass claims processes are usually analysed under the umbrella of international law, both the UNCC and the EECC were administrated by non-judicial bodies. In addition, de Greiff has submitted that mass claims processes present more fairness concerning reparations than courts. In this light, it is deemed important to explore the way they deal with reparations.[168] Finally, in a discussion paper written by the Cambodian Human Rights Action Committee (CHRAC) and REDRESS it has been acknowledged that administrative processes to address gross violations of human rights are Truth and Reconciliation Commissions, Compensation Commissions, Special governmental directives (programmes, services), and symbolic governmental acts (monuments).[169] Accordingly, analysing compensation commissions and national programmes stemming from TRCs or political agreements seems justified.

---

166 Suchova, M., "The importance of a Participatory Reparations Process and Its Relationship to the Principles of Reparations", *Briefing Paper No. 5, Reparations Unit, Essex University* (2011), p. 13; Díaz Gómez, C., "Elementos para un programa administrativa de reparaciones colectivas en Colombia" in C. Díaz Gómez (ed.), *Tareas Pendientes: Propuestas para la formulación de políticas públicas de la reparación en Colombia* (Bogotá, ICTJ 2010), p. 287. See also: ICC (Filing) *Prosecutor* v. *Lubanga*, Filing on Reparations and Draft Implementation Plan, ICC-01/04-01/06-3177, 3 November 2015, para. 172.

167 Carrillo, A. J. and Palmer, J. S., "Transnational Mass Claim Processes (TMCPs) in International Law and Practice", 28 *Berkeley Journal of International Law* (2010), p. 415-419. However, Carrillo and Palmer also point out several differences among TRCs and mass claim processes such as the funding and the adversarial nature of the latter.

168 de Greiff, *supra* n. 26, p. 459.

169 CHRAC and REDRESS, Considering Reparations for Victims of the Khmer Rouge Regime: A Discussion Paper, November 2009, p. 6.

Chapter II
Developments Concerning the Right to Reparation

1 Introduction

Reparations play an important role in upholding the rule of law, restoring equality, and providing remedial justice to those harmed as a result of a breach of an international obligation.[1] The essential role and importance of reparations within any legal system is perhaps best described by Justice Guha Roy: '[t]hat a wrong done to an individual must be redressed by the offender himself or by someone else against whom the sanction of the community may be directed is one of those timeless axioms of justice *without which social life is unthinkable*'.[2] Although the idea that the consequences of a wrongdoing should be adequately redressed was first established under domestic jurisdiction, the international legal framework has extensively developed the content and scope of redressing wrongful acts.[3] Primarily, the laws of state responsibility,[4] as interpreted and developed by the International Court of Justice (ICJ)[5] that is the 'supreme public international law tribunal',[6] have played a major role in shaping the content of reparations. The laws of state responsibility codified the most common forms of reparation used under international law during the last 200 years.[7] In addition to the ICJ's key role in the creation and interpretation of international law in general,

---

1 Shelton, D., *Remedies in International Human Rights Law* (Oxford, OUP 2015, 3rd ed.), p. 30-31, 38; Shelton, D., "Reparations for Indigenous Peoples: The Present Value of Past Wrongs", in F. Lenzerini (ed.), *Reparations for Indigenous Peoples: International and Comparative Perspectives* (Oxford, OUP 2008), p. 60.

2 Guha-Roy, S.N., "Is the law of responsibilities of states for injuries to aliens a part of a universal international law?", 55 *The American Journal of International Law* (1961), p. 863 (emphasis added).

3 Wolfe, S., *The Politics of Reparations and Apologies* (New York, Springer 2014), p. 285.

4 The codification of the Articles on State Responsibility reinforced the existing law on remedies and has become the major tool for establishing reparations. See: Shelton, *Remedies in International Human Rights Law, supra* n. 1, p. 37; Babu, R., *Remedies Under the WTO Legal System* (Leiden/Boston, Martinus Nijhoff 2012), p. 60-61.

5 Although the ICJ has not been very vocal in elaborating upon issues concerning reparations, the principles established through its jurisprudence have been embraced by many international courts. See: Gray, C., "Remedies", in C. Romano, K. Alter and Y. Shany (eds.), *The Oxford Handbook of International Adjudication* (Oxford, OUP 2015), p. 875.

6 Mendelson, M., "The International Court of Justice and sources of international law" in V. Lowe and M. Fitzmaurice (eds.), *Fifty Years of the International Court of Justice: Essays in honour of Sir Robert Jennings* (Cambridge, CUP 1996), p. 83.

7 Brown, C., *A Common Law of International Adjudication* (Oxford, OUP 2007), p. 186, 192.

international human rights law[8] has significantly influenced the international legal framework governing reparations.[9]

This chapter provides an overview of the main characteristics of reparations and their development as both a state obligation stemming from internationally wrongful acts and as an individual human right. The chapter opens with a brief explanation of how reparations form one of the two elements of the right to a remedy within the framework of both public international law and international human rights law. It continues with a discussion on the most important developments of the law and practice that underpin reparations in public international law. In particular, it focuses on the law of state responsibility and the landmark cases related to reparations from the International Court of Justice.[10] The chapter also takes a human rights perspective to discuss the most relevant law on and the practice of awarding reparations. In doing so, it focuses primarily on the jurisprudence of the two main regional judicial bodies: the Inter-American Court of Human Rights and the European Court of Human Rights.[11] These two courts have each produced a vast body of case law on remedies and reparations.[12] Finally, it addresses the current trend of judicial bodies at the international level to award collective reparations in cases of gross violations of human rights.

It is important to emphasise that this chapter does not examine all of the jurisprudence on contentious cases produced by the ICJ and the aforementioned regional human rights courts. Since the primary aim of the chapter is to provide a general overview of the main developments regarding reparations, it only focuses on landmark cases obtained from secondary sources.

---

8 Evans, C., *The Right to Reparation in International Law for Victims of Armed Conflict* (Cambridge, CUP 2012), p. 125-127.

9 In addition, Gray has noted that there is a blossoming jurisprudence on reparations in the field of public international law developed by other international judicial arbitral tribunals but that in general it is difficult to draw a set of coherent rules which are applicable to reparations. In light of this, I have chosen to only look at the word court and the ILC's Articles on State Responsibility (hereinafter ILC's ASR). See: Gray, *supra* n. 5, p. 871. Developments under international humanitarian law and international criminal law have also influenced the international legal framework on reparations. See: Evans, *supra* n. 8, p. 125-128.

10 As explained in Chapter I, the analysis in Chapter II will not address the jurisprudence of international arbitration courts and tribunals, nor will it look at the conclusions of the United Nations Compensation Commissions.

11 The research conducted on jurisprudence consists of all of the judgments of the IACtHR up until 2014 and relevant landmark cases from the ECtHR.

12 Shelton, *Remedies in International Human Rights Law, supra* n. 1, p. 146-152. When relevant, some references to the developments concerning the right to reparation within the framework of the African Commission on Peoples' and Human Rights and UN supervisory treaty bodies are made.

1.1 Right to a Remedy

The concept of *ubi jus ibi remedium* (there is no right without a remedy) means that a right can only protect a person insofar as that person has access to a remedy following a violation of that right.[13] It is part of the classical liberal theory of justice,[14] and the concept is central to most legal systems around the world.[15] There are many interpretations of what a 'remedy' exactly entails, but it is commonly understood to be a 'range of measures that may be taken in response to an actual or threatened violation'[16] in order to compensate or redress it.[17]

In general, remedies are composed of two elements: one procedural and one substantive. Under public international law, the procedural element refers to the avenues by which claims concerning a breach of an international obligation may be brought. This may include, for instance, proceedings before the International Court of Justice or the International Court of Arbitration. The substantive element refers to the measures available to the injured party, i.e. measures of reparation.[18] Under public international law, the measures available are restitution, compensation and satisfaction, and they can be afforded either singularly or in combination.[19]

Within the context of the law on state responsibility, states bear the obligation vis-à-vis other states to provide remedies, including full reparation for the infringement of an international obligation.[20] As a consequence of the development of international human rights law, this obligation has been extended vis-à-vis individuals. In fact, under international human rights law, the right to a remedy is crucial for victims to realise justice.[21] Furthermore, no derogation from the right to a remedy is permitted in relation to violations of non-derogable rights, such as the right to life or the

13 Thomas, T.A., "*Ubi Jus, Ibi Remedium*: The Fundamental Right to a Remedy", 41 *San Diego Law Review* (2004), p. 1633.

14 Freeman, *supra* n. 14, p. 37.

15 Bantekas, I. and Oette, L., *International Human Rights: Law and Practice* (Cambridge, CUP 2016, 2nd ed.), p. 601.

16 Shelton, *Remedies in International Human Rights Law, supra* n. 1, p. 17.

17 Babu, *supra* n. 4, p. 51.

18 Ibid., p. 52.

19 Article 34, ILC's ASR. Furthermore, Gray usually refers to these three measures of reparation as 'judicial remedies'. See: Crawford, J., *State Responsibility: The General Part* (Cambridge, CUP 2013), p. 506.

20 In addition to full reparation, states are obliged to cease the violation and, when necessary, to offer guarantees of non-repetition. See: Article 30 of the ILC's ASR.

21 Bassiouni, M.C., "International Recognition of Victims' Rights", 6 *Human Rights Law Review* (2006), p. 231. Sometimes, the right to a remedy is referred to as the right to justice. See: Danieli, Y., "Massive Trauma and the Healing Role of Reparative Justice" in C. Ferstman, M. Goetz and A. Stephens (eds.), *Reparations for Victims of, War Crimes and Crimes Against Humanity: Systems in Place and Systems in the Making* (Leiden, Martinus Nijhoff 2009), p. 44.

prohibition of torture.[22] This is because fundamental rights can only be guaranteed by effective remedies, whether they are judicial or non-judicial.[23]

Similar to the concept of remedies under public international law, the right to a remedy under international human rights law is composed of two key elements.[24] The first component is procedural; it refers to equal access to justice or effective domestic remedies consisting of either formal or informal mechanisms, before which victims can bring their claims.[25] In other words, it entails access to procedures related to the investigation, prosecution, and eventual punishment of those responsible for the violations.[26] The second component is substantive (reparations).[27] It refers to adequate, effective, and prompt reparation measures that aim to erase or mitigate the harm suffered. In fact, these two elements are also considered to be independent rights: the right to have access to justice and the right to reparation.

Regarding gross violations of human rights, a trend appears to have surfaced that suggests that the procedural aspect of remedies is limited to remedies of a judicial nature.[28] Without disregarding the existence of effective non-judicial remedies, judicial remedies are becoming increasingly crucial to protecting human rights.[29] It could therefore be concluded that the type of effective remedy, whether judicial or otherwise, is determined by the type of violation suffered.[30] Although the right

---

22 HRC General Comment No. 29, States of Emergency (Article 4) 31 August 2001, UN Doc. CCPR/C/21/Rev.1/Add.11, para. 14; Francioni, F., "The Rights of Access to Justice under Customary International Law", in F. Francioni (ed.) *Access to Justice as a Human Right* (Oxford, OUP 2007), p. 42-55.

23 Judicial remedies are awarded by judicial bodies (e.g. courts) while non-judicial remedies are awarded by non-judicial bodies (e.g. UN human rights treaty bodies). See: van Boven, T., "Victims' Rights to a Remedy and Reparations: The New United Nations Principles and Guidelines", in C. Ferstman, M. Goetz and A. Stephens (eds.), *Reparations for Victims of Genocide, War Crimes and Crimes Against Humanity: Systems in Place and Systems in the Making* (Leiden, Martinus Nijhoff 2009), p. 21; Francioni, *supra* n. 22, p. 1-8; International Commission of Jurists, "The Right to a Remedy and to Reparations for Gross Human Rights Violations", *Practitioner's Guide Series 2* (Geneva, International Commission of Jurists 2006), p. 44.

24 Shelton, *Remedies in International Human Rights Law, supra* n. 1, p. 16-19; van Boven, *supra* n. 23, p. 22; Rombouts, H., Sardaro, P. and Vandeginste, S., "The Right to Reparation for Victims of Gross and Systematic Violations of Human Rights", in K. de Feyter et al. (eds.), *Out of the Ashes: Reparations for Gross Violations of Human Rights* (Antwerp, Intersentia 2005), p. 368-370.

25 Principles 4, 5, 7, UNGA (Declaration on Basic Principles of Justice for Victims of Crimes and Abuse of Power) 29 November 1985, UN Doc A/RES/40/34 (Victims' Declaration).

26 Shelton, *Remedies in International Human Rights Law, supra* n. 1, p. 18.

27 Ibid., p. 16-19; van Boven, *supra* n. 23, p. 22.

28 Bantekas and Oette, *supra* n. 15, p. 615; Shelton, *Remedies in International Human Rights Law, supra* n. 1, p. 126; See: HRC (View) 27 October 1995, *Bautista de Arellana* v. *Colombia*, Comm. No. 563/1993, para. 8.2.

29 REDRESS, *Reparation: A sourcebook for victims of torture and other violations of human rights and international humanitarian law* (London, The REDRESS Trust 2003), p. 14.

30 REDRESS, *Reaching for Justice: The Right to Reparation in the African Human Rights System* (Geneva, The REDRESS Trust 2013), p. 9.

to a remedy is most commonly referred to as comprising just two elements,[31] it is important to mention that the Principles on Reparations recognise a third element of the right to a remedy: the right to be informed. It refers to the access to relevant information concerning the violations and the right to be informed about ongoing judicial or non-judicial processes and mechanisms of reparation.[32]

1.1.1 Procedural Aspect: Access to Justice

States have created several avenues to deal with claims of violations of international obligations in order to establish state responsibility and to identify the states' obligations arising from such responsibility. For instance, under the auspices of the United Nations, states created the ICJ, which deals with disputes submitted by the UN member states.[33] In one of its landmark cases, the Permanent Court of International Justice (PCIJ) established that international tribunals that have jurisdiction over a dispute have the intrinsic power to afford reparations.[34]

In addition, states have established several international arbitral tribunals to address claims for damages resulting from an international injury. In principle, each tribunal's remedial power is derived from the statute that established it, and most of them do specify the kind of remedies they are entitled to award.[35] For instance, some tribunals have been given the authority to interpret the applicable law and to issue declaratory judgments, while others may also have the power to issue mandatory judgments and to grant specific remedies.[36]

Under human rights law, access to justice is also referred to by some authors as the 'right to judicial protection',[37] which indicates the possibility to bring a claim before an independent and impartial competent body, and to have that claim heard in accordance with the law.[38] A state is under an obligation to establish a framework that enables and protects an individual's right to bring such a claim. The state obligation

---

31 Although most human rights bodies agree on these two elements of the right to a remedy, the African Commission on Human and Peoples' Rights has upheld that remedies are composed of three elements: availability, effectiveness, and efficiency. See: Musila, G.M., "The right to an effective remedy under the African Charter on Human and Peoples' Rights", 6 *African Human Rights Law Journal* (2006), p. 446, citing ACmHPR (Decision) 11 May 2000, *Sir Dawda K. Jawara* v. *Gambia,* Comm. No. 147/95-149/96.

32 Principles 11 and 24, Principles on Reparations.

33 The ICJ is the successor of the Permanent Court of International Justice which had been established by the League of Nations.

34 Shelton, *Remedies in International Human Rights Law, supra* n. 1, p. 33-34; PCIJ (Judgment) 26 July 1927, *Factory at Chorzów* (*Germany* v. *Poland*), p. 21.

35 Gray, *supra* n. 5, p. 873.

36 Gray, C., *Judicial Remedies in International Law* (Oxford, OUP 1990), p. 11-12.

37 Francioni, *supra* n. 22, p. 3. However, the content of right to judicial protection is borader. See: Article 25, American Convention on Human Rights.

38 Shelton, *Remedies in International Human Rights Law, supra* n. 1, p. 16; Francioni, *supra* n. 22, p. 3-25.

to provide avenues to facilitate victims' access to justice is emphasised particularly in the context of gross violations of human rights. It is believed that bringing justice in the context of gross abuses to some extent contributes to preventing the growth of a culture of impunity and might therefore aid the transition to a more democratic state.[39] Judge Cançado Trindade has gone so far as to state that the right to have access to justice belongs within the realm of *jus cogens* in the context of violations of *jus cogens* norms.[40]

The right to have access to justice is key to the enforceability of rights and thus constitutes an essential part of the protection of any human right.[41] The right to have access to justice is to be guaranteed primarily by domestic legal systems;[42] the possibility to access international remedies is subsidiary. Even though the right to have access to justice is an essential component of the protection of fundamental rights, it is not an absolute right when it is not connected to non-derogable rights such as gross violations of human rights. The right to have access to justice in the context of violations of derogable rights can therefore be indirectly limited, as long as this does not have an 'unduly restrictive' effect.[43] Examples include enacting a statute of limitations,[44] derogations made in times of emergency, and granting immunities. In addition, whilst states are also permitted to suspend some *non*-derogable rights in the case of an emergency or war, such restrictions are subject to certain conditions. For instance, the restriction should be in accordance with the principle of non-discrimination, it should be temporary, and it should be subjected to a proportionality and reasonableness test, among others.[45] When it comes to the issue of immunities

39 Almeida, I., "Compensation and Reparation for Gross Violations of Human Rights: Advancing the International Discourse and Action", in C.C. Joyner and M.C. Bassiouni (eds.), *Reining in Impunity for International Crimes and Serious Violations of Fundamental Human Rights: Proceedings of the Siracusa Conference, 14-21 September 1998, International Review of Penal Law 14* (Toulouse, Erès 1998), p. 401.

40 Contreras-Garduño, D. and Alvarez-Rios, I., "A Barren Effort? The Jurisprudence of the Inter-American Court of Human Rights on *Jus Cogens?*" in Y. Haeck et al. (eds.) *The Realisation of Human Rights: When Theory Meets Practice. Studies in Honour of Leo Zwaak* (Cambridge, Intersentia 2013), p. 187, citing IACtHR (Judgment) 31 January 2006, *Pueblo Bello Massacre* v. *Colombia*, Separate Opinion Judge Cançado Trindade, para. 13.

41 Shelton, *Remedies in International Human Rights Law, supra* n. 1, p. 18.

42 Article 5 (2) (b) Optional Protototol to the International Covenant of Civil and Political Rights (OP-ICCPR); Article 46 (2) (a) American Convention on Human Rights (ACHR); Article 35 (1) European Convention on Human Rights (ECHR).

43 Principle 7, Principles on Reparations. Notably, a statute of limitations does not apply in the case of gross violations of human rights that amount to international crimes.

44 Capone, F. et al., "Education and the Law of Reparations in Insecurity and Armed Conflicts", *British Institute of International Law* (2013), p. 9.

45 Francioni, *supra* n. 22, p. 42-45.

there are some exceptions, primarily with respect to international crimes and *jus cogens* rights, but not regarding any non-derogable right.[46]

1.1.2 Substantive Aspect: Reparations

While a detailed historical account of the chronological development of the legal concept of reparations[47] is not within the purview of this chapter, it is important to note that providing reparations to victims of crimes has its roots in Roman law.[48] Under Roman law, reparatory justice was a common feature of the courts: any victim could seek restitution and reparation, mostly in a pecuniary dimension, for the damage suffered from a wrongdoing.[49] However, the classical legal concept of providing reparation is grounded in tort law and the laws of state responsibility.[50]

Reparation is an 'umbrella concept'.[51] It is understood as 'payment for an injury or damage; redress for a wrong done';[52] or measures that lead to either the restoration of the state of affairs prior to the commission of the wrongdoing, or to compensation for the loss or damage suffered.[53] For instance, in a domestic context Wright understands reparation to amount to the money, service, or apology afforded to a victim by an offender.[54] Reparation is a 'generic term' that refers to different measures to which states may resort in order to discharge their responsibility following the breach of an international obligation, including a human rights obligation.[55]

---

46 Ibid., p. 48-49; Article 27, ICC's Rome Statute. See: Schabas, W., "International Criminal Courts", in C. Romano, K. Alter and Y. Shany (eds.), *The Oxford Handbook of International Adjudication*, (Oxford, OUP 2015), p. 206.

47 The term 'reparations' is also a concept that is used in religious, political, ethical and philosophical discourse. See: REDRESS, *Torture Survivor's Perceptions of Reparations: Preliminary Survey* (Mitcham, The REDRESS Trust 2001), p. 11.

48 Bassiouni, M.C., "International Criminal Law: International Enforcement", 3 *Brill* (2008), p. 637; The concept of reparation can also be found in cultural thoughts and practices of tribes and ancient communities, See: Bottigliero, I., *Redress for Victims of Crimes under International Law* (Leiden, Martinus Nijhoff 2004), p. 14-23.

49 McCarthy, C., "Reparations under the Rome Statute of the International Criminal Court' and Reparative Justice Theory", 3 *The International Journal of Transitional Justice* (2009), p. 251-252.

50 Roht-Arriaza, N., "Reparations in International Law and Practice", in M. C. Bassiouni (ed.), *The pursuit of international criminal justice: a world study on conflicts, victimization and post conflict justice* (Antwerp, Intersentia 2010, Vol.1), p. 656; Roht-Arriaza, N., "Reparations Decisions and Dilemmas", 27 *Hastings International and Comparative Law Review* (2004), p. 160.

51 Brown, *supra* n. 7, p. 186.

52 Shelton, "Reparations for Indigenous Peoples: The Present Value of Past Wrongs", *supra* n. 1, p. 59, citing Campbell Black, H., (ed.), *Black's Law Dictionary* (Saint Paul, West Publishing 1979, 5th ed.), p. 1167.

53 Stern, B., "The Obligation to Make Reparation", in J. Crawford, A. Pellet and S. Olleson (eds.), *The Law on International Responsibility* (Oxford, OUP 2010), p. 564.

54 REDRESS, *supra* n. 47, p. 11, citing Wright, M. "The impact of Victim/Offender Mediation on the Victim", 10 *Victimology* (1985), p. 631-645.

55 Shelton, *Remedies in International Human Rights Law, supra* n. 1, *supra* n. 1, p. 33.

Already in 1927, the PCIJ stated that the state has the obligation to provide reparation for the commission of an internationally wrongful act and that this is a principle of law.[56] In addition, it established that measures of reparation must, to the extent possible, erase the consequences of the state's wrongful act[57] and include measures of restitution, compensation, and satisfaction. The PCIJ's approach to reparations has been endorsed by the ICJ as well as by other international and national tribunals.[58] It is also endorsed by the principal law governing the consequences of internationally wrongful conduct, which was drafted and codified by the International Law Commission (ILC) in the Draft Articles on Responsibility of States for Internationally Wrongful Acts (the ILC's Articles on State Responsibility).[59]

Reparations also refer to an individual right – the right to reparation – which evolved from the international obligation to provide reparation after the infringement of an international obligation. The right to obtain reparation is well recognised under international human rights law through binding[60] and non-binding documents.[61] In fact, it has been acknowledged that unless reparation is provided, the state obligation to provide a remedy is not discharged.[62] Furthermore, under international human rights law a victim of a gross violation of human rights is a right-holder of full, effective, adequate, and prompt measures of reparation.[63] In this way, reparations aim to 'make a victim whole again' by attempting to restore the situation that existed before the violation occurred. This is facilitated through measures of restitution, compensation, satisfaction, and rehabilitation, and through guarantees of non-repetition.[64]

---

56 PCIJ, *Factory at Chorzów* (*Germany* v. *Poland*), *supra* n. 34, p. 21.

57 PCIJ (Judgment) 13 September 1928, *Factory at Chorzów* (*Germany* v. *Poland*), p. 47.

58 Babu, *supra* n. 4, p. 55.

59 Shelton, *Remedies in International Human Rights Law, supra* n. 1, p. 32.

60 ICJ (Judgment) 3 February 2012, *Jurisdictional Immunities of the State* (*Germany* v. *Italy: Greece intervening*), Dissenting Opinion Judge Cançado, para. 51, 59. See: Articles 3 and 9 (5), ICCPR; Articles 13 and 14, International Convention Against Torture and Other Cruel, Inhuman or Degrading Treatment or Punishment (CAT); Article 6, International Convention on the Elimination of All Forms of Racial Discrimination (CERD); Article 39, UN Convention on the Rights of the Child (CRC); Articles 5 and 50, ECHR; Articles 10, 25 and 63 (1), ACHR; Article 2 (c) CEDAW; Articles 13 and16, Convention on the Rights of Persons with Disabilities (CRPD); Article 24 (4) (5), Convention for the Protection of All Persons from Enforced Disappearance (ICED). It must be noted that the African Charter on Human and Peoples' Rights (ACHPR) does not contain any reference to the right to compensation; however, the Protocol to the ACHPR on the Establishment of the African Court on Human and Peoples' Rights (P-ACHPR) does so in its Article 27 (1).

61 Article 8, Universal Declaration of Human Rights (UDHR); Principles 5-13, Victims' Declaration; Preamble, para. 10 and Principles 11-18, Principles on Reparations.

62 HRC General Comment No. 31, Nature of the General Legal Obligation Imposed on States Parties to the Covenant 26 May 2004, UN Doc. CCPR/C/21/Rev.1/Add.13, para. 16.

63 International Commission of Jurists, *supra* n. 23, p. 44; Principles 11, 15, 18, Principles on Reparations.

64 Principle 18, Principles on Reparations.

However, since most serious violations of human rights are by their very nature irreparable,[65] the ideal to 'make a victim whole again' is difficult to achieve, if not impossible. No remedies or measures of reparation can revive a deceased loved one; nor can they restore the time that one has been held under unlawful detention or undo the torture suffered thereby. In this light, '[n]o single form of reparation is likely to be satisfactory to victims.'[66] Nevertheless, measures of reparation are an important element of any justice process as they can mitigate the suffering caused,[67] and they can provide relief in proportion to both the harm suffered and 'the gravity of the violations.'[68] Reparations can therefore play a role in restoring public order, preventing future violations, and even in reconstructing the fabric of society.[69]

2 Reparations: A State Obligation

2.1 Concept of Reparation

Although 'reparation' is often used interchangeably with, *inter alia*, the terms 'redress', '(financial) compensation', and 'remedies', there are some distinctions between these concepts. 'Redress' may refer to either measures of reparation[70] or remedies,[71] but it is more commonly understood as synonymous with 'remedies'.[72] 'Remedies' can be distinguished from reparations as a remedy encompasses both the procedural avenues to enforce a right, as well as the substantive element of the reparations themselves.[73] 'Compensation' is one of the three forms of reparations recognised by the law of state responsibility, alongside restitution and satisfaction.[74]

---

65 UNHRC (Final Report of the Special Rapporteur, Theo Van Boven, on the right to restitution, compensation and rehabilitation for victims of gross violations of human rights and fundamental freedoms to the 45th Session of the United Nations Commission on Human Rights) 2 July 1993, UN Doc. E/CN.4/Sub.2/1993/8.

66 UNSC (Report of the Secretary-General: The rule of law and transitional justice in conflict and post-conflict societies) 23 August 2004, UN Doc S/2004/616, para. 55. See: UNSC (Security Council Letter dated 14 December 2000 from Secretary-General addressed to the President of the Security Council) 15 December 2000, UN Doc S/2000/1198, para. 55.

67 Freeman, *supra* n. 4, p. 30.

68 Principles 13 and 15, Principles on Reparations.

69 Reisman, W.M., "Compensation for Human Rights Violations: The Practice of the Past Decade in the Americas" in A. Randelzhofer and C. Tomuschat (eds.), *State Responsibility and the Individual: Reparation in Instances of Grave Violations of Human Rights* (The Hague, Martinus Nijhoff 1999), p. 65.

70 Crawford, *supra* n. 19, p. 542, 773; Shelton, *Remedies in International Human Rights Law, supra* n. 1, p. 17.

71 Evans, *supra* n. 8, p. 13.

72 Ibid.

73 Shelton, *Remedies in International Human Rights Law, supra* n. 1, p. 16-19; van Boven, *supra* n. 23, p. 22; Rombouts, Sardaro and Vandeginste, *supra* n. 24, p. 368-370.

74 Article 34, ILC's ASR.

Public international law first defined the provision of reparation as a principle of law and a state duty arising from the breach of an international obligation[75] that exists even when it is not stipulated in a particular treaty.[76] Therefore, having to provide reparations is an immediate consequence of the breach of a primary obligation,[77] including violations of international human rights law and the commission of an international crime committed by the state or its agents by either an act or omission.[78] Obtaining reparation is also a right enjoyed by an injured state.[79]

The principal aim of providing reparation is to make good the injury caused by an internationally wrongful act.[80] At the same time, reparations have other purposes: they may deter the commission of further crimes, restore the rule of law, and to some extent contribute to achieving peace and reconciliation.[81] Reparations also play a role in sanctioning a responsible state and emphasising that a certain conduct amounts to a wrongful act.[82] Although the obligation of providing reparation belongs to the set of secondary rules of obligations,[83] some scholars consider it to pertain to the realm of *jus gentium* and *droit de gens*,[84] forming proof of the 'humanisation' of international law.[85] The secondary character of this obligation is also reflected in the notion of obtaining reparation as a secondary right, which is discussed in Section 3 of this chapter.

Last but not least, both the jurisprudence of the ICJ and the ILC's Articles on State Responsibility are silent on whether the state obligation to make reparations *vis-à-vis* other states is an absolute right. However, limitations to this obligation are also omitted. In previous versions of the ILC's Articles on State Responsibility a limitation on this obligation was proposed: '[i]n no case shall reparation result in depriving the

75 PCIJ, *Factory at Chorzów* (*Germany* v. *Poland*), *supra* n. 34, p. 21.

76 'It is a principle of international law that the breach of an engagement involves an obligation to make reparation in an adequate form. Reparation [is] indispensable complement of a failure to apply a convention and there is no necessity for this to be stated in the convention itself.' See: PCIJ, *Factory at Chorzów* (*Germany* v. *Poland*), *supra* n. 34, p. 21.

77 Following a breach of an international obligation, a state is required to cease the violation, to make guarantees of non-repetition, and to provide reparations. See: Stern, *supra* n. 53, p. 564-565.

78 Articles 6 and 33, ILC's ASR.

79 Crawford, *supra* n. 19, p. 507.

80 Shelton, *Remedies in International Human Rights Law, supra* n. 1, p. 33.

81 Shelton, *Remedies in International Human Rights Law, supra* n. 1, p. 20-27.

82 Expert Seminar on "Reparation for Victims of Gross and Systematic Human Rights Violations in the Context of Political Transitions", *Leuven, Catholic University of Leuven*, March 10, 2002, p. 21.

83 According to Articles 30 and 31 of the ILC's ASR the main secondary obligations stemming from a wrongful act are: i) the obligation to continue to fulfil its international obligations, ii) the cessation of the violation, iii) guarantees of non-repetition, and iv) reparations. See: Stern, *supra* n. 53, p. 563.

84 ICJ (Judgment) 19 June 2012, *Ahmadou Sadio Diallo* (*Republic of Guinea* v. *Democratic Republic of the Congo*), Separate Opinion of Judge Cançado Trindade, para. 15, 32.

85 Ibid., para. 40, 42.

population of a state of its own means of subsistence,'[86] but this limitation was not adopted in the final version.[87]

2.2 Types of Reparations

The law of state responsibility that applies to reparations, which was developed within the jurisprudence of the PCIJ and the ICJ, clearly states the different forms that reparation can assume and the hierarchy between them. Priority is given to restitution, followed by compensation and, finally, satisfaction. As stated previously, restitution seeks to re-establish the situation that existed before the wrongful act occurred. On the other hand, compensation refers to a payment that is equivalent to the damage incurred or suffered, while satisfaction is non-material and moral reparation, such as apologies, expressions of regret, and the recognition of the breach. These three forms of reparation are not mutually exclusive and can be granted either independently or cumulatively.[88] Lastly, it deserves to be mentioned that these three forms of reparation are not necessarily available in all inter-state disputes.[89]

2.2.1 Restitution

Restitution can be divided into three forms. Restitution in kind is the traditional form of reparation,[90] and although it has primacy over the other two forms it is scarcely awarded in practice.[91] The second type of restitution is material restitution, despite the fact that restitution is often comprised of both material and legal elements.[92] Material restitution refers to a wide range of different measures, such as property restoration and the restoration of rights, for instance the restoration of the right to liberty through the release of unlawfully detained individuals. It is often assumed

86 Stern, *supra* n. 53, p. 566.

87 Crawford affirms that states were concerned that this provision would be abused. See: Crawford, *supra* n. 19, p. 482.

88 Kerbat, Y., "Interaction between the forms of reparation", in J. Crawford, A. Pellet and S. Olleson (eds.), *The Law on International Responsibility* (Oxford, OUP 2010), p. 573. As explained earlier, the Commentary to Article 34 suggests that three forms of reparations should be granted in combination in some cases. See: Commentary to Article 34, International Law Commission, Draft Articles on Responsibility of States for Internationally Wrongful Acts, with commentaries, *Yearbook of the International Law Commission 2001 Volume 2 Part 2* (New York and Geneva, United Nations 2008), (hereafter ILC's Commentaries to ASR), p. 96, para. 5.

89 Brown, *supra* n. 7, p. 223.

90 Ibid., p. 191; Echeverria, G., "Do victims of torture and other serious human rights violations have an independent and enforceable right to reparations?", 16 *The International Journal of Human rights* (2012), p. 706.

91 Brown, *supra* n. 7, p. 195.

92 Gray, C., "The different forms of reparation: restitution", in J. Crawford, A. Pellet and S. Olleson (eds.), *The Law on International Responsibility* (Oxford, OUP 2010), p. 593.

that property restitution is more likely or possible to be achieved. However, it is important to note that when property is destroyed or altered, such restitution becomes impossible.[93]

The ICJ's landmark case on the restitution of property is the case of *Temple of Preah Vihear*, which concerned Thailand's unlawful occupation of a temple that belonged to Cambodia. The ICJ ordered Thailand to withdraw any military forces and to return all religious objects it might have removed from the temple.[94] However, Gray notes that Cambodia had not submitted any evidence indicating that Thailand had actually removed religious objects. He argues instead that the restitution was ordered because the claim was not contested by Thailand.[95] The ICJ also referred to the obligation of the restitution of property in the advisory opinion on the *Wall* case, when it stated that Israel bore the obligation to 'return the land, orchards, olive groves and other immovable property seized from any natural or legal person for purposes of construction of the wall in the Occupied Palestinian Territory' insofar as this was materially possible.[96]

Restitution can also take a legal form. This refers to the abrogation or non-applicability of a law or judicial decision and is closely related to cessation: it is sometimes difficult to distinguish between the two. For instance, in the *Arrest Warrant* case, which dealt with Belgium's arrest warrant against the Minister of Foreign Affairs of the Democratic Republic of the Congo, the ICJ ruled that Belgium had failed to respect the immunity from criminal jurisdiction that the Minister enjoyed under international law.[97] Accordingly, the ICJ ordered Belgium to cancel the arrest warrant based on the obligation to repair by means of returning the injured party to a situation demanded by law. This order both ceased the breach and restored the legal situation which existed prior to its occurrence.

Finally, the *LaGrand* case provides a good example of a case in which legal restitution has been sought.[98] In this case, Germany initiated proceedings against the United States before the ICJ, alleging a violation of the Vienna Convention on Consular Relations (VCCR). In particular, Germany alleged that the United States had violated international law by detaining, trying, and issuing the death penalty against two German nationals without informing them of their rights to consular access.[99] Since the German nationals had already been executed by the time the

93 Ibid., p. 593; Shelton, *Remedies in International Human Rights Law, supra* n. 1, p. 42-43.

94 ICJ (Judgement) 15 June 1962, *Temple of Preah Vihear* (*Cambodia* v. *Thailand*), p. 37.

95 Gray, *supra* n. 36, p. 106-107; ICJ, *Temple of Preah Vihear* (*Cambodia* v. *Thailand*), *supra* n. 94, p. 36.

96 ICJ (Advisory Opinion) 9 July 2004, *Legal Consequences of the Construction of a Wall in the Occupied Palestinian Territory*, para. 153.

97 ICJ (Judgment) 14 February 2002, *Arrest Warrant of 11 April 2000* (*Democratic Republic of the Congo* v. *Belgium*).

98 ICJ (Judgment) 27 June 2001, *LaGrand* (*Germany* v. *United States of America*).

99 Gray, *supra* n. 92, p. 593; ICJ, *LaGrand* (*Germany* v. *United States of America*), *supra* n. 98.

ICJ rendered its judgment, material restitution was not possible. Instead, Germany sought 'to ensure that German nationals will be provided with adequate consular assistance in the future.'[100] Germany therefore requested legal restitution measures that amounted to assurances of non-repetition. However, the ICJ understood these measures to be purely guarantees of non-repetition and did not award them, as it could not be presumed that the United States would repair such wrongful acts in the future.[101]

Despite its importance, realising restitution often faces the hurdles of disproportionality and material impossibility.[102] Disproportionality refers to 'a burden out of all proportion to the benefit deriving from restitution instead of compensation.'[103] The disproportionality of restitution is usually an issue when the wrongful act involves a breach of a procedural norm.[104] Material impossibility refers to 'permanently lost or destroyed' material.[105] In addition to these two limitations, restitution might not be possible, it may have little value to the injured state,[106] or it may be an inadequate measure of reparation for the damage inflicted,[107] especially with regard to moral damages.[108] Thus, restitution remains a little-used remedy, not only because of the difficulties in realising it, but also due to the reluctance of some courts to grant it. For instance, restitution is often requested before, yet rarely awarded by, the ICJ.[109]

2.2.2 Compensation

Compensation is the monetary payment provided for the harm suffered; however, it should not be understood as punishment, nor should it express any condemnatory or exemplary character.[110, 111] It can be considered a secondary form of reparation, as its primary function is to fill any gap not covered by restitution when restitution is either not possible or not appropriate. In principle, the amount of compensation should be equal to the value of restitution in kind.[112] Compensation is also subject to

100 ICJ (Memorial of the Federal Republic of Germany) 16 September 1999, *LaGrand* (*Germany* v. *United States of America*), para. 6.24.
101 Gray, *supra* n. 5, p. 880.
102 Gray, *supra* n. 92, p. 593, Shelton, *Remedies in International Human Rights Law, supra* n. 1, p. 40.
103 Article 35(b), ILC's ASR.
104 Crawford, *supra* n. 19, p. 514.
105 Ibid., p. 513.
106 Gray, *supra* n. 92, p. 593; Shelton, *Remedies in International Human Rights Law, supra* n. 1, p. 40.
107 Gray, *supra* n. 36, p. 16.
108 Ibid., p. 15.
109 Gray, *supra* n. 92, p. 593; Shelton, *Remedies in International Human Rights Law, supra* n. 1, p. 40.
110 Babu, *supra* n. 4, p. 84.
111 Commentary to Article 36, ILC's Commentaries to ASR, p. 99, para. 4.
112 PCIJ, *Factory at Chorzów* (*Germany* v. *Poland*), *supra* n. 34, p. 47.

the limitations of proportionality[113] and the requirement of causation.[114] In addition, states have argued that compensation should take into account national economic realities,[115] although no existing rule upholds this practice.

Despite its secondary character, practice shows that in the context of inter-state disputes, compensation is more often sought[116] and awarded than restitution.[117] It should cover pecuniary (material) and non-pecuniary (non-material) injuries,[118] loss of profits,[119] and incidental expenses.[120] Importantly, non-material harm 'includes such terms as individual pain and suffering, loss of loved ones or personal affront associated with an intrusion on one's home or private life.'[121] In addition, compensation should be granted in a 'reasonable manner' in which punitive compensation is excluded.[122] It is also possible to add interest to an amount of compensation.[123] In principle, compensation is awarded for any assessable financial damage,[124] which includes medical expenses and pensions.[125] However, it has also been awarded in cases in which it was *prima facie* not possible to define the assessable damages. For instance, in cases of unlawful killings or of unlawfully detained individuals, the personal injury suffered by the victims (whether direct or indirect) has been calculated and awarded.[126]

Brown has upheld that there are three key elements that shape compensation: i) availability, ii) types of harm, and iii) the method of calculating the harm.[127] However, Brown also signals the lack of a common standard of compensation in international public law.[128] He states that even if common grounds were to be found, the methods to calculate harm would remain contested.[129] States traditionally (and commonly) decide between themselves what amounts to a 'reasonable manner', and are encouraged to reach an agreement to define the amount of compensation to be

113 Commentary to Article 34, ILC's Commentaries to ASR, p. 96, para. 5.
114 Crawford, *supra* n. 19, p. 482.
115 Brown, *supra* n. 7, p. 204.
116 Brown, *supra* n. 7, p. 191; Commentary to Article 36, ILC's Commentaries to ASR, p. 99, para. 2.
117 Gray, *supra* n. 92, p. 593; Shelton, *Remedies in International Human Rights Law, supra* n. 1, p. 34.
118 Barker, J., "The different forms of reparation: compensation", in J. Crawford, A. Pellet and S. Olleson (eds.), *The Law on International Responsibility* (Oxford, OUP 2010), p. 599.
119 Article 36, ILC's ASR.
120 Brown, *supra* n. 7, p. 201. These categories are not closed.
121 Commentary to Article 31, ILC's Commentaries to ASR, p. 92, para. 5.
122 Shelton, *Remedies in International Human Rights Law, supra* n. 1, p. 38.
123 Crawford, *supra* n. 19, p. 531.
124 Article 36, ILC's Article on State Responsibility.
125 Brown, *supra* n. 7, p. 199-200.
126 Commentary to Article 36, ILC's Commentaries to ASR, p. 102, para. 18; Shelton, *Remedies in International Human Rights Law, supra* n. 1, p. 146-152.
127 Brown, *supra* n. 7, p. 199.
128 It is important to mention that Brown's statement is based on the jurisprudence of international tribunals including arbitral ones.
129 Brown, *supra* n. 7, p. 205, 224.

paid, usually within six months.[130] The period in which states are encouraged to reach an agreement is decided on a case-by-case basis: it may be more than six months,[131] or even undetermined.[132] The ICJ only intervenes if an agreement cannot be reached; to date, it has only determined the measure of compensation in two cases.[133] These were the *Corfu Channel* case, which was concerned with Albania's failure to warn the UK of mines in Albanian waters which resulted in damage to UK ships,[134] and the *Diallo* case, which concerned violations of the rights of a Guinean businessman, Ahmadou Sadio Diallo, and his diplomatic protection.[135] In the *Corfu Channel* case, the ICJ appointed experts and established an amount for compensation, whereas in the *Diallo* case only when the states had failed to come to an agreement did the Court establish an amount by relying on equitable considerations.[136]

2.2.3 Satisfaction

The precise legal concept of satisfaction cannot be found anywhere in international law.[137] However, it is acknowledged that measures of satisfaction deal with 'the

---

130 ICJ (Judgment) 30 November 2010, *Ahmadou Sadio Diallo* (*Republic of Guinea* v. *Democratic Republic of the Congo*), para. 163-164. It is important to note that the parties could be given up to eighteen months to reach an agreement. See: Wellens, K., *Negotiations in the Case Law of the International Court of Justice: A Functional Analysis* (Oxford/New York, Routledge 2016), p. 314-316. This approach also resonated in the practice of the ECtHR and the ACmHPR. See: Musila, *supra* n. 31, p. 455; Mouyal, L., *International Investment Law and the Right to Regulate: A Human Rights Perspective* (Oxford/New York, Routledge 2016), p. 112; Malcolm, E. and Murray, R., (eds.), *The African Charter on Human and Peoples' Rights: The System in Practice 1986-2006* (Cambridge, CUP, 2008), p. 82.

131 The ICJ has ordered 12 months as a period to reach an agreement. See: ICJ (Judgment) 16 December 2015, *Construction of a Road in Costa Rica along the San Juan River* (*Nicaragua* v. *Costa Rica*), para. 229 (5) (a).

132 ICJ (Judgment) 19 December 2005, *Armed Activities on the Territory of the Congo* (*Democratic Republic of the Congo* v. *Uganda*), para. 345 (6).

133 Crawford, *supra* n. 19, p. 518-519; ICJ, *Ahmadou Sadio Diallo* (*Republic of Guinea* v. *Democratic Republic of the Congo*), *supra* n. 130, para. 163-164. The PCIJ also awarded damages in the *SS Wimbledon case* for not allowing the steamship "Wimbledon" to pass through the Kiel Canal. However, the Court did not explain how it had assessed the damages. See: PCIJ (Judgment) 17 August 1923, *S.S. "Wimbledon"* (*United Kingdom* v. *Japan*), p. 32.

134 ICJ (Judgment) 15 December 1949, *Corfu Channel* (*United Kingdom of Great Britain* and *Northern Ireland* v. *Albania*).

135 ICJ, *Ahmadou Sadio Diallo* (*Republic of Guinea* v. *Democratic Republic of the Congo*), *supra* n. 84, para. 11.

136 Crawford, *supra* n. 19, p. 519; ICJ (Judgment) 9 April 1949, *Corfu Channel* (*United Kingdom of Great Britain* and *Northern Ireland* v. *Albania*); ICJ, *Ahmadou Sadio Diallo* (*Republic of Guinea* v. *Democratic Republic of the Congo*), *supra* n. 84, para. 7.

137 This form of reparation under public international law is even said to be 'lesser known' in comparison to restitution and compensation. See: Falk, R., 'Reparations, International Law, and Global Justice: A New Frontier' in P. de Greiff (ed.), *The Handbook of Reparations* (Oxford, OUP 2006), p. 483.

affront or injury caused by a violation of rights not associated with actual damage to property or persons.'[138] Judge Garcia-Amador has even considered satisfaction to be the punitive element of reparations in the context of public international law.[139] This stance nonetheless opposes the existing law of remedies.

The ILC's Articles on State Responsibility leave the definition of what constitutes a measure of satisfaction open for interpretation,[140] but satisfaction can be understood as a form of reparation for damage that is not financially assessable.[141] Measures of satisfaction include apologies and statements of regret, the punishment of responsible persons, monetary compensation, and declarations of responsibility from the respondent state.[142] It is subject to limitations which include adherence to the principle of proportionality, and the requirement that satisfaction is not presented in such a way as to humiliate the state responsible for the wrongful act.[143]

Historically in inter-state litigation, a declaratory judgment is commonly sought.[144] Declarations of responsibility are obtained by a judicial judgment.[145] The major objective of such a declaration is to repair the moral damage caused by the injury.[146] Declaratory judgments are of great importance, because they serve as a reminder of the responsible state's obligations and thereby help states to abide by the rule of law.[147] Interestingly, the ICJ awards this remedy more often than others, due to its belief that a declaratory judgment can often provide adequate satisfaction for the harm done to a state.[148] This can be attributed to the fact that, traditionally, 'satisfaction was intended to redress the moral and political injuries caused to the honour, dignity or reputation of the state.'[149] However, it is left to the discretion of

---

138 Commentary to Article 36, ILC's Commentaries to ASR, p. 98-99, para. 1.

139 The second element was a compensatory one by means of restitution or compensation. See: Shelton, *Remedies in International Human Rights Law, supra* n. 1, p. 34.

140 Article 37 (2), ILC's ASR.

141 Commentary to Article 37, ILC's Commentaries to ASR, p. 106, para. 3; Shelton, *Remedies in International Human Rights Law, supra* n. 1, p. 156-157.

142 Wyler, E. and Papaux, A., "The different forms of reparation: satisfaction", in J. Crawford, A. Pellet and S. Olleson (eds.), *The Law on International Responsibility* (Oxford, OUP 2010), p. 623-631.

143 Article 37 (3), ILC's ASR; Crawford, *supra* n. 19, p. 531; Wyler and Papaux, *supra* n. 142, p. 635.

144 Shelton, *Remedies in International Human Rights Law, supra* n. 1, p. 285.

145 Kerbat, *supra* n. 88, p. 578; ICJ (Judgment) 26 February 2007, *Application of the Convention on the Prevention and Punishment of the Crime of Genocide* (*Bosnia and Herzegovina* v. *Serbia* and *Montenegro*), para. 462; ICJ, *Corfu Channel* (*United Kingdom of Great Britain* and *Northern Ireland* v. *Albania*), *supra* n. 136, p. 35-36; quoted in ICJ (Judgment) 26 February 2007, *Application of the Convention for the Prevention and Punishment of the Crime of Genocide* (*Bosnia and Herzegovina* v. *Serbia* and *Montenegro*), para. 463.

146 Zyberi, G., "The International Court of Justice and applied forms of reparations for international human rights and humanitarian law violations", 7 *Utrecht Law Review* (2011), p. 207.

147 Brown, *supra* n. 7, p. 192.

148 Gray, *supra* n. 5, p. 876; ICJ, *Corfu Channel* (*United Kingdom of Great Britain* and *Northern Ireland* v. *Albania*), *supra* n. 136, p. 35-36.

149 Wyler and Papaux, *supra* n. 142, p. 625.

the wrongdoing state to take appropriate measures to comply with international obligations.[150]

Of further importance is that this measure has also been awarded when the causality requirement of an alternative measure of reparation, such as compensation, has not been met. As will be elaborated upon in the section on causality, the necessity of a sufficient causal link in the context of satisfaction is highlighted in the case of *Bosnia and Herzegovina against Serbia and Montenegro*. In this case, the ICJ first ruled that the respondent state had breached its international obligation to prevent and punish genocide, and then decided that the declaration of state responsibility in the judgment (measure of satisfaction) was an adequate form of reparation for the applicant. The ICJ deemed this to be adequate, because the causal link requirement to justify awarding compensation had not been met.[151]

2.2.4 Cessation and Guarantees of Non-Repetition

The ILC's Articles on State Responsibility draw a distinction between the obligation to afford full reparation (by means of restitution, compensation or rehabilitation) and the obligations of cessation, assurances of non-repetition (ANR) and guarantees of non-repetition (GNR).[152] Significantly, these three obligations could be awarded not only in the interest of the injured states, but also in the collective interest.[153] Furthermore, measures of cessation, ANR and GRN are future oriented, as opposed to measures of reparation which are inherently restorative or backward-looking. Accordingly, the ILC has stated that cessation is 'the negative aspect of future performance [and is] concerned with securing an end to continuing wrongful conduct, whereas assurances and [GNR] serve a preventive function [...] of future performance.'[154]

According to Babu, the obligation to cease a violation enjoys primacy in public international law when a state has breached an international obligation.[155] Cessation is required when the wrongful act 'is continuing',[156] which encompasses wrongful acts of a continuing character and 'where the State has violated an obligation on a series of occasions.'[157] It should be mentioned that the fulfilment of this obligation cannot always be distinguished from the reparation measure called restoration.[158] For

150 Gray, *supra* n. 5, p. 876.
151 ICJ, *Application of the Convention on the Prevention and Punishment of the Crime of Genocide* (*Bosnia and Herzegovina* v. *Serbia and Montenegro*), *supra* n. 145, para. 459-463.
152 Article 30, ILC's ASR.
153 Crawford, *supra* n. 19, p. 476; Commentary to Article 30, ILC's Commentary to ASR, p. 89-90, para. 5, 11.
154 Commentary to Article 30, ILC's Commentary to ASR, p. 88, para. 1.
155 Babu, *supra* n. 4, p. 89.
156 Article 30, ILC's ASR.
157 Commentary to Article 30, ILC's Commentary to ASR, p. 89, para. 3.
158 Babu, *supra* n. 4, p. 71-72.

instance, in the *LaGrand* case a restoration of rights would have consisted of granting the German detainees access to consular protection – provided they had not been executed before the ICJ issued its judgment. In this case, the restoration of rights would have also constituted a measure aimed at the cessation of violations.

The *United States Diplomatic and Consular Staff in Tehran* case also illustrates the close relationship between restitution and cessation. In this case, the ICJ ordered the release of US diplomatic and consular staff being held in Iran, as well as their safe departure from Iranian territory.[159] While this order was based on the obligation of cessation,[160] it can also be perceived as a restoration of rights. As previously explained, in the *Arrest Warrant* case the ICJ ordered Belgium to cancel an arrest warrant as a form of *restitutio in integrum*. However, it also subsequently resulted in Belgium ceasing the violation of its international obligation to respect the immunity of the Minister of Foreign Affairs of the Democratic Republic of the Congo.

Two distinctions between cessation and restitution can be identified. First, whilst restitution is subject to proportionality limitations, cessation is not.[161] Second, although restitution is not always possible, cessation is.[162] This is evident in the ILC's Articles on State Responsibility, which establish that an order of cessation can even be granted in cases in which an international obligation has been breached on several occasions.[163] However, in practice this does not always occur. In the *Avena* case, Mexico claimed that the United States had violated the Vienna Convention on Consular Relations several times, and, referring to the *LaGrand* case, sought measures of cessation.[164] The ICJ however dismissed the claim of the existence of repeated violations.[165]

Regarding the obligation to provide assurances and guarantees of non-repetition, it is first important to distinguish them. The former refers to a verbal commitment, whereas the latter refers to specific actions that aim to prevent further violations.[166] Nevertheless, both 'are concerned with the restoration of confidence in a continuing relationship,'[167] and both possess an 'exceptional character'.[168] The ICJ

159 ICJ (Judgment) 24 May 1980, *United States Diplomatic and Consular Staff in Tehran* (*United States of America* v. *Iran*), para. 95 (3) (a-b).

160 The ICJ noted that Iran's breaches of its obligations towards the United States under the Vienna Conventions of 1961 and 1963 were continuous and hence that Iran had an obligation to cease the violations. Ibid., para. 80, 90.

161 Commentary to Article 30, ILC's Commentaries to ASR, p. 90, para. 12; Babu, *supra* n. 4, p. 72; Crawford, *supra* n. 19, p. 476.

162 Crawford, *supra* n. 19, p. 465.

163 Commentary to Article 30, ILC's Commentaries to ASR, p. 89, para. 3.

164 ICJ (Judgment) 31 March 2004, *Avena and other Mexican nationals* (*Mexico* v. *United States of America*), para. 146.

165 Ibid., para. 148.

166 Babu, *supra* n. 4, p. 73.

167 Commentary to Article 30, ILC's Commentaries to ASR, p. 89, para. 9.

168 Ibid., p. 90-91, para. 13.

has implied that assurances of non-repetition are met when a state can demonstrate its best efforts to prevent further violations.[169] According to the ICJ, guarantees of non-repetition are owed 'if circumstances so require', which indicates their 'exceptional character'.[170] To date, there is no clear definition of which would be the circumstances under which these measures are to be awarded. However, some commentators believe that two factors could be taken into account in deciding whether to award guarantees of non-repetition: i) whether the obligation breached is of a *jus cogens* or peremptory nature, and ii) whether the wrongful act amounts to a grave breach.[171]

Contrary to the distinction made by the ILC's Articles on State Responsibility, states have requested the ICJ to award guarantees of non-repetition as a form of reparation. The ICJ has accordingly dealt with these measures as forms of reparation, although it has been reluctant to grant them.[172] This reluctance appears to be based upon the Court's consideration that a state's obligation to act in good faith must prevail:[173] if a state has committed a wrongful act, it should not be presumed that it would commit such an act again.[174]

For instance, in the *LaGrand* case, Germany requested the ICJ to determine 'that the [US] shall provide Germany an assurance that it will not repeat its unlawful acts and that, in any future cases of detention of or criminal proceedings against German nationals, the [US would] ensure in law and practice the effective exercise of the rights under Article 36 of the Vienna Convention on Consular Relations.[175] The ICJ did not grant the requested GNR, but it did recognise their need. The reason for this was that the Court took into account the fact that the US had implemented a national programme to ensure that its authorities complied with its international obligation under the Vienna Convention.[176] As a consequence, the ICJ stated 'that the commitment expressed by the United States to ensure the implementation of [...] its obligations under Article 36, paragraph 1 *(b),* must be regarded as meeting Germany's request for a general assurance of non-repetition.'[177] Furthermore, in the *Avena* case, Mexico requested both assurances and guarantees of non-repetition against the US

169 Crawford, *supra* n. 19, p. 476.
170 Commentary to Article 30, ILC's Commentaries to ASR, p. 90-91, para. 13.
171 D'Argent, P., "Reparation, Cessation, Assurances and Guarantees of Non-Repetition", 24 *SHARES Research Paper* (2014), p. 9. Grave breaches usually involve violations of humanitarian law. See: Solis, G.D., *The Law of Armed Conflict: International Humanitarian Law in War* (New York, CUP 2016, 2nd ed.), p. 109-110.
172 Gray, *supra* n. 5, p. 880; Crawford, *supra* n. 19, p. 473.
173 ICJ, (Judgment) 16 December 2015, *Certain Activities carried out by Nicaragua in the Border Area* (*Costa Rica* v. *Nicaragua*), para. 227; ICJ, *Jurisdictional Immunities of the State* (*Germany* v. *Italy: Greece intervening*), *supra* n. 60, para. 138.
174 Gray, *supra* n. 5, p. 880-881.
175 ICJ, *LaGrand* (*Germany* v. *United States of America*), *supra* n. 98, para. 117.
176 Ibid., para. 123.
177 Ibid., para. 124.

in order to achieve compliance with obligations under Article 36 of the VCCR.[178] However, the ICJ found that the commitment expressed by the US since the *LaGrand* case should be considered sufficient to provide assurances.[179]

It is relevant to mention that the Special Rapporteur on State Responsibility, Willem Riphagen, initially understood assurances and guarantees of non-repetition as a form of satisfaction.[180] In addition, whilst the ILC's Articles on State Responsibility distinguish between them and measures of reparation, they do acknowledge that such assurances and guarantees of non-repetition can also amount to a form of satisfaction.[181] On the other hand, Crawford maintains that distinguishing assurances and guarantees of non-repetition from measures of satisfaction allows for the possibility to seek them in a collective interest. If this were not possible, then assurances and guarantees of non-repetition could only be sought if other measures of satisfaction could not repair the injury.[182]

2.3 Main Characteristics of Reparations

In public international law, four criteria of reparations can be identified: *restitutio in integrum*,[183] adequacy,[184] full reparations[185] and proportionality.[186] These four criteria relate to each of the three forms of reparations identified in the previous section (restitution, compensation and satisfaction). When state responsibility is established, full reparation, which aims to provide *restitutio in integrum,* is owed to the injured state. Full reparation can consist of restitution, compensation, or satisfaction, either on their own or in combination. When deciding in a given case upon which measures could amount to full reparation, the principles of adequacy and proportionality are taken into account.

The International Court of Justice, as well as its predecessor, the Permanent Court of International Justice, have developed the content and scope of these characteristics in their jurisprudence. The ILC's Articles on State Responsibility also expand upon these principles,[187] as will be explained in the following sections.

---

178 ICJ, *Avena and other Mexican Nationals* (*Mexico* v. *United States of America*), *supra* n. 164, para. 146.

179 Ibid., para. 148-149.

180 Crawford, *supra* n. 19, p. 475.

181 Commentary to Article 30 and 37, ILC's Commentaries to ASR, p. 90 and 106, para. 11 and 5 respectively.

182 Crawford, *supra* n. 19, p. 476.

183 PCIJ, *Factory at Chorzów* (*Germany* v. *Poland*), *supra* n. 57, p. 47; Stern, *supra* n. 53, p. 564.

184 ICJ (Judgment) 20 April 2010, *Pulp Mills on the River Uruguay* (*Argentina* v. *Uruguay*), para. 274.

185 Article 31 (1), ILC's ASR.

186 Ibid., Articles 35 (b) and 37 (3).

187 Shelton, D., "Righting Wrongs: Reparations in the Articles on State Responsibility", 96 *The American Journal of International Law* (2002).

2.3.1 Restitutio in Integrum

The principle of '*restitutio in integrum*', also known as the 'rule of priority', finds its roots in Roman law, and refers to the restoration of a situation *ex ante.*[188] Since the *Factory at Chorzów* case before the PCIJ, it has been established that the main objective of providing reparations is to 'as far as possible, wipe out all the consequences of the illegal act and re-establish the situation which would, in all probability, have existed if that act had not been committed.'[189] However, it is often impossible to achieve this ideal, because its realisation depends on 'the concrete circumstances surrounding each case and the precise nature and scope of the injury.'[190] It also requires ample speculation as to what would have been the situation if the wrongdoing had not taken place;[191] it is this *hypothetical* or speculative situation that is supposed to be restored.

This principle was not only established in the *Factory at Chorzów* case; remarkably it was also put aside. Neither party, including the injured state, sought *restitutio in integrum*. The focus of the injured state was in fact on compensation, not restitution.[192] In fact, although the rule of priority in reparations privileges restitution as the ideal form of reparation, this is rarely followed in practice.[193] In addition, in some cases *restitutio in integrum* may not be appropriate; however, there are no guidelines that indicate in which circumstances it is suitable to use this principle to repair damage which has been done.[194] Notably, the *restitutio in integrum* rule applies to all wrongdoings. However, when developing the ILC's Articles on State Responsibility, the ILC attempted to make a distinction based on whether this rule is compulsory or optional. It was proposed that the rule should only be compulsory in relation to violations of *jus cogens* norms. In relation to 'ordinary' violations, the rule would be optional. However, this approach was not included in the final version of the Articles.[195]

2.3.2 Full Reparations

The terms 'full' and 'adequate' are often used interchangeably when referring to reparations.[196] Although the principle of full reparations differs from the principle of adequacy, this difference is not always clear. Full reparations are defined as 'restitution,

188 Shelton, *Remedies in International Human Rights Law, supra* n. 1, p. 145.
189 PCIJ, *Factory at Chorzów* (*Germany* v. *Poland*), *supra* n. 57, p. 47; Stern, *supra* n. 53, p. 564.
190 ICJ, *Avena and other Mexican Nationals (Mexico* v. *United States of America), supra* n. 164, para. 119.
191 Gray, *supra* n. 92, p. 590.
192 Gray, C., "The Choice between Restitution and Compensation", 10 *European Journal of International Law* (2009), p. 414.
193 Kerbat, *supra* n. 88, p. 579.
194 Gray, *supra* n. 36, p. 15-16.
195 Kerbat, *supra* n. 88, p. 580.
196 Barker, *supra* n. 118, p. 601.

compensation and satisfaction, either singly or in combination,'[197] which covers *all* the material and moral injury caused by the wrongdoing.[198] Restitution is the measure most likely to achieve full reparation. If restitution is (totally or partially) impossible or if it fails to make good the damage that has been caused, then compensation for the damage should be awarded.[199] If neither can make good the damage, measures of satisfaction should be awarded.[200] Significantly, the Commentary on the ILC's Articles on State Responsibility states that full reparation 'may only be achieved in particular cases by the combination of different forms of reparations.'[201] This suggests that the three forms of reparations complement each other. It could therefore be reasonably assumed that it is unlikely that states can provide full reparation by granting only one of the three measures.[202] Interest can also be awarded in some cases to provide full reparation,[203] with the aim to bridge the gap between the loss and its financial consequences.[204] The determination of the interest is left to the discretion of the tribunal and respective parties;[205] there are no guidelines on how to calculate the interest.[206] Importantly, providing full reparation can be limited by the principle of proportionality,[207] and the 'wilful or negligent action or omission' of the respondent state.[208]

Finally, Tomuschat contends that the concept of providing full reparation stems from human rights law and not from public international law. He claims that the IACtHR first articulated the principle of full reparations when it incorrectly read the obligation to grant *restitutio in integrum* as the obligation to grant *full* reparations by referring to the *Factory at Chorzów* case.[209] While Tomuschat may indeed be correct, the ILC's Articles on State Responsibility later embraced this concept and it is now more accurate to refer to the principle of full reparation as belonging to the field of public international law.[210]

---

197 Article 34, ILC's ASR.

198 Article 31, ILC's ASR.

199 Ibid., Article 36; Kerbat, *supra* n. 88, p. 578.

200 These include, *inter alia*, acknowledging the breach, an expression of regret and a formal apology, Article 37 (1) (2), ILC's ASR.

201 International Commission of Jurists, *supra* n. 23, p. 27, citing the Commentary to Article 34, ILC's Commentaries to ASR, p. 95, para. 2

202 Ibid., p. 26.

203 Article 38, ILC's ASR; Shelton, *Remedies in International Human Rights Law, supra* n. 1, p. 156.

204 Lauterpacht, E. and Nevill, P. , "The different forms of reparation", in J. Crawford, A. Pellet and S. Olleson (eds.), *The Law on International Responsibility* (Oxford, OUP 2010), p. 617.

205 Shelton, *Remedies in International Human Rights Law, supra* n. 1, p. 42.

206 Brown, *supra* n. 7, p. 195.

207 Babu, *supra* n. 4, p. 79.

208 Article 39, ILC's ASR.

209 Tomuschat, C., *Human Rights: Between Idealism and Realism* (Oxford, OUP 2008, 2nd ed.), p. 363.

210 Article 31, ILC's ASR.

2.3.3 Adequacy and Appropriateness

Brown has submitted that the principle of appropriateness guiding the provision of reparations is a contested matter, and therefore the courts should decide, through jurisprudential developments, on adequate, just, fair, or appropriate measures of reparation.[211] The PCIJ understood adequacy to be '[r]estitution in kind, or, if this is not possible, payment of a sum corresponding to the value which a restitution in kind would bear.'[212] This definition overlaps with that of full reparations; in fact, the principle of adequacy helps to facilitate the awarding of full reparation The ICJ in the *Pulp Mills* case articulated adequacy more clearly, stating that the forms of reparation 'must be appropriate to the injury suffered, taking into account the nature of the wrongful act having caused it.'[213] In other words, it relates to the form of reparation that would make good the damage.[214]

Since the consequences of a violation vary, the appropriate measures to remedy that violation also differ. It has been argued that the adequacy of reparations depends on 'the nature of the court, the type of dispute, the identity of the parties, [...] the particular relief sought by the claimant,'[215] and 'the concrete circumstances surrounding each case and the precise nature and scope of the injury.'[216] What amounts to 'adequate' should therefore be decided on a case-by-case basis.[217] However, it is not always clear whether adequacy is a purely legal matter, or whether it allows some room for political influence. The reason for this is that after a judicial body hands down a judgment on responsibility, the matter of determining an adequate form of reparation is generally addressed through political means. In principle, the injured state may choose the form of reparation it prefers or considers the most appropriate.[218] Traditionally, the parties to the dispute arrive at a mutual agreement on the measures of reparation. In addition, even if a court decides on the measures of reparation, the parties to the case need to agree on the specific measures that are necessary to implement such a decision. For example, even if a court orders a responsible state to provide compensation, the parties might agree between themselves on the precise amount.[219] Another example is the ICJ practice to order that full reparation is to be provided, while allowing the

211 Brown, *supra* n. 7, p. 187-189.

212 PCIJ, *Factory at Chorzów* (*Germany* v. *Poland*), *supra* n. 57, p. 47.

213 ICJ, *Pulp Mills on the River Uruguay* (*Argentina* v. *Uruguay*), *supra* n. 184, para. 274.

214 Kerbat, *supra* n. 88, p. 579.

215 Brown, *supra* n. 7, p. 192.

216 ICJ, *Avena and other Mexican Nationals (Mexico* v. *United States of America)*, *supra* n. 164, para. 119.

217 Ibid.

218 Article 34 (2) (b), ILC's ASR.

219 In the case of *Factory Chorzow*, the Court indicated that compensation should cover (amongst other things) the loss of profits. However, since the parties had already agreed on the amount of compensation, they had the freedom to choose whether to include loss of profits. See: PCIJ, *Factory at Chorzów* (*Germany* v. *Poland*), *supra* n. 57, p. 49, 51.

responsible state to determine the measures that it considers most appropriate.[220] A recent example is found in the *Jurisdictional Immunities of the State* case, where the ICJ found Italy responsible for having violated Germany's sovereign immunity. The Court ruled that Italy had the duty to provide for *restitutio in integrum* by 'enacting appropriate legislation or by resorting to other means of its choosing.'[221] On the other hand, in cases where the ICJ has found that a violation of international obligations resulted from a state's national legislation or decision, it has ordered the state to undertake specific measures to remedy the situation.[222]

In principle, adequacy refers to the capacity of certain measures of reparations to repair the damage caused, but according to the ICJ's case law, it could be interpreted as the form of reparation preferred and deemed appropriate by the injured state. This choice is grounded in Article 43 (2) (b) of the ILC's Articles on State Responsibility, which states that the 'injured state may specify in particular … what form reparation should take'.[223] Crawford also refers explicitly to the right of the injured state to request a specific form of reparation.[224]

2.3.4 Proportionality

It is crucial that the reparation awarded is proportional to the injury caused.[225] Proportionality is closely linked to adequacy, as it establishes both the need to adopt certain measures to attain the objective of reparations and the limitations of the three recognised forms of reparations under public international law. Although the ILC's Articles on State Responsibility refer only to proportionality in relation to the injury and the measures of restitution and satisfaction awarded, its commentary extends the principle of proportionality to each of the three forms of reparations, including the measure of compensation.[226]

It has been argued that proportionality not only serves as a limitation on the forms of reparations, but it can also 'permit the increase in the award of damages in satisfaction,' in particular when dealing with gross violations of human rights.[227]

---

220 In this regard, the ICJ decides on reparations by taking into account the form of reparation requested by the injured State (it refuses to consider other forms). The ICJ also considers any motivated objections made by the responsible state on the form of reparation requested by the injured state. See: Kerbat, *supra* n. 88, p. 576-578.

221 ICJ (Judgment) 3 February 2012, *Jurisdictional Immunities of the State (Germany* v. *Italy: Greece intervening)*, *supra* n. 60, p. 154, para. 137.

222 ICJ (Judgment) 31 March 2014, *Whaling in the Antarctic* (*Australia* v. *Japan: New Zealand intervening*), para. 247 (7).

223 ICJ, *Avena and other Mexican Nationals (Mexico* v. *United States of America)*, *supra* n. 164, para. 119.

224 Crawford, *supra* n. 19, p. 508.

225 Article 35 (b), 37 (3), ILC's ASR.

226 Commentary to Article 34, ILC's Commentaries to ASR, p. 96, para. 5

227 Shelton, *Remedies in International Human Rights Law, supra* n. 1, p. 34.

It is worth noting that in some cases equitable considerations are invoked instead of the principle of proportionality.[228] For instance, it might be difficult to assess an amount of compensation in light of the proportionality principle, so judges might therefore use the principle of equity to guide their decision on a specific measure of reparation.[229]

Finally, it is important to recall that certain breaches of international obligations may be considered grave and the remedy should thus be proportional to such gravity. However, the concept of gravity within public international law is not well defined.[230] In this context, the proportionality of a given award should be defined with a certain degree of flexibility.

2.4 Other Substantive and Procedural Aspects of Reparations

2.4.1 Liability to Repair

A state that breaches an international obligation by an act or omission must erase all negative consequences that arise from it,[231] unless there is an insufficient causal link between the wrongful act and the resulting harm.[232] This is confirmed by the ILC's Articles on State Responsibility, which recognise that in inter-state complaints, states are liable to provide reparations once international responsibility has been established.[233] State responsibility in the context of an international violation cannot be established by another state. In fact, public international law dictates that no state may 'punish' or 'judge' another state.[234]

As international obligations lie predominantly with states, the obligation to repair also generally pertains to the responsible state. However, in the ICJ's advisory opinion on *Reparation for Injuries Suffered in the Service of the United Nations*, the Court recognised that states are not the only subjects of international law:[235] subjects

---

228 Ibid., p. 38.

229 The principle of equity 'involves flexibility and an objective consideration of what is just, fair and reasonable in all circumstances of the case'. See: ICJ, *Ahmadou Sadio Diallo* (*Republic of Guinea* v. *Democratic Republic of the Congo*), *supra* n. 84, para. 24.

230 Mavroidis, P. C., "Remedies in the WTO Legal System: Between a Rock and a Hard Place", 764 *EJIL* (2000), p. 772-773.

231 Article 1, ILC's ASR.

232 See the previous section on causality and the example ICJ, *Application of the Convention on the Prevention and Punishment of the Crime of Genocide* (*Bosnia and Herzegovina* v. *Serbia and Montenegro*), *supra* n. 145.

233 REDRESS, *supra* n. 29, p. 12.

234 Tomuschat, C., "The Responsibility of Other Entities: Private Individuals" in J. Crawford, A. Pellet and S. Olleson (eds.), *The Law on International Responsibility* (Oxford, OUP 2010), p. 320.

235 ICJ (Advisory Opinion) 11 April 1949, *Reparation for Injuries Suffered in the Service of the United Nations*; Crawford, J., "The System of International Responsibility", in J. Crawford, A. Pellet and S. Olleson (eds.), *The Law on International Responsibility* (Oxford, OUP 2010), p. 17-18.

also include legal persons, such as the United Nations. It could therefore be inferred that such legal persons also bear the duty to repair a breach of an international obligation for which they were found to have been responsible.[236]

2.4.2 Beneficiaries

Traditionally, the primary beneficiaries of reparations under public international law are states that have suffered an injury. Initially, states could only issue claims for internationally wrongful acts through inter-state complaints, as individuals could not enjoy rights without the intermediation of their respective states.[237] Based on this, the ILC's Articles on State Responsibility consider states to be the only 'affected subjects of international law,'[238] despite the fact that in cases in which nationals suffered injuries, the Court considered those injuries when calculating the damages.[239] The reason behind this is that in such cases the state whose nationals were directly affected could seek reparation for the internationally wrongful breach suffered by the state itself. In other words, the state claims reparations for its own injury and not for the injuries suffered directly by individual victims.[240] However, Article 33 (2) of the ILC's Articles on State Responsibility suggests that the state obligation to pay reparations can extend to individuals: 'the obligations of the responsible state' are to be understood 'without prejudice to any right, arising from the international responsibility of a state, which may accrue directly to any person or entity other than a state.'[241]

In its advisory opinion on the *Reparation for Injuries Suffered in the Service of the United Nations,* the ICJ recognised that international organisations, meaning non-state actors, are entitled to claim and receive reparations in an international dispute with a state.[242] In its subsequent advisory opinion on the *Wall*, the ICJ affirmed that

---

236 Crawford, *supra* n. 235, p. 17-18.

237 Echeverria, *supra* n. 90, p. 700-702.

238 Article 42, ILC's ASR; Tomuschat, C., "Individual Reparation Claims in Instances of Grave Human Rights Violations: The Position under General International Law", in A. Randerlzhofer and C. Tomuschat (eds.), *State Responsibility and the Individual: Reparations in Instances of Grave Violations of Human Rights* (Dordrecht, Kluwer Law International 1999), p. 3; Babu, *supra* n. 4, p. 65-66.

239 REDRESS, *supra* n. 29, p. 10; Shelton, *Remedies in International Human Rights Law, supra* n. 1, p. 32-33.

240 Where individuals have suffered harm as a resulf of violations of international law, the injury claimed is not that of the harmed individual but rather that of the state. Shelton, *Remedies in International Human Rights Law, supra* n. 1, p. 146; PCIJ (Judgment) 30 August 1924, *Mavrommatis Palestine Concessions* (*Greece* v. *United Kingdom*), p. 12.

241 Article 33 (1) (2), ILC's Article on State Responsibility. Similarly, Article 19 (c) of the Draft Articles on Diplomatic Protection states that it is the injured person who should receive any compensation obtained for the injury from the responsible State.

242 ICJ, *Reparation for Injuries Suffered in the Service of the United Nations, supra* n. 235, p. 17.

individuals can be beneficiaries of reparations. In this opinion, the Court ruled that Israel should pay compensation directly to individuals for property damage that arose as a consequence of Israel's construction of a wall.[243] In addition, the Court also extended the state duty to repair to any legal person.[244] These two advisory opinions of the ICJ appear to have opened the door for private individuals and both natural and legal persons to be considered beneficiaries of reparations in the context of inter-state complaints.

However, in contentious cases, the ICJ has not discussed at length the issue of who can be a beneficiary of reparations. Instead, the Court has referred to subjects of international law that can invoke the right to receive reparation; from this it could be inferred that a subject able to invoke the right to receive reparation is also entitled to benefit from that reparation. At first, the Court asserted that only states are able to invoke the right to receive reparation, and not a private individual who had suffered an injury or whose rights had been violated.[245] This approach changed in 2010 with the ICJ's judgment in *Guinea* v. *Democratic Republic of the Congo* (the *Diallo* case) where the ICJ granted compensation to an individual.[246] Although the claimant was the State of Guinea, the beneficiary of the reparations in this case was an individual.[247] For the first time in its history, the ICJ expanded the scope of a 'state' dimension to the individual,[248] due in large part to developments in international human rights law.[249] Significantly, the ICJ considered international human rights to be 'the substantive law

243 With regard to the fact 'that the construction of the wall in the Occupied Palestinian Territory has, *inter alia*, entailed the requisition and destruction of [property], the Court finds that Israel has the obligation to make reparation for the damage caused to all the natural or legal persons concerned'. See: ICJ, *Legal Consequences of the Construction of a Wall in the Occupied Palestinian Territory, supra* n. 96, para. 152. However, it has been argued that the ICJ's ruling may have been influenced by the fact that Palestine has not yet been recognised as a state, leaving natural and legal persons as the only viable recipients of measures of reparation. See: D'Argent, P., "Compliance, Cessation, Reparation and Restitution in the Wall Advisory Opinion" in P.M Dupuy et al. (eds.) Common values in International Law, Essays in Honour of Christian Tomuschat (Kehl, Engel Verlag 2006), p. 475.

244 ICJ, *Legal Consequences of the Construction of a Wall in the Occupied Palestinian Territory, supra* n. 96, p. 198, para. 152.

245 Stern, *supra* n. 53, p. 567, citing the ICJ, (Judgment) 19 December 2005, *Armed Activities on the Territory of the Congo (Democratic Republic of the Congo* v. *Uganda)*, Separate Opinion of Judge Simma, para. 37; Zyberi, *supra* n. 146, p. 207.

246 ICJ, *Ahmadou Sadio Diallo* (*Republic of Guinea* v. *Democratic Republic of the Congo*), *supra* n. 130, para. 161, 165 (7).

247 Ibid., Separate Opinion of Judge Cançado Trindade, para. 232.

248 ICJ, *Ahmadou Sadio Diallo* (*Republic of Guinea* v. *Democratic Republic of the Congo*), Separate Opinion of Judge Cançado Trindade, *supra* n. 84, para. 12.

249 ICJ, *Ahmadou Sadio Diallo* (*Republic of Guinea* v. *Democratic Republic of the Congo*), *supra* n. 130, para. 68; ICJ, *Ahmadou Sadio Diallo* (*Republic of Guinea* v. *Democratic Republic of the Congo*), Separate Opinion of Judge Cançado Trindade, *supra* n. 130, para. 237; ICJ, *Ahmadou Sadio Diallo* (*Republic of Guinea* v. *Democratic Republic of the Congo*), *supra* n. 84, para. 13.

applicable' to the case.[250] This approach seems to be in line with Article 33 (2) of the ILC's Articles on State Responsibility.[251]

Furthermore, when it comes to violations of peremptory norms and *erga omnes* obligations,[252] 'all states can be held to have a legal interest,' because those violations affect the international community as a whole.[253] However, the ICJ has clarified that even when there is evidence of damage, this neither implies nor creates a right for each state to claim reparations.[254] Similarly, the ILC's Articles on State Responsibility establish that where there is a violation of an *erga omnes* obligation, states are exceptionally entitled to invoke the responsibility of another state,[255] and to request the fulfilment of reparation 'in the interest of the injured state or the beneficiaries of the obligation breached.'[256] It is thus possible for a third state to seek reparation on behalf of the injured state.[257] Finally, beneficiaries are entitled to waive their right to reparation if they so wish.[258]

2.4.3 Assessment of Harm

Although the ILC's Articles on State Responsibility stipulate that upon the establishment of state responsibility there is 'an obligation to compensate for the damage caused,'[259] the Articles provide no explanation of how to quantify those damages. However, Article 36 defines damage as any non-material and material harm, the latter of which includes the loss of profits.[260]

By and large, assessing the harm caused by an internationally wrongful act is a complex task, which in general requires that several factors are considered depending upon, *inter alia,* whether the harm caused is pecuniary (material) or non-pecuniary (non-material).[261] It is important to note that in order to assess the harm caused, it

---

250 ICJ, *Ahmadou Sadio Diallo* (*Republic of Guinea* v. *Democratic Republic of the Congo*), Separate Opinion of Jugde Cançado Trindade, *supra* n. 130, para. 223.

251 Rombouts, Sardaro and Vandeginste, *supra* n. 24, p. 367.

252 For a distinction between peremptory norms and *erga omnes* obligations see: Vos, J.A., *The Function of Public International Law* (The Hague, T.M.C. Asser Press 2013), p. 249-273.

253 It is important to mention that while the breach of *erga omnes* obligations does not establish automatic jurisdiction over the issue by an international tribunal, it does with *jus cogens* violations. See: ICJ (Judgment) 30 June 1995, *Case concerning East Timor* (*Portugal* v. *Australia*), para. 29.

254 ICJ (Judgment) 5 February 1970, *Barcelona Traction, Light and Power Company, Limited (Belgium* v. *Spain)*, p. 32, 36, para. 33, 46.

255 Article 48, ILC's ASR.

256 Ibid., Article 54.

257 Crawford, *supra* n. 19, p. 503.

258 D'Argent, *supra* n. 171, p. 12.

259 Article 36, ILC's ASR.

260 Ibid.

261 The assessment of damages is also determined by the causal link between the wrongful act and the injury. A further explanation of the causal link is addressed in the section addressing causality.

must first be determined whether or not the damage in question can be assessed financially. If so, the manner of achieving this may vary, as changes in the market and methods of valuation directly affect financially assessable damage.[262] This is further complicated by the fact that 'value is not an absolute or unitary concept.'[263] It is furthermore accepted that the quantification formula for assessable damage will vary depending on, for instance, the nature of the primary obligation breached and the wrongful conduct involved.[264]

In relation to material harm, factors to be considered include the causal link between the damage and the harm; interest and costs; and the value of the material injury, the loss of profits (possible future income), and incidental expenses.[265] Additional and more specific criteria may also apply, depending on the type of material harm caused. For instance, in assessing harm to property the value of such property at both the time prior to its destruction and following its destruction is also considered.[266] As far as non-material harm is concerned, tribunals usually decide, within their own discretion, whether such harm is to be assessed financially or otherwise. The ICJ had never financially assessed non-material harm such as pain and suffering[267] until its decision in the *Diallo* case where the Court relied on the principle of an equitable basis[268] and made use of presumptions. In this case, the ICJ stated that psychological suffering and the loss of reputation were 'inevitable consequences' of the violation.[269]

It is difficult to identify any concrete guiding principles for the ICJ's approach to assessing damages, as it has only done so in two cases: in *Corfu Channel* and *Diallo*. In *Corfu Channel,* experts made the assessment,[270] and concluded that the value of the damage was greater than the amount claimed by the United Kingdom.[271] In *Diallo*, the ICJ made its own assessment of the damages by applying the principle of equity to determine the amount of money to be paid, although the Court provided

262 Shelton, *Remedies in International Human Rights Law, supra* n. 1, p. 41.

263 Barker, *supra* n. 118, p. 607.

264 Crawford, *supra* n. 19, p. 519; Shelton, *supra* n. 1, p. 41, citing Commentary to Article 36, ILC's Commentaries to ASR.

265 Shelton, *Remedies in International Human Rights Law, supra* n. 1, p. 42-44, 146-456; Barker, *supra* n. 118, p. 609.

266 Shelton, *supra* n. 1, p. 152-155. In addition, to engage in the assessment of the loss of lives also implies the consideration of different factors.

267 Zyberi, *supra* n. 146, p. 209.

268 It must be recalled that non-material harm in an international context is not usually assessed. Instead, measures of satisfaction are granted for this kind of harm. ICJ, *Ahmadou Sadio Diallo* (*Republic of Guinea* v. *Democratic Republic of the Congo*), *supra* n. 84, para. 33.

269 Ibid., para. 21.

270 ICJ, *Corfu Channel* (*United Kingdom of Great Britain* and *Northern Ireland* v. *Albania*), *supra* n. 134, p. 246-249.

271 Crawford, *supra* n. 19, p. 519.

no further explanation. Instead, the Court mentioned that the principle of equity is used by several judicial and non-judicial human rights bodies.[272]

Finally, it must be pointed out that a great deal of inconsistency surrounds the way in which international courts decide upon the type of damages and the way(s) in which they are financially assessed.[273] From this it can be concluded that courts exercise both discretion and flexibility in their assessment of damages. While flexibility and discretion may allow for the consideration of more claims for reparation, such an approach has its drawbacks. For instance, international courts, including the ICJ, usually decide on a discretionary basis whether expert opinions are required.[274] Expert opinions can also be used to assess damages, and in this context it is not yet clear why in some cases the ICJ acts as a financial expert in quantifying damages, whereas in others it does not.

2.4.4 Standard of Proof

At present, under international law there are no common evidentiary procedural laws except for the general principle of law establishing that claimants must prove their assertions (*actori incumbit onus probandi).*[275] This general principle applies to the merits as well as to reparations, but is subject to some flexibility. First, the burden of proof can be shared. A case in point is *Armed Activities on the Territory of the Congo,* in which the applicant alleged the use of illegal force while the respondent alleged the justification of such force on the grounds of self-defence.[276] In this case, both parties bore the burden of proof concerning their allegations. In addition, in establishing the compensation awarded in the *Diallo* case, the ICJ upheld that the *onus probandi* could be shifted to the respondent state if it were 'in a better position to establish certain facts.'[277] The ILC's Articles on State Responsibility provide no guidance on the evidentiary laws governing claims including reparations.[278] However, international adjudicative bodies generally rely on their founding treaties or agreements as guidelines regarding the standard of proof required to prove a claim such as an injury or damage.[279]

272 ICJ, *Ahmadou Sadio Diallo* (*Republic of Guinea* v. *Democratic Republic of the Congo*), *supra* n. 84, para. 24.

273 Gray, *supra* n. 5, p. 881.

274 Riddell, A., "Evidence, Fact-Finding, and Experts", in C. Romano, K. Alter and Y. Shany (eds.), *The Oxford Handbook of International Adjudication* (Oxford, OUP 2015), p. 852.

275 Ibid., p. 858.

276 Thienel, T., "The Burden and Standard of Proof in the European Court of Human Rights", 50 *German Yearbook of International Law* (2007), p. 550-551.

277 ICJ, *Ahmadou Sadio Diallo* (*Republic of Guinea* v. *Democratic Republic of the Congo*), *supra* n. 84, p. 5.

278 Shelton, *supra* n. 187, p. 854.

279 Riddell, *supra* n. 274, p. 853.

In general, international courts tend to be flexible when it comes to the application of some evidentiary rules, including those on the burden and standard of proof.[280] The underlying reason for this is their desire to respect the sovereignty of the states that are parties to the proceedings, and to reduce procedural hurdles that might prevent the settlement of disputes. A flexible approach towards the rules regulating the standard of proof may also be justified in an international context as there is often a significant period of time between the act alleged and the proceedings that follow. In addition, flexibility is necessary in order to allow for the diverse legal systems represented on international benches. Against this background, international tribunals tend to adopt different approaches towards evidence and, thereby, different standards of proof.[281]

Some consistency can be observed in the use of standards by international courts. Standards that are commonly employed include: i) the 'preponderance of evidence' also called the 'balance of probabilities', 'more likely than not', and 'more probable than not'; ii) 'beyond reasonable doubt'; and iii) '*l'intime conviction du juge*' also known as the 'sufficiency of evidence'. Whilst both the preponderance of evidence and the standard of beyond reasonable doubt stem from common law legal systems, the former is a lower standard more commonly associated with civil proceedings, which is met when a claim is more likely than not to be true. The latter is a higher standard which is predominantly applicable in criminal proceedings, and requires that the evidence presented is so convincing that a plausible reason to believe contrary to that evidence cannot be found. '*L'intime conviction du juge*', or the sufficiency of evidence, is a standard of proof used in both civil and criminal proceedings, and it refers to convincing or persuading the judge of a given affirmation. Riddell claims that the standard of proof is better understood in national rather than international contexts, and that international courts usually struggle in adopting one standard or another. The practice of the ICJ exemplifies this: the Court has made use of the three standards in different cases without explaining its reasons for doing so.[282]

For instance, regarding the merits, in the *Corfu Channel* case the ICJ required a degree of certainty from the United Kingdom to prove the 'exceptional gravity' of the allegations put forward;[283] in other words, the evidence should leave '*no room* for reasonable doubt'[284] However, in the *Bosnia and Herzegovina* v. *Serbia and Montenegro* case, the Court upheld that the allegations must be 'fully conclusive'[285]

280 A detailed discussion on the burden of proof falls outside the scope of this section. For further insights on this topic, see: Riddell, *supra* n. 274, p. 853.

281 Ibid., p. 850-852.

282 Ibid., p. 861-863.

283 ICJ, *Corfu Channel* (*United Kingdom of Great Britain* and *Northern Ireland* v. *Albania*), *supra* n. 136, p. 17.

284 Ibid., p. 18.

285 ICJ, *Application of the Convention on the Prevention and Punishment of the Crime of Genocide* (*Bosnia and Herzegovina* v. *Serbia and Montenegro*), *supra* n. 145, p. 17.

and that the Court must be 'fully convinced' that the allegations have been clearly established. This reference seems to suggest that, in this case, the Court used the standard of *'l'intime conviction'*.

Finally, 'judicial notice' can also be considered sufficient to meet the standard of proof required. Judicial notice refers to a court's acceptance of notorious or well-known facts as proven and indisputable facts. In general, judicial notices stem from the precedents created from Court dockets.[286] In the case of *Bosnia and Herzegovina* v. *Serbia and Montenegro* the ICJ used cross-court judicial notice by upholding that the commission of genocide was proven, as the ICTY, a different international court of a different nature, had previously determined this.[287]

Thus, the standard of proof applied to demonstrate a specific injury varies between international tribunals, and, to some extent, the nature of the tribunal is decisive for the approach adopted. In general, flexibility prevails when it comes to choosing a standard of proof.[288] Although flexibility might at times bring uncertainty for the parties, it might be more effectual in proceedings than a clear and strict standard. Compensation cases provide a useful example: if the standard were strict, the amount of compensation could be negatively impacted if the assessment of damages were reduced to the minimum. In such cases, some flexibility may facilitate a higher award of monetary compensation.[289]

2.4.5 Causality

Regardless of which standard of proof a tribunal adopts, there must be a causal link between the wrongful act and the damage claimed for a state to be obliged to provide reparation.[290] This is confirmed by Article 31 (1) of the ILC's Articles on State Responsibility:

The responsible state is under an obligation to make full reparation for the injury caused by the internationally wrongful act.[291]

Although causality is closely related to the principle of providing full reparation,[292] public international law does not provide a uniform definition of what

286 Judicial notice is an important tool for expediting trials because it allows a judge to accept facts without corroborating evidence. These facts are usually taken from other judgments. See: 'judicial notice' in Law, J., *Oxford Dictionary of Law* (Oxford, OUP 2015, 8th ed.). It should be state that a judicial notice can also cover uncontested information outsourced from a non-judicial body.

287 Riddell, *supra* n. 274, p. 862-864.

288 Ibid., p. 865, 868.

289 Gray, *supra* n. 5, p. 888.

290 Article 31 (2), ILC's ASR; Shelton, *supra* n. 1, p. 144.

291 Ibid., Article 31 (1).

292 Babu, *supra* n. 4, p. 76. In addition, causality is a requirement for obtaining compensation. See: Crawford, *supra* n. 19, p. 482.

constitutes a causal link.[293] Crawford has even stated that there is no such thing as a general principle of causality within public international law.[294] Several scholars have furthermore criticised the ILC's Articles on State Responsibility for not addressing the issue of causation in more detail.[295] In fact, all documents that deal with reparations avoid the establishment of a causal link test that could determine the measure of reparation.[296] The reason behind this reluctance is partially explained by the ILC's Commentaries to the Articles on State Responsibility, which clearly state that the 'causal link is not necessarily the same in relation to every breach of an international obligation.'[297] The Commentaries thus bestow tribunals and states with significant discretionary powers to adopt and develop appropriate causality tests.[298] Finally, this wording suggests that causal link tests should be decided on a case-by-case basis.[299]

In general, the damages claimed should not be too inconsequential, indirect or remote from the wrongful act.[300] Causation therefore also limits the extent to which the harm is to be repaired,[301] and is thus of crucial importance when establishing reparations.[302] Although this importance is not contested, the exact content and meaning of causality is a matter of contention. Some scholars have argued that the discretion surrounding causality reflects a policy choice for a tribunal,[303] with the aim 'to provide the victim with equitable compensation for the harm suffered.'[304]

Two types of causation can be identified: factual causation (also known as the '*sine qua non test*', 'cause-in-fact', and the 'but-for test') and legal causation, and both should be proven simultaneously. While the tests for factual causation are strict, requiring the commission of the wrongful act to be essential or indispensable

293 Gattini, A., "Breach of the Obligation to Prevent and Reparation Thereof in the ICJ's Genocide Judgment", 18 *The European Journal of International Law* (2007), p. 708; Commentary to Article 31 (2), ILC's Commentaries to ASR, p. 92, para. 10.

294 UN, ILC (Third report of the Special Rapporteur, James Crawford, on State Responsibility) 15 March, 15 June, 10 and 18 July and 4 August 2000, UN. Doc. A/CN.4/507, para. 28-29.

295 Crawford, *supra* n. 19, p. 494.

296 Stern, *supra* n. 53, p. 569-570; Shelton, *supra* n. 1, p. 39; McCarthy, C. "Reparation for Gross Violations of Human Rights law and International Humanitarian Law at the International Court of Justice", in C. Ferstman, M. Goetz and A. Stephens (eds.), *Reparations for Victims of Genocide, War Crimes and Crimes Against Humanity: Systems in Place and Systems in the Making* (Leiden, Martinus Nijhoff 2009), p. 291.

297 Commentary to Article 31, ILC's Commentaries to ASR, p. 93, para. 10.

298 Shelton, *supra* n. 187, p. 846-847; Shelton, *supra* n. 1, p. 144.

299 McCarthy, *supra* n. 296, p. 291.

300 Shelton, *supra* n. 1, p. 33, 39.

301 Gattini, A. "The UN Compensation: Old Rules, New Procedures on War Reparations", 13 *European Journal of International Law* (2002), p. 172; Barker, *supra* n. 118, p. 605; D'Argent, *supra* n. 171, p. 15.

302 D'Argent, *supra* n. 171, p. 12

303 Ibid., p. 15.

304 Parisi, F. and Fon, V., "Causation and Responsibility: The Compensation Principle from Grotius to Calabresi", 64 *Maryland Law Review* (2005), p. 114.

to the harm suffered, the legal standard of causality requires the commission of the wrongful act to be substantial but not necessarily indispensable.[305] The 'but-for' test, or factual causation, is a precondition for establishing if the harm is attributable to the state. If we consider the following example: x is driving and fails to stop at a red traffic light, colliding with y's car. Y claims that, as a result of the accident, her car is damaged beyond repair, and that she has suffered psychological harm. The test for factual causation requires that *but for* x's actions, the harm suffered by *y* would not have occurred.

The test for legal causation requires the presence of a link between *x*'s actions and the harm(s) suffered by *y*; in other words, the establishment of a link between the car accident and *y*'s claims. Several tests can be applied to establish legal causality but the most commonly applied are directness, foreseeability, and proximity.[306] In addition, presumptions of injuries can also be used to establish causality in an international dispute.[307] Directness refers to the chain of events that result from a wrongful act.[308] According to Arangio-Ruiz, the legal causation of directness is very difficult to prove and it has been used by arbitrarial tribuanls to justify the rejection of compensation claims.[309] The foreseeability test examines whether the respondent state could have foreseen a specific injury before engaging in an act or omission that led to the wrongful act.[310] As such, it has been preferred by some arbitral tribunals in the belief that foreseeability 'provides some discipline and predictability in assessing proximity.'[311] The proximity test, on the other hand, relates to indirect losses that are not too remote. This test is met when one of the two following questions is answered positively: i) 'Is the harm a natural consequence of the violation?' or ii) '[W]ere the damages reasonably contemplated by both parties when they [adopted the international agreement] as being a probable result of the breach?'[312]

The issue of causality is further complicated by the fact that the scope of each test depends on the rules and traditions of the jurisdiction within which the

---

305 McCarthy, *supra* n. 296, p. 297.

306 McCarthy, *supra* n. 296, p. 292. In addition, there are some other causation tests that are rarely used such as 'ambit of the purpose' and 'natural and normal sequences' and 'adequate causation'. See: Gattini, *supra* n. 293, p. 708-109; Capone et al., *supra* n. 44, p. 115-116; Babu, *supra* n. 4, p. 77-78.

307 Shelton, *supra* n. 1, p. 33.

308 Castellanos-Jankiewicz, L., "Causation and International State Responsibility", 5 *SHARES Research Paper* (2012), p. 52.

309 Fox, M.B., "Imposing Liability for Losses from Agrresive War: An Economic Analyis of the UN Compensation Commission", 13 *European Journal of International Law* (2011), p. 203.

310 McCarthy, *supra* n. 296, p. 297.

311 EECC Decision Number 7: *Guidance Regarding Jus ad Bellum Liability* (2007), para. 13.

312 Justice Yaw Appau, "Justice of the Court of Appeal in Ghana: Assessment of Damages", *Paper Presented at Induction Course for Newly Appointed Circuit Judges at the Judicial Training Institute*, p. 3. Available at: <http://jtighana.org/new/links/papers/ASSESSMENT%20OF%20DAMAGES%20-Justice%20Yaw%20Appau.pdf>.

test is applied.[313] The approach of the ICJ illustrates these complexities: the Court applies the criteria of 'sufficient directness' and a 'certain causal nexus' between the wrongful act and the injury suffered. In other words: it seeks to establish a 'sufficient degree of certainty'.[314] The way in which the Court has applied such criteria appears to resemble the *causa sine qua non* test. This becomes clear in the case of *Bosnia and Herzegovina* v. *Serbia and Montenegro* in which the ICJ ruled that Serbia had violated its international obligations under the Genocide Convention to prevent and punish genocide. Consequently, the Court decided that Serbia was under an obligation to provide reparation. However, the ICJ upheld that there was not a 'sufficiently direct and certain causal nexus' between the illegal conduct and the damage.[315] Since causality is crucial in establishing a claim for financial compensation,[316] it did not grant compensation for the harm claimed by Bosnia. Instead, the Court ruled that acknowledging state responsibility in the judgment (a measure of satisfaction) was a sufficient form of reparation for the applicant state.[317] In other words, the ICJ required the applicant state to prove that the respondent state's wrongful act amounted to a substantial and significant contribution to the occurrence of the act of genocide, and that if such a wrongful act had not been committed, the genocide would not have occurred.[318] The ICJ thus applied a *sine qua non* test with a *sui generis* verbal formula.

This judgment raises several concerns. First, while the ILC's Articles on State Responsibility allow the causal link to change from case to case, they do not provide for the link to vary according to the modality of the reparation. In this case, the ICJ decided otherwise. The Court seems to have applied a lower causality test with regard to the measure of satisfaction, and a higher causality test with regard to the claim for compensation. Second, it is not clear whether the causal link varies if the wrongful act is an act or an omission; if this is the case, then the legal grounds for such an approach are also unclear, as[319] the ILC's Articles on State Responsibility do not distinguish between an act and an omission.[320] Third, it is clear that the Court's stance was the result of the applicant's failure to meet the standard of proof required for the compensation claimed.[321] Fourth, it must be acknowledged that it was Bosnia

---

313 Barker, *supra* n. 118, p. 605.

314 ICJ, *Ahmadou Sadio Diallo* (*Republic of Guinea* v. *Democratic Republic of the Congo*), *supra* n. 84, para. 61.

315 ICJ, *Application of the Convention on the Prevention and Punishment of the Crime of Genocide* (*Bosnia and Herzegovina* v. *Serbia and Montenegro*), *supra* n. 145, para. 459-463.

316 Gray, *supra* n. 5, p. 875.

317 ICJ, *Application of the Convention on the Prevention and Punishment of the Crime of Genocide* (*Bosnia and Herzegovina* v. *Serbia and Montenegro*), *supra* n. 145, para. 459-463.

318 McCarthy, *supra* n. 296, p. 294.

319 Ibid., p. 288-289.

320 Article 2, ILC's ASR.

321 ICJ, *Application of the Convention on the Prevention and Punishment of the Crime of Genocide* (*Bosnia and Herzegovina* v. *Serbia and Montenegro*), *supra* n. 145, para. 462.

that limited the reparation by asking the Court for a declaratory judgment in its memorial.[322]

2.5 Compliance with Judgments on Reparations

Compliance with judgments is essential to uphold the rule of law and thereby the principle of legality. However, neither conceptualising nor measuring compliance is a simple task. In fact, there is a growing need to define compliance as well as to develop a method by which to measure it. Compliance can be anything between a single act or a long and slow process, and factors such as the clarity or ambiguity of a court's order, state capacity, and the complexity of the remedial order must be taken into account,[323] as well as the potential need for negotiations among the state parties to the dispute to find a remedy[324] 'of [their] own choosing.'[325]

For instance, in contentious cases involving state responsibility for violations of international law the ICJ is generally reluctant to specify the means of compliance. In the *Gabcíkovo-Nagymaros Project* case, the ICJ ruled that *restitutio in integrum* would be achieved if both Hungary and Slovakia resumed their cooperation in the utilisation of their shared water resources.[326] In addition, the ICJ acknowledged that while both states had suffered financial losses from the wrongdoing performed by the other, a settlement would have been achieved had both parties retracted their claims for monetary compensation.[327] However, the parties were unable to come to an agreement, and Slovakia requested an additional judgment.[328] In this case, two obstacles to compliance can be identified: the lack of a political will on the part of both the applicant and respondent state, and the lack of clarity from the Court. Another example is the *Haya de la Torre* case. The ICJ stated with respect to the issue of how to implement its judgment that 'it is not part of the Court's judicial function to make such a choice'.[329] Since a lack of compliance can decrease the legitimacy of a court, it is desirable that judgments, including those concerning reparations, are as clear as possible.[330] Perhaps the lack of clarity stems from the Court's willingness to abide

322 Gattini, *supra* n. 293, p. 707; D'Argent, *supra* n. 171, p. 15.
323 Huneeus, A., "Compliance with Judgments and Decisions", in C. Romano, K. Alter and Y. Shany (eds.), *The Oxford Handbook of International Adjudication* (Oxford, OUP 2015), p. 437-445.
324 Schulter, C., *Compliance with decisions of the International Court of Justice* (New York, OUP 2004), p. 405.
325 Brown, *supra* n. 7, p. 213.
326 ICJ (Judgment) 25 September 1997, *Gabčíkovo-Nagymaros Project* (*Hungary* v. *Slovakia*), para. 150.
327 Ibid., para. 153.
328 Gray, *supra* n. 5, p. 877-878.
329 ICJ (Judgment) 13 June 1951, *Haya de la Torre* (*Colombia* v. *Peru*), para. 79-83; ICJ (Judgment) 20 December 1974, *Nuclelar Test* (*Australia* v. *France*); ICJ, *Arrest Warrant of 11 April 2000* (*Democratic Republic of the Congo* v. *Belgium*), *supra* n. 97.
330 Huneeus, *supra* n. 323, p. 442.

by declaratory judgments and not by mandatory ones. Mandatory judgments are not traditionally seen as appropriate judicial remedies in public international law.[331]

Assessing compliance can be influenced by the period of time that a state takes to fully comply with a judgment; for instance, complying with a judgment within six months has a different impact than complying with a judgment within twenty years. Lastly, it is important to note that enforcement mechanisms can sometimes be decisive in achieving state compliance. The PCIJ for instance asserted in the *Factory at Chorzów* case that it did not have the power to monitor compliance with its judgments: who 'neither can nor should contemplate the contingency of [a] judgment not being complied with.'[332] Compliance with the ICJ's judgments was originally envisaged as a task for the UN Security Council (UNSC) through its Article 94(2):[333] in cases of non-compliance with an ICJ ruling, the creditor party may resort to the UNSC. Yet the ICJ has a – albeit limited – role in compliance with its judgments, as it 'may require previous compliance with the terms of the judgment' as a condition for admitting proceedings in revision.[334] In addition, the matter of compliance with the judgments of the ICJ is confidential, and if a case remains in the ICJ's docket, it is possible to infer that the parties have not reached an agreement.

Significantly, Schulter has stated that the compliance record for judgments on contentious cases is 'generally satisfactory'.[335] If Article 94(2) is triggered by a creditor state, the UNSC may 'make recommendations or decide on measures to be taken to give effect to the judgment.'[336] The underlying reason for delegating the compliance task to the UNSC and not to the ICJ was that non-compliance can generate new political tensions among states and thus requires political action.[337] Significantly, no practice of the UNSC regarding states' non-compliance with the ICJ's judgments in contentious cases exists.[338] Despite this, some creditor states have brought cases of non-compliance before the UNSC, yet the UNSC did not take action, nor did states follow up through requests for a Council meeting.[339] Finally, while Schulter has stated that the compliance record for judgments on contentious cases is 'generally satisfactory',[340] whether a state may institute proceedings as a consequence of non-compliance remains unclear, as this has not yet been affirmed by the ICJ.

---

331 Gray, *supra* n. 36, p. 159-160.
332 PCIJ, *Factory at Chorzów* (*Germany* v. *Poland*), *supra* n. 57, p. 63.
333 Huneeus, *supra* n. 323, p. 444-445, 449.
334 Article 61 (3), ICJ's Statute.
335 Schulter, *supra* n. 324, p. 403.
336 Article 94 (2), UN Charter.
337 Schulter, *supra* n. 324, p. 19.
338 Ibid., p. 5.
339 Schulter, *supra* n. 324, p. 39 citing the ICJ case on Military and paramilitary activities in and against Nicaragua. What is interesting in this case is that Nicaragua brought to the attention of the UNSC the lack of compliance on the part of the US, which is a permanent member of the UNSC.
340 Schulter, *supra* n. 324, p. 403.

3 Reparations: A Human Right for Victims

As with violations of public international law, the issue of state responsibility is central when a state breaches an international human rights obligation.[341] However, the nature of state obligations stemming from human rights violations differs from that of state obligations based on violations of public international law.[342] As a result, the nature of the associated proceedings differs, as well as the reparations approach adopted.[343] This section will address the evolution of reparations from a state obligation to an individual human right.

Although the obligation to provide reparations was initially limited to inter-state disputes, individuals now enjoy the right to reparation for breaches of human rights obligations. States parties to international human rights instruments are therefore obliged to provide an effective remedy, including reparations, to the individual whose protected rights have been violated.[344] In this light, reparations are perceived as a requirement for justice.[345]

The shift from a state-oriented focus of reparations towards a victim-oriented focus can be attributed to several developments that precede the adoption of human rights treaties.[346] An example is the Final Act of the Paris Conference on Reparations, which obliged Germany to pay reparations and compensation to the Allied forces on behalf of the individual victims of the Holocaust.[347] This act arguably acknowledged, indirectly, the individual right to reparations for a crime committed by a state. In addition, the inadequacy of the inter-state reparations following the Second World War and the subsequent disappointment of its victims contributed significantly to the shift to victim-oriented reparations, as well as the pursuit of the legal protection of individuals against states.[348]

The adoption of a *corpus juris* designed to protect all individuals from human rights abuses was undoubtedly an important step in consolidating the individual right to reparation.[349] This right has since been recognised by various non-binding[350]

341 Shelton, *supra* n. 1, p. 32; van Boven, *supra* n. 23, p. 24-27; van Boven, T., "The need to repair?", 16 *The International Journal of Human Rights* (2012), p. 694; REDRESS, *supra* n. 29, p. 13.

342 Shelton, *supra* n. 1, p. 59.

343 Ibid., p. 60-61.

344 Article 2 (3) ICCPR; Article 13 ECHR; Articles 2, 25 ACHR; Articles 2, 7 ACHPR.

345 van Boven, *supra* n. 341, p. 694.

346 Wolfe, *supra* n. 3, p. 36-37.

347 Peté, S. and du Plessis, M., "Reparations for Gross Violations of Human Rights in Context", in M. du Plessis and S. Peté (eds.), *Repairing the Past? International Perspectives on Reparations for Human Rights Abuses* (Antwerp, Intersentia 2007), p. 11; Wolfe, *supra* n. 3, p. 36-37; Final Act of the Paris Conference on Reparation as adopted on 21 December 1945.

348 Buxbaum, R. M., "From Paris to London: The Legal History of European Reparation Claims: 1946-1953", 31 *Berkeley Journal of International Law* (2013), p. 324.

349 REDRESS, *supra* n. 29, p. 11.

350 1985 Victims' Declaration, 2005 Principles on Reparations.

and binding[351] international and regional human rights instruments. Most human rights instruments employ different terms to refer to reparation, including 'effective remedy',[352] 'compensation',[353] 'adequate compensation',[354] 'fair compensation',[355] 'redress',[356] 'rehabilitation',[357] and 'physical and psychological recovery and integration'.[358] Although, strictly speaking, each term has a different meaning, these differences are often negligible and the terms are regularly used interchangeably.[359] Despite the lack of terminological consistency, the individual right to reparation is well established under international human rights law and is considered to be part of customary international law.[360]

It is worth mentioning that the recognition of the right to reparation is further supported by the vast jurisprudence of regional and international judicial and non-judicial bodies.[361] In addition, this right has also been recognised under instruments of

351 The recognition of a victim's right to reparation has a long history, which began with Article 8 UDHR, followed by several binding international human rights instruments that include, *inter alia*, Articles 3, 9 (5) ICCPR; Articles 13, 14 CAT; Article 6 CERD; Article 39 CRC; Articles 5, 50 ECHR; Articles 10, 25, 63 (1) ACHR; Article 2 (c) CEDAW; Articles 13, 16 CRPD; Article 24 (4) (5) ICED; and Article 27(1) P-ACHPR.

352 Article 8 UDHR, Article 13 ECHR.

353 Article 10 American Declaration on Human Rights (ADHR); Article 14 ICCPR, Article 3 (5) ECHR; Article 3 (5) Protocol 7 to the ECHR; Article 91 Additional Protocol 1 to the Geneva Conventions.

354 Principle 47, Draft Principles on the Allocation of Loss in the case of Transboundary Harm arising out of Hazardous Activities.

355 Article 63 (1) ADHR, Article 9 (5) ICCPR.

356 Article 14, CAT.

357 Articles 13, 16, CRPD.

358 Article 39, CRC.

359 Haasdijk, S., "The Lack of Uniformity in the Terminology of the International Law of Remedies", 5 *Leiden Journal of International Law* (1992), p. 245-263.

360 van Boven, *supra* n. 23, p. 21; Letter dated 12 October 2000 from the President of the International Tribunal for the Former Yugoslavia Addressed to the Secretary-General, UN Doc. S/2000/1063, 3 November 2000, para. 47; Letter dated 9 November 2000 from the President of the International Criminal Tribunal for Rwanda Addressed to the Secretary-General, UN Doc. S/2000/1198, 15 December 2000, para. 6; Evans, *supra* n. 8, p. 40; Lenzerini, F. and Vrdoljak, A. (eds.), *International Law for Common Goods: Normative Perspectives on Human Rights, Culture and Nature* (Oxford/Portland, Hart 2014); Peters, A., *Beyond Human Rights: The Legal Status of the Individual in International Law* (Cambridge, CUP 2016), p. 186. In addition, the following sections will reinforce this statement.

361 ICJ, *Legal Consequences of the Construction of a Wall in the Occupied Palestinian Territory supra* n. 96, para. 152-153; HRC, *supra* n. 62, para. 16, establishing that Article 2 (3) 'requires that States Parties make reparation to individuals whose Covenant rights have been violated'; Report by the Special Rapporteur on the promotion of truth, justice, reparation and guarantees of non-recurrence, Pablo de Greiff, UN Doc A/69/518, 8 October 2014, para. 17; Evans, *supra* n. 8, p. 30-31 and 52; McCarthy, C., *Reparations and Victim Support in the International Criminal Court* (Cambridge, CUP, 2012), p. 13-18.

different branches of international law such as humanitarian law[362] and international criminal law.[363] Finally, states' practice[364] and *opinio juris* also appear to support the right to reparations.[365]

Although it is generally asserted that the individual right to reparation is recognised globally,[366] whether it is based on treaty or international customary law,[367]

362 Zegveld, L., "Remedies for Victims of Violations of International Humanitarian Law", 85 *International Review of the Red Cross* (2003), p. 525; Gillard, E., "Reparations for violations of international humanitarian law", 85 *International Review of the Red Cross* (2003), p. 529. In addition, Kalshoven has argued that the *travaux prḗparatoires* of Article 3 of the Hague Convention confer on individuals the right to compensation once it is established that there has been a violation of humanitarian law. See: Kalshoven, F., "State Responsibility for Warlike Acts of the Armed Forces: From Article 3 of the Hague Convention IV of 1907 to Article 91 of Additional Protocol I of 1977 and beyond", 40 *The International and Comparative Law Quarterly* (1991), p. 827. However, the remaining challenge is determining who is liable to make the reparation and the body to which the reparations claim should be made.

363 Article 75, ICC's Rome Statute, Rules 94-98 ICC's Rules of Procedure and Evidence; Rules 23*quinquies* and 80*bis*, ECCC Internal Rules as revised on 16 January 2015.

364 Several State reparation programmes and peace agreements have also recognised that victims are entitled to reparations. See: Evans, *supra* n. 8, p. 4. However, it must be highlighted that peace agreements might also include amnesties and the absence of reparations. See also: Slye, R.C., "A Limited Amnesty? Insights from Cambodia" *Seattle University School of Law Research Paper No. 12-24,* (2012), p. 2.

365 When the Principles on Reparations were debated and adopted, the States' comments and reactions did not 'question the existence of an international right to reparation owned by the victims', but rather focused on their content. See: Expert Seminar on "Reparation for Victims of Gross and Systematic Human Rights Violations in the Context of Political Transitions", *supra* n. 82, p. 17.

366 Zegveld, L., "Victims's Reparations Claims and International Criminal Courts: Incompatble Values?", 8 *Journal of International Criminal Justice,* (2010), p. 85; Buyse, A., "Lost and Regained? Restitution as a Remedy for Human Rights Violations in the Content of International Law", 68 *Heidelberg Journal of International Law* (2008), p. 134, citing Kamminga, M., "Legal Consequences of an Internationally Wrongful Act of a State against an Individual", in: M.L. van Emmerik, P. Hein van Kempen and T. Barkhuysen (eds.), *The Execution of Strasbourg and Geneva Human Rights Decisions in the National Legal Order* (The Hague: Martinus Publishers 1999), p. 65-74; van Boven, *supra* n. 23, p. 21.

367 Shelton, *supra* n. 1, p. 238; Bassiouni, *supra* n. 21, p. 217-218; OHCHR, *Rule-of-Law Tools for Post-Conflict States, Reparations Programs* (New York/Geneva, UN 2008), p. 6; Rose, C., "An Emerging Norm: The Duty of States to Provide Reparations for Human Rights Violations by Non-State Actors", 33 *Hastings International and Comparative Law Review* (2010), p. 307; Pisillo-Mazzeschi, R., "International Obligation to Provide Reparation Claims?", in A. Randelzhofer and C. Tomuschat (eds.), *State Responsibility and the Individual: Reparation in Instances of Grave Violations of Human Rights* (The Hague, Martinus Nijhoff 1999), p. 171; Rombouts, Sardaro and Vandeginste, *supra* n. 24, p. 367.

some scholars have challenged this view.[368] For instance, Tomuschat argues that reparations are a secondary state obligation that has not yet evolved into an individual right. He states that while the right to a remedy is well recognised under international human rights law, its recognition is limited to its procedural aspect (available recourses to bring a claim).[369] In addition, he asserts that while some human rights instruments allow for reparation or compensation for victims, they face two major limitations. First, the decision on whether to grant reparations is highly discretionary; and second, reparations are usually limited to certain violations. These are not necessarily those considered gross,[370] but rather the violations indicated in each instrument.

3.1 Concept of Reparation

Under international human rights law, the primary purpose of reparations is to help to deliver justice to victims of human rights violations. They aim to address and ameliorate the victims' suffering[371] by providing compensation for all material and non-material damages incurred,[372] thus enabling them to resume their lives and overcome the trauma endured.[373] As such, the right to reparation is a cornerstone of the protection of human rights.[374]

In addition, reparations issued in the context of human rights not only benefit the victims of the violation: they may also have a socio-political impact. Reparations facilitate accountability by conveying a message of disapproval for the violation. They also have the potential to both impact public policies[375] and prevent

---

368 Letschert, R. and van Boven, T., "Providing Reparation in Situations of Mass Victimization: Key Challenges Involved", in R. Letschert et al. (eds.), *Victimological Approaches to International Crimes: Africa* (Cambridge, Intersentia 2011), p. 167, citing International Law Association, *Draft Declaration of International Law Principles on Reparation for Victims of Armed Conflict (Substantive Issues)*, Conference Report, 74th ILA Conference (15-20 August 2010), p. 2; Tomuschat, *supra* n. 209, p. 358-372; Tomuschat, C., "Darfur: Compensation for the Victims", 3 *Journal of International Criminal Justice* (2005), p. 579-589; Evans, *supra* n. 8, p. 40-41. Similarly, Seibert-Fohr contests the existence of the right to reparations, See: Seibert-Fohr, A., *Prosecuting Serious Human Rights Violations* (Oxford, OUP 2009), p. 244.

369 Tomuschat, *supra* n. 209, p. 359-360.

370 Tomuschat, C., "Reparations for victims of gross human rights violations", 10 *Tulane Journal of International and Comparative Law* (2002), p. 183; Evans, *supra* n. 8, p. 41.

371 IACtHR (Judgment) 18 September 2003, *Bulacio* v. *Argentina*, Separate Opinion of Judge Cançado Trindade, para. 25.

372 IACtHR (Judgment) 27 November 1998, *Loayza Tamayo* v. *Peru*, para. 90.

373 Evans, *supra* n. 8, p. 3.

374 UNHRC, *supra* n. 65.

375 REDRESS, *supra* n. 47, p. 22-27.

further violations.[376] This is especially true in relation to measures of satisfaction and guarantees of non-repetition. These include the cessation of the violation; the reform of existing laws; institutional reforms guaranteeing that civilian and military proceedings are in accordance with due process standards; the training of police personnel; and the memorialisation of the crimes, for instance the building of museums and the renaming of public buildings.[377]

The concept and content of the right to reparation are constantly evolving and expanding. This can largely be attributed to the complexities encountered in repairing the damage caused by human rights violations. Against this background, it is acknowledged that an important aspect of reparations is that they exceed financial compensation.[378] The Inter-American Court of Human Rights (IACtHR) has played an important role in shaping the content and scope of this right through its jurisprudence. Compared to its European counterpart (the ECtHR), the IACtHR is bestowed with greater reparatory powers. While the ECtHR – through Article 41 of its constituent document – possesses the power to grant 'just satisfaction' for the victims of human rights violations,[379] the IACtHR is empowered to restore and ensure the enjoyment of the rights violated and provide fair compensation, if appropriate.[380]

In this context, the IACtHR has awarded a wide range of monetary and non-monetary remedies to individual victims.[381] It is important to note that most of the cases administered by the IACtHR are related to large-scale victimization. The nature of these cases, as well as the victims' claims for specific reparations, have to some

376 'Reparation, beyond the purpose of relieving the suffering of an affording justice to victims [...] has an inherent preventive and deterrent aspect'. See: UNHRC (Report of the Special Rapporteur, Sir Nigel Rodley, on Question of torture and other cruel, inhuman or degrading treatment or punishment) 11 August 2000, UN Doc A/55/290, p. 28; Ferstman, C., "Reparation as Prevention: Considering the Law and Practice of Orders for Cessation and Guarantees of Non-Repetition in Torture Cases" 6 *Essex Human Rights Review* (2010), p. 7.

377 Ferstman, *supra* n. 376, p. 22-25; Principle 23, Principles on Reparations; Guarnizo-Peralta, D., *Guarantees of non-repetition and the right to health: Review of the law and evolving practice of judicial and semi-judicial bodies at the global and regional levels.* An unpublished thesis submitted for the Degree of Doctor of Philosophy, University of Essex, 2016, p. 18-19.

378 Principles 19-23, Principles on Reparations.

379 Article 41, European Convention on Human Rights. Importantly, 'just satisfaction' has a broader meaning than that of satisfaction within the ICJ's jurisprudence and the ILC's ASR. Under Article 41 of the ECHR 'the award of satisfaction is not an automatic consequence of a finding by the European Court of Human Rights'. See: Just Satisfaction claims – European Court of Human Rights, 1 January 2016. Available at: <http://www.echr.coe.int/Documents/PD_satisfaction_claims_ENG.pdf>.

380 Article 63, ACHR. Despite the lack of certainty regarding its remedial powers, the African Commission has also granted more than a declaratory relief of compensation. This human rights body is expanding its path in regional reparations doctrine mirroring, to some extent, the IACtHR's approach.

381 Cassel, D., "The Expanding Scope and Impact of Reparations Awarded by the Inter-American Court of Human Rights" in K. De Feyter et al. (eds.), *Out of the Ashes: Reparations for Gross Violations of Human Rights* (Antwerp, Intersentia 2005), p. 193.

extent influenced the IACtHR's progressive approach towards reparations.[382] It is important to mention that the IACtHR's approach also inspired the ECtHR, which despite its apparently limited remedial powers has moved from a very conservative position taking a more progressive stance. This can be observed in some of the court's recent judgments, in which it has been willing to grant measures beyond 'just satisfaction' to achieve full restitution.[383] Another example is the adoption of pilot judgments. Although these judgments were primarily adopted to deal with the large number of cases pending before the court, as they address systemic underlying causes of violations they inherently allow the court to address violations beyond the particular merits of a given case.[384]

The forthcoming sections will expound the main characteristics of reparations as interpreted by the IACtHR and the ECtHR. However, it is worth mentioning that their approaches have tended to differ. In general, the ECtHR has been inclined to provide reparations by means of declaratory judgments and compensation while the IACtHR has gone beyond compensation and granted a large variety of non-monetary awards, some of a collective nature.

3.2 Types of Reparations

The types of reparations recognised under human rights law are largely modelled on public international law. Accordingly, reparations for human rights violations include restitution, compensation and satisfaction. In addition, and unlike reparations within public international law, they also include measures of rehabilitation and guarantees of non-repetition, adding up to a total of five types of reparations recognised under human rights law. Considering that, contrary to public international law, reparations can also take place on a collective basis,[385] it is important to mention that measures of satisfaction and guarantees of non-repetition not only aim to redress individual harm, but also the damage inflicted on society as a whole.

The scope and content of each of the five types of reparations have been defined predominantly by the jurisprudential developments of human rights supervisory bodies, with a key role for both the ECtHR and the IACtHR. These two human rights courts were initially cautious in their approach to reparations – they principally

382 Antkowiak, T., "An emerging mandate for international courts: Victim-centered remedies and restorative justice", 47 *Standford Journal of International Law* (2011).

383 Colandrea, V., "On the Power of the European Court of Human Rights to Order Specific Non-Monetary Measures: Some Remarks in Light of the Assanidze, Broniowski and Sejdovic Cases", 7 *Human Rights Law Review* (2007), p. 396.

384 McKay, F., "What Outcome for Victims?", in D. Shelton (ed.), *The Oxford Handbook of International Human Rights Law* (Oxford, OUP 2013), p. 940.

385 Some scholars refer to collective or moral reparations as synonyms. Bantekas and Oette, *supra* n. 15, p. 621, 631.

focus on providing declaratory judgments and financial compensation.[386] However, the IACtHR ever since its first case already included a non-monetary remedy. In *Velásquez Rodríguez*, the IACtHR ordered Honduras to pay fair compensation to the victims,[387] and demanded that those responsible for the violation would be investigated, prosecuted and punished.[388] On the other hand, the ECtHR adopted a very conservative approach until very recently, when it decided to include measures of non-monetary relief in its orders for reparations.[389]

3.2.1 Restitution

Restitution is the original and most preferred measure of reparation under human rights law.[390] Its main objective is a reversion to the *status quo ante*: to reinstate the situation that a person or community would have enjoyed had the violation not occurred.[391] It encompasses a variety of measures including the restoration of legal rights[392] and liberties,[393] such as the release of an unlawfully detained person;[394] the facilitation of the return of individuals or communities to their land or place of residence;[395]

386 Aldana-Pindell, R., "An Emerging Universality of Justiciable Victims' Rights in the Criminal Process to Curtail Impunity for State-Sponsored Crimes", 26 *Human Rights Quarterly* (2004), p. 615-616.

387 In addition, the IACtHR also ruled that the compensation was to be agreed upon by the parties subject to its approval within six months, IACtHR (Judgment) 29 July 1988, *Velásquez Rodríguez* v. *Honduras*, para. 194 (5)-(7). Since the parties could not reach an agreement the Court set a fixed amount. See: IACtHR (Judgment) 21 July 1989, *Velåsquez Rodríguez* v. *Honduras*, para. 60 (1).

388 IACtHR (Judgment) 29 July 1988, *Velåsquez Rodríguez* v. *Honduras*,para. 174; IACtHR (Judgment) 21 July 1989, *Velásquez Rodríguez* v. *Honduras*, para. 34.

389 Shelton, *supra* n. 1, p. 386.

390 Shelton, *supra* n. 1, p. 298.

391 ECtHR (Judgment) 31 October 1995, Case No.14556/89, *Papamichalopoulos and Others* v. *Greece (Article 50)*, para. 34.

392 IACtHR (Judgment) 17 September 1998, *Loyza Tamayo* v. *Peru*, para. 122.

393 ECtHR (Judgment) 8 April 2004, Appl. No. 71503/01, *Assanidze* v. *Georgia*, para. 202-203; ECtHR (Judgment) 8 July 2004, Appl. No. 48787/99, *Ilaşcu and Others* v. *Moldova and Russia*, para. 490; IACtHR, *Loayza Tamayo* v. *Peru*, *supra* n. 372, para. 5.

394 This measure, however, can overlap with the State obligation to cease a continuing violation. See: IACtHR, *Loyza Tamayo* v. *Peru*, *supra* n. 392, para. 84; ECtHR (Judgment) 8 April 2004, Appl. No. 71503/01, Assanidze v. *Georgia*, para. 202-203; ECtHR, *Ilaşcu and Others* v. *Moldova And Russia*, *supra* n. 393, para. 482.

395 IACtHR (Judgment) 15 June 2005, *Moiwana Community* v. *Suriname*, para. 4; IACtHR (Judgment) 15 September 2005, *Masaccre Mapiripán* v. *Colombia*, para. 11; IACtHR (Judgment) 27 November 2008, *Valle Jaramillo et al.* v. *Colombia*, para. 20; ACmHPR (Decision) 6 November 2000, *John D. Ouko* v. *Kenya*, Comm. No. 232/99.

the reinstatement of an individual to a previous position of employment;[396] and the restoration of property.[397]

Despite its importance, restitution is not always applicable. First, restitution may be impossible. This can be illustrated by the *Akdivar and Others v Turkey* case brought before the ECtHR, in which the claimants had been evicted from their homes which were subsequently burnt.[398] In this case, restitution was materially impossible as the houses had been destroyed. Secondly, not all human rights supervisory bodies may have the remedial power to order restitution. The ECtHR, for instance, maintained for several decades that it lacked competence to order this modality of reparations, as its judgments were declaratory in nature.[399] Nevertheless, the court has referred to restitution in some of its recent judgments by stating that '[i]f the nature of the breach allows of *restitutio in integrum,* it is for the respondent State to effect it, the Court having neither the power nor the practical possibility of doing so itself.'[400] Finally, as victims might not always deem restitution to be desirable they might request the courts for another measure of reparation.[401]

Restoration of property

Regarding the restoration of property, the IACtHR has mainly been concerned with issues related to the land of indigenous peoples. The court has interpreted the individual right to property under the American Convention as including the protection of communal land, especially when related to indigenous or tribal people.[402] In this context, in the IACtHR's landmark decision in the *Mayagna (Sumo) Awas Tingni Community* case the court ruled that indigenous communities have the right to live on

396 ECtHR (Judgment) 9 January 2013, Appl. No. 21722/11, *Oleksandr Volkov* v. *Ukraine*, para. 208; HRC (View) 26 July 2002, *Félix Enrique Chira Vargas-Machuca* v. *Peru*, Comm. No. 906/2000, para. 9; IACtHR, *Loyza Tamayo* v. *Peru, supra* n. 392, para. 113-116; IACtHR (Judgment) 2 February 2001, *Baena-Ricardo et al.* v. *Panama*, para. 203; ACmHPR (Decision) 11 May 2000, *Malawi African Association et al.* v. *Mauritania,* para. 142 (4), Comm. No. 54/91-61/91-96/93-98/93-164/97-196/97-210/98.

397 ECtHR, *Papamichalopoulos and Others* v. *Greece (Article 50), supra* n. 391, para. 38; ECtHR (Judgment) 23 January 2001, Appl. No. 28342/95, *Brumarescu* v. *Romania*, para. 22. It is important to mention that when the restoration of property cannot be done, compensation is awarded. See: ECtHR (Judgment) 23 January 2001, Appl. No. 28342/95, *Brumarescu* v. *Romania*; ECtHR (Judgment) [GC] 22 June 2004, Appl. No. 31443/ 96, *Broniowski* v. *Poland.*

398 ECtHR (Judgment) [GC] 1 April 1998, Appl. No. 99/195/605/693, *Akdivar and Others* v. *Turkey*, para. 18.

399 ECtHR (Judgment) 14 September 1987, Appl. No. 9063/80, *Gillow* v. *United Kingdom*, para. 9; Antkowiak, T., "Remedial Approaches to Human Rights Violations: The Inter-American Court of Human Rights and Beyond", 46 *Columbia Journal of Transnational Law* (2008), p. 357.

400 ECtHR, *Papamichalopoulos and Others* v. *Greece (Article 50)*, *supra* n. 391, para. 34.

401 REDRESS, *supra* n. 47, p. 16.

402 IACtHR (Judgment) 31 August 2001, *Mayagna (Sumo) Awas Tingni* v. *Nicaragua*, para. 149.

their traditional and communal lands, including in the absence of a property title.[403] It is important to highlight that the IACtHR has acknowledged that the restoration of land for indigenous or tribal peoples also implies that the right to cultural identity is respected. It thus helps to 'preserv[e] cultural identities in a democratic and pluralistic society.'[404]

As opposed to the IACtHR, the ECtHR has never ordered the restoration of property. Instead, it has only recommended such restitution in cases related to violations of property rights. For instance, in the *Papamichalopoulos* case that relates to the *de facto* expropriation of the private land of fourteen individuals, the ECtHR found Greece to be in violation of property rights and 'ordered' Greece to return the land to the fourteen applicants.[405] However, the ruling was limited in the sense that in case the state was not capable of executing this order within six months, Greece was obliged to compensate the victims for their properties.[406] Similarly, in the *Brumarescu* case in which the applicant issued a complaint for the expropriation of his house without having received any compensation, the court upheld that 'the State *should* [...] restore the applicant's title to the rest of the house within six months.'[407] If the state failed or if it was not possible to restore the property, it would have to ensure compensation.[408]

Perhaps the ECtHR's reluctance to explicitly order the restoration of property could be partially explained by its statutory remedial powers, and the states' freedom to execute the court's rulings by the means that they decide, 'provided that such means are compatible with the conclusions set out in the Court's judgments.'[409] Finally, it is important to note that the ECtHR has challenged the following generally accepted limitations to restitution: materially impossibility and disproportionality.[410] The court appeared to suggest that if a state fails to restore property within a reasonable time, in this case within six months, then compensation should apply.

403 Ibid., para. 164, Operative para. 4. See also: IACtHR, *Moiwana Community* v. *Suriname*, *supra* n. 395, para. 3; ACmHPR (Desicion) 25 November 2009, *Centre for Minority Rights Development (Kenya) and Minority Rights Group (on behalf of Endorois Welfare Council)* v. *Kenya,* Comm. No. 276/03, para. 1(a).

404 IACtHR, *Mayagna (Sumo) Awas Tingni* v. *Nicaragua*, *supra* n. 402, para. 147-148; IACtHR (Judgment) 17 June 2005, *Yakye Axa Indigenous Community* v. *Paraguay,* para.147-149.

405 ECtHR (Judgment) 24 June 1993, Appl. No.14556/89, *Papamichalopoulos and Others* v. *Greece*, para. 41.

406 ECtHR, *Papamichalopoulos and Others* v. *Greece (Article 50)*, *supra* n. 391, para. 39, 54 (2) (3).

407 ECtHR (Judgment) [GC] 23 January 2001, Appl. No. 28342/95, *Brumărescu* v. *Romania*, para. 22-23, 31(1). Emphasis added.

408 Ibid., para. 23, 31 (2).

409 ECtHR (Judgment) [GC],13 July 2000, Appl. Nos. 39221/98 and 41963/98, *Scozzari and Giunta* v. *Italy*, para. 249.

410 See: Article 35, ILC's ASR.

Return to one's land

The IACtHR has ordered guarantees to be given that victims will be able to safely return to their land, community or even their country.[411] An example is the *Moiwana Community* case, which relates to the massacre of 39 members of the *N'djuka* tribe and the forced displacement of its survivors. The IACtHR ordered Suriname to redress violations and to ensure the restitution of the community's traditional lands as well as to guarantee the safety of those who decided to return.[412] Similar guarantees have been ordered in cases in which the commitment of gross violations of human rights has forced inhabitants to be displaced. A case in point is the *Mapiripán Massacre* that relates to the massacre – and other violations – of 49 inhabitants of a town called Mapiripán. The IACtHR ruled that the State must provide guarantees of safe return for those who wanted to return.[413] Similarly, in the *19 Merchants* case, the IACtHR ordered Colombia not only to create the necessary safe conditions to allow victims to return to their country but also to cover the associated costs thereof.[414]

Restoration of employment

In cases in which the complainants have been unlawfully dismissed, the IACtHR has ordered that they be reinstated in their previous positions of employment. An example of this is the *Loayza Tamayo* case, which concerned the unlawful detention and torture of *Ms. Loayza Tamayo*. The IACtHR ordered Peru to reinstate the victim in her previous job and to provide 'full retirement benefits, including those owed for the period transpired since the time of her detention', inter alia.[415]

The IACtHR has also ordered states to reinstate judges of the lower courts in their previous positions or positions corresponding to the same rank, salary and benefits, provided that the victim agrees to this.[416] Mindful of a reinstatement's legal complexities, the IACtHR has provided states with the option to pay compensation instead, albeit only in the case of well-founded arguments that prevented such reinstatement. Nevertheless, in the *Quintana Coello et al.* case that dealt with the unlawful dismissal of 27 judges of the Ecuador Supreme Court, the IACtHR ordered monetary compensation to be paid, but not the reinstatement of the judges.[417] The

411 IACtHR, *Valle Jaramillo et al.* v. *Colombia*, *supra* n. 395, para. 20. A similar approach has been taken by the African Commission. See: ACmHPR, *John D. Ouko* v. *Kenya*, *supra* n. 395.

412 IACtHR, *Moiwana Community* v. *Suriname*, *supra* n. 395, para. 4.

413 IACtHR, *Masaccre Mapiripán* v. *Colombia*, *supra* n. 395, para. 11.

414 IACtHR (Judgment) 5 July 2004, *19 Merchants* v. *Colombia*, para. 279.

415 IACtHR, *Loayza Tamayo* v. *Peru*, *supra* n. 372, para. 1-2.

416 IACtHR (Judgment) 5 August 2008, *Apitz Barbera et al. ("First Court of Administrative Disputes")* v. *Venezuela*, para. 246; IACtHR (Judgment) 30 June 2009, *Reverón Trujillo* v. *Venezuela*, Operative para. 7; IACtHR (Judgment) 1 July 2011, *Chocrón Chocrón* v. *Venezuela*, para. 152-153.

417 IACtHR (Judgment) 23 August 2013, *The Supreme Court of Justice (Quintana Coello et al.)* v. *Ecuador*, para. 214-215.

court came to this decision as it was impossible to order their reinstatement without disrupting the composition of the Supreme Court and the laws regarding the tenure of judges in Ecuador.[418] Remarkably, a similar case heard by the ECtHR culminated in a different and even more progressive decision. In the *Oleksandr Volkov* case, which concerned the unlawful dismissal of a judge of the Supreme Court of Ukraine, the ECtHR issued its decision ordering a person's reinstatement: it ordered that Mr. Volkov be reinstated as a Supreme Court judge as soon as possible.[419] In this case the ECtHR adopted a very progressive approach, but it did not indicate how Ukraine would have to comply with this order without disruptions to the composition of the Supreme Court of Ukraine.

Restoration of rights

In several cases the IACtHR has ordered states to restore violated rights. For example, when a person has been unlawfully detained, the court has orderedthat person's release within a reasonable time.[420] Furthermore, in cases in which a person was tried before a court without respect being given to due process rights, the IACtHR has ordered, within a reasonable time, either a new trial which provides full guarantees of due process[421] or that the verdict be overturned as well as the nullification of any criminal record.[422]

The ECtHR has also ordered that certain rights be restored. Although the ECtHR has stated that 'it lack[s] authority to issue explicit directions on remedial matters, such as the reversal of convictions,'[423] it has indirectly ordered the release of an unlawfully detained person. An example is the *Assanidze* case in which the applicant had remained in detention despite having been acquitted of criminal charges. While the court reiterated that its judgments are declaratory in nature, it 'considered that the respondent State must secure the applicant's release at the earliest possible date.' The court explained that the nature of the violation '[did] not leave any real choice as to the measures required to remedy it.'[424] Similarly, in the case of *Ilaşcu and others,* the court ordered the immediate release of the three applicants.[425]

---

418 Some former judges also expressed their desire to renounce the possibility of reinstatement. See: Ibid., para. 214.

419 ECtHR, *Oleksandr Volkov* v. *Ukraine*, *supra* n. 396, para. 208.

420 Interestingly, such restitution has been ordered in a judgment regarding the merits of the case instead of reparations. See: IACtHR, *Loyza Tamayo* v. *Peru*, *supra* n. 392, para. 84.

421 IACtHR (Judgment) 30 May 1999, *Castillo Petruzzi et al.* v. *Peru*, para. 221.

422 IACtHR, *Loyza Tamayo* v. *Peru*, *supra* n. 392, para. 122; IACtHR (Judgment) 3 December 2001, *Cantoral Benavides* v. *Peru*, para. 4-5.

423 Antkowiak, *supra* n. 399, p. 357.

424 ECtHR, *Assanidze* v. *Georgia*, *supra* n. 393, para. 202-203.

425 ECtHR, *Ilaşcu and Others* v. *Moldova And Russia*, *supra* n. 393, para. 285.

Furthermore, the ECtHR has determined that due process rights must be restored by ordering the respondent state to open a new investigation.[426]

3.2.2 Compensation

Compensation refers to the financial reimbursement or indemnification for material and non-material harm 'that cannot otherwise be remedied.'[427] Although it cannot erase the violations suffered, it does help to alleviate victims' suffering by contributing to satisfying their material needs.[428] In addition, it could even aid in fulfilling the 'personal life project' of the victims.[429] Financial compensation is particularly relevant when victims are unable to work as a consequence of the violations that they have suffered.[430]

In general, compensation should be substantial rather than symbolic, and proportional to the harm inflicted.[431] This makes financial compensation something of a paradigm.[432] Compensation, however, can extend beyond monetary awards to address situations of poverty and marginalisation, which may have contributed to victimisation.[433] In addition, compensating victims could also be considered to be a symbolic act as it has the potential to convey a tangible recognition of state responsibility

---

426 ECtHR (Judgment) [GC], 30 June 2009, Appl. No. 32772/02, *Verein Gegen Tierfabriken Schweiz (VgT)* v. *Switzerland* (No. 2).

427 ECtHR, *Scozzari and Giunta* v. *Italy*, *supra* n. 409, para. 250; Principle 20, Principles on Reparations; van Boven, T. et al., "Seminar on the Right to Restitution, Compensation and Rehabilitation for Victims of Gross Violations of Human Rights and Fundamental Freedoms", 12 *SIM Special* (1992), p. 6-7.

428 REDRESS, *supra* n. 47, p. 14, citing Zedner, L. "Reparation and Retribution: are they reconcilable", 57 *Modern Law Review* (1994), p. 238.

429 It is important to note that in the *Loayza Tamayo* v. *Peru* case, the IACtHR developed this concept but did not order financial compensation. In later cases, the IACtHR decided to make an economic assessment of the damage to the life project of the victim (e.g. *Cantoral Benavides* case). In recent cases, the Court has not dealt with this sort of damage. See: Shelton, *Remedies in International Human Rights Law*, *supra* n. 1, p. 19, 315; Verdeja, E., "A Critical Theory of Reparative Justice", 15 *Constellations* (2008), p. 212.

430 Verdeja, *supra* n. 429, p. 212.

431 Danieli, *supra* n. 21, p. 60; HRC (View) 7 November 2003, *Albert Wilson* v. *Philippines*, Comm. No. 868/1999, para. 5.14.

432 IACtHR (Judgment) *Loayza-Tamayo* v. *Peru*, Joint Separate Opinion of Judges Cançado Trindade and Abreu-Burelli, *supra* n. 372, para. 5, 8-10.

433 Carranza, R., "The Right to Reparations in Situations of Poverty", *International Center for Transitional Justice Briefing* (2009), p. 2. In addition, through collective compensation by means of the creation of trust funds, the Court has not only attempted to repair the violation suffered by a large number of victims but also to improve the social conditions of marginalization in which victims were forced to live. See: Uprimny, M. R., "Between Corrective and Distributive Justice: Reparations of Gross Human Rights Violations in Times of Transition", 25 *Netherlands Quarterly of Human Rights* (2009).

In practice, international courts, including human rights courts, prefer to grant compensation as opposed to other forms of reparation.[434] This practice may reflect a common and traditional understanding that has developed within legal systems around the world: when damage occurs, financial compensation is granted.[435] Consequently, reparation is often confused with compensation; this can result in the importance of other forms of reparations being neglected.[436] Compensation has played a dominant role in the IACtHR's and ECtHR's jurisprudence, and the former is known for awarding generous and large sums of money.[437] However, in its very first contentious case, *Velásquez Rodríguez,* the IACtHR adopted a very conservative approach and decided that compensation needed to be agreed upon by the parties themselves, subject to the approval of the court.[438] This approach appeared to correspond to the traditional stance of the ICJ, as well as the ECtHR's position during its initial decades of operation. While allowing the parties to agree on an adequate amount of compensation appears to be in line with the principle of state sovereignty, it also opens the door to lengthy negotiations between the parties involved. This may delay the materialization of this measure of reparation.

Finally, in the *Guiso-Gallisay* case the ECtHR suggested that compensation should be substantial: it 'must be such as to create a serious and effective means of dissuasion with regard to the repetition of unlawful conduct of the same type, without however assuming a punitive function.'[439]

General rules governing compensation

Determining the amount of compensation for a human rights violation is highly complex. To begin with, existing rules governing compensation are general and, to some extent, vague. Most human rights treaties only stipulate that compensation 'should be provided for any economically assessable damage, as appropriate and proportional to the gravity of the violation and the circumstances of each case.'[440] Human rights supervisory bodies are thus implicitly bestowed with extensive discretionary powers to decide on the rules surrounding compensation. They are left to decide which harm is economically assessable, and what sum of money is

434 Aldana-Pindell, *supra* n. 386, p. 615-616.

435 Danieli, *supra* n. 21, p. 60; Brodney, M., "Implementing Criminal Court-Ordered Collective Reparations: Unpacking Present Debates", 1 *Journal of the Oxford Centre for Socio-Legal Studies* (2016), p. 5.

436 Bantekas and Oette, *supra* n. 15, p. 621.

437 Shelton, *supra* n. 1, p. 326; This is not the case during the last years.

438 Reisman, *supra* n. 69, p. 75; IACtHR (Judgment) 29 July 1988, *Velásquez Rodríguez* v. *Honduras*, para. 191. Similar approaches are to be found in the decisions of the African Commission on Human and Peoples' Rights. See: Musila, *supra* n. 31, p. 455.

439 ECtHR (Judgment) 22 December 2009, Appl. No. 58858/00, *Guiso-Gallisay* v. *Italy,* para. 85.

440 Principle 20, Principles on Reparations.

considered to be proportional to the gravity of the violation, among other things.[441] While human rights courts have tailored compensation on a case-by-case basis,[442] this has resulted in a dearth of 'coherent and consistent theory and practice regarding damages.'[443]

Under public international law, compensation aims to cover *only* assessable damages, and excludes moral damage as this is usually remedied by measures of satisfaction.[444] Human rights courts, on the other hand, usually award compensation for both material losses resulting from a violation (loss of earnings and consequential damages, such as the costs incurred while searching for victims who have disappeared) and moral harm (subjective elements such as emotional distress, pain and suffering), as well as legal costs and expenses.[445] In addition, compensation can include the payment of interest – this could for example cover the time 'from the date of violation to the date of the judgment.'[446]

While both the ECtHR and the IACtHR usually grant compensation for material and non-material damages, the former has failed to provide any details on how such damages are quantified.[447] In contrast, the IACtHR specifies the category of harm to which a sum of money to be awarded belongs.[448] Furthermore, the ECtHR has established that compensation cannot be granted on its own motion,[449] while the IACtHR does grant reparations including compensation *proprio motu*.[450] Finally, the IACtHR maintains that compensation should not be a punitive or exemplary

---

441 These questions are equally applicable to any form of reparation. UNSC, *supra* n. 66.

442 Rubio-Marin, R., Sandoval, C. and Diaz, C., "Repairing Family Members: Gross Human Rights Violations and Communities of Harm" in R. Rubio-Marin, (ed.), *The Gender of Reparations, Unsettling Social Hierarchies while Redressing Human Rights Violations* (New York, CUP 2009), p. 217.

443 McKay, *supra* n. 384, p. 936.

444 Brown, *supra* n. 7, p. 191.

445 McKay, *supra* n. 384, p. 935; Oette, L., "Bringing Justice to Victims? Responses of Regional and International Human Rights Courts and Treaty Bodies" in C. Ferstman, M. Goetz & A. Stephens, *Reparations for Victims of Genocide, War Crimes and Crimes Against Humanity: Systems in Place and Systems in the Making* (Leiden, Martinus Nijhoff 2009), p. 235.

446 IACtHR (Judgment) 19 September 1996, *Neira Alegría et al.* v. *Peru*, para. 50.

447 ECtHR (Judgment) 10 May 2007, Appl. No. 40464/02, *Akhmadova and Sadulayeva* v. *Russia*, para. 146.

448 Roht-Arriaza, "Reparations in International Law and Practice", *supra* n. 50, p. 661-662.

449 Pellonpää, M., "Individual Reparation Claims under the European Convention on Human Rights" in A. Randelzhofer and C Tomuschat (eds.), *State Responsibility and the Individual: Reparation in Instances of Grave Violations of Human Rights* (The Hague, Martinus Nijhoff 1999), p. 112.

450 In the *Rochela Massacre* case, the Court ordered four additional measures of satisfaction and guarantees of non-repetition which had not been requested by the victims. See: IACtHR (Judgment) 11 May 2007, *Rochela Massacre* v. *Colombia*, para. 286. Similarly in the *Plan de Sánchez* case, the IACtHR ordered, as part of the measures on non-repetition, that parts of the judgment be published in the language of the community as well as the provision of financial funding for programmes to improve the living conditions of the community. See: IACtHR (Judgment) 19 November 2004, *Plan de Sánchez Massacre* v. *Guatemala*, para. 102, 105.

measure against the state[451] and that it must be accompanied by other measures.[452] This is because victims may perceive compensation to be nothing more than 'blood money' or a means to buy their suffering.[453] To avoid this, compensation should be accompanied by measures of satisfaction[454] aimed at addressing emotional and moral damage.[455] Other human rights supervisory bodies have adopted a similar approach.[456]

In general, compensation is calculated either through a discretionary assessment of the damages or is based on equitable considerations (the principle or criterion of equity),[457] also known as 'fairness'.[458] The principle of equity refers to a 'prudent estimate' of the monetary equivalent of the damage. It takes into account the specific circumstances of a case, the nature of the violation, and all factors and information which are available.[459] This principle evidently allows for great discretion on the part of the courts[460] and it is often used in the absence of sufficient evidence to support a claim.

Compensation granted for non-material damage is usually based on equitable considerations.[461] According to the ECtHR, equity is '[i]ts guiding principle' as it warrants 'flexibility and an objective consideration of what is just, fair and reasonable' in determining compensation.[462] However, it can also be applied to material damages. For instance, in the *Vera Vera* case, the IACtHR was faced with the challenge of calculating the material damage, including the loss of future earnings, of the deceased victim who happened to earn his living through illegal activities. In cases in which there is no evidence of a specific salary, the court usually provides an estimation based on the minimum wage;[463] yet in this particular case, the representatives failed to provide evidence of the minimum wage in Ecuador. Nonetheless, the court

---

451 IACtHR (Judgment) 21 July 1989, *Velásquez-Rodríguez* v. *Honduras*, para. 38.

452 Gray, *supra* n. 5, p. 895.

453 Verdeja, *supra* n. 429, p. 212-213; Danieli, *supra* n. 21, p. 60-61.

454 Significantly, when measures of satisfaction are granted without remuneration, they are considered insufficient. This example demonstrates the level of complementarity between the measures of reparation. REDRESS, *supra* n. 47, p. 15.

455 Danieli, *supra* n. 21, p. 62.

456 CAT through its General Comment No. 3 has stated that 'monetary compensation alone may not be sufficient redress for a victim of torture and ill-treatment.' See: CAT General Comment No. 3, Implementation of Article 14 by States parties, U.N. Doc. CAT/C/GC/3 (2012), 16 November 2012.

457 ECtHR (Judgment) 10 January 2006, Appl. No. 67881/01, *Gruais and Bousquet* v. *France*, para. 32-34; IACtHR (Judgment) 22 February 2002, *Bámaca Velásquez* v. *Guatemala*, para. 51 (b), 54 (a).

458 IACtHR (Judgment) 27 November 2003, *Maritza Urrutia* v. *Guatemala*, para. 158.

459 Pasqualucci, J.M., *The Practice and Procedure of the Inter-American Court of Human Rights* (New York, CUP 2013, 2nd ed.), p. 243.

460 However, the IACtHR has denied that it has complete discretion in deciding on compensation. IACtHR (Judgment) 10 September 1993, *Aloeboetoe et al.* v. *Surinam*, para. 87.

461 Brown, *supra* n. 7, p. 207; Oette, *supra* n. 445, p. 235.

462 ECtHR (Judgment) [GC] 7 July 2011, Appl. No. 27021/08, *Al-Jedda* v. *the United Kingdom*, para. 114.

463 IACtHR (Judgment) 14 September 1996, *El Amparo* v. *Venezuela*, para. 28-29.

determined that the amount to be compensated for the loss of earnings should be based on the principle of equity.[464]

Economically assessable damages

The Principles on Reparations establish that economically assessable damages include the following non-exhaustive list: i) physical harm, including medicinal and medical services; ii) moral or psychological harm; iii) loss of opportunities, including employment, education, and social benefits; iv) material damages including loss of earnings; v) costs incurred for legal or expert assistance, and vi) social services.[465] In addition, the IACtHR has included expenses related to the search for a disappeared victim and funeral costs.[466] Factors such as age, life expectancy and a person's relationship with the immediate victim, as well as a person's current salary may also be taken into account.[467] Similarly the ECtHR takes into account, inter alia, the seriousness of a violation, a person's age, and the contextual background in which the violation took place when calculating damages.[468]

At first sight, compensation for someone's death or for the suffering, distress or anxiety inflicted appears to be economically unquantifiable. Yet the practice of human rights courts has demonstrated that these cases can, to a certain extent, be assessed financially.[469] In addition, the IACtHR has occasionally also provided compensation for two peculiar categories of harm: harm to the 'project of life'[470] and to 'family assets'.[471]

The 'project of life' concept refers to the conditions that are necessary to achieve reasonable standards of personal fulfilment and self-development.[472] It was first employed in the *Loayza Tamayo* case, although the court refused to translate such harm into economic terms.[473] It was not until the *Cantoral Benavides* case

464 IACtHR (Judgment) 19 May 2011, *Vera Vera* v. *Ecuador*, para. 131. A further explanation of the assessment of compensation is given in section related to the assessment of harm.

465 Principle 20, Principles on Reparations. See also: Commentary to Article 36, ILC's Commentaries to ASR, p. 101, para. 16.

466 IACtHR (Judgment) 29 August 2002, *Caracazo* v. *Venezuela*, para. 84-85.

467 Shelton, *supra* n. 1, p. 146-147.

468 Altwicker-Hámori, S., Altwicker, T. and Peters, A., "Measuring Violations of Human Rights: An Empirical Analysis of Awards in Respect of Non-Pecuniary Damage under the European Convention on Human Rights", 76 *Heidelberg Journal of International Law* (2016), p. 18-20.

469 Shelton, *supra* n. 1, p. 315-376.

470 IACtHR, *Loayza Tamayo* v. *Peru*, *supra* n. 372.

471 IACtHR (Judgment) 3 July 2004, *Molina-Theissen* v. *Guatemala*, para. 59-61.

472 IACtHR, *Loayza Tamayo* v. *Peru*, *supra* n. 372, para. 150.

473 Ibid., para. 153.

that the court assessed this damage financially.[474] As compensation, it awarded the victims a fellowship at a recognized university, covering all the costs involved.[475] This having been said, it must be noted that this category of harm has not been included in the court's most recent jurisprudence. Similar to this concept, the ECtHR has developed the concept of 'loss of opportunities', such as the full development of intellectual capabilities or being able to acquire a profession.[476] The IACtHR has only ruled on harm to family assets in one case: *Molina Thiessen*, which concerned the disappearance of a minor and the constant threat posed by the State to the minor's family. Consequently, the family were forced to leave their home country, with half of the family members emmigrating to Mexico and the other half to Ecuador.[477]

Limitations to compensation

There are several factors that can limit compensation. One of these is proportionality, since compensation should be proportional to the harm suffered. Notably, no guidelines exist, or at least they are not available to the public, to explain the methods used by international human rights courts to assess when compensation is to be considered proportional. Secondly, Gray has argued that the use of the principle of equity could limit compensation. According to him, this principle allows courts to award compensation that is inferior to the damage caused.[478] Gray's assertion is highly contested, however, as it appears to contradict the practice of the international human rights courts. As was stated previously, international human rights courts have applied the principle of equity to award reparations when the evidence was insufficient to support a compensation claim.

Finally, the financial situation of a given country could limit compensation. For instance, when granting reparations, the ECtHR takes the economic and social reality of the government into consideration.[479] The IACtHR maintains, on the other hand, that it does not take this into account. In the *Aloeboetoe v Suriname* case, for instance, the Court rejected the objections raised by Suriname against the sum of money awarded by the IACommHR on the grounds that it was not in line with the social and economic reality in Suriname.[480] In light of this, it could be concluded that

474 In recent cases, the Court has not discussed this sort of damage. The last case in which the Court referred to this category of damage was the *Gómez Palomino* v. *Perú* case in 2005 – on this occasion the Court applied the concept of the Project of life in an intergenerational perspective. See: Shelton, *supra* n. 1, p. 19, 315; Verdeja, *supra* n. 429, p. 212.

475 IACtHR, *Cantoral Benavides* v. *Peru*, *supra* n. 422, para. 80.

476 ECtHR (Judgemt) 6 April 2000, Appl. No. 34369/97, *Thlimmenos* v. *Greece*, para. 70.

477 IACtHR, *Molina-Theissen* v. *Guatemala*, *supra* n. 471, para. 59-61.Similar to the 'project of life' category of harm, the harm to family assets is not part of the current case law.

478 Gray, *supra* n. 5, p. 891.

479 Gray, *supra* n. 5, p. 891.

480 IACtHR, *Aloeboetoe et al.* v. *Suriname*, *supra* n. 460, para. 34, 37, 88.

the IACtHR awards compensation for the victims' suffering regardless of whether the amount can be paid by the state in question.

3.2.3 Rehabilitation

Rehabilitation does not exist under public international law and is thus inherently related to reparations provided to victims of human rights violations. To date, the concept's definition and the way rehabilitation can be provided has not been universally established, nor has it been subject to extensive scholarly debate.[481] The first international document that referred to rehabilitation for victims was the 1985 Victims' Declaration. Although the document uses the term 'assistance' instead of rehabilitation, it highlights the need for victims to receive medical, psychological, social and legal assistance.[482]

Furthermore, the Principles on Reparations define rehabilitation as all measures related to 'medical and psychological care as well as legal and social services' provided to the victims.[483] And according to Sandoval Villalba, these measures could also be provided to any given community as a whole.[484] Human rights bodies have adopted a similar definition, interpreting it as the restoration of capabilities or the acquisition of new skills to maximise the victim's self-sufficiency.[485] In this light, rehabilitation requires 'multidisciplinary and interdisciplinary' measures.[486]

Rehabilitation is, in almost all cases, an acute necessity for each victim[487] and it acquires particular importance in cases related to violations of personal integrity[488] or any gross violation of human rights.[489] Its importance lies in the fact that measures of rehabilitation have the potential to assist victims to 'recuperate their self-esteem

---

481 Sandoval Villalba, C., *Rehabilitation as a form of reparations under international law* (London, The REDRESS Trust 2009), p. 6-10.

482 Principles 14-17, Victims' Declaration.

483 Principle 21, Principles on Reparations. CAT General Comment No. 3 *supra* n. 456, para. 11-12.

484 Sandoval Villalba, *supra* n. 481, p. 9, citing WHO Expert Committee on Disability Prevention and Rehabilitation, *Technical Report on Disability Prevention and Rehabilitation,* (Geneva, WHO 1981) p. 9.

485 See: CAT General Comment No. 3 *supra* n. 456, para. 11-12; Working Group on Enforced or Involuntary Disappearances, General Comment on Article 19 of the Declaration on the Protection of All Persons from Enforced Disappearance, 12 January 1998, E/CN.4/1998/43, para. 75.

486 Sandoval Villalba, *supra* n. 481, p. 6.

487 ICJ, *Ahmadou Sadio Diallo* (*Republic of Guinea* v. *Democratic Republic of the Congo*), Separate Opinion of Judge Cançado Trindade, *supra* n. 84, para. 83.

488 Ibid., para. 84, special emphasis is made on Article 14 (1) CAT.

489 Amezcua-Noriega, O., "Reparation Principles under International Law and their Possible Application by the International Criminal Court: Some Reflections", *Briefing Paper No. 1, Reparations Unit, Essex University* (2011), p. 8; Sveaass, N., "Gross human rights violations and reparation under international law: approaching rehabilitation as a form of reparation", 4 *European Journal of Psychotraumatology* (2013), p. 1.

and their capacity to live in harmony with others',[490] and to reinstate the victim's reputation.[491] Therefore, rehabilitation can contribute to the social reintegration of victims and should be available to the victim on a long-term basis.[492] In fact, several human rights instruments refer to this measure of reparation as a right in and of itself: the right to rehabilitation.[493]

Measures of rehabilitation are often considered alongside financial compensation, as the State may be obliged to pay the costs of past and future rehabilitation measures.[494] In addition to financial payments, measures of rehabilitation may also be afforded as in-kind services, such as providing access to long-term medical or psychological treatment.[495] In this context, the ECtHR and IACtHR have awarded compensation for past and future medical expenses. It is important to note that, in comparison to the IACtHR, the ECtHR rarely awards compensation for future medical expenses, but instead focuses on expenses incurred in the past.[496] Considering the extent to which these awards overlap with measures of compensation, the two are often confused: both courts have failed to explicitly state that such medical reimbursement constitutes a measure of rehabilitation.[497]

Unlike its European counterpart, the IACtHR has not only repeatedly awarded medical and psychological treatment to victims and their closest relatives,[498] but also to communities as a whole. In the *Plan de Sánchez Massacre* case, the court ordered that specific programmes be created to provide victims with free psychological and psychiatric treatment at the collective, family and individual level.[499] In addition, a health centre was to be established so that the victims could receive medical and psychological care in their own village.[500] In the *Aloeboetoe* case, the court ordered

490 ICJ, *Ahmadou Sadio Diallo* (*Republic of Guinea* v. *Democratic Republic of the Congo*), Separate Opinion of Judge Cançado Trindade, *supra* n. 84, para. 85.

491 Shelton, *supra* n. 1, p. 394.

492 Danieli, *supra* n. 21, p. 60; In the *Barrios Altos* case, the IACtHR awarded rehabilitation measures such as free access for life. See: IACtHR (Judgment) 30 November 2001, *Barrios Altos* v. *Peru*, para. 42.

493 Article 14, CAT; Articles 23, 24, CRC; Article 7, CRC's Optional Protocol; Article 24 (5) (b), ICCPED.

494 International Commission of Jurists, *supra* n. 23, p. 144.

495 Sandoval Villalba, *supra* n. 481; IACtHR (Judgment) 31 January 2006, *Massacre of Pueblo Bello* v. *Colombia;* IACtHR (Judgment) 1 July 2006, *Ituango Massacres* v. *Colombia;* IACtHR (Judgment) 25 November 2006, *Miguel Castro-Castro Prison* v. *Peru.*

496 The ECtHR has not even awarded such compensation in cases of enforced disappearances. See: Scovazzi, T. and Citroni, G., *The Struggle against Enforced Disappearances and the 2007 United Nations Convention* (Leiden, Martinus Nijhoff 2007), p. 372.

497 Sandoval Villalba, *supra* n. 481, p. 45-57, 62.

498 IACtHR, *Massacre of Pueblo Bello* v. *Colombia*, *supra* n. 495, para. 274 ; IACtHR, *Ituango Massacres* v. *Colombia*, *supra* n. 495, para. 403; IACtHR, *Miguel Castro-Castro Prison* v. *Peru*, *supra* n. 495, para. 449.

499 IACtHR, *Plan de Sánchez Massacre* v. *Guatemala*, *supra* n. 450, para. 106-108, 117.

500 Ibid., para. 110, 117.

the reopening of a medical dispensary in a village affected by gross human rights violations.[501] While these measures are related to rehabilitation measures, they are also considered to be collective reparations.

3.2.4 Satisfaction

Satisfaction refers to the restoration of dignity through a variety of mostly symbolic measures[502] that are predominantly of a collective nature. However, these measures can also target individual needs, such as measures aimed at addressing moral damages including frustration,[503] the reputation of the victim,[504] or the truth in a given case.[505]

Traditionally, declaratory judgments have been the most common form of satisfaction, and were for decades the only measures adopted by the ECtHR.[506] The IACtHR, on the other hand, has interpreted the concept of satisfaction more broadly, and has ruled that solely a declaratory judgment does not constitute full reparation.[507] It also considers judgments acknowledging state responsibility a form of satisfaction,[508] as well as measures directed at the cessation of the violation.[509] However, such measures could overlap with the category of restitution. For instance, the release of a person who was unlawfully detained ends a violation, but also restores the right to freedom of the individual.[510]

---

501 IACtHR, *Aloeboetoe et al.* v. *Suriname*, *supra* n. 460, para. 96.

502 Bantekas and Oette, *supra* n. 15, p. 629-630.

503 McCarthy, *supra* n. 296, p. 290.

504 Pasqualucci, *supra* n. 459, p. 228, 307. However, addressing the moral reputation of the victim can also be considered as a part of rehabilitation measures. See also: Pasqualucci, *supra* n. 459, p. 107, 225.

505 This is especially relevant in cases of enforced disappearances and extrajudicial killings. However, the right to truth has both an individual and a collective dimension. See: OHCHR, Study on the Right to the Truth: Report of the Office of the United Nations High Commissioer for Human Rights, 8 February 2006, UN. Doc. E/CN.4/2006/91, p. 11, para. 36.

506 Gray, *supra* n. 5, p. 890; ECtHR (Judgment) [GC], 17 December 1996, Appl. No. 19187/91, *Sauders* v. *The United Kingdom*, para. 89.

507 Gray, *supra* n. 5, p. 894; IACtHR (Judgment) 25 May 2001, *"White Van" (Paniagua-Morales et al.)* v. *Guatemala*, para. 105; IACtHR (Judgment) 26 May 2001, *"Street Children" (Villagrán-Morales et al.)* v. *Guatelama*, para. 88; IACtHR (Judgment) 29 November 2006, *La Cantuta* v. *Peru*, para. 219; IACtHR (Judgment), 28 November 2012, *Artavia Murillo et al. ("in vitro fertilization")* v. *Costa Rica*, para. 323.

508 IACtHR, *Castillo Petruzzi et al.* v. *Peru*, *supra* n. 421, para. 225; IACtHR (Judgment) 28 November 2002, *Cantos* v. *Argentina*, para. 71.

509 IACtHR, *Loayza Tamayo* v. *Peru*, *supra* n. 372, Operative para. 3; IACtHR (Judgment) 20 January 1999, *Suárez-Rosero* v. *Ecuador*, para. 76; IACtHR (Judgment) 6 February 2001, *Ivcher-Bronstein* v. *Peru*, Operative para. 8; IACtHR (Judgment) 2 July 2004, *Herrera-Ulloa* v. *Costa Rica*, para. 195. Under Article 30 of the ILC's ASR, the cessation of a violation is considered as an independent legal obligation. This measure is also considered as a restitution of rights. See: ICJ, *United States Diplomatic and Consular Staff in Tehran* (*United States of America* v. *Iran*), *supra* n. 159.

510 IACtHR (Judgment) 17 September 1997, *Loayza Tamayo* v. *Peru*, Res. 5.

Other measures the IACtHR considers as satisfaction relate to rendering acknowledgement, justice and truth. In light of this, the court has ordered apologies;[511] investigation of the facts; identification, prosecution and punishment of those responsible;[512] publication of the outcome of the investigation and trial in national newspapers;[513] and the promotion of truth-telling, among others.[514] Significantly, the IACtHR has asserted that the right to truth is an important form of reparation with an individual and collective dimension[515] that aims to restore the victim's reputation and honour.[516]

The ECtHR has been limited in awarding measures of satisfaction in some of its cases.[517] It is important to note that in cases of enforced disappearances, the ECtHR has stated that states are obliged to conduct 'effective investigation[s] capable of leading to the identification and punishment of those responsible.'[518] However, it has not ordered states to conduct such investigations as part of its reparations. In similar cases, the IACtHR has ordered the following measures of satisfaction: an investigation into the whereabouts of the disappeared;[519] the location of the victim's remains;[520] the granting of educational benefits such as scholarships and educational

511 IACtHR, *Cantoral Benavides* v. *Peru, supra* n. 422, para. 81; IACtHR, *Moiwana Community* v. *Suriname, supra* n. 395, para. 2-7, 216.

512 IACtHR, *Velásquez Rodríguez* v. *Honduras, supra* n. 438, para. 174; IACtHR, (Judgment) 21 July 1989, *Velásquez Rodríguez* v. *Honduras*, para. 34; IACtHR, *El Amparo* v. *Venezuela, supra* n. 463, Res. 4; IACtHR (Judgment) 12 November 1997, Suárez-Rosero v. Ecuador, para. 107; IACtHR, *Maritza Urrutia* v. *Guatemala, supra* n. 458, para. 194 (5); IACtHR (Judgment) 12 September 2005, *Gutiérrez-Soller* v. *Colombia*, para. 96; IACtHR, *Masaccre Mapiripán* v. *Colombia, supra* n. 395, para. 335 (7).

513 IACtHR, *Maritza Urrutia* v. *Guatemala, supra* n. 458; IACtHR, *Gutiérrez-Soller* v. *Colombia, supra* n. 512; IACtHR, *Masaccre Mapiripán* v. *Colombia, supra* n. 395.

514 Shelton, *supra* n. 1, p. 396.

515 IACtHR, *Moiwana Community* v. *Suriname, supra* n. 395, para. 204.

516 IACtHR (Judgment) 26 January 2000, *Trujillo-Oroza* v. *Bolivia*; IACtHR, *Barrios Altos* v. *Peru, supra* n. 492; IACtHR, *Bámaca Velásquez* v. *Guatemala, supra* n. 457; IACtHR (Judgment) 25 November 2003, *Myrna Mack Chang* v. *Guatemala*; IACtHR, *19 Merchants* v. *Colombia, supra* n. *414*; IACtHR (Judgment) 22 November 2004, *Carpio Nicolle et al.* v. *Guatemala*; IACtHR (Judgment) 1 March 2005, *Serrano-Cruz Sisters* v. *El Salvador*; IACtHR (Judgment) 3 March 2005, *Huilca-Tecse* v. *Peru*; IACtHR, *Moiwana Community* v. *Suriname, supra* n. 395, para. 204; IACtHR, *Miguel Castro-Castro Prison* v. *Peru, supra* n. 495, para. 440.

517 Mégret, F., "The International Criminal Court and the Failure to Mention Symbolic Reparations", 16 *International Review of Victimology* (2009), p. 131.

518 ECtHR (Judgment) 19 February 1998, Appl. No. 158/1996/777/978, *Kaya* v. *Turkey*, para. 107; ECtHR (Judgment) [GC], 28 July 1999, Appl. No. 25803/94, *Selmouni* v. *France*, para. 79; ECtHR (Judgment) 28 March 2000, Appl. No. 22535/93, *Mahmut Kaya* v. *Turkey*, para. 124; ECtHR (Judgment) 11 April 2000, Appl. No. 32357/96, *Sevtap Veznedaroğlu* v. *Turkey*, para. 32; ECtHR (Judgment) 31 May 2005, Appl. No. 25165/94, *Akdeniz* v. *Turkey*, para. 139.

519 IACtHR, *Moiwana Community* v. *Suriname, supra* n. 395, para. 193.

520 IACtHR, *Neira Alegría et al.* v. *Peru, supra* n. 446; IACtHR, *Moiwana Community* v. *Suriname, supra* n. 395; IACtHR, *Neira Alegría et al.* v. *Peru, supra* n. 446, para. 69.

materials;[521] and the burial of the mortal remains in accordance with the victims' 'religious beliefs and customs.'[522] The court's understanding of satisfaction has been comprehensive, as it has gone as far as to order the creation of a DNA information system to allow the identification and, eventually, family reunification of the children who disappeared during El Salvador's internal conflict.[523]

Finally, any ritual revolving around memory is also considered a measure of satisfaction. Its objective is to heal the social fabric damaged by gross violations of human rights, and therefore must be conducted with dignity and respect.[524] Along these lines, the IACtHR has considered commemorations and tributes as part of the measures of satisfaction, especially following collective victimization. This includes constructing museums and (memorial) monuments,[525] erecting plaques, naming streets[526] or educational establishments after the victim(s),[527] and building education centres in memory of the victims and the community itself.[528] Significantly, when the IACtHR grants these measures of satisfaction, it orders the State to consult with the victims regarding important practicalities, such as the design and location of the memorial.[529]

All in all, measures of satisfaction can serve an important preventive and educative purpose.[530] Consequently, they are commonly awarded to victims of gross violations of human rights by human rights bodies.[531] For example, monuments can be erected to 'allow future generations to learn' about specific violations that form part of the history of a given state.[532] In this light, monuments can become symbolic

521 IACtHR, *Barrios Altos* v. *Peru, supra* n. 492, para. 43; IACtHR, *Cantoral Benavides* v. *Peru, supra* n. 422, para. 6, 80; IACtHR, *Myrna Mack Chang* v. *Guatemala, supra* n. 516, Res. 11; IACtHR, *Valle Jaramillo et al.* v. *Colombia, supra* n. 395, para. 19.

522 IACtHR, *"Street Children" (Villagrán-Morales et al.)* v. *Guatelama, supra* n. 507, para. 102.

523 IACtHR, *Serrano-Cruz Sisters* v. *El Salvador, supra* n. 516, para. 103.

524 Danieli, *supra* n. 21, p. 63.

525 IACtHR (Judgment) 30 November 2001, *Barrios Altos* v. *Peru,* para. 5; IACtHR (Judgment) 30 November 2001, *Barrios Altos* v. *Peru*, para. 50, Operative para. 5(7); IACtHR, *Moiwana Community* v. *Suriname, supra* n. 395, para. 2-7; IACtHR, *Masaccre Mapiripán* v. *Colombia, supra* n. 395, para. 10, 13.

526 Pasqualucci, *supra* n. 459, p. 206; IACtHR, *Myrna Mack Chang* v. *Guatemala, supra* n. 516, para. 286.

527 IACtHR, *"Street Children" (Villagrán-Morales et al.)* v. *Guatelama, supra* n. 507, para. 103, Operative para. 7; IACtHR (Judgment) 27 February 2002, *Trujillo-Oroza* v. *Bolivia*, para. 122. Operative para. 6.

528 IACtHR, *Aloeboetoe et al.* v. *Suriname, supra* n. 460; IACtHR, *"Street Children" (Villagrán-Morales et al.)* v. *Guatelama, supra* n. 507; IACtHR, *Cantoral Benavides* v. *Peru, supra* n. 422, para. 42; IACtHR, *Trujillo-Oroza* v. *Bolivia, supra* n. 527.

529 IACtHR, *Moiwana Community* v. *Suriname, supra* n. 395, para. 218.

530 Danieli, *supra* n. 21, p. 63-64.

531 Mégret, *supra* n. 517, p. 128-129.

532 IACtHR, *Trujillo-Oroza* v. *Bolivia, supra* n. 527, para. 46.

reparations for the individual victim and a given society as a whole.[533] This also implies that some measures constitute both measures of satisfaction and guarantees of non-repetition.[534] In addition, Mégret has asserted that when measures of satisfaction are future-oriented, they are in fact guarantees of non-repetition.[535]

3.2.5 Guarantees of Non-Repetition

One of the main foundations underpinning the establishment of international human rights instruments and institutions is the prevention of human rights violations. To this end, guarantees of non-repetition are essential, as they aim to prevent further violations and facilitate the re-establishment of the rule of law. Against this background, several human rights instruments devote special attention to the state's obligation to prevent human rights violations.[536] Guarantees of non-repetition are measures that 'look forward', as they aim to prevent further violations both in relation to the victims who may fear retaliation or harm, and in relation to society as a whole.[537] They usually 'go beyond the individual case' because they do not only seek to restore the *status quo ante* of a victim, but rather to prevent 'certain violations, particularly by bringing about systemic changes,'[538] Measures geared towards transforming social, political, cultural or economic structural conditions with the aim of preventing further violations are usually referred to as 'transformative reparations', but they are in essence guarantees of non-repetition.[539] Thus, guarantees of non-repetition can be seen as collective reparation measures as they benefit society as a whole.[540]

The IACtHR is considered a pioneer in shaping the content of guarantees of non-repetition.[541] Measures that the court has ordered include the following: providing international human rights and international humanitarian law training

533 Mégret, F., "Of Shrines, Memorials and Museums: Using the International Criminal Court's Victim Reparations and Assistance Regime to Promote Transitional Justice", 16 *Buffalo Human Rights Law Review* (2010), p. 26-31.

534 Shelton, *supra* n. 1, p. 397; REDRESS, *supra* n. 29, p. 20; Annex to the UN ECOSOC, Question of the Human Rights of all Persons Subjected to any form of Detention or Imprisonment, 16 January 1997, UN. Doc. E/CN.4/1997/104, p. 5.

535 Mégret, *supra* n. 517, p. 130-132.

536 Some examples of these instruments are the Inter-American Convention on the Prevention of Violence against Women (the 'Convention of Belém do Pará'); the ICPED; and CAT and its Optional Protocol, See: Ferstman, *supra* n. 376, p. 9-12.

537 When human rights violations take place, society as a whole is also harmed, see: Shelton, *supra* n. 1, p. 60-61.

538 Bantekas and Oette, *supra* n. 15, p. 631.

539 Chappell, L., "The gender injustice cascade: 'transformative' reparations for victims of sexual and gender-based crimes in the Lubanga case at the International Criminal Court", 21 *The International Journal of Human Rights* (2017), p. 1225-1226.

540 Mégret, *supra* n. 517, p. 130-132.

541 The Human Rights Committee has also ordered these measures, however. See: Crawford, *supra* n. 19, p. 474.

to police forces, the military, state agents, and society in general;[542] strengthening the independence and autonomy of the judiciary; establishing mechanisms to help prevent and monitor social conflicts; and promoting the observance of the existing norms that are compliant with international obligations.[543]

Guarantees of non-repetition are regarded as an exceptional form of remedy, and have become crucial for victims who have suffered through continuous periods of conflict.[544] Likewise, the IACtHR has often resorted to guarantees of non-repetition in cases involving gross violations of human rights, as they can produce significant national policy changes.[545] In this light, the IACtHR has ordered pervasive legal reforms,[546] including of constitutional law.[547] It is important to mention that when the IACtHR has ordered reforms to the law, it does not only rely on Article 63 of the ACHR, which describes its remedial powers, but also on Article 2. The latter Article deals with the state's obligation to adapt and adopt any national legislative or other measure that is necessary to fully protect the rights enshrined by the ACHR.[548]

In contrast, the ECtHR has traditionally demonstrated a reluctance to order guarantees of non-repetition.[549] Nevertheless, the adoption of pilot judgments in its

---

542 IACtHR, *Castillo Petruzzi et al.* v. *Peru, supra* n. 421; IACtHR, *Barrios Altos* v. *Peru, supra* n. 492; IACtHR (Judgment) 7 September 2004, *Tibi* v. *Ecuador,* Res. 7; IACtHR, (Judgment) 1 February 2006, *Lopez-Alvarez* v. *Honduras*, Operative para. 9; IACtHR, *La Cantuta* v. *Peru, supra* n. 507, Operative para. 15.

543 Principle 23, Principles on Reparations.

544 Sierra Leone Truth and Reconciliation Report, *Witness to Truth: Report of the Sierra Leone Truth and Reconciliation*, Vol. II, Chapter 4, November 2004, p. 232. <http://www.sierra-leone.org/Other-Conflict/TRCVolume2.pdf>.

545 Hillebrecht, C., "The power of human rights tribunals: Compliance with the European Court of Human Rights and domestic policy change", 20 *European Journal of International Relations* (2014), p. 1101.

546 IACtHR, *Loayza Tamayo* v. *Peru, supra* n. 372, Res. 5; IACtHR, *Castillo Petruzzi et al.* v. *Peru, supra* n. 421, para. 226, Operative para. 14; IACtHR (Judgment) 21 June 2002, *Hilaire, Constantine and Benjamin et al.* v. *Trinidad and Tobago*, para. 212; IACtHR (Judgment) 26 September 2006, *Almonacid-Arellano et al.* v. *Chile*, Operative para. 3, 5; IACtHR, (Judgment) 14 May 2013, *Mendoza et al.* v. *Argentina*, Operative para. 20-23.

547 IACtHR, *Loayza Tamayo* v. *Peru, supra* n. 372, Res. 5; IACtHR (Judgment) 5 February 2001, *"The Last Temptation of Christ" (Olmedo-Bustos et al.)* v. *Chile*, para. 98, Operative para. 4.

548 Interestingly, these orders appear in the section on reparations but aim at reinforcing Artile 2 of the ACHR. See: IACtHR, *"White Van" (Paniagua-Morales et al.)* v. *Guatemala, supra* n. 507, para. 203; IACtHR (Judgment) 24 November 2009, *"las Dos Erres" Massacre* v. *Guatemala*, para. 238-242; IACtHR (Judgment) 27 April 2012, *Pacheco Teruel et al.* v. *Honduras,* para. 92-98; IACtHR, *Mendoza et al.* v. *Argentina, supra* n. 546, para. 323-325. Significantly, in cases in which the reform relates to Article 21 of the ACHR, the IACtHR does not invoke Article 2. See: IACtHR, *Moiwana Community* v. *Suriname, supra* n. 395, para. 209.

549 ECommHR (Report) 13 July 1983, Case No. 9017/80, *Anthony McGoff* v. *Sweden*, para. 31.

jurisprudence has opened the door to ordering guarantees of non-repetition.[550] This is because pilot judgments were designed to cope, in an effective and prompt manner, with huge numbers of cases that arise as a result of systemic human rights violations within a member state.[551] In this context, the prevention of further violence and legal cases is one of the priorities of these judgements' measures of reparation. As such, in the *Broniowski*[552] and *Hutten-Czapaska* cases,[553] the ECtHR first identified systemic problems in the State's legal order that precluded many individuals from obtaining compensation for properties that belonged to the former Polish territory.[554] Subsequently, in both cases the court ordered the State to employ appropriate legal and administrative measures to secure the right to property,[555] in such a way that a fair balance would be struck between the interests of individuals and those of the community.[556] In addition, the court declared that in cases of systematic violations, the State could not limit itself to providing only compensation, but rather had the obligation to ensure that its domestic legal system would redress the situation and thereby prevent further violations.[557] It thus appears that in pilot judgments, states are usually ordered to undertake domestic legal reforms.[558] Since those reforms have the purpose of protecting the victim of a violation and society as a whole, they could be perceived as guarantees of non-repetition.

This said, it must be noted that pilot judgments have thus far been predominantly, but not exclusively, concerned with property restitution,[559] the length

550 However, even in these judgments the Court has stated that States remain free to choose the manner in which they will discharge their obligations under its judgments. See: ECtHR, *Broniowski* v. *Poland*, *supra* n. 397, para, 191; ECtHR (Judgment) 16 June 2006, Appl. No. 35014/97, *Hutten-Czapska* v. *Poland*, para. 239.

551 Antkowiak, *supra* n. 399, p. 354.

552 ECtHR, *Broniowski* v. *Poland*, *supra* n. 397, para. 189-194.

553 ECtHR, *Hutten-Czapska* v. *Poland*, *supra* n. 550, para. 235-356.

554 Ibid., para. 239, quoted in Antkowiak, T., "Remedial Approaches to Human Rights Violations: The Inter-American Court of Human Rights and Beyond", 46 *Columbia Journal of Transnational Law* (2008), p. 439.

555 ECtHR, *Broniowski* v. *Poland*, *supra* n. 397, para. 194.

556 ECtHR, *Hutten-Czapska* v. *Poland*, *supra* n. 550, para. 239.

557 ECtHR, *Papamichalopoulos and Others* v. *Greece (Article 50)*, *supra* n. 391, para. 34.

558 Oette, *supra* n. 445, p. 237.

559 ECtHR, *Broniowski* v. *Poland*, *supra* n. 397; ECtHR, *Hutten-Czapska* v. *Poland*, *supra* n. 550; ECtHR (Judgment) 7 December 2006, Appl. No. 46347/99, *Xenides-Arestis* v. *Turkey*; ECtHR (Judgment) 13 November 2007, Appl. No. 33771/02, *Driza* v. *Albania*; ECtHR (Judgment) 27 November 2007, Appl. No. 74258/01, *UrbáRska Obec Trenčlanske Biskupice* v. *Slovakia;* ECtHR (Judgment) 3 November 2009, Appl. No. 27912/02, *Suljagić* v. *Bosnia and Herzegovina*; ECtHR (Judgment) 12 October 2010, Appl. No. 30767/05 and 33800/06, *Maria Atanasiu and Others* v. *Romania*; ECtHR (Judgment) 31 July 2012, Appl. Nos. 604/07, 43628/07, 46684/07 and 34770/09, *Manushaqe Puto and Others* v. *Albania*; ECtHR (Judgment) 3 September 2013, Appl. No. 5376/11, *M.C. and Others* v. *Italy*; and ECtHR (Judgment) [GC], 26 July 2014, Appl. No. 60642/08, *Ališić and Others* v. *Bosnia and Herzegovina, Croatia, Serbia, Slovenia and "The Former Yugoslav Republic of Macedonia"*.

of proceedings[560] and widespread overcrowding in prisons.[561] It is therefore difficult to predict whether pilot judgments will also be used in cases where the systematic issue relates to gross violations of human rights, but this possibility exists.[562]

3.3 Main Characteristics of Reparations

Reparations in human rights law share the same characteristics as those in public international law: *restitutio in integrum*, full reparations,[563] adequacy[564] and proportionality.[565] These characteristics relate to all forms of reparations. Accordingly, the Principles on Reparations state that reparations should be adequate, effective and prompt as well as full and proportional to the gravity of the violations suffered.[566] Within the umbrella of proportionality, reparations should not enrich or impoverish the victim.[567] Furthermore, human rights law adds a few additional elements to the

560 ECtHR (Judgment) [GC], 29 March 2006, Appl. No. 36813/97, *Scordino* v. *Italy* (No. 1); ECtHR (Judgment) 7 July 2015, Appl. Nos. 72287/10, 13927/11 and 46187/11, *Rutkowski and others* v. *Poland*.

561 ECtHR (Judgment) 10 January 2012, Appl. Nos. 42525/07 and 60800/08, *Ananyev and Others* v. *Russia*; ECtHR (Judgment) 8 January 2013, Appl. Nos. 43517/09, 46882/09, 55400/09, *Torreggiani and Others* v. *Italy;* ECtHR (Judgment) 27 January 2015, Appl. Nos. 36925/10, 21487/12, 72893/12, 73196/12, 77718/12 and 9717/13, *Neshkov and Others* v. *Bulgaria*; ECtHR (Judgment) 10 March 2015, Appl. Nos. 14097/12, 45135/12, 73712/12, 34001/13, 44055/13, and 64586/13, *Varga and Others* v. *Hungary*.

562 It must be pointed out that Kamminga has stated that the European Court is effectively unable to deal with gross human rights violations. See: Kamminga, M., "Is the European Convention on Human Rights Sufficiently Equipped to Cope with Gross and Systematic Violations?", 12 *Netherlands Quarterly of Human Rights* (1994), p. 153. Yet at first the Court seemed to be unable to deal with systematic violations of human rights. Reforms to its main legal framework allowed for it to adopt pilot judgments. The same could happen in the future should the Court decide to take one step forward towards respect for human rights by tackling GVHR.

563 Amezcua-Noriega, *supra* n. 489, p. 7.

564 Principle 10, Principles on Reparations.

565 Principle 15, Principles on Reparations.

566 Principles 15, 18 Principles on Reparations.

567 Shelton, *supra* n. 1, p. 123; Guideline 1, Principal Guidelines for a Comprehensive Reparations Policy, OEA/Ser/L/V/II.131 (2008), (Hereinafter, OAS Reparations Principal Guidelines 2008). Available at: <http://www.cidh.org/pdf%20files/Lineamientos%20Reparacion%20Administrativa%2014%20mar%202008%20ENG%20final.pdf>; IACtHR, *"Street Children" (Villagrán-Morales et al.)* v. *Guatelama*, *supra* n. 507, para. 63. The ECtHR has stated that reparations are not 'intended to give financial comfort or sympathetic enrichment' to the victim. See also: ECtHR (Judgment) [GC], 18 September 2009, Appl. Nos. 16064/90, 16065/90, 16066/90, 16068/90, 16069/90, 16070/90, 16071/90, 16072/90 and 16073/90, *Varnava and others* v. *Turkey*, para. 224.

previous four characteristics: reparations should be i) in line with the principle of non-discrimination,[568] ii) gender sensitive,[569] and iii) victim-oriented.[570]

The notion that reparations should be in line with the principle of non-discrimination is based on two main reasons. This is because, firstly, the application of human rights should always be in line with this principle[571] and, secondly, it is clearly entrenched in the most authoritative document regarding reparations, the Principles on Reparations.[572] As for the principle of victim-orientedness, although it was initially included in the drafting of the Principles on Reparations, which stated that reparations 'should respond to the needs and wishes of the victims',[573] this clause was not adopted in the final version of the Principles. Finally, the characteristic of gender-sensitivity has been mentioned in some international human rights documents and case law.[574]

The following sections will discuss the four core characteristics of reparations in the context of international human rights. As the principles of international human rights law were drafted on the premises developed under public international law, some of this information may overlap with that provided in Section 2.3.[575]

568 Principle 25, Principles on Reparations; Amezcua-Noriega, *supra* n. 489, p. 6.

569 Gender reparations specifically emphasise the need for psychological and physical rehabilitation. See: Urban Walker, M., "Gender and Violence in Focus: A Background for Gender Justice in Reparations", in R. Rubio-Marin, *The Gender of Reparations: Unsettling Sexual Hierarchies While Redressing Human Rights Violations* (New York, CUP 2009), p. 18-62.

570 Amezcua-Noriega, *supra* n. 489, p. 6; Preamble of the Principles on Reparations; Roht-Arriaza, "Reparations Decisions and Dilemmas", *supra* n. 50, p. 164. This characteristic may well include the idea that victims should be consulted when determining the reparation in order to bring justice to their claims. See: Expert Seminar on "Reparation for Victims of Gross and Systematic Human Rights Violations in the Context of Political Transitions", *supra* n. 82, p. 23.

571 Article 7, UDHR; Article 4, ICCPR; Article 2 (2), ICESRC; Article 1 (3), ICERD; Article 1, CEDAW; Article 2, CRC; Article 1, ACHR; Article 2(2), ECHR.

572 Principle 25, Principles on Reparations.

573 Principle 4, Proposed Basic Principles and Guidelines, Sub-Commission on Prevention of Discrimination and Protection of Minorities, Study concerning the right to restitution, compensation and rehabilitation for victims of gross violations of human rights and fundamental freedoms. Final Report submitted by Mr. Theo van Boven, Special Rapporteur, E/CN.4/Sub.2/1993/8, 2 July 1993, p. 56.

574 African Commission on Human and Peoples' Rights, Resolution on the Right to a Remedy and Reparation for Women and Girls Victims of Sexual Violence, IACmHPR, Access to Justice for Women Victims of Sexual Violence in Mesoamerica, 9 December 2011, OEA/Ser.L/V/II. Doc. 63; IACmHR, Access to Justice for Women Victims of Violence in the Americas, 20 January 2007, OEA/Ser. L/V/II. doc. 68; CEDAW General Recommendation No. 25 on Article 4, paragraph 1 of CEDAW, 30 January 2004, UN Doc./CEDAW/C/2004/I/WP. 1/Rev.1, Section II; IACtHR (Judgment) 16 November 2009, *González et al. ("Cotton Field")* v. *Mexico,* para. 450-455.

575 Tomuschat, *supra* n. 370, p. 160-161.

3.3.1 *Restitutio in Integrum*

This principle aims to undo the harm inflicted – a utopian ideal when it comes to almost all human rights violations. No measure of reparation can erase the suffering that ensues from most human rights violations. Consequently, international human rights bodies have recognised that its application depends on the nature of the violation: if the nature of the violation allows for this, states should aim at providing *restitutio in integrum*.[576] In all other cases, reparations should aim to contribute to alleviating the distress and suffering of victims.[577]

While most international tribunals accept *restitutio in integrum* as the guiding principle on reparations, each tribunalhas given it a different content.[578] Since its first case, the IACtHR has drawn inspiration from the *Factory at Chorzów* case, defining this principle as 'the restoration of the prior situation, the reparation of the consequences of the violation, and indemnification for patrimonial and non-patrimonial damages, including emotional harm.'[579] On the other hand, the ECtHR has defined it as 'restor[ing] as far as possible the situation existing before the breach',[580] covering both direct loss (*damnum emergens*) and loss of profits (*lucrum cessans*).[581] This suggests that for the ECtHR full reparation is a synonym of *restitutio in integrum*.[582]

3.3.2 *Full Reparation*

The IACtHR was the first body ever to refer to this term.[583] Full reparation is aimed at indemnifying all material and non-material harm that a violation has caused. It is thus evident that it shares the same aim as the principle of *restitutio in integrum* as defined by the ECtHR. Similarly, the Set of Principles for the Protection and Promotion of Human Rights through Action to Combat Impunity (Principles against Impunity) states that full reparations 'shall cover all injuries suffered by the victim.' and 'shall include individual measures [of] restitution, compensation and rehabilitation, and

576 Shelton, *supra* n. 1, p. 212; ECtHR, *Papamichalopoulos and Others* v. *Greece (Article 50)*, *supra* n. 391, para. 34.
577 REDRESS, *supra* n. 47, p. 26.
578 Amezcua-Noriega, *supra* n. 489, p. 3.
579 IACtHR (Judgment) 21 July 1989, *Velásquez-Rodríguez* v. *Honduras*, para. 26.
580 ECtHR, *Papamichalopoulos and Others* v. *Greece (Article 50)*, *supra* n. 391, para. 34.
581 ECtHR, *Papamichalopoulos and Others* v. *Greece (Article 50)*, *supra* n. 391; ECtHR, *Assanidze* v. *Georgia*, *supra* n. 393; ECtHR, *Ilaşcu and Others* v. *Moldova And Russia*, *supra* n. 393, para. 489.
582 Brown, *supra* n. 7, p. 198, 204; Nifosi-Sutton, I., "The Power of the European Court of Human Rights to Order Specific Non-Monetary Relief: A Critical Appraisal from a Right to Health Perspective", 23 *Harvard Human Rights Journal* (2010), p. 54.
583 Tomuschat, *supra* n. 209, p. 363.

general measures of satisfaction.'[584] Thus, the Principles against Impunity dictate that full reparations include all measures of reparations, with the exception of guarantees of non-repetition.

3.3.3 Adequacy and Appropriateness

Human rights treaties and related texts usually refer to 'fair', 'adequate', 'appropriate' and 'effective' reparations, without distinguishing between the meanings of these adjectives.[585] In fact, the term 'adequate' is used interchangeably with the terms 'fair', 'just' and 'appropriate'.[586] Like many other aspects of reparations, the issue of adequacy is complex. To date, there are no guidelines in existence that indicate which measures are considered appropriate for specific human rights violations, nor is it desirable to formulate such precise guidelines. Since victims are not homogenous (socially, culturally, psychologically, etc.), what may be adequate for some would not necessarily be adequate for others.

Furthermore, it is difficult to maintain that reparations, regardless of their type, can ever be adequate to repair the harm suffered by a violation of human rights, especially those that are considered gross. Despite the complexity involved in defining adequate reparations, some human rights bodies have considered some measures to be more adequate (or 'just') than others.[587] For instance, the IACtHR has contended that just reparations should include measures of satisfaction,[588] while the ECtHR usually considers monetary compensation to be just reparation.[589] On the other hand, scholars have argued that an adequate form of reparation usually includes a combination of financial and non-financial measures. However, no guidelines on how to balance such measures have been provided.[590]

When determining what constitutes adequate reparations, some of the following factors should be taken into account: the gravity of the violations;[591] the

584 Principle 36, Annex II, UNHCR, *Question of the Impunity of Perpetrators of Human Rights Violations (Civil and Political): Revised Final Report Prepared by Mr. Joinet Pursuant to Sub-Commission Decision 1996/119*, 2 October 1997, UN Doc. E/CN.4/Sub.2/1997/20/Rev. 1; Principle 34, Addendum, UCHCR, Report of the independent expert to update the Set of principles to combat impunity, Diane Orentlicher, 8 February 2005, UN Doc E/CN.4/2005/102/Add.1. An earlier draft of the Principles on Reparations defined 'full reparations' as any restitution, compensation, satisfaction and guarantees of non-repetition. See: Proposed Basic Principles and Guidelines, *supra* n. 573, para. 48.

585 Principles 10 and 11, Principles on Reparations.

586 Oette, *supra* n. 445, p. 219.

587 Pasqualucci, *supra* n. 459, p. 233.

588 IACtHR (Judgment) 26 November 2008, *Tiu Tojín* v. *Guatemala*; IACtHR (Judgment) 27 November 2008, *Ticona Estrada et al.* v. *Bolivia*.

589 ECtHR (Judgment) 16 November 1999, Appl. No. 31127/96, *E.P.* v. *Italy*, para. 75-77.

590 REDRESS, *supra* n. 47, p. 17.

591 IACtHR, *Massacre of Pueblo Bello* v. *Colombia*, *supra* n. 495, para. 258.

views, needs, and wishes of the victims;[592] and the potential of the reparations to erase the effects of the violation.[593] The fact that reparations should neither enrich nor impoverish the victim or his or her children also needs to be taken into account.[594] Finally, the passing of time may influence which forms of reparations are adequate and relevant.[595] As Buyse has pointed out, if a person occupies a home illegally, the passing of time will make the restitution of such property to its legitimate owner more difficult and morally unjustified, rendering this measure inadequate.[596]

Similar to public international law, the issue of adequacy in the context of human rights leaves some room for politics. Like the ICJ, the ECtHR usually allows states to decide what is to be considered an adequate reparation measure. For instance, in some pilot judgments, the court has indicated the need for guarantees of non-repetition. Yet the state is free to choose which are the most appropriate measures to be adopted in order to fulfil this obligation.[597] Previously, the same approach was taken by the IACtHR when granting compensation by not specifying the exact amount to be compensated, leaving the parties involved to agree on the adequate amount to be paid.[598]

Lastly, another important factor that is of extreme importance, but that ironically is not commonly discussed in the reparations scholarship, is whether some reparation measures can put victims in danger if provided without measures of protection. For instance, after the ruling of the IACtHR in the *Plan de Sánchez* case, the government of Guatemala was under an obligation to pay individual compensation to the victims. After several victims had received their monetary compensation, they were robbed.[599] Thus, even when a measure of reparation is deemed to be the most adequate to the victim's suffering, it might also put the victim in harm's way.

---

592 For instance, in the context of the compensation awarded to victims of the atrocities committed during the dictatorship in Argentina, the victims of forced disappearances saw compensation as an attempt to buy their suffering. Thus, they rejected the compensation, whereas victims of political imprisonment considered compensation to be a rightful form of reparation. REDRESS, *supra* n. 47, p. 43. See also: Hamber, B., "Repairing the Irreparable: Dealing with double-binds of making reparations for crimes of the past", 5 *Ethnicity and Health* (2000), p. 219.

593 Shelton, *supra* n. 1, p. 31.

594 OAS Reparations Principal Guidelines 2008, *supra* n. 567; IACtHR, *"Street Children" (Villagrán-Morales et al.)* v. *Guatelama*, *supra* n. 507, para. 63.

595 REDRESS, *supra* n. 47, p. 64.

596 Buyse, *supra* n. 366, p. 132.

597 Antkowiak, *supra* n. 399, p. 411.

598 IACtHR, *Velásquez Rodríguez* v. *Honduras*, *supra* n. 438, para. 191. In addition, the Human Rights Committee (HRC), when granting compensation, does not specify an amount of money to be awarded to the victim; instead, it affirms that compensation must be 'adequate' and allows the State to decide thereon. HRC (View) 31 July 2003, *S. Jegatheeswara Sarma* v. *Sri Lanka*, Comm. No. 950/2000, para. 11. International Commission of Jurists, *supra* n. 23, p. 126.

599 Evans, *supra* n. 8, p. 72.

3.3.4 Proportionality

In general, proportionality in the context of reparations refers to their correspondence to the gravity and consequences of the human rights violation.[600] Hence, a precondition for proportionality is the assessment of the seriousness of the violations and the harm that they have inflicted. While material harm is generally easy to measure, it is extremely challenging, if not impossible, to quantify the physical and moral suffering of a victim. Even when the extent of physical and moral suffering can be established, it must be calculated on a case-by-case basis because one particular human rights violation has the potential to inflict different degrees of physical and psychological harm to different victims.

The question thus remains how human rights supervisory bodies can affirm that the principle of proportionality is guaranteed. The ECtHR claims that it considers the 'gravity of the violations' when granting reparations (mostly monetary compensation). However, the court applies 'equitable considerations' when establishing the amount granted,[601] which generally results in omitting an assessment of the harm and the gravity of the violation. This compromises the principle of proportionality. The IACtHR also states that reparations need to be proportional, but fails to explain how this is to be implemented.[602] It is noteworthy that as a consequence of the principle of proportionality, reparations should neither enrich nor improverish the victims.[603]

Although assessing the proportionality of reparations is highly dependent on the victims' perceptions, some guidelines are desirable in order to afford realistic expectations to victims who are waiting to be awarded reparations. To date, human rights bodies have not yet attempted to formulate such guidelines, at most, the ECtHR have rejected aggravated damages when dealing with serious crimes.[604] However, it is clear that when it comes to mass or gross violations of human rights (GVHR), the State and its population would be rendered eternal debtors when having to attempt to repair all the harm done to every victim of GVHR.[605] As a result, victims of GVHR are generally awarded more symbolic reparations, thereby raising the question of how this could be considered proportional to the victims' suffering.[606]

600 ECtHR (Judgment) 18 December 1996, Appl. No. 21987/93, *Aksoy* v. *Turkey*, para. 113.

601 ECtHR (Judgment) [GC],8 July 1999, Appl. No. 23657/94, *Çakici* v. *Turkey*, para. 130.

602 IACtHR, *Castillo Petruzzi et al.* v. *Peru*, *supra* n. 421, para. 51.

603 Amezcua-Noriega, *supra* n. 489, p. 5.

604 ECtHR (Judgment) 24 April 1998, Appl. No. 12/1997/796/998-999 *Selçuk* v. *Turkey*, para. 119; ECtHR (Judgment) 25 July 2005, Appl. No. 31417/96; 32377/96, *Lustig-Prean and Beckett* v. *The United Kingdom*, para. 12.

605 A detailed discussion on reparations for mass violations is further provided in Section 4.

606 A further detailed explanation of this matter is given in Chapter III.

3.4 Other Substantive and Procedural Aspects of Reparations

3.4.1 Liability to Repair

As in public international law, under human rights law states are responsible for providing victims with reparations for their acts and omissions that resulted in human rights violations from which these victims suffered harm.[607] In addition, it must be stated that, at the domestic level, human rights violations are attributed to a person, whether legal or natural, and consequently the responsible party is liable to provide reparations to the victims. If the liable party is unable or unwilling to provide reparations, the state should act as a subsidiary, for instance by establishing reparation programmes and assisting victims as required.[608]

3.4.2 Beneficiaries

Under international human rights law, the beneficiaries of reparations are, first of all, the direct victims of a violation (the injured parties).[609] However, when the immediate victim has disappeared or is dead, the beneficiaries can be the victim's family members. In this light, the IACtHR has established that the right to reparation for the harm endured by the victims 'up to the time of their death is transmitted to their heirs by succession,'[610] with spouses and children being the most common successors.[611] In defining successors, the IACtHR generally relies on national law,[612] but it has also considered the traditions or customs of the victims when this approach is more victim-inclusive.[613] For instance, in the *Bámaca-Velásquez* case, the court acknowledged that the disappeared person adhered to the cultural traditions of the Mam ethnic group. Thus, it was decided to distribute the compensation between the spouse, children and other siblings,[614] even though national law only included ascendants and descendants. Likewise, in the *Aloeboetoe* case the IACtHR took into account the tribal customary law of the Maroons, which allows for polygamy, to award reparations to all the wives of the deceased victims. This contradicts Suriname national law as this does not recognise polygamy, and thus would have allowed only one wife (the first one) to receive reparations.[615]

---

607 Principle 15, Principles on Reparations.
608 Principle 16, Principles on Reparations.
609 IACtHR (Judgment) 26 November 2010, *Cabrera García and Montiel Flores* v. *Mexico*, para. 211.
610 IACtHR, *Aloeboetoe et al.* v. *Suriname*, *supra* n. 460, para. 62; IACtHR (Judgment) 27 August 1998, *Garrido and Baigorria* v. *Argentina*, para. 50; IACtHR (Judgment) 18 September 2003, *Bulacio* v. *Argentina*, para. 85.
611 IACtHR, *Aloeboetoe et al.* v. *Suriname*, *supra* n. 460, para. 62.
612 Ibid., para. 62.
613 Ibid., para. 62, 63; IACtHR, *Bámaca Velásquez* v. *Guatemala, supra* n. 457, para. 52.
614 IACtHR, *Bámaca Velásquez* v. *Guatemala, supra* n. 457, para. 52.
615 IACtHR, *Aloeboetoe et al.* v. *Suriname*, *supra* n. 460, para. 62, 63.

Not only direct victims can be beneficiaries of reparations: it is acknowledged that victims' relatives are generally profoundly affected by the violations suffered by their loved ones.[616] Accordingly, indirect victims 'may be regarded as an 'injured party,'[617] which implies that their own rights have been directly violated.[618] Thus, a victim's relative could not only be entitled to be the beneficiary of reparations as an heir or successor of the direct victim, but also as a victim him/herself as a result of the suffering which has ensued from the violstion of the direct victim's rights.[619] To identify the indirect victims or the next of kin, the IACtHR has made use of presumptions[620] by examining, inter alia, the 'closeness of the family relationship', as well as the efforts made by the family member to seek justice for the violations suffered by the direct victim.[621] The court has also presumed that grave or gross violations of human rights directed towards a victim inherently affect the victim's immediate family, making them indirect victims or beneficiaries.[622] It is important to mention that it is sometimes difficult to distinguish direct from indirect victims when discussing GVHR. These violations involve many victims who may have suffered to a different degree and from different violations.

Dependants of the victim may also become the beneficiaries of reparations.[623] For instance, the IACtHR has asserted that beneficiaries of reparations can be 'extended to cover persons who, though not successors of the victims, have suffered some consequence of the unlawful act.'[624] Dependants, however, must meet the following criteria to be recognized as beneficiaries of reparations: i) proof of effective and regular payments in cash or in kind, 'made by the victim to the claimant regardless of whether or not they constituted a legal obligation to pay support'; ii) 'the nature of the relationship between the victim and the claimant should [provide] the assumption that the payments would have continued had the victim not been killed' or had not disappeared; and iii) 'the claimant must have experienced a financial need.'[625]

---

616 IACtHR (Judgment) 19 November 1999, *"Street Children" (Villagrán-Morales et al.)* v. *Guatelama*, para. 173-177; ECtHR, *Varnava and others* v. *Turkey*, *supra* n. 567.

617 ECtHR, Çakici v. *Turkey*, *supra* n. 601, para. 130.

618 ECtHR, *Aksoy* v. *Turkey*, *supra* n. 600, para. 113.

619 IACtHR, *Garrido and Baigorria* v. *Argentina*, *supra* n. 610, para. 50.

620 IACtHR, *"Street Children" (Villagrán-Morales et al.)* v. *Guatelama*, *supra* n. 507, para. 68.

621 IACtHR, *Bámaca Velásquez* v. *Guatemala*, *supra* n. 457, para. 163.

622 IACtHR (Judgment) 31 May 2001, *Cesti-Hurtado* v. *Peru*, para. 54.

623 The wording 'dependant as a right holder of reparation' at the international level has only been explicitly found in The Robben Island Guidelines, para. 50 which states that 'all States should ensure that all victims of torture and their dependents' receive reparation.

624 IACtHR, *Aloeboetoe et al.* v. *Suriname*, *supra* n. 460, para. 67-68.

625 Ibid., para. 68.

Finally, the jurisprudence of the IACtHR has demonstrated that groups can also be beneficiaries of – collective – reparations.[626] In sum, it may be concluded that beneficiaries could include direct and indirect victims[627] (also known as third persons),[628] such as the next of kin,[629] the dependants of direct victims, family groups,[630] successors of victims,[631] and collectivities.[632] Similarly, the ECtHR identifies any victim who is 'the person directly affected by the act or omission' which constitutes a human rights violation as the beneficiary of this violation.[633] This may include the next of kin.[634] The court does not distinguish between direct and indirect victims; instead, the next of kin can be considered victims of the violation of other rights such as ill-treatment or access to justice.[635] The ECtHR has also recognized that legal persons can be victims and, as such, has awarded them reparations.[636]

3.4.3 Assessment of the Harm

A multitude of legal rules and qualifications provide guidance on how to assess the harm suffered. Rules related to eligibility, causation, attribution, mitigation, dealing with risk, and indeterminacy can help to determine if a given damage is measurable and compensable.[637] Evidently, the assessment of material harm such as property loss differs significantly from that of non-material harm such as a victim's suffering.[638]

626 IACtHR (Judgment) 28 November 2007, *Saramaka People* v. *Suriname*, para. 188. The African Commission has also recognized collectivities as holders of rights. See: ACmHPR, *Centre for Minority Rights Development (Kenya) and Minority Rights Group (on behalf of Endorois Welfare Council)* v. *Kenya*, *supra* n. 403, para. 150-151.

627 IACtHR, *"las Dos Erres" Massacre* v. *Guatemala*, *supra* n. 548, para. 292; IACtHR (Judgment) 25 May 2010, *Chitay Nech y Otros* v. *Guatemala*, para. 278.

628 The HRC has usually referred to third persons instead of indirect victims. See: HRC, *S. Jegatheeswara Sarma* v. *Sri Lanka*, *supra* n. 598.

629 IACtHR, *Cesti-Hurtado* v. *Peru*, *supra* n. 622, para. 54. See also: ICJ, *Ahmadou Sadio Diallo* (*Republic of Guinea* v. *Democratic Republic of the Congo*), Separate Opinion of Judge Cançado Trindade, *supra* n. 84, para. 55.

630 IACtHR (Judgment) 27 November 1998, *Castillo-Páez* v. *Peru*, para. 76.

631 ECtHR (Judgment) 18 October 1982, Appl. No. 7215/75, *X* v. *United Kingdom*, para. 18-19; IACtHR (Judgment) 28 February 2003, *"Five Pensioners"* v. *Peru*, para. 180; Article 14 CAT.

632 IACtHR, *Mayagna (Sumo) Awas Tingni Community* v. *Nicaragua*, Separate Opinion of Judge Sergio García Ramírez, *supra* n. 402, para. 15; IACtHR, *Moiwana Community* v. *Suriname*, *supra* n. 395; IACtHR, *Yakye Axa Indigenous Community* v. *Paraguay*, *supra* n. 404, para. 6-9.

633 ECtHR (Judgment) 25 June 1996, Appl. No.19776/92, *Amuur* v. *France*, para. 36.

634 ECtHR (Judgment) 2 September 1998, Appl. No. 63/1997/847/1054, *Yaşa* v. *Turkey*, para. 66.

635 ECtHR (Judgment) 25 May 1998, Appl. No. 15/1997/799/1002, *Kurt* v. *Turkey*, para. 134.

636 Altwicker-Hámori, Altwicker and Peters, *supra* n. 468, p. 15. At present, only once has the IACtHR recognized such a legal person (an indigenous political party in Nicaragua) as a victim and the beneficiary of reparation. See: IACtHR (Judgment) 23 June 2005, *YATAMA* v. *Nicaragua*, para. 248.

637 Barker, *supra* n. 118, p. 603.

638 Ibid., p. 603-604.

While it is generally acknowledged that material damage may be assessed more easily than moral harm,[639] both remain a highly complex matter.

Attempting to assess material losses resulting from violations of the right to life or personal integrity is particularly difficult. This is because human rights violations produce different kinds of harm, which may be assessed using several economic methods.[640] In general, when human rights courts assess damages, some common factors can be identified. Regarding the right to life, these include age; health; the life conditions of a deceased individual; the life expectancy of the deceased; and the particular relationship between the deceased and the beneficiary.[641] In relation to the deprivation of liberty, the following factors are usually taken into account: the arbitrariness of the arrest; any physical or moral suffering related to the imprisonment; and the duration of the imprisonment.[642] However, the factors on this list are neither exhaustive nor compulsory.

Both the ECtHR and the IACtHR include loss of earnings in the category of material harm. The ECtHR usually bases this upon the victim's last salary; if the exact salary cannot be substantiated by a document, the court will establish it on the basis of equity,[643] taking into account the length of the violation and work experience.[644] In a similar fashion, the IACtHR, in the absence of proof of the victim's salary, takes into account the average life expectancy in the country in question;[645] the minimum wage established in national law;[646] as well as the social benefits granted under national legislation. In addition, it usually deducts 25% for personal expenses.[647] Importantly, in *the Chaparro Álvarez and Lapo Íñiguez* case, the IACtHR refused to calculate the material loss that resulted from the State's seizure of the victim's company. Instead, it ruled that an arbitration tribunal should determine the value of the loss.[648] In the meantime, the court awarded compensation 'based on the equity principle', whilst deciding that if the arbitration tribunal were to order a greater amount of compensation, the government could deduct the money already awarded by the court. However, if it was less, the victim could keep the money.[649]

---

639 Bottigliero, *supra* n. 48, p. 29.
640 Shelton, *supra* n. 1, p. 331.
641 Ibid., p. 147.
642 Shelton, D., *Remedies in International Human Rights Law* (Oxford, OUP 2005, 2nd ed.), p. 71.
643 ECtHR (Judgmet) 13 November 2003, Appl. Nos. 23145/93 and 25091/94, *Elci and others* v. *Turkey*, para. 721-722.
644 Ibid., para. 721-722.
645 IACtHR, *Loayza Tamayo* v. *Peru, supra* n. 372, para. 129; IACtHR, *Bámaca Velásquez* v. *Guatemala, supra* n. 457, para. 51 (b); IACtHR, *Caracazo* v. *Venezuela, supra* n. 466, para. 29.
646 IACtHR, *Neira Alegría et al.* v. *Peru, supra* n. 446, para. 49-52; IACtHR (Judgment) 26 May 2001, *"Street Children" (Villagrán-Morales et al.)* v. *Guatelama,* para. 79.
647 IACtHR, *"Street Children" (Villagrán-Morales et al.)* v. *Guatelama, supra* n. 507, para. 81.
648 IACtHR (Judgment) 21 November 2007, *Chaparro Álvarez and Lapo Íñiguez* v. *Ecuador*, para. 232.
649 Ibid., para. 232.

Regarding moral damage, the ECtHR has stated that providing compensation for moral harm has the purpose of acknowledging that the harm has occurred, but it cannot be awarded as a 'financial comfort or sympathetic enrichment at the expense of the Contracting Party concerned.'[650] Therefore, harm is assessed on an equitable basis,[651] because this criterion implies 'flexibility and an objective consideration of what is just'.[652] Nevertheless, the ECtHR has claimed that it takes the gravity of the violations into consideration when appraising the harm suffered by the victims.[653]

While the IACtHR usually follows the ECtHR's approach regarding the use of equitable considerations when it comes to moral damage,[654] it has granted higher awards to more immediate relatives. For example, spouses and children are usually granted higher sums of money than siblings.[655] Furthermore, as explained in the section on compensation, the IACtHR has developed some very creative concepts that have sometimes been considered when assessing the harm suffered by the victims: harm to the 'project of life'[656] and to 'family assets'.[657] Whilst both categories represent a comprehensive and holistic approach to reparations for human rights violations, they have been applied inconsistently, and in only a few cases.[658]

In general, it is fair to conclude that assessing moral damage is a matter of judicial discretion[659] and in some instances this applies equally to the assessment of material damages. According to Crawford, this is because human rights supervisory bodies 'award damages more as a vindication of the rights infringed than as an economic evaluation of what was lost'.[660] The assessment of the damage, according to him, is purely discretionary and without the aim of ever being proportional to the harm inflicted. In this light, Shelton asserts that human rights courts could be influenced by the nature of the victim and the degree of sympathy evoked when assessing the damage caused by a given violation.[661]

---

650 ECtHR, *Varnava and others* v. *Turkey, supra* n. 567, para. 225.

651 Ibid., para. 224.

652 Altwicker-Hámori, Altwicker and Peters, *supra* n. 468, p. 15.

653 ECtHR, Çakici v. *Turkey*, *supra* n. 601, para. 130; Altwicker-Hámori, Altwicker and Peters, *supra* n. 468, p. 17-18.

654 IACtHR, *Cantoral Benavides* v. *Peru*, *supra* n. 422, para. 53.

655 IACtHR (Judgment) 21 January 1994, *Gangaram-Panday* v. *Suriname*, para. 49.

656 IACtHR, *Loayza Tamayo* v. *Peru*, *supra* n. 372.

657 IACtHR, *Molina-Theissen* v. *Guatemala*, *supra* n. 471, para. 59-61.

658 Antkowiak, *supra* n. 399, p. 371.

659 Bottigliero, *supra* n. 48, p. 29; Gray, *supra* n. 5, p. 891.

660 Crawford, J., 'State Responsibility', Max Planck Encyclopedia of Public International Law [MPEPIL], September 2006, para. 34. Available at: <http://opil.ouplaw.com/view/10.1093/law:epil/9780199231690/law-9780199231690-e1093>.

661 Gray, *supra* n. 5, p. 891, citing Shelton, D., *Remedies in International Human Rights Law* (Oxford, OUP 2005, 2nd ed.), p. 345-348.

3.4.4 Standard of Proof

Like domestic courts, international courts need evidentiary rules to establish facts in a dispute. Evidentiary rules, essential for a court's functioning, belong to the cluster of procedural law and are applicable throughout the whole judicial process, including the reparation stage. Significantly, Thienel contends that despite their importance, less attention has been paid to procedural rules in the context of international human rights law when compared to public international law.[662] In general, international courts adopt a flexible approach to evidentiary rules such as the burden and standard of proof.[663] While the former determines which party must bring evidence that proves certain assertions, the latter determines 'how heavy the burden of proof is' and the test that a court requires in order to accept or reject a finding of facts.[664] The flexibility of these rules allows the courts to decrease procedural obstacles that could prevent them from adjudicating a claim.[665] In the context of human rights law, this flexibility is beneficial to victims in their search for justice.

When it comes to the burden of proof, the basic general principle of law that states that who asserts must prove their affirmations (*actori incumbit onus probandi* or *onus probandi)*[666] is also applicable in international human rights law. The ECtHR's Rules explicitly support this principle, but they have failed to establish the standard of proof required to prove a claim.[667] While the IACtHR's Rules are silent regarding both the burden and standard of proof required,[668] the IACtHR has acknowledged the *onus probandi* principle and established its standard of proof in its rulings.[669]

Despite their acceptance of the *onus probandi* principle, both the IACtHR and the ECtHR have shifted the burden of proof at times, in relation to both the merits and the reparations stage. Regarding the former, the courts have shifted the burden of proof in cases in which the State was in possession of the evidence, and thus had the power to hide or destroy it. As stated by the IACtHR, 'the State cannot rely on the defense that the complainant has failed to present evidence when it cannot be obtained without the State's cooperation.'[670] Good examples of this are cases related

662 Thienel, *supra* n. 276, p. 543.

663 Riddell, *supra* n. 274, p. 853.

664 Thienel, *supra* n. 276, p. 557.

665 Riddell, *supra* n. 274, p. 851-852.

666 Ibid., p. 858.

667 Rule 60 (2) (3) Rules of the ECtHR. It must be added that this rule does not apply at the admissibility stage as establishing a violation would *prima facie* be sufficient.

668 See: Rules of Procedure of the IACtHR (hereinafter IACtHR's Rules) approved by the IACtHR during its LXXXV Regular Period of Sessions, held from November 16 to 28, 2009.

669 IACtHR, *Aloeboetoe et al.* v. *Suriname*, *supra* n. 460, para. 71; IACtHR, *"White Van" (Paniagua-Morales et al.)* v. *Guatemala*, *supra* n. 507, para. 86; IACtHR (Judgment) 26 May 2001, *"Street Children" (Villagrán-Morales et al.)* v. *Guatelama*, para. 68.

670 IACtHR, *Gangaram-Panday* v. *Suriname, supra* n. 655, para. 49; IACtHR, *Caracazo* v. *Venezuela*, *supra* n. 466, para. 50.

to enforced disappearances, ill-treatment and deaths while in police custody,[671] as well as cases in which the court's finding of procedural violations during domestic procedures has evoked the presumption of a substantive human rights violation.[672] A shift of the burden of proof in these cases intends to ameliorate the inherent inequalities between the individual(s) and the state machinery.[673] Besides this, the burden of proof can also be shared. This is especially relevant in cases in which interference with a right might have been permissible; in this case, the State would need to prove that the interference was justified.[674] Finally, the IACtHR has also shifted the burden of proof in the reparations stage, especially when establishing moral harm: 'it is the State who shall invalidate [the presumption of mental and emotional harm]' resulting from human rights violations towards the relatives.[675] Under the ECtHR, this is not the case, as this Court has upheld that moral harm (non-pecuniary damage) does not require any proof as long as material damage has been found.[676]

Regarding the issue of the standard of proof, it is pertinent to recall that it is better understood under domestic law. Despite maintaining a different understanding of the concept, the major legal traditions (common and civil law) require a higher standard of proof in criminal law processes than in those of a civil or administrative nature. This general rule has also been espoused at the international level.[677] The three standards that are most commonly used by the ECtHR and the IACtHR are i) the preponderance of evidence, also called the balance of probabilities; ii) beyond reasonable doubt; and iii) *l'intime conviction du juge,* also known as the sufficiency of evidence.[678]

At present, the IACtHR has used, without any consistency, all three standards when it comes to the proving of facts – the preponderance of evidence having been applied the most.[679] The court invoked the *l'intime conviction du juge* especially

671 Ambrus, M., "The European Court of Human Rights and Standards of Proof: An Evidentiary Approach towards the Margin of Appreciation" in L. Gruszczynski and W. Werner (eds.), *Deference in International Courts and Tribunals* (Oxford, OUP 2014), p. 239; Contreras-Garduño, D., "The Inter-American System of Human Rights" in A. Mihr and M. Gibney (eds.), *The SAGE Handbook of Human Rights* (London, SAGE 2014), p. 610; Kinsch, P., "On the Uncertainties Surrounding the Standard of Proof in Proceedings Before International Courts and Tribunals" in G. Venturini & S. Bariatti, (eds.), *Diritti Individuali e Giustizia Internationale: Liber Fausto Pocar* (Milan, Giuffrè 2009), p. 438.

672 Ambrus, *supra* n. 671, p. 239.

673 Riddell, *supra* n. 274, p. 859.

674 Thienel, *supra* n. 276, p. 552-553.

675 IACtHR, *Aloeboetoe et al.* v. *Suriname*, *supra* n. 460, para. 71, 76; IACtHR, *Loayza Tamayo* v. *Peru*, *supra* n. 372, para. 140.

676 ECtHR (Judgment) 01 June 2006, Appl. No. 64890/01 *Gridin* v. *Russia*, para. 20; ECtHR (Judgment) 07 July 2014, Appl. No. 42119/04. *Firstov* v. *Russia*, para. 49.

677 Ambrus, *supra* n. 671, p. 252.

678 Riddell, *supra* n. 274, p. 861-863.

679 Paúl, A., "In search of the standards of proof applied by the Inter-American Court of Human Rights", 55 *Revista Instituto Interamericano de Derechos Humanos* (2012), p. 73, 82-84.

during its first cases;[680] and although it has stated that the beyond reasonable doubt standard is not applicable to disputes under its jurisdiction, it has nevertheless applied this standard in a few cases.[681] With respect to the standard of proof that is required for a reparation claim, the IACtHR generally *presumes* the existence of pecuniary damage, even if this is not supported by documentary evidence. As a result, when assessing the presumed harm, it applies the principles of equity or fairness.

On the other hand, some scholars have often stated that the ECtHR uses the standard of beyond reasonable doubt only in relation to the proving of facts,[682] especially in cases related to violations of Articles 2 and 3.[683] Yet the ECtHR has even maintained that the standard of beyond reasonable doubt 'may follow from the coexistence of sufficiently strong, clear and concordant inferences or of similar unrebutted presumptions of fact.'[684] Interestingly, the court has asserted that this standard is not in conformity with the beyond reasonable doubt standard employed by domestic courts in criminal cases.[685] In criminal trials, this standard is closely associated with the presumption of innocence; this creates a high threshold that, if applied under human rights law, would likely prevent plaintiffs from proving their allegations.[686] In light of this, it appears that the ECtHR has constructed a different definition of the standard of beyond reasonable doubt that facilitates its application in a human rights context.[687] The ECtHR's understanding of this standard is unprecedented and innovative; as the court has never explained why it has chosen to refer to the standard of beyond reasonable doubt nor exactly what it means, this remains open to discussion.[688]

---

680 Ibid., p. 74, citing the IACtHR, *Velásquez Rodríguez* v. *Honduras*, *supra* n. 438; Riddell, *supra* n. 274, p. 861-862.

681 Ibid., p. 70, 97-101. See also: IACtHR, *Apitz Barbera et al. ("First Court of Administrative Disputes")* v. *Venezuela*, *supra* n. 416, para. 108.

682 The same standard was also previously used by the abolished ECmmHR. See: Thienel, *supra* n. 276, p. 564.

683 Ibid., p. 556, 564-565, 582. See: In relation to Article 2: ECtHR (Judgment) [GC], 8 July 1999, Appl. No. 23763/94, *Tanrikulu* v. *Turkey*, para. 97; ECtHR, *Mahmut Kaya* v. *Turkey*, *supra* n. 518, para. 87; ECtHR (Judgment) [GC] 11 July 2006, Appl. No. 54810/00, *Jalloh* v. *Germany*, para. 67; and in relation to Article 3: ECtHR (Judgment) [GC], 5 September 1995, Appl. No. 18984/91, *McCann and others* v. *Great Britain*, para. 148-150.

684 ECtHR, *Tanrikulu* v. *Turkey*, *supra* n. 683, para. 97; ECtHR, *Mahmut Kaya* v. *Turkey*, *supra* n. 518, para. 87; ECtHR, *Jalloh* v. *Germany*, *supra* n. 683, para. 67.

685 Thienel, *supra* n. 276, p. 566, citing ECtHR (Judgment) 6 July 2005, Appl. Nos. 43577/98 and 43579/98, *Nachova and Others* v. *Bulgaria*, para. 147.

686 Ibid., p. 578-579.

687 Kinsch, *supra* n. 671, p. 435-441; ECtHR (Judgment) 18 January 1978, Appl. No. 5310/71, *Ireland* v. *The United Kingdom*; ECtHR (Judgment) 6 April 2000, Appl. No. 26772/95, *Labita* v. *Italy*; ECtHR (Judgment) 26 February 2009, Appl. No. 63997/00, *Fedorov* v. *Russia*.

688 ECtHR (Judgment) 13 June 2002, Appl. No. 38361/97, *Anguelova* v. *Bulgaria,* Dissentig Opinion of Judge Bonello, para. 10; Thienel, *supra* n. 276, p. 566, 575.

In some cases, the ECtHR has indirectly applied the standard of *l'intime conviction du juge* by using the wording 'must be convincingly established'.[689] One factor that may influence the adoption of a given standard of proof by the ECtHR is its doctrine of the margin of appreciation (MoA),[690] which requires that the factual and moral questions involved are taken into account.[691] Some scholars have argued that given the nature of its proceedings, the ECtHR should adopt the standard of the preponderance of evidence instead of the two standards used by the court (beyond reasonable doubt and *l'intime conviction du juge*).[692] Finally, the ECtHR appears to have established a new standard of proof in relation to pilot judgments. In these cases, the ECtHR refers to 'well-founded' cases. While this is more sympathetic towards the victims,[693] it implies a lower standard of proof.

Interestingly, Ambrus has noted that the ECtHR's terminology used to define the standard of proof varies. The court appears to use these terms interchangeably: 'standard of proof' when facts need to be proven; 'MoA' when the justification of state interference needs to be proven; and the 'level of scrutiny' in cases related to discrimination.[694] Finally, in relation to the reparations stage, in addition to the standard of beyond reasonable doubt, the ECtHR also makes use of presumptions in combination with the guiding principle of equity.[695]

Use of presumptions

Both the IACtHR and the ECtHR apply the use of presumptions as the underlying standard of proof to assess non-material or moral damage, such as grief, anguish and sadness, especially in cases related to gross violations of human rights.[696] This applies both to the victims and their next of kin;[697] thus, both courts presume that the suffering of the victim's relatives is a natural and inevitable consequence of the volation of the direct victim's rights.[698]

---

689 Thienel, *supra* n. 276, p. 582.
690 Ibid., p. 554.
691 Ambrus, *supra* n. 671, p. 240-253.
692 Thienel, *supra* n. 276, p. 584-585.
693 Oette, *supra* n. 445, p. 230.
694 Ambrus, *supra* n. 671, p. 238.
695 Gray, *supra* n. 5, p. 891.
696 Rombouts, Sardaro and Vandeginste, *supra* n. 24, p. 384; Madrigal-Borloz, V., "Damage and Redress in the jurisprudence of the Inter-American Court of Human Rights (1979-2001)", in G. Urlich and L. Krabbe Boserup (eds.), *Human Rights in Development Yearbook 2001: Reparations: redressing past wrongs* (The Hague, Kluwer Law International 2003); See: IACtHR, *Masaccre Mapiripán* v. *Colombia*, *supra* n. 395, para. 146; ECtHR (Judgment) 29 March 2006, Appl. No. 64890/01, *Apicella* v. *Italy*, para. 93.
697 IACtHR, *Caracazo* v. *Venezuela*, *supra* n. 466, para. 50 (e).
698 ECtHR, Çakici v. *Turkey*, *supra* n. 601, para. 98; IACtHR, *Caracazo* v. *Venezuela*, *supra* n. 466, para. 50 (e); IACtHR, *Masaccre Mapiripán* v. *Colombia*, *supra* n. 395, para. 146.

Besides moral damages, both courts have also invoked the use of presumptions when assessing material damages. For instance, the IACtHR usually presumes that a victim who has attained the age of majority 'carries out productive activities and perceives, at least, an income equivalent to the minimum legal wage in the country involved'.[699] In line with this, if the plaintiffs cannot prove that they have received a given income, the IACtHR will calculate the damage presuming that the victims' income was at least the minimum wage. Another case in point is *Akdivar and Others*, in which the 'applicants' houses were burnt by the security forces.'[700] In this case, the ECtHR was challenged by the fact that there was no documentary evidence proving the ownership of one plaintiff's house nor its value, because the house had been 'passed from generation to generation, and was acquired by prescriptive use.'[701] Despite this, the ECtHR awarded compensation based on the principle of equity.[702]

The IACtHR has expounded its use of presumptions in detail. In general, the court presumes the following: i) the death of a person who has disappeared in the middle of violent events; ii) 'adults who receive income and have a family spend most of that income providing for the needs of its members'; iii) the relatives of the dead person paid the costs of his funeral; iv) adults usually carry out remunerated work activities at at least the minimum wage even if the victim was unemployed at the time of the violation; v) human rights violations and 'a situation of impunity regarding those violations cause grief, anguish and sadness, both to the victims and to their next of kin.'[703] The use of presumptions as a crucial element in the 'preponderance of evidence' may also be observed in cases involving widespread violations of human rights in which the court does not request a higher standard of proof to establish a link between the widespread violations and a particular case.[704] On the other hand, the ECtHR also made use of presumptions in relation to widespread violations of human rights. For instance, in cases of enforced disappearances, it presumes that the victim's relatives have suffered 'distress and anguish' if the state has not undertaken an investigation.[705] Nowadays, it does use a 'rebuttable presumption' of non-pecuniary damage in relation to any right that has been violated by a given state.[706]

Although it is a rather abstract criterion, the presumption principle is believed to be in the interest of promoting justice.[707] In this light, when the claimant cannot prove his/her reparation claim with documentary evidence, the IACtHR and the

699 IACtHR, *Caracazo* v. *Venezuela*, *supra* n. 466, para. 50 (d).
700 ECtHR, *Akdivar and Others* v. *Turkey*, *supra* n. 398, para. 18.
701 Ibid., para. 17-18.
702 Ibid., para. 19.
703 IACtHR, *Caracazo* v. *Venezuela*, *supra* n. 466, para. 50.
704 Paúl, *supra* n. 679, p. 88-90.
705 ECtHR (Judgment) 18 December 2012, Appl. Nos. 2944/06 and 8300/07, 50184/07, 332/08, 42509/10, *Aslakhanova and others* v. *Russia*, para. 133.
706 Altwicker-Hámori, Altwicker and Peters, *supra* n. 468, p. 11-12.
707 Barker, *supra* n. 118, p. 602.

ECtHR could presume the existence of damage based on the merits and assess this damage based on the principle of equity.[708] The ECtHR and the IACtHR apply the use of presumptions regardless of the standard of proof used, especially with respect to cases related to mass violations. It can therefore be concluded that the ECtHR and the IACtHR regularly make use of a 'relaxed standard of proof' regarding both the merits and reparations.[709]

Finally, as in public international law, under human rights law 'judicial notice' can suffice as the standard of proof. It is pertinent to recall that judicial notice can occur when the court does not know all the relevant facts and cannot conduct investigations *proprio motu*. Even though the ECtHR is capable of conducting its own investigations, it has made use of judicial notice from domestic courts in relation to national security concerns.[710] The IACtHR has gone as far as using the information of truth commission reports as judicial notices to prove certain facts. However the information provided int those reports is, at times, contested.[711]

3.4.5 Causality

As mentioned previously, this principle of reparations refers to a causal connection between a violation and the harm caused. Its purpose is to avoid repairing any harm that is considered to be too indirect, inconsequential or remote from the violation.[712] In the same vein, the IACtHR has stated that: '[t]o compel the perpetrator of an illicit act to erase all the consequences produced by his action is completely impossible, since that action caused effects that multiplied to a degree that cannot be measured.'[713]

---

708 ECtHR (Judgment) 17 February 2004, Appl. No. 25760/94, *Ipek* v. *Turkey*, para. 227; IACtHR, *Chaparro Álvarez and Lapo Íñiguez* v. *Ecuador*, *supra* n. 648.

709 The REDRESS Trust, *Report: Reparations for victims of genocide, crimes against humanity and war crimes: Systems in place and systems in the making, The Hague, 1-2 March 2007* (The Hague, The REDRESS Trust 2007), p. 34; Paúl, *supra* n. 679, p. 71.

710 Thienel, *supra* n. 276, p. 546-547.

711 IACtHR, *Myrna Mack Chang* v. *Guatemala*, *supra* n. 516, para. 131; IACtHR, *Maritza Urrutia* v. *Guatemala*, *supra* n. 458, para. 56; IACtHR (Judgment) 18 November 2004, *De la Cruz-Flores* v. *Peru*, para. 61; IACtHR (Judgment) 6 April 2006, *Baldeón-García* v. *Peru*, para. 72(1); IACtHR, *Almonacid-Arellano et al.* v. *Chile*, *supra* n. 546, para. 82; IACtHR, *Miguel Castro-Castro Prison* v. *Peru*, *supra* n. 495, para. 197; IACtHR, *La Cantuta* v. *Peru*, *supra* n. 507, para. 80 (1)-(16), 86-95; and IACtHR (Judgment) 4 July 2007, *Zambrano Vélez et al.* v. *Ecuador*, para. 128. See also: Ferrara, A., *Assessing the Long-term Impact of Truth Commissions: The Chilean Truth and Reconciliation Commission in Historical Perspective* (Abingdon/ New York, Routledge 2014), p. 131-138; Rodríguez-Pinzón, D., "The Inter-American human rights system and transitional processes" in A. Buyse, and M. Hamilton (eds.), *Transitional Jurisprudence and the ECHR: Justice, Politics and Rights*, (Cambridge, CUP 2011), p. 247-248. In addition, the Inter-American Commission of Human Rights has also adopted this practice. See: IACommHR (Report) 1 March 1996, *Comadres* v. *El Salvador*, para. 24.12.

712 Shelton, *supra* n. 1, p. 279.

713 IACtHR, *Aloeboetoe et al.* v. *Suriname*, *supra* n. 460, para. 48.

Similarly, the ECtHR has maintained that the obligation of providing just satisfaction stemming from Article 41 is 'to provide reparation *solely for damage suffered* by those concerned *to the extent that such events constituted a consequence of the violation.*'[714] Thus, in order to be granted reparations it is necessary that sufficient connections are established between the damage and the actual violation.[715]

As explained in section 2.4.5, there are two main groups of causation: factual causation and legal causation (also known as proximate cause). As each group has different tests to prove causation. Causality tends to be very flexible in human rights law. Both the IACtHR and the ECtHR have used legal causation or proximate cause when awarding reparations. However, when applying legal causation, three tests are available to the courts: directness, foreseeability and proximity.[716] Although the IACtHR has determined that 'reparations must have a causal link with the facts of the case, the alleged violations, the proven damages, as well as with the measures requested to repair the resulting damages,'[717] it has not adopted any specific test. On the other side of the globe, the ECtHR has asserted that 'there must be a clear causal connection between the damage claimed by the applicant and the violation.'[718] However, the ECtHR usually applies different tests without justifying its reasons for doing so. It may however be possible to assume that the test depends on whether the harm claimed is material or non-material.[719]

Regarding non-material harm, the ECtHR has acknowledged the need to establish 'a causal link between the anxiety and distress suffered' and the human rights violations in a given case.[720] At the same time, it was reluctant, at least initially, to reach more than a declaratory judgment concerning such harm.[721] As a result, during the first decades of its existence it was difficult to determine how the ECtHR applied the causal link to claims related to moral harm. Currently, the ECtHR makes use of

---

714 ECtHR, *Scozzari and Giunta* v. *Italy*, *supra* n. 409, para. 248-250. Emphasis added.

715 Rombouts, Sardaro and Vandeginste, *supra* n. 24, p. 380-382. (It is important to note that causality also applies to the calculation of compensation).

716 For the definitions of these tests see Section 2.4.5 of this Chapter.

717 IACtHR, *Ticona Estrada et al.* v. *Bolivia*, *supra* n. 588, para. 110; IACtHR, *González et al. ("Cotton Field")* v. *Mexico, supra* n. 574, para. 450-451.

718 ECtHR, *Ipek* v. *Turkey*, *supra* n. 708, para. 223; ECtHR (Judgment) 13 April 2011, Appl. No. 17792/07, *Kallweit* v. *Germany*, para. 87; Pellonpää, *supra* n. 449, p. 113.

719 It must be recalled that material damage is usually presumed by the Court. See: Bydlinski, F., "Methodological Approaches to the Tort Law of the ECHR" in A. Fenyves, E. Karner, and H. Koziol (eds.), *Tort Law in the Jurisprudence of the European Court of Human Rights* (Vienna, De Gruyter 2011), p. 72: Bydlinski, F., "Can the Reparation Awarded to Victims of Violations under the ECHR be Considered a Real 'Just' Satisfaction? in A. Fenyves, E. Karner, and H. Koziol (eds.), *Tort Law in the Jurisprudence of the European Court of Human Rights* (Vienna, De Gruyter 2011), p. 390. ECtHR (Judgment) 11 July 2002, Appl. No. 28957/95, *Christine Goodwin* v. *The United Kingdom*.

720 Ibid.

721 Pellonpää, *supra* n. 449, p. 117, citing ECtHR (Judgment) 27 March 1996, Appl. No. 17488/90, *Goodwin* v. *United Kingdom*, para. 50.

presumptions to confirm a causal link.[722] Thus, the need to establish a causal link is stricter in relation to material damage compared to non-material damage. Finally, contrary to public international law, the mere finding of a violation in international human rights law is sufficient to grant reparations, even if the causal link is not clear.[723] This may be the result of strong reliance on the use of presumptions.[724]

3.5 Compliance with Judgments on Reparations

Compliance with judgments is essential within any legal order as it not only upholds the rule of law and the principle of legality, but it can also enhance the effective protection of human rights at the domestic level. Additionally, states' compliance helps prevent an endless inflow of cases. Compliance is also 'a useful proxy for the effectiveness' of a given court, including regional human rights courts.[725] Within the realm of human rights, most scholars have distinguished two levels of a state's compliance: partial compliance and full compliance.[726] In order to determine or measure compliance, different factors need to be considered, including the degree of clarity of a court's order; the consistency of the court's rulings; the complexity of the remedial order; the state's capacity to comply with specific measures;[727] and its domestic politics, including those aimed at maintaining a good international reputation.[728] Other factors that might influence compliance are the nature of the human rights bodies (judicial or non-judicial) that have upheld the ruling, as well as their individual follow-up procedures.[729] In addition, the issue of time also plays an important role in measuring compliance; there is a difference between a state complying with the ordered measures in a timely fashion as opposed to many years later. That having been said, it is worth mentioning that scholars have not always taken all of these factors into account when assessing states' compliance.

Despite its importance, compliance is a challenging matter for international human rights courts[730] as states appear to prefer to only partially comply with court rulings.[731] This á la carte compliance attitude pertains to both the ECtHR and the

722 Gray, *supra* n. 5, p. 891.
723 McCarthy, *supra* n. 296, p. 295.
724 Capone et al., *supra* n. 44, p. 117.
725 Hawkins, D. and Jacoby, W., "Partial Compliance: A Comparison of the European and Inter-American Courts for Human Rights", 6 *Journal of International Law and International Relations* (2010), p. 39.
726 Ibid.
727 Huneeus, *supra* n. 323, p. 437-445.
728 Hawkins and Jacoby, *supra* n. 725, p. 41.
729 Gori, G., "Compliance", in D. Shelton (ed.), *The Oxford Handbook of International Human Rights Law* (Oxford, OUP 2013), p. 893.
730 Hillebrecht, C., "Implementing International Human Rights Law at Home: Domestic Politics and the European Court of Human Rights", 13 *Human Rights Review* (2012), p. 298.
731 Hawkins and Jacoby, *supra* n. 725, p. 83.

IACtHR,[732] although it is generally recognised that the ECtHR enjoys a higher compliance rate.[733] Hawkins and Jacoby contend that in order to understand the difference in states' compliance within the two systems it is important to consider the differences that are inherent in the courts' functioning.[734]

First, there exists a stark difference in the courts' power to oversee their judgments. While Article 46 of the ECHR establishes that the specific body in charge of overseeing states' compliance with ECtHR judgments is the Committee of Ministers, the ACHR is silent in this regard.[735] The IACtHR has however recognised that 'the effectiveness of the judgments depends on compliance with them,' and has interpreted the ACHR in such a way that gives it the authority to monitor states' compliance.'[736] Thus, while the ECtHR relies on a third (political) body to oversee the execution of its judgments, the IACtHR's oversight is direct and of a judicial nature.[737]

Secondly, in most of its cases the ECtHR leaves it up to the states to determine the measures of reparations that are required to meet their obligation under Article 46 of the ECHR,[738] whereas the IACtHR explicitly orders states to take specific measures and actions.[739] Hawkins and Jacoby have called these different approaches a 'check-list' versus 'delegated' compliance.[740] At first sight, it appears that states called before the ECtHR would find it easier to comply with the court's judgments for the simple reason that they are the ones who decide which measures to implement as part of their obligations.

Finally, the measures that states are ordered to take by the IACtHR are usually far more complex and specific than the ones ordered by the ECtHR, which may influence the time that it takes for states to comply with them.[741] An example of

732 Hawkins and Jacoby, *supra* n. 725, p. 37-38, 83-84.

733 McKay, *supra* n. 384, p. 936; See: Ebobrah, S., "International Human Rights Courts", in C. Romano, K. Alter and Y. Shany (eds.), *The Oxford Handbook of International Adjudication*, (Oxford, OUP 2015), p. 247.

734 In both regimes States tend to partially comply with the Courts' rulings. Within the IASHR, States' compliance varies from State to State whereas in the European scenario compliance varies depending on the right violated. See: Hawkins and Jacoby, *supra* n. 725, p. 37-38, 83.

735 Huneeus, *supra* n. 323, p. 451; Brown, *supra* n. 7, p. 213.

736 IACtHR (Judgment) 28 November 2003, *Baena-Ricardo et al.* v. *Panama*, para. 129.

737 Gori, *supra* n. 729, p. 911, 917. It is not clear after how many years the Court follows up its judgments. It seems that the Court is not consistent in this repect. However, it is claimed that the Court's financial resources might be insufficient. See also: Basch, F. et al., "The Effectiveness of the Inter-American System of Human Rights Protection: A Quantitative Approach to its Functioning and Compliance with its Decision", 7 *SUR – International Journal on Human Rights* (2010), p. 19.

738 ECtHR, *Assanidze* v. *Georgia*, *supra* n. 393, para. 202.

739 Hawkins and Jacoby, *supra* n. 725, p. 37. However, we must note that the ECtHR spells out specific reparation in two instances: when the nature of the violation requires this and in its pilot judgments. See: Gray, *supra* n. 5, p. 893.

740 Hawkins and Jacoby, *supra* n. 725, p. 37, 43-44.

741 Gori, *supra* n. 729, p. 916.

this is the IACtHR order to states to investigate human rights violations and punish those responsible. State compliance with these kinds of orders is very low,[742] which may be partially explained by the fact that these orders require states to investigate past abuses for which, given the passage of time, evidence might be difficult, if not impossible, to obtain. Similarly, the IACtHR has also ordered states to implement other costly and complex measures such as the creation of a genetic bank, the reform of national laws and the creation of funds for the development of a given community.[743] These measures require actions from several institutions and branches of the government such as the judiciary, the legislature and the executive. Thus, the government will need to ensure that these institutions cooperate in order to be able to fully comply with the measures. In countries where democracy is weak or the political environment is difficult, such cooperation is unlikely to take place. Finally, the courts differ in their remedial approaches. This is mostly the result of the fact that the IACtHR's remedial power[744] is far greater than that of the ECtHR:[745] while the latter is expected to provide 'just satisfaction', the former is expected to remedy the consequences of the violation of human rights and to pay fair compensation to the victims.

By the same token, some scholars have noticed that states before the IACtHR usually comply with half of all the reparations ordered by the court[746] mostly individual reparations that are relatively simple to carry out.[747] Regarding complex measures such as those of satisfaction and guarantees of non-repetition, it appears that states are more inclined to comply with those related to the training of public officials, legal reforms and the creation or reform of institutions, and less likely to comply with an order to investigate, prosecute and eventually punish the perpetrators of a given violation.[748] Furthermore, complex measures also affect the time during which they are supposed to take place. While it is assumed that the longer it takes for victims' reparations to materialize, the feebler atonement becomes,[749] it is therefore important to acknowledge that complex measures such as enacting or reforming laws[750] or

742 McKay, *supra* n. 384, p. 938; Bailliet, C. M., "Measuring Compliance with the Inter-American Court of Human Rights: The Ongoing Challenge of Judicial Independence in Latin America", 31 *Nordic Journal of Human Rights* (2013), p. 483.

743 Hillebrecht, C., "The Domestic Mechanisms of Compliance with International Human Rights Law: Case Studies from the Inter-American Human Rights System", 34 *Human Rights Quaterly* (2012), p. 959.

744 Article 63, ACHR.

745 Article 41, ECHR.

746 Basch et al., *supra* n. 737, p. 18.

747 McKay, *supra* n. 384, p. 945; Hawkins and Jacoby, *supra* n. 725, p. 37, 77.

748 McKay, *supra* n. 384, p. 940.

749 In some cases, the victim has died before the reparation orders are fully complied with. See: IACtHR (Judgment) 22 November 2004, *Carpio-Nicolle* et al. v. *Guatemala*, para. 115 (h).

750 Hillebrecht, *supra* n. 545, p. 1113.

investigating and punishing past human rights violations[751] will inherently take a long time to be realized. Perhaps this is the reason why in some of its judgments the IACtHR requires states to carry out a particular action 'within a reasonable time',[752] instead of setting a specific deadline for this.[753] Finally, it should be emphasised that full compliance with the IACtHR's judgments usually takes several years, or even a decade.[754] If we acknowledge that the average length of a process is between six and seven years (from the complaint to the judgment),[755] it follows that it may take almost two decades for victims to see justice materialize.

Finally, it is worth mentioning that both the European and the Inter-American System have enforcement mechanisms to ensure state compliance. The Council of Europe (CoE) can suspend the membership of states on the grounds of non-compliance with the ECtHR's judgments.[756] Compliance with the IACtHR's judgments can be enforced by means of the OAS General Assembly (OAS-GA).[757] The ACHR requires the court to inform the OAS-GA about cases of non-compliance and to submit its recommendations.[758] However, it has been claimed that neither of these mechanisms has been effective;[759] and if compliance does not take place, it is the victims that areimmediately affected.[760]

While the overseeing capacity of the courts and their enforcement mechanisms influence state compliance – less diligent court oversight may result in partial or lower state compliance –[761] it is essentially a matter of domestic politics.[762] As a result, the strongest and most democratic states are more compelled to comply with their obligations.[763] In addition, Hillebrecht has noted that certain domestic institutions are crucial in the implementation of judgments. For instance, compliance is higher if the judiciary is strongly independent,[764] and if the executive is able to forge coalitions with the executive and the legislature.[765] In addition, Huneeus agrees that judicial

---

751 IACtHR, *Pacheco Teruel et al.* v. *Honduras, supra* n. 548, para. 128; IACtHR (Judgment) 20 August 2013, *Garcia Lucero et al.* v. *Chile*, para. 220.
752 IACtHR (Judgment) 4 July 2006, *Ximenes-Lopes* v. *Brazil*, para. 262 (6).
753 Hawkins and Jacoby, *supra* n. 725, p. 41.
754 Ibid., p. 51.
755 McKay, *supra* n. 384, p. 945; Baillet, *supra* n. 742, p. 478-479.
756 Huneeus, *supra* n. 323, p. 450.
757 Ibid., p. 449-450.
758 Article 65, ACHR.
759 Huneeus, *supra* n. 323, p. 450; Baillet, *supra* n. 742, p. 479-480.
760 Hillebrecht, *supra* n. 545, p. 1103.
761 Hawkins and Jacoby, *supra* n. 725, p. 38; Gori, *supra* n. 729, p. 910.
762 Hillebrecht, *supra* n. 545, p. 1117.
763 Hillebrecht, *supra* n. 730, p. 279.
764 Hillebrecht, *supra* n. 545, p. 1107.
765 Hillebrecht, *supra* n. 743, p. 959.

independence – which is generally weak in the IACtHR context –[766] is decisive for compliance, and highlights the importance of a state's legal culture.[767]

It is precisely judicial independence which is key for what is commonly referred to as *indirect* compliance.[768] The Argentinian experience is illustrative: a few months after the IACtHR's judgment on *Barrios Altos* v. *Peru*, Argentina's domestic courts struck down two amnesty laws because they were not compatible with the ACHR. This decision was followed by the Argentine Congress which repealed the same laws.[769] In this case, it can be maintained that the IACtHR's rulings are effective, despite partial state compliance, as they have resulted in the promotion of a new legal culture in the continent.

4 Conclusions

In public international law, reparations were initially understood as a principle of law and a state obligation *vis-à-vis* another state when breaching an international duty.[770] Since the adoption of international human rights instruments, this state obligation has been extended to individuals.[771] As a matter of fact, reparations are not only considered to be state obligations but also individual human rights,[772] which empower natural persons whose rights – as protected by international human rights instruments– have been violated to seek reparations.[773]

Reparations under public international law and human rights law share some of the same characteristics; they should be full, adequate and proportional to the damage incurred, and they should aim for *restitutio in integrum*. However, there are no guidelines in either field as to when reparations are to be considered adequate, proportional and full. As a result, courts have had complete discretion to decide on these matters. In theory, under both public international law and human rights law, *restitutio in integrum* has been the guiding factor, and restitution has been the primary measure of reparations. In practice, this does not hold true, however. Over the last two

766 Baillet, *supra* n. 742, p. 478.

767 Huneeus, *supra* n. 323, p. 454-455.

768 Ibid., p. 455-456.

769 Gori, *supra* n. 729, p. 917; Hillebrecht, *supra* n. 743, p. 975-976.

770 Buti, A., "International Law Obligations to Provide Reparations for Human Rights Abuses", 6 *Murdoch University Electronic Journal of Law* (1999); IACtHR, *"White Van" (Paniagua-Morales et al.)* v. *Guatemala*, *supra* n. 507, para. 78.

771 ICJ, *Legal Consequences of the Construction of a Wall in the Occupied Palestinian Territory*, *supra* n. 96, p. 152-153; International Commission of Jurists, *supra* n. 23, p. 9.

772 Shelton, *supra* n. 1, p. 58; ICJ, *Ahmadou Sadio Diallo* (*Republic of Guinea* v. *Democratic Republic of the Congo*), Separate Opinion of Judge Cançado Trindade, *supra* n. 84, para. 33.

773 HRC, *supra* n. 62, para. 16.

centuries, modern arbitral practice and the ICJ's jurisprudence have rarely awarded restitution.[774]

Restitution is also rarely awarded under human rights law, the main reason being that the nature of human rights violations does not allow for this. Nevertheless, the IACtHR appears to be determined to order *restitutio in integrum* by all means necessary. In this light, the court's approach to reparations is usually to grant as many measures as possible, including restitution where possible. Consequently, the IACtHR has provided the most important case law for victims of human rights violations.[775] Furthermore, the IACtHR has also referred to *restitutio in integrum* as *integral reparations,* which means that victims should receive measures of rehabilitation and satisfaction in addition to monetary compensation.[776] This is especially emphasized when it comes to redressing gross violations of human rights. In contrast, the ECtHR was initially reluctant to acknowledge that it had the power to order restitution measures. Despite this, the ECtHR has ordered restitution measures in a few cases, mainly when there was no other way of achieving restitutio in integrum (e.g. the reopening of unfair criminal proceedings).[777]

The main difference between the remedial approaches of the ECtHR and the IACtHR is that the former has little interest in responding to the needs of the victims.[778] The ECtHR tends to deal with 'just satisfaction' in a couple of lines, simply ordering a lump sum by way of pecuniary and/or non-pecuniary damages. It typically declares that it has decided 'on an equitable basis,' and rarely substantiates the amounts with calculations.[779] The remedial approach of the IACtHR not only aims to address the needs of a particular individual, but also to prevent further violations.

The ECtHR's preferred measure of reparation has been compensation. The IACtHR has also granted monetary compensation in most of its cases, although usually accompanied by other measures. Similarly, the ECtHR has categorically recognized that compensation is not sufficient to remedy human rights violations. In this light, the Grand Chamber has reminded states that the ECHR 'imposes [...] a legal obligation not just to pay those concerned the sums awarded by way of just satisfaction, but also to choose, [...] if appropriate, individual measures to be adopted in their domestic legal order to put an end to the violation found by the Court and to redress so far as possible [its] effects.'[780]

---

774 Gray, *supra* n. 192, p. 416.

775 Oette, *supra* n. 445, p. 237.

776 IACtHR, *"Street Children" (Villagrán-Morales et al.)* v. *Guatelama*, Separate Opinion of Judge A.A. Cançado Trindade, *supra* n. 507, para. 28, 35 and 37.

777 Committee of Ministers, 'Recommendation on the re-examination or reopening of certain cases at domestic level following judgments of the European Court of Human Rights' (19 January 2000), Recommendation No. R (2000) 2; Gori, *supra* n. 729, p. 906-907.

778 McKay, *supra* n. 384, p. 936.

779 ECtHR, (Judgment) 8 April 2004, Appl. No. 26307/95, *Tahsin Acar* v. *Turkey,* para. 264.

780 ECtHR, *Scozzari and Giunta* v. *Italy*, *supra* n. 409, para. 249.

Under public international law, reparations are subject to a high degree of flexibility. First, states have the right to elect, which means that they can choose the reparation that they deem the most appropriate. In addition, they enjoy the freedom to determine how to discharge an order of reparation. Similarly, the ECtHR has stated that its judgments are 'essentially declaratory and leaves to the state the choice of means to' comply with its obligations.[781] However, the ECtHR also has the discretion to award monetary compensation to victims.[782]

Declaratory judgments are the most common remedy before the PICJ and the ICJ.[783] In contrast, the IACtHR and the ECtHR tend to accompany such judgments with compensation and other orders[784] – perhaps in the hope of achieving *restitutio in integrum*. Significantly, the ECtHR has acknowledged that its rulings are essentially declaratory, but in some cases the reparations ordered suggested that the judgments are, in fact, mandatory.[785] The IACtHR, on the other hand, has a robust understanding of its mandatory powers. Recent developments, including at the ICJ, suggest that international courts are moving towards more mandatory judgments.[786]

Human right law (HRL) has created new forms of reparations within international law that are collective awards. Collective awards belong to the realm of human rights law. In this regard, the IACtHR has been a pioneer. The court has ordered different collective awards that are related to measures of satisfaction, but that sometimes go beyond satisfaction, such as the reopening of a school and a medical dispensary in a village affected by GVHR;[787] the establishment of a health centre so that the victims can obtain medical and psychological care in their own village;[788] ordering a specific amount of money to be invested in works or services in the collective interest;[789] and the creation of specific programmes to provide free psychological and psychiatric treatment at the collective, family and individual level.[790]

Although collective reparations do not exist under public international law, both the obligation of cessation and assurances and guarantees of non-repetition

781 Brown, *supra* n. 7, p. 211-213; ECtHR (Judgment) 13 June 1979, Appl. No. 6833/74, *Marckx* v. *Belgium*, para. 58; Gray, *supra* n. 36, p. 152; ECtHR, *Assanidze* v. *Georgia*, *supra* n. 393, para. 202.

782 Rule 75 of the RoP ECtHR; van Dijk et al., *Theory and Practice of the European Convention on Human Rights* (Antwerpen/Oxford, Intersentia 2006), p. 248-249.

783 Brown, *supra* n. 7, p. 208-209.

784 Ibid., p. 209.

785 See: ECtHR, *Assanidze* v. *Georgia*, *supra* n. 393, para. 202-203. The Court first held that 'its judgments are essentially declaratory in nature' but that the only means of implementing the judgment was the release of the applicants. Also in pilot judgments, the Court spells out specific measures to be taken by the State. See: Gray, *supra* n. 5, p. 893.

786 Brown, *supra* n. 7, p. 223.

787 IACtHR, *Aloeboetoe et al.* v. *Suriname*, *supra* n. 460, para. 96.

788 IACtHR, *Plan de Sánchez Massacre* v. *Guatemala*, *supra* n. 450, para. 110, 117.

789 IACtHR, *Mayagna (Sumo) Awas Tingni* v. *Nicaragua*, *supra* n. 402, para. 167.

790 IACtHR, *Plan de Sánchez Massacre* v. *Guatemala*, *supra* n. 450, para. 93, 106-108, 117.

indirectly protect the collective interests of the international community,[791] and may be seen as collective awards. These measures, however, are considered to be state obligations when a wrongful act has been committed rather than measures of reparations.[792] As a result, they can be ordered independently of reparations.[793] However, if these measures could eventually be dealt with as reparations, it could be assumed that collective awards of this sort are available under public international law. Furthermore, according to the commentaries of the ILC's Articles of State Responsibility, guarantees of non-repetition can constitute a form of satisfaction. However, they go beyond satisfaction, as they can be granted in the collective interest and not only to restore the moral damage of the injured state that could not be restored otherwise.[794] By means of its pilot judgments, the ECtHR has ordered states to create national mechanisms that can provide redress to victims.

In general, guarantees of non-repetition are measures which 'look forwards' and are more often awarded in the context of international human rights law.[795] In repetitive cases and via pilot judgments, the ECtHR has issued general orders that benefit not only the victims in a case, but society itself.[796] They aim to address and remedy the structural problem identified by the pilot decision.[797] In this respect, pilot judgments could be perceived as a collective reparation award, because they benefit a group: a given society. Yet, the ECtHR has never referred to them as such.

Legal causation is commonly applicable to reparations, both within public international law and human rights law. However, the tests employed by the courts vary. International human rights courts usually rely on a flexible approach towards causality, in particular when it comes to GVHR involving a large number of victims. This is because victims of these crimes are usually faced with the problem of compiling evidence. Similarly, mass claims also tend to make use of a flexible approach.[798] In addition, there appears to be a close relationship between the use of presumptions, flexible causality and the principle of equity. A flexible burden of proof and the principle of equity are more victim-oriented.

791 Crawford, *supra* n. 19, p. 460.

792 Article 30, ASR.

793 Kerbat, *supra* n. 88, p. 573-574.

794 Crawford, *supra* n. 19, p. 475-476.

795 Shelton, *Remedies in International Human Rights Law, supra* n. 1, p. 39-40; Commentary to Article 30, ILC's Commentaries to ASR.

796 Gori, *supra* n. 729, p. 907.

797 ECtHR, *Maria Atanasiu and Others* v. *Romania, supra* n. 559, para. 237.

798 Oette, *supra* n. 445, p. 229.

Chapter III
Collective Reparations at the Inter-American Court of Human Rights

1 Introduction

While it is true that collective reparations were initially associated with transitional justice mechanisms, the IACtHR's innovative approach to reparations has resulted in the awarding of collective reparations under this legal human rights framework.[1] Although international human rights courts are designed to address isolated cases of individual violations in individual cases and thus to grant individual reparations, most of the cases dealt with by the Inter-American Court of Human Rights (IACtHR or the Court) involve situations of mass repression or civil conflict that affect large numbers of victims.[2] In 2004, the IACtHR became the first international court to order reparations for more than 260 victims in a case concerning the mass murder of a huge number of indigenous community members.[3] While the majority of the cases brought before this Court show a pattern of systematic and widespread violations of human rights, not all cases have involved multiple victims.[4] In cases with large numbers of victims, the IACtHR has granted collective reparations that resemble those granted under transitional justice mechanisms.[5]

1 Most recently, the ICC's legal framework has allowed collective reparations to be related to international criminal law. A detailed discussion of this will take place in Chapter IV.

2 Antkowiak, T., "Remedial Approaches to Human Rights Violations: The Inter-American Court of Human Rights and Beyond", 46 *Columbia Journal of Transnational Law* (2008), p. 418; Roht-Arriaza, N., "Reparations in International Law and Practice", in M. C. Bassiouni (ed.), *The pursuit of international criminal justice: a world study on conflicts, victimization and post conflict justice* (Antwerp, Intersentia 2010, Vol.1), p. 661; Pasqualucci, J.M, "Victim Reparations in the Inter-American Human Rights System: A Critical Assessment of Current Practice and Procedure", 18 *Michigan Journal of International Law* (1996), p. 6.

3 Antkowiak, *supra* n. 2, p. 353-353.

4 For instance, the first contentious case dealt with the systematic practice of enforced disappearances in Honduras, but the direct victim was only Mr. Mandredo Velásquez.

5 Contreras-Garduño, D. and Rombouts, S., Collective Reparations for Indigenous Communities Before the Inter-American Court of Human Rights, 27 *Merkourios Utrecht Journal of International and European Law* (2010), p. 6-10; Mayeux, B. and Mirabal, J., "Collective and Moral Reparations in the Inter-American Court of Human Rights" *University of Texa's Human Rights Clinic* (2009), p. 1; Roht-Arriaza, *supra* n. 2, p. 662.

Globally, the IACtHR's jurisprudence on reparations has been recognized by several scholars as being the most advanced, comprehensive and creative of its kind.[6] The Court has been challenged by the types of violations that it has had to address, as well as by the specific cultural and individual perspectives of some victims who succeeded in bringing their cases forward, particularly when those cases involved indigenous and tribal peoples. This has, to a great extent, influenced the Court's innovative approach,[7] which involves orders of material and symbolic measures ranging from ordering the State to issue public apologies to mandating the State to investigate human rights violations and to identify, prosecute, and punish those responsible for the said violations.

When dealing with large number of victims, dvantage of allowing victims to define the exact content and detailse violations).vi Furthermore, the IACtHR has granted individual reparations, collective reparations, and a combination of both in cases involving gross violations of human rights affecting large numbers of victims, such as massacres, as well as in cases where collective violations affected indigenous or tribal communities.[8] This chapter analyses the practice of the IACtHR regarding cases dealing with GVHR and involving large numbers of victims, including indigenous peoples. Through this analysis, the chapter aims to understand the patterns underlying the Court's choice of individual, collective or combined reparations. Furthermore, this chapter aims to define the content, scope and procedural aspects of collective reparations before the IACtHR, the first international tribunal to incorporate this type of reparations within the realm of international human rights law. Finally, it seeks to provide an overview of the challenges that collective reparations present in this field of law, including in their implementation.

---

6 McKay, F., "What Outcome for Victims?", in D. Shelton (ed.), *The Oxford Handbook of International Human Rights Law* (Oxford, OUP 2013), p. 935; Alvarez, I., et al., "Conference: Reparations in the Inter-American System: A Comparative Approach", 56 *American University Law Review* (2007), p. 1375-1377.

7 Pasqualucci, *supra* n. 2, p. 6-7.

8 Oette, L., "Bringing Justice to Victims? Responses of Regional and International Human Rights Courts and Treaty Bodies", in C. Ferstman, M. Goetz & A. Stephens, Reparations for victims of genocide, war crimes and crimes against humanity: systems in place and systems in the making (Leiden, Martinus Nijhoff 2009), p. 233; IACtHR (Judgment) 15 September 2005, *Mapiripán Massacre* v. *Colombia*, para. 183.

1.1 Selection of Cases

Although both the Inter-American Commission on Human Rights (IACommHR or the Commission)[9] as well as the IACtHR have granted collective reparations, this chapter solely focuses on the jurisprudence of the IACtHR. The IACtHR is known for ordering collective reparations in cases of GVHR and cases involving collective harm, especially with regard to indigenous and tribal peoples.[10] As such, the following exhaustive analysis covers 40 cases selected from among the entire jurisprudence of the Court (from its first contentious case in July 1988 up until December 2017).[11] These 40 cases meet the following criteria: i) they deal with gross violations of human rights,[12] or with collective rights of indigenous and tribal peoples,[13] and ii) the victims are natural persons and iii) there are a large number of victims (more than 5 direct victims).

The decision to rely on the above-mentioned criteria is not only grounded on scholarship, but also on the Court's developing jurisprudence. First of all, the first case in which the IACtHR awarded collective reparations was the *Aloeboetoe* case, the first case before the Court dealing with violations against a tribal group.[14] It related to the arbitrary arrest, inhuman treatment and subsequent murder of a group of 7 members of the Maroon tribe by the national armed forces of Suriname. After finding the state to be in violation of the ACHR, the Court ordered Suriname, as part of the reparations, to reopen a school and make it operational on a permanent basis as well as to establish a dispensary and to also make it operational.[15] Antkowiak claims that the Court's approach in this case was influenced by the *in situ* visit conducted by a Court representative, which allowed the Court to have a general view of the precarious living conditions of the Maroon community.[16]

---

9 The Commission have referred to collective reparations when addressing measures aimed at commemorating the memory of the victims. See: IACmHR (Report) 27 October 2005, *Villatina Massacre* v. *Colombia*, Case 11.141, Report No. 105/05, para. 25. It has also referred to service-based collective reparations for indigenous peoples as 'social reparations.' See: IACmHR (Report) 13 April 2000, *Caloto Massacre* v. *Colombia*, Case 11.101, Report No. 36/00, para. 59, 62, 72, 75(3).

10 Contreras-Garduño, D., Defining Beneficiaries of Collective Reparations: The experience of the IACtHR, 4 *Amsterdam Law Forum* (2012); Shelton, D., *Remedies in International Human Rights Law*, OUP (2015), p. 251-252.

11 When necessary, references are made to cases beyond the 40 which are the subject of this analysis.

12 The cases selected deal with torture, enforced disappearances and/or killings.

13 Three cases related to indigenous peoples were excluded from the analysis: the case of *Yatama* v. *Nicaragua* because the beneficiary was a legal entity (an indigenous political party). In addition, the cases of *Norín Catrimán et al.* v. *Chile* and *Escué Zapata* v. *Colombia* were also excluded. The former was excluded because it dealt with a violation that is not considered to be a GVHR. The latter was excluded because although it dealt with a GVHR, there was only one direct victim.

14 IACtHR (Judgment) 10 September 1993, *Aloeboetoe et al.* v. *Suriname*.

15 Roht-Arriaza, *supra* n. 2, p. 662.

16 Antkowiak, *supra* n. 2, p. 366, footnote 70.

Secondly, the IACtHR seems to have developed two main approaches regarding cases dealing with GVHR, with the choice of approach depending on whether the victims in a given case are numerous or not. For instance, the Court's first contentious case, *Velásquez Rodríguez,* was related to the kidnapping, torture and forced disappearance of Mr. Velásquez by state agents. In this case, the Court ordered the state to pay fair compensation to the victim and his next of kin,[17] and to investigate, prosecute and punish those responsible for the violations.[18] The latter is a measure of satisfaction. Yet, in the case of the *Pueblo Bello massacre* that related to the enforced disappearance of 37 people by paramilitary groups,[19] the Court not only awarded individual compensation, measures of satisfaction and guarantees of non-repetition,[20] but also collective reparations, including the implementation of a housing programme.[21] Significantly, neither the victims nor the Commission requested that the housing programme be granted – this measure was granted at the behest of the Court. Hence, the IACtHR seems to grant collective reparations in cases of GVHR only when the number of victims in the case is large, as is evident in the *Pueblo Bello massacre* case.

Finally, the IACtHR has usually ordered states to implement general measures whose benefits extend beyond the victims in a given case. Since the majority of the cases brought before the Court indicate underlying systematic problems, in almost all cases the Court has ordered states to implement measures designed to avoid future occurrences of similar violations.[22] It has likewise ordered measures aimed at combating impunity, such as ordering the state to investigate, prosecute and punish the perpetrators of a given violation as well as to prohibit the application of amnesties and statutes of limitation in domestic proceedings when dealing with GVHR.[23] Although such measures may be seen as collective ones, not all cases in which the Court has ordered them were included in this analysis.

As such, the following exhaustive analysis covers 40 cases selected from among the entire jurisprudence of the Court (from its first contentious case in July 1988 up until December 2017).

17 IACtHR (Judgment) 29 July 1988, *Velásquez Rodríguez* v. *Honduras*, para. 194 (5)-(7); IACtHR (Judgment) 21 July 1989, *Velásquez Rodríguez* v. *Honduras*, para. 60 (1).

18 IACtHR (Judgment) 29 July 1988, *Velásquez Rodríguez* v. *Honduras*, para. 174; IACtHR (Judgment) 21 July 1989, *Velásquez Rodríguez* v. *Honduras*, para. 34.

19 It also related to the murder of 6 people.

20 IACtHR (Judgment) 31 January 2006, *Pueblo Bello Massacre* v. *Colombia*, para. 258, 265-279.

21 Ibid., para. 276.

22 Alvarez et al., *supra* n. 6, p. 1383-1384.

23 Ibid., p. 1375, 1393.

1.2 Table of the 40 Cases Selected from the IACtHR's Jurisprudence

No.	Case	GVHR	I&TP's	Collective right: traditional lands	Number of victims >5
1	*Aloeboetoe et al.* v. *Suriname*	X	X		X
2	*El Amparo* v. *Venezuela*	X			X
3	*"White Van" (Paniagua-Morales et al.)* v. *Guatemala*	X			X
4	*Mayagna (Sumo) Awas Tingni Community* v. *Nicaragua*		X	X	X
5	*Barrios Altos* v. *Peru*	X			X
6	*Caracazo* v. *Venezuela*	X			X
7	*Las Palmeras* v. *Colombia*	X			X
8	*19 Merchants* v. *Colombia*	X			X
9	*Juvenile Reeducation Institute* v. *Paraguay*	X			X
10	*Plan de Sánchez Massacre* v. *Guatemala*	X	X		X
11	*Moiwana Community* v. *Suriname*	X	X	X	X
12	*Yakye Axa Indigenous Community* v. *Paraguay*		X	X	X
13	*Mapiripán Massacre* v. *Colombia*	X			X
14	*Pueblo Bello Massacre* v. *Colombia*	X			X
15	*Sawhoyamaxa Indigenous Community* v. *Paraguay*		X	X	X
16	*Ituango Massacres* v. *Colombia*	X			X
17	*Montero-Aranguren et al. (Detention Center of Catia)* v. *Venezuela*	X			X
18	*Miguel Castro-Castro Prison* v. *Peru*	X			X
19	*La Cantuta* v. *Peru*	X			X
20	*The Rochela Massacre* v. *Colombia*	X			X

No.	Case	GVHR	I&TP's	Collective right: traditional lands	Number of victims >5
21	*Saramaka People* v. *Suriname*		X	X	X
22	*"Las Dos Erres" Massacre* v. *Guatemala*	X	X		X
23	*Xákmok Kásek Indigenous Community* v. *Paraguay*		X	X	X
24	*Gomes Lund et al. ("Guerrilha Do Araguaia")* v. *Brazil*	X			X
25	*Contreras et. al.* v. *El Salvador*	X			X
26	*The Barrios Family* v. *Venezuela*	X			X
27	*The Kichwa Indigenous People of Sarayaku* v. *Ecuador*		X	X	X
28	*The Río Negro Massacres* v. *Guatemala*	X	X		X
29	*Massacres of El Mozote and neighboring locations* v. *El Salvador*	X			X
30	*Gudiel Álvarez et al. ("Diario Militar")* v. *Guatemala*	X			X
31	*Santo Domingo Massacre* v. *Colombia*	X			X
32	*Afro-descendant communities displaces from the Cacarica River Basin (Operation Genesis)* v. *Colombia*	X			X
33	*Kuna Indigenous People of Madungandí and the Emberá Indigenous People of Bayano and their Members* v. *Panama*		X	X	X
34	*Rodríguez Vera et al. (the disappeared from the Palace of Justice)* v. *Colombia*	X			X

No.	Case	GVHR	I&TP's	Collective right: traditional lands	Number of victims >5
35	*Peasant Community of Santa Bárbara* v. *Peru*	X			X
36	*Garífuna Punta Piedra Community and its Members* v. *Honduras*		X	X	X
37	*Garífuna Triunfo de la Cruz Community and its Members* v. *Honduras*		X	X	X
38	*The Kaliña and Lokono Peoples* v. *Suriname*		X	X	X
39	*Members of the Village of Chichupac and Neighboring Communities of the Municipality of Rabinal* v. *Guatemala*	X			X
40	*Vereda La Esperanza* v. *Colombia*	X			X

2 The IACtHR's Legal Framework for Reparations

The Inter-American Court, one of the two main supervisory bodies of the American Convention on Human Rights, is based in San José, Costa Rica. Created by means of the adoption of the American Convention on Human Rights of 1969 (ACHR), the Court was only established in 1979 and despite being a permanent judicial body, its bench consists of part-time judges.[24] Judgments involving reparations are 'final and not subject to appeal'.[25] However, States could ask for a judgment to be clarified when they deem that it is not sufficiently clear. States are obliged 'to comply with the judgment of the Court in any case to which they are parties'.[26] Although the Convention does not confer the Court with the power to monitor compliance with its judgments, the Court has declared that this power is part of its 'inherent judicial authority'.[27] Monitoring compliance is conducted through reports submitted by the State, whereupon victims may submit observations on those reports.[28] When

24 Ruiz Chiriboga, O., "The Independence of the Inter-American Judge" 11 *The Law and Practice of International Courts and Tribunals* (2012), p. 131.
25 Article 67, ACHR.
26 Article 68 (1), ACHR.
27 IACtHR (Judgment) 28 November 2003, *Baena-Ricardo et al.* v. *Panama*, para. 129.
28 Article 69 (1), IACtHR's Rules.

appropriate, the Court may hold compliance hearings.[29] However, the Court has not indicated a specific yearly timeline according to which the monitoring of compliance is to take place. This is decided on a case-by-case basis and at the discretion of the Court.

The IACtHR's legal basis for granting reparations is found in Article 63 (1) of the ACHR, which confers it with wide reparatory powers.[30]

> If the Court finds that there has been a violation of a right or freedom protected by its Convention, the Court *shall* rule that the injured party be ensured the enjoyment of his right or freedom that was violated. It shall also rule, *if appropriate*, that the consequences of the measure or situation that constituted the breach of such right or freedom be remedied and that fair compensation be paid to the injured party (emphasis added).

Accordingly, upon declaring a state's responsibility, the IACtHR shall i) restore the enjoyment of the rights violated when possible. In addition, and if appropriate, the Court has the authority to decide, on a discretionary basis, to: ii) repair all the consequences of the damage caused, and iii) award fair compensation. The former suggests that the IACtHR has the power to grant reparation measures that it considers adequate even if the victims have not requested them. Finally, while it has acknowledged in its jurisprudence that fair compensation for the loss suffered should be awarded discretionally,[31] the IACtHR has refrained from defining why a specific sum of money is deemed 'fair' in a given case. According to García Ramírez, a fair or just compensation is a sum of money that is equal to the material and non-material damage suffered.[32] Yet, this determination of proportionality is not always evident.

Since its first decision the IACtHR has decided that 'the objective of human rights law', including the IASHR, is to protect victims and to afford reparations for the suffering and damage caused by the violations.[33] True to this statement, the Court has sought to afford as many reparation measures as possible and to protect victims and societies as a whole from further violations of human rights.[34] In general, the Court has attempted to grant the reparations that have been sought by victims. For instance, the reparations that are most often sought by GVHR victims are symbolic measures. As such, the Court has granted commemorations, memorials, the recovery

29 Article 69 (3), IACtHR's Rules.

30 Pasqualucci, *supra* n. 2, p. 10-11.

31 IACtHR (Judgment Interpretation) 17 August 1990, *Velásquez Rodríguez* v. *Honduras*, para. 27; IACtHR (Judgment Interpretation) 17 August 1990, *Case of Godínez-Cruz* v. *Honduras*, para. 27.

32 García Ramírez, S., "Las Reparaciones en el Sistema Interamericano de Protección de los Derechos Humanos", in *El Sistema Interamericano de Protección de los Derechos Humanos en el Umbral del Siglo XXI, Memoria del Seminario* (San José, Corte IDH 2003, 2nd ed.), p. 338.

33 IACtHR (Judgment) 29 July 1988 *Velásquez-Rodríguez* v. *Honduras*, para. 134.

34 Antkowiak, T.M., "An Emerging Mandate for International Courts: Victim-Centered Remedies and Restorative Justice" 47 *Standford Journal of International Law* (2011), p. 281.

of disappeared persons (or their remains).[35] By doing this, the IACtHR has adopted a 'victim-centred approach'.[36]

3 Principles on Reparations

The IACtHR has upheld that the right to reparations recognized by the ACHR 'codifies a rule of customary law', a view with a parallel principle in the field of international law.[37] While the Court has upheld that the main purpose of reparations is 'to eliminate the effects of the violation committed' (*restitutio in integrum*),[38] it has also recognized that such an ideal is neither always materially possible nor appropriate.[39] In light of this recognition, reparations should help victims by making their suffering more bearable.[40] In addition, *restitutio in integrum* may be insufficient to properly redress the wrong in some cases, as it may be necessary to go beyond restoration.[41] In this light, Uprimny has submitted that in cases where the victim of the crime, who happened to live in poverty, is provided with measures of restitution as a form of reparation, this would imply: restoring the harm inflicted by a certain violation, and also placing the victim back in a situation of poverty, and most likely, discrimination. Consequently, the reparation measure should go beyond *restitutio in integrum*.[42]

Further, the Court has highlighted that reparations should aim to prevent the repetition of violations.[43] In addition, the Court has clarified that reparations shall not enrich or impoverish the beneficiary of the award (victim).[44] Also, reparations are non-punitive, as they should compensate the victim whilst not punishing the

35 Ibid., p. 282-283.
36 Ibid., p. 289-292.
37 IACtHR, *Aloeboetoe et al.* v. *Suriname*, *supra* n. 14, para. 43.
38 IACtHR (Judgment) 21 July 1989, *Velásquez-Rodríguez* v. *Honduras*, para. 26; IACtHR (Judgment) 2 September 2004, *"Juvenile Reeducation Institute"* v. *Paraguay*, para. 261.
39 IACtHR, *Aloeboetoe et al.* v. *Suriname*, *supra* n. 14, para. 49.
40 IACHR, *Velásquez Rodríguez* v. *Honduras*, *supra* n. 31, para. 27.
41 IACtHR, *Aloeboetoe et al.* v. *Suriname*, *supra* n. 14, para. 49.
42 Uprimny, M.R., Between Corrective and Distributive Justice: Reparations of Gross Human Rights Violations in Times of Transition, 25 *Netherlands Quarterly of Human Rights* (2009), p. 633-634.
43 IACtHR (Judgment) 25 May 2001, *"White van" (Paniagua-Morales et al.)* v. *Guatemala*, para. 80; IACtHR (Judgment) 29 August 2002, *Caracazo* v. *Venezuela*, para. 94; IACtHR (Judgment) 5 July 2004, *19 Merchants* v. *Colombia*, para. 222.
44 IACtHR (Judgment) 15 June 2005, *Moiwana Community* v. *Suriname*, para. 171; IACtHR (Judgment) 17 June 2005, *Yakye Axa Indigenous Community* v. *Paraguay*, para. 182; IACtHR, *"Juvenile Reeducation Institute"* v. *Paraguay*, *supra* n. 38, para. 261; IACtHR, *Mapiripán Massacre* v. *Colombia*, *supra* n. 8, para. 245.

State.[45] Reparations must only repair the damage that has been done.[46] Accordingly, compensation should cover material and non-material losses and be geared primarily towards the principle of equity.[47] Although the Court has upheld that national law does not play a role in calculating reparations and cannot restrict the right to reparations before the IACtHR,[48] the Court has, at times, taken into account reparations that victims may have obtained at the national level when calculating the reparations to be granted by the Court.[49] Finally, reparations ordered by the Court are not exclusive, as they could be supplemented by the states later on.[50] In addition, if it is proven that the state supported, tolerated or facilitated public authorities' violation of rights protected by the ACHR, the State is liable for these violations themselves.[51] Finally, the IACtHR has stated that in cases involving indigenous peoples, reparations need to address the damage on both individual and community levels.[52] In such cases, the Court has taken into account the indigenous peoples' culture and perspectives in order to interpret all rights enshrined by the ACHR, including the right to reparation.[53]

4 Types of Reparations

Collective reparations have been granted in cases related to GVHR involving large numbers of victims as well as in cases related to collective rights violations that affected indigenous and tribal peoples (I&TP).[54] In some cases, however, CRs are granted along with individual measures. The following sections aim to analyse the different individual and collective measures that the IACtHR has awarded to victims of GVHR and collective rights violations.

---

45 IACtHR, *Velásquez-Rodríguez* v. *Honduras, supra* n. 38, para. 27, 38, 52; Yet, Judge Cançado Trindade has stated that some reparations ordered by the Court have an exemplary character and indeed punish the state. See: IACtHR (Judgment) 19 November 2004, *Plan de Sánchez Massacre* v. *Guatemala*, Separate Opinion of Judge A.A. Cançado Trindade, para. 25.

46 IACtHR (Judgment) 26 November 2002, *Las Palmeras* v. *Colombia,* para. 96; IACtHR, *Aloeboetoe et al.* v. *Suriname*, *supra* n. 14, para. 46.

47 IACtHR (Judgment) 31 August 2001, *Mayagna (Sumo) Awas Tingni Community* v. *Nicaragua,* para. 168; IACtHR, *Aloeboetoe et al.* v. *Suriname*, *supra* n. 14, para. 86, 87.

48 Donoso, G., 'Inter-American Court of Human Rights' reparation judgments: Strengths and challenges for a comprehensive approach', 49 *Revista IIDH* (2009), p. 42.

49 IACtHR (Judgment) 24 November 2010, *Gomes Lund et al. ("Guerrilha do Araguaia")* v. *Brazil*, para. 303.

50 IACtHR (Judgment) 1 July 2006, *Ituango Massacres* v. *Colombia,* Separate Opinion of Judge Sergio Garcia Ramirez, para. 22.

51 IACtHR, *Mapiripán Massacre* v. *Colombia, supra* n. 8, para. 110.

52 IACtHR, *Yakye Axa Indigenous Community* v. *Paraguay, supra* n. 44, para.188; IACtHR, *Plan de Sánchez Massacre* v. *Guatemala*, *supra* n. 45, para. 86.

53 IACtHR, *Yakye Axa Indigenous Community* v. *Paraguay, supra* n. 44, para. 51.

54 Contreras-Garduño, D., *supra* n. 10, p. 41; Oette, *supra* n. 8, p. 233.

4.1 Individual Measures

Individual measures of reparation include restitution, compensation, rehabilitation, satisfaction and guarantees of non-repetition.[55] Individual reparation measures present an opportunity to provide a personal harm-tailored approach. However, an individualistic approach to reparations, and to human rights in general, does not cater for the specific social, spiritual and cultural dimension of certain groups, namely indigenous and tribal peoples.[56]

4.1.1 Restitution

Within international human rights law, measures of restitution seem to be the ideal reparation as restitution measures aim to restore the victims to their situation prior to the occurrence of violations. However, this measure is mostly impossible to realize, especially in cases dealing with GVHR.[57]

Cases related to GVHR

The Court has attempted to restore some of the material losses resulting from GVHR, especially measures to guarantee the safe return of victims who wish to return to their lands and country. This measure was ordered in the *Mapiripán Massacre* case.[58] In addition, in the *19 Merchants* case the IACtHR ordered Colombia also to cover the associated costs necessary for the victims to return to the country.[59] Further, in the *Peasant Community of Santa Bárbara* case, the Court ordered the restitution of domestic animals and the reconstruction of houses that had been raised to the ground. However, the Court provided the state with the alternative to provide compensation for this.[60] And in the case of *Contreras et al.*, which dealt with the abduction and forced disappearance of several children by the Salvadorian military forces during the civil war, the Court ordered the state to take all the measures that were necessary to restore the original identity of one of the victims, including the correction of her name and surname in accordance with those of her biological parents.[61]

---

55 See Chapter II.

56 Citroni, G. and Quintana Osuna, K.I., 'Reparations for Indigenous Peoples in the Case Law of the Inter-American Court of Human Rights', in F. Lenzerini (ed.), *Reparations for Indigenous Peoples: International & Comparative Perspectives* (Oxford OUP 2008), p. 318, 340.

57 For a detailed discussion on these measures see Chapter II.

58 IACtHR, *Mapiripán Massacre* v. *Colombia, supra* n. 8, para. 11.

59 IACtHR, *19 Merchants* v. *Colombia, supra* n. 43, para. 279.

60 IACtHR (Judgment) 1 September 2015, *Peasant Community of Santa Bárbara* v. *Peru,* para. 304.

61 IACtHR (Judgment) 31 August 2011, *Contreras et al.* v. *El Salvador*, para. 195-196.

Cases related to I&TPs' traditional lands

In all cases related to violations of the right to property (Article 21 of the ACHR) in relation to the traditional lands of indigenous and tribal peoples, the Court has ordered states to restore the their lands collectively rather than individually. The Court has stressed that such restitution needs to be conducted in accordance with I&TPs' customary law and values as well as with the full participation of the given community.[62]

4.1.2 Compensation

Compensation measures aim to financially reimburse victims for the damage that they have suffered. The monies in compensation awards are usually symbolic, as no monetary sum could ever repair GVHR such as the murder or torture of a person. Although monetary compensation may not always be adequate,[63] it is a measure that is commonly awarded by the Court.

Cases related to GVHR

In cases dealing with massacres and extrajudicial killings, the IACtHR's compensation orders are largely granted on an individual basis, even in cases that concern indigenous or tribal peoples.[64] Cases in point are *Aloeboetoe, Moiwana community* and the *Rio Negro massacre*.[65] In addition, in the *Plan de Sánchez* case, the Court also ordered individual compensation for the more than 250 victims of the massacre.[66] Significantly, the amounts ordered are influenced by the number of victims in a given case, in addition to other factors. As such, Antkowiak has submitted that the Court usually grants lower compensation awards than for violations in isolated cases.[67] According to him, this approach makes it feasible for a state to comply with the compensation order.[68]

Avoidance of double compensation

Furthermore, the Court has not granted compensation to victims who have received reparations (financial and/or symbolic) at the national level. For instance, in the

62 IACtHR, *Mayagna (Sumo) Awas Tingni Community* v. *Nicaragua*, *supra* n. 47, para. 164.
63 Antkowiak, *supra* n. 2, p. 388.
64 Oette, *supra* n. 8, p. 236.
65 IACtHR (Judgment) 4 September 2012, *Río Negro Massacres* v. *Guatemala,* para. 309; IACtHR, *Aloeboetoe et al.* v. *Suriname*, *supra* n. 14, para. 50, 100-108; IACtHR, *Moiwana Community* v. *Suriname*, *supra* n. 44, para.187.
66 IACtHR, *Plan de Sánchez Massacre* v. *Guatemala, supra* n. 45, para. 72-89.
67 Antkowiak, *supra* n. 2, p. 396-399.
68 Ibid., p. 397-399.

Rodríguez Vera case, the Court first analysed whether the compensation received by some of the victims at the national level in Colombia had been based on 'objective and reasonable' criteria.[69] Since this requirement had been met, the Court decided not to grant financial compensation for either the material or the moral damage suffered by victims who had already received national compensation.[70] Yet, four victims in this case had not received reparations and thus the IACtHR decided to award financial compensation to these four victims.[71] In the *Santo Domingo Massacre* case, most of the relatives of the direct victims had already received reparations at the domestic level.[72] The Court did not therefore order any additional monetary reparations for moral and material damage in favour of those who had received reparations from the Colombian domestic system.[73] With regard to those victims who had not received compensation at the national level, the Court requested the state to employ a domestic mechanism, within one year, in order to compensate them.[74]

Cases related to I&TPs' traditional lands

The IACtHR has not ordered individual compensation for victims in cases related to violations of indigenous and tribal peoples' right to property over their traditional or ancestral lands. This may be a result of the Court's understanding of the particular collective approach that I&TPs adopt with regard to their lands.

4.1.3 Rehabilitation

According to the Principles on Reparations, measures of rehabilitation refer to all measures related to 'medical and psychological care as well as legal and social services' provided to victims.[75] In general, the Court has stated that victims are entitled to individual and collective medical, psychological and psychiatric assistance.[76]

---

69 IACtHR (Judgment) 12 November 2014, *Rodríguez Vera et al. (the disappeared from the Palace of Justice)* v. *Colombia,* para. 595.
70 Ibid., para. 592.
71 Ibid., para. 596.
72 IACtHR (Judgment) 30 November 2012, *Santo Domingo Massacre* v. *Colombia,* para. 334-335.
73 Ibid., para. 336.
74 Ibid., para. 337.
75 Principle 21, Principles on Reparations; CAT (General Comment No. 3 of the Committee against Torture, Implementation of Article 14 by States parties) 16 November 2012, UN Doc. CAT/C/GC/3 para. 11-12.
76 IACtHR, *Plan de Sánchez, Massacre* v. *Guatemala, supra* n. 45, para. 106-108.

Cases related to GVHR

Rehabilitation measures are commonly part of the reparations awarded to victims of GVHR as well as to their next of kin and the survivors, especially in those cases related to massacres, enforced disappearances and/or torture.[77] In general, the Court orders the respondent state to provide victims with free medical, psychological and psychiatric assistance through its healthcare institutions. However, in cases where the victims no longer reside within the territory of the state, the Court has ordered the state to pay a certain amount of money to cover victims' healthcare expenses in their new country of residence.[78]

Cases related to I&TPs' traditional lands

The Court has never granted individual measures of health or psychological rehabilitation in a case related to indigenous and tribal peoples and their right to their traditional lands.

4.1.4 Satisfaction and GNR

The Court has not been consistent in classifying different measures of reparation. For instance, measures of non-repetition are classified under the heading of satisfaction.[79] This may respond to the fact that there are measures such as apologies that are both measures of satisfaction and GNR.[80] Both measures of satisfaction and GNR are predominantly of a collective nature. However, some measures of satisfaction may well address individual needs, for instance the delivery of truth in a given case.[81] On a collective basis, there are several measures that could be classified as both measures of satisfaction and GNR. For example, monuments, the publication of a judgment,

---

77 IACtHR (Judgment) 30 November 2001, *Barrios Altos* v. *Peru*, para. 42, 50 (3); IACtHR (Judgment) 25 November 2006, *Miguel Castro-Castro Prison* v. *Peru*, para. 448-450; IACtHR (Judgment) 29 November 2006, *La Cantuta* v. *Peru*, para. 238; IACtHR, *19 Merchants* v. *Colombia*, *supra* n. 43, para. 278-280, 295(9); IACtHR, *Plan de Sánchez Massacre* v. *Guatemala*, *supra* n. 45, para. 106-108; IACtHR, *Mapiripán Massacre* v. *Colombia*, *supra* n. 8, para. 312; IACtHR, *Pueblo Bello Massacre* v. *Colombia*, *supra* n. 20, para. 274, IACtHR, *Ituango Massacres* v. *Colombia*, *supra* n. 50, para. 403.

78 IACtHR (Judgment) 20 November 2012, *Gudiel Álvarez et al. ("Diario Militar")* v. *Guatemala* para. 340.

79 IACtHR, *Plan de Sánchez Massacre* v. *Guatemala*, *supra* n. 45, para. 93. In addition, in some cases, under the heading of other measures, it has ordered measures of rehabilitation, satisfaction, and guarantees of non-repetition. See: IACtHR (Judgment) 24 November 2009, *"Las Dos Erres" Massacre* v. *Guatemala*, para. 255-274.

80 IACtHR, *Moiwana Community* v. *Suriname*, *supra* n. 44, para. 124.

81 The right to truth has both an individual and collective dimension. See: Groome, D., The Right to Truth: The Evolution of a Right (2015). Available at: <https://ssrn.com/abstract=2660889>.

or orders to investigate, prosecute and eventually punish the perpetrators of a given violation.

Cases related to GVHR

The IACtHR has emphasized the obligation to investigate, prosecute and punish those responsible for a violation, especially in cases related to gross violations of human rights (e.g. enforced disappearances, torture and killings).[82] This measure is both one of satisfaction for victims and a guarantee of non-repetition that tackles impunity issues. In addition, the Court has consistently ordered states to prosecute, investigate and punish those responsible for human rights violations suffered by the victims in a given case. This measure is both an individual and a collective one, as it delivers justice in individual cases while also being crucial in the fight against impunity.[83] It must be stated, however, that the Court sometimes orders this measure as part of reparation measures[84] and at other times as part of a state's general obligation under the ACHR.[85]

The IACtHR has also ordered educational materials as a form of satisfaction for some individual victims.[86] In the *19 Merchants* case, the Court, with the aim of repairing the honour and reputation of the victims, ordered the State to publicly recognize its responsibility for the violations.[87] Similarly, in the *Gomes Lund* case, the Court ordered a public act of acknowledgment of international responsibility to be held with high-ranking state officials and victims, including the latter's next of kin.[88] In the *Ituango massacre* case, the Court went as far as to specify that such a ceremony needed to be covered by the media.[89] In cases of GVHR involving I&TP, the Court has ordered the state to exhume, identify and return human remains to the deceased's relatives for proper burial in accordance with their customs and beliefs.[90]

82 Shelton, *supra* n. 10, p. 109-110.
83 IACtHR (Judgment) 27 November 1998, *Loayza Tamayo* v. *Peru*, Joint-Concurring Opinion of Judges A.A. Cançado Trindade and A.A. Abreu-Burelli, para. 3.
84 IACtHR (Judgment) 11 May 2007, *La Rochela Massacre* v. *Colombia*, para. 277.
85 IACtHR (Judgment) 25 October 2012, *Massacres of El Mozote and neighboring locations* v. *El Salvador*, para. 312-321; IACtHR (Judgment) 21 August 2017, *Vereda La Esperanza* v. *Colombia*, para. 266-269; IACtHR, *Rodríguez Vera et al. (the disappeared from the Palace of Justice)* v. *Colombia*, *supra* n. 69, para. 553-559; IACtHR, *Santo Domingo Massacre* v. *Colombia*, *supra* n. 72, para. 295-297; IACtHR, *Gudiel Álvarez et al. ("Diario Militar")* v. *Guatemala*, *supra* n. 78, para. 326-330.
86 IACtHR, *Barrios Altos* v. *Peru*, *supra* n. 77, Operative para. 5.
87 IACtHR, *19 Merchants* v. *Colombia*, *supra* n. 43, para. 274.
88 IACtHR, *Gomes Lund et al. ("Guerrilha Do Araguaia")* v. *Brazil*, *supra* n. 49, para. 274-277.
89 IACtHR, *Ituango Massacres* v. *Colombia*, *supra* n. 50, para. 406.
90 IACtHR, *Aloeboetoe et al.* v. *Suriname*, *supra* n. 14, para. 109; IACtHR, *Moiwana Community* v. *Suriname*, *supra* n. 44, para. 208.

Cases related to I&TPs' traditional lands

Measures of satisfaction and GNR awarded on an individual basis to members of an I&TP are very uncommon. However, in the *Moiwana* case, which deals also with GVHR, the Court ordered Suriname, as a measure of satisfaction and a GNR, to 'issue a public apology to the whole nation with regard to the occurrences that took place in the Village of Moiwana and to the survivors and family members in particular'.[91]

4.2 Collective Measures

Although there is no single definition of 'collective reparations', the IACtHR is well known for awarding these measures of reparation.[92] According to De Greiff, collective reparations refer to both the types of goods or benefits distributed to certain victims, as well as to measures aimed at redressing collectivities (groups of people) or communities.[93] Furthermore, a well-known study conducted by Essex University defines collective reparations as being subject to at least one of the following three criteria: i) they pertain to violations of a collective right or to rights violations that impact a community; ii) the beneficiary is a group or a group of people; iii) the measures are not individually tangible.[94] This study also provides some examples of collective reparations: measures of satisfaction and rehabilitation, funds, apologies, services, the translation of a judgment and environmental and social impact assessments.[95] In this light, and based on the Court's labelling when granting reparations, this section breaks down collective measures of reparation into three main categories: i) symbolic, ii) material, and iii) collective reparations.

4.2.1 Symbolic (Satisfaction & GNR)

Symbolic reparations and measures of satisfaction of a collective nature are commonly considered to be synonymous.[96] In addition, scholars have affirmed that guarantees of non-repetition are to be considered as measures of satisfaction that have a preventive nature.[97] Likewise, the IACtHR seems to accept, more often than not, that certain

---

91 IACtHR, *Moiwana Community* v. *Suriname*, *supra* n. 44, para. 216.

92 Mayeux and Mirabal, *supra* n. 5, p. 1.

93 Report by the Special Rapporteur on the promotion of truth, justice, reparation and guarantees of non-recurrence, Pablo de Greiff, UN Doc A/69/518, 8 October 2014, para. 38.

94 Aubry, S. and Henao-Trip, M.I., "Collective Reparations and the International Criminal Court", *Briefing Paper No.2, Reparations Unit, Essex University* (2011), p. 2-3.

95 Ibid., p. 5.

96 Mégret, F., "The International Criminal Court and the Failure to Mention Symbolic Reparations", 16 *International Review of Victimology* (2009), p. 122; Dudai, R., "Closing the gap: symbolic reparations and armed groups", 93 *International Review of the Red Cross* (2011), p. 6.

97 Mégret, *supra* n. 96, p. 129-132; Roht-Arriaza, N., "Reparations Decisions and Dilemmas", 27 *Hastings International and Comparative Law Review* (2004), p. 159-160.

measures are both measures of satisfaction and GNR. For instance, it has asserted that monuments have a twofold purpose: to memorialize the events of the violation and to prevent further violations.[98]

Cases related to GVHR

Measures of satisfaction and GNR have been a common feature of IACtHR judgments in relation to GVHR.[99] The IACtHR has ordered a wide range of different measures aiming to prevent further violations.[100] These include training the public, the judiciary, and even the military regarding human rights, international humanitarian law and human rights law.[101] In addition, the Court has ordered commemorative measures, the investigation and punishment of those responsible for human rights violations,[102] and the interpretation of the ACHR regarding the prohibition of amnesties and the non-prescription of GVHR.[103]

Furthermore, in a case related to enforced disappearances, the Court ordered the creation of a website to assist in the search for the abducted children with the purpose of reuniting them with their families.[104] The Court has also ordered states to apologise. For instance, in the *Plan de Sánchez,* case, and despite the fact that the State had already apologised on its own motion during the proceedings,[105] the Court ordered such an apology to be offered in a public ceremony.[106] In cases involving massacres, the Court has ordered states to create a commemorative plaque in a public place,[107] or a monument.[108] The Court has also ordered states to publish the Court's judgment in their official state gazette.[109]

---

98 IACtHR, *Moiwana Community* v. *Suriname*, *supra* n. 44, para. 218.

99 Antkowiak, *supra* n. 2, p. 380.

100 Basch, F. et al., "The Effectiveness of the Inter-American System of Human Rights Protection: A Quantitative Approach to its Functioning and Compliance with its Decision", 7 *SUR – International Journal on Human Rights* (2010), p. 13-14.

101 IACtHR, *La Rochela Massacre* v. *Colombia, supra* n. 84, para. 303; IACtHR, *Ituango Massacres* v. *Colombia*, *supra* n. 50, para. 409.

102 IACtHR (Judgment) 11 November 1999, *Caracazo* v. *Venezuela*, para. 143-(4)(a); IACtHR, *Gomes Lund et al. ("Guerrilha Do Araguaia")* v. *Brazil*, *supra* n. 49, para. 283.

103 IACtHR, *La Rochela Massacre* v. *Colombia, supra* n. 84, para. 303; IACtHR, *Ituango Massacres* v. *Colombia*, *supra* n. 50, para. 409.

104 IACtHR, *"Las Dos Erres" Massacre* v. *Guatemala*, *supra* n. 79, para. 271-274; IACtHR, *Contreras et al.* v. *El Salvador*, *supra* n. 61, para. 209-210.

105 IACtHR (Judgment) 29 April 2004, *Plan de Sánchez* v. *Guatemala,* para. 9.

106 IACtHR, *Plan de Sánchez, Massacre* v. *Guatemala*, *supra* n. 45, para. 125 (2) (3).

107 IACtHR, *Ituango Massacres* v. *Colombia*, *supra* n. 50, para. 408.

108 IACtHR, *Moiwana Community* v. *Suriname*, *supra* n. 44, para. 218; IACtHR, *Mapiripán Massacre* v. *Colombia, supra* n. 8, para. 315; IACtHR, *Pueblo Bello* v. *Colombia*, *supra* n. 20, para. 278.

109 IACtHR, *Barrios Altos* v. *Peru*, *supra* n. 77, Operative para. 5 (d).

Cases related to I&TPs' traditional lands

The Court has ordered states to undertake the necessary domestic legislative and institutional reforms in order to recognise indigenous and tribal peoples' lands.[110] In addition, it has ordered the creation of 'an effective mechanism for the delimitation, demarcation, and titling' of traditional and ancestral lands of I&TP,[111] and has furthermore prohibited states and private parties from using those lands that should undergo titling.[112] Furthermore, the Court has also ordered states to apologise to I&TP communities[113] in a public ceremony in accordance with the latter's traditions and uses and language,[114] as well as to broadcast the judgment in the language of the IP community.[115]

4.2.2 Material

4.2.2.1 Restitution

Cases related to GVHR

Measures of restitution on a collective basis were not identified in any cases related to GVHR. This seems to be logical as it is not possible to erase and restore violations of this kind.

Cases related to I&TPs' traditional lands

In all cases related to violations of indigenous and tribal peoples' right to property over their traditional lands, the Court has ordered states to restore the said I&TPs' lands. In this regard, the Court has acknowledged that indigenous peoples have a special and important relationship with their lands and territories. This relationship includes productive activities and is thereby necessary for both the I&TPs' survival as well as for a 'material and spiritual relationship' which is required to preserve their culture.[116] The IACtHR has upheld that I&TP are entitled to live freely in their territory, despite

---

110 IACtHR, *Moiwana Community* v. *Suriname*, *supra* n. 44, para. 209-211; IACtHR, *Yakye Axa Indigenous Community* v. *Paraguay, supra* n. 44, para. 225.

111 IACtHR (Judgment) 29 March 2006, *Sawhoyamaxa Indigenous Community* v. *Paraguay*, para. 146; IACtHR, *Mayagna (Sumo) Awas Tingni Community* v. *Nicaragua*, *supra* n. 47, para. 164, 173; IACtHR, *Yakye Axa Indigenous Community* v. *Paraguay, supra* n. 44, para. 242(6).

112 IACtHR, *Moiwana Community* v. *Suriname*, *supra* n. 44, para. 211.

113 Ibid., para. 216.

114 IACtHR, *Plan de Sánchez Massacre* v. *Guatemala, supra* n. 45, para. 100-101; IACtHR, *Moiwana Community* v. *Suriname*, *supra* n. 44, para. 216-217; IACtHR, *Yakye Axa Indigenous Community* v. *Paraguay, supra* n. 44, para. 226.

115 IACtHR (Judgment) 23 June 2005, *Yatama* v. *Nicaragua*, para. 252-253.

116 IACtHR, *Mayagna (Sumo) Awas Tingni Community* v. *Nicaragua*, *supra* n. 47, para. 149.

not having a title over it.[117] In the *Kichwa Indigenous People of Sarakuya* case, the Court, as part of the restoration of the IP lands, ordered the removal of explosives and the reforestation of the said lands.[118] Furthermore, the Court has also attempted to restore Maya culture through measures such as carrying out instructions in Maya-Achí in the affected communities.[119]

4.2.2.2 Compensation

Cases related to GVHR

Measures of compensation on a collective basis were not identified in any cases related to GVHR, not even in cases related to GVHR committed against indigenous or tribal peoples.

Cases related to I&TPs' traditional lands

In the majority of cases related to land rights of indigenous and tribal peoples, the Court has ordered financial compensation on a collective basis.[120] For instance, in the *Saramaka* case, the Court ordered the state to pay USD 75, 000 for the damage caused to the Saramaka's traditional land by mining activities carried out under a state-granted concession. This concession had been granted without consulting the tribe. In the remaining cases, the Court granted a specific amount of money, intended to be invested in a community development fund, as compensation for both pecuniary and non-pecuniary damages.[121] This monetary sum has ranged from USD 50,000 to

117 IACtHR (Judgment) 28 November 2007, *Saramaka People* v. *Suriname*, para. 95; IACtHR, *Plan de Sánchez Massacre* v. *Guatemala, supra* n. 45, para. 85; IACtHR, *Mayagna (Sumo) Awas Tingni Community* v. *Nicaragua, supra* n. 47, para. 149.

118 IACtHR (Judgment) 27 June 2012, *The Kichwa Indigenous People of Sarayaku* v. *Ecuador*, para. 289-295. Similar measures were ordered in the case of *Kaliña and Lokono Peoples*. Yet here the Court labelled those measures as rehabilitation. See: IACtHR (Judgment) 25 November 2015, *The Kaliña and Lokono Peoples* v. *Suriname*, para. 290.

119 IACtHR, *Plan de Sánchez Massacre* v. *Guatemala, supra* n. 45, para. 110.

120 The only two exceptions to this is the case of *Moiwana*, which deals also with GVHR and the case of Yakye Axa. In the later, the Court granted a specific sum of money as compensation to the identified members of the community. Here the Court did not specify the distribution of monies. See: IACtHR, *Yakye Axa Indigenous Community* v. *Paraguay, supra* n. 44, para. 189, 195.

121 See cases: IACtHR (Judgment) 24 August 2010, *Xákmok Kásek Indigenous Community* v. *Paraguay*, para. 323-324; IACtHR, *Mayagna (Sumo) Awas Tingni Community* v. *Nicaragua, supra* n. 47, Operative para. 173 (6-7); IACtHR, *Moiwana Community* v. *Suriname, supra* n. 44, para. 213-215; IACtHR, *Yakye Axa Indigenous Community* v. *Paraguay, supra* n. 44, para. 205-206; IACtHR, *Sawhoyamaxa Indigenous Community* v. *Paraguay, supra* n. 111, para. 224-225; IACtHR, *Saramaka People* v. *Suriname, supra* n. 117, para. 199-202; IACtHR, *The Kichwa Indigenous People of Sarayaku* v. *Ecuador, supra* n. 118, para. 317, 323.

USD 1,500,000.[122] Although the Court, when granting these measures, has commonly referred to them as collective compensation,[123] they will be addressed in section 4.2.3.

4.2.2.3 Rehabilitation

Cases related to GVHR

In the *Barrios Altos* case, the Court ordered the State to provide all beneficiaries with free health care, including diagnostic procedures, hospitalization, surgery, medicines, and childbirth, as well as psychological healthcare at the healthcare centre where the victims resided.[124] Significantly, special measures were ordered for children and women in the *Pueblo Bello* case.[125] In the *Plan de Sánchez Massacre* case, the Court even ordered the creation of specific programmes to afford victims with psychological and psychiatric treatment at the collective, family and individual levels, all completely free of charge.[126]

Cases related to I&TPs' traditional lands

The Court has not granted measures of rehabilitation in cases related to the traditional lands of indigenous and tribal peoples. It has rather granted health services and the construction of medical centres for the benefit of the communities in question. However, in the *Kaliña and Lokono Peoples* case, the Court has ordered the state of Suriname to rehabilitate the territory which was taken away from the tribal community and, instead, given to a company by means of a mining concession. Such rehabilitation included measures of reforestation in the affected areas.[127] Interestingly, a similar measure ordered in the *Kichwa* case was labelled by the Court as a measure of land restoration.[128]

---

122 IACtHR (Judgment) 8 October 2015, *Garífuna Punta Piedra Community and its Members* v. *Honduras*, para. 335; IACtHR (Judgment) 8 October 2015, *Garífuna Triunfo de la Cruz Community and its Members* v. *Honduras*, para. 298; IACtHR, *The Kaliña and Lokono Peoples* v. *Suriname*, *supra* n. 118, para. 298.

123 In the Moiwana case, the Court referred to this measure as a form of satisfaction and GnR. See: IACtHR, *Moiwana Community* v. *Suriname*, *supra* n. 44, para. 213-215.

124 IACtHR, *Barrios Altos* v. *Peru*, *supra* n. 77, Operative para. 3.

125 In the case of Pueblo bello that concerned IPs, special measures of reparation for pregnant women. See: IACtHR, *Pueblo Bello Massacre* v. *Colombia*, *supra* n. 20, para. 239, 258.

126 IACtHR, *Plan de Sánchez Massacre* v. *Guatemala*, *supra* n. 45, para. 93, 106-108, 117.

127 IACtHR, *The Kaliña and Lokono Peoples* v. *Suriname*, *supra* n. 118, para. 290.

128 IACtHR, *The Kichwa Indigenous People of Sarayaku* v. *Ecuador*, *supra* n. 118, para. 289.

4.2.3 Collective Reparations

Under different labels, the Court has ordered various measures aimed at providing social services by means of a community development fund or state-guided projects. In this light, the Court has sometimes granted these measures as measures of satisfaction,[129] compensation for non-pecuniary damage,[130] collective compensation for non-pecuniary damage,[131] collective compensation through a community development fund,[132] and restitution development programmes.[133] While the Court's classification does not seem to be consistent, the content of the measures is the same: social services for a large number of victims without the need to identify each beneficiary individually.

Projects and funds with the purpose of creating community health, housing or education programmes have been referred to by some scholars as 'non-monetary economic compensation' ordered by the IACtHR as collective reparations.[134] Thus, it seems to be logical to also refer to those measures as collective reparations in this study.

Significantly, the Court has awarded these measures in cases related to massacres (*Aloeboetoe, Ituango, Moiwana Community, Plan de Sánchez, Pueblo Bello, Río Negro and El Mozote and neighbouring locations)* and in cases related to traditional lands of indigenous and tribal peoples communities (*Mayagna (Sumo) Awas Tingni, Moiwana, Yakye Axa, Sawhoyamaxa, Saramaka People, Xámok Kásek, Kichwa Indigenous Peoples of Sarayaku, Garífuna Punta Piedra, Garífuna Triunfo de La Cruz* and *Kaliña and Lokono People*). Finally, the Court has not ordered collective reparations in cases related to enforced disappearances and/or torture, even if these cases involved large numbers of victims.

---

129 IACtHR, *Ituango Massacres* v. *Colombia*, *supra* n. 50, para. 407; IACtHR, *Pueblo Bello Massacre* v. *Colombia*, *supra* n. 20, para. 276; IACtHR, Río Negro Massacres v. *Guatemala*, *supra* n. 65, para. 281-284; IACtHR, *Moiwana Community* v. *Suriname*, *supra* n. 44, para. 213-215.

130 IACtHR, *Aloeboetoe et al.* v. *Suriname*, *supra* n. 14, para. 116 (5).

131 IACtHR, *Mayagna (Sumo) Awas Tingni Community* v. *Nicaragua*, *supra* n. 47, para. 167; IACtHR, *Yakye Axa Indigenous Community* v. *Paraguay*, *supra* n. 44, para. 205-206; IACtHR, *Sawhoyamaxa Indigenous Community* v. *Paraguay*, *supra* n. 111, para. 224-225; IACtHR, *Saramaka People* v. *Suriname*, *supra* n. 117, para. 199-202; IACtHR, Xákmok Kásek Indigenous Community v. *Paraguay*, *supra* n. 121, para. 323-324; IACtHR, *The Kichwa Indigenous People of Sarayaku* v. *Ecuador*, *supra* n. 118, para. 323.

132 IACtHR, *Garífuna Punta Piedra Community and its Members* v. *Honduras*, *supra* n. 122, para. 335; IACtHR, *Garífuna Triunfo de la Cruz Community and its Members* v. *Honduras*, *supra* n. 122, para. 298; IACtHR, *The Kaliña and Lokono Peoples* v. *Suriname*, *supra* n. 118, para. 298.

133 IACtHR, *Massacres of El Mozote and neighboring locations* v. *El Salvador*, *supra* n. 85, para. 336-340.

134 Calderón Gamboa, J.F., *La reparación integral en la jurisprudencia de la Corte Interamericana de Derechos Humanos: estándares aplicables al nuevo paradigma mexicano* (México, CNDD 2013), p. 61-63; Basch et al., *supra* n. 100, p. 13.

4.2.3.1 Definition

Finally, although the Court has not provided a definition of collective reparations, its jurisprudence demonstrates that they are composed of service-based measures. Significantly, in 12 cases out of the 16 cases in which the Court has ordered these types of reparations, the Court has ordered the creation of a community development fund tasked with providing services and infrastructure. The Court usually orders states to allocate a specific amount of money to investments in such development funds. These funds' services and infrastructure projects include providing communities with water, housing, medical assistance, food, and financial and human resources for schools, among others.[135] It is important to mention that in some cases the Court has identified the services that the fund is supposed to deliver based on the victims' requests,[136] while in others the victims were given the possibility to choose the nature of the services during the implementation phase.[137]

In addition, the Court has ordered housing projects[138] and the reopening of a school and a medical dispensary in a village affected by the commission of GVHR[139] as well as the improvement of the road systems.[140] In these cases, the Court has defined neither the amount of money to be invested nor the time frame in which such services are to be provided. A case in point is the *Pueblo Bello* case where the Court ordered the state of Colombia to implement a housing program without further specifications.[141]

Finally, it must be stated that the IACtHR has ordered these collective reparations to be granted on either a permanent basis (e.g. the reopening of a school or the establishment of human rights training for the police and the military) or on the basis of a specific budget devoted to their operation. When the budget has been exhausted or invested in the collective reparations projects, then the state is considered to have complied with the collective reparations order.[142]

---

135 IACtHR, *Saramaka People* v. *Suriname*, *supra* n. 117, para. 201; IACtHR, *Sawhoyamaxa Indigenous Community* v. *Paraguay*, *supra* n. 111, para. 230-233; IACtHR, *Plan de Sánchez Massacre* v. *Guatemala*, *supra* n. 45, para. 105-110.

136 IACtHR, *Plan de Sánchez Massacre* v. *Guatemala*, *supra* n. 45, para. 90; IACtHR, *Saramaka People* v. *Suriname*, *supra* n. 117, para. 192.

137 IACtHR (Judgment) 31 August 2001 Magayama Sumo, Operative para. 173 (6).

138 IACtHR, *Ituango Massacres* v. *Colombia*, *supra* n. 50, para. 407; IACtHR, *Plan de Sánchez Massacre* v. *Guatemala*, *supra* n. 45, para. 105, 117.

139 IACtHR, *Aloeboetoe et al.* v. *Suriname*, *supra* n. 14, para. 96.

140 IACtHR, *Plan de Sánchez Massacre* v. *Guatemala*, *supra* n. 45, Operative para. 9.

141 IACtHR, *Pueblo Bello Massacre* v. *Colombia*, *supra* n. 20, para. 276.

142 IACtHR, *Moiwana Community* v. *Suriname*, *supra* n. 44, para. 218; IACtHR (Monitoring Compliance Order) 22 November 2010, *Moiwana Community* v. *Suriname*, para. 39.

5 Substantive and Procedural Aspects of Collective Measures and Reparations

5.1 Adequacy

In general, human rights violations affect each victim's life in a different way.[143] With this view, adequate reparation measures are usually chosen on a case-by-case basis. Although victims may never be satisfied with any reparation,[144] the IACtHR has traditionally taken into account certain factors to help ensure that the Court's ordered reparations are adequate.[145] Such factors include, for instance, the gravity of the violations (whether they constitute a GVHR),[146] the views and wishes of the victims (as expressed in the remedies sought),[147] the potential of the reparations to erase the effects of the violation,[148] the particular conditions of the victim (age, gender, needs),[149] and any relevant cultural and political convictions of the victims, particularly in the case of indigenous peoples.[150] For example, in cases related to property rights and indigenous or tribal peoples, the Court has acknowledged that the latter groups do have a 'collective understanding of the concepts of property and possession',[151] among others. In addition, the Court has made clear that the adequacy of a type of measure depends on the specific violation suffered and on the material and non-material damage caused.[152]

Antkowiak has argued that in GVHR cases, judgments solely awarding compensation and acknowledging the responsibility of the state are inadequate. This is because GVHR give rise to myriad consequences and, as such, an adequate form of reparation should consist of a combination of multiple measures, i.e. a holistic approach involving material and symbolic measures.[153] While this may be the best

---

143 McKay, *supra* n. 6, p. 946.
144 Ibid., p. 947.
145 See Chapter II, Sections 2.3.3 and 3.3.3.
146 IACtHR, *Pueblo Bello Massacre* v. *Colombia, supra* n. 20, 258; Laplante, L.J., "Bringing Effective Remedies Home: The Inter-American Human Rights System, Reparations, and the Duty to Prevention", 22 *Netherlands Quarterly of Human Rights* (2004).
147 For instance, in its first case, the victims asked the Court to order Honduras to investigate and prosecute those responsible, and this was granted. See: IACtHR, *Velásquez-Rodríguez* v. *Honduras, supra* n. 38, para. 7.
148 Shelton, *supra* n. 10, p. 31.
149 Citroni and Quintana Osuna, *supra* n. 56, p. 321.
150 Antkowiak, *supra* n. 34, p. 283. It is important to highlight that each group of indigenous peoples is different from another and so their needs are also different. See: Citroni and Quintana Osuna, *supra* n. 56, p. 340.
151 IACtHR, *Sawhoyamaxa Indigenous Community* v. *Paraguay, supra* n. 111, para. 120; IACtHR, *Saramaka People* v. *Suriname, supra* n. 117, para. 91.
152 IACtHR, *La Cantuta* v. *Peru, supra* n. 77, para. 202; IACtHR, *"White Van" (Paniagua-Morales et al.)* v. *Guatemala, supra* n. 43, para. 79.
153 Antkowiak, *supra* n. 34, p. 284, 355.

approach, it is anything but easy to balance such measures in an award. For instance, monetary awards may create ambivalence as victims may perceive them to be blood money, hence they can be detrimental to the victims' healing process.[154] Yet, money is a symbolic measure that can give victims the freedom to spend it for what they consider to be the best redress for a violation.[155] Having said that, monetary compensation may put victims at risk, as recipients may be robbed. Consequently, the contextual background of victims' living conditions needs to be taken into account.[156]

Furthermore, based on his research, Antkowiak asserts that the majority of victims before the IACtHR usually prefer symbolic (non-monetary) reparations such as apologies, the acknowledgement of state responsibility or monuments, inter alia.[157] Yet, these measures are not always appropriate per se. A case in point is the *Miguel Castro-Castro Prison* case that dealt with the violent deaths of convicted and incarcerated members of the Shining Path. The Court ordered Peru to include the names of the victims on the monument called *El ojo que llora* (the eye that cries).[158] This monument, however, had been built to honour the victims of Peru's internal conflict where the majority of the violations had been committed by the Shining Path. Hence, this order was received very negatively by civil society, as victims and perpetrators were to be honoured on the same monument.[159] The government of Peru conveyed to the Court the huge discontent and confusion that this measure elicited. In the interpretation of the judgment, the Court revised and altered its approach by allowing for the commemoration of the victims through other means.[160] Balancing the awards also implies deciding whether the measures would be granted on an individual or collective basis. To date, the Court has not indicated when individual, collective or combined measures are deemed to be adequate.

Significantly, the Court's approach of granting collective reparations by means of a community development fund or a single service project seems to respond to the victims' needs and wishes. In almost all cases, victims' representatives and/or the IACmmHR requested these measures.[161] Although not requested in the *Mayagna (Sumo) Awas Tingni* case, it could be inferred that the Court based its decision to grant

154 Antkowiak, *supra* n. 2, p. 388.

155 Hamber, B., "Repairing the Irreparable: Dealing with double-binds of making reparations for crimes of the past", 5 *Ethnicity and Health* (2000), p. 222 citing the South African TRC's final report.

156 See Chapter II, Section 3.3.3.

157 Antkowiak, *supra* n. 2, p. 388.

158 IACtHR, *Miguel Castro-Castro Prison* v. *Peru, supra* n. 77, para. 454.

159 Burgorgue-Larsen, L., 'The right to determine reparations' in L. Burgorgue-Larsen and A. Úbeda de Torres, *The Inter-American Court of Human Rights: Case Law and Commentary* (New York, OUP 2011), p. 237-328.

160 IACtHR (Judgment Interpretation) 2 August 2008, *Miguel Castro-Castro Prison* v. *Peru*, para. 57.

161 From the 16 cases where the Court granted reparations only in the following cases were these measures not requested: *Aloeboetoe*, *Mayagna (Sumo) Awas Tingni Community, Ituango and Pueblo Bello.*

CR on expert opinions which asserted that the 'physical health, mental health, and social health of indigenous peoples is linked to the concept of the land.'[162] Since the Court found a violation of the right to property of IP with regards to their traditional land, it seems that the Court tried to repair the harm incurred by such a violation.[163] Interestingly, in *Xákmok Kásek Indigenous Community* the Court ordered CR based on both the Commission's allegations regarding basic social services, namely health and educational ones, and the state's willingness to continue providing social services to ensure the living conditions of the community.[164]

5.1.1 Victims' Participation

Victims' participation is a precondition for the Court to listen to their needs and wishes. Victims do not have direct access to the IACtHR. The Commission, however, has the power to refer and litigate a case on behalf of the victims before the IACtHR.[165] Yet, victims' participatory rights have developed within the system[166] since 2009 and victims have been recognized as parties to the proceedings with the ability to present claims and arguments that do not need to be in line with those presented by the Commission in its case referral.[167]

Not only have victims presented their wishes regarding reparations before the IACtHR, but the Court has often taken these wishes into account. In adjudicating land rights for indigenous and tribal peoples, the Court took these peoples' worldview into consideration, and the reparations were accordingly granted.[168] However, sometimes it has also awarded measures that have not been requested. A case in point is *Plan de Sánchez*, where the Court awarded financial compensation to restore and maintain the community chapel without the victims having requested this.[169] Antkowaiak has stated that in *Aloeboetoe,* the IACtHR took a paternalistic approach by not involving the victims (the community) when deciding on the types of social services it would

162 IACtHR, *Mayagna (Sumo) Awas Tingni Community* v. *Nicaragua, supra* n. 47, para. 83 (d).

163 In this case, the Court allowed the indigenous people community to decide about the nature of services that would benefit the entire community.

164 IACtHR, Xákmok Kásek Indigenous Community v. *Paraguay, supra* n. 121, para. 203-215, 322.

165 Article 61(2), ACHR.

166 Contreras-Garduño, D. and Fraser, J., "The Identification of Victims before the Inter-American Court of Human Rights and the International Criminal Court and its impact on Participation and Reparations: A Domino Effect?", 7 *Inter-American and European Human Rights Journal* (2014), p. 185.

167 Article 25, IACtHR's Rules of Procedure as approved by the Court during its LXXXV Regular Period of Sessions, held from November 16 to 28, 2009 (hereafter 2009 IACtHR's RoP).

168 IACtHR, *Mayagna (Sumo) Awas Tingni Community* v. *Nicaragua, supra* n. 47, para. 149.

169 Antkowiak, *supra* n. 2, p. 393.

award.[170] However, after this case, the Court seemed to have listened to victims when grading social services.[171]

Design of reparations

Throughout its jurisprudence, the Court has acknowledged the need to adopt a participatory approach in the design of collective reparations when granting them to indigenous or tribal peoples. In the first case where the Court granted collective reparations, the Court simply ordered the exact social services that it wanted to see realized (the reopening of a specific school and the establishment of a dispensary).[172] Later, in the *Plan de Sánchez* case, the Court ordered specific social services and infrastructure programmes after taking the victims' petitions into account.[173] In the *Moiwana* case, developmental programmes were ordered to be directed at health, housing, education and other priority areas. For this, the Court ordered the allocation of USD 1.2 million and the establishment of a committee composed of victims and state representatives who, in conjunction, would determine how to invest the resources.[174] In the *Mayagna (Sumo) Awas Tingni* case, the Court changed its approach by requiring the members of the affected community to participate in the design of the fund's programmes and decide freely on the nature of the 'works or services of collective interest'.[175] A similar approach was adopted in the *Sawhoyamaxa* and *Yakye Axa* cases, where the Court granted collective reparations and ordered the creation of a committee to develop comparable social projects. However, in these two cases the Court ordered the community development programme to be directed at educational, housing, agricultural, health projects and drinking water services as well as sanitation infrastructure.[176] Unfortunately, the Court has not adopted a participatory approach when granting collective reparations in all of the massacre cases. In both the *Ituango*

170 Antkowiak, *supra* n. 2, p. 385.

171 IACtHR, *Plan de Sánchez Massacre* v. *Guatemala, supra* n. 45, para. 90; IACtHR, *Moiwana Community* v. *Suriname*, *supra* n. 44, para. 197, 199; IACtHR, *Yakye Axa Indigenous Community* v. *Paraguay, supra* n. 44, para. 196-197; IACtHR, *Sawhoyamaxa Indigenous Community* v. *Paraguay, supra* n. 111, para. 201(g); IACtHR, *Saramaka People* v. *Suriname*, *supra* n. 117, para. 192; IACtHR, *The Kichwa Indigenous People of Sarayaku* v. *Ecuador*, *supra* n. 118, para. 320; IACtHR, Río Negro Massacres v. *Guatemala, supra* n. 65, para. 281; IACtHR, *Massacres of El Mozote and neighboring locations* v. *El Salvador*, *supra* n. 85, para. 337; IACtHR, *Garífuna Punta Piedra Community and its Members* v. *Honduras*, *supra* n. 122, para. 330, IACtHR, *Garífuna Triunfo de la Cruz Community and its Members* v. *Honduras*, *supra* n. 122, para. 287; IACtHR, *The Kaliña and Lokono Peoples* v. *Suriname*, *supra* n. 118, para. 292.

172 Roht-Arriaza, *supra* n. 2, p. 662.

173 IACtHR, *Plan de Sánchez Massacre* v. *Guatemala, supra* n. 45, s. 90.

174 IACtHR, *Moiwana Community* v. *Suriname*, *supra* n. 44, para. 218.

175 IACtHR, *Mayagna (Sumo) Awas Tingni Community* v. *Nicaragua*, *supra* n. 47, para. 167.

176 IACtHR, *Sawhoyamaxa Indigenous Community* v. *Paraguay*, *supra* n. 111, para. 224, 248; IACtHR, *Yakye Axa Indigenous Community* v. *Paraguay, supra* n. 44, para. 205, 242.

and *Pueblo Bello* cases, the Court left it to the discretion of the state to decide on the operational details of the housing programmes granted without ensuring the participation of the victims.[177]

5.1.2 Agreement

In some cases, the reparations granted have been the result of an agreement among the parties. For instance, in the *Barrios Altos* case, upon its recognition of responsibility, the State sought a friendly settlement regarding reparations. The Court considered it 'appropriate that reparations are determined by mutual agreement between' the parties and established a period of 3 months to reach such an agreement. Otherwise, the Court would determine the reparations.[178] An agreement was reached after the 3-month period but there was no controversy regarding the reparations and the court decided to accept the agreement.[179] The agreement included provisions on the identification of victims as well as measures of material and non-material reparations.[180]

And in some other cases the parties have reached partial agreements regarding reparations. For instance, in *La Rochela Massacre* case, the parties reached a 'partial agreement in relation to some reparation measures'.[181] And in the *Ituango Massacres* case, the state reached agreements with some of the victims and the Court approved them.[182] Yet, agreements on reparations (either partial or full) have proved to be difficult to reach.[183]

5.2 Liability to Repair

States that have ratified the American Convention on Human Rights and that have accepted the jurisdiction of the IACtHR do have the obligation to comply with the Court's judgments.[184] As such, states are responsible for providing victims with reparations for their acts and omissions that resulted in violations of one or more rights enshrined in the Convention when these violations were against one or more

177 Antkowiak, *supra* n. 2, p. 387; IACtHR, *Ituango Massacres* v. *Colombia*, *supra* n. 50, para. 407; IACtHR, *Pueblo Bello Massacre* v. *Colombia*, *supra* n. 20, para. 276.

178 IACtHR (Judgment) 14 March 2001, *Barrios Altos* v. *Peru*, para. 35, 50, 51(6).

179 Ibid., 22, 46.

180 Ibid., para. 26-44.

181 IACtHR, *La Rochela Massacre* v. *Colombia*, *supra* n. 84, para. 8, 20, 22, 227, 281.

182 IACtHR, *Ituango Massacres* v. *Colombia*, *supra* n. 50, para. 184, 368.

183 IACtHR (Judgment) 4 December 1991, *Aloeboetoe et al.* v. *Suriname*, para. 17; IACtHR (Judgment) 18 January 1995, *El Amparo* v. *Venezuela*, para. 21; IACtHR (Judgment) 14 September 1996, *El Amparo* v. *Venezuela*, para. 7; IACtHR, *Aloeboetoe et al.* v. *Suriname*, *supra* n. 14, para. 42; IACtHR, *Caracazo* v. *Venezuela*, *supra* n. 102, para. 10, 37, 42; IACtHR, *Miguel Castro-Castro Prison* v. *Peru*, *supra* n. 77, para. 143, 197(34); IACtHR, *Contreras et al.* v. *El Salvador*, *supra* n. 61, para. 12,17.

184 Articles 62, 65 and 68, ACHR.

individuals within their territory.[185] Accordingly, the Court has repeatedly upheld that states bear 'the duty to make reparation for and remove the consequences of the violation'.[186]

5.3 Beneficiaries

The beneficiaries of reparations are those persons recognized as victims (injured parties) of a violation of any human right protected by the ACHR.[187] Although the concept of a victim is not fully defined, victimhood is limited to natural persons.[188] It comprises the direct victims of a violation and any indirect victims.[189] On the one hand, a direct victim is a person who has directly suffered harm.[190] On the other hand, indirect victims are the direct victims' next of kin,[191] any dependants, or any third parties who could prove that they suffered harm as a consequence of the violation(s) inflicted upon the direct victim.[192] In light of these concepts, the Court has recognized the direct victim's children, spouse or permanent companion,[193] stepfather and half-siblings,[194] step-children,[195] and children born outside of wedlock as indirect

185 Articles 1 (1) and 65 ACHR.

186 IACtHR, *La Cantuta* v. *Peru, supra* n. 77, para. 200; IACtHR, *Miguel Castro-Castro Prison* v. *Peru, supra* n. 77, para. 414.

187 IACtHR, *Ituango Massacres* v. *Colombia*, Separate Concurring Opinion of Judge S. Garcia Ramirez, *supra* n. 50, para. 10.

188 Yet, the Court has once recognized a legal person (an indigenous political party in Nicaragua) as a victim and beneficiary of reparation. See: IACtHR, *Yatama* v. *Nicaragua, supra* n. 115, para. 248.

189 This might also include potential victims. See: Úbeda de Torres, A., "Determination of Victims", in L. Burgorgue-Larsen and A. Úbeda de Torres, *The Inter-American Court of Human Rights: Case Law and Commentary* (New York, OUP 2011), p. 113-114.

190 IACtHR, *Ituango Massacres* v. *Colombia*, Separate Concurring Opinion of Judge S. Garcia Ramirez, *supra* n. 50, para. 11.

191 According to Article 2(16) of the IACtHR's Rules of Procedure as amended by the Court during its LXXXII Ordinary Period of Sessions, held from January 19 to 31, 2009, the next of kin 'refers to "immediate family", that is, the direct ascendants and descendants, siblings, spouses or permanent companions, or those determined by the Court, if applicable'. However, this definition was removed from the current IACtHR Rules as approved by the Court during its LXXXV Regular Period of Sessions, held from November 16 to 28, 2009.

192 IACtHR, *Moiwana Community* v. *Suriname*, *supra* n. 44, para. 178; IACtHR, *Mapiripán Massacre* v. *Colombia, supra* n. 8, para. 257; IACtHR, *Pueblo Bello Massacre* v. *Colombia*, *supra* n. 20, para. 237; IACtHR, *Ituango Massacres* v. *Colombia*, *supra* n. 50, para. 356.

193 IACtHR, *Pueblo Bello Massacre* v. *Colombia, supra* n. 20, para. 240; IACtHR, *El Amparo* v. *Venezuela, supra* n. 183, para. 41(c).

194 IACtHR (Judgment) 7 June 2003, *Juan Humberto Sánchez* v. *Honduras,* para. 175.

195 IACtHR (Judgment) 1 February 2006, *López-Álvarez* v. *Honduras*, para. 187

victims.[196] Lastly, the recognition of indirect victims does not depend on and is not linked to whether they participate in the proceedings before the IACtHR.[197]

Furthermore, beneficiaries not only include the direct and indirect victims but also their heirs and successors, and collectivities. Heirs come into play when the victim has died – they inherit the reparation owed to the direct victim. The IACtHR has been quite progressive in defining heirs and successors. Although national law is the guiding principle in the determination of successors,[198] the Court has also followed customary family law when the latter is more victim-inclusive.[199] The Court has also recognised certain groups and communities as injured parties and beneficiaries of reparations.[200] In addition, the Court has also upheld that the next of kin of victims of GVHR, such as enforced disappearances, murders or torture, can also be considered to be direct victims of a violation of the right to humane treatment. To determine such victimization, the Court will analyse the particularly close connection between the said next of kind and the victims of GVHR to decide whether a violation of Article 5 has occurred.[201] Finally, the Court has also recognised collectivities as beneficiaries, mainly in the form of indigenous and tribal peoples,[202] but also some communities.[203] These collectivities, however, are not expressly recognised as injured parties.

Identification of Victims

In principle, alleged victims who have not been identified in the proceedings cannot subsequently be granted reparations. Victims are to be identified by the Commission and their names need to have already been mentioned in the report referring the

---

196 IACtHR (Judgment) 27 August 1998, *Garrido and Baigorria* v. *Argentina*, para. 54, 56.

197 IACtHR (Judgment) 25 November 2003, *Myrna Manck Chang* v. *Guatemala*, para. 245. (Also the proceedings before the IACmHR).

198 IACtHR, *La Rochela Massacre* v. *Colombia, supra* n. 84, para. 308.

199 IACtHR, *Aloeboetoe et al.* v. *Suriname*, *supra* n. 14, para. 62, 63.

200 IACtHR, *Saramaka People* v. *Suriname*, supra n. 117, para. 189; IACtHR, *The Kichwa Indigenous People of Sarayaku* v. *Ecuador*, *supra* n. 118, para. 284; IACtHR, *Garífuna Triunfo de la Cruz Community and its Members* v. *Honduras*, *supra* n. 122, para. 257; IACtHR, *Garífuna Punta Piedra Community and its Members* v. *Honduras*, *supra* n. 122, para. 317.

201 IACtHR, *Gomes Lund et al. ("Guerrilha Do Araguaia")* v. *Brazil*, *supra* n. 49, para. 235; IACtHR, *Santo Domingo Massacre* v. *Colombia, supra* n. 72, para. 242-243; IACtHR, *Rodríguez Vera et al. (the disappeared from the Palace of Justice)* v. *Colombia, supra* n. 69, para. 533; IACtHR (Judgment) 17 April 2015, *Cruz Sánchez et al.* v. *Peru,* para. 444.

202 IACtHR, *Saramaka People* v. *Suriname*, *supra* n. 117, para. 188; IACtHR, *Mayagna (Sumo) Awas Tingni Community* v. *Nicaragua*, Separate Opinion of Judge Sergio García Ramírez, *supra* n. 47, para. 15; IACtHR, *Moiwana Community* v. *Suriname*, *supra* n. 44; IACtHR, *Yakye Axa Indigenous Community* v. *Paraguay, supra* n. 44, para. 6-9.

203 IACtHR, *Plan de Sánchez Massacre* v. *Guatemala, supra* n. 45, para. 109-111; IACtHR, *Ituango Massacres* v. *Colombia*, *supra* n. 50, para. 407; IACtHR, Río Negro Massacres v. *Guatemala*, *supra* n. 65, para. 284.

case.[204] However, in cases of massive or collective violations, such identification may be done even within a year or two after the judgment has been delivered.[205] Identification after the delivery of the judgment is a response to the fact that it is not always possible to identify all victims of certain violations due to the specific circumstances of their cases.[206] Accordingly, Amaya Úbeda has stated that the Court's current legal framework takes into account that certain violations not only affect individuals but also collectivities, as well as that the members of certain groups, namely indigenous and tribal peoples, are difficult to identify.[207] Thus, the Court usually applies a flexible approach to this identification.

5.3.1 Collectivities as Beneficiaries

McKay has stated that the Court usually grants collective reparations to indigenous and tribal peoples because the violations suffered by them are directed against and suffered by a community as a whole, rather than just by individuals.[208] Even so, the Court has not always recognised the community or peoples as an injured party. For instance, in its first case dealing with GVHR against members of a tribal people, the *Aloeboetoe* case, the Court did not grant the Commission's request to recognize the whole community as a 'family' and, thereby, as an injured party.[209] Yet, the IACtHR provided awards for the benefit of the whole community. However, in its later jurisprudence, the Court has acknowledged several indigenous and tribal communities as injured parties.[210] In addition, the Court has recognised some 'geographic' communities that are not necessarily composed of indigenous or tribal peoples as beneficiaries of collective reparations.[211] For instance, in the *Ituango Massacre* case, the Court ordered collective reparations for the benefit of the inhabitants of the municipal communities of *El Aro* and *La Granja*.[212]

---

204 Article 35 (1), IACtHR's Rules; IACtHR, *Mapiripán Massacre* v. *Colombia, supra* n. 8, para. 289.

205 IACtHR (Judgment) 20 November 2013, *Afro-Descendant Communities displaced from the Cacarica River Basin (Operation Genesis)* v. *Colombia*. para. 435; IACtHR, *Gomes Lund et al. ("Guerrilha Do Araguaia")* v. *Brazil, supra* n. 49, para. 252. However, sometimes the Court does not establish a specific time frame. Instead it requires states to conduct such identification within a 'reasonable time'. See: IACtHR, *Mapiripán Massacre* v. *Colombia, supra* n. 8, para. 335 (8).

206 IACtHR, *Sawhoyamaxa Indigenous Community* v. *Paraguay, supra* n. 111, para. 73; IACtHR, *Saramaka People* v. *Suriname, supra* n. 117, para. 188.

207 Úbeda de Torres, *supra* n. 189, p. 118.

208 McKay, *supra* n. 6, p. 935.

209 IACtHR, *Aloeboetoe et al.* v. *Suriname, supra* n. 14, para. 19, 83.

210 IACtHR, *Sawhoyamaxa Indigenous Community* v. *Paraguay, supra* n. 111, para. 204; IACtHR, Xákmok Kásek Indigenous Community v. *Paraguay, supra* n. 121, para. 278; IACtHR, *The Kaliña and Lokono Peoples* v. *Suriname, supra* n. 118, para. 273.

211 Antkowiak, *supra* n. 2, p. 385.

212 IACtHR, *Ituango Massacres* v. *Colombia, supra* n. 50, para. 361, 407.

5.3.2 Society as a Beneficiary

The IACtHR has also recognised 'society as a whole' as a beneficiary of reparations.[213] The Court usually goes beyond the individual-centric doctrine of human rights to embrace a wider set of beneficiaries when the cases at hand indicate an evident pattern of systematic violations.[214] Consequently, in these cases, the Court usually orders measures in the form of guarantees of non-repetition, whose main aim is to repair beyond the harm suffered by the direct victims and to attempt to serve as both a remedy for society and a means for combating impunity.[215]

5.4 Assessment of Harm

Although the IACtHR's Rules do not offer guidelines as to how to assess the harm, the Court has developed different techniques and established some relevant factors to widen its assessment. First of all, the Court has established that the principle of 'sana *crítica*' guides the assessment of evidence, including the assessment of evidence related to the reparations stage. The Court considers this principle to be an adequate one in the field of international human rights because it provides for broad flexibility in the assessment of evidence.[216] The *sana crítica*, which is common to the Hispanic civil legal traditions, refers to 'a system for evaluating the weight of evidence [...] in accordance with the rules of logic and experience'.[217] The *sana crítica* is commonly used when a tribunal lacks specific rules prescribing a particular weight to certain pieces of evidence, as in the case of the IACtHR.[218] This principle requires judges to explain the considerations, based on which they weighed evidence, and thereby represents a middle point between rigidity regarding evidentiary rules on one hand and arbitrary decisions on the other.[219] In order to refer to this principle, the Court sometimes uses different wording,[220] such as 'sana crítica',[221] 'sound judicial

213 Schönsteiner, J., "Dissuasive Measures and the "Society as a Whole": A Working Theory of Reparations in the Inter-American Court of Human Rights", 23 *American University International Law Review* (2011), p. 164.

214 Ibid., p. 138.

215 Ibid., p. 129, 141-144, 149.

216 IACtHR, *Mapiripán Massacre* v. *Colombia, supra* n. 8, para. 73.

217 Paúl, A., "Sana Crítica: The System for Weighing Evidence Utilized by the Inter-American Court of Human Rights", 18 *Buffalo Human Rights Law Review* (2012), p. 193.

218 Ibid., p. 205, 212.

219 Ibid., p. 208, 212-213, 220.

220 Ibid., p. 193-194.

221 IACtHR (Judgment) 30 November 2016, *Members of the Village of Chichupac and Neighboring Communities of the Municipality of Rabinal* v. *Guatemala*, para. 74; IACtHR, *Vereda La Esperanza* v. *Colombia, supra* n. 85, para. 49; IACtHR, *Garífuna Triunfo de la Cruz Community and its Members* v. *Honduras, supra* n. 122, para. 36, 38.

discretion',[222] 'sound criticism',[223] 'competent analysis',[224] 'reasonable credit',[225] and 'reasoned judgment'.[226] The Court also pays attention to the specific circumstances of the case and 'to the limits imposed by respect for legal certainty and the equality of the parties'.[227] Furthermore, the Court also takes into account the traditions and culture of the victims. For instance, in cases related to indigenous and tribal victims, the Court has taken into account their culture, communal understanding, intergenerational relations with the members of the community and their worldview.[228]

In assessing the harm, the rules related to causation, the standard of proof and beneficiaries' eligibility provide some degree of guidance.[229] As such, the Court has upheld that in assessing the harm, it takes into consideration the evidence and arguments brought before it by the parties, as well as its case law.[230] Although the principle of equity[231] is widely used by the Court in assessing material and non-material damage, the Court uses it in line with the clear evidence of the damage

---

222 IACtHR, *The Kaliña and Lokono Peoples* v. *Suriname*, *supra* n. 118, para. 24, 27; IACtHR, *Rodríguez Vera et al. (the disappeared from the Palace of Justice)* v. *Colombia*, *supra* n. 69, para. 50, 74-75; IACtHR, *Afro-Descendant Communities displaced from the Cacarica River Basin (Operation Genesis)* v. *Colombia*, *supra* n. 205, para. 43; IACtHR, *Santo Domingo Massacre* v. *Colombia*, *supra* n. 72, para. 41; IACtHR, *Gudiel Álvarez et al. ("Diario Militar")* v. *Guatemala*, *supra* n. 78, para. 35.

223 IACtHR (Judgment) 8 March 1998, *"White Van" (Paniagua-Morales et al.)* v. *Guatemala*, para. 76; IACtHR, *Saramaka People* v. *Suriname*, *supra* n. 117, para. 63, 70-711; IACtHR, *Ituango Massacres* v. *Colombia*, *supra* n. 50, para. 109, 113-117; IACtHR, *Pueblo Bello Massacre* v. *Colombia*, *supra* n. 20, para. 63-64.

224 IACtHR, *"Las Dos Erres" Massacre* v. *Guatemala*, *supra* n. 79, para. 55, 60; IACtHR, *Yakye Axa Indigenous Community* v. *Paraguay*, *supra* n. 44, para. 32, 43, 45; IACtHR, *Mapiripán Massacre* v. *Colombia*, *supra* n. 8, para. 73; IACtHR, *"Juvenile Reeducation Institute"* v. *Paraguay*, *supra* n. 38, para. 64; IACtHR, *Miguel Castro-Castro Prison* v. *Peru*, *supra* n. 77, para. 166,185; IACtHR, *Caracazo* v. *Venezuela*, *supra* n. 43, para. 39; IACtHR, *Mayagna (Sumo) Awas Tingni Community* v. *Nicaragua*, *supra* n. 47, para. 88, 90, 102.

225 IACtHR, *La Cantuta* v. *Peru*, *supra* n. 77, para. 59, 64; IACtHR, *Sawhoyamaxa Indigenous Community* v. *Paraguay*, *supra* n. 111, para. 33.

226 IACtHR, *La Rochela Massacre* v. *Colombia*, *supra* n. 84, para. 55; IACtHR, *"Juvenile Reeducation Institute"* v. *Paraguay*, *supra* n. 38, para. 65.

227 IACtHR, "*White Van" (Paniagua-Morales et al.)* v. *Guatemala*, *supra* n. 43, para. 51.

228 Rodríguez-Garavito, C., "Ethno Reparations: Collective Ethnic Justice and the Reparation of Indigenous Peoples and Black Communities in Colombia", in M. Bergsmo et al, *Distributive Justice in Transitions* (Oslo, Torkel Opshal Academic EPublisher 2010), p. 349, 360.

229 Barker, J., "The different forms of reparation: compensation", in J. Crawford, A. Pellet and S. Olleson (eds.), *The Law on International Responsibility* (Oxford, OUP 2010), p. 603.

230 IACtHR, *19 Merchants* v. *Colombia*, *supra* n. 43, para. 236; IACtHR, *Yakye Axa Indigenous Community* v. *Paraguay*, *supra* n. 44, para. 193; IACtHR, *La Cantuta* v. *Peru*, *supra* n. 77, para. 213; IACtHR, *Garífuna Triunfo de la Cruz Community and its Members* v. *Honduras*, *supra* n. 122, para. 289.

231 As explained in Chapter II section 3.2.1, the principle of equity refers to a prudent and discretional estimate of the monetary equivalent of the damage.

suffered and its relationship with the violations which have been proven.[232] Finally, in some cases, the Court has requested the assistance of an actuarial expert in order to make an informed decision regarding the amount of reparations to be granted.[233] In the *Miguel Castro-Castro Prison* case, upon the determination of four categories of harm and their respective compensation, the Court delegated the assessment of injuries and handicaps to domestic bodies specializing in such assessments.[234]

Types of harm

The IACtHR has recognized that certain violations, such as the prolonged denial of justice (impunity), produce different forms of harm, such as individual material and non-material harm, as well as harm in social relations within families and communities.[235] As such, the Court has recognised material damage and moral damages,[236] as well as collective harm[237] and even cultural harm, particularly in cases related to indigenous and tribal peoples.[238] Since the assessment of different harms requires different techniques, the following sections will elaborate on this process. For instance, when awarding compensation for material damages, the Court adopts an objective approach in assessing the damages,[239] while it applies the principle of equity in the case of non-material damages.[240]

5.4.1 Moral Harm

Moral harm includes the suffering, grief, anguish and sadness experienced by the direct victim and his or her immediate relatives,[241] the impairment of values that have great significance for an individual, as well as the non-pecuniary changes in the living conditions of the victim or his or her family.[242] In general, moral damage cannot be calculated mathematically by using a fixed formula.[243] The Court is sometimes

---

232 IACtHR, *The Kichwa Indigenous People of Sarayaku* v. *Ecuador*, *supra* n. 118, para. 314.

233 IACtHR, *El Amparo* v. *Venezuela, supra* n. 183, para. 12.

234 IACtHR, *Miguel Castro-Castro Prison* v. *Peru, supra* n. 77, para. 424-433.

235 IACtHR, *"Las Dos Erres" Massacre* v. *Guatemala, supra* n. 79, para. 226.

236 Roht-Arriaza, *supra* n. 2, p. 661-662.

237 IACtHR, *Afro-Descendant Communities displaced from the Cacarica River Basin (Operation Genesis)* v. *Colombia, supra* n. 205, para. 459.

238 IACtHR (Judgment) 24 April 2004, *Plan de Sánchez Massacre* v. *Guatemala*, para. 47 (2); IACtHR, *Plan de Sánchez Massacre* v. *Guatemala, supra* n. 45, para. 49 (12).

239 IACtHR, *Plan de Sánchez Massacre* v. *Guatemala,* Separate Opinion of Judge Garcia-Ramirez, *supra* n. 45, para. 14-17.

240 Antkowiak, *supra* n. 2, p. 396.

241 IACtHR, *Caracazo* v. *Venezuela, supra* n. 43, para. 50.

242 IACtHR, *Members of the Village of Chichupac and Neighboring Communities of the Municipality of Rabinal* v. *Guatemala, supra* n. 221, para. 324.

243 Pasqualucci, *supra* n. 2, p. 34.

guided by expert opinions in order to understand the magnitude of the emotional consequences suffered by the next of kin.[244] In general, the Court determines the moral damage stemming from the suffering of victims by means of a rebuttable presumption,[245] especially in cases related to GVHR and their impunity.[246] If the state does not rebut it, the Court considers the presumption to be well grounded.[247]

According to the Court, moral damages can be repaired by means of monetary compensation, the delivery of goods or services, and other measures to commemorate and dignify victims, as well as measures aiming to ensure that similar violations will not reoccur.[248] If the chosen measure is compensation, it is calculated in terms of 'fairness' (the principle of equity)[249] and it takes the circumstances of the case into account.[250] It must be stated that the principle of equity is a subjective notion that is interpreted in accordance with the composition of the bench.[251] Furthermore, Pasqualucci affirms that the Court decreases the amount of reparations awarded for moral damages when the state accepts its responsibility.[252] And according to Antkowiak, the Court also reduces the amount awarded for moral damages in cases involving multiple victims.[253]

5.4.2 Material Harm

The Court has asserted that material damage entails the loss of a victim's income,[254] the expenses incurred as a result of the violations, and any other pecuniary consequences

244 IACtHR, *Las Palmeras* v. *Colombia, supra* n. 46, para. 50; Pasqualucci, *supra* n. 2, p. 232.

245 IACtHR, *Gudiel Álvarez et al. ("Diario Militar")* v. *Guatemala, supra* n. 78, para. 286-288; IACtHR, *Peasant Community of Santa Bárbara* v. *Peru, supra* n. 60, para. 274; IACtHR, *Members of the Village of Chichupac and Neighboring Communities of the Municipality of Rabinal* v. *Guatemala, supra* n. 221, para. 161.

246 IACtHR, *Caracazo* v. *Venezuela, supra* n. 43, para. 50.

247 IACtHR, *Peasant Community of Santa Bárbara* v. *Peru, supra* n. 60, para. 276; IACtHR, *Members of the Village of Chichupac and Neighboring Communities of the Municipality of Rabinal* v. *Guatemala, supra* n. 221, para. 162.

248 IACtHR, *Moiwana Community* v. *Suriname, supra* n. 44, para. 191; IACtHR (Judgment) 26 May 2001, *"Street Children" (Villagrán-Morales et al.)* v. *Guatemala*, para. 84.

249 IACtHR, *19 Merchants* v. *Colombia, supra* n. 43, para. 250.

250 IACtHR, *El Amparo* v. *Venezuela, supra* n. 183, para. 73.

251 Donoso, *supra* n. 48, p. 44.

252 Pasqualucci, *supra* n. 2, p. 35.

253 Antkowiak, *supra* n. 2, p. 396.

254 In cases concerning deceased victims, this becomes the income that the deceased would have received during the remainder of their expected lives.

that have a causal link with the facts of the case.[255] While the Court has claimed that it does not have full discretion in determining financial awards,[256] it has not adopted a single method of quantifying material damage. Yet, the Court has referred to the need to 'carefully examine' the evidence available to it[257] and consequently to make a 'prudent estimate' based on a case's factual circumstances. Furthermore, the Court has attempted to develop criteria to calculate certain material harm, yet these criteria are not rigid.[258]

For instance, in assessing the compensation for violations of the right to life, the Court takes into account factors such as the deceased's age, health, living conditions, life expectancy, place of residence, as well as the extent of the relationship between the deceased and the beneficiary, if applicable.[259] First of all, the Court uses the information provided by the parties to conduct its assessment.[260] In the absence of proof of a victim's salary, the Court takes into account the average life expectancy in the country in question,[261] as well as the minimum wage established by national law.[262]

In addition, the Court has acknowledged that, in certain cases, reasonable and sufficient evidence does not exist and, consequently, the Court first presumes material harm and thus affords compensation based on the principle of equity.[263] The Court

255 IACtHR (Judgment) 24 November 2011, *Barrios Family* v. *Venezuela*, para. 359; IACtHR, *19 Merchants* v. *Colombia*, *supra* n. 43, para. 236; IACtHR, *Yakye Axa Indigenous Community* v. *Paraguay, supra* n. 44, para. 193; IACtHR, *La Cantuta* v. *Peru*, *supra* n. 77, para. 213; IACtHR, Xákmok Kásek Indigenous Community v. *Paraguay, supra* n. 121, para. 325; IACtHR, *Gomes Lund et al. ("Guerrilha Do Araguaia")* v. *Brazil*, *supra* n. 49, para. 298; IACtHR, *The Kichwa Indigenous People of Sarayaku* v. *Ecuador*, *supra* n. 118, para. 309; IACtHR, *Rodríguez Vera et al. (the disappeared from the Palace of Justice)* v. *Colombia*, *supra* n. 69, para. 591; IACtHR, *Peasant Community of Santa Bárbara* v. *Peru*, *supra* n. 60, para. 342; IACtHR, *Members of the Village of Chichupac and Neighboring Communities of the Municipality of Rabinal* v. *Guatemala*, *supra* n. 221, para. 324; IACtHR, *Garífuna Triunfo de la Cruz Community and its Members* v. *Honduras*, *supra* n. 122, para. 289.

256 IACtHR, *Aloeboetoe et al.* v. *Suriname*, *supra* n. 14, para. 87; IACtHR, *The Kichwa Indigenous People of Sarayaku* v. *Ecuador*, *supra* n. 118, para. 314.

257 IACtHR (Judgment) 6 December 2001, *Las Palmeras* v. *Colombia*, para. 47; IACtHR, *19 Merchants* v. *Colombia*, *supra* n. 43, para. 71, 72; IACtHR, *Plan de Sánchez Massacre* v. *Guatemala*, *supra* n. 45, para. 38; IACtHR, *Mapiripán Massacre* v. *Colombia*, *supra* n. 8, para. 75,76; IACtHR, *Members of the Village of Chichupac and Neighboring Communities of the Municipality of Rabinal* v. *Guatemala*, *supra* n. 221, para. 66.

258 Pasqualucci, *supra* n. 2, p. 26, footnote 142.

259 IACtHR, *Las Palmeras* v. *Colombia*, *supra* n. 46, para. 56, 58; IACtHR, *Montero-Aranguren et al. (Detention Center of Catia)* v. *Venezuela*, *supra* n. 345, para. 127; IACtHR, *El Amparo* v. *Venezuela*, *supra* n. 183, para. 28; Shelton, *supra* n. 10, p. 147; Pasqualucci, *supra* n. 2, p. 230.

260 IACtHR, *El Amparo* v. *Venezuela*, *supra* n. 183, para. 49.

261 IACtHR (Judgment) 22 February 2002, *Bámaca Velásquez* v. *Guatemala*, para. 51 (b); IACtHR, *Caracazo* v. *Venezuela*, *supra* n. 43, para. 29.

262 IACtHR, *"Street Children" (Villagrán-Morales et al.)* v. *Guatelama*, *supra* n. 248, para. 79.

263 IACtHR, "*White Van" (Paniagua-Morales et al.*) v. *Guatemala*, *supra* n. 43, para. 119.

also presumes the following in order to assess material harm: i) adult persons with a regular income 'spend most of that income providing for the needs' of their families; ii) a deceased victim's relatives cover the costs of the funeral; and iii) an adult person carries out economic activities that allow him/her to earn at least the minimum legal wage.[264] Finally, upon finding a violation, especially one of a GVHR nature, expenses and costs on the part of the family can be inferred regardless of clear evidence.[265]

5.4.3 Collective Harm

Several scholars have upheld that collective reparations aim to redress collective harm.[266] However, the IACtHR seems to have ordered collective reparations both in cases where collective harm has been recognized[267] and in cases where it has not.[268]

For instance, in the *Aloeboetoe* case, the Court only recognised the individual harm inflicted on the direct victims and their next of kin. Yet, it ordered measures aimed at benefiting the whole tribal people.[269] In contrast, in the *Plan de Sánchez Massacre* case, the Court recognized the collective harm suffered by the members of the communities affected by the massacre and, accordingly, it granted collective reparations.[270] At times, the Court has not awarded collective reparations despite having acknowledged collective harm in a given case, such as in the *Afro-descendant communities displaced from the Cacarica River Basin* case.[271]

Significantly, the Court refers to collective harm by means of stating that a given violation has inflicted harm on members of certain communities,[272] on a

---

264 IACtHR, *Caracazo* v. *Venezuela, supra* n. 43, para. 50.

265 IACtHR (Judgment) 29 May 2014, *Norín Catrimán et al. (Leaders, members and activist of the Mapuche Indigenous People)* v. *Chile,* para. 444.

266 Rosenfeld, F., "Collective Reparations for Victims of Armed Conflicts", 92 *International Review of the Red Cross* (2010), p. 732; Roht-Arriaza, N. and Orlovsky, K., *A Complementary Relationship: Reparations and Development,* International Center for Transitional Justice, 3 (July 2009), Available at: <https://www.ictj.org/sites/default/files/ICTJ-Development-Reparations-ResearchBrief-2009-English.pdf>; Mayeux and Mirabal, *supra* n. 5, p. 1.

267 IACtHR, *Mayagna (Sumo) Awas Tingni Community* v. *Nicaragua, supra* n. 47, Operative para. 173 (1-7); IACtHR, *Moiwana Community* v. *Suriname, supra* n. 44, Operative para. 233 (1-4) and 213-215.

268 IACtHR, *Aloeboetoe et al.* v. *Suriname, supra* n. 14, para. 83-84.

269 Ibid., para. 96.

270 IACtHR, *Plan de Sánchez Massacre* v. *Guatemala, supra* n. 45, para. 110.

271 IACtHR, *Afro-Descendant Communities displaced from the Cacarica River Basin (Operation Genesis)* v. *Colombia, supra* n. 205, para. 459, 476. However, general measures of reparation were awarded. See: para. 444-447, 459.

272 IACtHR, *Saramaka People* v. *Suriname, supra* n. 117, para.188, 189; IACtHR, *Mayagna (Sumo) Awas Tingni Community* v. *Nicaragua, supra* n. 47, para. 139, 153-155; IACtHR, Xákmok Kásek Indigenous Community v. *Paraguay, supra* n. 121, para. 278.

community itself,[273] or by declaring a community to be the injured party in a given case.[274] Significantly, the Court usually infers this harm without further elaborating on how it assesses it. Consequently, victims are not required to prove the existence of harm.

5.5 Standard of Proof

Neither the burden of proof nor the standard of proof required to prove an alleged damage are clarified by the IACtHR's Rules. Yet, the IACtHR has stated that the *onus probandi* principle applies as a matter of the general principle of law.[275] Furthermore, the Court has established a flexible standard of proof through its rulings.[276] Although it embraces the *onus probandi* principle, in some cases the IACtHR has shifted the burden of proof during the reparations stage,[277] especially when establishing moral harm.[278] Such a shifting of the burden of proof is intended to ameliorate the inequalities of the parties in gathering evidence.[279] As such, the Court has affirmed that 'the State's defense cannot rest on the impossibility for the plaintiff to provide evidence, when it is the State that controls the means to clarify incidents that took place within its territory'.[280]

The Court has neither adopted a clear standard of proof nor applied one systematically throughout its jurisprudence.[281] This seems to correspond to the fact that, in general, international tribunals do not use the notion of standard of proof.[282] However, Paúl has submitted that the Court uses, implicitly, a common standard of

---

273 IACtHR (Judgment) 14 October 2014, *Indigenous Communities Kuna of Madungandí and Emberá of Bayano and its members* v. *Panama*, para. 209; IACtHR, *The Kichwa Indigenous People of Sarayaku* v. *Ecuador*, *supra* n. 118, para. 284; IACtHR, *Garífuna Punta Piedra Community and its Members* v. *Honduras*, *supra* n. 122, para. 317, 372 (6).

274 IACtHR, *Moiwana Community* v. *Suriname*, *supra* n. 44, para. 176; IACtHR, *Sawhoyamaxa Indigenous Community* v. *Paraguay*, *supra* n. 111, para. 204.

275 IACtHR, *Las Palmeras* v. *Colombia, supra* n. 257, para. 41.

276 IACtHR, *Aloeboetoe et al.* v. *Suriname*, *supra* n. 14, para. 71; IACtHR, *"Street Children" (Villagrán-Morales et al.)* v. *Guatelama*, *supra* n. 248, para. 68; IACtHR, "*White Van" (Paniagua-Morales et al.*) v. *Guatemala*, *supra* n. 43, para. 86.

277 The Court has also shifted the burden of proof in relation to the merits. See: Chapter 2.

278 IACtHR, *Aloeboetoe et al.* v. *Suriname*, *supra* n. 14, para. 71, 76; IACtHR, *Loayza Tamayo* v. *Peru*, *supra* n. 83, para. 140.

279 Riddell, A., "Evidence, Fact-Finding, and Experts", in C. Romano, K. Alter and Y. Shany (eds.), *The Oxford Handbook of International Adjudication* (Oxford, OUP 2015), p. 859.

280 IACtHR, *Barrios Family* v. *Venezuela*, *supra* n. 255, para. 141; IACtHR, *Afro-Descendant Communities displaced from the Cacarica River Basin (Operation Genesis)* v. *Colombia*, *supra* n. 205, para. 270; IACtHR, *Rodríguez Vera et al. (the disappeared from the Palace of Justice)* v. *Colombia*, *supra* n. 69, para. 81, 230.

281 Instead, the Court has applied several standard of proof in different cases.

282 Paúl, A., "In search of the standards of proof applied by the Inter-American Court of Human Rights", 55 *Revista Instituto Interamericano de Derechos Humanos* (2012), p. 62.

proof in the majority of its cases: the standard of preponderance of evidence.[283] This standard is lower than the standards of 'beyond reasonable doubt' and of 'clear and convincing evidence'.[284]

The Court determines the applicable standard by taking into account the nature, characteristics and seriousness of the cases.[285] In addition, Paúl suggests that the composition of the bench may play a role in deciding the applicable standard of proof in a given case.[286] The Court has also stated that the 'standards of proof are less formal in an international legal proceeding than in a domestic one'.[287] Further, the Court has affirmed that it has the power 'to evaluate evidence freely' and does not need 'to adopt a rigid determination of the amount required' to prove a fact.[288] This suggests a great degree of flexibility for the Court to adopt different standards of proof.

In this light Neuman has asserted that the standard of proof has been very informal and flexible, especially during the IACtHR's early jurisprudence.[289] Perhaps the informality to which Neuman refers is due to the fact that the Court has avoided any excessive burden of proof in some cases, although not always in a consistent manner. In light of this, Judge Cançado Trindade has upheld that an excessive burden of proof or 'probatio diabolica' is incompatible with international human rights law.[290] In addition, the Court has generally used presumptions and the criteria of probabilistic reasoning when assessing evidence. Both judicial notions directly impact the standard of proof applicable by the Court (balance of probabilities) and may help to give the wrong impression that the Court uses a lower standard of proof.[291]

Despite the Court's flexibility regarding the standard of proof that is applicable to reparations, the Court has usually stated that allegations regarding violations need to meet certain evidentiary standards in relation to the 'degree of quality, certainty and sufficiency';[292] in other words, they need to meet a certain standard of proof. As

---

283 This standard is usually applied when a tribunal faces the absent of explicit rules: Ibid., p. 57, 60, 63.

284 Ibid., p. 63.

285 IACtHR, *Velasquez Rodriguez* v. *Honduras*, *supra* n. 33, para. 128; IACtHR, *Rodríguez Vera et al. (the disappeared from the Palace of Justice)* v. *Colombia*, *supra* n. 69, para. 81.

286 Paúl, *supra* n. 282, p. 75.

287 IACtHR, *Velasquez Rodriguez* v. *Honduras*, *supra* n. 33, para. 128.

288 IACtHR, *Barrios Family* v. *Venezuela*, *supra* n. 255, para. 141; IACtHR, *Rodríguez Vera et al. (the disappeared from the Palace of Justice)* v. *Colombia*, *supra* n. 69, para. 81.

289 Neuman, G.L., "Import, Export and Regional Consent in the Inter-American Court of Human Rights" 19 *European Journal of International Law* (2008), p. 108.

290 IACtHR (Judgment Interpretation) 30 November 2007, *La Cantuta* v. *Peru,* Concurring opinion of Judge A.A. Cançado Trindade, para. 45; IACtHR, *Sawhoyamaxa Indigenous Community* v. *Paraguay*, Separate opinion by Judge A.A. Cançado Trindade, *supra* n. 111, para. 21. *Probatio diabolica* refers to a requirement of evidence that it is impossible to meet.

291 Paúl, *supra* n. 282, p. 75-76, 82-84.

292 IACtHR, *Norín Catrimán et al. (Leaders, members and activist of the Mapuche Indigenous People)* v. *Chile, supra* n. 265, para. 113.

will be discussed below, such a standard depends on whether the damage is moral or material.

In relation to the determination and assessment of the harm

The IACtHR generally uses rebuttable presumptions (*iuris tantum*) as a standard of proof to establish and assess moral harm. As a general rule, the Court presumes that moral harm has been suffered by the direct victims and their next of kin in cases related to GVHR[293] and their impunity.[294] This presumption is based on the ground that such suffering is evident.[295] While the presumption of harm extends to close relatives, other siblings or dependents would have to prove the moral damage that they allege.[296] The Court requires, however, that the identity of the said relatives be proven in order for them to be able to claim moral harm stemming from the direct victim.[297]

It is important to mention that when such moral harm is presumed, the Court shifts the burden of proof onto the state, which may rebut such a presumption.[298] In order to establish and assess the harm alleged by distant relatives or dependants, evidence needs to be adduced. In particular, the Court requires dependants to meet the following criteria: i) proof of regular payments in cash or in kind, 'made by the victim to the claimant regardless of whether or not they constituted a legal obligation to pay support', as well as ii) a close relationship between the victim and the claimant and iii) proof that the claimant is in financial need.[299] Furthermore, the Court has considered that presumptions, testimonies and expert reports are sufficient to prove

293 IACtHR, *Aloeboetoe et al.* v. *Suriname*, *supra* n. 14, para. 71, 76; IACtHR, "*White Van" (Paniagua-Morales et al.*) v. *Guatemala*, *supra* n. 43, para. 125, 158; IACtHR, "*White Van" (Paniagua-Morales et al.*) v. *Guatemala*, Separate opinion Judge De Roux Rengifo, *supra* n. 43, p. 1; IACtHR, *Mapiripán Massacre* v. *Colombia*, *supra* n. 8, para. 146; IACtHR, *La Cantuta* v. *Peru*, *supra* n. 77, para. 217-218; IACtHR, *Caracazo* v. *Venezuela*, *supra* n. 43, para. 50 (e); IACtHR, *Pueblo Bello Massacre* v. *Colombia*, *supra* n. 20, para. 257; Pasqualucci, J.M., *The Practice and Procedure of the Inter-American Court of Human Rights* (New York, CUP 2do edition, 2013), p. 194.

294 IACtHR, *Las Palmeras* v. *Colombia*, *supra* n. 46, para. 55; IACtHR, *Rodríguez Vera et al. (the disappeared from the Palace of Justice)* v. *Colombia*, *supra* n. 69, para. 534.

295 IACtHR, *Río Negro Massacres* v. *Guatemala*, *supra* n. 65, para. 307; IACtHR, *Rodríguez Vera et al. (the disappeared from the Palace of Justice)* v. *Colombia*, *supra* n. 69, para. 533; IACtHR, *Members of the Village of Chichupac and Neighboring Communities of the Municipality of Rabinal* v. *Guatemala*, *supra* n. 221, para. 324. Recently, the Court has stated that the presumption of moral harm can be applied to any human rights violation regardless of whether it is grave or not. See: IACtHR, *Members of the Village of Chichupac and Neighboring Communities of the Municipality of Rabinal* v. *Guatemala*, *supra* n. 221, para. 324.

296 IACtHR, *Aloeboetoe et al.* v. *Suriname*, *supra* n. 14, para. 71.

297 IACtHR, "*White Van" (Paniagua-Morales et al.*) v. *Guatemala*, *supra* n. 43, para. 143.

298 IACtHR, *Aloeboetoe et al.* v. *Suriname*, *supra* n. 14, para. 71; IACtHR, "*White Van" (Paniagua-Morales et al.*) v. *Guatemala*, *supra* n. 43, para. 125.

299 IACtHR, *Aloeboetoe et al.* v. *Suriname*, *supra* n. 14, para. 68.

moral damage.[300] The Court has also emphasised that not only is documentary evidence needed to prove a fact. In addition, the parties need to demonstrate the relationship between those documents and the harm claimed.[301]

On the other hand, the Court usually requires sufficient evidence[302] or reasonable and satisfactory evidence to prove material damage.[303] This implies that the Court accepts the sufficiency of evidence as the standard of proof (*l'intime conviction du juge*) in relation to material damage.[304] Significantly, the Court requires the parties to provide clear evidence of 'the relationship between the pecuniary claim and the facts of the case and the violations alleged.'[305] In this light, victims must substantiate the relevance of the claimed measure. Finally, the Court sometimes uses presumptions to determine and assess material damage, even if the latter is not supported by documentary evidence. For instance, the IACtHR usually presumes that an adult victim 'carries out productive activities and perceives, at least, an income equivalent to minimum legal wage in the country involved'.[306]

In relation to victims' identification

The identification of victims is closely related to the determination of both the facts and the harm. Direct victims are usually identified through evidence proving certain violations, whereas most of the indirect victims are identified under the 'presumption test'.[307] Since the IACtHR mainly uses two standards of proof with regard to the merits of the cases, namely the sufficiency of evidence[308] and the preponderance of evidence,[309] it could be concluded that these two standards are mostly used when identifying direct victims.[310] When using presumptions to determine indirect victims, the Court prevents the victims from adducing any other evidence besides that which

300 IACtHR, *Plan de Sánchez Massacre* v. *Guatemala, supra* n. 45, para. 78; IACtHR, *Santo Domingo Massacre* v. *Colombia, supra* n. 72, para. 242, 244.

301 IACtHR, *Indigenous Communities Kuna of Madungandí and Emberá of Bayano and its memebrs* v. *Panama, supra* n. 273, para. 250.

302 IACtHR, *Ituango Massacres* v. *Colombia, supra* n. 50, para. 257; IACtHR, *Gudiel Álvarez et al. ("Diario Militar")* v. *Guatemala, supra* n. 78, para. 43; IACtHR, *Afro-Descendant Communities displaced from the Cacarica River Basin (Operation Genesis)* v. *Colombia, supra* n. 205, para. 337; IACtHR, *Rodríguez Vera et al. (the disappeared from the Palace of Justice)* v. *Colombia, supra* n. 69, para. 159.

303 IACtHR, *Afro-Descendant Communities displaced from the Cacarica River Basin (Operation Genesis)* v. *Colombia, supra* n. 205, para. 279.

304 This is a higher standard than that of balance of probabilities.

305 IACtHR, *The Kichwa Indigenous People of Sarayaku* v. *Ecuador*, *supra* n. 118, para. 314.

306 IACtHR, *Caracazo* v. *Venezuela, supra* n. 43, para. 50 (d).

307 Pasqualucci, *supra* n. 293, p. 194.

308 Riddell, *supra* n. 279, p. 861-863.

309 Paúl, *supra* n. 282, p. 73, 82-84.

310 Although the Court has rejected the standard of beyond reasonable doubt, the Court has used it in relation to the merits in few cases. See: Paúl, *supra* n. 282, p. 70, 78.

proves the 'closeness of the family relationship', as well as evidence showing the efforts made by the family member to seek justice for the violations suffered by the direct victim.[311] For distant family members to be also recognized as victims, they need to prove that they have endured harm.[312] In its more recent jurisprudence, the Court has extended the presumption of harm to other siblings who are not direct relatives.[313] Finally, in cases related to IP, the Court allows statements to be used to prove the identity of victims and the existence of the alleged harm. Such statements need to be made by a recognized leader of the community together with two additional persons.[314]

Evidence

Despite being silent on the quality and the quantity of evidence that is required, the IACtHR's Rules establish that the parties need to offer evidence that is 'properly organized'[315] and 'opportune' 'so that [the Court] has the maximum information to evaluate the facts and substantiate its decisions'.[316] In addition, the Court may obtain evidence on its own motion and/or it may request additional evidence from the parties or from a specific body or authority.[317] From its jurisprudence, it becomes evident that the Court accepts not only documents and testimonies as evidence but also circumstantial evidence and presumptions,[318] but only when 'consistent conclusions about the facts can be inferred from them.'[319]

In general, the evidence presented by the parties to the cases is composed of documentary, expert and testimonial evidence.[320] Documentary evidence has included photographs,[321] videotapes,[322] the testimony of witnesses and expert witnesses,

311 IACtHR, *Bámaca Velásquez* v. *Guatemala, supra* n. 261, para. 163.

312 IACtHR, *Gomes Lund et al. ("Guerrilha Do Araguaia")* v. *Brazil, supra* n. 49, para. 235; IACtHR, *Barrios Family* v. *Venezuela, supra* n. 255, para. 302; IACtHR, *Gudiel Álvarez et al. ("Diario Militar")* v. *Guatemala, supra* n. 78, para. 286, 288; IACtHR, *Santo Domingo Massacre* v. *Colombia, supra* n. 72, para. 242; IACtHR, *Cruz Sánchez et al.* v. *Peru, supra* n. 201, para. 444; IACtHR, *Members of the Village of Chichupac and Neighboring Communities of the Municipality of Rabinal* v. *Guatemala, supra* n. 221, para. 161-162.

313 IACtHR, *Rodríguez Vera et al. (the disappeared from the Palace of Justice)* v. *Colombia, supra* n. 69, para. 533.

314 IACtHR, *Moiwana Community* v. *Suriname, supra* n. 44, para. 178.

315 Articles 40 (2) (b) and 41 (1) (b), IACtHR Rules.

316 IACtHR, *Velasquez Rodriguez* v. *Honduras, supra* n. 33, para. 148.

317 Article 58, IACtHR's Rules.

318 IACtHR, *Rodríguez Vera et al. (the disappeared from the Palace of Justice)* v. *Colombia, supra* n. 69, para. 81, 230.

319 IACtHR, *Afro-Descendant Communities displaced from the Cacarica River Basin (Operation Genesis)* v. *Colombia, supra* n. 205, para. 269.

320 IACtHR, *Ituango Massacres* v. *Colombia, supra* n. 50, para. 109.

321 IACtHR, *Caracazo* v. *Venezuela, supra* n. 102, para. 26.

322 IACtHR, *Caracazo* v. *Venezuela, supra* n. 43, para. 41.

whether in written or oral form,[323] the Court's observations upon an *in situ* visit,[324] and copies of birth certificates, as well as marriage and death certificates.[325] For instance, in the *Mayagna (Sumo) Awas Tingni* case, it could be inferred that the Court based its decision to grant CR on expert opinions which asserted that the 'physical health, mental health, and social health of indigenous peoples is linked to the concept of the land.'[326] Since the Court found a violation of the IPs' right to property with in regard to their traditional lands, it seems that the Court tried to repair the harm resulting from the violation by means of granting collective reparations even when the victims did not request them.

In addition, the Court has attributed special significance to reports of truth commissions as relevant evidence in the determination of facts and of states' international responsibility,[327] especially, but not only, in relation to Peru and Guatemala. In light of this, the Court has determined the existence of systematic practices, the political and historical backgrounds surrounding cases and even the living conditions of victims based on reports from truth commissions.[328]

Significantly, the Court has acknowledged that the claimants sometimes cannot prove the claimed harm due to the circumstances of the case. In the *Mapiripán Massacre* case, for instance, the Court acknowledged that the victims had been displaced from their community, due to which they could not provide enough documentation to prove certain material harm.[329] In cases related to indigenous and tribal peoples, the Court is usually flexible regarding the type of evidence needed to prove facts and damages. This is because indigenous and tribal peoples' perspectives

---

323 IACtHR, *Mayagna (Sumo) Awas Tingni Community* v. *Nicaragua, supra* n. 47, para. 83; IACtHR, *"White Van" (Paniagua-Morales et al.)* v. *Guatemala, supra* n. 43, para. 66-67; IACtHR, *Las Palmeras* v. *Colombia, supra* n. 46, para. 26-27; IACtHR, *Pueblo Bello Massacre* v. *Colombia, supra* n. 20, para. 65–66; IACtHR, *Miguel Castro-Castro Prison* v. *Peru, supra* n. 77, para. 86-87; IACtHR, Xákmok Kásek Indigenous Community v. *Paraguay, supra* n. 121, para. 16-17.

324 IACtHR, *Garífuna Punta Piedra Community and its Members* v. *Honduras, supra* n. 122, para. 70.

325 IACtHR, *Caracazo* v. *Venezuela, supra* n. 43, para. 63; IACtHR, *Plan de Sánchez Massacre* v. *Guatemala, supra* n. 45, para. 63.

326 IACtHR, *Mayagna (Sumo) Awas Tingni Community* v. *Nicaragua, supra* n. 47, para. 83 (d).

327 Ferrara, A., *Assessing the Long-term Impact of Truth Commissions: The Chilean Truth and Reconciliation Commission in Historical Perspective* (Abingdon/ New York, Routledge 2014), p. 131-138; Rodríguez-Pinzón, D., "The Inter-American Human Rights System and Transitional Processes" in A. Buyse, and M. Hamilton (eds.), *Transitional Jurisprudence and the ECHR: Justice, Politics and Rights* (Cambridge, CUP 2011), p. 247-248.

328 IACtHR, *Miguel Castro-Castro Prison* v. *Peru, supra* n. 77, para. 197; IACtHR, *La Cantuta* v. *Peru, supra* n. 77, para. 80 (1)-(16), 86-95; IACtHR, *Cruz Sánchez et al.* v. *Peru, supra* n. 201, para. 139; IACtHR, *Plan de Sánchez Massacre* v. *Guatemala, supra* n. 45, para. 45; IACtHR, *"Las Dos Erres" Massacre* v. *Guatemala, supra* n. 79, para. 70-83, 170-172; IACtHR, Río Negro Massacres v. *Guatemala, supra* n. 65, para. 56-67, 82-85; IACtHR, *Gudiel Álvarez et al. ("Diario Militar")* v. *Guatemala, supra* n. 78, para. 54-58, 199; IACtHR, *Members of the Village of Chichupac and Neighboring Communities of the Municipality of Rabinal* v. *Guatemala, supra* n. 221, para. 74-81, 84.

329 IACtHR, *Mapiripán Massacre* v. *Colombia, supra* n. 8, para. 266.

regarding their lives, including their respective economic capacities, differ greatly from the remainder of the population.[330] For instance, in the *Aloeboetoe* case, the Court took into consideration that the case related to a tribal 'community that lives in the jungle, whose members are practically illiterate and do not utilize written documents.'[331]

Furthermore, it is worth noting that some states have frustrated the work of the Court by not providing evidence or documentation, or by sending samples of low-quality evidence. These actions have been carried out with the intention of allowing the state to escape accountability for certain violations.[332] Such tactics, along with the nature of the violations and the fact that some victims cannot gather evidence, may be the reason for the Court to have adopted a flexible approach regarding the standard of proof. Finally, it must be stated that, in some cases, the Court remains silent with regard to the standard of proof or evidence that is required.[333] This is partially due to the fact that a state's acknowledgement of responsibility is enough for the Court to consider that the moral damages suffered by the direct victims have been proved.[334]

5.6 Causality

The causal connection is a principle of reparations that requires a connection between the claimed harm and the proven violations. As already mentioned in Chapter 2, there are two main groups of causation: factual causation (also known as '*sine qua non test*', 'cause-in-fact', and the 'but-for test') and legal causation, which is generally identified through three tests: directness, proximity and foreseeability.[335] Factual causation establishes whether the defendant state is responsible for certain violations, whilst legal causation establishes whether a responsible state has the obligation to repair a certain claimed harm.

The IACtHR does not require the responsible state to repair all possible consequences of a violation,[336] but rather the 'immediate effects'[337] or damage that

330 Pasqualucci, *supra* n. 2, p. 27.

331 IACtHR, *Aloeboetoe et al.* v. *Suriname*, *supra* n. 14, para. 72.

332 Tan, M.H., "Upholding Human Rights in the Hemisphere: Casting Down Impunity Through the Inter-American Court of Human Rights" 43 *Texas International Law Journal* (2008), p. 278.

333 IACtHR, *Mayagna (Sumo) Awas Tingni Community* v. *Nicaragua*, *supra* n. 47; IACtHR, *Barrios Altos* v. *Peru*, *supra* n. 77; IACtHR, *Plan de Sánchez Massacre* v. *Guatemala*, *supra* n. 45; IACtHR, *Mapiripán Massacre* v. *Colombia*, *supra* n. 8; IACtHR, *La Rochela Massacre* v. *Colombia*, *supra* n. 84; IACtHR, *Saramaka People* v. *Suriname*, *supra* n. 117; IACtHR, *"Las Dos Erres" Massacre* v. *Guatemala*, *supra* n. 79; IACtHR, Xákmok Kásek Indigenous Community v. *Paraguay*, *supra* n. 121; IACtHR, *Río Negro Massacres* v. *Guatemala*, *supra* n. 65.

334 IACtHR, *Aloeboetoe et al.* v. *Suriname*, *supra* n. 14, para. 52.

335 See Chapter II, Section on Causality.

336 IACtHR, *Aloeboetoe et al.* v. *Suriname*, *supra* n. 14, para. 48.

337 Ibid., para. 49.

is 'directly caused' by the violations.[338] Accordingly, only the damage that has a causal link with the facts of the case is to be repaired.[339] In addition, the Court has determined that 'reparations must have a causal link with the facts of the case, the alleged violations, the proven damages, as well as with the measures requested to repair the resulting damages.'[340] Yet, the Court has not adopted a uniform test or a standard of causality.[341] Instead, the Court uses different tests depending on whether the harm claimed is material or non-material. The Court implies the use of the proximity test for material harm, whereas it usually presumes causality in cases of non-material harm.[342]

It seems that the Court determines the required level of causality on a case-by-case basis and based on the available evidence. This is because similar violations do not always lead to similar consequences. For instance, in the *Diario Militar* case, the Court did not grant reparations for the allegation that the forced disappearances had led to the displacement of the victims' family members on the grounds of a lack of causality and available evidence.[343] In contrast, in the *Pueblo Bello* case which dealt with a massacre and enforced disappearances, the Court did find that

338 IACtHR, *Saramaka People* v. *Suriname*, *supra* n. 117, para. 199.

339 IACtHR, *19 Merchants* v. *Colombia*, *supra* n. 43, para. 236; IACtHR, *Yakye Axa Indigenous Community* v. *Paraguay*, *supra* n. 44, para. 193.

340 IACtHR, *"Las Dos Erres" Massacre* v. *Guatemala*, *supra* n. 79, para. 227; IACtHR, *Barrios Family* v. *Venezuela*, *supra* n. 255, para. 316; IACtHR, *The Kichwa Indigenous People of Sarayaku* v. *Ecuador*, *supra* n. 118, para. 281; IACtHR, *Río Negro Massacres* v. *Guatemala*, *supra* n. 65, para. 247; IACtHR, *Massacres of El Mozote and neighboring locations* v. *El Salvador*, *supra* n. 85, para. 304; IACtHR, *Gudiel Álvarez et al. ("Diario Militar")* v. *Guatemala*, *supra* n. 78, para. 322; IACtHR, *Santo Domingo Massacre* v. *Colombia*, *supra* n. 72, para. 291; IACtHR, *The Kaliña and Lokono Peoples* v. *Suriname*, *supra* n. 118, para. 270; IACtHR, *Afro-Descendant Communities displaced from the Cacarica River Basin (Operation Genesis)* v. *Colombia*, *supra* n. 205, para. 411; IACtHR, *Indigenous Communities Kuna of Madungandí and Emberá of Bayano and its memebrs* v. *Panama*, *supra* n. 273, para. 205; IACtHR, *Rodríguez Vera et al. (the disappeared from the Palace of Justice)* v. *Colombia*, *supra* n. 69, para. 544; IACtHR, *Cruz Sánchez et al.* v. *Peru*, *supra* n. 201, para. 453; IACtHR, *Peasant Community of Santa Bárbara* v. *Peru*, *supra* n. 60, para. 283; IACtHR, *Garífuna Punta Piedra Community and its Members* v. *Honduras*, *supra* n. 122, para. 314; IACtHR, *Garífuna Triunfo de la Cruz Community and its Members* v. *Honduras*, *supra* n. 122, para. 254; IACtHR, *Members of the Village of Chichupac and Neighboring Communities of the Municipality of Rabinal* v. *Guatemala*, *supra* n. 221, para. 267.

341 Contreras-Garduño and Fraser, *supra*. n. 166, p. 196.

342 Yet, in some cases the Court uses presumptions to meet the proximity case. For instance, in the *El Mozote and neighbouring locations* case, the Court stated that it did not 'not have any evidence to prove the loss of earnings and the consequential losses suffered by the victims in this case. However, the Court considers it logical that, in cases such as this one, gathering evidence to prove this type of material loss and submitting it to the Court is a complex task'. Thus, the Court assumed that the violations declared in the judgment implied 'serious pecuniary consequences'. See: IACtHR, *Massacres of El Mozote and neighboring locations* v. *El Salvador*, *supra* n. 85, para. 383.

343 IACtHR, *Gudiel Álvarez et al. ("Diario Militar")* v. *Guatemala*, *supra* n. 78, para. 307.

the violations had led to several victims having to flee.[344] Furthermore, the Court does not always explicitly refer to the need for a causal link between the violations and the damage claimed. Hence, an analysis of causality is sometimes omitted in its judgments.[345] When the Court omits such an analysis, in most cases the state has already acknowledged its full or partial responsibility for the claimed violations.[346] This may explain why, in some cases, there is no assessment of causality.

Finally, throughout the cases, it is clear that most discussions on causation are led by the parties and chiefly relate to factual causation (whether the actions or omissions of a given state have a causal link to the alleged violations).[347] In addition, some Judges' separate opinions have also addressed factual causation at length. For instance, in the *Yakye Axa Indigenous Community* case, Judges Cançado Trindade and M.E. Ventura Robles stated that there existed a clear causal link between the community being deprived of its traditional lands and the death of some of the community's members. This causality arose from the state's lack of due diligence regarding the living conditions of all members of the aforementioned community.[348] Significantly, when it comes to legal causation, most of the discussion is led by the respondent states, which usually demand that the victims must prove a causal link between an alleged harm and the actions for which the state has been found responsible.[349]

---

344 [344] IACtHR, *Pueblo Bello Massacre* v. *Colombia, supra* n. 20, para. 95(161) and 159.

345 IACtHR (Judgment) 29 June 2006, *Ituango Massacres* v. *Colombia*; ; IACtHR (Judgment) 5 July 2006; *Montero-Aranguren et al. (Detention Center of Catia)* v. *Venezuela* IACtHR, *Barrios Altos* v. *Peru, supra* n. 77; IACtHR, *Moiwana Community* v. *Suriname, supra* n. 44; IACtHR, *Mapiripán Massacre* v. *Colombia, supra* n. 8; IACtHR, *Pueblo Bello Massacre* v. *Colombia, supra* n. 20; IACtHR, *Miguel Castro-Castro Prison* v. *Peru, supra* n. 77; IACtHR, *La Rochela Massacre* v. *Colombia, supra* n. 84.

346 IACtHR, *Barrios Altos* v. *Peru, supra* n. 178, para. 31; IACtHR, *Ituango Massacres* v. *Colombia, supra* n. 345, para. 63, 70; IACtHR; *Montero-Aranguren et al. (Detention Center of Catia)* v. *Venezuela, supra* n. 345, para. 26; IACtHR, *Miguel Castro-Castro Prison* v. *Peru, supra* n. 77, para. 129-144; IACtHR, *La Rochela Massacre* v. *Colombia, supra* n. 84, para. 8-22.

347 IACtHR, *19 Merchants* v. *Colombia, supra* n. 43, para. 89, 169; IACtHR, *Yakye Axa Indigenous Community* v. *Paraguay, supra* n. 44, para. 157, 159; IACtHR, *Santo Domingo Massacre* v. *Colombia, supra* n. 72, para. 176, 179, 254; IACtHR, *Afro-Descendant Communities displaced from the Cacarica River Basin (Operation Genesis)* v. *Colombia, supra* n. 205, para. 215, 306. In addition, an expert witness has referred to factual causation. See: IACtHR, *Plan de Sánchez Massacre* v. *Guatemala, supra* n. 45, para. 32.

348 IACtHR, *Yakye Axa Indigenous Community* v. *Paraguay,* Separate dissenting opinion of judges A.A. Cançado Trindade and M.E. Ventura Robles, *supra* n. 44, para. 11, 13. See also: IACtHR, *Sawhoyamaxa Indigenous Community* v. *Paraguay*, Separate opinion, Judge A.A. Cançado Trindade, *supra* n. 111, para. 25.

349 IACtHR, *Las Palmeras* v. *Colombia, supra* n. 46, para. 52; IACtHR, *19 Merchants* v. *Colombia, supra* n. 43, para. 246.

5.7 Implementation of Collective Reparations

According to Article 68 of the ACHR, states are obliged to comply with the Court's judgments. The IACtHR is in charge of monitoring compliance with its reparation orders.[350] If states are unwilling to cooperate, the Court may resort to the OAS General Assembly (OAS-GA) to enforce its orders.[351] Article 65 of the ACHR vests the Court with the power to refer to the non-compliance of a state in its annual report to the OAS-GA.[352] The GA can then discuss, if appropriate, the adoption of measures against the state.[353] However, this enforcement mechanism is not considered to be very effective.[354] Since 2004, the Court has barely made use of its power under Article 65, thereby precluding any significant collaborative work between the Court and the OAS.[355] And even if the Court did resort to its Article 65 powers, Antkowiak asserts that the OAS usually does not exert sufficient pressure upon states to ensure compliance.[356] Yet, if too much pressure is exerted, states could be led to denounce the Convention and, thus, to leave the system altogether.[357]

Monitoring procedure

The Court has strengthened its compliance monitoring system over the years. It first started by issuing orders on compliance monitoring as early as 1999, spurred by several states' lack of compliance with its orders.[358] This practice only became institutionalised at the end of 2009, however.[359] The Court has also introduced more guidelines regarding the implementation process. For instance, the Court must already indicate within its judgments the timeframe during which states should report their compliance progress. This timeframe varies – the Court has indicated periods of

350 Article 69, IACtHR's Rules.

351 Huneeus, A., "Compliance with Judgments and Decisions", in C. Romano, K. Alter and Y. Shany (eds.), *The Oxford Handbook of International Adjudication* (Oxford, OUP 2015), p. 449-450.

352 Article 65, ACHR.

353 Pasqualucci, *supra* n. 2, p. 18.

354 Huneeus, *supra* n. 351, p. 450; Bailliet, C. M., "Measuring Compliance with the Inter-American Court of Human Rights: The Ongoing Challenge of Judicial Independence in Latin America", 31 *Nordic Journal of Human Rights* (2013), p. 479-480.

355 Cançado Trindade, A.A., "Compliance with Judgments and Decisions- the Experience of the Inter-American Court of Human Rights: a reassessment", *13 Revista – Instituto Brasileiro de Direitos Humanos* (2014), p. 31; Baluarte, D.C., "Strategizing for Compliance: The Evolution of a Compliance Phase of Inter-American Court Litigation and the Strategic Imperative for Victims' Representatives", 27 *American University International Law Review* (2012), p. 283-286.

356 Antkowiak, *supra* n. 34, p. 304-307.

357 Tan, *supra* n. 332, p. 281.

358 The Court issued its first compliance decision in a case against Peru, possibly as a result of the refusal of Fujimori to comply with the court's orders. See: Baluarte, *supra* n. 355, p. 266, 276-277.

359 Article 69, IACtHR's Rules.

6 months,[360] 1 year,[361] 18 months,[362] or even a recurring report every 6 months.[363] The determination of this reporting period is not regulated by the IACtHR's Rules; it is therefore left to the discretion of the Court to decide thereon. Furthermore, the Court has adopted a resolution explaining its practice on compliance.[364]

In addition, since 2008, the Court has held compliance monitoring hearings (closed or public).[365] These hearings may be with respect to either a single case or to different cases against a single state.[366] Despite all these efforts by the Court, the majority of the states only partially comply with the judgments. In light of this, Hunneus has pointed out the need for more dialogue between the Court and the states' internal organs, which are the ones that are eventually in charge of materialising the states' obligations under the ACHR, including reparation orders.[367] Finally, in order to further strengthen compliance with the Court's orders, Baluarte has submitted that states should create national bodies/mechanisms specialising in overseeing and implementing the Court's orders against their parent states.[368]

Actual compliance with collective symbolic measures (satisfaction and GnR)

The IACtHR has ordered symbolic collective measures in all the 40 cases studied. The most common symbolic collective measures ordered by the Court are: the publicity of a judgment, apologies, publics acts of recognition of the state's responsibility, legislative reforms, and the investigation, prosecution and punishment of the perpetrators of the violations.[369] Significantly, the Court has labelled the latter

---

360 IACtHR, *Barrios Altos* v. *Peru, supra* n. 77, para. 50; IACtHR, Xákmok Kásek Indigenous Community v. *Paraguay, supra* n. 121, para. 337.

361 IACtHR, *Gomes Lund et al. ("Guerrilha Do Araguaia")* v. *Brazil, supra* n. 49, para. 325; IACtHR, *Río Negro Massacres* v. *Guatemala, supra* n. 65, para. 324.

362 IACtHR, *Miguel Castro-Castro Prison* v. *Peru, supra* n. 77, para. 470.

363 IACtHR, *Mayagna (Sumo) Awas Tingni Community* v. *Nicaragua, supra* n. 47, Operative para. 173 (8); IACtHR, *Caracazo* v. *Venezuela, supra* n. 43, para. 143.

364 IACtHR (Resolution) 29 June 2005, Supervisión de cumplimiento de sentencias: Aplicabilidad del artículo 65 de la Convención Americana sobre Derechos Humanos.

365 Baluarte, *supra* n. 355, p. 278.

366 Article 30 (5), IACtHR's Rules.

367 Huneeus, A., "Courts Resisting Courts: Lessons from the Inter-American Court's Struggle to Enforce Human Rights" 44 *Cornell Internal Law Journal* (2011), p. 529.

368 Baluarte, *supra* n. 355, p. 283-286; Cançado Trindade, *supra* n. 355, p. 30.

369 In some cases, the Court has also ordered the state to provide training in human rights and in the rights of indigenous peoples for state officials. See: IACtHR, *The Kichwa Indigenous People of Sarayaku* v. *Ecuador, supra* n. 118, para. 302; IACtHR, *Río Negro Massacres* v. *Guatemala, supra* n. 65, para. 291; IACtHR, *Massacres of El Mozote and neighboring locations* v. *El Salvador, supra* n. 85, para. 369. In some other cases, the Court has also ordered the state to provide training in international humanitarian law. See: IACtHR, *Ituango Massacres* v. *Colombia, supra* n. 50, para. 409; IACtHR, *Mapiripán Massacre* v. *Colombia, supra* n. 8, para. 316.

measure as a general duty of the states in relation to the ACHR and as a measure of reparation.[370]

While compliance with the publicity of the judgment, apologies and publics acts of recognition of the state's responsibility is comparatively higher than those measures aimed at investigating, prosecuting and punishing those responsible for the violations where compliance is very low. This seems to hold true not only in relation to the 40 cases under study but also in relation to the majority of the Court's cases.[371] According to Gonzalez-Salzberg, measures related to the investigation, prosecution and punishment of those responsible for the violations as well as legislative reform have a lower degree of compliance due to their complexity and lengthy process.[372] In this light, it is important to point out that from the cases in which the Court has ordered the responsible states to amend their national legislation in order to protect the lands of indigenous and tribal peoples, only the state of Nicaragua has done so in the case of *Magayna(Sumo) Awas Tingui Community.*[373]

Actual compliance with collective reparations (service-based projects and community development funds)

Out of the 16 cases where the Court has ordered CR, states have only fully complied with the orders in two cases. The *Aloeboetoe* case, which is the first case where the Court ordered CR, was declared closed in 1997. Interestingly, although the state of Suriname had complied with all the points in the *Aloeboetoe* judgment, including the order to reopen and make operational a school and a dispensary, the State did not relay this information to the Court but rather to the Commission.[374] The other case marked by full compliance is the *Mayagna (Sumo) Awas Tingni* case, which was declared closed in 2009.[375]

---

370 Since *El Amparo* case, the Court has labelled as a measure of reparation. See: Gonzalez-Salzberg, D.A., "Do States comply with the compulsory judgments of the Inter-American Court of Human Rights? An empirical study of the compliance with 330 measures of reparations", 13 *Revista do Instituto Brasileiro de Direitos Humanos* (2014), p. 19.

371 McKay, *supra* n. 6, p. 938; Bailliet, *supra* n. 354, p. 483; Tan, *supra* n. 332, p. 262.

372 Gonzalez-Salzberg, *supra* n. 370, p. 21-22.

373 IACtHR (Monitoring Compliance Order) 3 April 2009, *Mayagna (Sumo) Awas Tingni* v. *Nicaragua*. However, neither Suriname nor Paraguay have complied with this measure. See: IACtHR (Monitoring Compliance Order) 23 November 2011, *Saramaka People* v. *Suriname;* IACtHR (Monitoring Compliance Order) 30 August 2017, *Cases of Indigenous Communities Yakye Axa Indigenous, Sawhoyamaxa* y *Xákmok Kásek Indigenous Community* v. *Paraguay.*

374 Tan, *supra* n. 332, p. 258.

375 IACtHR, *Mayagna (Sumo) Awas Tingni* v. *Nicaragua, supra* n. 373.

5.8 Main challenges of Implementation

Collective reparations are usually composed of several elements and are thus more complex in their implementation.[376] One factor that may affect the implementation of measures of reparation is the state's own understanding of how these measures should be implemented, especially in cases where the Court has not provided clear implementation guidelines to accompany its orders. For instance, in the *Sawhoyamaxa* case, the Court ordered the state of Paraguay to establish a community development fund and to allocate USD 1,000,000 to it. The fund had the objective of establishing educational, housing, agricultural and health projects, as well as building the necessary infrastructure for drinking water and sanitation in the lands of the affected community. However, the Court ordered these projects to be implemented by an implementation committee.[377] While the Court indicated the composition of the committee, it neglected to indicate the amount, out of the USD 1,000,000, that was to serve as the committee's operational budget.[378] This meant that whenever the state decided on a specific amount to be invested in a project, it could not be certain whether the IACtHR would agree with its decision. Hence, the state did not have clarity as to how to comply with the Court's judgment.

Having said that, this situation may also represent an opportunity for the government and the victims to engage in dialogue and to agree on a budget, as well as on other technical issues related to running the services and infrastructure projects. This dialogue, in turn, may guarantee not only the implementation of the reparations but also the victims' sense of achieved justice, as they themselves have played a role in the design of their reparation projects. In addition, if the Court were to give precise and strict guidelines to be followed when running a community development fund or projects aimed at providing social services, this act may be perceived as intrusive, especially considering that the Court is unlikely to know the difficulties in implementing a given collective reparation measure in a specific cultural, economic and geographic context. In light of this, Antkowiak proposes that the Court should provide a platform for states and victims to agree on exact services and goods to be delivered as part of the collective reparation orders. While he affirms that this would result in a few months' delay in the proceedings and elicit a need to provide a facilitator for the platform, these efforts may be seen as an investment in greater compliance rates.[379]

Furthermore, orders of collective reparations usually omit a specific timeframe in which the reparations' beneficiaries may enjoy the service projects. For instance, in the *Aloeboetoe* case, the state had complied with the orders to reopen a school and to

376 Antkowiak, *supra* n. 34, p. 304.
377 IACtHR, *Sawhoyamaxa Indigenous Community* v. *Paraguay*, *supra* n. 111, para. 224.
378 Ibid., para. 225.
379 Antkowiak, *supra* n. 34, p. 309-316.

make a dispensary operational. Yet, it is unclear whether the case could be reopened if the state discontinues the operation of the school and the dispensary.[380] However, in the judgment in the *Mayagna (Sumo) Awas Tingni* case, the second CR judgment that was fully complied with, it could be presumed that the state's obligation to provide the CR would expire when the USD 50,000 ordered to be invested in services in the collective interest would be spent by common agreement with the affected community and would thereby be exhausted. Whilst this presumption seems logical, it remains a question whether the Court could be willing to reopen the case if victims complain about not having agreed upon a given service that has already been provided.

5.8.1 Other Challenges & Dilemmas

Taking into consideration that collective awards were originally considered to be the most adequate type of reparations for groups such as indigenous and tribal peoples, awarding collective reparations raises three main dilemmas. First of all, collective reparations may imply the recognition of groups other than indigenous and tribal peoples under the American Convention on Human Rights. Secondly, the following question will arise: who, exactly, is the holder of rights in the context of collective reparation 'groups' (people targeted collectively with no shared identity) and 'members' of indigenous and tribal peoples (people sharing an identity and other links). Third, some critics argue that the IACtHR actually awards collective reparations when a violation concerns *collective rights.*[381] Thus, there comes the question of whether the AC protects collective rights, and if so, which ones.

Regarding the issue of the recognition of groups, it is important to highlight that, at present, it seems that there are only two well-recognized groups under international law. Namely, indigenous peoples (IPs) and tribal peoples have been accepted as group subjects of international law.[382] This recognition helped the IACtHR to elaborate on their rights and special protection.[383] Yet, the Court has implicitly recognised that GVHR create groups entitled to collective redress. This seems to be in line with the recognition of groups as victims of international crimes.[384] Yet, the methodology and boundaries of grouping victims are yet to be clarified (i.e. whether to group victims according to the kind of violation or according to the consequences endured).

380 Tan, *supra* n. 332, p. 258.

381 Bantekas, I. and Oette, L., *International Human Rights: Law and Practice* (Cambridge, CUP 2016, 2nd ed.), p. 631.

382 López-Cárdenas, C.M., "Aproximación a un estándar de reparación integral en procesos colectivos de violación a los derechos humanos. Jurisprudencia de la Corte Interamericana de Derechos Humanos" 11 *Revista Estudios Socio-Jurídicos* (2009), p. 309.

383 Ibid., p. 309.

384 In addition, Pasqualucci has maintained that the commission or tolerance of GVHR by a given state makes the whole community a victim (indirectly). See: Pasqualucci, *supra* n. 2, p. 21.

According to Judge García Ramírez, indigenous peoples possess collective rights as a community and, in addition, the members of the community possess rights as individuals. Both sets of rights are 'deeply and closely interrelated' but 'retain their own character', and both are protected by the ACHR through specific measures.[385] Similarly, tribal communities also possess collective and individual rights as these peoples share similar characteristics as those of IP.[386] In addition, Judge Ramírez has affirmed that there is an 'inextricable link between individual and collective rights'.[387] However, if we consider victims of GVHR as a group, the question of who are the rights holders concerning collective reparations is raised.

Whilst it is silent with respect to the protection of collective rights, the Court has interpreted some individual rights protected by the AC as principally collective rights, but not exclusively with respect to the right to property (Article 21 of the ACHR) in cases related to indigenous and tribal communities.[388] Although the ACHR was not intended to protect collective rights, their protection may well be derived from an evolving interpretation of the ACHR. In this light, we must recall that the IACtHR has upheld that human rights treaties are living instruments and that, therefore, their interpretation must evolve over time so that they reflect current and pressing situations.[389] In addition, Judge Sergio García Ramírez has submitted that the AC does not deny collective rights. He has even stated that individual rights 'originate from, and acquire existence, effectiveness and significance in, the context of collective rights', hence protecting individual rights implies the protection of collective rights and vice versa.[390]

385 IACtHR, *Plan de Sánchez Massacre* v. *Guatemala,* Separate Opinion of Judge García Ramírez which Judge Medina Quiroga also signed, *supra* n. 45, para. 5.

386 IACtHR, *Moiwana Community* v. *Suriname*, *supra* n. 44, para. 86(5); IACtHR, *Saramaka People* v. *Suriname*, *supra* n. 117, para. 80-82 and 84.

387 IACtHR, *Mayagna (Sumo) Awas Tingni Community* v. *Nicaragua*, Concurring Opinion of Judge Sergio García Ramírez, *supra* n. 47, para. 14; IACtHR, *Plan de Sánchez Massacre* v. *Guatemala,* Separate opinion of Judge Sergio García Ramírez, *supra* n. 45, para. 10.

388 In reaching this conclusion, the IACtHR relied on different international instruments. See: IACtHR, *Mayagna (Sumo) Awas Tingni Community* v. *Nicaragua*, Concurring Opinion Garcia Ramirez, *supra* n. 47, para. 148; The Court has also interpreted the right of 'Freedom of Movement and Residence' enshrined in Article 22 of the AC as a collective right. This holds true in cases related to the issue of the 'internal displacement' of populations. Hence, it seems that the Court is willing to interpret different rights protected by the ACHR as collective. See: IACtHR, *Moiwana Community* v. *Suriname*, *supra* n. 44, para. 120.

389 IACtHR, *The Kichwa Indigenous People of Sarayaku* v. *Ecuador*, *supra* n. 118, para. 161.

390 IACtHR, *Sawhoyamaxa Indigenous Community* v. *Paraguay*, Separate Opinion of Judge Sergio García-Ramírez, *supra* n. 111, para. 11.

Transitional Justice

In 2008, the IACommHR issued some guidelines regarding the relationship between collective reparations programmes, as part of national transitional justice mechanisms, and the states' obligations under the ACHR. While the Commission recognised that victims are entitled to individual reparations in conjunction with collective measures such as satisfaction and GNR,[391] it also affirmed that 'in situations of transitional justice [...] administrative reparation programs are a legitimate way to comply with the obligation of reparation'.[392] In contrast, the Court has not elaborated upon the compatibility of collective reparations with the individual right to receive reparations as enshrined by the ACHR. While the Court's jurisprudence may well serve as an implicit answer, questions of legal certainty are raised by the lack of coherence regarding the circumstances under which an award consisting solely of collective reparations is compatible with the ACHR.

6 Conclusions

The IACtHR has created new paradigms to redress victims and groups. On the one hand, these paradigms entail continuously granting measures of satisfaction and guarantees of non-repetition, which provide a collective benefit.[393] On the other hand, the Court offers redress through serviced-based collective reparations. From the research conducted in this chapter, it is possible to conclude that the Court distinguishes between general measures of collective benefits (satisfaction and GNR) and collective reparations.[394]

The Court's understanding of CR differs from the current stream of scholarly thought, which is clearly represented by De Greiff. According to De Greiff, collective reparations refer to both symbolic and social services measures, awarded to groups of people regardless of whether those groups enjoy legal personality.

If the Court were to embrace De Greiff's understanding of CR, it could be concluded that, first, the Court has ordered both individual and collective reparations in all cases related to both GVHR that involve a large number of victims (>5), and in all cases related to the ancestral lands of indigenous and tribal peoples. From the

391 OAS, *Principal Guidelines for a Comprehensive Reparations Policy,* Doc. No. OEA/Ser/L/V/II.131, 19 February 2008, para. 1.

392 On the Colombian reparations programmes, see further the March 2014 hearing of the IACHR, discussing the implementation of Law 906/2004; Shelton, *supra* n. 10, p. 232.

393 The Court has granted measures of satisfaction and GNR in all 40 cases studied. Yet, the Court does not only grant these measures in cases related to GVHR and I&TP involving a large number of people as it is well known that the Court has granted similar measures in cases where the claimant is a singular person. See: Antkowiak, *supra* n. 2, p. 355.

394 In its most recent jurisprudence, the Court has implied that collective reparations are those measures aiming to provide services for a given community, whether through a community development fund or a specific service project.

Court's understanding of collective reparations and based on the findings of section 4 of this Chapter, it is possible to conclude that:

In cases related to enforced disappearances and/or torture that involve a large number of victims, the Court grants a combination of individual reparations and measures of satisfaction and GNR.

Likewise, in cases of massacres, the Court usually grants a combination of individual reparations and measures of satisfaction and GNR. The exceptions to this are the *Aloeboetoe, Plan de Sánchez, Pueblo Bello* and *Ituango* cases, where the Court granted a combination of individual and collective reparations, as well as measures of satisfaction and GNR.

In cases related to land violations suffered by indigenous or tribal peoples, the Court awards collective reparations and measures of satisfaction and GnR. The exception to this, however, are the *Moiwana* case, which also dealt with a massacre and in which the Court also awarded individual reparations, and the *Indigenous Communities Kuna of Madungandí and Emberá of Bayano* case. Here, the Court granted the collective measure of financial compensation in addition to measures of satisfaction and GnR, but did not award collective reparations.[395]

Finally, while collective reparations are complex and not very different from development aid programmes, they offer the advantage of addressing both basic and structural problems of marginalisation and poverty. According to Laurence Burgorgue-Larsen, the IACtHR has used reparations to help in the 'personal reconstruction of the person as a human being' and, in society as a whole, to help improve the protection of human rights. In this light, the Court has made extensive use of orders of satisfaction and guarantees of non-repetition.[396] By the same token, it can be concluded that the Court has awarded collective reparations to transform the living conditions of the members of given communities.

However, the IACtHR has awarded collective reparations to underprivileged communities, namely those composed of indigenous and tribal peoples. These awards may respond better to the specific cultural background and worldview of the said groups.[397] Thus, such collective reparations are evidence of the IACtHR's readiness to go beyond the traditional approach when adjudicating rights under the ACHR. Collective reparations require such an open-content approach as their content depends on the balance between several factors, of which available resources and the wishes and needs of victims play a central role. However, Antkowiak has submitted that this approach may also be discriminatory and even paternalistic unless victims have explicitly requested this.[398]

395 IACtHR, *Indigenous Communities Kuna of Madungandí and Emberá of Bayano and its memebrs* v. *Panama, supra* n. 273, para. 214-233.

396 Burgorgue-Larsen, *supra* n. 159, p. 232-234.

397 Citroni and Quintana Osuna, *supra* n. 56, p. 318.

398 Antkowiak, *supra* n. 2, p. 384, 398.

Antkowiak's statement referring to collective reparations being discriminatory becomes stronger when taking into account that the Court has stated that collective reparations are part of the individual right to receive reparations. This approach is evidenced in cases related to indigenous and tribal peoples. For instance, in the *Yakye Axa* case, the Court upheld that 'an important component of the individual reparation is the reparation that this Court will subsequently grant to the members of the communities as a whole'.[399] Similarly, in the *Moiwana* case, the Court stated that 'the individual reparations to be awarded must be supplemented by communal measures'.[400] From the above analysis, it can be concluded that, on the one hand, the Court has indeed recognised that collective reparations are part of the right to individual reparations. On the other hand, despite the partial nature of collective reparations in relation to the individual right to reparation, the Court has decided to grant CR as standalone awards to victims in certain cases. The Court has not explained why granting a partial reparation is justified in such instances. Yet, in most cases where the Court has granted collective reparations, victims' representatives and/or the IACmmHR have explicitly asked for them.[401]

---

399 IACtHR, *Yakye Axa Indigenous Community* v. *Paraguay, supra* n. 44, para. 188; IACtHR, *Plan de Sánchez Massacre* v. *Guatemala, supra* n. 45, para. 86.

400 IACtHR, *Moiwana Community* v. *Suriname, supra* n. 44, para. 194.

401 From the 16 cases where the Court granted reparations, only in the following 4 cases were these measures not specifically requested: *Aloeboetoe*, *Mayagna (Sumo) Awas Tingni Community, Ituango and Pueblo Bello.*

CHAPTER IV
COLLECTIVE REPARATIONS IN INTERNATIONAL CRIMINAL LAW

Today's conflicts are often
rooted in the failure to
repair yesterday's injury'
Roy S. Lee[1]

1 INTRODUCTION

International criminal law was originally based on the tenets of retributive justice and thus assumed an offender-driven approach.[2] This changed with the establishment of the permanent International Criminal Court (ICC or the Court), which marked a significant advancement in the recognition of the rights of victims in international criminal law proceedings. This includes the right to reparations.[3] The ICC was the first international permanent criminal tribunal that had the power to deliver justice beyond retributive justice, as it recognises 'the need to provide effective remedies for victims.'[4] It thus affords victims the right to seek and receive reparations,[5] including

1 Lee, R.S., "The Rome Conference and its Contributions to International Law", in R.S. Lee (ed.), *The international Criminal Court: The Making of the Rome Statute: Issues, Negotiation and Results* (The Hague, Martinus Nijhoff 1999), p. 1.

2 McCarthy, C., "Victim Redress and International Criminal Justice", 10 *Journal of International Criminal Law* (2012), p. 351-355; O'Shea, A., "Reparations under International Criminal Law", in M. du Plessis and S. Peté (eds.), *Repairing the Past?: International Perspectives on Reparations for Human Rights Abuses* (Antwerp, Intersentia 2007), p. 181.

3 The three main victims' rights recognized by the ICC's Rome Statute are: right to participation (Article 68 (3)); right to receive protection (Article 68 (1) and Article 43 (6)); the right to request reparations (Article 75 (1)). It must be acknowledged that the *ad hoc* tribunals did open the door to the recognition of victims' rights within the realm of international criminal law. See: Cryer, R., et al. (ed.), *An Introduction to International Criminal Law and Procedure* (Cambridge, CUP 2014, 3rd ed.), p. 3.

4 ICC (Decision) 7 August 2012, *Prosecutor* v. *Thomas Lubanga Dyilo*, Decision establishing the principles and procedures to be applied to reparations, ICC-01/04-01/06-2904, para. 177.

5 Before the establishment of the ICC, victims' reparations at the international level were only possible in the context of state responsibility within the international human rights law framework. See: Fischer, P., "The Victims' Trust Fund of the International Criminal Court – Formation of a Functional Reparations Scheme", 17 *Emory International Law Review* (2003), p. 200.

restitution, compensation, rehabilitation and collective awards,[6] as well as 'other forms of reparations.'[7] The ICC's redress mandate was further enhanced by the creation of the Trust Fund for Victims (TFV or Trust Fund), an institution tasked with implementing reparations and providing humanitarian assistance to victims in cases appearing before the ICC.[8]

Following the establishment of the ICC, the Extraordinary Chambers in the Courts of Cambodia (ECCC or the Extraordinary Chambers), an internationalised hybrid criminal tribunal, also recognised the right of victims to seek and receive reparations.[9] The tribunal is "internationalised" in the sense that it is a national institution that requires international participation:[10] although its legal framework is national law,[11] the ECCC emerged out of an international agreement between the Cambodian government and the United Nations to prosecute the crimes committed by the leaders of the Khmer Rouge.[12] The ECCC's reparations mandate is more limited than that of the ICC: it can only grant collective and moral measures of reparation.[13] Since 2010, the ECCC's redress mandate has been reinforced by the Victims Support Section (VSS), which has the power to create and implement non-

6 Article 75 (1), ICC's Rome Statute; Rule 98 (2), ICC's Rules of Procedure and Evidence (ICC's RoPE).

7 Rule 94 (1) (f), ICC's RoPE.

8 Article 79, ICC's Rome Statute; Rule 98, ICC's RoPE.

9 Under the ECCC victims have the possibility to be recognized as civil parties. If so, they are entitled to two rights: the right to participate (Rule 23) and the right to request collective or moral reparations (Rule 23*quinquies*) under the Internal Rules as revised on 16 January 2015, (Rev. 9) (hereafter 'ECCC's Internal Rules'). In addition, victims, whether they are recognized as civil parties or as witnesses, enjoy the right to protection (Rule 29).

10 Half of its staff, judges and prosecutors are international and are appointed by the UN. See: Zegveld, L., "Victims' Reparations Claims and International Criminal Courts: Incompatible Values?", 8 *Journal of International Criminal Justice* (2010), p. 89-90; Schabas, W., "International Criminal Courts", in C. Romano, K. Alter and Y. Shany (eds.), *The Oxford Handbook of International Adjudication* (Oxford, OUP 2015), p. 206, 212; Shelton, D., *Remedies in International Human Rights Law* (Oxford, OUP 2015, 3rd ed.), p. 126-127.

11 Its laws are rooted in Cambodian procedures with some elements of international law. See: Jeffery, R., "Beyond Repair?: Collective and Moral Reparations at the Khmer Rouge Tribunal", 13 *Journal of Human Rights* (2014), p. 106. In addition, the ECCC may seek guidance 'from procedural rules established at the international level, where appropriate.' See: ECCC (Judgment) 26 July 2010, *Prosecutor* v. *Kaing Guek Eav* alias '*Duch*' (Case 001), Judgment, No. 001/18-07-2007-ECCC/TC, para. 35.

12 From 1975 up until 1979, the Khmer Rouge massively abused more than three million people in Cambodia by forcing them into slave labour, torture and killing anyone who did not agree with their policies as they were considered to be enemies. See: Phan, H.D., "Reparation to Victims of Gross Human Rights Violations: The case of Cambodia", 4 *East Asia Law Review* (2009), p. 277-278; Path, K., and Kanavaou, A., "Converts, not ideologues? The Khmer Rouge practice of thought reform in Cambodia, 1975-1978", 20 *Journal of Political Ideologies* (2015).

13 Rule 23 (1) *quinquies*, ECCC's Internal Rules. It is also important to note that Article 39 of the ECCC's Internal Rules foresees the restitution of property acquired unlawfully or by criminal conduct to the state but not to the legitimate victims.

judicial programmes for the benefit of victims. In addition, it can design, implement and secure external funding for reparation projects.[14]

Of the existing international criminal tribunals,[15] only the ICC and the ECCC are empowered to award collective reparations to victims upon the accused's conviction.[16] This chapter analyses the normative framework for reparations with regard to both of these international criminal tribunals, as well as their emerging practice regarding collective reparations. Although the two tribunals' statutes and rules do not provide a definition of collective reparations, both courts have exercised their remedial powers. Through this comparative analysis, this chapter aims to define the content, scope and procedural aspects of collective reparations within international criminal law. Furthermore, it seeks to unveil the challenges that collective reparations present in this field of international law.

2 Legal Framework of Reparations

The use of reparations in criminal proceedings is not a common feature of all criminal systems in the world. This is because the main objective of criminal proceedings has been to provide retributive justice. However, the inclusion of reparations in the ICC's Rome Statute appears to be justified by three main reasons. First, reparations ensure that perpetrators can be held accountable for their crimes. Second, they provide justice by addressing the suffering of the victims, and thus have the potential to prevent future crimes and to contribute to lasting peace. Third, they contribute to processes of rehabilitation and reconciliation at both the individual and community level.[17]

These reasons are also relevant in the context of the ECCC.[18] Significantly, reparations were only included in the ECCC's legal framework after it had already been established. Reparations for victims were neither incorporated in the agreement between the UN and the Cambodian Government, nor in the national legislation upon

14 Rule 12*bis* (2), Rule 12*bis* (3), Rule 23 *quinquies* (3) (b); ECCC's Internal Rules (Rev. 5).

15 Other existing international – hybrid – criminal tribunals include the Special Court for Sierra Leone (SCSL), the Special Tribunal for Lebanon (STL), the Bosnian War Crimes Chamber (WCC), the Regulation 64 Panels in Kosovo, and the Extraordinary African Chambers (EAC). See: Ciorciari, J.D., and Heindel, A., "Experiments in International Criminal Justice: Lessons from the Khmer Rouge Tribunal", 35 *Michigan Journal of International Law* (2014), p. 370.

16 Zegveld, *supra* n. 10, p. 91; McKay, F., "What Outcome for Victims?", in D. Shelton (ed.), *The Oxford Handbook of International Human Rights Law* (Oxford, OUP 2013), p. 937.

17 Lee, *supra* n. 1, p. 1, 39; Muttukumaru, C., "Reparation to Victims", in R.S. Lee (ed.), *The International Criminal Court: The Making of the Rome Statute. Issues, Negotiations, Results* (The Hague, Martinus Nijhoff 1999), p. 264; ICC *Lubanga* Principles on Reparations, *supra* n. 4, para. 179; Preamble, ICC's Rome Statute.

18 Ramil-Nogales J., and van Schaak, B.,, "A Collective Response to Mass Violence: Reparations and Healing in Cambodia, in Brining the Khmer Rouge to Justice: Prosecuting Mass Violence before the Cambodian Courts" *Santa Clara University School of Law,* Legal Studies Research Papers Series, Working Paper No. 06-02 (2006), p. 369-373.

which the ECCC was based. Instead, they were introduced by the ECCC's judges when adopting its Internal Rules.[19]

2.1 The ICC's Legal Framework

Before the ICC, individual victims of the most heinous crimes may obtain redress by either acquiring reparations through a court order or by receiving assistance through the Trust Fund.[20] While the ICC's reparation orders are contingent upon the conviction of a given perpetrator on specific charges (case-based reparations), the TFV can provide support to victims of crimes under the jurisdiction of the ICC regardless of whether they are associated with an ongoing case. Importantly, the ICC's reparation orders are part of the procedures that are separate from those of the conviction of the perpetrator, and they are also subject to appeals.[21]

The ICC's reparations are based primarily on the principle of the perpetrator's liability for reparations. Yet very few perpetrators, if any, will possess sufficient resources to afford to pay reparations for every single victim of their crimes, especially considering that international crimes generally involve large numbers of victims.[22] In light of this, the ICC's reparations framework contains a complementary mechanism: the TFV. Its reparations system can thus be perceived as a hybrid system.[23] The Trust Fund complements the reparation mandate of the ICC in multiple ways: i) it provides assistance to victims; ii) it supports the ICC as a depositary for fines or forfeiture; iii) it acts as an intermediary for collective reparations; and iv) it supplements case-based reparations when the TFV's Board of Directors so requires.[24]

The ICC's Rome Statute lays down the Court's power to grant reparations,[25] including restitution, compensation, rehabilitation and collective awards against the convicted person.[26] It also indicates that collective awards are to be made through the TFV. However, it provides no details on the substantive and procedural aspects underlying reparations. Instead, the ICC is given full discretion to define those aspects

19 The first version of the ECCC's Internal Rules was adopted on 12 June 2007. Several revisions of these rules have followed.

20 Articles 75 and 79, ICC's Rome Statute; Rule 98, ICC's RoPE.

21 Cryer et al., *supra* n. 3, p. 495; Article 76 (3) and 82(4), ICC's Rome Statute; Rules 91 (4), 94-97, ICC's RoPE.

22 Henselin, M., Heiskanen, V. and Mettraux, G., "Reparations to Victims before the International Criminal Court: Lessons from International Mass Claims Processes", 17 *Criminal Law Forum* (2006), p. 339.

23 Mégret, F., "Justifying Compensation by the International Criminal Courts" 36 *Brook Journal of International Law* (2010), p. 125.

24 These functions will be explained in the following section.

25 This power is merely permissive, as the ICC is not compelled to grant reparations in each case. Thus, Article 75 merely grants victims a potential right to reparation, in other words, a non-absolute right.

26 However, this list is not exhaustive and reparations may therefore also take the form of satisfaction or guarantees of non-repetition.

through the establishment of the 'principles relating to reparations'. These principles are supposed to clarify the modalities, scope and extent of any damage to be repaired; the standard of proof that is required in a reparations claim; the causality test that is required to prove the relationship between the crime and the loss or injury sustained; the mechanism(s) to identify the victims; the criteria to establish the appropriate modalities of reparations in a given case; and the forms of and the times within which these reparations are to be implemented.

Finally, the ICC may award reparations upon request[27] and of its own motion when exceptional circumstances so require.[28] In both scenarios, it must consider the views of the convicted person, the victims, and other interested persons or states.[29] Applications for reparations are individual and allow victims to communicate their needs and wishes. However, this does not necessarily mean that the ICC will rule on each individual application when it orders collective reparations. This occurred in the *Lubanga* case, where the Court ordered the Registry to transfer the individual applications to the TFV.[30] In contrast, in the *Katanga* case the ICC decided to analyse all the individual applications that it had received.[31] Compared to individual applications, *motu proprio* reparations can benefit a greater number of victims. It opens the door to reparations for victims who are either unaware of the possibility of receiving reparations or who, due to their geographical and financial situation, are unable to submit an individual application.[32]

2.1.1 The Trust Fund for Victims

The Trust Fund is an independent body that strengthens the ICC's reparative justice mandate, as it was established 'for the benefit of victims of crimes within the jurisdiction of the Court, and the families of such victims.'[33] Besides, it is aimed at 'ensuring empowerment, hope and dignity for victims.'[34] The Trust Fund has two

27 The requests must be submitted before the reparations' hearing.

28 Rule 94 (1), 95(1), ICC's RoPE.

29 Article 75 (3), ICC's Rome Statute.

30 In addition, the TFV was given the authority to decide whether to include the victims who applied for reparation in any of the reparations programmes. See: ICC *Lubanga* Principles on Reparations, *supra* n. 4, para. 284.

31 ICC (Order) 24 March 2017, *Prosecutor* v. *Germain Katanga,* Ordonnance de réparation en vertu de l'article 75 du Statut, ICC-01/04-01/07-3728, 24 March 2017, para. 33.

32 Dannenbaum, T., "The International Criminal Court, Article 79, and Transitional Justice: The case for an Independent Trust Fund for Victims" 28 *Wisconsin International Law Journal* (2010), p. 274.

33 Article 79(1), ICC's Rome Statute.

34 TFV's Background Summary, August 2008, p. 2. Available at <https://www.icc-cpi.int/NR/rdonlyres/E582AE21-D718-4798-97ED-C6C9F0D9B42D/0/TFV_Background_Summary_Eng.pdf> (All links were accessed on 7 June 2017 unless otherwise stated).

primary mandates: the role of assisting victims (humanitarian relief, so to speak) and a reparation mandate.[35]

In its assistance role, the TFV provides support to victims who have suffered physical, psychological or material harm as a result of crimes within the Court's jurisdiction.[36] It should be mentioned that this assistance is targeted at communities or groups of victims rather than individual victims.[37] The TFV possesses great flexibility:[38] it determines independently when and where to implement diverse projects and to use its resources for the benefit of victims.[39] As the TFV is an independent body, the ICC has limited authority over its activities.[40] First, the Trust Fund only assists victims in cases where the Court has already opened an investigation.[41] Second, the TFV needs to notify the ICC of its intention to carry out assistance projects. The Court may curtail those projects when i) they have the potential to interfere with its work in relation to an ongoing investigation or prosecution of crimes, or ii) the projects are inconsistent with the rights of the accused in a given case.[42]

The TFV has received the ICC's approval to initiate over thirty projects in three out of the ten cases currently under its investigation: Northern Uganda, the Democratic Republic of Congo (DRC) and the Central African Republic (CAR).[43] Thus far, the Trust Fund's projects[44] have mainly focussed on i) physical rehabilitation measures such as reconstructive surgery, prosthetics and HIV/Aids treatment and support; ii) psychological rehabilitation measures at the individual and group level through different activities, such as music and dance; and iii) material support at both the individual and community level, such as livelihood activities and vocational

35 Article 75 (2) and Article 79 (2), ICC's Rome Statute; Rule 98 (2) (3) (4), ICC's RoPE.

36 Regulation 48, 49, TFV's Regulations.

37 ICC (Decision) 05 March 2008, *Situation in Uganda*, Notification of the Board of Directors of the Trust Fund for Victims in accordance with Regulation 50 of the Regulations of the Trust Fund, Case No. ICC-02/04-120, p. 39; ICC (Decision) 11 April 2008, *Situation in Democratic Republic of Congo*, Notification of the Board of Directors of the Trust Fund for Victims in accordance with Regulation 50 of the Regulations of the Trust Fund, Case No. ICC-01/04-492, p. 38.

38 Rule 98 (5), ICC's RoPE.

39 The TFV's assistance is determined by the TFV's Board of Directors after an assessment of the harm inflicted within a situation, the available services or programmes benefiting victims and recourse allocation. See: TFV, Programme Progress Report 2015, *Assistance & Reparations: Achievements, Lessons Learned, and Transitioning*, p. 12.

40 ICC, *DRC Situation* TFV Notification, *supra* n. 37.

41 TFV, Programme Progress Report November 2009, p. 10-11.

42 Regulation 50(a)(ii)-(iii), TFV's Regulations.

43 ICC, Uganda TFV's Notification, *supra* n. 37; ICC, DRC TFV's Notification, *supra* n. 37; ICC (Decision) 23 October 2012, *Situation in Central Africa*, Decision on the "Notification by the Board of Directors in accordance with Regulation 50 a) of the regulations of the Trust Fund for Victims to undertake activities in the Central African Republic", Case No. ICC-01/05-41.

44 It currently operates fifteen projects in the DRC, nine in northern Uganda, and has six projects planned for the CAR.

training;[45] and iv) activities addressing sexual gender-based violence (SGBV) and discrimination designed to promote community reconciliation and healing.[46] Special attention is devoted to vulnerable victims such as women, children and victims of sexual violence.[47] Up until 2016, the TFV's projects in the DRC and Northern Uganda directly benefited 104,548 and 358,498 victims respectively.[48] The majority of these beneficiaries received a combination of physical and psychological rehabilitation and material support.[49] Projects in the Central African Republic were planned to start in 2013, but they have been suspended due to security reasons.[50]

The TFV identifies its beneficiaries through interviews[51] on the basis of demographic data.[52] The beneficiaries must fulfil certain criteria.[53] Priority is given to vulnerable victims such as women, children, the elderly, victims with a medical emergency, and direct victims (as opposed to indirect ones).[54] Where the number of victims is too high, beneficiaries are selected according to ranking priorities.[55] The kind of assistance to be provided depends on the assessment of the harm suffered.[56] Finally, the TFV requires a causal link where the 'harm is an immediate result' of the crime, meaning that there is no other cause between the harm and the crime.[57]

The FV's reparation mandate includes a *depositary* and an *intermediary* role, as well as a potential s*upplementary* (or *complementary*) role when case-based reparations are assigned. Regarding the *depositary* role, the ICC can order the awards for reparations to be deposited with the Trust Fund when individual reparations are

45 TFV (Report) 16 August 2016, Report to the Assembly of States Parties on projects and activities of the Board of Directors of the Trust Fund for Victims for the period 1 July 2015 to 30 June 2016, ICC-ASP/15/14, para. 36 (a) (b) (c).

46 TFV, Strategic Plan 2014-2017, August 2014, p. 6; TFV, Programme Progress Report 2015, *supra* n. 39, p. 21.

47 TFV, Report to the ASP, *supra* n. 45, para. 36 (d), 37 (a); TFV, Programme Progress Report 2015, *supra* n. 39, p. 13.

48 TFV, Summary of Annual Report 2016, p. 2.

49 TFV, Report to the ASP, *supra* n. 45, para. 37.

50 TFV's Press Release, ICC-TFV-20120325-PR891, 26 March 2013, Available at <https://reliefweb.int/report/central-african-republic/trust-fund-victims-suspends-its-activities-central-african-republic>.

51 TFV, Programme Progress Report 2015, *supra* n. 39, p. 14.

52 Regulation 60, TFV's Regulations.

53 The criteria are: the beneficiary must i) be a direct or indirect victim; ii) demonstrate existing harm; iii) demonstrate that the harm is an immediate result of crimes that fall under the ICC's jurisdiction and that were committed after 1 July 2002. See: Regulations 61-88, TFV's Regulations; McCarthy, C., *Reparations and Victim Support in the International Criminal Court* (Cambridge, CUP 2012), p. 233.

54 TFV, Programme Progress Report 2015, *supra* n. 39, p. 13.

55 TFV, Annual Report 2015, p. 13-14.

56 TFV, Programme Progress Report 2015, *supra* n. 39, p. 12.

57 TFV, Programme Progress Report 2015, *supra* n. 39, p. 13.

'impossible or impracticable' at that time.[58] These awards are to be separated from the TFV's other resources. The *intermediary* role entails the Trust Fund's potential to distribute reparation awards to the victims 'where the number of the victims and the scope, forms and modalities of reparations make a collective award more appropriate.'[59] Finally, its *supplementary* role provides the TFV with the discretion to use part of its voluntary contributions to complement case-based reparations.[60] Significantly, according to its regulations, the Trust Fund can complement case-based reparations only when the reparation order happens to be of a collective nature, or when the award for reparations is transferred by the TFV in order to be implemented by an intergovernmental or (inter)national organisation.[61] Despite this, in the *Katanga* case the TFV decided to provide funds for both the individual and collective awards ordered by the ICC.[62]

Finally, it is important to mention that the TFV's financial resources consist mainly of voluntary contributions from governments, international organizations, individuals, corporations and other entities.[63] Contributions should be refused if they are inconsistent with the TFV's independence and aims, or when the donor requests earmarking which may give rise to an inequitable distribution of the available funds and property among the different groups of victims.[64] Despite the financial difficulties that usually confront funds that are dependent upon voluntary contributions,[65] the Trust Fund has significant monetary resources at its disposal. Contributions from several states had totalled € 25,124,750 by mid-2016,[66] and the Fund has a reserve of € 5 million for reparations.[67]

---

58 Rule 98 (2), ICC's RoPE. In addition, Article 79 (2) of the Rome Statute allows the ICC to order money and any other property collected through fines or forfeiture to be transferred to the TFV.

59 Article 75 (2), ICC's Rome Statute; Rule 98 (3), ICC's RoPE.

60 Regulation 56, TFV's Regulations.

61 Regulation 56, TFV's Regulations.

62 ICC, Press Release, 18 May 2017. Available at: <https://www.icc-cpi.int/legalAidConsultations?name=pr1305>; ICC (Notification) 17 May 2017, *Prosecutor* v. *Germain Katanga*, Notification pursuant to regulation 56 of the TFV Regulation regarding the Trust Fund Board of Directors Decision Relevant to complement the payments of individual and collective reparations awards, ICC-01/04-01/07-3740. The TFV took a different stance in the Lubanga case. See: ICC (Observations) 25 April 2012, *Prosecutor* v. *Thomas Lubanga Dyilo*, Observations on Reparations in Response to the Scheduling Order of 14 March 2012, ICC-01/04-01/06-2872, para. 250.

63 Regulation 21 (a), TFV's Regulations.

64 Regulation 30, TFV's Regulations.

65 Schwager, E., "The Right to Compensation for Victims of an Armed Conflict", 4 *Chinese Journal of International Law* (2005), p. 427.

66 TFV, Programme Progress Report 2015, *supra* n. 39, p. 57; TFV, Annual Report 2015, p. 57; TFV, Report to the ASP, *supra* n. 45, p. 14.

67 Decision 5, TFV (Decisions) Lists of Decisions by the Board of Directors, adopted 14th Annual Meeting, 18-21 April 2016. Available at < https://www.trustfundforvictims.org/sites/default/files/imce/List%20of%20Decisions%20-%20ENGLISH.pdf>.

2.2 The ECCC's Legal Framework

Like the ICC, the ECCC can also award measures of reparation against the convicted person for the benefit of the victims of a crime within its jurisdiction.[68] These measures are limited to those of a collective and moral nature. However, it does not define the content or scope of collective and moral reparations. The ECCC's reparation framework explicitly 'excludes individual awards, whether or not of a financial nature, and privileges those measures that benefit as many victims as possible.'[69] It is important to note that the reparation mandates of the ICC and the ECCC differ in some respects.

First, unlike the ICC,[70] the possibility for victims to claim reparations did not feature in the ECCC's laws of establishment.[71] Instead, the ECCC's reparation mandate was introduced in its Internal Rules, which were drafted by the Extraordinary Chamber's judges.[72] Second, unlike the ICC, the ECCC may only award reparations at the request of civil parties;[73] the Chambers are not empowered to award reparations *motu proprio*. Third, the ECCC limits reparations to collective and moral measures while the ICC allows for both individual and collective measures. Furthermore, as opposed to the ICC, the ECCC's Internal Rules do not only limit the reparations award, they also specify the aim of collective and moral reparations which is twofold: i) to 'acknowledge the harm suffered by [the victims]' and ii) to provide benefits, other than monetary payments, to address the victims' harm.[74]

In addition, the first revision of the ECCC's Internal Rules went as far as to provide examples of collective and moral reparations: i) publishing the judgment in any news or other media; b) funding any activity or service to the benefit of the victims; and iii) other appropriate comparable forms of reparation.[75] Although these examples were deleted from the final version of the ECCC's Internal Rules, the ECCC has affirmed that they provide guidelines regarding the content of collective and moral reparations.[76]

There appear to be several justifications for the limitation on collective and moral reparations in the ECCC's mandate. First, the magnitude of the crimes committed by

68 Rules 23 *quinquies*, (1), (3) (a), ECCC's Internal Rules.

69 ECCC (Judgment) 13 February 2012, *Prosecutor* v. *Kaing Guek Eav* alias '*Duch*' (Case 001), Appeal Judgment, No. 001/18-07-2007-ECCC/SC, para. 659.

70 Article 75 of the ICC's Rome Statute affords victims the right to seek and receive reparations.

71 The Law on the Establishment of the Extraordinary Chambers as amended did not envisage a right for victims to claim reparations. It was not until 2007 that the judges of the ECCC included this right within its Internal Rules.

72 Ciorciari and Heindel, *supra* n. 15, p. 372.

73 It must be noted that a precondition for obtaining reparations before the ECCC is that victims must have been accepted as civil parties.

74 Rules 23*quinquies* and 80*bis*, ECCC's Internal Rules.

75 Rule 23 (12), ECCC's Internal Rules (Rev. 1).

76 ECCC, *Duch* Appeal Judgment, *supra* n. 69, para. 658.

the Khmer Rouge is immeasurable, with almost the entire population being affected. In this light, collective reparations have the potential to benefit more victims than individual measures.[77] Second, the prosecution of crimes committed almost four decades ago yields many evidentiary constraints, and collective reparations require a lower standard of proof than those of an individual nature, including compensation. Third, the outcome of several population-based surveys indicates that the majority would prefer to receive collective or community-based reparations, especially those related to social services.[78] Finally, it must be stated that, since 2010, the VSS is empowered to develop and implement non-judicial programmes for the benefit of victims and to ensure external funding for reparations.[79]

2.2.1 Victims Support Section

The Victims Support Section was initially called the Victims Unit, and its primary mandate was to support the ECCC by reaching out to the general public and victims, as well as by helping victims who wanted to participate as civil parties in the proceedings.[80] During the initial years of the VSS's existence, it could not operate effectively due to a lack of funding. Instead, several local NGOs filled the void by providing services and legal representation for victims.[81] In 2010, after the *Duch* judgment, the ECCC expanded its mandate to include two additional tasks: i) the development and implementation of victims' assistance programmes in collaboration with governmental and non-governmental entities,[82] and ii) designing, implementing and securing sufficient external funding for reparation projects in conjunction with Lead Co-Lawyers.[83] Thus, while in the case of the ECCC reparations are primarily borne by those who have been convicted, it also allows for external funding.

The VSS's assistance programmes are non-judicial and are therefore expected to benefit victims beyond the civil parties in a given case. This VSS mandate resembles that of the TFV's assistance role, although the main difference is that the VSS does not

77 CHRAC and REDRESS, "Considering Reparations for Victims of the Khmer Rouge Regime: A Discussion Paper" (2009), p. 7.

78 Ramil-Nogales and van Schaak, *supra* n. 18, p. 368, 370-371.

79 ECCC (Memorandum) 23 September 2011, *Prosecutor* v. *Nuon Chea and Khieu Samphan* (Case 002/01), Memorandum: Initial Specification of the Substance of Reparations Awards Sought by the Civil Party Lead Co-Lawyers Pursuant to Internal Rule 23*quinquies* 3, No. E125, p. 2; Ciorciari Heindel, *supra* n. 15, p. 424.

80 Rule 12, ECCC's Internal Rules.

81 Ciorciari and Heindel, *supra* n. 15, p. 424; Sperfeldt, C., "The Role of Cambodian Civil Society in the Victim Participation Scheme of the Extraordinary Chambers in the Courts of Cambodia" in T. Bonacker and C. Safferling, *Victims of International Crimes: An Interdisciplinary Discourse* (The Hague, Asser Press 2013), p. 350-351.

82 Rule 12*bis* (3), ECCC's Internal Rules (Rev. 6).

83 Rules 12*bis* (2) and 23*quinquies* (3) (b), ECCC's Internal Rules (Rev. 6).

require the ECCC's approval to carry out its assistance programmes.[84] Nevertheless, the VSS has not yet identified any assistance project to be implemented; at most, it has approved a few NGO reparative projects in Cambodia.[85] Therefore, it appears that the NGO partners have thus far assumed the task of implementing restorative projects, with no immediate relationship with the judicial processes against the Khmer Rouge leaders.[86] According to Ciorciari and Heindel, the VSS will continue to link those NGO projects to the ECCC by providing its stamp of approval but it is unlikely that it will implement non-judicial measures.[87]

Regarding the design, implementation and securing of funding for reparation projects, this is to be performed in conjunction with Lead Co-Lawyers, in collaboration with governmental and non-governmental organisations[88] and in parallel with the ongoing trial.[89] Finally, the reparation projects allow for external funding,[90] but the ECCC's Internal Rules do not specify who can provide this external funding. The *Nuon Chea and Khieu Samphan* case however demonstrated that funding is most likely to derive from states and international organisations.[91]

2.3 Overview of the Cases

Before delving into the issue of reparation principles, it is necessary to provide a brief overview of the cases that will be addressed in the following sections. At present, the ICC has ordered reparations in three different cases. This Chapter will however only analysed the *Lubanga* and the *Katanga* cases.[92] At the time of writing, only the verdict in the *Lubanga* case is final, as the *Katanga* reparation judgment is being appealed. Likewise, the ECCC has issued two judgments on reparations: in the *Duch* case (case 001) and in the *Nuon Chea and Khieu Samphan* case (case 002). While the

84 ECCC, Reparation Program 2013-2017 for the victims of the Khmer Rouge Regime 1975-1979, Power point presentation, Slide 16 Available at: <http://vss.eccc.gov.kh/images/stories/2014/Reparation.pdf>.

85 Ciorciari and Heindel, *supra* n. 15, p. 425. The VSS has approved several projects with NGOs such as the Cambodian Defenders Project and the Transcultural Psychosocial Organization.

86 Sperfeldt, *supra* n. 81, p. 353-354.

87 Ciorciari J.D, and Heindel, A., *Hybrid Justice: The Extraordinary Chambers in the Courts of Cambodia* (Ann Arbor, University of Michigan Press 2014), p. 228.

88 Rules 12*bis* (3) and 23*quinquies* (3)(b), ECCC's Internal Rules; ECCC (Judgment) 7 August 2014, *Prosecutor* v. *Nuon Chea and Khieu Samphan* (Case 002/01), Judgment, No.002/19-09-2007/ECCC/TC.

89 ECCC, *Nuon Chea et al.* Memorandum E125, *supra* n. 79.

90 Rule 23*quinquies* (3)(b), ECCC's Internal Rules.

91 ECCC, *Chea and Shamphan* Judgment, *supra* n. 88, para. 1125-1152.

92 The Court has also ordered reparations in the *Al Mahdi* case. As explained in the introductory chapter of this book, this case is not analysed because it deals with crimes against cultural properties in Timbuktu, a crime that does not fall within the concept of GVHR. See: ICC (Order) 17 August 2017, *Prosecutor* v. *Ahmad Al Faqi Al Mahdi*, Reparations Order, ICC-01/12-01/15-236, para. 1.

Duch case is final, *Nuon Chea and Khieu Samphan* is not. It is important to mention that case 002 has been sub-divided into two mini-trials: 002/01 and 002/02. Both are against the two perpetrators. Of these two subcases, only 002/01 is final; 002/02 is still ongoing and a judgment has not yet been rendered.

ICC case law

On 14 March 2012, *Thomas Lubanga Dyilo* was found guilty of being a co-perpetrator of war crimes pertaining to the enlistment and conscription of children under the age of fifteen to actively participate in the hostilities of the armed conflict in the eastern Democratic Republic of the Congo.[93] The number of victims of these crimes committed by *Lubanga* was significant, as the involvement of children under the age of 15 in hostilities was widespread.[94] On 10 July 2012, *Lubanga* was sentenced to a total of fourteen years' imprisonment.[95] On 7 August 2012, the ICC Trial Chamber (ICC-TC) established the relevant principles on reparations and delivered its first decision on reparations and ordered collective reparations for the victims to be administered through the TFV.[96] On 1 December 2014, the Appeals Chamber (ICC-AC) confirmed the judgment and its respective sentencing.[97] On 3 March 2015, the ICC-AC amended the previous decision, improving/perfecting the approach of the ICC-TC, and instructed the TFV to present a draft of the reparations' implementation plan.[98] On 3 November 2015, the TFV filed a Draft Implementation Plan that included both service-based and symbolic collective reparation programmes.[99] On 21 October 2016, the ICC-TC approved the symbolic collective reparations proposed in the TFV plan.[100] As of December 2017, the service-based collective reparations have still not

93 ICC (Judgment) 14 March 2012, *Prosecutor* v. *Thomas Lubanga Dyilo,* Judgment pursuant to Article 74 of the Statute, ICC-01/04-01/06-2842.

94 ICC (Judgment) 3 March 2015, *Prosecutor* v. *Thomas Lubanga Dyilo*, Judgment on the appeals against the "Decision establishing the principles and procedures to be applied to reparations" of 7 August 2012, ICC-01/04-01/06-3129, para. 153.

95 ICC (Decision) 10 July 2012, *Prosecutor* v. *Thomas Lubanga Dyilo,* Decision on Sentence pursuant to Article 76 of the Statute, ICC-01/04-01/06-2901.

96 ICC, *Lubanga* Principles on Reparations, *supra* n. 4.

97 ICC (Judgment) 01 December 2014, *Prosecutor* v. *Thomas Lubanga Dyilo,* Judgment on the appeals of the Prosecutor and Mr. Lubanga Dyilo against the "Decision on Sentence pursuant to Article 76 of the Statute", ICC-01/04-01/06-3122. This decision was confirmed in 2015. See: ICC (Decision) 22 September 2015, *Prosecutor* v. *Thomas Lubanga Dyilo,* Decision on the review concerning the reduction of the sentence of Mr. Thomas Lubanga Dyilo, ICC-01/04-01/06-3173.

98 ICC, *Lubanga* Principles on Reparations' Appeal Judgment, *supra* n. 94.

99 ICC (Filing) 3 November 2015, *Prosecutor* v. *Thomas Lubanga Dyilo*, Filing on Reparations and Draft Implementation Plan, ICC-01/04-01/06-3177-Red.

100 ICC (Order) 21 October 2016, *Prosecutor* v. *Thomas Lubanga Dyilo*, Order approving the proposed plan of the Trust Fund for Victims in relation to symbolic collective reparations, ICC-01/04-01/06-3251.

been fully approved, with only the first stage (programmatic framework) receiving approval.[101]

On 7 March 2014, *Germain Katanga* was found guilty as an accessory[102] in the commission of a crime against humanity (murder) and the war crimes of murder, attacking a civilian population, the destruction of property, and pillaging in the Bogoro massacre on 24 February 2003 during the armed conflict in the eastern Democratic Republic of the Congo.[103] *Katanga* was acquitted of rape and sexual slavery as crimes against humanity and of the war crimes of sexual slavery, rape, and the use of children under the age of fifteen years to participate actively in hostilities.[104] On 23 May 2014, *Katanga* was sentenced to twelve years' imprisonment.[105] On 13 November 2015, this sentence was reduced by 3 years and 8 months.[106] On 24 March 2017, the ICC-TC II ordered individual and collective reparations.[107] Finally, 341 victims filed reparation applications.[108]

ECCC case law

Case 001: on 26 July 2010, *Kaing Guek Eav*, alias *Duch*, a former head of the *Tuol Sleng* prison site (S-21), was found to have been directly responsible for the planning, instigating and ordering[109] of crimes against humanity and violations of humanitarian law as well as aiding and abetting therein. He was sentenced to 35 years' imprisonment, minus five years because of his unlawful detention.[110] Of the 28 reparation requests brought by the civil parties, only two were granted: i) the inclusion of the names of the admitted civil parties and their deceased family members in the judgment, and ii) the publication of all statements of apology and an

101 The programmatic part refers to the selection and finalising of contracts with the implementing partners. ICC (Order) 6 April 2017, *Prosecutor* v. *Thomas Lubanga Dyilo*, Order approving the proposed programmatic framework for collective service-based reparations submitted by the Trust Fund for Victims, ICC-01/04-01/06-3289.

102 It must be pointed out that the accessory liability for which Mr. Katanga was found guilty is within the meaning of Article 25 (3)(d), ICC's Rome Statute that deals with residual liability.

103 ICC (Judgment) 7 March 2014, *Prosecutor* v. *Germain Katanga*, Judgment pursuant to Article 74 of the Statute, ICC-01/04-01/07-3436-tENG, 7 March 2014, para. 1691.

104 Ibid., para. 1088, 1693.

105 ICC (Decision) 23 May 2014, *Prosecutor* v. *Germain Katanga*, Decision on Sentence pursuant to article 76 of the Statute, ICC-01/04-01/07-3484.

106 ICC (Decision) 13 November 2015, *Prosecutor* v. *Germain Katanga*, Decision on the review concerning the reduction of the sentence of Mr. Germain Katanga, ICC-01/04/01/07-3615.

107 ICC, *Katanga* Reparations Order, *supra n.* 31.

108 Ibid., para. 32. It must be stated that 297 out of the 341 applicants have proven themselves to be victims on the balance of probabilities and therefore are entitled to become beneficiaries of reparations.

109 ECCC, *Duch* Trial Judgment, *supra* n. 11, para. 521, 526, 531 and 537.

110 Ibid., para. 567-568, 631-633.

acknowledgement of responsibility made by *Duch*.[111] On 13 February 2012, the ECCC Supreme Court Chamber (SCC) increased *Duch's* sentence to life imprisonment in its appeals judgment,[112] and confirmed the reparation measures granted by the ECCC Trial Chamber (ECCC-TC).[113] During this case, 93 victims were recognised as civil parties of whom only 66 were identified as beneficiaries of reparations.[114]

Case 002:[115] the case was split into two sections on 22 September 2011,[116] with the aim of enhancing the expeditiousness of the trials. However, this caused many uncertainties and to some extent complicated the trials even further.[117] On 7 August 2012, *Nuon Chea and Khieu Samphan* (case 002/01) were found guilty on accounts of crimes against humanity and were sentenced to life imprisonment.[118] The former was found to be directly responsible and as a superior,[119] and the latter was found responsible through a Joint Criminal Enterprise (JCE) and directly for planning, instigating, and aiding and abetting.[120] In the same judgment the ECCC-TC approved seven out of the thirteen reparation projects.[121] On 23 November 2016, the SCC confirmed the sentence against both convicted persons but overturned the conviction for the crime against humanity: extermination and persecution on political grounds.[122] Since there was no appeal against these reparations, the projects approved

111 Ibid., para. 667-668.

112 ECCC, *Duch* Appeal Judgment, *supra* n. 69, para. 383.

113 Ibid., para. 68.

114 ECCC, *Duch* Trial Judgment, *supra* n. 11, para. 636-650.

115 Initially the case related to four senior Khmer Rouge leaders: *Nuon Chea*, former Deputy Secretary of the Communist Party of Kampuchea; *Khieu Samphan*, former President of the State Presidium; *Ieng Thirith*, former Minister for Social Affairs; and *Ieng Sary*, former Deputy Prime Minister and Foreign Minister. However, *Ieng Thirith* was released after the Trial Chamber found her unfit to stand trial. See: ECCC (Decision) 13 September 2012, *Prosecutor* v. *Nuon Chea et al.* (Case 002), Decision on Reassessment of Accused IENG Thirith's Fitness to Stand Trial following Supreme Court Chamber Decision on 13 December 2011, No. E138/1/10. In addition, *Ieng Sary* died on 14 March 2013 and the proceedings against him were thereby terminated. See: Available at < https://www.eccc.gov.kh/en/indicted-person/ieng-sary-fomer-accused>.

116 ECCC (Order) 22 September 2011, *Prosecutor* v. *Nuon Chea et al.* (Case 002), Severance order pursuant to internal rule 89ter, No.002/19-09-2007/ECCC-E124.

117 Heindel, A., "Managing Enormous Mass Crimes Indictments: The ECCC Severance Experiment' in in S. M. Meisenberg and I. Stegmiller, *The Extraordinary Chambers in the Courts of Cambodia: Assessing their Contribution to International Criminal Law* (The Hague, Asser Press 2016), p. 435-459; Williams, S., "The Severance of *Case 002* at the ECCC: A Radical Trial Management Technique or a Step Too Far", 13 *Journal of International Criminal Justice* (2015).

118 ECCC, *Chea and Shamphan* Judgment, *supra* n. 88, para. 1106-1107.

119 Ibid., para. 941.

120 Ibid., para. 1053-1054.

121 Ibid., para. 1160.

122 ECCC (Judgment) 23 November 2016, *Prosecutor* v. *Nuon Chea and Khieu Samphan* (Case 002/01), No.002/19-09-2007/ECCC/SC, para. 1120-1121.

by the ECCC-TC were considered to be final. During this case, 3,866 civil parties participated in the trial.[123]

3 Principles on Reparations

The ICC's legal framework establishes a few general rules regarding reparations, but it does not specify all the substantive and procedural aspects. Instead, the ICC is given wide discretion to define those aspects through the adoption of the *Principles on Reparations*. Similarly, the ECCC's legal framework remains silent with respect to most procedural and substantive aspects governing its reparations. Even though the ECCC is not explicitly mandated to create a set of general principles, it has started to clarify the principles and rules that govern its reparation system through its case law.

The absence of principles or clear rules concerning substantive and procedural regulations governing the reparations mandate of the two tribunals is partially explained by the fact that reparations under international criminal law had no precedent before the establishment of the ICC and the ECCC. While domestic law, public international law and human rights law have established principles regarding reparations, these cannot as such be borrowed by international criminal tribunals because the nature of their legal regimes differs.[124] Nonetheless, the principles established within these fields have provided some limited guidance or inspiration to both tribunals.[125]

The following sections will describe the principles on reparations as stipulated by the legal frameworks of both the ICC and the ECCC, and as developed through its case law. In this regard, it is noteworthy to highlight that special attention will be devoted to substantive and procedural issues of collective reparations.

3.1 ICC's General Principles

The ICC has recognised that the right to reparation is a well-established victims' right.[126] The ICC's Principles on Reparations were first established by the ICC-AC in the *Lubanga* case, and they may 'be applied, adapted, expanded upon, or added to by

123 ECCC (Decision) 24 June 2011, *Prosecutor* v. *Nuon Chea et al.* (Case 002), Decision on Appeals Against Orders of the Co-investigating Judges on the Admissibility of Civil Party Applications, No. D411/3/6, para. 60; Sperfeldt, *supra* n. 81, p. 358.

124 Dwertmann, E., *The Reparation System of the International Criminal Court* (Leiden/Boston Martinus Nijhoff 2010), p. 295.

125 McCarthy, C., "Reparations under the Rome Statute of the International Criminal Court and Reparative Justice Theory", 3 *The International Journal of Transitional Justice* (2009), p. 256; ECCC, *Duch* Appeal Judgment, *supra* n. 69, para. 65.

126 ICC, *Lubanga* Principles on Reparations, *supra* n. 4, para. 185.

future Trial Chambers.'[127] Accordingly, the ICC-TC II applied them in the *Katanga* case.[128] They concern the following principles:

- *Purposes of reparations*: These are twofold: to 'oblige those responsible for serious crimes to repair the harm they caused to the victims' and to 'enable the Chamber to ensure that offenders account for their acts.'[129]
- Reparations should *foster reconciliation* between victims, perpetrators and communities.[130]
- *The principle of liability to remedy harm*: This principle is derived from the individual criminal responsibility of the perpetrator and it complements the ICC's justice mandate.[131]
- *Reparations are part of the ICC judicial process*:[132] Nevertheless, their implementation may be conducted through a non-judicial body, the TFV.[133]
- *Elements of an order for reparations*: An order must include five essential elements: it must i) be made against the convicted person; ii) inform the convicted person of his/her scope of liability with respect to the reparations awarded; iii) specify and provide reasons for the type of reparation; iv) define the harm caused and identify the appropriate modalities of reparations accordingly; and v) identify the victims eligible to be beneficiaries, or set out the criteria for eligibility, based on causality between the harm and the crimes.[134]
- *Victims are to be heard: By means of their participation,* victims have a voice throughout the entire process.[135]

---

127 ICC (Order) 3 March 2015, *Prosecutor v. Thomas Lubanga Dyilo*, Annex to the Judgment on the appeals against the "Decision establishing the principles and procedures to be applied to reparations" of 7 August 2012, ICC-01/04-01/06-3129-AnxA, para. 5.

128 ICC, *Katanga* Reparations Order, *supra n.* 31, para. 29-31.

129 ICC, *Lubanga* Principles on Reparations, *supra* n. 4, para. 179; ICC, *Lubanga* Principles on Reparations' Appeal Judgment, *supra* n. 94, para. 151; ICC, *Lubanga* Appeal Judgment on Reparations Order, *supra* n. 127, para. 2; ICC, *Katanga* Reparations Order, *supra* n. 31, para. 15.

130 ICC, *Lubanga* Principles on Reparations, *supra* n. 4, para. 193, 244; ICC, *Lubanga* Appeal Judgment on Reparations Order, *supra* n. 127, para. 46, 71-72; ICC, *Katanga* Reparations Order, *supra n.* 31, para. 268, 317.

131 ICC, *Lubanga* Principles on Reparations' Appeal Judgment, *supra* n. 94, para. 99, 101

132 ICC, *Lubanga* Principles on Reparations' Appeal Judgment, *supra* n. 94, para. 237; ICC, *Katanga* Reparations Order, *supra* n. 31, para. 18.

133 ICC, *Lubanga* Principles on Reparations, *supra* n. 4, para. 260

134 ICC, *Lubanga* Principles on Reparations' Appeal Judgment, *supra* n. 94. para. 1, 32; ICC, *Katanga* Reparations Order, *supra* n. 31, para. 31.

135 ICC, *Lubanga* Principles on Reparations, *supra* n. 4, para. 267; ICC, *Lubanga* Appeal Judgment on Reparations Order, *supra* n. 127, para. 76.

- *Non-discrimination and equal access to reparations*: Victims must be treated equally.[136]
- *Affirmative action* measures may be adopted in order to guarantee equal, effective and safe access to reparations for vulnerable victims.[137]
- *Respect and protection of victims*: Victims are to be treated with humanity and respect, and should receive measures to ensure their safety, well-being and privacy.[138]
- *Transformative*: Reparations need to address underlying injustices and inequalities and avoid perpetuating existing stigmatisation.[139]
- *Gender-inclusive approach*: The principles and procedures of reparations should be guided by gender-inclusivity.[140]
- *Voluntariness*: Reparations are voluntary, and the informed consent of the recipient is necessary prior to the award.[141]
- *Transparency*: Reparation proceedings should be transparent.[142] The registry bears responsibility for publicity and outreach during the reparation proceedings.[143]
- When victims are awarded reparations, the ICC should take into account whether those victims have previously received reparation awards by other bodies.[144]

---

136 ICC, *Lubanga* Principles on Reparations, *supra* n. 4, para. 187, 191; ICC, *Lubanga* Appeal Judgment on Reparations Order, *supra* n. 127, para. 12, 16, 18; ICC, *Katanga* Reparations Order, *supra* n. 31, para. 30.

137 ICC, *Lubanga* Principles on Reparations, *supra* n. 4, para. 200; ICC, *Lubanga* Appeal Judgment on Reparations Order, *supra* n. 127, para. 19.

138 ICC, *Lubanga* Principles on Reparations, *supra* n. 4, para. 190; ICC, *Lubanga* Appeal Judgment on Reparations Order, *supra* n. 127, para. 15; ICC, *Katanga* Reparations Order, *supra* n. 31, para. 30.

139 ICC, *Lubanga* Principles on Reparations, *supra* n. 4, para. 192; ICC, *Lubanga* Appeal Judgment on Reparations Order, *supra* n. 127, para. 17; ICC, *Katanga* Reparations Order, *supra* n. 31, para. 310.

140 ICC, *Lubanga* Principles on Reparations, *supra* n. 4, para. 202; ICC, *Lubanga* Appeal Judgment on Reparations Order, *supra* n. 127, para. 18.

141 ICC, *Lubanga* Principles on Reparations, *supra* n. 4, para. 204; ICC, *Lubanga* Principles on Reparations' Appeal Judgment, *supra* n. 94, para. 159; ICC, *Lubanga* Appeal Judgment on Reparations Order, *supra* n. 127, para. 30.

142 ICC, *Lubanga* Principles on Reparations, *supra* n. 4, para. 251; ICC, *Lubanga* Appeal Judgment on Reparations Order, *supra* n. 127, para. 51.

143 ICC, *Lubanga* Principles on Reparations, *supra* n. 4, para. 258; ICC, *Lubanga* Appeal Judgment on Reparations Order, *supra* n. 127, para. 52

144 ICC, *Lubanga* Appeal Judgment on Reparations Order, *supra* n. 127, para 9; ICC, *Katanga* Reparations Order, *supra* n. 31, para. 319.

In addition, reparations should i) take into account the needs and priorities of the victims;[145] iii) be preventive;[146] iv) be culturally-sensitive;[147] v) be adequate, appropriate,[148] and meaningful;[149] vi) be proportionate to the harm caused; and vii) support self-sustaining programmes.[150]

All in all, it can be concluded that the principles highlight the first and most important purpose of reparations within the ICC, which is to render perpetrators accountable for their crimes and to exact payment for these crimes. The other principles may even be considered to be secondary to the ultimate goal of reparations within the ICC.

3.2 ECCC's General Principles

To date, the ECCC has not clarified the principles or precepts underlying reparations under its jurisdiction; at most, it has referred to the purposes of collective and moral reparations:

- *The purposes of moral and collective reparations*: These are twofold: to acknowledge the harm suffered by the Civil Parties due to the crimes for which the accused was convicted, and to provide benefits to the Civil Parties that address this harm.[151]
- Reparations 'are intended to be *essentially symbolic* rather than compensatory'.[152]
- Reparations are to 'be awarded *against, and be borne by the convicted persons*,'[153] yet external funding for reparations is allowed[154] (emphasis added).

---

145 ICC *Lubanga* Principles on Reparations, *supra* n. 4, para. 189; ICC, *Lubanga* Appeal Judgment on Reparations Order, *supra* n. 127, para. 32; ICC, *Katanga* Reparations Order, *supra* n. 31, para. 30.

146 ICC *Lubanga* Principles on Reparations, *supra* n. 4, para. 240; ICC, *Katanga* Reparations Order, *supra* n. 31, para. 297.

147 ICC *Lubanga* Principles on Reparations, *supra* n. 4, para. 245; ICC, *Lubanga* Appeal Judgment on Reparations Order, *supra* n. 127, para. 47; ICC, *Katanga* Reparations Order, *supra* n. 31, para. 168.

148 ICC, *Lubanga* Principles on Reparations, *supra* n. 4, para. 242; ICC, *Lubanga* Appeal Judgment on Reparations Order, *supra* n. 127, para. 44; ICC, *Katanga* Reparations Order, *supra* n. 31, para. 15, 268.

149 In this light, the ICC has strived to grant meaningful reparations. See: ICC, *Katanga* Reparations Order, *supra* n. 31, para. 15.

150 ICC, *Lubanga* Principles on Reparations, *supra* n. 4, para. 246; ICC, *Lubanga* Appeal Judgment on Reparations Order, *supra* n. 127, para. 48; ICC, *Katanga* Reparations Order, *supra* n. 31, para. 268.

151 Rule 23*quinquies* (1), ECCC's Internal Rules; ECCC, *Chea and Shamphan* Judgment, *supra* n. 88, para. 1114.

152 ECCC, *Duch* Appeal Judgment, *supra* n. 69, para. 644.

153 ECCC, *Duch* Appeal Judgment, *supra* n. 69, para. 656. Rule 23*quinquies* (3) (a), ECCC's Internal Rules.

154 ECCC, *Chea and Shamphan* Judgment, *supra* n. 88, para. 1112-1113.

4 Types of Reparations

The ICC can award reparations including restitution, compensation, rehabilitation and collective awards[155] in a 'symbolic, preventative or transformative' manner.[156] Significantly, individual and collective reparations are not mutually exclusive.[157] On the other hand, the ECCC can only award collective and moral reparations. Its legal framework explicitly excludes individual and monetary awards.[158] It therefore gives preference to 'measures that benefit as many victims as possible' as opposed to individual measures.[159] The ECCC's categorical denial of financial compensation relies on three main objections: i) compensation may be problematic because victims may perceive it as the buying of their suffering;[160] ii) it may create or exacerbate tensions within communities;[161] and iii) following the commission of international crimes, it is unlikely that societies will have the necessary funds to finance individual reparations.

4.1 Individual Reparations

Individual measures may take the form of restitution, compensation, rehabilitation, satisfaction and guarantees of non-repetition.[162] While the advantages of individual reparations include the fact that they may be tailored to victims' personal harm, they present many challenges within the context of international crimes. For instance, it is unlikely that all the harm suffered by the victims can be addressed; it is also unlikely that sufficient funds will be available. In addition, they disregard the social harm inflicted by the commission of crimes, which is especially relevant in the context of international crimes.[163]

Of the five types of individual reparations, restitution is very unlikely to be granted by the ICC as the majority of the harm inflicted by international crimes is

155 Article 75 (1), ICC's Rome Statute; Rule 98 (2), ICC's RoPE.

156 ICC, *Lubanga* Principles on Reparations, *supra* n. 4, para. 222; ICC, *Lubanga* Appeal Judgment on Reparations Order, *supra* n. 127, para. 34.

157 ICC, *Lubanga* Principles on Reparations, *supra* n. 4, para. 220.

158 Rules 23*quinquies* and 80*bis*, ECCC's Internal Rules; ECCC, *Nuon Chea et al.* Decision on the Civil Party Applications' Appeals, *supra* n. 123, para. 70.

159 ECCC, *Duch* Appeal Judgment, *supra* n. 69, para. 659.

160 Roht-Arriaza, N., "Reparations Decisions and Dilemmas", 27 *Hastings International and Comparative Law Review* (2004), p. 180; Mégret, F., "The International Criminal Court and the Failure to Mention Symbolic Reparations", 16 *International Review of Victimology* (2009), p. 131.

161 This was acknowledged by the ICC. See: ICC *Lubanga* Principles on Reparations, *supra* n. 4, para. 108.

162 See: Chapter II, section 3.2.

163 Mégret, F., "The case for collective reparations before the International Criminal Court" in J.M. Wemmers (ed.) *Reparations for Victims of Crimes against Humanity* (Abingdon, Routledge 2014), p. 175-176.

inherently irreparable.[164] In addition, most measures of satisfaction and guarantees of non-repetition are actually of a collective nature, and most cannot be implemented by the perpetrator, as they are understood as measures that can only be implemented by the State. For instance, common guarantees of non-repetition include the adoption or modification of certain laws, as well as human rights training for police or military personnel. As for measures of satisfaction, the naming of streets after victims or the erection of a monument or memorial requires the consent and involvement of state authorities. Thus, if the ICC is to grant individual measures, it will most likely award either compensation or rehabilitation. However, the Court is not prevented from ordering satisfaction and guarantees of non-repetition measures and invoking the states parties' obligations to cooperate with the Court as means to ensure their implementation.[165]

Although compensation may take the form of both individual and collective awards, it is usually granted on an individual basis.[166] Scholars have emphasised the importance of complementing financial measures with symbolic or moral reparations,[167] because these have an important function that compensation cannot always provide: acknowledging the harm.[168] Without additional measures, some victims may consider compensation to be nothing more than blood money and it may even create further tensions in society. In addition, compensation may be substantial or symbolic, meaning that it may aim to compensate the loss in its entirety or bring modest relief that, while not compensating all losses, will provide victims with some remedy. Compensation granted in the context of a conflict or post-conflict situation is likely to be of a symbolic nature. The reason for this is twofold: firstly, substantial amounts given to victims may put the recipients at risk, and, secondly, resources may be very limited, so much so as to preclude even any consideration of substantial compensation.[169] Against this background, in the *Katanga* case the ICC awarded symbolic individual monetary reparations of USD 250 per victim accompanied by collective reparations, including moral, development and economic measures.[170] While the ICC recognized the importance of individual reparations in conveying an

164 ICC, *Lubanga* Principles on Reparations, *supra* n. 4, para. 204; ICC, *Lubanga* Principles on Reparations' Appeal Judgment, *supra* n. 94, para. 223; ICC, *Lubanga* Appeal Judgment on Reparations Order, *supra* n. 127, para. 67.

165 Articles 86 and 87, ICC's Rome Statute.

166 ICC, *Lubanga* Draft Implementation Plan, *supra* n. 99, para. 204; ICC, *Katanga* Reparations Order, *supra* n. 31, para. 271.

167 Roht-Arriaza, *supra* n. 160, p. 180; Mégret, *supra* n. 160, p. 131.

168 Roht-Arriaza, *supra* n. 160, p. 159, 181; Cryer et al., *supra* n. 3, p. 581.

169 McKay, *supra* n. 16, p. 945; Iliff, F., Maitre-Muhl F., and Sirel, A., "Adverse Consequences of Reparations", *Briefing Paper No.6, Reparations Unit, Essex University* (2011), p. 3-4; Evans C., *The Right to Reparation in International Law for Victims of Armed Conflict* (Cambridge, CUP 2012), p. 72.

170 ICC, *Katanga* Reparations Order, *supra* n. 31, para. 300, 306.

acknowledgment of the harm suffered,[171] it also highlighted that symbolic monetary awards would avoid further tension in the victims' communities.[172] Finally, it is important to point out that the ICC's approach in the *Lubanga* case, where it ruled that compensation would only be granted if sufficient funds were available,[173] was rendered moot by the fact that Mr. Katanga's victims had obtained individual compensation even after he was declared indigent for the purpose of reparations.

4.2 Moral Reparations

As already referred to in Chapter 3, symbolic reparations, moral reparations or measures of satisfaction of a collective nature are commonly considered to be synonymous.[174] In addition, scholars have affirmed that guarantees of non-repetition are to be considered as measures of satisfaction that have a preventive nature.[175] Accordingly, throughout this chapter we will refer to moral reparations, symbolic reparations, measures of satisfaction of a collective nature and guarantees of non-repetition as being synonymous.[176]

Moral reparations are awarded to victims in order to respond to their non-material needs,[177] or for the kind of harm that cannot be easily quantified.[178] Moral reparations aim to redress the dignity of victims[179] and are also targeted at a wide range of victims.[180] Following Mégret and Roht-Arriaza's approach, moral reparations[181] can be clustered into five groups: i) an acknowledgement of responsibility (declaratory judgments and apologies); ii) truth-seeking (an investigation of the facts and the identification, prosecution and punishment of those responsible, a search for the whereabouts of those who have disappeared, locating the remains of victims); iii) dissemination of the truth by mass media (publishing the outcome of the investigation and trial); iv) the reintegration of victims through measures aimed at memoralisation (memorials, commemorations, tributes, the naming of buildings or streets after the victims, the granting of educational benefits such as scholarships and educational materials as well as the burial of mortal remains in accordance with the

171 Ibid., para. 285.
172 Ibid., para. 299.
173 ICC *Lubanga* Principles on Reparations, *supra* n. 4, para. 226.
174 Mégret, *supra* n. 160, p. 122; Dudai, R., "Closing the gap: symbolic reparations and armed groups", 93 *International Review of the Red Cross* (2011), p. 6.
175 Mégret, *supra* n. 160, p. 129-132; Roht-Arriaza, *supra* n. 160, p. 159-160.
176 Dudai, *supra* n. 174, p. 6.
177 Ibid., p. 6.
178 Jeffery, *supra* n. 10, p. 104.
179 Principle 22, Principles on Reparations; Bantekas, I., and Oette, L., *International Human Rights Law and Practice* (Cambridge, CUP 2016, 2nd ed.), p. 629-630.
180 Mégret, *supra* n. 160, p. 131.
181 Scholars however refer to measures of satisfaction.

victims' religious beliefs and customs); and v) measures to prevent future violations (institutional reforms, training, and memorials).[182]

Moral reparations have particular importance under the ECCC's legal framework for reparations; they are one of the two forms of relief that the Extraordinary Chambers can award. The ICC is equally empowered to grant these measures of reparation; in fact, the ICC's first approval of a TFV proposal for collective reparations in the *Lubanga* case concerned moral reparations.[183] Their importance does not however diminish their problematic nature with regard to their implementation in the context of international criminal law. These measures usually require state involvement, and in international criminal law states are not parties to the cases.[184] Yet, not all moral measures require state involvement, such as apologies by the perpetrator and the dissemination of the truth (which can be achieved through the dissemination of a judgment).[185]

4.2.1 Acknowledgment of Responsibility

The most common acknowledgment of responsibility is achieved through a judgment. However, under human rights law states can additionally be ordered to publicly acknowledge their responsibility for human rights violations and to apologise to the victims.[186] This approach cannot be immediately translated into international criminal law. As far as the ICC is concerned, apologies need to be voluntary. In this light, the ICC-TC I invited Mr. Lubanga to apologise to the victims of his crime whether on a public or confidential basis.[187] It appears that while the ICC acknowledges the restorative utility of apologies in situations of mass violence,[188] it also recognises that

182 See: Chapter II, sections. 3.2.3 and 3.2.4.

183 ICC, *Lubanga* Approval on Collective Symbolic Reparations, *supra* n. 100.

184 Birchall, E., Francq, E., and Pijnenburg, A., "The International Criminal Court and Reparations for Child Victims of Armed Conflict", *Briefing Paper No.4, Reparations Unit, Essex University* (2011), p. 25.

185 Ramil-Nogales and van Schaak, *supra* n. 18, p. 364.

186 See the following cases from the Inter-American Court of Human Rights. IACtHR (Judgment) 15 June 2005, *Moiwana Community* v. *Suriname*, para. 2-7, 216; IACtHR (Judgment) 3 December 2001, *Cantoral Benavides* v. *Peru*, para. 81.

187 ICC *Lubanga* Principles on Reparations, *supra* n. 4, para. 241.

188 Urban Walker, M., "Restorative Justice and Reparations", 37 *Journal of Social Philosophy* (2006), p. 388; Mégret, *supra* n. 160, p. 141; Jones, S., "Apology Diplomacy: Justice for All?", *Issue 122, Discussion papers in diplomacy,* Netherlands Institute of International Relations 'Clingendael', 2011, p. 5. Available at: <http://www.clingendael.nl/sites/default/files/20110900_cdsp_discussionpapersindiplomacy_122_jones.pdf>. Significantly, Tomuschat challenges the utility of apologies given by an individual. According to him, apologies offered by individuals 'are no more than a gesture of courtesy and do not have the same weight as official apologies offered by a State'. See: Tomuschat, C., "The Responsibility of Other Entities: Private Individuals" in J. Crawford, A. Pellet and S. Olleson, *The Law on International Responsibility* (Oxford, OUP 2010), p. 320. In addition to the ICC, the TFV has also recognised the relevance of a voluntary apology to the process of reconciliation. See: ICC, *Lubanga* Draft Implementation Plan, *supra* n. 99, para. 261.

ordering a convicted person to apologise may raise some human rights issues. For instance, it can be perceived as a cruel or inhumane act.[189] However, it is possible to overcome these human rights issues and it seems that the benefits of apologies, regardless of whether they have been ordered or are sincere, outweigh their apparent problems.[190]

Similarly, the ECCC has emphasised that apologies contribute to satisfying victims indefinitely, as they transcend time and the particular audience at which they are targeted;[191] however, the ECCC has refrained from ordering a convicted person to apologise. In addition, in the *Duch* case the victims sought an official statement of apology from the government of Cambodia, but this measure was denied because the ECCC lacked jurisdiction to issue orders of reparations against the government of Cambodia.[192]

Significantly, defendants sometimes voluntarily apologise during the trial, as was the case in *Duch,*[193] *Katanga*[194] and *Lubanga*[195] Mr. Katanga also declared his willingness to offer an apology to his victims, whether publicly or privately, in a ceremony or by letter in the reparation stage.[196] The TFV considered a public apology to be the preferred option, but this does not appear to be possible as Katanga is in prison, serving his sentence. Alternatively, the TFV, which was tasked with the implementation of reparations in both cases, has foreseen the possibility of delivering an apology by way of a video.[197] Although apologies 'must be given voluntarily in

189 Mégret, *supra* n. 160, p. 127-135-136.

190 van Dijck, G., "The Ordered Apology", 37 *Oxford Journal of Legal Studies* (2017), p. 586-587; White argues thee need of ordered apologies as means to provide complete remedies to plaintiffs. See: White, B., "Say you're Sorry: Court-Ordered Apologies as a Civil Rights Remedy", 91 *Cornell Law Review* (2006), p. 1311.

191 ECCC, *Duch* Appeal Judgment, *supra* n. 69, para. 677.

192 ECCC, *Duch* Trial Judgment, *supra* n. 11, para. 671; ECCC, *Duch* Appeal Judgment, *supra* n. 69, para. 680.

193 ECCC, *Duch* Trial Judgment, *supra* n. 11, para. 659.

194 ICC (Notice) 25 June 2014, *Prosecutor* v. *Germain Katanga,* Annex A to Defence Notice of Discontinuance of Appeal against the 'Jugement rendu en application de l'article 74 du Statut' rendered by Trial Chamber II on 7 April 2014, ICC-01/04-01/07-3497-AnxA.

195 Mr. Lubanga apologised in an open session held for a review of his sentence reduction. See: ICC (Transcript) 21 August 2015, *Prosecutor* v. *Thomas Lubanga Dyilo*, Sentence Review Session, ICC-01/04-01/06-T-366-Red-ENG, p. 27.

196 ICC, *Katanga* Reparations Order, *supra* n. 31, para. 315, 318.

197 ICC (Filing) 25 July 2017, *Prosecutor* v. *Germain Katanga,* Draft implementation plan relevant to Trial Chamber II's order for reparations of 24 March 2017 (ICC-01/04-01/07-3728) with Confidential Annex 1: Detailed Overview of beneficiary categories, proposed awards within each category, and estimated values and budget costs thereto, Public Annex 2: Defence correspondence regarding Mr Katanga's potential participation, Confidential, ex parte available to the Registry only Annex 3: Table of harm categorizations on an individual basis of all 297 victims, Confidential, ex parte available to OPCV Legal Representative only Annex 4: Table of harm categorization of victims represented, Confidential, ex parte available to the Legal Representative only Annex 5: Table of harm categorization of victims represented, ICC-01/04-01/07-3751-Red, para. 132-133.

order to be genuine,'[198] it is difficult to assert the sincerity of apologies provided by defendants. Victims may therefore perceive those apologies as being motivated by self-interest.[199]

4.2.2 Truth-Seeking

One of the purposes of international trials is that victims find the 'truth' with regard to what happened in relation to the crimes suffered. However, the truth that is uncovered in international trials may be controversial, as it may be forcefully disputed among different groups.[200] In addition, the truth that emerges from an international trial is merely partial, as a specific case is limited to the specific charges that the prosecutor has initiated. In the *Katanga* case, however, the ICC specifically excluded searching for the whereabouts of those who disappeared as part of the collective reparations,[201] because it was deemed inappropriate within the socio-cultural context of the case and could put victims at risk.[202]

4.2.3 Dissemination of a Judgment

Nonetheless, for many victims the truth that has resulted from an international trial is of great importance. The ECCC has therefore acknowledged 'that the dissemination of materials of the ECCC proceedings is an appropriate form of reparation.'[203] However, in the *Duch* case, the victims' request to publish parts of the judgment was not granted due to a 'lack of specificity' and *Duch's* financial resources. Instead, the ECCC assured the victims that the *Duch* trial judgment would be made available on its website and that outreach activities would be organised to inform society about the judgment, as this would contribute to the reconciliation process in Cambodia.[204]

In addition, in the *Nuon Chea and Khieu Samphan* case, the victims proposed, through their Lead Co-Lawyers, both the publication of a booklet explaining the trial and the publication and distribution of the trial judgment in the Khmer language as

198 Jones, *supra* n. 188, p. 6.

199 ICC (Filing) 21 January 2015, *Prosecutor* v. *Germain Katanga,* Registry Report on Applications for Reparations in accordance with Trial Chamber II's Order of 27 August 2014, ICC-01/04-01/07-3512-Anx1-Red2, para. 13.

200 Ramji-Nogales, J., "Bespoke transitional justice at the International Criminal Court" in C. De Vos, S. Kendall and C. Stahn (eds) *Contested Justice: The Politics and Practice of International Criminal Court Interventions* (Cambridge, CUP 2015) p. 107, 110.

201 Disappeared people need to be understood as missing people and not as enforced disappeared people.

202 ICC, *Katanga* Reparations Order, *supra* n. 31, para. 301.

203 ECCC, *Duch* Appeal Judgment, *supra* n. 69, para. 709.

204 ECCC, *Duch* Trial Judgment, *supra* n. 11, para 669; ECCC, *Duch* Appeal Judgment, *supra* n. 69, para. 709.

a form of reparation.[205] Both of these reparation measures were approved,[206] and it is important to mention that these two reparation measures were not ordered against those who had been convicted, but were measures to be implemented by means of external funding.[207] On the other hand, in the *Katanga* case the dissemination of information on the process was excluded as part of the collective reparations programmes. This was based on the consultation of victims, the socio-cultural context, and the risk of creating an unsafe environment for those victims.[208]

4.2.4 Memory-related Measures

The ICC approved memory-related measures in the *Lubanga* case as part of the symbolic collective reparations to be implemented by the TFV.[209] The measures included a two-year project monitored by the ICC through quarterly reports issued by the TFV.[210] On the other hand, in the *Katanga* case the ICC specifically excluded memory-related measures such as commemorative events and the construction of monuments. This decision was based on the consultation of victims, the socio-cultural context, and the risk of creating an unsafe environment for the victims and/or social turbulence.[211]

Regarding the ECCC, in the *Duch* case the victims requested the adoption of a national commemoration day and the construction of pagodas and other memorials as part of their moral reparations. However, both requests were denied due to the lack of detail regarding the nature, location and cost of the reparations. In addition, ordering the Cambodian government to provide reparations was not within the jurisdiction of the ECCC, while the measures would inevitably require government involvement.[212] The Supreme Chamber reiterated this judgment and emphasised that these kinds of measures are the prerogative of administrative governmental authorities.[213] In addition, in the *Duch* case the victims also sought the preservation of 'the S-21 archives, Vann Nath's paintings and the S-21 and S-24 sites,' which is a type of preventive measure directed against similar crimes. The request was denied, however, as the ECCC was

205 ECCC, *Chea and Shamphan* Judgment, *supra* n. 88, para. 1138-1139.
206 Ibid., para. 1160.
207 Rule 23 *quinques* (3) (b) of the ECCC's Internal Rules, recognized another alternative path to obtain reparations in addition to the one borne by convicted persons.
208 ICC, *Katanga* Reparations Order, *supra* n. 31, para. 301.
209 ICC (Filing) 19 September 2016, *Prosecutor* v. *Thomas Lubanga Dyilo*, Public Redacted version of Filing regarding symbolic collective reparations projects with confidential Annex: Draft Request for Proposals, ICC-01/04-01/06-3223-Conf, ICC-01/04-01/06-3223-Red, para. 29-43; ICC, *Lubanga* Approval on Collective Symbolic Reparations, *supra* n. 100.
210 ICC, *Lubanga* Approval on Collective Symbolic Reparations, *supra* n. 100. para. 17.
211 ICC, *Katanga* Reparations Order, *supra* n. 31, para. 301.
212 ECCC, *Duch* Trial Judgment, *supra* n. 11, para. 671-672.
213 ECCC, *Duch* Appeal Judgment, *supra* n. 69, para. 712-713.

not mandated to order reparations against the government of Cambodia, and because it was unclear who the legal owners of these sites were.[214]

In the *Nuon Chea and Khieu Samphan* case, four memory-related measures were requested: a national remembrance day, public memorials, the construction of a memorial on Phnom Penh, and the construction of a memorial for the victims living in France.[215] Although the ECCC Chamber considered that all four measures were appropriate to address the harm suffered and that they had the potential to provide moral and collective reparations, it only approved the two that had secured sufficient external funding for their implementation.[216] These were to be implemented as envisaged by the organisations which had obtained the funding. Finally, it must be emphasised that the four reparation orders were sought under Rule 23 *quinques* (3) (b) of the ECCC's Internal Rules and were not to be ordered against those who had been convicted.

4.2.5 Preventive Measures

Under international criminal law victims do not commonly request preventive measures because their implementation requires direct State involvement. Preventive measures (often referred to as transformative measures) are forward-looking guarantees of non-repetition, which aim to transform social, political, economic or cultural structures in order to prevent future victimisation. Nevertheless, the ICC has embraced preventive measures as part of the collective reparations that can be obtained by victims.[217] However, in the *Lubanga* case the preventive measures envisaged were actually those memory-related activities mentioned in the previous section.[218] In addition, the ICC recognised that, through rehabilitation programmes, social transformation could be achieved.[219] Regarding the EECC, preventive measures were also adopted through memory-related measures.

214 ECCC, *Duch* Trial Judgment, *supra* n. 11, para. 673; ECCC, *Duch* Appeal Judgment, *supra* n. 69, para. 680.

215 ECCC, *Chea and Shamphan* Judgment, *supra* n. 88, para. 1126-1130.

216 Ibid., para. 1161.

217 ICC *Lubanga* Principles on Reparations, *supra* n. 4, para. 222, 236; ICC, *Lubanga* Principles on Reparations' Appeal Judgment, *supra* n. 94. para. 202; ICC, *Lubanga* Appeal Judgment on Reparations Order, *supra* n. 127, para. 67; ICC (Filing) 3 November 2015, *Prosecutor* v. *Thomas Lubanga Dyilo*, Annex A to Filing on Reparations and Draft Implementation Plan, ICC-01/04-01/06-3177-AnxA.

218 ICC, *Lubanga* TFV's Symbolic Reparations Proposal, *supra* n. 209, para. 41.

219 ICC, *Lubanga*, Annex A to the Draft Implementation Plan, *supra* n. 217, para. 23.

4.2.6 *Other Measures of Satisfaction*

In the *Duch* case, of all the collective and moral reparations requested, only two were granted: i) the inclusion of the names of the civil parties and the immediate victims of the crimes committed in the detention centre S-21 in the judgment and ii) the publication of all the statements of apology made by *Duch* during the trial.[220] In the *Nuon Chea and Khieu Samphan* case, the ECCC granted the inclusion of the civil parties' names on the ECCC website.[221]

4.3 Collective Reparations

There is no legal definition of collective reparations.[222] While collective reparations can be granted by both the ICC and the ECCC, neither of the two tribunals' legal framework provides a clear definition of these types of reparations. Nevertheless, the first revision of the ECCC's Internal Rules included some examples of moral and collective reparations.[223] Furthermore, through the tribunals' case law it is possible to infer the definition and content of collective reparations within the realm of international criminal law, as will be discussed at length in the subsequent section.

4.3.1 *Definition*

'Collective reparations' is an ambiguous concept. According to De Greiff, 'collective' is used to qualify both the reparations (the types of goods distributed or the method of distributing them) and the persons who receive them, namely collectivities (groups of people).[224] Mégret states that in the ICC's RoPE the definition of collective reparations is implied as: i) individual reparations whose disbursement is done collectively (Rule 98 (4)); ii) reparations awarded to a collectivity, meaning a legal entity (Rule 85 (b)); or iii) reparations awarded to a large number of victims and therefore to a group (Rule 98 (3)).[225] However, the latter can also be interpreted as the ICC having the authority to apply a mass claim procedure; it does not necessarily refer to collective reparations.

In addition, a study by Essex University defines collective reparations as being subject to at least one of the following three criteria: i) they pertain to violations of

220 ECCC, *Duch* Trial Judgment, *supra* n. 11, para. 667-668; ECCC, *Duch* Appeal Judgment, *supra* n. 69, para. 629, 678.

221 ECCC, *Chea and Shamphan* Judgment, *supra* n. 88, para. 1140.

222 Brodney, M., "Implementing Criminal Court-Ordered Collective Reparations: Unpacking Present Debates", 1 *Journal of the Oxford Centre for Socio-Legal Studies* (2016), p. 11.

223 Rules 23 (12), ECCC's Internal Rules.

224 UN, Report by the Special Rapporteur on the promotion of truth, justice, reparation and guarantees of non-recurrence, Pablo de Greiff, UN Doc. A/69/518, 8 October 2014, para 38.

225 Mégret, *supra* n. 163, p. 171-172.

a collective right or rights violations that impact a community; ii) the beneficiary is a group or a group of people; iii) the measures are not individually tangible.[226] This study also provides some examples of collective reparations: measures of satisfaction and rehabilitation, funds, apologies, services, the translation of a judgment and environmental and social impact assessments.[227] In addition, Rosenfeld has proposed a definition that is very similar to the one provided by the Essex University study. The main difference is that Rosenfeld adds a fourth criterion to its definition: the existence of collective harm.[228]

In the *Lubanga* case, the TFV, based on expert consultations, promoted a concept of collective reparations similar to De Greiff and Rosenfeld's definitions. The ICC has echoed this definition. The TFV stated that collective reparations encompass both collective awards and collective beneficiaries. The latter referred to i) victims of a collective right's violation; ii) victims of collective harm; iii) violations affecting a group or collective (whether tied to a geographical area or self-defined); and iv) violations that affect society as a whole. Collective benefits referred to serviced-based measures targeting a group or community.[229] The ECCC similarly appears to support Rosenfeld's view, as it has stated that collective reparations stem from collective injury.[230]

Despite the lack of a clear definition, it is widely acknowledged that collective reparations aim to provide redress for large numbers of victims, groups and communities directly or indirectly through the implementation of a wide range of social and symbolic programmes.[231] Whereas 'social programmes' refer to service-based benefits to victims (improving livelihoods, infrastructures or even institutions), symbolic programmes aim to restore victims' dignity (truth-seeking, acknowledgement of the violation, memory-related measures).[232] Collective reparations thus include a wide set of measures that can respond to different harms.[233] Furthermore, collective reparations are usually associated with administrative measures that are future-oriented, moving beyond merely repairing past harm.[234] Whether serviced-based or symbolic, collective reparations may not always be tangible for all victims, although

226 Aubry, S., and Henao-Trip, M.I., "Collective Reparations and the International Criminal Court", *Briefing Paper No. 2, Reparations Unit, Essex University* (2011), p. 2-3.

227 Ibid., p. 5.

228 Rosenfeld, F., "Collective Reparations for Victims of Armed Conflicts", 92 *International Review of the Red Cross* (2010), p. 732.

229 ICC, *Lubanga* Draft Implementation Plan, *supra* n. 99, para. 173-175.

230 "Collective reparations also stem from collective injury which has an individual effect as well". ECCC, *Nuon Chea et al.* Decision on the Civil Party Applications' Appeals, *supra* n. 123, para. 70

231 Magarrell, L., "Reparations in Theory and Practice", *ICTJ* (2007), p. 5-6.

232 In addition, there is a claim that collective reparations may also be restitutive in addition to service-based and symbolic ones. See: CHRAC and REDRESS, *supra* n. 77, p. 8.

233 Ramil-Nogales and van Schaak, *supra* n. 18.

234 Phan, *supra* n. 12, p. 295.

the ECCC has asserted that collective reparations provide individual benefits to victims.[235]

From the above-mentioned definitions, several challenges emerge. First, how should a group be defined? For instance, Rosenfeld argues that collective reparations should only be granted to recognised groups, and not to a mere plurality of individuals.[236] However,

the ICC has clarified that a group of people may be a beneficiary of reparations even when that group is not vested with legal personality.[237] This means that the ICC embraces De Greiff's understanding of groups: groups of people may be linked based on ethnic, social, racial, political, or religious grounds or because they have either suffered a collective harm or have suffered from the same crimes.[238]

In addition, the content and scope of collective reparations are rather unspecified, considering that they can include many different measures.[239] The next section will discuss the scope and content of collective awards as have become apparent from ICC and ECCC practice.

4.3.2 Scope

4.3.2.1 Scope of the ICC's Collective Reparations

The ICC has awarded collective reparations in both cases under discussion and has stated that collective reparations may include both service-based and symbolic measures.[240] In the *Lubanga* case, upon awarding collective reparations to be implemented by the TFV,[241] the ICC-TC provided indications of the most adequate forms of collective reparations. These included measures of restitution, compensation and rehabilitation, as well as symbolic, preventative or transformative measures.[242] Notwithstanding this, determining the exact nature and the amount of the award was left to the TFV's discretion.[243] This discretion was, however, limited, as the TFV was

235 ICC (Filing) 18 April 2012, *Prosecutor* v. *Thomas Lubanga Dyilo*, OPCV Observations on issues concerning reparations, ICC-01-04/01-06-2863, para. 83.

236 Rosenfeld, *supra* n. 228, p. 736.

237 ICC, *Katanga* Reparations Order, *supra* n. 31, para. 276.

238 de Greiff's report, *supra* n. 224, para. 38.

239 Rosenfeld, *supra* n. 228, p. 743.

240 ICC, *Katanga* Reparations Order, *supra* n. 31, para. 279.

241 ICC, *Lubanga* Principles on Reparations, *supra* n. 4, para. 270; ICC, *Lubanga* Principles on Reparations' Appeal Judgment, *supra* n. 94, para. 143; ICC, *Lubanga* Appeal Judgment on Reparations Order, *supra* n. 127, para. 53.

242 ICC, *Lubanga* Principles on Reparations, *supra* n. 4, para. 222-241; ICC, *Lubanga* Principles on Reparations' Appeal Judgment, *supra* n. 94, para. 202; ICC, *Lubanga* Appeal Judgment on Reparations Order, *supra* n. 127, para. 67.

243 ICC, *Lubanga* Principles on Reparations' Appeal Judgment, *supra* n. 94, para. 203; ICC, *Lubanga* Appeal Judgment on Reparations Order, *supra* n. 127, para. 68-70.

given a six-month deadline, which could have been extended if necessary in order to provide scope to the collective reparations by way of projects, which in turn had to be approved by the ICC-TC II.[244] The TFV, based on expert and victim consultations in 22 localities in Ituri, thus proposed the content of the collective reparations in a Draft Implementation Plan (DIP).[245] In the *Katanga* case, the ICC likewise ordered collective reparations through the TFV.[246] The main difference in comparison with the *Lubanga* case was that the ICC-TC II guided the TFV by identifying four appropriate collective reparation measures, mainly of a service-based nature: i) housing; ii) income-generating activities; iii) education; and v) psychological rehabilitation measures.[247]

a) Service-based Measures

In the *Lubanga* case, the TFV proposed four categories of collective projects: i) rehabilitation (psychological and physical); ii) formal and informal education; iii) socio-economic development measures and vocational training; iv) measures to promote community reconciliation and to raise awareness of child soldier enlistment.[248] In addition, it included v) transformative measures aimed at addressing the underlying causes of violence, such as gender inequality and social stigma.[249] Of these measures, those that are service-based are categories i), ii) and iii), while the remaining categories iv) and v) are symbolic measures. The Court has not approved the service-based projects because the exact timeframe, cost and limitations of each project were not clearly specified in the DIP.[250] While the TFV has argued that it cannot provide the Court with such a level of detail because the exact number of victims remains uncertain and the task of identifying them is complex,[251] the Court has approved the first stage of the DIP's implementation, which concerns the selection and the contract of the implementing partners.[252] In the *Katanga* case, the TFV presented

---

244 Initially, the ICC-TC omitted to establish any precise deadline regarding the five-step plan for the implementation of reparations. See: ICC, *Lubanga* Principles on Reparations' Appeal Judgment, *supra* n. 94, para. 240-242; ICC, *Lubanga* Appeal Judgment on Reparations Order, *supra* n. 127, para. 75-79.

245 ICC, *Lubanga* Draft Implementation Plan, *supra* n. 99, para. 46-53, 180-181.

246 In addition, individual reparations were also granted. See: ICC, *Katanga* Reparations Order, *supra* n. 31, para. 30.

247 ICC, *Katanga* Reparations Order, *supra* n. 31, para. 302, 304.

248 ICC, *Lubanga*, Annex A to the Draft Implementation Plan, *supra* n. 217, para. 61-94.

249 Ibid., para. 82-94.

250 ICC (Order) 9 February 2016, *Prosecutor* v. *Thomas Lubanga Dyilo*, Order instructing the Trust Fund for Victims to supplement the draft implementation plan, ICC-01/04-01/06-3198-tENG, para. 10, 21-22.

251 ICC (Filing) 7 June 2016, *Prosecutor* v. *Thomas Lubanga Dyilo*, TFV's Additional Programme Information Filing, ICC-01/04-01/06-3209, para. 29, 63.

252 ICC, *Lubanga* Approval on Collective Service-Based Reparations, *supra* n. 101.

a DIP containing concrete proposals regarding the four collective reparations that the ICC ordered (housing, income-generating activities, education, and psychological rehabilitation measures).[253] The DIP is still to be approved, however.

b) Symbolic Measures

In the *Lubanga* case, the TFV's DIP mentioned the possibility of establishing symbolic measures.[254] Yet the ICC-TC, cognisant of the importance of symbolic reparations for the communities in question, requested the TFV to study the feasibility of designing concrete symbolic reparation projects, by means of 'a commemoration and/or building a statue for child soldiers'. The TFV was also requested to produce specific information regarding the costs of and the timeframe for such projects.[255] In response, the TFV submitted a separate proposal for symbolic collective reparations, consisting of symbolic structures (commemoration centres in three communities) and mobile memorialisation (initiatives in five additional communities).[256] After two hearings, this proposal was approved and the ICC highlighted that symbolic reparations would create the necessary environment within the affected communities for service-based reparations to be carried out.[257]

Here, two concerns have been raised. The first is that it is not possible to analyse the degree of specification regarding the costs and location of the symbolic measures approved, as that information has been treated as confidential. Consequently, the standard of specificity that the ICC requires in order to approve collective reparations is left unclear. Secondly, the TFV has emphasised the need to implement both service-based and symbolic collective reparations simultaneously so that victims could not become disconnected from the collective reparations programme.[258] Despite the stated importance of simultaneous implementation and the fact that symbolic reparations in the *Lubanga* case have been approved, they will most likely be implemented before the service-based ones. Finally, as stated earlier, symbolic collective reparations were considered to be unsuitable in the *Katanga* case, thereby precluding simultaneous implementation.[259]

---

253 ICC *Katanga* DIP, para. 124-131.

254 Measures to promote community reconciliation and to raise awareness of child soldier enlistment and transformative measures aimed at addressing the underlying causes of violence, such as gender inequality and social stigma.

255 ICC (Request) 15 July 2016, *Prosecutor* v. *Thomas Lubanga Dyilo*, TC II's Request Concerning the Feasibility of Applying Symbolic Collective Reparations, ICC-01/04-01/06-3219, para. 12.

256 CC, *Lubanga* TFV's Symbolic Reparations Proposal, *supra* n. 209, para 29.

257 ICC, *Lubanga* Approval on Collective Symbolic Reparations, *supra* n. 100, para. 12.

258 ICC, *Lubanga* TFV's Symbolic Reparations Proposal, *supra* n. 209, para. 14.

259 ICC, *Katanga* Reparations Order, *supra* n. 31, para. 301.

4.3.2.2 Scope of the ECCC's Collective Reparations

In the *Duch* case, the civil parties presented a joint submission on reparations, which included 28 different requests that can be divided into three categories: i) individual and monetary measures; ii) symbolic measures such as the dissemination of the judgment and preventive measures; and iii) service-based measures such as rehabilitation.[260] Out of all these requested measures, only two symbolic measures were granted.[261]

In the *Nuon Chea and Khieu Samphan* case, the civil parties submitted a joint application for reparations. They requested 13 projects pertaining to two main categories: i) symbolic measures such as the dissemination of the judgment, commemoration, and preventive measures; and ii) service-based reparations by means of rehabilitation measures.[262] Contrary to the *Duch* case, the majority of the reparation requests were granted.

a) Service-Based Measures

The ECCC addressed only two service-based reparation measures in the *Duch* judgment: i) vocational and business skills training and micro-enterprise loans, and ii) free access to medical care and education.[263] Neither of these measures were granted.[264] The ECCC cited four main reasons for this decision: i) the latter fell outside the scope of its reparations mandate;[265] ii) the awards lacked specificity[266];

260 The ECCC's legal framework uses the terms 'moral' to refer to 'symbolic reparations' and 'collective reparations' to refer to 'service-based reparations'. See: ECCC (Filing) 14 September 2009, *Prosecutor* v. *Kaing Guek Eav* alias '*Duch*'(Case 001) Civil Parties' Co-Lawyers' Joint Submission on Reparations, No. E159/3.

261 ECCC, *Duch* Trial Judgment, *supra* n. 11, para. 667-668; ECCC, *Duch* Appeal Judgment, *supra* n. 69, para. 629, 678.

262 The projects sought were: i) a national remembrance day, ii) a public memorial initiative, iii) construction of a memorial in Phnom Penh; iv) memorial for the victims living in France; v) testimonial therapy; vi) group therapy; vii) a permanent exhibition; viii) a mobile exhibition and an educational project; ix) a chapter on forced population in the national curriculum; x) the construction of a peace learning centre; xi) the dissemination of the facts of the case 002/01; xii) the dissemination of the trial judgment; xiii) inclusion of the civil parties' names in the trial judgment. See: ECCC, *Chea and Shamphan* Judgment, *supra* n. 88, para. 1126-1140.

263 ECCC, *Duch* Trial Judgment, *supra* n. 11, para. 670-675.

264 ECCC, *Duch* Trial Judgment, *supra* n. 11, para. 670, 674; ECCC, *Duch* Appeal Judgment, *supra* n. 69, para. 703.

265 The ECCC considered that not only individual and monetary awards were outside the scope of its mandate but also measures such as 'vocational training, micro-enterprise loans and business skills training'. See: ECCC *Duch* Judgment, 26 July 2010, para. 670.

266 ECCC, *Duch* Trial Judgment, *supra* n. 11, para. 665-674; ECCC, *Duch* Appeal Judgment, *supra* n. 69, para. 694, 704.

iii) the accused was indigent and thus incapable of providing these reparations;[267] and iv) the involvement of the Cambodian government was required for implementation, and this did not fall within the ECCC's jurisdiction.[268]

Two aspects of the ECCC's decision deserve further mention. First, the Chamber appeared to reduce the concept of collective and moral reparations to those of symbolic value only. Regarding free access to medical care and education it stated that '[r]equests of this type – which by their nature are not *symbolic* but instead designed to benefit a large number of *individual victims* – are outside the scope of available reparations before the ECCC.'[269]

Second, in the *Duch* trial judgment the ECCC created a prerequisite for obtaining reparations that did not exist within its legal framework at the time when the victims filed their applications: applications had to include 'a clear specification of the nature of the relief sought, its link to the harm caused by the Accused that it seeks to remedy, and the quantum of the indemnity or amount of reparation sought from the Accused.'[270] It was only after the *Duch* trial judgment that the ECCC's Internal Rules were modified accordingly.[271]

In its appeal judgment, the ECCC Supreme Court Chamber (SCC) reaffirmed most of the judgement of the ECCC with one exception. The SCC found that measures of physical and psychological rehabilitation (or access to medical health) were adequate measures of collective reparation.[272] However, it added that these kinds of reparations require an administrative structure to implement the awards, which was not available at the ECCC. In addition, it found that the claims omitted the exact costs, the number of beneficiaries and the duration of the treatment, and that this information could not be amended by the SSC. Therefore, the measures were not granted.[273]

The ECCC amended its restrictive interpretation of collective reparations in its second judgment on reparations in case 002/01. In the *Nuon Chea and Khieu Samphan*

267 ECCC, *Duch* Trial Judgment, *supra* n. 11, para. 664-665; ECCC, *Duch* Appeal Judgment, *supra* n. 69, para. 668.

268 ECCC, *Duch* Trial Judgment, *supra* n. 11, para. 663-675; ECCC, *Duch* Appeal Judgment, *supra* n. 69, para. 664, 680.

269 ECCC, *Duch* Trial Judgment, *supra* n. 11, para 674.

270 Ibid., para. 665.

271 Rule 23*quinquies* (2), ECCC's Internal Rules (Rev. 7), established the following criteria as prerequisites for granting moral and collective reparations: a) the nature of the claim must be clear; b) there must be a link between the harm caused and the conviction of the accused; and c) the amount of reparation and the method of implementation must be specified.

272 ECCC, *Duch* Appeal Judgment, *supra* n. 69, para. 701, 704.

273 Ibid., para. 704.

case, service-based reparations in the form of rehabilitation were requested,[274] and psychological assistance projects were granted in the trial judgment.[275] However, these measures would not be paid for by those who had been convicted, but instead would be implemented by different organisations with funding from either other states or (international) organisations.[276]

b) Symbolic Measures

The symbolic measures granted by the ECCC were already discussed at length in part 4.2.

4.3.2.3 Scope of Collective Reparations in General

The most important conclusion that emerges from the above study of the ICC's and ECCC's practice and framework regarding the scope of collective reparations is that their content and scope are situation-specific.[277] In the case of the ICC, the decision on the exact scope of collective reparations may be delegated to the TFV. Nevertheless, it is clear that collective reparations are granted either as symbolic or service-based measures. The most frequently sought measures of service-based collective reparations appear to be those related to rehabilitation, while the most frequently sought symbolic measures are those related to commemoration and the prevention of future crimes. These may include educational measures; although, at first glance, these may appear to be service-based reparations, in some scenarios where they aim to prevent similar crimes by disseminating information on past violations, they are considered to be symbolic measures, because they aim to guarantee the non-repetition of crimes.

5 Substantive and Procedural Aspects of Collective Reparations

Unlike the ECCC, the ICC has the authority to award both individual and collective reparations. This raises the question of when awarding collective reparations is deemed to be adequate. Other substantive aspects also remain unclear: who bears the

274 The projects sought were: i) a national remembrance day, ii) a public memorial initiative, iii) the construction of a memorial in Phnom Penh; iv) a memorial for the victims living in France; v) testimonial therapy; vi) group therapy; vii) a permanent exhibition; viii) a mobile exhibition and an educational project; ix) a chapter on forced population in the national curriculum; x) the construction of a peace learning centre; xi) the dissemination of the facts of the case 002/01; xii) the dissemination of the trial judgment; xiii) inclusion of the civil parties' names in the trial judgment. See: ECCC, *Chea and Shamphan* Judgment, *supra* n. 88, para. 1126-1140.

275 ECCC, *Chea and Shamphan* Judgment, *supra* n. 88, para. 1131-1133, 1135-1137.

276 Rule 23 *quinques* (3) (b) of the ECCC's Internal Rules, allows for this alternative.

277 Aubry and Henao-Trip, *supra* n. 226, p. 11.

liability to repair, and who are the beneficiaries of collective awards? Furthermore, procedural aspects such as who is supposed to assess the harm and how, and what the appropriate causality test and the standard of proof are for collective reparations also require clarification. To this end, the following sections aim to shed some light on the main substantial and procedural aspects of collective reparations.[278]

5.1 Adequacy

According to the ICC's Rome Statute, there are two main elements that the ICC should consider when determining whether individual, collective or both awards are deemed to be adequate: the assessment of the damage or loss, and the number of victims. If the number of victims is large, collective reparations would be considered appropriate.[279] In addition, while individual reparations may appear to be more appropriate because they are tailored to the particular suffering endured by the victims as a result of the crime inflicted upon them, they might not be able to repair the harm in a meaningful and sufficient way.[280] This is because they would not address the collective harm. In this light, collective reparations are 'a necessary response to collective harm.'[281] However, scholars have argued that collective reparations should always be complementary to individual ones,[282] as they only address collective harm. The commission of international crimes also implies the infliction of individual harm,[283] which subsequently may give rise to a collective effect. Accordingly, the most adequate forms of reparations combine individual and collective awards, as approved by the ICC in the *Katanga* case.[284] As for the ECCC, its Internal Rules do not specify when collective reparations, moral reparations, or both should be granted, leaving this decision to the ECCC's discretion.

In addition, the issue of adequacy is closely related to whether a reparation measure is responsive to victims' needs,[285] and hence can be considered to be a meaningful measure.[286] In this light, in addition to their needs, victims' perspectives, which may vary depending on several factors such as gender, age, socio-economic or

278 The substantive and procedural aspects discussed in this section are those that are commonly identified in academic literature related to reparations.

279 Article 75 (1) Rule 97 (1), ICC's RoPE.

280 Dwertmann, *supra* n. 124, p. 121-122.

281 Rosenfeld, *supra* n. 228, p. 746.

282 Aubry and Henao-Trip, *supra* n. 226, p. 17.

283 Rosenfeld, *supra* n. 228, p. 744.

284 ICC, *Katanga* Reparations Order, *supra* n. 31, para. 298-302.

285 Sub-Commission on the Promotion and Protection of Human Rights, *Study Concerning the Right to Restitution, Compensation and Rehabilitation for Victims of Gross Violations of Human Rights and Fundamental Freedoms: Final Report*, 2 July 1993, UN Doc. E/CN.4/Sub.2/1993/8, para. 133,137. It is important to highlight that victims' needs vary greatly as victims do not comprise homogenous groups.

286 McKay, *supra* n. 16, p. 923.

political backgrounds,[287] should be considered when deciding on adequate measures of reparations in a given case. According to the author, the victims' perspective should be the key element considered by the Court when deciding which measures of reparations are to be awarded. The perspective of the victims who personally suffered the crimes should be more important than what scholars, as outsiders, submit regarding whether individual or collective reparations are appropriate. Studies have shown that victims usually prioritise responses to 'problems of security, poverty and livelihood,'[288] and consequently prefer measures related to shelter, schools and education and medical care.[289] Indeed, before the ECCC victims prioritised community measures that positively affect these aspects of their daily lives. Similarly, before the ICC many victims in the *Lubanga* and *Katanga* cases had requested vocational training, education, employment opportunities, and income-generating measures as well as rehabilitation measures.[290]

Significantly, in the *Lubanga* case the ICC took into account the age, gender and best interests of the children involved when awarding reparations,[291] but it appeared to have disregarded the fact that the victims had explicitly favoured individual reparations[292] over community awards, since it was the community that supported and facilitated the crimes. The ICC-AC confirmed that collective reparations were adequate,[293] and supported the reasons put forward by the ICC-TC to justify this decision: i) the number of victims affected by those crimes was large, and not all victims had been identified at the time of the reparation judgment;[294] and ii) the

287 Ibid., p. 924.

288 Ibid., p. 926.

289 Correa, C., "Reparations for Victims of Massive Crimes. Making Concrete a Message of Inclusion", in R. Letschert et al. (eds.), *Victimological Approaches to International Crimes: Africa* (Cambridge, Intersentia 2011), p. 196.

290 ICC (Observations) 18 April 2012, *Prosecutor* v. *Thomas Lubanga Dyilo*, Observations on the sentence and reparations by Victims a/0001/06, a/0003/06,a/0007/06, a/00049/06, a/0149/07, a/0155/07, a/0156/07, a/0162/07, a/0149/08, a/0404/08, a/0405/08, a/0406/08, a/0407/08, a/0409/08, a/0523/08, a/0610/08, a/0611/08, a/0053/09, a/0249/09, a/0292/09, a/0398/09 and a/1622/10, ICC-01/04-01/06-2864-tENG, para 20-22; ICC, *Katanga* Reparations Order, *supra* n. 31, para. 301-302.

291 ICC *Lubanga* Principles on Reparations, *supra* n. 4, para. 210-211; ICC, *Lubanga* Principles on Reparations' Appeal Judgment, *supra* n. 94. para. 160; ICC, *Lubanga* Appeal Judgment on Reparations Order, *supra* n. 127, para. 23-24.

292 ICC *Lubanga* Principles on Reparations, *supra* n. 4, para. 220; ICC, *Lubanga* Victims' Observations on the sentence and reparations, *supra* n. 290,s para. 15; ICC (Observations) 18 April 2012, *Prosecutor* v. *Thomas Lubanga Dyilo*, Observations du groupe de victimes V02 concernant la fixation de la peine et des réparations, ICC-01/04-01/06-2869, para. 16.

293 ICC, *Lubanga* Principles on Reparations' Appeal Judgment, *supra* n. 94, para. 130-157. It must be stated that victims also requested some measures of collective nature in addition to individual ones. See: ICC, *Lubanga* V02 Victims' Observations on the sentence and reparations, *supra* n. 292, para. 19-20.

294 ICC *Lubanga* Principles on Reparations, *supra* n. 4, para. 219-220; ICC, *Lubanga* Principles on Reparations' Appeal Judgment, *supra* n. 94, para. 153.

available resources were limited, and collective awards require a lower quantity of resources.[295] Therefore, it determined that collective awards would be 'more beneficial and have greater utility',[296] as long as the beneficiaries could demonstrate a link between the harm they had suffered and the crimes committed.[297]

In the *Katanga* case, the victims requested individual reparations, thereby opposing collective reparations. These applications arose from a distrust of the programme's implementation and sustainability, as well as a belief that collective reparations might result in a conflict among the beneficiaries and an unfair distribution of the award.[298] Accordingly, the majority of the victims preferred individual compensation, accompanied by individual physical and psychological medical care.[299] The ICC, however, granted individual reparations in the form of symbolic compensation, and collective reparations in the form of housing, income-generating activities, education, and psychological measures.[300] It is important to point out that the TC categorically took into consideration the wishes of the victims to exclude symbolic collective reparations.[301]

In the *Duch* case, the ECCC upheld that collective and moral reparations were adequate, because they are inclusive and would benefit the unspecified number of victims.[302] A similar approach was taken in the *Nuon Chea* case, where the ECCC stated that collective reparations could benefit many victims other than the civil parties.[303] Thus, for the ECCC it seems that adequacy is understood in relation to the number of victims who benefit from specific reparation: the greater the number, the more adequate that measure will be.

5.1.1 Victims' Participation

Whilst victims' participation in the proceedings relates to the reparations process, the present research does not address the right to participate. However, as stated previously, adequacy refers to reparations' responsiveness to the victims' needs and wishes. This implies that victims need to have a voice during the whole reparations

295 ICC *Lubanga* Principles on Reparations, *supra* n. 4, para. 274; ICC, *Lubanga* Principles on Reparations' Appeal Judgment, *supra* n. 94. para. 213 (while it did not explicitly state that it presumed that the AC did not contest this issue).

296 ICC *Lubanga* Principles on Reparations, *supra* n. 4, para. 274; ICC, *Lubanga* Principles on Reparations' Appeal Judgment, *supra* n. 94, para. 213.

297 ICC, *Lubanga* Appeal Judgment on Reparations Order, *supra* n. 127, para. 214 -215.

298 ICC, *Katanga* Report on Reparation Applications, *supra* n. 199, para. 30, 57, 60.

299 Ibid., para. 42, 49.

300 ICC, *Katanga* Reparations Order, *supra* n. 31, para. 298-306.

301 Ibid., para. 301.

302 ECCC, *Duch* Appeal Judgment, *supra* n. 69, para. 659.

303 ECCC (Filing) 12 March 2012, *Prosecutor* v. *Nuon Chea et al.* (Case 002) Initial specification of the substance of the awards that the Civil Party Lead Co-lawyers intend to seek-Hearing of 19 October 2011, No. E125/2, para. 84.

process – from the application, to the design phase, to its implementation, indicating that the participation of victims is desirable.

According to the ICC's legal framework, victims may be heard in matters of reparation by different means. Firstly, by submitting applications for reparations along with any supporting documentation (evidence) to the Registrar at any moment of the proceedings.[304] Nevertheless, there is no clear understanding of what the ICC is supposed to do with the victims' applications. The *Lubanga* and *Katanga* cases demonstrate two very different approaches. In the *Lubanga* case, the ICC upheld that it did not rule on the individual applications because it was granting collective reparations,[305] whilst in the *Katanga case* the Court did rule on the individual applications and granted collective reparations. This suggests that whether these applications are taken into account is up to the ICC's discretion.

Similarly, the possibility of holding a reparations hearing in which victims can participate is also subject to the Court's discretion.[306] Victims can also be heard through observations – prior to delivering a reparations order, the Court may invite the convicted person, the victims and other interested parties to submit their observations.[307] Additionally, the Registry can also be a channel for victims' views to be heard – the Registry can provide the Court with a mapping of the victims, which is an estimation of the potential victims.[308] With this mapping, the said victims can be invited to present their views and to participate in the design and implementation of reparations. However, this is only feasible when a representative sample of the victims has been identified.

Finally, victims are also heard by being able to lodge an appeal, like defendants, against any Court order, including those orders relating to reparations. In this light, victims appealed against the approval of the TFV's symbolic collective reparations plan separately, without having approved the full DIP.[309] However, this appeal was rejected on the ground that the order of collective reparations had apparently been

---

304 Rule 94, ICC's RoPE; Regulation 56, ICC's Regulations.

305 ICC, *Lubanga* Principles on Reparations' Appeal Judgment, *supra* n. 94, para. 185.

306 Article 76 (3), ICC's Rome Statute.

307 Rule 97 (2), ICC's RoPE.

308 REDRESS, Moving Reparation forward at the ICC: Recommendations, November 2016, p. 14, 16.

309 It must be recalled that the TFV's DIP should include all measures of reparation to be implemented by the TFV. However, in the *Lubanga* case, measures concerning symbolic collective reparations were dealt with separately from the DIP which included mainly service-based collective reparation measures. See: ICC (Filing) 28 October 2016, *Prosecutor* v. *Thomas Lubanga Dyilo,* Application from the V01 group of victims requesting leave to appeal the "Orderrelating to the request of the Office of Public Counsel for Victims of 16 September 2016" and the "Order approving the proposed plan of the Trust Fund for Victims in relation to symbolic collective reparations" of 21 October 2016, ICC-01/04-01/06-3254-tENG, para. 19.

misunderstood.[310] Against this background, it is important to mention that the TFV is devoid of the power to appeal against decisions of the Court in general, including those related to the DIP.[311] While observations by the victims, the defence, and the TFV are allowed, the ICC possesses very ample powers to approve the design and implementation of any measures of reparation – whether framed in the DIP or not.

All in all, victims' voices should be a key element in considering measures of reparation that are adequate in a given case and the ICC provides different venues for victims to be heard. By providing adequate support to make victims' participation substantial, the legal representatives of the victims (LRV),[312] as well as the Office of Public Counsel for the Victims (OPCV)[313] and the Registry,[314] may play a vital role in ensuring that victims' voices reach the ICC.[315]

5.2 Liability to Repair

According to the ICC's and ECCC's legal framework, reparations are inherently linked to the conviction of the defendant, and thus under both tribunals reparations should be borne by the convicted person.[316] However, in the case of the ICC the TFV can step in when the convicted person lacks the financial resources to cover reparations. The ECCC similarly retains the option of implementing a project with external funding by third parties.[317] These considerations are important, as the principle of 'the defendant must pay' appears to be unrealistic when reality clearly demonstrates that most

310 ICC (Decision) 17 January 2017, *Prosecutor* v. *Thomas Lubanga Dyilo,* Decision rejecting the application for leave to appeal of the Legal Representatives of the 01 Group of Victims, ICC-01/04-01/06-3263-tENG, para. 15-17.

311 The TFV sought leave of appeal when the DIP in the Lubanga case was first rejected by the ICC. However, the ICC pointed out that the TFV had no *locus standi*. See: ICC (Decision) 18 April 2016, *Prosecutor* v. *Thomas Lubanga Dyilo,* Decision on the request of the Trust Fund for Victims for leave to appeal against the order of 9 February 2016, ICC-01/04-01/06-3202-tENG, para. 15-17.

312 In principle, vvictims can participate in in the different phases of the proceedings usually through their lawyers (LRV). They are to present the victims' views and concerns. See: Article 68 (3), ICC's Rome Statute.

313 The OPCV is an independent office at ICC responsible for providing legal assistance to victims and their legal representatives. The OPCV can also be appointed by the ICC's judges to represent victims in court. See: Regulation 81 (4), ICC's Regulations.

314 The Registry assists victims in participating in the different phases of the proceedings. Such assistance includes helping victims to choose their legal representation. If victims are unable to choose, the Registry is allowed to appoint counsel for victims. See: RoPE Rule 16.1 (c) and Article 90, The ICC's RoPE.

315 ICC, *Lubanga* Appeal Judgment on Reparations Order, *supra* n. 127, para. 29.

316 ECCC, *Duch* Appeal Judgment, *supra* n. 69, para, 656; ECCC, *Chea and Shamphan* Judgment, *supra* n. 88, para. 1123; ICC, *Lubanga* Principles on Reparations' Appeal Judgment, *supra* n. 94, para. 65, 99; ICC, *Katanga* Reparations Order, *supra* n. 31, para. 16, 252.

317 In this case, this funding must be secured by the Co-Lawyers and the VSS, and the project must provide remedial benefits. Rule 23*quinquies* (3) (a) (b), ECCC's Internal Rules; ECCC, *Chea and Shamphan* Judgment, *supra* n. 88, para. 1123.

defendants before the two tribunals have been declared indigent and are thus in need of legal aid themselves.[318]

5.2.1 Liability and Indigence

In the *Lubanga* case, the ICC-TC I ordered reparations to be funded by the TFV as a result of Lubanga*'s* indigence.[319] However, the ICC-AC overturned this decision, and emphasised that reparation orders have 'to be issued in *all* circumstances against the convicted person.'[320] According to the Court, an indigent convicted person may be ordered to make symbolic reparations,[321] or alternatively, the TFV's Board of Directors may be invited, but not obliged, to 'advance' some resources to enable the implementation of the ordered reparations.[322] Thus, Lubanga was declared liable for reparations irrespective of his indigence.[323]

It is important to highlight that the ICC, through its reparations order and appeals judgment on reparations, found Lubanga indigent based on his declaration of indigence issued at the start of the case for the purpose of receiving legal aid, which, according to the ASP, 'b[ore] no relevance to the ability of the accused to provide reparations.'[324] Only in 2016 was Lubanga declared indigent for the purposes of reparations.[325] The ICC was more decisive in the *Katanga* case, where it had already declared the defendant indigent for the purposes of reparations in its reparations order.[326] In *Katanga,* the ICC reaffirmed that indigence is not an obstacle to liability for reparations[327] and thus asserted Katanga*'s* liability to repair.

---

318 van den Wyngaert, C., "Victims before International Criminal Courts: some views and concerns of an ICC Trial Judge", 44 *Case Western Reserve Journal of International Law* (2012), p. 490; ECCC, *Duch* Appeal Judgment, *supra* n. 69, para. 668.

319 ICC, *Lubanga* Principles on Reparations, *supra* n. 4, para. 269-273.

320 ICC, *Lubanga* Principles on Reparations' Appeal Judgment, *supra* n. 94. para. 76.

321 ICC, *Lubanga* Principles on Reparations' Appeal Judgment, *supra* n. 94. 241.

322 ICC, *Lubanga* Principles on Reparations' Appeal Judgment, *supra* n. 94. para. 116; ICC, *Lubanga* Appeal Judgment on Reparations Order, *supra* n. 127, para. 62. This however sounds more like a credit institution.

323 ICC, *Lubanga* Principles on Reparations' Appeal Judgment, *supra* n. 94. para. 105, 117; ICC, *Lubanga* Appeal Judgment on Reparations Order, *supra* n. 127, para. 60.

324 ICC-ASP (Resolution) 20 December 2011, Adopted at the 7th plenary meeting by consensus, ICC-ASP/10/Res.3, para. 3.

325 ICC (Decision) 15 December 2017, *Prosecutor* v. *Thomas Lubanga Dyilo,* Décision fixant le montant des reparations auxquelles Thomas Lubanga Dyilo est tenu, with two public annexes (Annex I and Annex III) and one confidential annex, *ex parte,* Registry, Trust Fund for Victims, Legal Representatives of V01 and V02 groups of Victims and Office of Public Counsel for Victims (Annex II) and confidential redacted version of Annex II, ICC-01/04-01/06-3379-Red, para. 287.

326 ICC, *Katanga* Reparations Order, *supra* n. 31, para. 328.

327 ICC, *Lubanga* Principles on Reparations' Appeal Judgment, *supra* n. 94, para. 102-105. ICC, *Katanga* Reparations Order, *supra* n. 31, para. 245.

Finally, the ICC stated that the convicted person's indigence may be temporary and that future earnings by Lubanga could be claimed by the TFV, which would in the meantime 'finance' the reparations.[328] The TFV, however, clarified that it is not a creditor institution and that Lubanga would become a direct debtor towards the ICC and not towards the TFV when the reparations are implemented with the TFV's resources.[329] In the *Katanga* case, the ICC implied that future earnings by the convicted person may also be claimed by directing the Presidency, with the help of the Registrar, to monitor Katanga's financial situation.[330] It remains unclear, however, what the ICC would do if any convicted person's financial situation were to improve during or after his/her time in prison and which mechanism the ICC would use to ensure that the said convicted person reimburses the ICC and/or the TFV for the money spent on reparations ordered against him/her.[331]

Contrary to the ICC, indigence is taken into account by the ECCC when assessing the defendant's liability for reparations. In the *Duch* case, the ECCC found that the perpetrator's indigence did not permit him to supplement the awards in any way.[332] Hence, the Extraordinary Chambers refrained from granting requests that would necessitate financial means from *Duch* to be implemented.[333] Furthermore, similar to the ICC, the ECCC recognised that indigence is temporary. The ECCC also recognised that victims could seek reparations from *Duch* in the future, although this would have to occur before national tribunals.[334] Such a national mechanism, however, is not available in ICC cases.

Finally, even when defendants are not found to be indigent, it is very unlikely that they would have 'deep pockets' for reparations. They may have spent all their assets on legal assistance during their trials,[335] or they may successfully hide their

---

328 ICC, *Lubanga* Principles on Reparations' Appeal Judgment, *supra* n. 94, para. 115.

329 ICC, *Lubanga* Draft Implementation Plan, *supra* n. 99, para. 123.

330 ICC, *Katanga* Reparations Order, *supra* n. 31, para. 329.

331 The legal framework provides that the Presidency of the Court must continually monitor the financial situation of the sentenced person even after the sentence. However, this legal framework does not state how the monitoring would take place. See: Article 75 (4), ICC's Rome Statute; Regulation 117, ICC's Regulations.

332 ECCC, *Duch* Trial Judgment, *supra* n. 11, para. 634, 666. ECCC, *Duch* Appeal Judgment, *supra* n. 69, para. 668.

333 ECCC, *Duch* Trial Judgment, *supra* n. 11, para. 664-668; ECCC, *Duch* Appeal Judgment, *supra* n. 69, para. 667.

334 ECCC, *Duch* Appeal Judgment, *supra* n. 69, para 692.

335 Keller, L.M., "Seeking Justice at the International Criminal Court: Victims' Reparations" 29 *Thomas Jefferson Law Review* (2007), p. 189.

assets during the trial.[336] For instance, Mr. Jean-Pierre Bemba, who was considered quite wealthy at the time the ICC proceedings against him started, was believed not to be able to afford the reparations for all the potential harm inflicted on the 5,000 victims identified in his case.[337] To counteract this situation, the ICC can order the confiscation and freezing of assets already at the pre-trial stage when issuing arrest warrants. The ECCC does not possess such a mechanism. However, this does not necessarily provide any guarantees:[338] in the *Bemba* case,[339] almost € 5 million were seized at the beginning of his trial, yet by 2014 over 60 percent of those assets had been spent on his defence.[340]

5.2.2 Liability and Proportionality to the Crime's Contribution

One of the inherent characteristics of international crimes is that they are committed by a plurality of persons. However, despite the collective nature of international crimes, international criminal law requires that the individual responsibility of the participants in an international crime is identified. This has prompted the adoption of

336 Jorda, C., and de Hemptinne, J., "The Status and Role of the Victim" in A. Cassese, P. Gaeta, and R.W. Jones, *The Rome Statute of the International Crimincal Court: A Commentary* (Oxford, OUP 2002), p. 1415; A case in point is the Special Court of Sierra Leone's trial against Charles Taylor who was believed to have a fortune in several foreign banks. At the time of writing the money has still not been found, however. See: Schabas, W., "The International Criminal Court at Ten" 22 *Criminal Law Forum* (2011), p. 501. It is important to mention that at the very beginning of their cases, all defendants need to declare whether they have sufficient financial means to pay for their legal defence. If they do not have the necessary financial means, the Tribunal is to grant financial legal aid. Interestingly, not everyone is willing to declare their "real" financial means for this purpose, as can be illustrated by the *Karadžić* case before the ICTY. *Karadžić,* at the very beginning of his case declared that he did not have enough financial means to afford the cost of his legal defence. Three years after he was arrested and after the ICTY had paid a considerable amount of money on his legal aid, the Registry of the ICTY discovered that although *Karadžić* had previously declared that he did not have sufficient means to pay for his defence, it was subsequently demonstrated that this was not true. Consequently, the ICTY requested that he should repay more than € 100,000 to the tribunal. ICTY (Registry Order) *Prosecutor* v. *Karadžić*, IT-95-5/18-T, 11 October 2012. See also: <http://www.sense-agency.com/icty/karadzic-gets-a-bill-from-tribunal.29.html?news_id=14255> [Accessed on 24 October 2012]. This case shows that if an accused is not willing to pay for his own defence, he will be less willing to declare his financial situation in order to pay reparations.

337 Dannenbaum, *supra* n. 32, p. 297.

338 Articles 57 (3)(e) and 77 (2)(b), ICC's Rome Statute. See: ICC (Decision) 10 February 2006, *Prosecutor* v. *Thomas Lubanga Dyilo,* Decision on the Prosecutor's Application for a Warrant of Arrest, Article 58, No. ICC-01/04-01/06-2-tEN, para. 130-141.

339 ICC (Case) *Prosecutor* v. *Jean-Pierre Bemba Gombo*, ICC-01/05-01/08.

340 ICC (Filing) 26 April 2016, *Prosecutor* v *Jean-Pierre Bemba Gombo*, Public Redacted Version of Submissions on Sentence ICC-01/05-01/08-3376-Conf, ICC-01/05-01/08-3376-Red, para. 101; ICC (Order) 17 November 2008, *Prosecutor* v. *Jean-Pierre Bemba Gombo*, Order to File in the Record of the Case a Public Redacted Version of a Decision, ICC-01/05-01/08-251, para. 8. See also: CICC, Latest News on Jean-Pierre Bemba Gombo, 30 July 2008, Available at <http://iccnow.org/?mod=newsdetail&news=3088>.

the theory of joint criminal enterprise (JCE) at the international criminal level. This theory of liability involves a plurality of individuals acting on different levels and following a common plan to commit a crime,[341] thereby giving rise to three forms of liability according to the criminal's participation in the crime.[342]

In this light, the ICC's Rome Statute constructed four different levels of criminal participation in Article 25 (3). This model may act as a guideline when awarding reparations: the higher the level of contribution to the crime, the higher is the liability to repair the harm caused. The first level of responsibility (principals or co-perpetrators)[343] requires an *essential* contribution to the commission of the crime.[344] In addition, co-perpetration requires the existence of a common plan, and that the essential contribution be coordinated.[345] The second and third levels (accessory)[346] require a *substantial* contribution,[347] and the fourth level (residual form of accessory or subsidiary)[348] requires that such contribution is *significant*.[349]

Significantly, at the domestic level, civil responsibility for crimes committed by a group of actors is addressed either i) proportionally or ii) *in solidum* (in solidarity). While the first refers to the perpetrator's liability in proportion to his/her factual contribution to the crime and hence to the harm caused, liability in solidarity means that the perpetrator is obliged to repair the total of the harm caused.[350] In this light, any victim could request reparations for the totality of the harm suffered from any of the perpetrators. In turn, the defendant may take civil action against the other perpetrators to recover their share of any joint liability. However, this mechanism does

341 Ciorciari and Heindel, *supra* n. 15, p. 380-381.

342 This theory was fist adopted by the ICTY and its applicability is justified under customary international law. There are three variants of JCE (basic or JCE I, systemic JCE II and extended JCE III). The three variants share three elements: the existence of a plurality of perpetrators, the existence of a common plan to commit the crime, and the participation of the accused in the common purpose. See: Yanev, L., "The Theory of Joint Criminal Enterprise at the ECCC: A Difficulty Relationship" in S.M. Meisenberg and I. Stegmiller, *The Extraordinary Chambers in the Courts of Cambodia: Assessing their Contribution to International Criminal Law* (Asser Press, The Hague 2016), p. 204-208.

343 Article 25 (3) (a), ICC's Rome Statute.

344 ICC, *Lubanga* Trial Judgment, *supra* n. 93, para. 999; Roxin C. *Autoria y Dominio del Hecho en Derecho Penal,* (Madrid, Marcial Pons 2000), p. 310.

345 ICC (Decision) 29 January 2007, *Prosecutor* v *Thomas Lubanga Dyilo*, Decision on the confirmation of charges, ICC-01/04-01/06-803-tEN, para. 322, 343.

346 Article 25 (3) (b) (c), ICC's Rome Statute.

347 ICC (Decision) 16 December 2011, *Prosecutor* v. *Callixte Mbarushimana,* Decision on the confirmation of charges, ICC-01/04-01/10-465-Red, para. 277-283.

348 Article 25 (3) (d), ICC's Rome Statute.

349 ICC, *Mbarushimana* Confirmation of Charges, *supra* n. 347; ICC, *Lubanga* Confirmation of Charges, *supra* n. 345, para. 335-337; ICC (Decision) 30 September 2008, *Prosecutor* v. *Germain Katanga and Mathieu Ngudjolo Chui,* Decision on the confirmation of charges, ICC-01/04-01/07-717, para. 483.

350 McCarthy, *supra* n. 53, p. 145.

not exist at the ICC.[351] The ICC itself has clarified that it is not bound by any national practice regarding civil responsibility *in solidium*.[352] Therefore, in both the *Lubanga* and the *Katanga* cases, the ICC established that liability must be proportionate to the individual criminal participation of the convicted person and to the resulting harm.[353] Thus, the convicted persons are not obliged to repair the entirety of the harm suffered by the victims.

While proportional liability appears to be a fair approach, its main challenge lies in determining the extent of the perpetrator's liability according to his/her contribution to the crime. Remarkably, although the ICC has stated that liability is dependent on proportionality, the ICC has not established any guidelines for calculating the perpetrator's liability in relation to the level of the contribution to the crime. In the *Lubanga* case, the ICC did not first establish the extent of Lubanga's liability due to the uncertainty surrounding the number of victims and hence the harm that they had suffered. Yet the ICC has acknowledged that it is the Trial Chamber that is the body that is charged with establishing the liability of the defendant[354] and that such a determination will not be subject to an appeal.[355]

In the *Lubanga case,* after more than five years since its first reparations order, the ICC determined the financial liability of Mr. Lubanga. The ICC considered a sample of 425 victims[356] to establish that the harm resulting from the commission of Mr. Lubanga's crimes amounted to USD 8,000 per victim *ex aequo et bono*.[357] Thus, Mr. Lubanga's financial liability towards the 425 victims amounted to USD 3,400, 000.[358] In addition, the ICC bore in mind that the number of Mr. Lubanga's victims was greater than the number presented in the sample of victims.[359] The court consequently calculated that Mr. Lubanga's liability towards those unidentified victims was amounted to USD 6,600, 000,[360] which implies that at least another 825 victims had yet to be identified. It was thus concluded that Mr. Lubanga's entire

351 Ibid., p. 145.

352 ICC, *Katanga* Reparations Order, *supra* n. 31, para. 263.

353 ICC, *Lubanga* Principles on Reparations' Appeal Judgment, *supra* n. 94, para. 118; ICC, *Lubanga* Appeal Judgment on Reparations Order, *supra* n. 127, para. 20-21; ICC, *Katanga* Reparations Order, *supra* n. 31, para. 252.

354 ICC, *Lubanga* Decision Setting the Liability for Reparations, *supra* n. 325, para. 23.

355 Ibid., para. 24.

356 473 dossiers were brought to the ICC, but only 425 passed the balance of probabilities test. See: ICC, *Lubanga* Decision Setting the Liability for Reparations, *supra* n. 325, para. 190. It must be stated that this sample was brought to the Chamber by the TFV, in conjunction with the OPCV and the LR of V01 and V02 victims on a rolling basis. See: ICC (Transcript) 15 December 2017, *Prosecutor* v. *Thomas Lubanga Dyilo*, Transcript of Delivery of a Reparations Order, ICC-01/04-01/06-T-369-ENG ET WT 15-12-2017 1-19 NB T, para. 21-25.

357 ICC, *Lubanga* Decision Setting the Liability for Reparations, *supra* n. 325, para. 190, 259.

358 Ibid., para. 279.

359 Ibid., para. 199.

360 Ibid., para. 280.

liability for his participation in the crimes committed was USD 10,000,000.[361] On the other hand, in the *Katanga* case the ICC had already determined in its reparations order that the defendant's liability amounted to USD 1,000,000 out of the total harm assessed at USD 3,752, 620.[362]

Unfortunately, the ICC has not explained how it reached this decision and, for the sake of transparency, it is desirable that the Court elaborates on the process of determining liability. However, one could conclude that Katanga was found liable for 27% of the total harm assessed due to his significant contribution to the crimes committed. In contrast, in the *Lubanga* case the ICC did suggest that Mr. Lubanga was liable for the total harm caused, where this said harm was calculated on equitable grounds. Accordingly, it could be concluded that the number of victims affected and the level of contribution to the crime are important factors in calculating liability in the reparations of a given perpetrator. In this light, it is important to highlight that while Mr. Lubanga was found guilty on the grounds of co-perpetration (Article 25 (3) (a)),[363] Mr. Katanga was found guilty on the grounds of a residual form of accessory perpetration (Article 25 (3)(d)).[364]

In the *Duch* case, the ECCC embraced the concept of proportional liability by stating that the nature of the criminal responsibility of the convicted person determines the extent of his obligation to repair.[365] In addition, the ECCC ruled in the *Nuon Chea and Khieu Samphan* case that the multiple accused had to jointly repair the harm caused. This judgment is based on a JCE form of liability;[366] according to JCE, each participant is equally responsible as a co-perpetrator of the crime(s).[367] In this light, the ECCC maintained that the consequences of the criminal act are shared among all perpetrators. However, the ECCC has not elaborated any further on how such proportionality in the liability for reparations is supposed to be understood. Perhaps this has not been deemed necessary because the ECCC considers that reparations are essentially symbolic.[368]

---

361 Ibid., para. 281.

362 ICC, *Katanga* Reparations Order, *supra* n. 31, para. 239, 264, 326.

363 ICC, *Lubanga* Confirmation of Charges, *supra* n. 345, para. 410; ICC, *Lubanga* Trial Judgment, *supra* n. 93, para. 1272.

364 ICC, *Katanga* Trial Judgment, *supra* n. 103, para. 1693.

365 ECCC, *Duch* Trial Judgment, *supra* n. 11, para. 513.

366 ECCC, *Nuon Chea et al.* Decision on the Civil Party Applications' Appeals, *supra* n. 123, para. 72

367 ICTY (Judgment) 28 February 2005, *Prosecutor* v. *Kvočka et al.*, Appeals Judgment, IT-98-30/1-A, para. 79-81; ICTY (Judgment) 15 July 1999, *Prosecutor* v. *Dusko Tadić,* Appeals Judgment, IT-94-1-A, para. 188, 191, 195-226; Bigi, G., "Joint Criminal Enterprise of the Jurisprudence of the International Criminal Tribunal for the Former Yugoslavia and the Prosecution of Senior Political and Military Leaders: The Krajišnik Case in, A. von Bogdandy and R. Wolfrum, (eds.), *Max Planck Yearbook of United Nations Law* (The Hague, Brill,Volume 14, 2010), p. 53-54.

368 ECCC, *Duch* Appeal Judgment, *supra* n. 69, para. 644.

5.3 Beneficiaries

Identifying beneficiaries is not only essential to implementing reparations: if victims are identified at an early stage, this can ensure their participation in the design and implementation of reparations, thus increasing their benefits. The following sections will discuss who may become a beneficiary of collective reparations, how victim identification is supposed to occur, as well as which body is charged with identifying victims.

5.3.1 Who Can Become a Beneficiary?

For the ICC, beneficiaries include direct and indirect victims, legal entities,[369] and also entire communities.[370] Importantly, 'a victim does not cease to be a victim because of his or her death;'[371] therefore, their successors can also be beneficiaries of reparations. Direct victims have to meet a fourfold set of criteria: i) they must be a natural or legal person; ii) they must have suffered harm; iii) the crime which caused the harm must be a crime for which the perpetrator was convicted; and iv) there must be a causal nexus between the harm suffered and the crime.[372] In addition, the ICC has established that beneficiaries of reparations are not restricted to those who participated in the proceedings.[373]

It is important to highlight that in the *Lubanga* case, the ICC ordered collective reparations for the benefit of communities and localities beyond the ones identified during the trial.[374] However, the community reparations were only meant to benefit those members of the community who had suffered harm as a consequence of the crimes for which the accused was convicted.[375] It appears that the ICC's approach regarding community reparations is narrower than the general understanding of collective reparations. To illustrate this, it is important to recall that the ICC Registry stated that the difference between individual and collective reparations lies in the fact that the former benefit specific victims, while the latter benefit a given community without the need to identify each member of the community as a victim.[376] However,

369 ICC *Lubanga* Principles on Reparations, *supra* n. 4, para.194-197; ICC, *Lubanga* Appeal Judgment on Reparations Order, *supra* n. 127, para. 6, 8.

370 ICC *Lubanga* Principles on Reparations, *supra* n. 4, para.179, 197.

371 ICC (Decision) 12 December 2008, *Prosecutor v Jean-Pierre Bemba Gombo*, Single Judge Hans-Peter Kaul, Fourth Decision on Victims' Participation, ICC-01/05-01/08-320, para. 40.

372 ICC, *Katanga* Reparations Order, *supra* n. 31, para. 36-37.

373 ICC *Lubanga* Principles on Reparations, *supra* n. 4, para. 187; ICC, *Lubanga* Appeal Judgment on Reparations Order, *supra* n. 127, para. 12.

374 ICC, *Lubanga* Principles on Reparations' Appeal Judgment, *supra* n. 94, para. 211, 214, 226; ICC, *Lubanga* Appeal Judgment on Reparations Order, *supra* n. 127, para. 56.

375 ICC, *Lubanga* Principles on Reparations, *supra* n. 4, para. 211-212; ICC, *Lubanga* Appeal Judgment on Reparations Order, *supra* n. 127, para. 54.

376 ICC, *Katanga* Report on Reparation Applications, *supra* n. 199, para. 89.

the ICC requires each individual beneficiary of collective awards to be identified. In the *Katanga* case, the collective reparations were to benefit each of the victims of Mr. Katanga.[377] This was feasible since the victims had already been identified in the ICC's reparations order.

Before the ECCC, only civil parties can become beneficiaries of reparations; 'a Civil Party has a right, as a member of a collective "class", to request moral reparations.' This right flows from joining the proceedings.[378] Any person who can clearly be identified and can prove that he/she have suffered physical, material or psychological injury as a direct consequence of at least one of the alleged crimes with which an accused is charged may become a civil party.[379] In addition, victims may be admitted under the presumption of harm.[380] Civil parties are composed of direct[381] and indirect victims[382] 'who [have] suffered personal injury as a result of the injury to his or her family member' (*iure proprio*), or those acting as successors of a direct victim who has deceased (*iure hereditatis*).[383] Significantly, indirect victims are not restricted to the immediate family, but include those with special bonds of affection or dependence.[384] Furthermore, the ECCC has upheld that the harm that victims must prove in order to be accepted as a civil party does not necessarily need to be individual, but could also be collective harm. Against this background, the ECCC has stated that it would be unrealistic to try to establish individual injury by the accused.[385]

Victims must file a civil party application as well as supporting evidence no later than fifteen days after the Co-investigating Judges' notification on the conclusion of the judicial investigation.[386] In addition, civil party victims are represented as a 'single, consolidated group' by the Co-Lead lawyers who are allowed to 'file a single claim for collective and moral reparations.'[387] Finally, being given the status of a civil party does not imply that victims will, by default, be beneficiaries of reparations. First, the ECCC would need to assess whether the alleged harm stems directly from the crimes for which the accused was convicted.

Finally, victims face several limitations to becoming a beneficiary of reparations before the ICC and the ECCC. Both courts only prosecute those who bear the greatest

377 ICC, *Katanga* Reparations Order, *supra* n. 31, para. 303.
378 ECCC, *Nuon Chea et al.* Decision on the Civil Party Applications' Appeals, *supra* n. 123, para. 99.
379 Rule 23*bis* (1) (a) (b), ECCC's Internal Rules.
380 ECCC, *Nuon Chea et al.* Decision on the Civil Party Applications' Appeals, *supra* n. 123, para. 72.
381 ECCC, *Duch* Appeal Judgment, *supra* n. 69, para. 416.
382 Ibid., para. 417.
383 Ibid., para. 419.
384 ECCC, *Duch* Trial Judgment, *supra* n. 11, para. 643.
385 ECCC, *Nuon Chea et al.* Decision on the Civil Party Applications' Appeals, *supra* n. 123, para. 77.
386 Rule 23*bis* (2) (a), ECCC's Internal Rules.
387 Ibid., Rule 23 (3).

responsibility for international crimes, which limits the number of prosecutions.[388] In this way, the system privileges victims of crimes that are actually prosecuted. Second, the Office of the Prosecutor has full discretion to select the charges to be brought, which cannot be changed or expanded upon by the victims.[389] Finally, victims must prove a causal link between the crimes and the harm allegedly suffered.[390] The latter is especially problematic in the context of the ECCC, as the crimes under its jurisdiction were committed more than three decades ago. In addition, before the ECCC, beneficiaries are limited to those who have been granted the status of civil parties.

5.3.2 Identification of Beneficiaries

To become a beneficiary, a victim must be identified as such. Yet the when, who, and how of carrying out such an identification is not always an easy task.

When and who?

In general, victims are identified at the end of the trial,[391] yet many more may have to be identified during and after the reparations stage as not all victims participate or submit reparations applications.[392] In the *Lubanga* case, the ICC-TC delegated victim identification to the TFV, without providing an eligibility criterion. However, the ICC-AC subsequently ruled that it is the Trial Chamber's responsibility to identify the victims or set eligibility criteria.[393] Consequently, the ICC-AC established the harm criteria and highlighted the importance of a causal link between the said harms and the victim. The ICC-AC tasked the TFV with identifying the victims without specifying any timespan.[394] However, it can be inferred that the ICC expected that

---

388 Aptel, C., "Prosecutorial Discretion at the ICC and Victim's Right to Remedy" 10 *Journal of International Criminal Justice* (2012), p. 1357; McCarthy, *supra* n. 53, p. 70; Ferstman, C., and Goetz, M., "Reparations before the International Criminal Court: The Early Jurisprudence on Victim Participation and its Impact on Future Reparations Proceedings" in C. Ferstman, M. Goetz and A. Stephens (eds.), *Reparations for Victims of Genocide, War Crimes and Crimes Against Humanity: Systems in Place and Systems in the Making* (Leiden, Martinus Nijhoff 2009), p. 318.

389 Kristjánsdóttir, E., "International Mass Claims Processes and the ICC Trust Fund for Victims" in C. Ferstman, M. Goetz and A. Stephens (eds.), *Reparations for Victims of, War Crimes and Crimes Against Humanity: Systems in Place and Systems in the Making* (Leiden, Martinus Nijhoff 2009), p. 181.

390 ICC, *Lubanga* Principles on Reparations' Appeal Judgment, *supra* n. 94, para. 63.

391 Henselin, Heiskanen and Mettraux, *supra* n. 22, p. 329.

392 ICC (Order) 25 January 2018, *Prosecutor* v. *Thomas Lubanga Dyilo,* Order Directing Further Information from the Trust Fund for Victims on the Procedure for Determining Victim Status at the Implementation Stage of Reparations, ICC-01/04-01/06-3391-tENG, para. 1.

393 ICC, *Lubanga* Principles on Reparations' Appeal Judgment, *supra* n. 94, para. 187.

394 ICC, *Lubanga* Appeal Judgment on Reparations Order, *supra* n. 127, para. 57-59.

the TFV would have identified all victims by the time the DIP was filed, based on the ICC's expectation that the TFV would take victims' wishes and needs into account when drafting the said DIP. This consideration by the TFV could only happen if the victims had been identified by then.[395]

The TFV estimated that approximately 3,000 victims were potentially eligible.[396] This estimation is based on reports on the ethnic conflict in Ituri,[397] the Registry's map of potential victims,[398] and interviews carried out by the TFV and the LRV.[399] Yet the TFV indicated that the individual identification of victims should be conducted during the implementation process and not beforehand.[400] This was further supported by the additional information that the DIP presented to the ICC, where it was concluded that victims' identification was a complex, expensive, and traumatising experience for the victims. It was thus requested once again that identification should only take place in the implementation process and not prior to the projects' design.[401] In this light, the TFV stated that the standard that is applicable to identifying beneficiaries should be lower than the one used to allow victims to participate in proceedings.[402]

Regardless of this, the ICC insisted that the TFV, assisted by the OPCV and the Registry, should continue its identification of victims before approving the design of the reparation measures.[403] This is the main reason why the service-based collective reparations were not approved in this case and were therefore not implemented.[404]

Nonetheless, the ICC seems to have taken a different approach regarding the identification of victims in relation to collective reparations of a symbolic nature, and in this approach there is no need for the previous identification of beneficiaries

---

395 Ibid., para. 79.

396 ICC, *Lubanga* TFV Additional Programme Information, *supra* n. 251, para. 13.

397 ICC, *Lubanga* Draft Implementation Plan, *supra* n. 99, para. 246-253.

398 Ibid., para. 35. The mapping came from the VPRS after conducting interviews and carrying out field missions. See: Ibid., para. 33-45.

399 ICC, *Lubanga,* Annex A to the Draft Implementation Plan, *supra* n. 217, para. 45-46.

400 ICC, *Lubanga* Draft Implementation Plan, *supra* n. 99, para. 147.

401 ICC, *Lubanga* TFV Additional Programme Information, *supra* n. 251, para. 19, 93; TFV, Report to the ASP, *supra* n. 45, para. 35.

402 ICC (Observations) 08 April 2013, *Prosecutor* v. *Thomas Lubanga Dyilo,* Observations of the Trust Fund for Victims on the appeals against Trial Chamber I 's "Decision establishing the principles and procedures to be applied to reparations", ICC-01/04-01/06-3009, para. 170.

403 ICC, *Lubanga* Approval on Collective Symbolic Reparations, *supra* n. 100, para. 21; ICC (Order) 7 November 2017, *Prosecutor* v. *Thomas Lubanga Dyilo,* Order Instructing the Trust Fund for Victims to Inform the Chamber of the Progress Made in the Implementation of Reparations, ICC-01/04-1/06-3376-tENG.

404 Not even the approved Symbolic reparations have been implemented due to security concerns. See: ICC (Filing) 15 November 2017, *Prosecutor* v. *Thomas Lubanga Dyilo* Third progress report on the implementation of collective reparations as per the Trial Chamber II orders of 21 October 2016 and 6 April 2017 with one confidential, ex parte Annex A available to the Registrar only, ICC-01/04-01/06.

for the collective reparations to be implemented.[405] Finally, in the *Katanga* case, the identification of victims was far less complicated when compared to the *Lubanga* case. In the *Katanga* case, victims were identified by the Court based on the 341 individual applications for reparations that it had received,[406] of which 297 were found to be eligible.[407]

How?

The ICC has established that victims may be identified using both official and unofficial documents (voting or refugee cards, ID certificates, certificates attesting to the loss of an ID card), including even 'a statement signed by two credible witnesses establishing their identity'.[408] As such the ICC in *Katanga* did identify victims by means of 'voter's cards, refugee cards, certificates serving as identification and certificates of loss of identification'.[409]

The TFV affirmed that it would use several documents to identify victims, such as identification cards, electoral cards, lists obtained from former commanders, demobilization cards, health clinic cards, school identification cards, or statements signed by two credible witnesses denoting a person's identity. In addition, it assured that it would take into account the difficulties that women usually face in accessing documents needed for their identification.[410]

Furthermore, in order to be eligible as a beneficiary, direct victims must prove a causal link between the harm suffered and the crimes for which the perpetrator was convicted.[411] In addition, indirect victims must demonstrate their personal relationship with the direct victim.[412] Indirect victims can prove their personal relationship with the direct victim by demonstrating their family relationship via different documents, such as their 'parents' names on a voter's card in accordance with those on a death certificate.'[413] In addition, the ICC highlighted that the concepts of a 'family' and a 'close relationship' must be understood in accordance with their social structures.[414]

---

405 ICC, *Lubanga* TC II's Request on Feasibility of Symbolic CR, *supra* n. 255, para. 11.

406 ICC, *Katanga* Reparations Order, *supra* n. 31, para. 32.

407 Ibid., para.168, 287.

408 ICC, *Lubanga* Principles on Reparations, *supra* n. 4, para. 198; ICC, *Lubanga* Appeal Judgment on Reparations Order, *supra* n. 127, para. 57; ICC, *Katanga* Reparations Order, *supra* n. 31, para. 71-72.

409 ICC, *Katanga* Reparations Order, *supra* n. 31, para. 72.

410 ICC, *Lubanga*, Annex A to the Draft Implementation Plan, *supra* n. 217, para. 47-48.

411 Rule 85, ICC's RoPE.

412 ICC, *Lubanga* Appeal Judgment on Reparations Order, *supra* n. 127, para. 53

413 ICC, *Katanga* Reparations Order, *supra* n. 31, para. 120.

414 ICC *Lubanga* Principles on Reparations, *supra* n. 4, para. 195; ICC, *Lubanga* Appeal Judgment on Reparations Order, *supra* n. 127, para. 7; ICC, *Katanga* Reparations Order, *supra* n. 31, para. 120.

Main challenges

In addition to the difficulties that many victims, especially women, face in obtaining the necessary documentation to identify themselves, the TFV has highlighted that the complexity in identifying victims is increased by the fear that many victims express regarding any reprisals. This fear also extends to the safety of victims if their identities happen to be disclosed.[415] This concern regarding safety is especially relevant because the ICC acknowledged Mr. Lubanga's right to screen the process of victim identification.[416] In the case of *Lubanga* the defence argued that the non-disclosure of the identity of the victims to the defence could block the rights of the defence, as well as blocking the rights of due process and equality of arms.[417] However, this position has been contested. On the one hand, the ICC has established that the victim's consent is required in order to disclose confidential information that the Registry possesses through the individual applications filed before it to the TFV.[418] In addition, the TFV must ensure the safety, privacy and well-being of the victims,[419] while Rule 98(3) of the RoPE also prescribes that the identity of victims should not be disclosed due to security issues.[420] On the other hand, Mr. Lubanga had the right to screen the individual identification of victims even though this right could lead to retaliation.

Against this background, it must be recalled that the ICC itself has recognised that reparations belong to a judicial process[421] that is different from the one establishing the responsibility of the accused. In this light, Zappalà argues that pursuant to Article 75 of the ICC's Rome Statute, the ICC is not obliged 'to preserve the rights of the accused since the establishment of guilt or innocence has already occurred'.[422] In addition, in the *Katanga* case, the ICC upheld that the defendant had the right to

415 ICC (Filing) 31 May 2016, *Prosecutor* v. *Thomas Lubanga Dyilo*, First submission of victim dossiers with Twelve confidential, *ex parte* annexes, available to the Registrar, and Legal Representatives of Victims V01 only, ICC-01/04-01/06-3208, para. 194.

416 ICC, *Lubanga* Principles on Reparations' Appeal Judgment, *supra* n. 94, para. 167; ICC, *Lubanga* Appeal Judgment on Reparations Order, *supra* n. 127, para. 66.

417 ICC, *Lubanga* Decision Setting the Liability for Reparations, *supra* n. 325, para. 54-55.

418 ICC, *Lubanga* Principles on Reparations' Appeal Judgment, *supra* n. 94, para. 162; ICC, *Lubanga* Appeal Judgment on Reparations Order, *supra* n. 127, para. 73-74.

419 ICC, *Katanga* Reparations Order, *supra* n. 31, para. 310, ICC, *Lubanga* Appeal Judgment on Reparations Order, *supra* n. 127, para. 34.

420 ICC (Decision) 14 December 2012, *Prosecutor* v. *Thomas Lubanga Dyilo*, Decision on the admissibility of the appeals against Trial Chamber I's "Decision establishing the principles and procedures to be applied to reparations" and directions on the further conduct of proceedings, ICC-01/04-01/06-2953, para. 31.

421 ICC, *Lubanga* Principles on Reparations' Appeal Judgment, *supra* n. 94, para. 237.

422 Zappalà, S., "The Rights of Victims v. the Rights of the Accused" 8 *Journal of International Criminal Justice* (2010), p. 143.

submit observations on the eligibility of each victim to receive individual reparations, but not on their eligibility to receive collective reparations.[423]

Consequently, it could be argued that Mr. Lubanga did not per se possess a full right to have the identities of all eligible victims for reparations disclosed. In addition, matters relating to individual beneficiaries are ideally to be regulated by the TFV's Regulations when the reparations are supplemented by the TFV. It is pertinent to add that the TFV does not have any obligation to protect the rights of the accused.[424] Thus, the identification of victims for the purposes of collective reparations should not allow the accused to intervene by screening the process.[425] Furthermore, such identification becomes an administrative process outside the rules of judicial proceedings.[426] Yet, the ICC still upheld that the process of screening victims by Mr. Lubanga at the implementation stage could be carried out subject to protective measures.[427] This contradictory state of affairs reflects the difficulties inherent in achieving a fair balance between the rights of defendants and victims.[428]

Similar to the ICC, the ECCC accepts official and unofficial documents when identifying victims.[429] In the *Duch* case, out of the 90 civil parties, only 76 were identified as beneficiaries because they could prove they had suffered psychological and physical harm as a direct consequence of the crimes for which the perpetrator was convicted.[430] Finally, in the *Nuon Chea and Khieu Samphan* case, the ECCC, based upon expert evidence, recognised all of the 3,866 civil parties as beneficiaries; hence all were awarded moral and collective reparations.[431] In its judgment, the ECCC omitted any mention of how victims should be identified and the causal link that is required.[432] It remains to be seen whether this implies that the ECCC applies a

---

423 ICC (Decision) 8 May 2015, *Prosecutor* v. *Germain Katanga*, Decision on the "Demande de clarification concernant la mise en œuvre de la Règle 94 du Règlement de procédure et de preuve" and future stages of the proceedings, ICC-01/04-01/07-3546-tENG, para. 21.

424 Brodney, *supra* n. 222, p. 16.

425 Ibid., p. 24.

426 ICC, *Lubanga* TFV Additional Programme Information, *supra* n. 251, para. 15.

427 ICC, *Lubanga* Appeal Judgment on Reparations Order, *supra* n. 127, para. 66.

428 Brodney, *supra* n. 222, p. 35.

429 ECCC, *Duch* Appeal Judgment, *supra* n. 69, para. 536, 544. The ECCC's admission of unofficial documents was based on the Cambodian Civil Code 2006, Art. 155 (4): "Unofficial documents signed by the principal or the principal's representative shall be presumed to have been authentically executed."

430 ECCC, *Duch* Trial Judgment, *supra* n. 11, para. 646-650; ECCC, *Duch* Appeal Judgment, *supra* n. 69, para. 537-629; Hughes, R., and Elander, M., "Justice and the Past: the Khmer Rouge Tribunal" in K. Brickell and S. Springer (eds.) *The Handbook of Contemporary Cambodia* (New York, Routledge 2016), p 48; Studzinsky, S., "Victim's Participation before the Extraordinary Chambers in the Courts of Cambodia" *Zeitschrift für Internationale Strafrechtsdogmatik* (2011), p. 887. Available at <http://www.zis-online.com/dat/artikel/2011_10_627.pdf>.

431 ECCC, *Chea and Shamphan* Judgment, *supra* n. 88, para. 1110-1111, 1150.

432 Ibid., para. 1114-1222.

less stringent identification of victims in cases where the reparations awarded are not to be borne by the convicted person.

5.4 Assessment of Harm

First of all, it should be clarified that harm, injury and damage are often considered to be synonymous.[433] Under the ICC, the personal harm[434] to be addressed by reparations may include physical, psychological or material harm that a victim has suffered either directly or indirectly.[435] In addition, harm can also be collective, and reparations should address both individual and collective harm.[436] As for defining reparations, the ICC-TC has the responsibility to 'clearly *define* the harms that result from the crimes for which the person was convicted,'[437] although the assessment of harm can be delegated to the TFV.[438] It is one of the most challenging issues in international criminal law;[439] it is 'already complex in the context of individual violations,'[440] and in cases of mass victimisation this complexity is further enhanced, as the harm is usually multidimensional and multi-layered.[441]

In the *Lubanga* case, the ICC-AC identified the harm to be repaired[442] and subsequently delegated the assessment of this harm to the TFV, which was assisted in this task by a team of experts that it had selected beforehand.[443] The two main reasons for delegating this task in the *Lubanga* case were that i) there was still uncertainty regarding the number of victims and, since the TFV was tasked with their identification, the ICC-AC was unable to assess the harm, and ii) the TFV was

433 ICC (Judgment) 11 July 2008, *Prosecutor* v. *Thomas Lubanga Dyilo*, Judgment on the Appeals of The Prosecutor and the Defence against Trial Chamber I's Decision on Victims' Participation, ICC-01/04-01/06, para. 31.

434 ICC, *Lubanga* Principles on Reparations' Appeal Judgment, *supra* n. 94, para. 10; ICC, *Katanga* Reparations Order, *supra* n. 31, para. 39.

435 ICC *Lubanga* Principles on Reparations, *supra* n. 4, para. 228-229; ICC, *Lubanga* Appeal Judgment on Reparations Order, *supra* n. 127, para. 10.

436 ICC, *Lubanga* Appeal Judgment on Reparations Order, *supra* n. 127, para. 33; ICC, *Katanga* Report on Reparation Applications, *supra* n. 199, para. 74; ICC, *Katanga* Reparations Order, *supra* n. 31, para. 274.

437 ICC, *Lubanga* Principles on Reparations' Appeal Judgment, *supra* n. 94, para. 187.

438 Ibid., para. 184.

439 McCarthy, *supra* n. 53, p. 134.

440 Dwertmann, *supra* n. 124, p. 167.

441 Studzinsky, S., "Reparations at the Extraordinary Chambers in Courts of Cambodia (ECCC)", in REDRESS, *Conference Report: Reparations before the International Criminal Court: Issues and Challenges, The Hague, 12 May 2011* (The Hague, The REDRESS Fund 2011), p. 12.

442 ICC, *Lubanga* Principles on Reparations' Appeal Judgment, *supra* n. 94, para. 191; ICC, *Lubanga* Appeal Judgment on Reparations Order, *supra* n. 127, para. 58.

443 ICC *Lubanga* Principles on Reparations, *supra* n. 4, para. 282-283.

considered to be better equipped to conduct this assessment.[444] Significantly, the TFV upheld that the assessment of harm allows for some presumptions to be mad. For instance, it is possible to presume psychological harm if it is established that the victim was indeed a child soldier.[445]

Contrary to *Lubanga,* in the *Katanga* case the ICC-TC II itself conducted the assessment of the harm, even doing so without the help of any experts.[446] The Court applied the technique of mass claims of standard valuation.[447] Instead of assessing individual losses, the ICC standardised the losses and the amount afforded to the victims. This technique is problematic as neither victims nor harm are homogenous[448] and its utilization may lead to victims receiving a standard amount of financial compensation regardless of how exceptional their loss has been. Nevertheless, clustering groups of victims has certain benefits, as it may accelerate the reparation process.[449] It must be noted that this technique was advanced by the LRV, which had filed a very comprehensive report on the different types of harm suffered by the 304 victims who had been identified at that time, with a table grouping these harms also being included in the report.[450] Similarly, the defence conducted a categorization of the alleged harm.[451] The grouping carried out by the LRV and defence seem to have influenced the ICC's decision to cluster the harms.

Furthermore, the ICC clarified that whilst the assessment of moral harm is independent from the economic context of the region,[452] the assessment of material harm is indivisible from the local economic situation.[453] Lastly, the ICC did not explain

444 McCarthy, C.,"The Rome Statute's Regime of Victim Redress Challenges and Prospects" in C. Stahn, (ed.), *The Law and Practice of the International Criminal Court* (Oxford, OUP 2015), p. 1217-1219.

445 ICC, *Lubanga*, Annex A to the Draft Implementation Plan, *supra* n. 217, para. 71.

446 ICC, *Katanga* Reparations Order, *supra* n. 31, para 191. It must be stated that such a clustering was possible because the majority of the damage endured by the victims was tangible (i. e. destruction of houses, pillaging of livestock and housewares, etc). See: ICC, *Katanga* Trial Judgment, *supra* n. 103, para. 942-948.

447 Niebergall, H., "Overcoming Evidentiary Weakness in Reparation Claims Programmes" in C. Ferstman, M. Goetz and A. Stephens (eds.), *Reparations for Victims of, War Crimes and Crimes Against Humanity: Systems in Place and Systems in the Making* (Leiden, Martinus Nijhoff 2009), p. 162, 164.

448 Moffet, L., "Elaborating Justice for Victims at the International Criminal Court", 13 *Journal of International Criminal Law* (2015), p. 5-6.

449 Niebergall, *supra* n. 447, p. 161.

450 ICC (Filing) 13 May 2016, *Prosecutor* v. *Germain Katanga,* Report on the implementation of Decision No. 3546, including the identification of harm suffered by victims as a result of crimes committed by Germain Katanga (article 75(1) of the Statute and regulation 38(1)(f) of the Regulations of the Court), ICC-01/04-01/07-3687-tENG.

451 ICC (Observations) 30 September 2016, *Prosecutor* v. *Germain Katanga*, Observations in response to the Trial Chamber's order of 15 July 2016 With Public redacted version of Annex A: Index of annexes, and public annexes 1-5 and 7-14, ICC-01/04-01/07-3714-Red, para. 15.

452 ICC, *Katanga* Reparations Order, *supra* n. 31, para. 189.

453 Ibid., para. 188.

the method on which it based its monetary calculations of the harm, yet it took into account the views of the victims, the convicted person, and the TFV.[454] According to Stahn, more than observations, hearings may be the best option to assess harm, especially those harms that were not previously included during the trial stage.[455] And when there are no specific particulars or data to consult, calculations are to be made on the basis of *ex aequo et bono* (the principle of equity).[456]

Similar to the ICC, the ECCC's Internal Rules establish that reparations should address 'physical, material or psychological injury'[457] of a personal but not necessarily direct nature.[458] In the *Duch* case, however, the ECCC referred exclusively to harm of a physical and psychological nature, omitting material harm.[459] In addition, the ECCC also recognises that the nature of crimes under its jurisdiction have a societal and cultural impact – because of their collective nature.[460]

5.5 Standard of Proof

The principle of law establishing that claimants must prove their assertions (*actori incumbit onus probandi* or *onus probandi* principle) also applies to reparations proceedings[461] and thus victims must substantiate their allegations.[462] Unlike human rights courts, the burden of proof cannot be reversed in international criminal law at any stage including reparations.[463] Nevertheless, the ICC could ask States to cooperate in finding evidence when victims are unable to provide it. Before the ICC, injured victims bear the burden of proving that they were affected in their personal interests as a result of the crimes committed by the convicted person[464] to the 'extent

454 ICC (Observations) 30 September 2016, *Prosecutor* v. *Germain Katanga,* Observations in response to the Trial Chamber's order of 15 July 2016 With Public redacted version of Annex A: Index of annexes, and public annexes 1-5 and 7-14, ICC-01/04-01/07-3714-Red.

455 Stahn, C., "Reparative Justice after the *Lubanga* Appeal Judgment: New Prospects for Expressivism and Participatory Justice or 'Juridified Victimhood' by Other Means?" 13 *Journal of International Criminal Justice,* p. 810.

456 ICC, *Katanga* Reparations Order, *supra* n. 31, para. 191.

457 Rule *23bis* (1) (b), ECCC's Internal Rules.

458 ECCC, *Nuon Chea et al.* Decision on the Civil Party Applications' Appeals, *supra* n. 123, para. 86.

459 ECCC, *Duch* Trial Judgment, *supra* n. 11, para. 641.

460 ECCC (Decision) 24 June 2011, *Prosecutor* v. *Nuon Chea et al.* (Case 002), Decision on Appeals Against Orders of the Co-investigating Judges on the Admissibility of Civil Party Applications, No. D404/2/4, para. 86.

461 Henselin, Heiskanen and Mettraux, *supra* n. 22, p. 328.

462 ICC, *Katanga* Reparations Order, *supra* n. 31, para. 59.

463 Article 67 (1) (i), ICC's Rome Statute; ECCC, *Duch* Appeal Judgment, *supra* n. 69, para. 33. Significantly, the EECC has explained that reversing the burden of proof could technically be possible but that this would be extremely unlikely to occur. See: ECCC, *Duch* Appeal Judgment, *supra* n. 69, para. 430.

464 Article 68 (3), ICC's Rome Statute.

possible'.[465] Similarly, civil parties bear the burden of proof before the ECCC.[466] The ICC has stated that it 'has a broad discretion in assessing the soundness of a given statement or other piece of evidence,'[467] and as such it has based its reparations findings on allegations that were similar and consistent despite the possible existence of minor discrepancies.[468] This is because, when it comes to reparations, the Court has adopted a more relaxed approach than that of 'beyond reasonable doubt'. In the *Lubanga* case, while rejecting a 'wholly flexible approach,'[469] the ICC applied the standard of on the balance of probabilities.[470] Thus, the ICC applied a less rigorous standard to reparations than that which is applicable to criminal responsibility.[471] The standard of on the balance of probabilities is also known as 'more likely than not', 'more probable than not' and the 'preponderance of evidence';[472] it is mainly used in common law traditions and is barely applied in civil law systems.[473] According to the ICC, it levels the playing field for the different parties and thus is in accordance with the right of the accused to a fair trial.[474] The same standard was applied in the *Katanga* case.[475]

The standard of on the balance of probabilities takes into account the general problems that victims face in collecting evidence to prove their claims as a consequence of the fact that the majority of the crimes are committed in the middle

465 Rule 94 (1) (g), ICC's RoPE.

466 ECCC (Decision) 27 August 2009, *Prosecutor v. Kaing Guek Eav alias 'Duch'* (Case 001), Direction on Proceedings Relevant to Reparations and on the Filing of Written Submissions No. E159, p. 2; Rule 23*bis* (1), ECCC's Internal Rules. ECCC (Order) 13 January 2010, *Prosecutor* v. *Nuon Chea et al.* (Case 002), Order on the Admissibility of Civil Party Applications Related to Request D250/3, No. D250/3/2, para. 11-18.

467 ICC (Decision) 10 August 2007, *Situation in Uganda,* Decision on Victims' Applications for Participation a/0010/06, a/0064/06 to a/0070/06, a/0081/06, to a/0104/06 and a/0111/06, a/0127/06, ICC- 02/04-101, para. 13.

468 ICC, *Katanga* Reparations Order, *supra* n. 31, para. 66-68.

469 ICC, *Lubanga* Principles on Reparations' Appeal Judgment, *supra* n. 94, para. 83.

470 ICC, *Lubanga* Principles on Reparations, *supra* n. 4, para. 253-254; I ICC, *Lubanga* Principles on Reparations' Appeal Judgment, *supra* n. 94, para. 118; ICC, *Lubanga* Appeal Judgment on Reparations Order, *supra* n. 127, para. 65.

471 ICC, *Lubanga* Principles on Reparations, *supra* n. 4, para. 251; ICC, *Katanga* Reparations Order, *supra* n. 31, para. 59. Article 66 (3) of the ICC's Rome Statute states: "In order to convict the accused, the Court must be convinced of the guilt of the accused beyond reasonable doubt."

472 Lewis, P., and Friman, H., "Reparations to Victims," in Roy R.S. Lee, (ed.), The International Criminal Court: Elements of Crimes and Rules of Procedure and Evidence (Transnational Publishers, Inc., 2001), p. 484.

473 Clermont, K., and Sherwin, E., "A Comparative View of Standards of Proof", 50 *American Journal of Comparative Law* (2002), p. 243.

474 ICC, *Lubanga* Principles on Reparations, *supra* n. 4, para. 387; Article 64(2) ICC's Rome Statute.

475 ICC, *Lubanga* Principles on Reparations, *supra* n. 4, para. 253; ICC, *Katanga* Reparations Order, *supra* n. 31, para. 50.

of conflicts, and evidence may have been destroyed or is unavailable.[476] Accordingly, indirect proof such as 'inferences of fact and circumstantial evidence' may be the only relevant and available proof supporting victims' claims.[477] In this light, as it mentioned previously in the section on the identification of victims, the ICC accepts as evidence to establish victims' identity both official and unofficial documents (voting or refugee cards, ID certificates, certificates attesting to the loss of an ID card) and even 'a statement signed by two credible witnesses establishing their identity'.[478]

Similar to the ICC's reparations proceedings, the ECCC's legal framework establishes that the standard of proof that is applicable to the proceedings as well as reparations[479] is 'more likely than not to be true',[480] also known as the 'preponderance of evidence' or on the 'balance of probabilities'.[481] In addition, mindful of the difficulties that victims face in providing evidence, the ECCC has 'show[n] flexibility and broadly accepted any documentary evidence capable of supporting the claim directly or indirectly.'[482] However, this does not imply that the ECCC relaxes the standard of on the balance of probabilities;[483] in fact, the ECCC's standard of proof is highly burdensome.[484] Finally, it deserves to be mentioned that the ICC-TC may consider evidence at different stages of the trial process, as long as it is not 'inappropriate, ineffective or inefficient to consider as part of the trial process' and does not undermine the defendants' right to a fair trial and the presumption of innocence.[485] Furthermore, victims may adduce new pieces of evidence during the reparations stage. For instance, if parties to the reparations proceedings present additional evidence identifying harms that are not mentioned in the convictions, the previously unmentioned harms may be accepted by the Court.[486] However, this cannot be used to prompt the ICC to review the facts upon which the judgment on criminal

---

476 ICC, *Lubanga* Principles on Reparations, *supra* n. 4, para. 251-252; ICC, *Lubanga* Appeal Judgment on Reparations Order, *supra* n. 127, para. 22; ICC, *Katanga* Reparations Order, *supra* n. 31, para. 84.

477 ICC, *Situation in Uganda,* Decision on Victims' Participation, *supra* n. 467, para. 15; ICC, *Katanga* Reparations Order, *supra* n. 31, para. 61.

478 ICC, *Lubanga* Principles on Reparations, *supra* n. 4, para. 198; ICC, *Lubanga* Appeal Judgment on Reparations Order, *supra* n. 127, para. 57; ICC, *Katanga* Reparations Order, *supra* n. 31, para. 71-72, 104.

479 ECCC, *Duch* Appeal Judgment, *supra* n. 69, para. 527, 531.

480 Rules 23*bis* (1) (b), ECCC's Internal Rules; ECCC, *Nuon Chea et al.* Decision on the Civil Party Applications' Appeals, *supra* n. 123, para. 56-57.

481 ECCC, *Duch* Appeal Judgment, *supra* n. 69, para. 523-524.

482 ECCC, *Duch* Appeal Judgment, *supra* n. 69, para. 527.

483 ECCC, *Duch* Appeal Judgment, *supra* n. 69, para. 531 and footnote 1079 attached to paragraph 645.

484 However, when the reparations are funded by external means, civil parties are not required to provide evidence of their own harm before the ECCC. See: ECCC, *Chea and Shamphan* Judgment, *supra* n. 88, para. 1110.

485 ICC (Decision) 18 January 2008, *Prosecutor* v. *Thomas Lubanga Dyilo*, Decision on victims participation, ICC-01/04-01/06-1119, para. 122.

486 ICC, *Lubanga* Principles on Reparations' Appeal Judgment, *supra* n. 94, para. 185.

responsibility was based.[487] Before the ECCC, 'initial specifications' of reparation requests must be provided at the start of the trial.[488]

Use of Presumptions

Presumptions are some of the most important means of assisting claimants in proving their claims.[489] The standard of on the balance of possibilities allows for a broad use of presumptions, and both the ICC and the ECCC have made use thereof. The ICC first used presumptions in relation to victims' participation, by applying the low threshold of 'grounds to believe'.[490] It has upheld that if indirect victims can provide proof of their close relationship with the direct victim of an international crime, victims are not required to introduce evidence regarding the harm caused.[491] Regarding reparation proceedings, the ICC appears to mirror its approach on victims' participation by allowing the use of presumptions as part of the evidence.[492] For instance, it can be presumed that an individual is succeeded by his/her spouse and children;[493] psychological harm is presumed in the case of indirect victims who have lost a family member as long as they are able to establish that they had a personal or familial link with the direct victim.[494] In this regard, 'family' must be understood in relation to the relevant family and social structures.[495] In addition, moral harm can be presumed when victims have proved material losses.[496]

On the other hand, the ECCC has stated that it has the power to formulate 'presumptions in the factual context of the cases before it' on a discretionary basis.[497] In addition, ECCC Judge March-Uhel has established two major presumptions: i) that the relatives of direct victims (i.e. parents, children, siblings, grandparents, in-laws, uncles, aunts and cousins) of crimes such as enslavement, murder, torture, rape

487 Rule 56, Rules of the Court; Rule 94, ICC's RoPE.

488 Rule 80*bis* (4), ECCC Internal Rules.

489 Niebergall, *supra* n. 447, p. 160.

490 Ferstman and Goetz, *supra* n. 388, p. 331.

491 ICC (Judgment) 23 February 2009, *Prosecutor* v. *Joseph Kony et* al., Judgment on the Appeals of the Defence against the decisions entitled 'Decision on victims' applications for participation a/0010/06, a/0064/06, a/0070/06, a/0081/06, a/0082/06, a/0084/06 to a/0089/06, a/0091/06 to a/0097/06, a/0099/06, a/0100/06, a/0102/06 to a/0104/06, a/0111/06, a/0113/06 to a/0117/06, a/120/06, a/021/06 and a/0123/06 to a/0127/06' of the Pre-Trial Chamber II, ICC-02/04-179.

492 ICC, *Katanga* Reparations Order, *supra* n. 31, para. 61.

493 ICC, *Lubanga* Appeal Judgment on Reparations Order, *supra* n. 127, para. 7; ICC, *Katanga* Reparations Order, *supra* n. 31, para. 121.

494 ICC, *Lubanga* Appeal Judgment on Reparations Order, *supra* n. 127, para. 58; ICC, *Katanga* Reparations Order, *supra* n. 31, para. 113.

495 ICC, *Lubanga* Appeal Judgment on Reparations Order, *supra* n. 127, para 7; ICC, *Katanga* Reparations Order, *supra* n. 31, para. 121.

496 ICC, *Katanga* Reparations Order, *supra* n. 31, para. 297.

497 ECCC, *Duch* Appeal Judgment, *supra* n. 69, para. 444

and other crimes against humanity, suffer psychological harm; and ii) that applicants who allege that they are part of a close-knit community, a member of whom suffered direct harm, suffer psychological harm as a consequence.[498] Furthermore, the ECCC has maintained that applicants alleging psychological injury in the absence of a close relationship to a direct victim could benefit, where appropriate, from a presumption of collective injury, 'as long as a civil party applicant submits that he/she was a member of the same targeted group or community as the direct victims.' This would derive from the very nature of the crimes under the ECCC's jurisdiction.[499]

5.6 Causality

Reparations are to be awarded for the harm suffered as a consequence of the commission of the crimes for which the accused was convicted. However, a causal relationship may not always be obvious. For instance, if *y* shoots *x* and *x* dies as a result, it is clear that *x*'s death is a consequence of *y*'s act. However, imagine that *y* had planned to kill *x* and puts a gun to *x*'s head, and *x* dies as a consequence of a heart attack. If *x* had a chronic heart condition, would *y* be responsible for *x*'s death? Or if *y* shoots *x* while he is hospitalised and doctors determine that *x* would have died of natural causes minutes after the shooting, then it is not entirely clear that *x* died because of *y*. Furthermore, not all the physical and psychological harm that victims attribute to a given crime can easily be linked to it. For instance, if the death of *x* is the consequence of *y* having shot him, could *x*'s mother receive reparations for the cancer she suffers as a consequence of the distress caused by *x*'s death?

When determining reparations, causality limits the liability of the defendant to the damage caused.[500] In order to determine causality, it is necessary to decide on the appropriate causality test, and subsequently, to determine whether the alleged damage satisfies this test.[501] However, establishing causality and its appropriate test is 'one of the most complex theoretical issues in criminal law.'[502] Besides, at present there is no 'settled view in international law' regarding the appropriate standard test for causation.[503]

498 ECCC, *Nuon Chea et al.* Decision on the Civil Party Applications' Appeals, *supra* n. 123, Separate and Partially Dissenting Opinion of Judge Marchi-Uhel, para. 68.

499 ECCC, *Nuon Chea et al.* Decision on the Civil Party Applications' Appeals, *supra* n. 460, para. 93.

500 McCarthy, *supra* n. 53, p. 135.

501 Wühler, N., "Causation and Directness of Loss as Elements of Compensability before the United Nations Compensation Commission", in R.B. Lillich (ed.), *The United Nations Compensation Commission: Thirteenth Sokol Colloquium*, (Irvington, Transnational Publishers 1995), p. 232.

502 ICC, *Situation in Uganda,* Decision on Victims' Participation, *supra* n. 467, para, 14.

503 Henselin, Heiskanen and Mettraux, *supra* n. 22, p. 325; See also: Chapter II.

Neither the ICC's nor the ECCC's legal framework establish the required test for causality to be applied to reparations.[504] Instead, this decision is at the tribunals' discretion. Before delving into the tribunals' understanding of causality, it is important to distinguish between factual causation (also known as the '*sine qua non test*', 'cause-in-fact', and the 'but-for test') and legal causation, which is generally identified through three tests: directness, proximity and foreseeability.[505] Factual causation establishes whether a defendant is criminally liable for a given harm – *is the harm attributable to the defendant?* In contrast, legal causation establishes whether the perpetrator is liable for repairing a given harm – *is the harm a result of the crimes for which the defendant is criminally responsible?*

Although proof of factual and legal causation is required simultaneously,[506] it has been argued that legal causation is more adequate for reparations than factual causation in the context of international criminal law. Since international crimes are usually committed by multiple actors who participate on different levels (principal, accessory and residual form of accessory) in the commission of the crimes,[507] it is usually impossible to conclude that a specific harm would have occurred *but for* the contribution of the convicted person. This is especially true regarding accessory and residual form of accessory. Therefore, the different modes of criminal liability require different standards of factual causation.[508]

Regarding causality before the ICC, the ICC-AC has affirmed that reparations should be closely linked to the individual criminal liability of the accused,[509] and that the exact requirements for causality are to be decided on a case-by-case basis.[510] In the case of *Lubanga,* the causal link required between the crime and the harm was 'but for', and the harm for which reparations were sought were the 'proximate cause' of the crimes for which the accused was convicted.[511] The majority of judicial systems around the world embrace the proximate cause test.[512] Similarly, in the *Katanga* case

504 Yet Rule 85 of the ICC's RoPE establishes that legal persons claiming to be victims of crimes must be prove 'direct harm'.

505 See: Chapter II, Section on Causality.

506 Pérez León Acevedo, J.P., *Victims' Status at International and Hybrid Criminal Courts: Victims' Status as Witnesses, Victim Participants/Civil Parties and Reparations Claimants,* (Åbo Akademi, UPÅ 2014), p. 601.

507 Article 25 (3) (b) (c) (d), ICC's Rome Statute.

508 McCarthy, *supra* n. 53, p. 142, 144.

509 ICC, *Lubanga* Principles on Reparations' Appeal Judgment, *supra* n. 94, para. 65, 118.

510 ICC, *Lubanga* Principles on Reparations' Appeal Judgment, *supra* n. 94, para. 80; ICC, *Lubanga* Appeal Judgment on Reparations Order, *supra* n. 127, para. 11; ICC, *Katanga* Reparations Order, *supra* n. 31, para. 166.

511 ICC *Lubanga* Principles on Reparations, *supra* n. 4, para. 249-250; ICC, *Lubanga* Principles on Reparations' Appeal Judgment, *supra* n. 94, para. 129; ICC, *Lubanga* Appeal Judgment on Reparations Order, *supra* n. 127, para. 59.

512 War Crimes Research Office, The Case-Based Reparations Scheme at the International Criminal Court, Legal Analysis and Edition Project, Washington College of Law, June 2010, p. 39.

the ICC applied the 'but for' test for harm and the test of proximate cause between the crimes and the harm to be repaired.[513] Stahn has pointed out that the ICC has opted for a stricter approach than that of the 'presumption of collective injury' which is usually applied to collective awards, yet not as strict as requiring a direct relation to the harm and the ' immediate link' test.[514]

Under the ECCC's legal framework, the causality standard for reparations is higher than that of the ICC, as the harm suffered must be a 'direct consequence of at least one of the crimes alleged against the Charged Person' in order for a claim to be valid.[515] Consequently, in the *Duch* case, the Extraordinary Chambers determined that the appropriate causal link test was 'direct causality',[516] despite the fact that this test is usually considered inadequate within the scholarship on reparations.[517] This causality requirement is almost impossible to meet for victims of mass crimes, because the harm caused may be immeasurable,[518] multidimensional and multi-layered. In addition, the crimes of the Khmer Rouge were committed more than three decades ago, which further complicates the issue of satisfying the causality test.[519] Remarkably, in the *Nuon Chea and Khieu Samphan* case, the causality test was not discussed by the ECCC. This may have been due to the fact that the civil parties requested various reparation projects that would be funded by external sources, and not by the convicted persons.[520]

5.7 Implementation of Collective Reparations

The ICC has stated that its success 'is, to some extent, linked to the success of its reparation system.'[521] This illustrates that the implementation of reparation orders is of the utmost importance to the ICC. Although the ECCC does not attach the same importance to reparations, it is undoubtedly concerned that its orders, including those relating to reparations, are complied with.

---

513 ICC, *Katanga* Reparations Order, *supra* n. 31, para. 162.

514 Stahn, *supra* n. 455, p. 808.

515 Rule 23*bis* (1)(b), ECCC's Internal Rules.

516 ECCC, *Duch* Trial Judgment, *supra* n. 11, para. 642; ECCC, *Duch* Appeal Judgment, *supra* n. 69, para. 642-643.

517 War Crimes Research Office, *supra* n. 512, p. 39.

518 Teitel, R., *Transitional Justice* (Oxford, OUP 2002), p. 134.

519 Studzinsky, *supra* n. 441, p. 12.

520 Yet, it must be noted that the requirement of direct causality was used by the ECCC in the *Nuon Chea and Khieu Samphan* case regarding victims' participation. See: ECCC, *Nuon Chea et al.* Decision on the Civil Party Applications' Appeals, *supra* n. 123, para. 71.

521 ICC, *Lubanga* Appeal Judgment on Reparations Order, *supra* n. 127, para. 3; ICC, *Lubanga* Prosecutor's Application for a Warrant of Arrest, *supra* n. 338, para. 136.

In principle, implementation is the only part of the reparations process that occurs outside the courtroom,[522] but similarly deserves a careful and rigorous approach. This is particularly important because collective reparations are usually awarded in post-conflict situations, and may easily generate additional tensions if not carried out prudently.[523] This is especially pertinent in case of the ICC. Both cases under examination are related to a conflict in Ituri in the DRC, where members of the 'Hema' and 'Lendu' people, the two largest ethnic groups in Ituri, clashed with each other.[524] However, in both cases the victims were members of the 'Hema', which could have resulted in the 'Lendu' not regarding the ICC as a totally impartial judicial body.[525] Consequently, the implementation of reparation orders ought to be sensitive to these circumstances in order to be successful.

5.7.1 ICC's Implementation of Collective Reparations

In both the *Lubanga* and *Katanga* cases, the ICC ordered reparations to be implemented through the TFV, with its activities subject to monitoring by the ICC.[526] The ICC's oversight ensures that reparations are implemented and are implemented fairly.[527] The ICC provides the TFV with guidelines concerning the implementation of the reparations ordered and, based on those guidelines, the TFV is expected to present a draft implementation plan (DIP) to be approved by the ICC.[528] In the *Lubanga* and *Katanga* cases, the TFV was given 6 months and 3 months, respectively, to present the DIP.[529] Upon its submission to the ICC, the parties concerned were to be provided

---

522 ICC, *Lubanga* Draft Implementation Plan, *supra* n. 99, para. 15. Yet, the Court has held some hearings regarding the implementation of reparations. See: ICC (Order) 6 October 2016, *Prosecutor* v. *Thomas Lubanga Dyilo,* "Order on the conduct of the hearing to be held on 11 and 13 October 2016', ICC-01/04-01/06.

523 ICC, *Lubanga*, Annex A to the Draft Implementation Plan, *supra* n. 217, para. 84.

524 The population of Ituri is composed of 18 different ethnic groups. ICC, *Katanga* Reparations Order, *supra* n. 31, para. 19-20.

525 Martinez Ventura, J.E., "Analisis del caso Lubanga: El procedimiento de reparations", in K. Ambos, E. Malarino and C. Steiner, *Analisis de la primera sentence de la Corte Penal Internacional: El caso Lubanga* (Konrad-Aadenauer-Stiftung e. V, Berlin, 2014), p. 360.

526 ICC *Lubanga* Principles on Reparations, *supra* n. 4, para. 286; ICC, *Lubanga* Appeal Judgment on Reparations Order, *supra* n. 127, para. 236; ICC, *Lubanga* Appeal Judgment on Reparations Order, *supra* n. 127, para. 76; ICC, *Katanga* Reparations Order, *supra* n. 31, para. 313.

527 McCarthy, *supra* n. 53, p. 242.

528 Regulation 98 (3); TFV's Regulations.

529 In the Lubanga case, the TFV had the possibility to obtain a 6-month extension if this was justified. ICC, *Lubanga* Principles on Reparations' Appeal Judgment, *supra* n. 94, para. 242; ICC, *Lubanga* Appeal Judgment on Reparations Order, *supra* n. 127, para. 75; ICC, *Katanga* Reparations Order, *supra* n. 31, para. 309.

with the opportunity to submit observations on the DIP.[530] It must be stated that the original time line for the implementation of reparations has been extended over and over as the process has proven to be more complicated than anticipated.

However, in comparison to the *Lubanga* case, the ICC in the *Katanga* case provided clear guidelines as to what the content of the DIP should be, as well as what the procedure for the approval of the DIP would be.[531] While this was a fine-tuned approach on the part of the ICC, the *Lubanga* case was far more complex in terms of securing the implementation of reparations. This is because the DIP was supposed to be filed while the identification of victims was still pending and the determination of the financial liability of Mr. Lubanga was also pending. The ICC guidelines to the TFV were to define the modalities for collective reparations through consultations with victims[532] and with the possible assistance of experts.[533] In addition, the TFV was advised to consider the implementation of services such as education, housing, and vocational training.[534]

Consequently, the approval of the DIP in the *Lubanga* case has been a long road that has not arrived at its expected destination. The TFV was asked to include in the DIP the specific projects constituting the collective reparations awarded, the amount of money needed to remedy the harm caused by *Lubanga,* as well as the amount with which the TFV would be willing to complement the awards.[535] It is important to mention that the ICC intended to use the TFV's assessment of the harm to determine the financial liability of Lubanga.[536] The TFV submitted the DIP on 3 November 2015, following an expert conference and victim and community consultation.[537]

530 ICC, *Lubanga* Principles on Reparations' Appeal Judgment, *supra* n. 94, para. 243; ICC, *Lubanga* Appeal Judgment on Reparations Order, *supra* n. 127, para. 77; ICC, *Katanga* Reparations Order, *supra* n. 31, para. 311.

531 ICC, *Katanga* Reparations Order, *supra* n. 31, para. 309-314.

532 ICC, *Lubanga* Principles on Reparations' Appeal Judgment, *supra* n. 94, para. 201; ICC, *Lubanga* Appeal Judgment on Reparations Order, *supra* n. 127, para. 79.

533 ICC *Lubanga* Principles on Reparations, *supra* n. 4, para. 260-266; ICC, *Lubanga* Appeal Judgment on Reparations Order, *supra* n. 127, para. 70.

534 ICC, *Lubanga* Appeal Judgment on Reparations Order, *supra* n. 127, para. 69-70.

535 ICC, *Lubanga* Principles on Reparations' Appeal Judgment, *supra* n. 94, para. 240; ICC, *Lubanga* Appeal Judgment on Reparations Order, *supra* n. 127, para. 78-79.

536 ICC, *Lubanga* Principles on Reparations' Appeal Judgment, *supra* n. 94, para. 241; ICC, *Lubanga* Appeal Judgment on Reparations Order, *supra* n. 127, para. 80.

537 TFV, Report to the ASP, *supra* n. 45, para. 28.

The DIP included five categories of collective projects.[538] It also indicated that the implementation of the collective reparations would take 3 years.[539]

Yet it was not approved for several main reasons: i) the victims were not clearly identified; ii) the liability of Lubanga was not determined; iii) there was a lack of specificity regarding the exact locations where the reparations would be implemented, as well as their costs and limitations; and iv) it did not indicate the amount that the TFV was able to contribute to the reparations.[540] Nevertheless, the DIP actually contained a detailed protocol and monitoring mechanisms for rehabilitation measures, including a number of life skills training sessions to be carried out within 3 years.[541] While the TFV has already indicated its decision to allocate one million euros to complement the reparation awards,[542] at the time of writing the Court has approved the first stage of the DIP's implementation, which concerns the selection and the contract of the implementing partners.[543] Significantly, the ICC requested the TFV to evaluate the designing of collective symbolic reparations in addition to the DIP.[544] In response, the TFV submitted a separate proposal for symbolic collective reparations, consisting of symbolic structures (commemoration centres in three communities) and mobile memorialisation (initiatives in five additional communities) to be implemented over the course of two years.[545] This proposal was approved on 21 October 2016 subject to the condition that a progress report would be presented every 3 months.[546] Its implementation already started in early 2017.[547] Yet by November 2017, the TFV was still in the process of selecting a partner organization for their implementation.[548]

In the *Katanga* case, following the ICC's approach that collective reparations must retain some flexibility,[549] the TFV has presented a DIP with concrete proposals regarding the four collective reparations that the ICC ordered (housing, income-generating activities, education, psychological rehabilitation measures) and with

538 The projects were: i) rehabilitation (psychological and physical); ii) formal and informal education; iii) socio-economic development measures and vocational training; iv) measures to promote community reconciliation and to raise awareness of child soldier enlistment; and v) transformative measures aimed at addressing the underlying causes of violence, such as gender inequality and social stigma. See: ICC, *Lubanga*, Annex A to the Draft Implementation Plan, *supra* n. 217, para. 61-94.

539 ICC, *Lubanga*, Annex A to the Draft Implementation Plan, *supra* n. 217, para. 173.

540 ICC, *Lubanga* Order to Supplement the DIP, *supra* n. 250, para. 10, 21-22.

541 ICC, *Lubanga*, Annex A to the Draft Implementation Plan, *supra* n. 217, para. 129-173.

542 ICC, *Lubanga* TFV Additional Programme Information, *supra* n. 251, para. 16.

543 ICC, *Lubanga* Approval on Collective Service-Based Reparations, *supra* n. 101.

544 ICC, *Lubanga* TC II's Request on Feasibility of Symbolic CR, *supra* n. 255, para. 12

545 ICC, *Lubanga* TFV's Symbolic Reparations Proposal, *supra* n. 209, para. 29, 65

546 ICC, *Lubanga* Approval on Collective Symbolic Reparations, *supra* n. 100.

547 ICC (Filing) 13 February 2017, *Prosecutor* v. *Thomas Lubanga Dyilo*, Information regarding Collective Reparations with Three public annexes, one confidential annex, and one confidential ex-parte annex available to Trial Chamber II only, ICC-01/04-01/06-3273.

548 ICC, *Lubanga* TFV's 3rd progress report on the implementation of CR, *supra* n. 404.

549 ICC, *Katanga* Reparations Order, *supra* n. 31, para. 305.

clustered awards packages in the five different categories of harm.[550] In addition, the TFV presented a plan on how to deliver the individual reparations of 250 USD to each eligible victim. In this regard, the TFV highlighted that this amount is not insignificant in the DRC and thus proposed that the victims should have the opportunity to have a financial advisor to evaluate the options to receive the money, as well as to ensure that such compensation would not only be given in a timely fashion but also transferred in a discreet manner.[551] Finally, the TFV stated that it would be able to contribute one million USD,[552] indicated that the reparations would be implemented over 2 years, and proposed a monitoring system that would produce a report every 6 months (rather than every 3 months as in *Lubanga*.)[553]

Furthermore, it is worth pointing out that Mr. Katanga himself has offered to contribute to the reparation awards by way of an apology, for instance.[554] Consequently, the TFV pointed out in its DIP that it is discussing his possible contribution with him.[555] In the same vein, the government of the Democratic Republic of Congo has asserted its willingness to participate in the reparations.[556] In response, the TFV has made concrete proposals for the DRC's possible participation, including: increasing its security presence in Bogoro while reparations are being implemented, releasing any of Katanga's outstanding salary for the payment of reparations, allowing Katanga to participate in a public apology, and providing plots of land free of charge in order to make housing available.[557] Importantly, the ICC has made it clear that the DRC's government is nonetheless not absolved of its obligations under international and domestic law to provide reparations to victims.[558]

Finally, the TFV's key role in the design and implementation of reparations has been demonstrated in both cases. It is therefore important to know the principles guiding the design and implementation of reparations. In this regard, the ICC has indicated that such activities need to be carried out by the TFV while affording safety, privacy, and well-being to the victims.[559] In addition, the TFV has adopted several principles regarding the design and implementation of reparations. In the *Lubanga* case those principles are: i) the 'do no harm' principle;[560] ii) the principle of non-

550 ICC, *Katanga* Draft Implementation Plan, *supra* n. 197, para. 2, 84.
551 Ibid., para. 115.
552 ICC, *Katanga* Draft Implementation Plan, *supra* n. 197, para. 46
553 Ibid., para. 116, 153.
554 ICC, *Katanga* Reparations Order, *supra* n. 31, para. 315.
555 ICC, *Katanga* Draft Implementation Plan, *supra* n. 197, para. 133-134.
556 ICC, *Katanga* Reparations Order, *supra* n. 31, para. 325.
557 ICC *Katanga* DIP, para 70.
558 ICC, *Katanga* Reparations Order, *supra* n. 31, para. 321.
559 Ibid., para. 310; ICC, *Lubanga* Appeal Judgment on Reparations Order, *supra* n. 127, para 34.
560 ICC *Lubanga* Principles on Reparations, *supra* n. 4, para. 57; ICC, *Lubanga* Appeal Judgment on Reparations Order, *supra* n. 127, para. 215; ICC, *Lubanga* Draft Implementation Plan, *supra* n. 99, para. 16; ICC, *Lubanga*, Annex A to the Draft Implementation Plan, *supra* n. 217, para. 87.

malfeasance;[561] iii) promoting individual and collective local narratives;[562] iv) the principle of mitigating stigma;[563] and v) affirmative action.[564]And in the *Katanga* case the principles are: i) to help victims to cope with livelihood, financial, and psychological trauma caused by the crimes committed by Katanga; and ii) that victims receive meaningful and tangible benefits from the reparations.[565] In addition, the TFV foresees the long-term objective of reparations in the following manner: a) that victims are able to cope with the livelihood, financial, and psychological trauma; and b) that victims are able to appreciate the symbolic value of the individual compensation awards.[566]

All in all, it can be concluded that the implementation of reparations in the *Lubanga* case has been more complex than what can be expected from the *Katanga* case. In the former case, not only is the number of victims greater, but also the guidelines given to the TFV by the ICC have not been entirely clear. In addition, the TFV has decided to contribute one million euros in each of the two cases, despite the fact that the number of victims in the *Lubanga* case could amount to at least 3 times the number of victims in the *Katanga* case. This carries the message that when there is a greater number of victims, the amount awarded to each will be less. It is also important to mention that the challenges in the implementation of reparations are exacerbated when the region is still facing a conflict.[567] Up to date, victims in either case have not seen their awarded reparations implemented.

It should be mentioned that Moffett, by citing Article 75(2) of the ICC,[568] has raised the argument that the ICC's legal framework does not explicitly state that reparations should be linked to charges against the perpetrators.[569] He further seeks to support this idea by referring to Judge Eboe-Osuji when the latter upheld that 'there is no general principle of law that required conviction as a prerequisite for reparation'.[570] Whilst this argument appears attractive given the possibility to eliminate tedious procedural requirements such as the identification of victims, the

561 ICC, *Lubanga*, Annex A to the Draft Implementation Plan, *supra* n. 217, para. 81, 87.

562 Ibid., para. 88.

563 Ibid., para. 81.

564 ICC, *Lubanga*, Annex A to the Draft Implementation Plan, *supra* n. 217, para. 56-57.

565 ICC, *Katanga* Draft Implementation Plan, *supra* n. 197, para. 3.

566 Ibid., para. 121.

567 Unfortunately both the *Lubanga* and *Katanga* cases involve the situation in the DRC which is still facing an ongoing conflict.

568 Article 75(2) reads as follows: "The Court may make an order directly against a convicted person specifying appropriate reparations to, or in respect of, victims, including restitution, compensation and rehabilitation."

569 Moffett, L., "Reparations for victims at the International Criminal Court: a new way forward?" 21 *The International Journal of Human* Rights (2017), p. 1206.

570 ICC (Decision) 5 April 2016, *Prosecutor* v. *William Samoei Ruto and Joshua Arap Sang*, Public redacted version of Decision on Defence Applications for Judgments of Acquittal, ICC-01/09-01/11-2027 Red-Corr.

lack of evidence in proving causality, the calculation of the perpetrator's liability, and even the assessment of the harm, Moffet's argument can be easily contested. In fact, the ICC emphasised in its reparations orders that reparations are inevitably linked to the crimes for which the perpetrator was convicted. A shift away from this approach may be desirable for the victims, but the rules would need to change and the reparations procedure part of an international civil procedure would have to be de-linked from the criminal procedure before the ICC.

5.7.2 ECCC's Implementation of Collective Reparations

As opposed to the ICC, the ECCC does not have the competence to enforce reparations; instead, this task is delegated to the ordinary Cambodian court system.[571] If reparations are ordered against the convicted person, the ECCC's Internal rules state that their enforcement is the responsibility of the 'appropriate national authorities [...] on the initiative of any member of the collective group, unless the verdict specifies that a particular award shall be granted in relation only to a specified group.'[572] However, if the reparations consist of externally funded projects, no specific rule exists on how to ensure their compliance. Nonetheless, H.E. Kranh, Acting Director of the ECCC's Office of Administration, has stated that most of the eleven endorsed reparation projects in the *Nuon Chea and Khieu Samphan* case[573] have been implemented successfully.[574] Everything considered, it appears that the implementation of reparations has received little attention at the ECCC.[575] However, some measures have been put in place. In relation to the *Duch* case the naming of civil parties in the published judgment and the compilation of the statement of apology by Mr. Duch has taken place. And in relation to the *Nuon Chea and Khieu Samphan* case the government of Cambodia has declared an annual day of remembrance.[576]

5.8 Main Challenges for Implementation

From the cases analysed above, it is possible to identify several important challenges regarding the design and implementation of collective reparation orders. First, since

571 ECCC, *Duch* Trial Judgment, *supra* n. 11, para. 661.

572 Rule 113 (1), ECCC's Internal Rules.

573 ECCC, *Chea and Shamphan* Judgment, *supra* n. 88, para. 1153, 1155 and 1160.

574 ECCC's Office of Administration Statement available at <https://www.eccc.gov.kh/en/articles/results-forum-developments-eccc%E2%80%99s-proceedings-and-reparations-case-00202> Accessed 10 May 2017.

575 Sperfeldt, C., "Collective Reparations at the Extraordinary Chambers in the Courts of Cambodia" 12 *International Criminal Law Review* (2012), p. 482.

576 Hughes, R., "Justice processes and discourses of post-conflict reconciliation in Southeast Asia: the experiences of Cambodia and Timor-Leste" in A. McGregor, L. Law, F. Miller (eds.) *Routledge Handbook of Southeast Asian Development* (New York, Routledge 2018), p. 96-108.

the concept of collective reparations remains ambiguous, it is essential that the guidelines for implementation are clearly defined[577] so as to avoid delays. In addition, it can be useful to establish deadlines in the judgments on the implementation of awards in order to afford victims a degree of certainty regarding when they will see justice materialise. However, as demonstrated by the *Lubanga* case, deadlines may not be feasible in complex situations, especially when victim stigmatisation and persisting violence impede victims from being identified or from receiving an award.

Second, it has been claimed that when it comes to reparations, the outcomes and the process are equally important.[578] In this light, victim participation in the crafting and implementation of collective reparations should be emphasised. This contributes to the creation of 'a sense of local ownership', and consequently promotes the healing and empowerment of the community.[579] Unfortunately, victim participation may be jeopardised as victims are usually divided regarding their needs and desires,[580] and they may also fear retaliation. To ameliorate this, the ICC and TFV have mechanisms to promote victim consensus while safeguarding the inclusion of vulnerable victims and providing them with safety measures.[581]

Third, it is essential to ensure that adequate funding is available for the implementation of reparations. The ICC is empowered to order state authorities or other third parties to confiscate, freeze or obtain information about the assets of the accused.[582] In addition, the ICC can order a convicted person to pay a fine in addition to imprisonment.[583] However, none of these measures were applied in the two ICC cases discussed.[584] Unlike the ICC, the ECCC does not allow for the imposition of fines or for the assets of the accused to be confiscated; the only penalty it can order is imprisonment.[585] Instead, the ECCC can confiscate any personal property, money, and real property that have been unlawfully acquired by the convicted persons in order to be returned to the government.[586]

Fourth, there are several conceptual and legal ambiguities that may prevent the effective implementation of reparation awards. For instance, with respect to the ICC,

577 Kristjánsdóttir, *supra* n. 389, p. 185.

578 Sperfeldt, *supra* n. 575, p. 475.

579 Suchova, M., "The importance of a Participatory Reparations Process and Its Relationship to the Principles of Reparations", *Briefing Paper No.5, Reparations Unit, Essex University* (2011), p. 2-3.

580 McKay, *supra* n. 16, p. 924.

581 Suchova, *supra* n. 579, p. 6.

582 Articles 77 (2) and 93(1)(k), ICC' Rome Statute; Henselin, Heiskanen and Mettraux, *supra* n. 22, p. 336; Article 57 (3)(e) and 93(l)(k).

583 Article 77 (2), ICC's Rome Statute; Rule 146, ICC's RoPE.

584 Mancini, M., "UN Sanctions Targeting Individuals and ICC Proceedings: How to Achieve a Mutually Reinforcing Interaction in N. Ronzitti (ed.) *Coercive Diplomacy, Sanctions and International Law,* (Leiden/Boston, Brill, 2016), p. 239.

585 Article 38, Law on the Establishment of the ECCC for the Prosecution of crimes committed during the period of democratic Kampuchea, 28 Oct. 2009.

586 Ibid., Article 39.

the degree of independence of the TFV in developing the DIP and its exact contents remain unclear. In addition, the degree of oversight by the ICC and the means by which it is to be enforced is still to be resolved.[587] What will the ICC do with the progress reports that the TFV is expected to hand in every three months? Will the ICC hold hearings to monitor compliance as the IACtHR does? Furthermore, it is unclear under what circumstances reparation applications are to be analysed individually by the court. The procedures should be clear to victims prior to submitting their applications, and they deserve to be informed if additional information may be requested at a later date.[588]

Regarding the ECCC, the most important concerns are related to compliance with the reparations, especially those that have external funding. Budgetary constraints have limited the ECCC's operational capabilities and this could hinder the monitoring of reparation projects, not to mention their financing.[589] Further challenges exist with regard to securing external funding for the projects, especially with a lack of leverage provided by the ECCC to secure political support.[590]

Fifth, under the ICC the implementation of collective reparations involves the collaboration of the Court with several actors such as the TFV,[591] states and intergovernmental organisations.[592] This cooperation is not only required at the time of their implementation, but also to employ measures to ensure funding for reparations such as confiscating or freezing the convicted person's assets within a given national jurisdiction.[593] Similarly, in the case of the ECCC, collective reparations require cooperation with the government of Cambodia, as well as international organisations and other governments willing to fund reparation projects. Yet, while the ICC has upheld that state parties have the obligation to cooperate fully with the ICC in order to enforce reparations orders, this is not the case for the ECCC.[594]

Furthermore, in addition to the states' cooperation, tribunals have encouraged governments to implement national reparation programmes to ensure full redress

---

587 Carayon G., and O'Donohue, J., "The International Criminal Court's Strategies in Relation to Victims", 15 *Journal of International Criminal Justice* (2017), p. 583.

588 REDRESS, Moving Reparation forward at the ICC, *supra* n. 308, p. 11.

589 Oeung, J., "Expectations, Challenges and Opportunities of the ECCC" in S.imon M. Meisenberg and I. Stegmiller, *Assessing the History, Establishment, Judicial Independence and Legacy: Assessing Their Contribution to International Criminal Law* (The Hague, T.M.C Asser Press 2016), p. 118.

590 Hughes and Elander, *supra* n. 430, p 49; Open Society Foundation, Briefing Paper, "The Funding Challenge for Reparations in Cambodia", September 2013. Available at:< https://www.opensocietyfoundations.org/briefing-papers/funding-challenge-reparations-cambodia>.

591 McCarthy, *supra* n. 444, p. 1206; Aubry and Henao-Trip, *supra* n. 226, p. 9.

592 Kristjánsdóttir, *supra* n. 389, p. 193.

593 Article 25, ICC's Rome Statute

594 ICC *Lubanga* Principles on Reparations, *supra* n. 4, para. 256; ICC, *Lubanga* Appeal Judgment on Reparations Order, *supra* n. 127, para. 50.

for victims.[595] Finally, a clear monitoring and oversight mechanism is essential for the implementation of reparations. While the ICC has retained judicial oversight concerning the implementation of collective reparations through the approval of the DIP and obligatory progress reports, the ECCC does not have this authority as the national Cambodian courts implement the reparations orders. The ECCC seems to be fairly disengaged with the actual implementation of reparations. After it has provided its endorsement, it mostly tries to convene funding meetings between project organizers, potential donors and the Cambodian government to promote the projects' realization.[596]

6 Conclusions

It is a principle of international criminal law that individual perpetrators are not only criminally responsible for the crimes they have committed, but are also liable for the harm caused to the victims.[597] In this light, the ICC and the ECCC afford justice beyond retributive tenets by providing measures of reparation and affirming the right of victims to reparations; the main challenge however lies in the materialisation of such a right.[598]

Although the ICC's legal framework suggests that individual reparations should be awarded by default, with collective reparations being the exception,[599] collective reparations feature consistently in the ICC's reparation orders. This is not only because collective reparations are generally more adequate and feasible, but also because they may be the only method that the Court has in order to avoid further unrest in post-conflict regions.[600] In general, collective reparations are believed to be adequate given the uncertainty surrounding the number of victims and the potential problems that may ensue from individual reparations among communities and victims themselves. They are also believed to be more feasible because of the likelihood of the convicted person's indigence, the TFV's limited resources to complement reparations, and the fact that collective reparations require fewer resources and allow for a greater number of victims to obtain remedial benefits. However, it should be added that – as

595 ICC *Lubanga* Principles on Reparations, *supra* n. 4, para. 239; ECCC, *Duch* Trial Judgment, *supra* n. 11, para. 66.

596 Ciorciari and Heindel, *supra* n. 87, p. 228; VSS Press Release *Wide Ranging Support for Reparation,* 17 March 2017; ECCC, VSS Fundraising Meeting on Case 002/02 Reparations, 3 April 2017, Available at <http://www.eccc.gov.kh/sites/default/files/media/Media_Alert_Eng_03.%20 04.2017%20.pdf>.

597 Zegveld, *supra* n. 10, p. 85.

598 Evans, *supra* n. 169, p. 3.

599 Mégret affirms that the ICC's legal framework regarding reparations seems to have been influenced by the individual approach of international human rights law. See: Mégret, *supra* n. 163, p. 173-174.

600 In this light, the TFV has stated that community reparations are the only kind of reparations that are meaningful in cases of mass atrocities. See: ICC, *Lubanga* TFV's Observations on the Principles on Reparations' Appeal Judgment, *supra* n. 402, para. 171.

is evident in the *Katanga* case – symbolic individual measures can also feasibly be ordered. Thus, the main challenge lies in finding the right balance between repairing each victim's individual harm and the limited resources available.[601]

Ideally, collective reparations should be awarded complementarily rather than as a substitute for individualised reparations,[602] considering that victims of international crimes suffer both individual and collective harm. Besides, individual and collective reparations are supposed to be different in substance and procedure,[603] the former being stricter in its methods, and the latter more flexible. In addition, combining the two measures of reparation could allow victims to distinguish collective reparations from general assistance provided by the TFV (development or humanitarian programmes).[604] This is of considerable importance because making a clear-cut distinction between assistance and collective reparations may be difficult.[605]

In this regard, we must recall that before the ICC redress is provided through two different bodies: the ICC and TFV. While having two venues for victims' redress enhances the ICC's credibility,[606] tensions between the two are likely to arise. Legally, the assistance provided by the TFV qualifies as humanitarian assistance rather than reparations which are always linked to an ICC order.[607] Nevertheless, its assistance has a reparative nature, and has the potential to empower victims and to provide recognition for the harm suffered.[608, 609] Consequently, assistance programmes clearly overlap with the content of a reparation order, which in turn may undermine the importance of the reparations.[610] To address this, the ICC would have to develop a strategy that allows victims to distinguish one from the other, so that reparations can be easily recognised.

That being said, for victims the distinction between reparations and assistance may be irrelevant in terms of the benefits obtained. In addition, the assistance is likely to be received much earlier than reparations, or it may be the only perceptible and materialised form of justice as not all victims of crimes under the ICC's jurisdiction are 'lucky' enough to have their crimes prosecuted.[611] As a consequence, the TFV's

---

601 REDRESS, Moving Reparation forward at the ICC, *supra* n. 308, p. 14.

602 Hamber, B., Repairing the Irreparable: dealing with the double-binds of making reparations from crimes of the past, 5 *Ethnicity and Health* (2000), p. 224-225.

603 ICC, *Lubanga* Draft Implementation Plan, *supra* n. 99, para. 159, 166,

604 Birchall, Francq and Pijnenburg, *supra* n. 184, p. 8; Ferstman and Goetz, *supra* n. 388, p. 343.

605 McKay, *supra* n. 16, p. 950.

606 See: Evans, *supra* no. 169, p. 110.

607 Kristjánsdóttir, *supra* n. 389, p. 21.

608 Dannenbaum, *supra* n. 32, p. 252.

609 ICC, *Lubanga* Draft Implementation Plan, *supra* n. 99, para. 154.

610 Moffet, L., "Reparations for 'Guilty Victims': Navigating Complex Identities of Victim-Perpetrators in Reparation Mechanisms", 10 *International Journal of Transitional Justice* (2010), p. 162.

611 REDRESS, Report on the Impact of the Rome Statute System on Victims and Affected Communities, 22 March 2010, p. 15.

assistance may be perceived as a symbol of the international community's solidarity with a large number of victims.[612]

Everything considered, it is important to acknowledge that regardless of the importance of reparations for victims,[613] reparations complement the ICC's primary duty as a criminal court: to bring justice to victims of the most heinous crimes.[614] In this light, collective reparations help to complement the symbolic justice that the ICC offers (considering that it can only focus on a handful of perpetrators or not all)[615] by providing reparations that, rather than addressing individual harms, offer relief of a more collective and symbolic nature.[616]

As opposed to the ICC, the ECCC's legal framework limits the measures of reparation that victims may seek to collective ones, whether symbolic or service-related. In theory, victims may seek redress through the VSS's assistance, similar to that provided by the TFV, as well as reparations. However, the VSS has implemented very limited assistance projects but it is planning to expand the projects.[617] For instance, a stupa was built to commemorate the victims of the Khmer Rouge genocide.[618] As a result, no debate on whether this assistance may overlap with reparations has arisen.

Furthermore, it is important to note that collective reparations appear to correspond more closely to the tribunals' purpose of contributing to a transitional justice and reconciliation process,[619] because they aim to enhance social solidarity, build civil trust, empower groups,[620] and contribute to the long-term goals of reconciliation.[621] In this light, the ICC, the TFV, and ECCC are also perceived as instruments for transitional justice and peace-building in post-conflict situations.[622] However, the potential of collective reparations to benefit many victims and thus to contribute to transitional justice is partly compromised, as both the ICC and ECCC

---

612 McCarthy, *supra* n. 125, p. 271.
613 van den Wyngaert, *supra* n. 318, p. 490.
614 Dwertmann, *supra* n. 124, p. 49; Zegveld, *supra* n. 10, p. 94.; McCarthy, *supra* n. 2, p. 353 -359; Dannenbaum, *supra* n. 32, p. 239.
615 Dannenbaum, *supra* n. 32, p. 276.
616 Moffet, L., "Reparative complementarity: ensuring an effective remedy for victims in the reparation regime of the International Criminal Court", 21 *The International Journal of Human Rights* (2012), p. 11.
617 The Phnom Penh Post's news, Khmer Rouge Tribunal reparations sought for large set of projects, 7 April 2017. Available at: <http://www.phnompenhpost.com/national/khmer-rouge-tribunal-reparations-sought-large-set-projects>.
618 Hughes, *supra* n. 576, p. 96-108.
619 Mégret, F., "Of Shrines, Memorials and Museums: Using the International Criminal Court's Victim Reparation and Assistance Regime to Promote Transitional Justice" 16 *Buffalo Human Rights Law Review* (2010), p. 28-35
620 Mégret, *supra* n. 163, p.179-180.
621 Rosenfeld, *supra* n. 228, p. 745.
622 Lee, *supra* n. 1, p. 39; Dannenbaum, *supra* n. 32, p. 298.

require the establishment of a causal link between the harm caused to victims and the crimes for which the accused was convicted.

From the analysis presented in this chapter, it also emerges that significant progress still needs to be made to ensure clarity and efficiency in giving effect to the right of victims to obtain reparations. Before the ICC, reparations principles are developed on a case-by-case basis. Although this approach has some notable benefits, as it aims to respond to the specific needs of victims, it also brings uncertainty, and sometimes even frustration for victims, as they do not know what to expect from reparations.[623] This approach is also likely to lead to inconsistencies,[624] although the Court has tried to establish consistency in its rulings by applying the *Lubanga* principles to the *Katanga* case.[625] While the Court started to establish and clarify some principles in its first decision on reparations in the *Lubanga* case, to date it has not developed a clear strategy or policy document that could help clarify its ambiguous legal framework.[626] Besides, such a document could reduce the time that victims need to wait before seeing reparation awards materialise and thereby contribute to both the satisfaction of victims[627] and the legitimacy of the ICC's work. In the *Lubanga* case, it has taken the ICC more than five years to implement its decision, although improvements on this front have been observed in the *Katanga* case.[628]

623 Carayon and O'Donohue, *supra* n. 587, p. 582.
624 Ibid., p. 582.
625 ICC, *Katanga* Reparations Order, *supra* n. 31, para. 29.
626 Carayon and O'Donohue, *supra* n. 587, p. 569.
627 REDRESS, Moving Reparation forward at the ICC, *supra* n. 308, p. 3.
628 Ibid., p. 9.

CHAPTER V
COLLECTIVE REPARATIONS & NON-JUDICIAL BODIES

1 INTRODUCTION

Collective reparations first emerged within the context of societies in transition: societies that have experienced either severe (internal) violent conflicts or authoritarian regimes that produced grave violations of human rights (GVHR) such as those that are protected under international human rights law and, in some cases, under international humanitarian law. These societies strive to deal with those past legacies while moving forward towards more democratic orders.[1] Although Tomuschat has submitted that in 'any process of transitional justice, the primary goal must be to re-establish security and respect for human rights as a matter of collective reparation',[2] thereby reducing reparations to the democratic 'transition itself', societies usually seek to provide reparations to the victims of past crimes through reparation programmes to facilitate such a transition and to bolster reconciliation processes.[3]

Reparations have become a 'leading response' in transitional justice processes (TJPs),[4] because they convey a message that the harm suffered is acknowledged and an attempt is being made to make amends for this harm.[5] Their importance is underscored by the fact that even the involvement of the United Nations Security Council (UNSC) in post-conflict situations includes the establishment of a *sui generis* mechanism of collective claims programmes to contribute to reconciliation.[6]

---

1 Odio Benito, E., "The International Criminal Court: possible contributions of the Rome Statute to judicial processes in transitional societies", in J. Almqvist and C. Espósito, *The Role of Court in Transitional Justice* (Abingdon/New York, Routledge 2012), p. 280.

2 Tomuschat, C., "Darfur: Compensation for the Victims", 3 *Journal of International Criminal Justice* (2005), p. 579-589, 587.

3 Niebergall, H., "Overcoming Evidentiary Weaknesses in Reparation Claims Programmes" in C. Ferstman, M. Goetz and A. Stephens (eds.), *Reparations for Victims of Genocide, War Crimes and Crimes Against Humanity: Systems in Place and Systems in the Making* (Leiden, Martinus Nijhoff 2009), p. 146-147.

4 Teitel, R., *Transitional Justice* (Oxford, OUP 2000), p. 127; van Boven, T., "Victims' Rights to a Remedy and Reparation: The New United Nations Principles and Guidelines" in C. Ferstman, M. Goetz and A. Stephens (eds.), *Reparations for Victims of Genocide, War Crimes and Crimes Against Humanity: Systems in Place and Systems in the Making* (Leiden, Martinus Nijhoff 2009), p. 237.

5 Magarrell, L., "Reparations in Theory and Practice", *ICTJ* (2007), p. 2.

6 The UNCC is also seen as a successful model for collective compensation for the crime of aggression. See: Gattini, A., "The UN Compensation Commission: Old Rules, New Procedures on War Reparations", 13 *European Journal of International Law* (2002), p. 161.

Although not necessarily exclusively, reparations as part of a TJP consist of collective reparations and most commonly focus on providing in-kind benefits such as medical or educational services as well as symbolic and satisfaction measures including apologies, monuments, or minimal financial awards. Reparations are usually demanded or established by Truth and Reconciliation Commissions (TRCs), but they can also emerge from national initiatives, often demanded by civil society. Alternatively, they may be provided by different non-judicial bodies.

This chapter will provide a comparative analysis of collective reparations as part of transitional justice mechanisms, with the aim of identifying similarities and differences among the substantive and procedural aspects of those reparations recommended or designed by different non-judicial bodies. The chapter commences by providing a definition of transitional justice and its most common mechanisms, as well as by commenting on the emergence of collective reparation programmes. Next, in-depth case studies will be discussed regarding the collective reparations recommended by the TRCs in Peru and Morocco. Both TRCs were a response to victims from oppressive government regimes and internal armed conflicts. The reason for studying these particular cases is straightforward: of all the collective reparations recommended by TRCs, the Moroccan and Peruvian ones are the most advanced in their implementation.[7] Hence, these case studies are uniquely positioned to illustrate the characteristics and restrictions of collective reparations under transitional justice processes.

Finally, this chapter also examines two mass claims reparation programmes (MCRs or Compensation Commissions): the United Nations Compensation Commission (UNCC) and the Eritrea-Ethiopia Compensation Commission (EECC). In contrast to the collective reparations in Peru and Morocco, the two MCRs are a response to victims of a war between two states, rather than an internal conflict or a repressive regime. The UNCC was established under the auspices of the UNSC in order to contribute to the reconciliation process between Iraq and Kuwait by providing compensation to a large number of victims in an expeditious manner.[8] The EECC, established through a bilateral agreement between Eritrea and Ethiopia, was part of the measures aimed at aiding the transition from open conflict to peace among these

---

7 Guillerot, J. and Carranza, R., *The Rabat Report: The Concept and Challenges of Collective Reparations* (ICTJ 2009), p. 14; Suchova, M., "The importance of a Participatory Reparations Process and Its Relationship to the Principles of Reparations", *Briefing Paper No. 5, Reparations Unit, Essex University* (2011), p. 13; Díaz Gómez, C., "Elementos para un programa administrativp de reparaciones colectivas en Colombia" in C. Díaz Gómez (ed.), *Tareas Pendientes: Propuestas para la formulación de políticas públicas de la reparación en Colombia* (Bogota, ICTJ 2010), p. 287. Other TRCs such as the Sierra Leone one have also recommended collective reparations. See: Report of the Sierra Leone Truth and Reconciliation Commission, Vol. 2, (2004).

8 van Zoelen, J.E.M. *The United Nations Compensation Commission: toward a new law state responsibility?*, PhD thesis, Utrecht University, 1996, p. 26.

countries.[9] Both commissions had the purpose of compensating victims of GVHR that also amounted to gross violations of humanitarian law. Furthermore, the UNCC is an administrative body which adopted quasi-judicial methods in the conduct of its proceedings, while the EECC is a quasi-judicial body.

The comparison between the two national collective reparation programmes, on the one hand, and the two MCRs, on the other, is grounded on three main reasons: i) all four programmes were established to provide benefits to a large number of victims; ii) all four programmes are concerned with justice in a post-conflict situation; iii) the distribution of the awards in each case is being carried out by non-judicial bodies. In addition, the techniques used in these MCRs have been referred to during the design of collective reparations in a legal process.[10] A caveat must be borne in mind, however. This chapter addresses the reparation responses to GVHR by non-judicial bodies without distinguishing the instances in which the said violations also constitute violations of international humanitarian law or international criminal law.

1.1 Definition of Transitional Justice

The term "transitional justice" (TJ) was coined in 1995 by Kritz.[11] TJ refers to a temporary and exceptional form of material and symbolic justice, aimed at responding to past GVHR and helping societies to come to terms with the legacies of past abuses and, consequently, to take steps towards democratization.[12] According to Đukić, TJ brings together the notions of *transition* and *justice* to conform to the challenges of each post-conflict situation.[13]

TJ takes the form of various judicial and non-judicial transitional justice mechanisms (TJMs) including: criminal trials, reparation programmes, truth

9 However, Healy and Plaut affirm that the creation of a Boundary Commission was the key mechanism provided by the Agreement, as it would end up with the border problem. See: Healy, S. and Plaut, M., "Ethiopia and Eritrea: Allergic to Persuasion", 7 *Briefing Paper Chatham House* (2007), p. 2.

10 ICC (Order) *Prosecutor* v. *Germain Katanga,* Ordonnance de réparation en vertu de l'article 75 du Statut, ICC-01/04-01/07-3728, 24 March 2017, para. 48, Footnote 92; ICC (Report) *Prosecutor* v. *Thomas Lubanga Dyilo,* Second Report of the Registry on Reparations, ICC-01/04-01/06-2806, 1 September 2011, para. 44; ICC (Decision) *Prosecutor* v. *Thomas Lubanga Dyilo*, Decision establishing the principles and procedures to be applied to reparations, ICC-01/04-01/06-2904, 7 August 2012, para. 248-249, Footnotes 433-434; ICC (Submission) *Prosecutor* v. *Thomas Lubanga Dyilo*, Prosecution's Response to the Defence Appeal against the "Decision establishing the principles and procedures to be applied to reparations", 21 September 2012, para. 33.

11 Sandoval Villalba, C., Transitional Justice: Key Concepts, processes and Challenges, *Institute for Democracy & Conflict Resolution* (2011), p. 2.

12 Wolfe, S., *The Politics of Reparations and Apologies* (New York, Springer 2014), p. 39; García-Godos, J., "Victim Reparations in Transitional Justice: What is at Stake and Why", 26 *Nordisk Tidsskrift for Menneskerettigheter,* (2008), p. 111; Teitel, *supra* n. 4, p. 4-5.

13 Đukić, D., "Transitional Justice and the International Criminal Court – in 'the interest of justice?'", 89 *International Review of the Red Cross* (2007), p. 692-693.

commissions, institutional reforms, memorialisation measures, historical documentation, vetting and dismissals, and lustration laws. All of these mechanisms have the purpose of establishing accountability, bringing justice to victims, and achieving reconciliation.[14] In this light, Sandoval refers to TJMs as peace-building mechanisms.[15] All TJMs are often combined to complement and support one another in order to reach the goals of the TJ process in a given country.[16] However, states lack concrete guidelines indicating the specific TJM combinations that are considered to be appropriate, the precise content thereof, and even the relationship between TJMs and international law.[17] Instead, governments decide, on a discretionary basis, which TJMs they will implement and in what manner this will be done. This decision may be based on a political agenda in peace accords at the end of a conflict, or on national decrees or laws.[18]

1.2 Truth and Reconciliation Commissions

Truth and Reconciliation Commissions (TRCs) are commonly established during the immediate post-transition period in countries emerging from a violent conflict or an authoritarian regime.[19] TRCs, perhaps the most common TJM,[20] are independent, temporary, and non-judicial fact-finding bodies that investigate and establish a record of past abuses and provide victims with a voice, acknowledgement, and the right to discover the truth.[21] Their work is intended to promote reconciliation, prevent future violations, vindicate the memory of victims, and help victims alleviate their suffering.[22] In this light, Wiebelhaus-Brahm even goes as far as to consider them as

---

14 UNSC, Report of the Secretary-General, The rule of law and transitional justice in conflict and post-conflict societies, No. S/2004/616, 23 August 2004, p. 4; ICJT, "What is Transitional Justice?", ICTJ 2009, p. 1; Tomuschat, *supra* n. 2, p. 580-581.

15 Sandoval Villalba, *supra* n. 11, p. 2.

16 ICJT, *supra* n. 14.

17 Other issues that may arise are the following: whether TJMs are necessary in a transitional process; where no GVHR have taken place, but a violation of fundamental rights such as freedom of speech has occurred. See: Sandoval Villalba, *supra* n. 11, p. 3.

18 OHCHR, *Rule of Law Tools for Post-Conflict States: Truth Commissions* (New York, UN 2006), p. 7-8.

19 Ibid., p 1.

20 Ibid., p. 11.

21 UNSC, *supra* n. 14; Wiebelhaus-Brahm, E., "Truth Commissions" in W. Schabas and N. Bernaz (eds.), *Routledge Handbook of International Criminal Law* (Abingdon, Routledge 2011), p. 369.

22 Hayner, P., *Unspeakable Truths: Confronting State terror and atrocity* (New York/London, Routledge 2001) p. 72, 85; Cryer, R. et al. (ed.), *An Introduction to International Criminal Law and Procedure* (Cambridge, CUP 2014, 3rd ed.), p. 579; Aldana, R., "A Victim-Centered Reflection on Truth Commissions and Prosecutions as a Response to Mass Atrocities" 5 *Journal of Human Rights* (2006), p. 109.

human rights bodies.[23] Yet the work of TRCs is not a substitute for justice derived from courts; in fact, TRCs have the potential to assist future prosecutions.[24]

Despite sharing the ultimate goal of helping society to understand past abuses, the TRCs' substantive and procedural aspects differ between countries.[25] Like other TJMs, TRCs are usually the result of political negotiations. Consequently, their mandate is limited to crimes committed within a specific timeframe, thereby restricting the scope of the truth that a TRC delivers.[26] Although the composition of commissions depends on their mandate and on the political compromises leading to their creation, commissioner bodies are generally gender-balanced groups of well-respected members of society, sometimes interspersed with foreign nationals who may be needed to guarantee the objectivity of the TRC's work.[27]

Usually, the TRCs' work involves four stages: i) a preparatory phase (the establishment of a strategic plan, procedures and policies); ii) an investigative phase (statements from victims and perpetrators); iii) public hearings; and iv) the issuing of a report.[28] If so empowered, the TRC may include in its final report recommendations for national reforms, prosecutions, or reparations.[29] However, TRCs do not have the mandate to oversee the implementation of such recommendations.[30] Despite their lack of direct oversight competence, TRCs have played an important role in promoting the creation and implementation of national collective reparation programmes.[31] One of their assets is their ability to identify patterns of widespread abuse[32] and victims' reality. Even if TRCs only survey a section of the total number of victims, the surveyed victims present their needs and pleas for compensation through hearings, allowing TRCs to recommend meaningful measures for reparations.[33]

---

23 Wiebelhaus-Brahm, *supra* n. 21, p. 369.
24 Hayner, *supra* n. 22, p. 29.
25 OHCHR, *supra* n. 18, p. 1.
26 OHCHR, *supra* n. 18, p. 21.
27 Wiebelhaus-Brahm, *supra* n. 21, p. 373.
28 Ibid., p. 374-375.
29 Cryer et al., *supra* n. 22, p. 578; Hayner, *supra* n. 18, p. 85.
30 Cryer et al., *supra* n. 22, p. 577.
31 Evans, C., *The Right to Reparations in International Law for Victims of Armed Conflict* (Cambridge, CUP 2012), p. 2.
32 Cryer et al., *supra* n. 22, p. 577-579; Hayner, *supra* n. 22, p. 30.
33 Hayner, *supra* n. 22, p. 172; Shelton, D., *Remedies in International Human Rights Law* (Oxford, OUP 2015, 3rd ed.), p. 9; OHCHR, *Rule of Law Tools for Post-Conflict States: Reparations programmes* (New York/Geneva, UN 2008), p. 9.

1.3 National Reparations Programmes

Under transitional justice, the adoption of administrative collective reparations programmes has become a common response to legacies of past violations.[34] Administrative collective reparations may either be recommended by TRCs or be established by national initiatives. They are believed to be a more adequate response to the large number of victims resulting from GVHR than the alternative of affected individuals claiming reparations before the courts. TRCs aim to address, but not necessarily restore, all individual and community harms by bringing direct benefits to victims.[35] Those benefits may be subdivided into material benefits and symbolic benefits, and into individual benefits and collective benefits.[36] In addition, reparation programmes may be based upon legislative or administrative measures, funded by national and/or international sources, and addressed to individuals and/or entire communities.[37]

It is important to point out that reparations are political projects that aim to bring about reconciliation and development while alleviating victims' suffering.[38] Reparation programmes face enormous challenges such as i) limited resources; ii) high demands by victims; and iii) underlying political needs. These challenges are further exacerbated by the fact that, in addition to issuing reparations, states in transition must aim to rebuild institutions, establish the rule of law, as well as achieving reconciliation and social healing.[39] While there are no specific guidelines for shaping reparations under TJ, the UN has tried to establish some principles and general guidelines through the adoption of documents such as the Principles on Reparations.[40] Significantly, TRCs have referred to the Principles on Reparations in their recommendations on collective reparation programmes. This demonstrates the

---

34 García-Godos, *supra* n. 12, p. 118; Laplante, L.J., "The Law of Remedies and the Clean Hand Doctrine: Exclusionary Reparation Policies in Peru's Political Transition", 23 *American University International Law Review* (2009), p. 57-58; Moffet, L., "Reparations for 'Guilty Victims': Navigating Complex Identities of Victim-Perpetrators in Reparation Mechanisms", 10 *International Journal of Transitional Justice* (2010), p. 148; Brodney, M., "Implementing Criminal Court-Ordered Collective Reparations: Unpacking Present Debates", 1 *Journal of the Oxford Centre for Socio-Legal Studies* (2016), p. 7.

35 de Greiff, P. , "Justice and Reparations", in P. de Greiff (ed.), *The Handbook of Reparations* (Oxford, OUP 2006), p. 452-453.

36 García-Godos, *supra* n. 12, p. 121.

37 Principle 32 of the Updated Set of Principles for the Protection and Promotion of Human Rights through Action to Combat Impunity: Human Rights Commission, *Updated Set of Principles for the Protection and Promotion of Human Rights through Action to Combat Impunity*, 8 February 2005, UN Doc. E/CN.4/2005/102/Add.1, p. 17 (hereinafter Principles to Combat Impunity).

38 de Greiff, *supra* n. 35, p. 454.

39 Shelton, *supra* n. 33, p. 121.

40 The three main documents are: the OHCHR Report on Rule of Law Tools: Reparations programmes, Principles to Combat Impunity, and the Principles on Reparations. See: ICJT, *Transitional Justice in the United Nations Human Rights Council* (ICTJ 2011), p. 1.

authority of this document,[41] and affirms that some national reparations programmes are framed under the body of *soft law* stemming from international law.

Finally, although TJMs and especially reparations are believed to be victim-centric,[42] both do not necessarily meet victims' rights standards as prescribed by international human rights standards. For example, it is possible that political decisions may lead to reparations being issued only to a specific group of victims rather than to all victims, and/or to reparation measures that, while carrying a message of recognition, may have little remedial effects. Finally, it is important to point out that, unlike other TJMs, reparations usually require the involvement of multiple governmental institutions, such as those concerned with healthcare, the economy, and housing.[43]

1.4 Mass Claims Reparations

Usually referred to as Mass Claims Processes, yet for the purposes of this research they will be mentioned as Mass Claims Reparations (MCRs or compensation commissions). Although not per se mechanisms of international law, MCRs are regarded as such. As such, MCRs have not been formally defined under international law but the term is generally accepted to include '*ad hoc* tribunals, quasi-judicial commissions or administrative programmes' created to resolve claims involving large numbers of claimants who have suffered an injury as a consequence of armed conflicts.[44] Generally, MCRs address limited injuries by providing financial compensation to victims (other forms of reparations are usually omitted).[45] Both the UNCC and the EECC are part of the more than 90 claims commissions that have been created during the last two centuries.[46] The UNCC and EECC are two modern

41 Correa, C., Guillerot, J., and Magarrell, L., "Reparations and Victim Participation: A Look at the Truth Commission Experience", in C. Ferstman, M. Goetz and A. Stephens (eds.), *Reparations for Victims of Genocide, War Crimes and Crimes Against Humanity: Systems in Place and Systems in the Making* (Leiden, Martinus Nijhoff 2009), p. 387.

42 Ramji-Nogales, J., "Bespoke transitional justice at the International Criminal Court" in C. de Vos, S. Kendall and C. Stahn (eds.) *Contested Justice: The Politics and Practice of International Criminal Court Interventions* (Cambridge, CUP 2015) p. 114.

43 Roht-Arriaza, N. and Orlovsky, K., "A Complementary Relationship: Reparations and Development" in P. de Greiff and R. Duthie (eds.), *Transitional Justice and Development: Making connections* (New York, Social Science Research Council 2009), p. 179-180.

44 Giroud, S. and Moss, S., "Mass Claims Processes under Public International Law" in Lein, E. et al. (eds.), *Collective Redress in Europe – Why and How?* (London, British Institute of International and Comparative Law 2015), p. 481.

45 Gray, C., "Remedies", in C. Romano, K. Alter and Y. Shany (eds.), *The Oxford Handbook of International Adjudication*, (Oxford, OUP 2015), p. 896.

46 Caron, D., "International Claims and Compensation Bodies", in C. Romano, K. Alter and Y. Shany (eds.), *The Oxford Handbook of International Adjudication*, (Oxford, OUP 2015), p. 280, 292-293.

mass claims processes,[47] each established to contribute to peacebuilding between two states and, in the case of the UNCC, to regional peace efforts as well.[48]

Similar to the case of collective reparations, Niebergall has submitted that MCRs usually share the need to strike a balance between three elements: i) the limited resources available to administer them; ii) pressure from victims with high expectations of obtaining redress; and iii) political pressure to deliver redress as expeditiously as possible.[49] Consequently, in fulfilling their mandate with a limited budget capacity, MCRs have developed innovative techniques such as the creation of multiple claims categories, whereby each category is characterized by a specific evidentiary standard and, for certain categories, a corresponding fixed lump-sum award.[50] This pragmatic approach adopted by the MCRs is, however, not without its flaws, since certain fraudulent practices can easily take place.[51] Nonetheless, Caron affirms that MCRs are an attractive reparations mechanism for states in either reaching a peace agreement or in dealing with the aftermath of a conflict. This is because they allow for the financial compensation of the harm suffered by thousands of victims, while at the same time limiting the harm to be compensated.[52]

2 Overview of the Case Studies

2.1 Peruvian TRC

The Peruvian Truth and Reconciliation Commission (known by its Spanish acronym, CVR)[53] was established in 2001 by Valentín Paniagua, the interim President of Peru at the time. The CVR was given the mandate to investigate, over the course of two years, serious violations of human rights committed during the twenty-year internal armed conflict (1980-2000) between armed groups and state forces.[54] The TRC was composed of seven persons of Peruvian nationality and known for their ethical

47 Giroud and Moss, *supra n.* 44, p. 486.

48 Caron, *supra* n. 46, p. 292. The UNSC established the UNCC under its mandate to restore international peace and security. See: Article 39, UN Charter.

49 Niebergall, *supra* n. 3, p. 147-148.

50 Caron, *supra* n. 46, p. 290-291; Dwertmann, E., *The Reparation System of the International Criminal Court* (Leiden/Boston Martinus Nijhoff 2010), p. 172-173; Kristjánsdóttir, E., "International Mass Claims Processes and the ICC Trust Fund for Victims" in C. Ferstman, M. Goetz and A. Stephens (eds.), *Reparations for Victims of, War Crimes and Crimes Against Humanity: Systems in Place and Systems in the Making* (Leiden, Martinus Nijhoff 2009), p. 179.

51 Niebergall, *supra* n. 3, p. 165; Singh, R., "Raising the Stakes: evidentiary issues in individual claims 61 before the United Nations Compensation Commission" in Permanent Court of Arbitration, *Redressing Injustices through Mass Claims Processes: Innovative Responses to Unique Challenges* (Oxford, OUP 2006), p. 89-91.

52 Caron, *supra* n. 46, p. 281-288.

53 Comisión de Verdad y Reconciliación.

54 Article 1, Supreme Decree, N° 065-2001-PCM.

prestige.[55] Its mandate was to investigate, in an in-depth manner, the causes of the conflict, to identify the responsibility of the actors involved, to identify the victims of the said actors, and to recommend both reparations for the victims and institutional reforms aimed at preventing similar violations in the future.[56] To this end, the CVR functioned in five working groups.[57] In 2003, the CVR submitted its final report, which consists of nine volumes. The report includes a set of recommendations for the Peruvian state aimed at providing reparations for victims and preventing similar violations.[58]

These recommendations are called the Comprehensive Plan of Reparations (known by its Spanish acronym, PIR), which became law in 2005. In 2006, the first step towards the implementation of reparation took place by means of the adoption of its Regulations.[59] According to the CVR, the PIR is composed of six programmes (the restitution of civil rights, reparations in education, reparations in health, collective reparations, symbolic reparations, and economic reparations).[60] However, according to its own Regulations, the PIR is composed of seven programmes. This is because the Regulations add another category: reparations in housing, which were originally part of the content of the economic reparations category, developed by the CVR.[61] In 2004, the government created a commission responsible for following up on the state policies in the areas of peace, collective reparations, and national reconciliation (known by its Spanish acronym CMAN).[62] Two years later, in 2006, the National Council of Reparations was formed (known by its Spanish acronym, NCR), which was in charge of registering victims so that beneficiaries could be identified.[63] In 2007, the implementation of collective reparations began, and, even ten years later,

55 Article 4, Supreme Decree, N° 065-2001-PCM.

56 Article 2, Supreme Decree, N° 065-2001-PCM.

57 Skaar, E., Malca, C.G. and Eide, T., *After Violence: Transitional Justice, Peace and Democracy* (Abingdon/New York, Routledge 2015), p. 109.

58 Guillerot and Carranza, *supra* n. 7, p. 30-32.

59 Ley No. 28592 (hereinafter 2006 PIR's law) and Supreme Decree Ds 015-2006-Jus: Reglamento de la Ley No. 28592 (hereinafter 2006 Regulations of PIR's law).

60 CVR's Final Report (Spanish version), Volume IX: Recommendations, national compromise to reconciliation (2003), p. 159-200 (hereinafter CVR's Final Report, Vol. IX).

61 Articles 13, 17, 22, 27, 32, 33 and 37, 2006 Regulations of PIR's law.

62 Comisión Multisectorial de Alto Nivel was created by Created by the Supreme Decree. No 003-2004-JUS.

63 ICTJ and APRODEH, *Perú ¿Cuánto se ha reparado en nuestras comunidades? Avances, percepciones y recomendaciones sobre reparaciones colectivas en Perú (2007–2011),* (ICTJ 2011), p. 7.

new measures of collective reparations were still being implemented.[64] Meanwhile, individual reparations began to be implemented starting from 2011. Individual financial compensation and the recovery of victims' mortal remains were the first measures to be implemented.[65] Although symbolic reparations had taken place since at least 2006,[66] only in 2013 were the guidelines on implementing symbolic reparations approved.[67]

Significantly, the CVR was tasked with identifying the actors responsible for the violations that occurred during the internal conflict. Yet this identification was not an alternative to national judicial prosecutions but, rather, an addition thereto.[68] Among the CVR's findings, it is important to mention that it established that the conflict resulted in more than 70,000 deaths and disappearances, hundreds of thousands of people being displaced by political violence, scores of communities being razed to the ground, and hundreds of people being unjustly imprisoned.[69] It also found that the Shining Path, one of the main armed groups involved in the conflict,[70] was responsible for approximately 54% of the deaths and disappearances,[71] while state armed forces were responsible for a further 45%.[72] The remaining 1% of the deaths

64 ICTJ, *Reparaciones en Perú: El largo camino entre las recomendaciones y la implementación* (ICTJ 2013), p. 25-26, 35-37; See also the CMAN wesbite where it is possible to see that as of 2018, collective reparations are still taking place: <https://cman.minjus.gob.pe/minjusddhh-inicia-proyectos-de-reparaciones-colectivas-en-145-comunidades-para-generar-desarrollo-sostenible/>, and <https://cman.minjus.gob.pe/minjusdh-acompano-en-tingo-maria-entrega-de-restos-de-26-victimas-del-periodo-de-violencia>.

65 Comisión Multisectorial de Alto Nivel (CMAN), Annual Report, 2013, I, p. 13; ICTJ, *supra* n. 64, p. 16, 22, 25

66 Garrido, K., Huerta, G. and Valencia, A., "Propuestas de reparaciones a las víctimas del conflicto armado interno: ¿qué hacer desde las regiones?: Región Junín", *Instituto de Defensa Legal* (2012), p. 7. Available at: <http://lum.cultura.pe/cdi/sites/default/files/rb/pdf/Libro%20Propuestas%20Reparaciones%20Regionales%20Junin.pdf> However, since 2003, NGOs and civil society in general had already implemented several symbolic measures. See: Robin Azevedo, V. and Delacroix, D., "Categorización étnica, conflicto armado interno y reparaciones simbólicas en el Perú post – Comisión de la Verdad y Reconciliación (CVR)", 2017, para. 25. Available at: <https://journals.openedition.org/nuevomundo/71688>.

67 CMAN, *supra* n. 65, p. 13; ICTJ, *supra* n. 64, p. 30-38.

68 Guillerot and Carranza, *supra* n. 7, p. 30-32.

69 Magarrell, L., "Reparations for Massive or Widespread Human Rights Violations: Sorting Out Claims for Reparations and the Struggle for Social Justice", 22 *Windsor Yearbook of Access to Justice* (2003), p. 87; Laplante, L.J., "Brining Effective Remedies Home: The Inter-American Human Rights System, Reparations, and the Duty to Prevention", 22 *Netherlands Quarterly of Human Rights* (2004), p. 363.

70 The main armed groups were the following paramilitary movements: The Communist Party group *Sendero Luminoso* (or 'Shining Path'), the Túpac Amaru Revolutionary Movement (MRTA), and the *Rondas Campesinas* (Armed Peasant Patrols).

71 CVR's Final Report (Spanish version), Volume II: Conflict actors, p. 13 (hereinafter, CVR's Final Report, Vol. II).

72 CVR's Final Report (Spanish versión), Volume III: Political and Institutional Actors, p. 1, (hereinafter, CVR's Final Report, Vol. III).

and disappearances were caused by other armed groups and other circumstances.[73] The Peruvian CVR also established that indigenous populations and rural and marginalised communities amounted to 75% of the victims during the conflict. In this light, the CVR emphasised that violence was suffered more by marginalised sectors of society and, therefore, the root causes thereof needed to be addressed in order to ensure lasting peace.[74]

2.2 Moroccan TRC

During King Hassan II of Morocco's authoritarian rule from 1956 to 1999, which came to be known as the 'Years of Lead', many human rights abuses took place, such as torture, enforced disappearances, arbitrary detentions, and extrajudicial killings. It is estimated that this period left more than 50,000 victims.[75] International and domestic criticism grew as time passed and the number of abuses increased.[76] In 1990, King Hassan II attempted to address some of those human rights abuses and to reinforce the protection of human rights by establishing the Advisory Council on Human Rights (known by its French acronym, CCDH). In 1998, the CCDH recommended that the king should establish an Independent Arbitration Commission (IAC) to compensate victims of arbitrary detention and enforced disappearances. In 1999, the IAC was established. It operated for four years and decided 7,000 cases of arbitrary detention and enforced disappearances,[77] as a result of which 3,700 victims were granted reparations.[78]

The IAC's financial compensations prompted Morocco's civil society to organise itself and demand a more comprehensive justice and reparations programme. In response to these demands, the CCDH recommended the establishment of a truth commission.[79] King Mohammed VI, who succeeded his father King Hassan II upon his death in 1999, saw in a TRC the possibility for a new social pact between the

73 Amnesty International, *Peru: Truth and Reconciliation Commission – a first step towards a country without* injustice (2004), p. 7.

74 CVR's Final Report (Spanish version), Vol. I: The process, the facts and the victims, p. 158-161(hereinafter, CVR's Final Report, Vol. I); Contreras-Garduño, D. and Rombouts, S., 'Collective Reparations for Indigenous Communities Before the Inter-American Court of Human Rights' 27 *Merkourios Utrecht Journal of International and European Law* 72, 2011, p. 6.

75 Loudiy, F., *Transitional Justice and Human Rights in Morocco: Negotiating the Years of Lead* (Routledge, New York 2014), p. 73.

76 Guillerot and Carranza, *supra* n. 7, p. 24-25.

77 Also cases of those who had died while in detention or shortly after their release, extrajudicial killings, torture, forced exile, and sexual violence. See: IER Final Report (English version), Volume 3: Justice And Reparation For Victims (2009), p. 22 (hereinafter, IER's Final Report, Vol. 3).

78 OHCHR, *supra* n. 33, p. 12, Footnote 22.

79 ICJT, "Truth and reconciliation in Morocco" (2009). Available at: <https://www.ictj.org/sites/default/files/ICTJ-Morocco-TRC-2009-English.pdf>.

inhabitants and institutions of Morocco.[80] Consequently, in December 2004, the Equity and Reconciliation Commission (known by its French acronym, IER) was established as the first ever TRC in an Islamic Arab society.[81] It was composed of 17 commissioners who were variously members of the CCDH, members of civil society, human rights activists, journalists and former detainees.[82] The IER was established as a non-judicial body whose mandate included establishing the nature of the GVHR constituting the enforced disappearances and arbitrary detentions during the Years of Lead, providing individual reparations to the victims thereof, recommending measures to guarantee non-repetition (GnRs), and promoting reconciliation.[83] To this end, the IER operated in three working groups.[84]

It is important to highlight that, in contrast to the CVR's mandate, the IER was not allowed to identify the individuals responsible for the violations but, rather, the institutions that permitted those GVHR. Although it was only competent to address forced disappearances and arbitrary detentions,[85] the IER interpreted its mandate in a progressive fashion. It decided to also focus on the following violations: extrajudicial executions, excessive uses of force against protestors, sexual violence, and forced exiles.[86] In 2005, the IER submitted its final report. Therein, it recommended individual reparations, community reparations, and certain symbolic reparations such as the preservation of memory and the adoption of guarantees of non-repetition.[87] The individual reparations included compensation and rehabilitation measures, among others. The collective reparations focused on building infrastructure, including schools, clinics, and women's centres in areas where such services had been purposely neglected.[88] Finally, the IER also recommended GnRs and a public apology from the Prime Minister.[89]

---

80 Hazan, P. , "Morocco: Betting on a Truth and Reconciliation Commission", USIP, Special Report 165. (2006), p. 2.

81 Ibid., p. 1.

82 Wiebelhaus-Brahm, E., "Truth Commissions and other Investigative Bodies" in M. C. Bassiouni (ed.), *The Pursuit of International Criminal Justice: A World Study on Conflicts, Victimization, and Post-Conflict Justice* (Antwerp/Oxford, Intersentia 2010), p. 524. An example of a former detainee who was appointed as a commissioner is Driss Benzekeri. See: Hazan, *supra* n. 80, p. 3-5.

83 Articles 6 and 9, IER's Statute.

84 The three working groups were: one in charge of investigations; another on reparations, and the last one in charge of studies and research. See: Article 15, IER's Statute.

85 Article 8, IER's Statute.

86 ICTJ Morocco Progress Report 2005, p. 13-15. See: IER Final Report (English version), Volumes 1-5 (2009).

87 Guillerot and Carranza, *supra* n. 7, p. 26.

88 Roht-Arriaza and Orlovsky, *supra* n. 43, p. 192.

89 IER's Final Report, Vol. 3, p. 49; Hazan, *supra* n. 80, p. 12.

2.3 The United Nations Compensation Commission

The United Nations Compensation Commission was established in 1991 as a subsidiary organ of the UNSC to address all compensation claims against Iraq as a result of its invasion of Kuwait. This invasion provoked the so-called 'Gulf War' (August 1990-February 1991).[90] The UNSC forced Iraq to withdraw from Kuwait and to accept its liability for 'any direct loss, damage, including environmental damage and the depletion of natural resources, or injury to foreign governments, nationals and corporations, as a result of Iraq's unlawful invasion and occupation of Kuwait.'[91]

The UNCC was a political and administrative body tasked with the 'fact-finding function of examining claims, verifying their validity, evaluating losses, assessing payment and resolving claims' for damages resulting from Iraq's unlawful invasion and occupation of Kuwait.[92] Those damages, as identified by the special rapporteur Walter Kälin, included GVHR suffered by Kuwaiti nationals, such as extrajudicial killings, torture, disappearances, mass arrests, and deportations to Iraq, and as such, warranted compensation.[93] To finance the reparation claims and cover the UNCC's costs, the UNSC decided to create a special fund (Compensation Fund) financed by the proceeds from the sale of Iraqi oil.[94]

The UNCC was set up in 1991 and it was composed of three organs: i) the Governing Council, whose membership mirrored that of the UNSC and was responsible for policymaking regarding the procedures before the Commission, approving compensation awards, and administrating the Compensation Fund; ii) The Secretariat, chaired by the Executive Secretary, was composed of 350 members, of whom the majority were lawyers and accountants. It was responsible for supporting the Governing Council and the Panels of Commissioners with legal, technical, and administrative assistance. The Secretariat was also delegated with the task of reviewing certain claims as well as grouping together larger claims with

---

90 Caron, D. and Morris, B., "The UN Compensation Commission: Practical Justice, not Retribution", 13 *European Journal of International Law* (2002), p. 193-194; Petrović, D. "Other Specific Regimes of Responsibility: The UN Compensation Commission" in J. Crawford, A. Pellet and S. Olleson (eds.), *The Law on International Responsibility* (Oxford, OUP 2010), p. 849-850.

91 UNSC, Resolution 662, Doc. S/RES/662, 9 August 1990, para. 1; UNSC, Resolution 674, Doc. S/RES/674, 29 October 1990, para. 8; UNSC, Resolution 687, Doc. S/RES/687, 3 April 1991, para. 16.

92 UN Secretary-General, Report pursuant paragraph 19 of the UNSC Resolution 687 (1991), Doc. S/22559, 2 May 1991. The UNCC is a hybrid body that combines the tasks of an administrative body and an international tribunal. See: van Houtte, H., Das, H. and Delmartino, B., "The United Nations Compensation Commission" P. de Greiff (ed.), *The Handbook of Reparations* (Oxford, OUP 2006), p. 327.

93 UN Economic and Social Council, *Report on the situation of human rights in Kuwait under Iraqi occupation, Walter Kälin,* 16 January 1992, UN Doc. E/CN.4/1992/26, para. 1.

94 This Fund was financed by 30% of the total sum received from the sale of petroleum and related products by Iraq. See: Singh, *supra* n. 51, p. 63; Petrović, *supra* n. 90, p. 850; UNSC, Resolution 687, *supra* n. 91, para. 18.

common legal and factual issues;[95] and iii) the Panels of Commissioners composed of 54 commissioners, each of whom was an expert in a field such as law, finance, accounting, insurance, or engineering.[96] There were 19 Panels of Commissioners, each of which consisted of three members and was responsible for deciding on the compensation claims before the UNCC.[97]

Although the UNCC was a political and administrative body, it did adopt some quasi-judicial methods.[98] Such methods were evident in the assessment of evidence, the sampling techniques, the making of determinations based on the applicable law and, sometimes, even in hearings.[99] Furthermore, the Commissioners could invoke international law.[100] The UNCC considered compensation claims for 14 years and handed down its final decision in June 2007.[101] It processed 2.6 million claims for a total of USD 370 billion filed by diverse states, international organisations, and UN special agencies.[102] The UNCC awarded compensation for 1.5 million claims amounting to USD 52 billion. By 2007, USD 27.6 billion had been made available to claimants.[103] By 2007, the UNCC had completed all payments pertaining to individual claimants (USD 11.7 billion).[104]

The creation of the UNCC is currently being questioned, especially the UNSC's competence to create and impose a compensation mechanism.[105] In this light, Gold has described the UNCC as 'a summary judgment holding Iraq responsible for a whole series of breaches of international law'.[106] In addition, during the Gulf War, both Iraq and Kuwait most likely engaged in unlawful activities that caused harm. In principle, both countries should be liable for their violations of international law.

95 It could verify claims under the categories 'A', 'B' and 'C'. See: Article 37(a), UNCC's *Provisional Rules for Claims Procedure*, UNCC Decision 10, Doc. No. S/AC.26/1992/10, 26 June 1992, (hereinafter UNCC's Rules).

96 Article 19 (2), UNCC's Rules.

97 Taylor, L.A., "The United Nations Compensation Commission" in C. Ferstman, M. Goetz and A. Stephens (eds.), *Reparations for Victims of Genocide, War Crimes and Crimes Against Humanity: Systems in Place and Systems in the Making* (Leiden, Martinus Nijhoff 2009), p. 198-199; Giroud and Moss, *supra n.* 44, p. 488.

98 Wassgren, H., "The UN Compensation Commission: Lessons of Legitimacy, State Responsibility, and War Reparations" 11 *Leiden Journal of International Law*, para. 479-484; Singh, *supra* n. 51, p. 63.

99 Taylor, *supra* n. 97, p. 199.

100 Article 31, UNCC's Rules.

101 Giroud and Moss, *supra* n. 44, p. 488.

102 Taylor, *supra* n. 97, p. 203.

103 Giroud and Moss, *supra* n. 44, p. 488.

104 See: UNCC, Important Notice. Available at: <https://www.uncc.ch/important-notice>.

105 van Zoelen, *supra* n. 8, p. 38; Gattini, *supra* n. 6, p. 161.

106 Gold, S., "International Claims Arising from Iraq's Invasion of Kuwait", 25 *The International Lawyer*, p. 715.

Yet only Iraq was declared liable for the harm that it had caused.[107] Furthermore, the UNSC's decision to create the UNCC constitutes its first ever measure aimed at dealing with an invasion and imposing a redress mechanism.

2.4 The Eritrea-Ethiopia Claims Commission

Between May 1998 and June 2000, a border conflict between Eritrea and Ethiopia arose from a dispute over a border demarcation. The conflict, which had several historical antecedents, resulted in thousands of deaths, as well as extensive human suffering and material destruction: more than 70,000 soldiers died, and more than a million people were forcibly displaced.[108] The war ended with a peace agreement between the governments of Eritrea and Ethiopia signed in December 2000 (the Algiers Agreement) that, among other provisions,[109] bilaterally established an arbitral mechanism called the Eritrea-Ethiopia Claims Commission (EECC).[110]

The EECC was given the mandate 'to decide, through binding arbitration, claims for loss, damage or injury' resulting from violations of international law or international humanitarian law during the conflict. International law and international humanitarian law also constituted part of the applicable law in the EECC's proceedings.[111] In order to fulfil its mandate, the EECC decided that financial compensation was the most adequate measure of reparation for resolving the claims, but the Commission did not omit the possibility of granting other measures, such as restitution or satisfaction.[112] In contrast to the UNCC, which had 54 commissioners,[113] the EECC consisted of 5 arbitrators nominated by the parties involved.[114] As opposed to the UNCC, the EECC was, in addition to dealing with claims, given the responsibility of establishing liability in respect of the claims. It resolved claims

107 The UNSC seemed to have addressed the issue of the crime of aggression committed by Iraq by invading and occupying Kuwait. Accordingly, Gattini believes that the UNCC set a precedent in interpreting such an invasion as part of an international wrongful act, and not international humanitarian law. See: Gattini, *supra* n. 6, p. 171.

108 Gray, C., "The Eritrea/Ethiopia Claims Commission Oversteps Its Boundaries: A Partial Award?", 17 *The European Journal of International Law* (2006), p. 700-703.

109 Dybnis, A., "Was the Eritrea-Ethiopia Claims Commission Merely a Zero-Sum Game? Exposing the Limits of Arbitration in Resolving Violent Transitional Conflict", 33 *Loyola Los Angeles International and Comparative Law Review* (2011), p. 259.

110 Article 5, Algiers Agreement. This Agreement in its Articles 3 and 4 also provided for the creation of an independent body 'to determine the origins of the conflict, and creation of neutral Boundary Commission to delimit the boundaries of the countries based on colonial treaties and international law'.

111 Article 5 (1), Algiers Agreement; Rule 19, EECC's Rules of Procedure.

112 EECC Decision 3, *Remedies,* 15 August 2001.

113 Petrović, *supra* n. 90, p. 850.

114 Article 5 (2), Algiers Agreement; Article 14, EEC's Rules of Procedure. The President of the EECC was Hans Van Houtte. Ethiopia appointed George Aldrich and James Paul, and Eritrea appointed Lucy Reed and John Crook. See: Gray, *supra* n. 108, p. 700-703.

regarding the treatment of prisoners and civilians, interferences with pensions, and also overstepped its mandate by trying to determine who was liable for starting the war.[115] This created more tensions in demarcating the Ethiopia-Eritrea border, the original subject of the two countries' dispute.

Despite struggling with limited resources, the EECC's accomplishments were considerable.[116] The EECC allowed for two types of procedures: individual claims and mass claims. The states, however, only made use of the individual procedure.[117] Perhaps this was a result of claimant governments aiming for higher compensation than the fixed-sum awards offered for mass claims.[118] When resolving claims, the EECC most frequently used international humanitarian law, since the majority of the claims involved, among other issues, the conduct of military operations or the treatment of prisoners of war, civilians, and of civilians' property.[119] International human rights law was only used to limit the claims from the governments. The EECC argued that both countries were state parties to the ICCPR and ICESCR and, as such, Article I (2), common to both covenants, explicitly forbade the states from depriving their people 'of its own means of subsistence'.[120] Consequently, the EECC recalled that large compensation awards would impose economic burdens on the governments that would undermine their capacity to provide their populations with basic social services.[121] Similar to the UNCC, which operated for 14 years, the EECC completed its work in about 10 years.[122]

3 Principles on Reparations in TJMs

The traditional approach to reparations derives from the notion of *restitutio in integrum*. According to Uprimny this *restitutio in integrum* is a synonym for full or integral reparations[123] and outlines that victims should receive the five types of modalities as outlined by the Principles on Reparations. However, reparation programmes as part of TJMs do have other goals besides compensating every single harm suffered by the victims and are unlikely to provide all five measures of reparation. Furthermore, it seems that the Principles on Reparations are sometimes misunderstood, since

115 Gray, *supra* n. 108, p. 703.
116 Dybnis, *supra* n. 109, p. 256.
117 Shelton, *supra* n. 33, p. 187.
118 According to the Rules of Procedure, the claimant had the right to choose which of the procedures to activate. See: Article 30(2), EECC's Rules of Procedure.
119 Giroud and Moss, *supra* n. 44, p. 490.
120 Shelton, *supra* n. 33, p. 188 citing Eritrea's Damages, Final Award, para. 18.
121 Ibid., p. 188.
122 Originally it was supposed to complete its mandate in 3 years but that was extended. See: Dybnis, *supra* n. 109, p. 262, 282.
123 Uprimny-Yepes, R., "Transformative Reparations of Massive Gross Human Rights Violations: Between Corrective and Distributive Justice", 27 *Netherlands Quarterly of Human Rights* (2009), p. 629.

Principle 18 allows states to decide what measures of reparation are 'appropriate' or fair in cases of GVHR.[124] Yet the discourse affirming that TJMs and, in particular, reparations are victim-centric may create expectations among victims regarding the possibility of being awarded full reparations. However, it is unlikely that such expectations will ever be fulfilled and may result in further frustration for victims.[125] This is because reparation programmes usually provide limited material and symbolic measures, and their benefits may be rather symbolic as far as victims are concerned.[126]

3.1 National Programmes

The UN and independent scholars have attempted to formulate some guiding principles for the design and implementation of fair and effective reparations programmes within the context of transitional justice. Some of the resulting principles are:

1) Reparations programmes need to be part of a holistic package of different TJMs.[127]
2) Governments should have discretion and flexibility when deciding on reparation programmes' content.[128]
3) Reparation programmes should aim to partially redress GVHR.[129]
4) They need to allow for the participation of victims.[130]
5) They need to make their processes accessible and adopt flexible evidentiary requirements.[131]

---

124 Principle 18 of the Principles on Reparations reads as follows: In accordance with domestic law and international law, and taking account of individual circumstances, victims of gross violations of international human rights law and serious violations of international humanitarian law should, as appropriate and proportional to the gravity of the violation and the circumstances of each case, be provided with full and effective reparation, as laid out in principles 19 to 23, which include the following forms: restitution, compensation, rehabilitation, satisfaction and guarantees of non-repetition.

125 Correa, C., "Reparations for Victims of Massive Crimes. Making Concrete a Message of Inclusion", in R. Letschert et al. (eds.), *Victimological Approaches to International Crimes: Africa* (Cambridge, Intersentia 2011), p. 187-188.

126 OHCHR, *supra* n. 33, p. 9.

127 de Greiff, P. , "Reparations Programs: Patterns, Tendencies, and Challenges" 50 *Politorbis* (2010), p. 59; OHCHR, *supra* n. 33, p. 1-3; Correa, Guillerot, and Magarrell, *supra* n. 41, p. 388.

128 OHCHR, *supra* n. 33, p. 7.

129 Ibid., p. 10.

130 Ibid., p. 15-18; Díaz Gómez, *supra* n. 7, p. 289; Correa, Guillerot, and Magarrell, *supra* n. 41, p. 385-414; Correa, *supra* n. 125, p. 209.

131 OHCHR, *supra* n. 33, p. 15-18.

6) They need to be grounded on three premises: the size of the victim population, the types of violations commonly suffered, and the consequences of the violations suffered by the victims.[132]
7) Reparation programmes should aim to foster civic trust and to recognize both victims' suffering and their standing as citizens.[133]
8) Reparations should be transformative, as they should prevent the victim from returning to a situation of marginalization, poverty, and exclusion.[134]
9) Reparations are not a replacement for public services.[135]
10) Reparations need to be gender sensitive: not only their accessibility,[136] but also their content should meet women's specific needs and preferences, which are usually household goods, livestock, and crops.[137]
11) Reparations should include affirmative action for vulnerable victims.[138]

Of all of these principles, the Peruvian national reparations programme was grounded on the following: a participative approach, affirmative action regarding the elderly, the orphaned, the widowed, and the disabled, respect for the dignity of the victims, equal treatment for those victims in similar situations, non-discrimination, and gender sensitivity.[139] The Moroccan national reparations programme followed a participative approach and adopted a gender-sensitive approach in both the methodology applied

---

132 Uprimny, R. and Camino Sánchez, N., "Propuestas para una restitución de tierras transformadora" in C. Díaz Gómez (ed.), *Tareas Pendientes: Propuestas para la formulación de políticas publicas de la reparación en Colombia* (Bogota, ICTJ 2010), p. 193-196; Correa, Guillerot, and Magarrell, *supra* n. 41, p. 387.

133 de Greiff, *supra* n. 127, p. 54; IER's Final Report, Vol. 3, p. 32.

134 Roht-Arriaza, N., "Reparations Decisions and Dilemmas", 27 *Hastings International and Comparative Law Review* (2004), p. 160; Villa Arcilla, L., "Reparación en y a través de la educación para víctimas de graves violaciones de los derechos humanos" in C. Díaz Gómez (ed.), *Tareas Pendientes: Propuestas para la formulación de políticas públicas de la reparación en Colombia* (Bogotá, ICTJ 2010), p. 68; Correa, *supra* n. 125, p. 196.

135 Díaz Gómez, *supra* n. 7, p. 312; Díaz Gómez, C., "Introduction" in C. Díaz Gómez (ed.), *Tareas Pendientes: Propuestas para la formulación de políticas públicas de la reparación en Colombia* (Bogota, ICTJ 2010), p. 8-10.

136 de Greiff, *supra* n. 127, p. 60; OHCHR, *supra* n. 33, p. 36; Rubio-Marin, R., *The Gender of Reparations: Unsettling Sexual Hierarchies While Redressing Human Rights Violations,* (Cambridge CUP 2009).

137 Roht-Arriaza, N., "Reparations in International Law and Practice", in M. C. Bassiouni (ed.), *The pursuit of international criminal justice: a world study on conflicts, victimization and post conflict justice* (Antwerp, Intersentia 2010, Vol.1), p. 691; IER's Final Report, Vol. 3, p. 32, 34.

138 Limón, P. and von Norman, J., "Prioritising Victims to Provide Reparations: Relevant Expertise", *Briefing Paper No. 3, Reparations Unit, Essex University* (2011), p. 2, 18; Guillerot and Carranza, *supra* n. 7, p. 48.

139 Article 6 and 7, Regulations of the PIR's law.

to its work[140] as well as in the distribution of its reparations.[141] This approach is much friendlier to women by far, compared to the one adopted by Peru, whose reparations have been criticized for a lack of female participation.[142]

3.2 Mass Claims Reparations

Mass claims reparations usually aim at repairing specific types of harm with financial compensation. From the UNCC and the EECC, the following principles could be drawn:

1) Affirmative action is justifiable on a humanitarian basis. The UNCC considered claims from categories 'A', 'B', and 'C' to be more pressing, thus these claims were dealt with more expeditiously.[143] Whilst the EECC did not give priority to claims from named individuals over government claims,[144] it was allowed to consider specific claims on a priority basis.[145] Although claims regarding rape were not prioritised, they received special attention.[146]
2) The EECC considered that the 'needs of the affected population' should determine the amount of financial compensation to be awarded in a post-war reparation process.[147]
3) Both the UNCC and the EECC adopted flexible evidentiary standards.
4) The UNCC established a system which allowed claimants who were disadvantaged, in principle due to their level of income, literacy, or education, to be afforded equal opportunities to prove their claims before the Commission. To this end, the UNCC, through its Secretariat, prepared country reports to help the Commissioners to understand the factual and legal issues faced by specific countries as well as to draw the Commissioners' attention to existing inequalities among claimants.[148]

---

140 IER's Final Report (English version), Volume 1: Truth, Equity and Reconciliation (2009), p. 75-76 (hereinafter IER's Final Report, Vol. 1).

141 IER's Final Report, Vol. 1, p. 86-87; IER's Final Report, Vol. 3, p. 112-114.

142 ICTJ and APRODEH, *supra* n. 63, p. 20, 31.

143 UNCC Decision 1, *Criteria for Expedited Processing of Urgent Claims*, Doc. S/AC.26/1991/1, 2 August 1991; Singh, *supra* n. 51, p. 69; Shelton, *supra* n. 33, p. 184.

144 Dybnis, *supra* n. 109, p. 68.

145 Article 5 (11), Algiers Agreement.

146 EECC Final Award, *Eritrea's Damages Claims*, 17 August 2009, para. 234; EECC Final Award, *Ethiopia's Damages Claims*, 17 August 2009, para. 104.

147 EECC Final Award, *Ethiopia's Damages Claims*, *supra* n. 146, para. 21; Crawford, J., *State Responsibility: The General Part* (Cambridge, CUP 2014), p. 484.

148 van Houtte, Das and Delmartino, *supra* n. 92, p. 343.

4 Types of Reparations

Reparations programmes within the context of transitional justice are benefits usually given outside legal proceedings that aim to address the suffering of individuals and communities.[149] The same holds true for mass claims reparations. While international law has established some guidelines regarding the forms in which reparations can be utilized, 'the exact content of any reparations programme for massive violations is not prescribed by law'.[150] Practice however shows that reparations programmes usually provide material and symbolic awards mostly on a collective basis, or in combination with some individual measures.[151]

Against this background, the Peruvian and Moroccan TRCs recommended collective and individual reparation measures.[152] While the individual reparations in Peru have since been delayed, individual reparations were the first to be implemented by the Moroccan government.[153] In contrast to the Peruvian CVR, the Moroccan IER focused on the implementation of both individual and community reparations. Yet it gave particular importance to community reparations in the regions and communities which suffered particular damage as a consequence of political violence.[154]

On the other hand, reparations programmes established by mass claims compensation commissions usually entail individual financial compensation. This compensation is, however, more symbolic than full monetary compensation for the harm suffered by the victims. Whilst the UNCC only provided financial reparations, the EECC adopted a broader approach. In principle, the EECC was to provide financial compensation, but, when appropriate, other forms of reparations could be awarded.[155] In this light, it also awarded measures of satisfaction, namely declarations of liability. Take, for instance, the Eritrean claim that dual citizens had arbitrarily lost their Ethiopian nationality and thereby suffered damage. The EECC decided that finding Ethiopia liable for dual citizens' arbitrary deprivation of citizenship was sufficient satisfaction in and of itself. Importantly, the EECC made this finding based on 'the paucity of evidence', suggesting that different measures of reparation require different levels of evidence.[156] In addition, the EECC also granted this measure of satisfaction in response to Ethiopia's claim that Eritrea had interfered with Ethiopia's chargé and

149 Correa, *supra* n. 125, p. 203.

150 Correa, Guillerot, and Magarrell, *supra* n. 41, p. 387.

151 Roht-Arriaza and Orlovsky, *supra* n. 43, p. 189.

152 CVR's Final Report, Vol. IX, p. 159-200. It must be noted that the IER used the terms collective reparations and community reparations indistinctively. See: IER's Final Report, Vol. 3, p. 33, 45, 49.

153 Waardt, M., "Are Peruvian Victims Being Mocked?: Politicization of Victimhood and Victims' Motivations for Reparations", 35 *Human Rights Quarterly* (2013), p. 838; IER's Final Report, Vol.1, p. 90; Follow-up Report on the Implementation of Equity and Reconciliation Commission Recommendations" Main Report, December 2009 (hereinafter IER Follow-up), p. 59.

154 Summary of the IER's Final Report, p. 27, 45.

155 Article 5 (17), Algiers Agreement; EECC Decision 3, *Remedies*, *Supra* n. 112.

156 EECC Final Award, *Eritrea's Damages Claims*, *supra* n. 146, para. 288.

official correspondence. The EECC's reasoning in granting this award was that the damage caused was non-material.[157] Although asked to award an apology as a form of satisfaction,[158] as well as additional measures of restitution,[159] the Commission did not grant any of the aforementioned awards on the grounds that they were neither customarily granted under international law nor were they appropriate as awards in general. This, unfortunately, did not hold true.[160]

4.1 Individual Reparations

Within a transitional justice context, individual reparations may tend to be granted in the form of symbolic financial compensation. The reason for this may be that it is seen as an easier way of approaching a reparations programme intended for a large number of victims.[161] Yet not only can financial compensation prove more expensive than other measures of reparation, but it also constitutes quite a controversial measure in itself. Victims may perceive the money awarded as a way to silence them for seeking justice.[162] Financial compensation may be suitable when it is part of a comprehensive reparations programme.[163] Against this background, individual reparations in the form of compensation were part of the recommendations made by the TRCs of both Peru and Morocco.

Peru's recommendation of individual reparations is not limited to financial compensation, but also includes measures of restitution (civil and political restoration of rights), rehabilitation (mental and physical health measures), and satisfaction (educational measures, in particular scholarships).[164] In contrast to the Peruvian CVR, the Moroccan IER focuses strongly on providing financial compensation. Yet, some other individual measures were also granted (i.e. reinsertion, legal settlement). It is pertinent to mention that some individuals received health assistance in the IER's Medical Unit. Yet such assistance qualifies as interim relief rather than as a measure of reparation itself. Unlike the CVR, the IER ordered individual reparations rather than recommending them.[165] These reparations included compensation, physical and psychological measures of rehabilitation, the restitution of jobs, social

157 EECC Final Award, *Ethiopia's Damages Claims*, *supra* n. 146, para. 269, 270.
158 EECC Partial Award, *Central Front – Eritrea's Claims 2, 4, 6, 7, 8 & 22*, 28 April 2004, para. 114.
159 EECC Partial Award, *Prisoners of War – Eritrea's Claim 17*, 28 April 2004, para. 78.
160 See: Chapter II.
161 OHCHR, *supra* n. 33, p. 22.
162 Iliff, F., Maitre-Muhl, F., and Sirel, A., "Adverse Consequences of Reparations", *Briefing Paper No.6, Reparations Unit, Essex University* (2011), p. 3.
163 OHCHR, *supra* n. 33, p. 12.
164 CVR's Final Report, Vol. IX, p. 168-193.
165 IER's Final Report (English version), Volume 5: The organisation of the work and activities of the Commission (2009), p. 62 (hereinafter IER's Final Report, Vol. 5); Alston, P. and Knuckey, S. (eds.), The transformation of human rights fact-finding (Oxford, OUP 2015), p. 197, Footnote 32.

reinsertion, the settlement of legal situations, and the recovery of property in cases of dispossession.[166] The IER devoted special attention to financial compensation. This is because it followed up on the work of the IAC, which was tasked with providing reparations to victims of enforced disappearance and arbitrary detention. Out of the almost 17,000 individual requests for reparations, the IER ordered that 9,779 victims needed to receive financial compensation. Furthermore, the IER's final report contains a list of persons out of those 9,779 victims who, in addition to compensation, are entitled to receive other measures of reparation.[167] Importantly, despite the special attention that the IER paid to compensation, the Commission made it a top priority to provide victims of GVHR with individual measures of rehabilitation through the collective reparations that it recommended.[168]

Individual financial compensation is the preferred form of reparation awarded by MCRs. The UNCC and the EECC are proof of this: the reparations they awarded are mainly concerned with financial compensation. However, in contrast to the UNCC, the EECC also granted statements of liability as a form of satisfaction.[169]

4.2 Collective Reparations

Collective reparations have gained increased support during recent years. Presumably, such support is due to the fact that these reparations recognise that 'collectivities have been the targets of violence' and thus deserve redress.[170]

4.2.1 Concept

As has already been explained in Chapters III and IV, 'Collective reparations' is a term that has been given different meanings in different contexts.[171] To reiterate for the sake of clarity, De Greiff's understanding is that it refers to certain types of goods, usually social services and symbolic measures, awarded to groups of people regardless of whether those groups enjoy legal personality. He also adds that the primary objective of collective reparations is to contribute to the process of reconciliation by rebuilding relationships among individuals, communities, as well as between separate communities and the government[172] In addition, Roht-Arrianza and Orlovsky affirm that collective reparations 'respond to collective harms and harms

166 IER's Final Report, Vol. 3, p. 45; HRW, "Morocco's Truth Commission: Honouring Past Victims during an Uncertain Present", 17 *Human Rights Watch* (2005), p. 20.

167 IER's Final Report, Vol.1, p. 88-91.

168 IER Follow-up, p. 59.

169 EECC Final Award, *Ethiopia's Damages Claims*, *supra* n.146, para. 270.

170 OHCHR, *supra* n. 33, p. 25.

171 In Chapter IV this definition has been discussed at length.

172 Report by the Special Rapporteur on the promotion of truth, justice, reparation and guarantees of non-recurrence, Pablo de Greiff, UN Doc A/69/518, 8 October 2014, para. 38.

to social cohesion' while maximizing available resources.[173] Still other scholars like Díaz have submitted that collective reparations are usually employed as a strategy to deny individual reparations.[174]

For the purposes of their work, the CVR and the IER each defined the concept of collective reparations. The CVR referred to the PIR, which includes collective reparations as concomitants of a state's moral and legal obligation to provide victims with substantial and meaningful benefits that help them to recover their confidence and trust in society. Accordingly, the PIR constituted a gesture by the Peruvian state on behalf of society as a whole, where the said gesture acknowledged the damage caused and reaffirmed the victims' dignity and their standing as citizens. In this light, collective reparations become an instrument to strengthen the formation of a new social pact that is needed to achieve democracy and reconciliation.[175] In addition, the CVR affirmed that the objective of collective reparations is to rebuild the social fabric, institutions, economy, and infrastructure of the families and the rural and urban communities affected by the violence.[176] The Moroccan IER's statute defined 'general and collective measures' as all measures 'put into practice through various measures such as compensation, readjustment, reintegration, rehabilitation, the preservation of memory and guarantees against the repetition of the violations'.[177] In addition, the IER established that the goal of these reparations is to help reinstate the regions that witnessed the occurrence of grave violations. These regions were held to have suffered harm due to the marginalization and exclusion resulting from the commission of grave violations.[178] Considering the views of both the CVR and the IER, collective reparations refer to all measures needed to remedy the harm suffered by communities and regions after the commission of numerous GVHR.

4.2.2 Scope

The exact content of collective reparations programmes is usually decided on a case-by-case basis. Generally, it includes material measures in the form of social services ('non-excludable goods' – goods that not only victims, but any member of society can access) and symbolic measures. Material measures are not restricted to social services but can also include measures of restitution, such the restoration of a name, the expunction of criminal records, or the restoration of passports or

173 Roht-Arrianza, N. and Orlovsky, K., "A Complementary Relationship: Reparations and Development", *ICTJ* (2009), p. 3.

174 Díaz Gómez, *supra* n. 7, p. 272.

175 Guillerot, J. and Magarrell, L., *Memorias de un proceso inacabado: reparaciones en la transición peruana* (Lima, APRODEH & ICTJ 2006), p. 31-32.

176 CVR's Final Report, Vol. IX, p. 195.

177 Article 5, IER's Statute.

178 IER's Final Report, Vol. 1, p. 86.

other documents.[179] Symbolic reparations include individual letters of apology sent to victims, an individual copy of a truth commission report, the inclusion of each victim in the final report of a truth commission,[180] as well as ceremonies, days of remembrance, public apologies, and the construction of monuments.[181] Public apologies in particular are usually considered the exception rather than the rule.[182] Yet President Toledo apologised on behalf of the state to those who suffered as a result of the conflict.[183]

In Peru, the CVR recommended a Comprehensive Plan of Reparations composed of six programmes (the restitution of civil rights, reparations in education, reparations in health, collective reparations, symbolic reparations, and economic reparations),[184] which then became law in 2005. In the PIR's law one initiative was distinguished as an additional, separate programme (the CVR had initially understood reparations in housing as part of the economic reparations).[185] Furthermore, the CVR's and PIR's Regulations established that collective reparations were to focus on four main areas: i) institutional strengthening of local authorities in the affected communities, as well as human rights and dispute resolution training; ii) productive capacity and economic infrastructure support; iii) support for the displaced to return; and iv) the strengthening of basic and cultural services, such as education, health, water, sanitation, and cultural heritage support projects.[186]

All in all, the CVR understands collective reparations as measures composed solely of diverse material measures. However, within the PIR, symbolic measures are foreseen as part of the CVR's comprehensive reparations approach. These measures aim to benefit both individual and collective beneficiaries, as well as society as a whole,[187] and are comprised of public acts, including a public apology from higher state officials, individual letters of apology to the victims, the explicit acknowledgment of all victims of violence, the creation of memorials, and the establishment of a national commemoration day to remember all victims of the armed conflict, among other such public acts.[188]

---

179 OHCHR, *supra* n. 33, p. 25.

180 OHCHR, *supra* n. 33, p. 23. This was the case of the Chilean Commission.

181 Correa, *supra* n. 125, p. 209.

182 Gray, D.C., "A no-excuse approach to transitional justice: reparations as tools of extraordinary justice" 87 *Washington University Law Review* (2010), p. 1082.

183 Wolfe, *supra* n. 12, p. 2-4, 307; Wiebelhaus-Brahm, *supra* n. 82, p. 501.

184 CVR's Final Report, Vol. IX, p. 159-202.

185 Articles 13, 17, 22, 27, 32, 33 and 37, 2006 Regulations of PIR's law.

186 CVR's Final Report, Vol. IX, p. 196-200; Article 27 of the Regulations of the PIR's law.

187 CVR's Final Report, Vol. IX, p. 161.

188 CVR's Final Report, Vol. IX, p. 161-163; Article 32, Regulations of the PIR's law.

In Morocco, the collective reparations comprise material and symbolic measures in regions that suffered violations and were socially and economically marginalized.[189]

Their content includes: i) strengthening civil society through human rights and democracy education; ii) symbolic measures, such as public memory sites, commemorations, and the conversion of former secret detention centres into additional sites of memory; iii) income-generating activities, with a special focus on women; iv) measures to guarantee the return of displaced people; and iv) the strengthening of basic services, including medical assistance.[190] In addition, the IER recommended GnR in the form of constitutional reforms, such as the recognition of fundamental rights and the strengthening of the separation of powers. It also recommended that the Prime Minister, but not the King, should acknowledge all past human rights abuses and offer an apology.[191]

It is important to point out that among the material measures, medical services assume a predominant position. The Peruvian and Moroccan TRCs included in-house medical units. While the Peruvian TRC's medical unit focused on working with victims before, during, and after public hearings and testimonies, the Moroccan TRC's medical unit focused on studying victims' conditions in order to better formulate its reparations recommendations in relation to victims' needs. As a result, it identified urgent cases that needed immediate reparations.[192]

5 Substantive and Procedural Aspects of Collective Reparations

5.1 Adequacy

Adequate reparations refer to the measures that are needed for a programme to be suitable for given victims, the violations they have suffered, and for their society as a whole.[193] As has already been mentioned, providing full reparations for large numbers of victims of GVHR is not possible.[194] In lieu of full reparations, collective reparations seem to have become a common response to GVHR. While the exact adequate measures must be decided on a case-by-case basis, scholars and the UN have developed general criteria to guide the devising of collective reparations (CR) within the context of TJMs. The following subsections aim to consider the principal elements of those criteria:

189 Guillerot and Carranza, *supra* n. 7, p. 26-28; HRW, *supra* n. 166, p. 20.

190 IER's Final Report, Vol. 3, p. 49; Díaz Gómez, *supra* n. 7, p. 288; Guillerot and Carranza, *supra* n. 7, p. 26-28.

191 IER's Final Report, Vol. 3, p. 49; Hazan, *supra* n. 80, p. 12.

192 OHCHR, *supra* n. 33, p. 24.

193 Ibid., p. 28-29.

194 Uprimny-Yepes, *supra* n. 123, p. 630.

5.1.1 *National Reparation Programmes*

(1) CR are political projects aiming to partially compensate the damage suffered

According to de Greiff, reparations programmes are adequate and fair if they achieve the following political objectives: acknowledgement, civil trust, and solidarity.[195] Similarly, Díaz supports the idea of CR being a political rather than legal project, due to the complexities and challenges of the harm to be repaired.[196] If reparations were to cover all the damage caused, then the repairing state would be left with insufficient funds to fulfil its other obligations towards its citizens, and, consequently, the entire society of the said state would itself become a victim of the state due to the awarded reparations.[197]

(2) CR aim to benefit a large number of victims and avoid tensions among victims

Collective reparations are deemed more adequate than individual reparations because the latter may put beneficiaries at risk, especially when only selected groups of victims are granted reparations. This could lead to conflict among victims and communities.[198] In addition, collective reparations may be the best option when low-level perpetrators and victims coexist in a given society.[199] CR allow a greater number of victims to access reparation benefits, as they do not require all beneficiaries to be identified individually.[200]

(3) CR maximise resources and are less costly

The OHCHR considers as adequate those reparations programmes that benefit the greatest number of victims and maximise resources. To this end, a reparations programme needs to combine symbolic and material reparations, as this combination is able to benefit more victims.[201] Here, it is important to add that CR are considered less costly and are thus preferred by states. The preference of states for CR arises from the fact that CR represent a fairer option for the whole of society, since their implementation would not greatly affect the remainder of a state's budget. Nevertheless, victims may perceive such measures as being less comprehensive than individual reparations.

---

195 de Greiff, *supra* n. 35, p. 461-466.
196 Díaz Gómez, *supra* n. 135, p. 6; Villa Arcilla, *supra* n. 134, p. 65.
197 Villa Arcilla, *supra* n. 134, p. 67.
198 Roht-Arriaza and Orlovsky, *supra* n. 43, p. 193-194; Magarrell, *supra* n. 5, p. 6.
199 Roht-Arriaza, *supra* n. 134, p. 197.
200 Magarrell, *supra* n. 69, p. 90; Roht-Arriaza and Orlovsky, *supra* n. 43, p. 192.
201 OHCHR, *supra* n. 33, p. 22.

(4) CR address primary needs and bring symbolic acknowledgement

Generally, victims prefer measures that will improve their living conditions, such as basic services related to health and education.[202] It is important, however, to make clear that the provision of social services by itself does not qualify as collective reparations. First, such social projects need to be accessible, accompanied by symbolic measures, and culturally sensitive.[203] For instance, communal unity is more valuable in some countries, regions, or communities,[204] such as in the rural and indigenous communities that were awarded CR by the CVR in Peru.[205] Thus, it is important to contribute to victims' quality of life and, at the same time, to keep in mind that providing social services to victims means acknowledging past abuses.[206]

(5) CR need to adopt a participative approach

Although all measures of reparation tend to 'always fall short of victims' expectations,'[207] reparations are better when victims participate in their design and implementation. Victim participation is a key component in designing CR.[208] It promotes the legitimacy of the adopted measures[209] and opens up dialogue between victims and the state.[210] Yet it also presents many challenges. First, governments tend to be not so receptive to victim participation because they are afraid of opening what they see as a door to countless demands for redress in the form of damages. Furthermore, it is unrealistic to hear all victims' voices, and thus selective representation is usually preferred. To make such representation effective, special attention needs to be given to adequate representation and communication channels between victims, representatives, and the bodies in charge of the design and implementation of the reparations.[211]

Participation may take place through direct consultations with all victims or their representatives as well as through workshops or conferences. In addition, in the long run, victims' participation provides room for debate as to how to include victims

---

202 Roht-Arriaza, *supra* n. 134, p. 199; de Greiff, *supra* n. 127, p. 62.
203 Roht-Arriaza, *supra* n. 134, p. 187, 200.
204 Ibid., p. 197.
205 Magarrell, *supra* n. 69, p. 93.
206 OHCHR, *supra* n. 33, p. 30.
207 Magarrell, *supra* n. 5, p. 4.
208 Guillerot and Carranza, *supra* n. 7, p. 52
209 Firchow, P., "The Implementation of the Institutional Programme of Collective Reparations in Colombia", 6 *Journal of Human Rights Practice* (2014), p. 15.
210 CVR's Final Report, Vol. IX, p. 157-158.
211 Correa, Guillerot, and Magarrell, *supra* n. 41, p. 385-394.

socially and politically within the new democratic society.[212] It may thus lead to institutional changes, and even serve to prevent future crimes.[213]

Both the CVR and the IER adopted a participatory approach in the design of their recommended collective reparations and advised that this approach should also be embraced during the implementation phase. In Peru, the CVR conducted consultations via workshops held throughout the whole country with the help of NGOs, particularly the ICTJ and APRODEH.[214] The consultations provided the CVR with information about victims' expectations and allowed an open discussion between victims and authorities, where political, legal, and financial viability were juxtaposed with the immediate needs and frustrations of victims.[215] Like Peru's CVR, the Moroccan IER encouraged victim participation beyond just the hearings stage. The IER established a national forum and held consultations with victims, civil society, NGOs, experts, and government institutions. This was a key element in the design of the Moroccan collective reparations.[216]

(6) CR should adopt transformative measures

CRs for victims of GVHR usually take place in societies with great economic and social inequality, extreme poverty, and weak institutions.[217] Within such societies, the poorest are usually more affected when GVHR take place. Two examples are the Colombian and Peruvian cases, where the majority of those affected during the internal conflicts were more marginalised members of society.[218] Yet poverty and marginalisation may come into play as both the causes and consequences of GVHR. In this light, Uprimny and Safon have emphasised the need to address social inequality and exclusion when repairing GVHR (transformative reparations). They see transformative reparations as a bridge for victims to receive recognition both as victims and as fully realized citizens who are able to access and enjoy their rights including economic, social and cultural rights (ESCR).[219] The content of transformative

212 Ibid., p. 389.

213 Ibid., p. 390, 404-405.

214 ICJT stands for: The International Center for Transitional Justice. See its main wesbite: <https://www.ictj.org/> and APRODEH stands for Asociación Pro Derechos Humanos. See its main website: <http://www.aprodeh.org.pe/>.

215 Correa, Guillerot, and Magarrell, *supra* n. 41, p. 402-403.

216 Guillerot and Carranza, *supra* n. 7, p. 26; Lefranc, S. and Vairel, F., "The emergence of Transitional Justice as a Professional International Practice" in L. Israël and G. Mouralis, *Dealing with Wars and Dictatorships: Legal Concepts and Categories in Action* (The Hague, TMC Asser Press -Springer 2014), p. 239.

217 Uprimny-Yepes, *supra* n. 123, p. 626.

218 Ibid., p. 631.

219 Saffon, M.P. , and Uprimny, R., "Distributive Justice and the Restitution of Disposed Land in Colombia" in M. Bergsmo et al., *Distributive Justice in Transitions* (Oslo, Torkel Opshal Academic EPublisher 2010), p. 387-397.

reparations embraces two state obligations: to repair and to afford ESCR services.[220] Furthermore, transformative reparations seem to be more adequate for vulnerable groups such as female victims of violence. This is because such reparations act on individual, communal, and structural levels.[221] Importantly, transformative measures should incorporate a 'symbolic dimension'.[222]

Accordingly, Manjoo contends that transformative reparations help to change conditions of marginalisation because they operate on three levels: individual, institutional, and structural.[223] However, transformative reparations may be confused with development programmes. Thus, they must be accompanied by symbolic measures to help victims differentiate them. Furthermore, transformative reparations can be difficult to distinguish from guarantees of non-repetition, as both measures try to make changes at the institutional level and thereby prevent future crimes. However, transformative reparations go beyond the prevention of similar crimes and try to empower vulnerable and marginalised people.[224]

5.1.2 Mass Claims Reparations

Finally, it is important to point out that adequacy plays a very small role within the work of compensation commissions, as their awards are mostly limited to financial compensation. However, the participation of claimants does take place, albeit in a very limited manner. More specifically, participation was mostly confined to personal statements which claimants attached to the official claim form.[225] In large and complex cases, when factual or legal questions were raised, individuals were invited to present their views in oral proceedings.[226] In such cases, a lawyer or legal representative of the claimant's choice would assist him or her.[227] In contrast to judicial proceedings, Iraq was not given any standing in the UNCC.[228] Foreign governments, international

---

220 Guillerot and Carranza, *supra* n. 7, p. 9.

221 Manjoo, R., "Introduction: reflections on the concept and implementation of transformative reparations" 21 *The International Journal of Human Rights*, p. 1193-1196; 'reparation must drive post-conflict transformation of socio-cultural injustices, and political and structural inequalities that shape the lives of women and girls' and 'must go above and beyond the immediate reasons and consequences of the crimes and violations; they must aim to address the political and structural inequalities that negatively shape women's and girls' lives'. See: 2007 Nairobi Declaration on Women's and Girl's Rights to a Remedy and Reparations, p. 2, 5.

222 Uprimny-Yepes, *supra* n. 123, p. 636-639.

223 Manjoo, *supra* n. 221, p. 1198-1199.

224 Uprimny-Yepes, *supra* n. 123, p. 644.

225 Taylor, *supra* n. 97, p. 204.

226 UNCC Decision 7, *Criteria for Additional Categories of Claims*, Doc. S/AC.26/1991/7/Rev.1, 17 March 1992, para. 3; Report of the Secretary-General, 2 May 1991, UN Doc. S/22559, para. 20; Articles 36(a) and 38(d), UNCC's Rules.

227 Article 38 (d), UNCC's Rules.

228 Gattini, *supra* n. 6, p. 168.

organisations, and the government of Iraq received regular written reports from the UNCC detailing the state of the claims process.[229] Consequently, Iraq was afforded a symbolic right to comment, within a short period of time, on claims and reports.[230] Yet the country was not given the right to appeal against decisions in the adjudication of claims by the UNCC. Although it seems that Iraq was not afforded fundamental due process in these quasi-judicial proceedings, the UNCC did invite Iraq to present its views in hearings regarding complex cases.[231] Within the EECC, victims' participation was even more limited than in the case of the UNCC. If at all, victims could participate by means of signing affidavits related to the conflict.[232]

5.2 Liability

In international law, liability refers to the legal duty to compensate victims or claimants for the harm suffered. Liability is usually determined by a judicial body. It is also a precondition for awarding reparations. However, under transitional justice, liability is treated differently.

5.2.1 National Reparation Programmes

First of all, we should recall that according to the Principles on Reparations, a state may be responsible for providing reparations to victims of GVHR when that state's actions or omissions resulted in human rights violations,[233] and when the person responsible for the harm is unable or unwilling to provide reparations.[234] The first scenario is termed direct liability while the second is known as subsidiary liability. In this light, after a period of democratization, new governments are responsible for violations committed by previous regimes because of the notion of continuity of state.[235] However, governments tend to create national reparations programmes guided by the idea of solidarity rather than state responsibility.[236] Although the international community may, in principle, bear responsibility for reparations to victims of GVHR, particularly if the community has ignored the commission of GVHR, there is no

229 Taylor, *supra* n. 97, p. 205.

230 Within 30 days Iraq may present its views and additional information regarding reports regarding claims under categories 'A', 'B' and 'C'. For claims of categories 'D', 'E' and 'F' within 90 days. See: Article 16 (1)-(3), UNCC's Rules.

231 Gattini, *supra* n. 6, p. 169.

232 Kidane, W., "Civil Liability for Violations of International Humanitarian Law: The Jurisprudence of the Eritrea-Ethiopia Claims Commission in The Hague," 25 *Wisconsin International Law Journal* (2007), p. 77.

233 Principle 15, Principles on Reparations.

234 Principle 16, Principles on Reparations.

235 Magarrell, *supra* n. 5, p. 10.

236 One example thereof is Colombia. See: Guillerot and Carranza, *supra* n. 7, p. 20.

legally binding mechanism against the international community.[237] Yet in some cases, the international community may help, on a discretionary basis, to make national reparations feasible. For instance, it could do so by accepting 'to exchange a certain amount of foreign debt' for victims' reparations, as it did in the case of Peru.[238] In addition to their legal obligation to repair victims of GVHR, states may also see some political benefit in carrying out reparations.

In the case of Peru, the CVR declared that it was the state's responsibility to repair all victims of the violence stemming from the internal conflict. According to the CVR, not only did the state bear responsibility to repair all victims under national and international law, but the state had also accepted such responsibility by empowering the CVR to propose reparations programmes.[239] In Morocco, the liability of the state is implied in the IER's Statute, which provides the Commission with a special budget to fulfil its mandate.[240] This mandate authorized the IER to order individual reparations and recommend collective ones.

5.2.2 Mass Claims Reparations

Liability within mass claims reparations differs from that of national reparations programmes. It should be recalled that the UNCC and the EECC were established to compensate the damage and suffering resulting from wars between two states. Yet the issue of liability for the engendered harm was handled very differently. On the one hand, within the UNCC's framework, the liability to bear the costs of the reparations was not decided by the UNCC but, rather, by the UNSC, which determined that Iraq was exclusively responsible for the 'direct' damage incurred as a consequence of the war between Iraq and Kuwait.[241] Thus, the UNCC was limited to assessing claims and distributing the compensation granted thereto. Iraq's liability was not only limited by the 'direct' harm criterion but also by the constraint that the United Nations Compensation Fund could dispose of no more than 30% of the country's export earnings from petroleum and petroleum-related products.[242] This 30% was reduced to 5% in 2003.[243]

In the EECC, on the other hand, an arbitration tribunal decided the liability issue. Ethiopia and Eritrea sought to hold each other accountable for all of the suffering and damage caused during the conflict by both parties. In its final decision, the EECC ordered each state to pay a specific amount of money: Ethiopia was awarded

237 Magarrell, *supra* n. 5, p. 11.
238 Ibid., p. 14; de Greiff, *supra* n. 127, p. 61.
239 CVR's Final Report, Vol. IX, p. 143-144.
240 Article 23, IER's Statute.
241 UNSC, *supra* n. 94, para. 16; van Zoelen, *supra* n. 8, p. 38.
242 UNSC Resolution 705, Doc. S/RES/705. 15 August 1991, para. 3.
243 UNSC Resolution 1483, Doc. S/RES/1483, 22 May 2003, para. 21.

USD 174,036,520 in monetary compensation and Eritrea was awarded a total of USD 163,520,865.[244] The sums were based on the commission of crimes, such as unprevented rape, the deprivation of property, the mistreatment of prisoners of war, and unlawful killings.[245] In addition, Ethiopia sought a measure of satisfaction for diplomatic infringements, which was awarded.[246] And Eritrea sought compensation for the same infringements, which was awarded.[247] In regard to compensation granted for the crime of rape, the EECC expressed the hope that both states would 'use the funds awarded to develop and support health programmes for women and girls in the affected areas.'[248] Even so, no exact order was given. Significantly, the overall awards represented a greater burden for Eritrea's economy, which is less developed than the comparatively stronger Ethiopian economy.[249]

5.3 Beneficiaries

The determination of beneficiaries is a key step in the reparatory process – it is a precondition for the adequacy and the implementation of reparations. Yet defining the victims and the beneficiaries of reparations is a rather complex task. Since all beneficiaries are victims but not all victims necessarily become beneficiaries of reparations, the definition of a beneficiary hinges on the conceptualization of a victim. According to de Greiff, governments tend to adopt the concept of a victim as defined by the Principles on Reparations when designating beneficiaries.[250] This concept involves persons who have individually or collectively suffered harm, as well as their immediate family or dependants.[251] In addition, collectivities (i.e. groups of persons who share a strong identity link, such as communities and indigenous peoples) may also be considered victims.[252]

However, under transitional justice, governments create categories of victims and discretionally limit the beneficiaries of reparations to some of those categories.[253] While such limitations seem to be a response to the issue of finite resources, they

244 EECC, *Ethiopia's Damages Claims*, *supra* n. 146, Award para. E; EECC, *Eritrea's Damages Claims*, *supra* n. 146, Award para. 1-21.

245 Ibid.

246 EECC, *Ethiopia's Damages Claims*, *supra* n. 146, para. 266, 269.

247 Yet, EECC did not award the total amounts claimed by Eritrea but a part of it. See: EECC *Eritrea's Damages Claims*, *supra* n. 146, para. 384-392.

248 EECC, *Eritrea's Damages Claims*, *supra* n. 146, para. 239.

249 EECC, *Ethiopia's Damages Claims*, *supra* n. 146, para. 18-23.

250 de Greiff, *supra* n. 127, p. 55.

251 Principles 8 and 9, Principles on Reparations.

252 Colombia has adopted the most progressive definition to define collectivities as victims and beneficiaries of reparations. It not only includes groups of natural persons who have suffered violations or share a strong link but also social and political organisations, as well as villages, communities and groups, regardless of their legal status. See: Firchow, *supra* n. 209, p. 4.

253 Magarrell, *supra* n. 5, p. 3-4; Shelton, *supra* n. 33, p. 122; Roht-Arriaza, *supra* n. 134, p. 158.

may instead appear to paint a picture of "winning" victims versus "losing" victims.[254] For instance, victims of GVHR (torture, enforced disappearances, or extrajudicial killings) are usually beneficiaries of reparations programmes. But victims of violations not considered to be 'grave', yet still fundamental, such as violations of freedom of speech or freedom of religion, are not eligible beneficiaries.[255] Contrary to the standards of international law, some states have excluded those considered to be victim-perpetrators from being beneficiaries. Although scholars usually argue that collective reparations may benefit victims and perpetrators alike,[256] this state of affairs may result in political tensions.[257]

5.3.1 National Reparations Programmes

In Peru, the CVR considered as victims all individuals or groups of people who suffered acts or omissions that gave rise to forced disappearances, abduction, extrajudicial killings, murder, forced displacement, arbitrary detention, violation of due process, forced recruitment, torture, and sexual violations and injuries amounting to violations of humanitarian law. The status of a victim would be awarded regardless of whether the damaging violation's perpetrator could be identified.[258] While its concept of victimhood extends to groups of people, such as groups of displaced peoples, the CVR also extended the concept of beneficiaries to include collectivities: peasants and indigenous communities, as well as any other town affected by the conflict by means of GVHR, property destruction, and the weakening of its local government, infrastructure, and local productive activities.[259]

However, not all victims were seen as beneficiaries. On the one hand, the Peruvian TRC acknowledged that the principles of non-discrimination and equality applied to the process of reparations and all victims without regard for whether they had 'clean hands'.[260] On the other hand, it acknowledged that public support for its work would be likely to be undermined if an ex-guerrilla were to receive reparations.[261] Consequently, and contrary to international law, victims suspected of

254 Gray, *supra* n. 182, p. 1065.

255 Usually civil and political rights violations. See: OHCHR, *supra* n. 33, p. 19.

256 Ramil-Nogales, J. and van Schaak, B., "A Collective Response to Mass Violence: Reparations and Healing in Cambodia, in Brining the Khmer Rouge to Justice: Prosecuting Mass Violence before the Cambodian Courts" Santa Clara University School of Law, *Legal Studies Research Papers Series, Working Paper No. 06-02, 2006*, p. 366.

257 Moffet, *supra* n. 34, p. 151.

258 CVR's Final Report, Vol. IX, p. 149.

259 CVR's Final Report, Vol. IX, p. 152-153, 195; Article 50, Regulations of the PIR's law; Article 7, Ley no. 28592 (PIR's law).

260 CVR's Final Report, Vol. IX, p. 149-50; Article 52, Regulations of the PIR's law. The doctrine of 'clean hands' is a common law doctrine/principle which is use to balance blame in determining the causation of injury and harm. See: Laplante, *supra* n. 34, p. 60, 72.

261 Laplante, *supra* n. 34, p. 74-76

being connected to armed insurgent groups were excluded.[262] Victims could have been members of the armed forces or the peasant patrols, but not of the guerrilla troops.[263]

The identification of individual and collective beneficiaries was neither conducted by the CVR, nor was a deadline given for this. Yet the deadline could be inferred to have been less than 6 years, as that is the deadline the CVR established for the PIR to take place.[264] The Regulations of the PIR's law establish that the National Council of Reparations is the body in charge of identifying all beneficiaries, including collectivities, through the National Victims Registry (Registro Único de Víctimas or RUV).[265] Collectivities are required to provide the following information: the name of the group, the name of the representative, the address or location, the type of violation suffered, the year and place where the violation took place, a description of the facts, and the names of people or sources that could support the provided information.[266] By 2009, the RUV had registered more than 58,000 out of the estimated 280,000 total of individual victims, as well as 5,000 out of the 9,000 collective victims.[267]

Furthermore, the CVR recommended the government to give priority to collectivities in receiving collective reparations. To this end, the CVR recommended certain criteria to identify the said collectivities.[268] Yet, the government was free to develop any other criteria to decide on such priority. Although, at first, the RUV established that beneficiaries were to be identified by December 2011, in 2016 the Peruvian government decided to reopen the registration of potential beneficiaries.[269] The reparations programme's funds were partitioned, with 96% going to projects and the remaining 4% being used to cover administrative costs.[270] Finally, it must be stated that the registration of some victims was done under the 'presumption of good faith'.[271]

According to the Moroccan IER's statute, victimhood under enforced disappearance or arbitrary detention automatically qualified a person and his or her

262 Guillerot and Carranza, *supra* n. 7, p. 30; Roht-Arriaza, *supra* n. 137, p. 686. The International Law Commission has rejected the doctrine of clean hands as a circumstance precluding wrongfulness. See: Laplante, *supra* n. 34, p. 64.

263 Articles 52 (a) and 47 (b), Regulations of the PIR's law; García-Godos, *supra* n. 12, p. 127.

264 CVR's Final Report, Vol. IX, p. 203.

265 Articles 51 and 64, Regulations of the PIR's law.

266 Article 75, Regulations of the PIR's law.

267 Guillerot and Carranza, *supra* n. 7, p. 30.

268 The criteria are: i) the magnitude and gravity of the damage suffered, ii) its degree of poverty, iii) its composition (percentage of women, children, the elderly, orphans, etc.), iv) its geographical location, v) its main productive activities, vi) whether they had received any support previously from the state or international cooperation. See: CVR's Final Report, Vol. IX, p. 201.

269 CMAN, *supra* n. 65, p. 13; ICTJ, *supra* n. 64, p. 3-4.

270 CMAN, *supra* n. 65, p. 13; ICTJ, *supra* n. 64, p. 10-11.

271 ICJ, *A Practitioner's Perspective on Forms of Justice in Peru and Colombia* (ICTJ 2017). Available at: <https://www.ictj.org/news/practitioners-perspective-forms-justice-peru-and-colombia>.

heirs or legal successors as beneficiaries of reparations.[272] Yet the IER went beyond its original mandate and extended the scope of beneficiaries to include victims of political killings, torture, injuries during urban riots, forced exile, and sexual violence. In addition, the IER also recognised as victims and beneficiaries of reparations those 'regions harmed as a result of the intensified occurrence of grave violations'.[273]

The Moroccan IER, pursuant to its finding that certain regions had been victimized, granted reparations to 11 communities where the whole of society had been affected by GVHR.[274] The communities selected as beneficiaries met at least one of the following criteria: i) where the clandestine centres of torture once operated; ii) where systematic violent events occurred; iii) where a great number of direct victims live; and iv) where victims suffered collective harm/punishment.[275] The notion of collective punishment refers to the deliberate deprivation of infrastructure and other forms of investment in communities that led to the said communities' marginalisation.[276] Like the Peruvian CVR, the Moroccan IER's deliberations support the idea of collective victimhood based on geographical ties.[277] Thus, while there is difficulty in defining collectivities, this difficulty can be overcome.[278]

With regard to individual victims, the IER's identification process was based on analogies. Essentially, it compared the facts described in the individual petitions with those facts established by its own investigations (field research, testimonies, etc.) aimed at unveiling the truth regarding the GVHR during the Years of Lead. Petitioners were sometimes invited and heard by the IER to clarify or complete information.[279] Individual petitions were submitted as a form that contained the full identity of the petitioners.[280]

5.3.2 Mass Claims Reparations

Beneficiaries were defined within the legal frameworks of the UNCC and the EECC.[281] In the case of the UNCC, beneficiaries could be individuals, legal persons, public sector entities, or international organisations that had suffered any direct loss,

272 Articles 5 and 7, IER's Statute.
273 IER's Final Report, Vol. 3, p. 50-53.
274 Figuig, Nador, El Hoceima, Errachidia, Khenifra, Ouarzazate, Zagora, Hay Mohammadi (Casablanca), Tantan, Azilal, and Khémissat. See: Guillerot and Carranza, *supra* n. 7, p. 27; IER's Final Report, Vol. 3, p. 48.
275 Díaz Gómez, *supra* n. 7, p. 281.
276 IER's Final Report, Vol. 3, p. 48; Guillerot and Carranza, *supra* n. 7, p. 26; de Greiff, P. , *supra* n. 511, p. 36-37.
277 Guillerot and Carranza, *supra* n. 7, p. 42, 44.
278 Ibid., p. 43.
279 IER's Final Report, Vol. 3, p. 62.
280 IER's Final Report, Vol. 3, p. 67.
281 Niebergall, *supra* n. 3, p. 149.

damage, or injury, including environmental damage, resulting from Iraq's invasion of Kuwait.[282] In other words, the eligible claimants were individuals (natural and legal persons) and corporations.[283] The privileged position of the individual, expressed in the ability to claim compensation against a state in an arbitrational setting, is considered by Gattini as the most remarkable contribution of the UNCC to the field of claims settlements.[284] The UNCC excluded certain individuals from being beneficiaries: no Iraqi national could be a beneficiary, unless they were also a national of another state,[285] and no member of the military forces could be a beneficiary unless they were a prisoner of war or could prove an injury that resulted from violations of international humanitarian law.[286] Due to pragmatic reasons, eligible claimants did not have the right to submit individual claims directly to the UNCC. Only governments could file claims, on behalf of individuals, corporations, international organisations, other entities belonging to foreign governments, or even on their own behalf. When governments refused or were unable to submit claims on behalf of individuals or corporations, an appointed agency would carry out the submission instead.[287] With this in mind, several UN organisations were appointed to bring claims.[288] Finally, a government could submit claims on behalf of foreign nationals or corporations seated in a foreign jurisdiction, provided that the relevant foreign governments gave their consent.[289]

In the EECC, beneficiaries could be either individuals or legal persons as well as the states of Ethiopia and Eritrea.[290] Here it must be stated that those individuals did not need to be nationals but persons of Eritrean or Ethiopian origin.[291]

The EECC allowed for individual and mass claims procedures. The individual procedures concerned claims brought by states on either their own behalf or on behalf of an individual.[292] And mass claims procedures concerned claims brought by

282 UNSC, *supra* n. 94, para. 16.

283 Wühler, N., "The United Nations Compensation Commission: A new contribution to the process of international claims resolutions", 2 *Journal of International Economic Law* (1999), p. 253.

284 Dispute mechanism resolutions at the international level, including arbitrational settings, were mainly created to deal with claims by states vis-à vis states. Yet, the UNCC opened the door for individuals to be able to claim compensation at the international level. See: Gattini, *supra* n. 6, p. 170-171.

285 UNCC Decision 1, *supra* n. 143, para. 17.

286 UNCC Decision 11, *Eligibility for Compensation of Members of the Allied Coalition Armed Forces*, Doc. No. S/AC.26/1992/11, 26 June 1992.

287 Article 5 (3), UNCC's Rules.

288 Some examples are: the UN Development Programme (UNDP), the UN High Commissioner for Refugees (UNHCR), and the UN Relief and Works Agency for Palestine Refugees in the Near East (UNRWA). See: Taylor, *supra* n. 97, p. 203.

289 Article 5 (1), UNCC's Rules.

290 Article 5 (8), Algiers Agreement.

291 Article 5 (9), Algiers Agreement.

292 Individual claims on behalf of an individual exceeded USD 100,000 Article 23, EECC Rules of Procedure.

individual that have suffered different violations as pursuant Article 30 of the EECC's Rules of Procedure. Yet no mass claims procedures took place. As with the UNCC, no individual person could file a claim directly to the EECC.[293] Within the individual claims framework, 6 claims on behalf of named individuals were submitted by Eritrea.[294] Besides those six submissions, all claims filed by Ethiopia and Eritrea were government claims alleging harm to unnamed persons and property.[295] Ethiopia filed 8 claims and Eritrea filed 32 claims on behalf of thousands of unspecified people.[296] Significantly, the compensation that the EECC awarded to both governments did not reach individual victims.

5.4 Assessment of Harm

Although the damage caused by GVHR is felt in different ways and degrees across individuals and communities,[297] and although it is in principle immeasurable, an assessment of harm is usually conducted in order to determine the most adequate measures of reparation.

5.4.1 National Reparations Programmes

Neither the Peruvian CVR nor the Regulations of the PIR's law establish the body in charge of conducting the assessment of harm or the methodology underlying the assessment. Neither did the CVR's report include an assessment of harm section. Nevertheless, the CVR referred, in general terms, to the type of harm reparations were supposed to address, namely social, economic and institutional damage.[298] The CVR also distinguished between the harm suffered between the displaced and the victims of death, disappearance, torture or sexual violence.[299]

In addition, the CVR accepts that to identify collectivities that should enjoy priority reparations, certain criteria need to be taken into account, notably the magnitude and gravity of the damage suffered and the level of poverty in which the community lives.[300] These two criteria imply that an assessment of harm is to be carried out. In addition, it could be presumed that such an assessment of harm may be

293 Kidane, *supra* n. 232, p. 39.

294 Dybnis, *supra* n. 109, p. 268; EECC, *Eritrea's Damages Claims*, *supra* n. 146, para. 393-436.

295 Giroud and Moss, *supra* n. 44, p. 489-490.

296 Shelton, *supra* n. 33, p. 187.

297 Guillerot and Carranza, *supra* n. 7, p. 10.

298 ICTJ and APRODEH, *Escuchando las voces de las comunidades: Un estudio sobre la implementación de las Reparaciones Colectivas en el Perú* (ICTJ 2010), p. 4.

299 Ibid., p. 27; Barrantes Segura, R., *Reparations and Displacement in Peru* (ICTJ 2012). Available at: <https://www.ictj.org/sites/default/files/ICTJ-Brookings-Displacement-Reparations-Peru-CaseStudy-2012-English.pdf>.

300 CVR's Final Report, Vol. IX, p. 201.

conducted by grouping the victims in accordance with the categories of beneficiaries and by assessing which communities were most affected by violations. Such an assessment is also possible by determining how marginalised the communities in question are, based on their access to basic social services. Yet, the body that is in charge of such an assessment remains unclear. However, the CVR recognises that it is up to the affected communities to decide on the type of measures of reparations that best compensate the harm suffered.[301] This may imply that the assessment of harm is carried out by the victims themselves, whether formally or informally. Finally, the CVR recommended that Peru should establish minimum and maximum amounts to be invested in projects in relation to the type of group of victims, poverty and the size of the community, but it did not go further into defining specific amounts.[302]

The Moroccan IER conducted the assessment of individual victims and community victims in parallel. The approach used in individual claims assessments mirrored that of the IAC.[303] Compensation was calculated using a fixed amount of money as a basic starting unit for all victims of the crimes to be compensated.[304] In cases of arbitrary detention or forced exile, this basic unit was multiplied by the number of months or years the person suffered the violation. In addition, other fixed amounts were added to the awards for loss of opportunity and income as well as for moral and physical harm. Remarkably, female victims were awarded increased monetary sums in acknowledgement of their 'special circumstances'.[305] In addition, the in-house medical unit established by the IER assessed the medical situation of victims and even handled pressing cases, which required immediate attention and could not wait until the implementation of reparations.[306] As such, when needed, the in-house unit provided victims with medicines and urgent treatment.[307]

In conducting a harm assessment, the IER first clustered all petitions into four categories according to the supporting evidence accompanying each petition. Then the Commission classified the petitions in accordance with the type and gravity of their underlying violations.[308] The IER prepared reports on the historical context of the violations, organized hearings in several regions to receive testimonies, and even held

301 ICTJ, *supra* n. 64, p. 14.
302 CVR's Final Report, Vol. IX, p. 195.
303 IER's Final Report, Vol. 5, p. 37.
304 Arbitrary detention, enforced disappearances, those who had died while in detention or shortly after their release, extrajudicial killings, torture, forced exile, and sexual violence.
305 IER's Final Report, Vol. 3, p. 36-45, 123-124.
306 Ferstman, C. and Goetz, M., "Reparations before the International Criminal Court: The Early Jurisprudence on Victim Participation and its Impact on Future Reparations Proceedings", in C. Ferstman, M. Goetz and A. Stephens (eds.), *Reparations for Victims of, War Crimes and Crimes Against Humanity: Systems in Place and Systems in the Making* (Leiden, Martinus Nijhoff 2009), p. 339.
307 IER's Final Report, Vol. 3, p. 47.
308 IER's Final report, Vol. 3, p. 61, 68.

consultative conferences.[309] Exceptional weight was given to analogies, testimonies, and to the congruence and context of the claims, especially when the petition lacked sufficient evidence.[310] Whilst the hearings helped to gather testimonies, they also served to make the IER's work visible to the public eye, to provoke public debate, and to promote a culture of dialogue.[311]

In order to determine the communities that should be regarded as victims, the IER first grouped individual victims according to the category of violations suffered and according to the region or community to which the said individuals belonged.[312] This allowed it to recognise the communities and regions that had suffered the most. In addition, the IER conducted detailed studies on the elements of proof that it had at hand, and held individual hearings for petitioners.[313] While the IER recommended some development projects as well as some symbolic projects for affected regions, its recommendations did not fix a specific general budget for all projects taken together. Instead the IER calculated a general cost for each of the programmes recommended. This cost, however, was calculated without indicating the number of victims involved in each project or the type of violations they had suffered.[314] Finally, it is important to note that the Moroccan IER adopted a 'gender approach' throughout its work, including its assessment of harm. In light of this approach, the TRC allowed as many women as possible to testify in hearings and conducted a qualitative study on gender and political violence during the Years of Lead. Furthermore, the IER obtained quantitative data related to violations suffered by women in order to draw conclusions on the broader patterns underlying gender and human rights violations.[315]

309 IER's Final Report, Vol. 5, p. 59-63.
310 IER's Final report, Vol. 3, p. 61, 68.
311 ICTJ Morocco Progress Report 2005, p. 17-18.
312 IER's Final Report, Vol. 3, p. 56-61.
313 IER's Final Report, Vol. 3, p. 68
314 The programmes covered a wide range of different service and memory measures such as educational, health and irrigation projects, an improvement to the existing infrastructure and the creation of a national history museum. See: IER's Final Report, Vol. 3, p. 87-102.
315 IER's Final Report, Vol. 1, p. 75-76.

5.4.2 *Mass Claims Reparations*

The UNCC decided to create six different categories of harm for the claims, and States were required to file their claims accordingly.[316]

Category	Type of claim
Category A	those forced to leave Iraq or Kuwait following the invasion (USD 2,500 for individuals and USD 5,000 for families)
Category B	those who suffered serious personal injury or the death of relatives (spouse, child or parents) (USD 5,000 for individuals and a maximum of USD 10,000 for families)
Category C	individuals claiming damages up to USD 100,000
Category D[317]	individuals claiming damages above USD 100,000
Category E	claims by corporations and legal entities, whether private or public
Category F	claims by states and international organisations related to the evacuation of refugees, environmental damage, and damages caused to properties belonging to governments.

In addition to these six categories, the UNCC adopted formulations and definitions of different types of injuries, under which mental and physical harm, as well as pecuniary losses, were covered.[318] Arising from these formulations, the concept of personal injuries included dismemberment, permanent or temporary disfigurement, a permanent or temporary significant limitation of the function of an organ or system, sexual assault, torture, as well as suffering caused to a spouse, child, or parent by the death of a relative.[319]

In carrying out its harm assessment, the UNCC relied on standard valuations, rather than attempting to assess all individual damages. Harm belonging to certain categories, namely 'A' and 'B', received the same standardised amount in compensation.[320] Categories 'A', 'B', and 'C' were given priority in the processing

316 UNCC Decision 1, *supra* n. 285; UNCC Decision 7, *supra* n. 226.

317 Claims C and D cover the same kinds of damages, the only difference seems to lie in the amount of money claimed. Damages covered by category 'C' are with 'respect to death or personal injury, or losses of income, support, housing or personal property, or medical expenses or costs of departure, as a result of Iraq's unlawful invasion and occupation of Kuwait'. See: UNCC Decision 1, *supra* n. 285, para. 14; and damages covered by category 'D' are with 'respect to any direct loss, damage, or injury (including death) to individuals as a result of Iraq's unlawful invasion and occupation of Kuwait'. See: UNCC Decision 7, *supra* n. 226, para. 6.

318 UNCC Decision 3, *Personal Injury and Mental Pain and Anguish*, Doc. S/AC.26/1991/3, 23 October 1991, p. 2.

319 Ibid., p. 2.

320 Niebergall, *supra* n. 3, p. 161, 164.

and payment of compensation[321] and, as such, they were resolved using mass claims techniques such as computerised data matching, 'sampling and additional verification as circumstances warranted'.[322] Wühler claims that these claims were also not assessed individually because of two main reasons: the small monetary amounts sought by the claimants and Iraq's acceptance of its liability.[323] Furthermore, for damages relating to mental pain and anguish, whether related to a physical injury or not, the UNCC established some award ceilings.[324] Offering compensation for mental pain and anguish without a corresponding physical injury was an innovative approach on the part of the UNCC.[325]

Furthermore, the manner in which assessments of property damage were carried out varied in accordance with the type of asset and the particular circumstances of the alleged damage. Two of the several valuation formulas used were the book value (an asset's costs minus accumulated depreciation) and the replacement value (the amount required to obtain an asset of the same kind and status as the asset damaged or lost).[326] In addition, claims under USD 100,000 were verified by being matched against information contained in a computerised database.[327] By grouping claims, relevant information could be carried over from one claim to another, making standardised valuation and quantification possible. As a result, common claims could be clustered and given similar benefits.[328] In addition, regarding claims in categories 'D', 'E', and 'F', the Commissioners conducted in situ missions to the claimant countries to

321 UNCC Decision 1, *supra* n. 285, para.1; UNCC Decision 17, *Priority of Payment and Payment Mechanism (Guiding Principles)*, UN Doc. S/AC.26/1994/17, 24 March 1994, para. 1; Singh, *supra* n. 51, p. 69; Shelton, *supra* n. 33, p. 184.

322 Taylor, *supra* n. 97, p. 205, 211.

323 Wühler, *supra* n. 283, p. 261.

324 For instance, up to USD 1,500 for having been a hostage; up to USD 15,000 for the death of a spouse, child or parent, up to USD 30,000 in cases of accumulated injuries. See: UNCC Decision 8, *Determination of Ceilings for Compensation for Mental Pain and Anguish*, Doc. S/AC.26/1992/8, 27 January 1992.

325 van Zoelen, *supra* n. 8, p. 42.

326 UNCC Decision 9, *Propositions and Conclusion on Compensation for Business Losses: Types of Damages and Their Valuation*, UN Doc. S/AC.26/1992/9, 6 March 1992; Shelton, *supra* n. 33, p. 186.

327 Giroud and Moss, *supra* n. 44, p. 488. In contrast, the review process for each higher category included techniques used in the previous ones, but also more individual attention. Category "C" claims could involve case-by-case determinations, as well as input from outside experts on the valuation of claims, all conducted under an inquisitorial approach. With claims in category "D" and above, the approach slowly became more arbitrational, with different parties being consulted for further evidence or observations. See: McGovern, F.E., "Dispute System Design: The United Nations Compensation Commission", 14 *Harvard Negotiation Law Review* (2009).

328 Niebergall, *supra* n. 3, p. 161-163; McCarthy, C., *Reparations and Victim Support in the International Criminal Court* (Cambridge, CUP 2012), p. 271.

gather information and assess the damage suffered.[329] These claims were individually reviewed.[330]

Within the EECC, as mentioned previously, two different types of claims procedures were foreseen: individual claims and mass claims. Accordingly, each would entail a different method of damage assessment. Mass claims would have required a lower standard of evidence and would have resulted in a fixed amount of financial compensation.[331] There were five different categories for mass claims:[332]

Category	**Type of claim**
Category 1	Claims by natural persons for unlawful expulsion from the country of their residence.
Category 2	Claims by natural persons for unlawful displacement from their residence.
Category 3	Claims by prisoners of war for injuries suffered as a result of unlawful treatment.
Category 4	Claims by civilians for unlawful detention and for injuries suffered as a result of unlawful treatment during detention.
Category 5	Claims by persons for loss, damage or injury other than those covered by the other categories.

Despite being accounted for, mass claims procedures did not take place. According to Dybnis, this was due to the limited resources and time faced by the EECC.[333] Individual claims, on the other hand, were filed by state parties either on their own behalf or on behalf of individuals.[334] These claims were individually considered.[335] The EECC compensated harms such as: human suffering and loss of income associated with the internal displacement of persons, death, and injury; damage to civilian property; damage to public buildings and infrastructure; and the looting and destruction of religious institutions.[336] Yet it refused to make 'a precise quantification of each type of harm suffered, because doing so would have been too difficult, given the scale of the injuries'. Instead, the Commission made a 'best assessment' through approximations.[337] Finally, in assessing the damages, the EECC considered four elements: i) whether liability for the acts had been established ii) whether the standard

329 Taylor, *supra* n. 97, p. 205.
330 Ibid., p. 213.
331 Brilmayer, L., Giorgetti, C., and Charlton, L., *International Claims Commissions: Righting Wrongs after Conflict* (Cheltenham, Edward Elgar Publishing, 2017), p. 117.
332 Article 30, EECC's Rules of Procedure.
333 Dybnis, *supra* n. 109, p. 269-270.
334 Claims by individuals needed to exceed USD 100,000.
335 Article 24, EECC's Rules of Procedure.
336 Dybnis, *supra* n. 109, p. 266-267.
337 Shelton, p. 189 Ethiopia's Damages, Final Award., paras 61-65.

of proof had been met; iii) whether there was causality between the wrongful act and the injury;[338] and iv) the economic capacity of the countries before the Commission, as both states were 'the poorest on earth'.[339]

5.5 Standard of Proof

The standard of proof adopted in the context of large-scale reparations is usually influenced by the fact that applicants typically submit incomplete evidence. One reason for submitting incomplete evidence is that victims might have fled the conflict area, thereby obstructing their access to evidence. A further complication comes in the form of the lengthy period of time that usually passes between a violation and the consequent reparations process. The nature of the said violation may also make proving it difficult in practice, as is the case with sexual violence, for instance. Finally, public records in affected countries tend to be inaccessible or of poor quality.[340] Since higher evidentiary requirements will discourage victims from applying, standards of proof are generally quite relaxed.

5.5.1 National Reparations Programmes

Both the Peruvian CVR's Final Report and the PIR are silent in respect of the standard of proof that victims needed to meet in order to prove the harm claimed.[341] The CVR however referred to the standard of proof used in gathering all the data that led to its final report. Contrary to judicial procedures that require certainty in the evidence, the CVR relied on the principle of 'rationality'.[342] At most, the Regulations of the PIR's law refer to the need for victims to provide supporting documents as well as the names of people who, by way of their testimony, could be able to confirm the claimed violations.[343] Considering the aforementioned requirements of the Regulations, it could be presumed that testimonies may have also been the main source used to prove claims. Furthermore, testimonies were the main sources for the Peruvian CVR's report – it was based on almost 17,000 private and public testimonies.[344] Finally,

---

338 EECC, *Eritrea's Damages Claims*, *supra* n. 146, para. 28; EECC, *Ethiopia's Damages Claims*, *supra* n. 146, para. 28.

339 EECC, *Eritrea's Damages Claims*, *supra* n. 146, para. 18; EECC, *Ethiopia's Damages Claims*, *supra* n. 146, para. 18.

340 Niebergall, *supra* n. 3, p. 148-150.

341 However, the CVR refers to the standard of proof for the authorities in charge of determining the bodily remains of victims in relation to the Protocol for the Excavation of Inhumated Human Remains, where the standard of the balance of probabilities relating to the quality and quantity of evidence is required to identify people. See: CVR's Final Report, Vol. IX, p. 275.

342 CVR's Final Report, Vol. I, p. 40.

343 Article 75, Regulations of the PIR's law.

344 Laplante, *supra* n. 34, p. 70.

in the identification of beneficiaries, a flexible approach was adopted with regard to evidence.[345] This seems to match the difficulties that victims have in providing documentation relating to their account of the violations, a difficulty that increases with the passing of time. Otherwise, imposing a high standard of proof in the context of mass victimization may imply re-victimization.[346]

On the other hand, the Moroccan IER adopted a very peculiar approach towards the burden of proof. It is a general principle of law that claimants must prove their assertion (*onus probandi* or the burden of proof). Yet, under certain circumstances, international human rights courts have shifted the burden of proof away from the claimant. The IER, however, neither held that the burden of proof was to be borne by the claimants, nor that it was the responsibility of the state. Instead, it decided that the IER itself was the body bearing the *onus probandi* in relation to checking the status of the petitioner, as well as proactively investigating the violation which was the subject of the petition and the injuries resulting from this violation.[347] Having established the body responsible for proving victims' claims, the IER decided to adopt an intimate conviction (also known as the sufficiency of evidence) as the standard of proof. The IER listed several elements that constituted acceptable proof, including communications, the testimonies of victims and officials, data from banks, judgments, available information concerning detention centres, and the reports stemming from its own in-depth investigations, both in situ and deriving from academic research.[348] Significantly, the IER was supported by international experts and more than 100 temporary staff.[349]

5.5.2 Mass Claims Reparations

The UNCC, in its Provisional Rules for Claims Procedures (UNCC Rules), clearly established that the burden of proof lay with the claimant.[350] Bearing in mind the challenges faced by claimants in providing sufficient evidence after a war where documentation is likely to have been destroyed, the UNCC decided to lower the required levels of evidence[351] and adopted a 'relaxed' standard.[352] In this light, it

345 ICTJ, *supra* n. 64, p. 9-10.

346 ICTJ, A Practitioners's Perspective on Forms of Justice in Peru and in Colombia. Available at: <https://www.ictj.org/news/practitioners-perspective-forms-justice-peru-and-colombia>.

347 IER's Final Report, Vol. 3, p. 68.

348 OHCHR, *supra* n. 33, p. 18, Footnote 31; IER's Final Report, Vol. 3, p. 68-69; IER's Final Report (English version), Volume 2: Establishing Truth and Responsibilities regarding Human Rights Violations (2009), p. 104 (Hereinafter CVR's Final Report, Vol. 2).

349 ICTJ, Morocco Progress Report 2005, p. 16-17.

350 Article 35 (1), UNCC's Rules.

351 Taylor, *supra* n. 97, p. 208.

352 van Houtte, Das and Delmartino, *supra* n. 92, p. 347.

adopted three standards of proof: 'simple documentation', 'reasonable minimum', and the 'balance of probability test'.[353]

Claims under Categories 'A' and 'B' were required to bring 'simple documentation', other appropriate evidence sufficient to prove the basic facts and the actual amount of loss claimed.[354] The evidence for claims under Category 'C' needed to meet the 'reasonable minimum'.[355] For example, claims for forced displacement (Category A) needed to bring simple documentation, such as a plane ticket, while Category C claims might be supported by proof of identity, personal statements, witness statements, and/or many other forms of documentary evidence, ranging from photographs to bank records.[356] The standard of proof applied to Categories 'D', 'E', and 'F' was even stricter than the one applied to the preceding categories. For these claims, the standard of proof was the 'balance of probability test'.[357] This indicates that claimants were required to prove in a flexible but convincing manner that they were entitled to compensation, rather than having to prove the occurrence of hard facts.[358]

The UNCC accepted a wide range of sources as evidence, including independent reports produced by the UN, government agencies, and by other international organisations, as well as academic research, medical reports, and witness and claimant statements.[359] These were particularly relevant for claims under Categories 'A', 'B', and 'C'.[360] With respect to Categories 'D', 'E', and 'F', the panels had full discretion to adopt special procedures in accordance with the particular characteristics of each claim.[361] The Commissioners were free to request additional evidence, including expert testimonies.[362] The UNCC has thus demonstrated that the standard of proof can be flexible and adjusted, so as to facilitate the process of reparations and ensure expeditiousness.[363] Likewise, it has been suggested that mass claims compensation

353 Article 35 (2) - (4), UNCC's Rules.

354 Article 35 (2) (a) - (b), UNCC's Rules.

355 Article 35 (2) (c), UNCC's Rules.

356 Kazazi, M., "An Overview of Evidence before the United Nations Compensation Commission", 1 *International Law Forum du droit international* (1999), p. 221-223; UNCC, *Report and Recommendations made by the Panel of Commissioners concerning the First Instalment of Individual Claims for Damages up to USD 100,000*, Doc. S/AC.26/1994/3, 21 December 1994, p. 24-26.

357 Niebergall, *supra* n. 3, p. 159. In addition, the UNCC decided that 'no loss shall be compensated by the Commission solely on the basis of an explanatory statement provided by the claimant'. See: UNCC Decision 46, *Explanatory Statements by Claimants in Categories "D", "E" and "F"*, Doc. S/AC.26/Dec.46, 3 February 1998.

358 van Haersolte-van Hof, J., "Innovations to Speed Mass Claims: New Standards of Proof" in Permanent Court of Arbitration (ed.) *Redressing Injustices through Mass Claims Processes: Innovative Responses to Unique Challenges* (Oxford, OUP 2006) p. 15.

359 McCarthy, *supra* n. 328, p. 271-272; Singh, *supra* n. 51, p. 73-75.

360 Singh, *supra* n. 51, p. 85.

361 Article 38, Rules.

362 Article 36, UNCC's Rules.

363 Niebergall, *supra* n. 3, p. 165; McCarthy, *supra* n. 328, p. 270.

commissions typically use a relaxed standard of proof, sometimes referred to as a standard of plausibility.[364] This invokes the idea of a trade-off, so to speak, between the adequacy of the evidence and the level of compensation.[365] For instance, suffering was presumed when a spouse, child, or parent had been killed, as well as when an individual was deprived of all economic resources, so as to threaten his or her survival and that of his or her spouse, children, or parents.[366] Presumptions were also used in determining the loss suffered (specifically, a presumption of the value).[367]

As was the case with the UNCC, claimants bore the burden of proof within the EECC.[368] But in contrast to the UNCC, the EECC applied a high standard of proof.[369] It adopted an 'amalgam' approach, located somewhere between the standard of 'clear and convincing evidence' and the 'balance of probabilities'.[370] However, in cases relating to rape or sexual abuse, the EECC recognized that it was unlikely to receive detailed and explicit proof of these violations, especially when taking into account the cultural context.[371] The EECC recognized the practical problems in gathering evidence and quantifying damages, as well as the complexity of the claims.[372] Hence, it often relied on inferences and logical analysis.[373] It also applied a lower standard of proof as a trade-off for a lower level of compensation.[374] The primary sources of evidence before the EECC were affidavits and testimonies;[375] other evidence also included documents, photographs, news reports, statements by officials, administrative and court documents, and medical reports, *inter alia*.[376]

5.6 Causality

Reparations are to be awarded for the harm suffered as a consequence of the commission of the crimes for which a person or state is liable. Understanding causality is a fairly complex matter. Under international law, causality is composed of two elements: factual causation (also known as '*sine qua non test*', 'cause-in-fact', and the 'but-for test') and legal causation, which is generally identified through three

364 van Haersolte-van Hof, *supra* n. 358, p. 22.
365 Gray, *supra* n. 45, p. 890.
366 UNCC Decision 3, *supra* n. 318, p. 2.
367 Taylor, *supra* n. 97, p. 209.
368 Article 14, EECC's RoP.
369 Kidane, *supra* n. 232, p. 71.
370 EECC, *Eritrea's Damages Claims*, *supra* n. 146, para. 36; EECC, *Ethiopia's Damages Claims*, *supra* n. 146, para. 36.
371 EECC, *Central Front – Eritrea's Claims 2, 4, 6, 7, 8 & 22, supra* n. 158, para. 39.
372 EECC, *Eritrea's Damages Claims*, *supra* n. 146, para. 34 and 36; EECC, *Ethiopia's Damages Claims*, *supra* n. 146, para. 34 and 36.
373 Kidane, *supra* n. 232, p. 84.
374 EECC, *Eritrea's Damages Claims*, *supra* n. 146, para. 38.
375 Kidane, *supra* n. 232, p. 77-78.
376 Ibid., p. 32-33.

tests: directness, proximity and foreseeability.[377] Factual causation refers to whether an injury is attributable a certain entity. There must be a clear, unbroken connection between the unlawful act or omission and the injury. Legal causation, on the other hand, concerns the liability for certain injuries. The entity which committed the unlawful act/omission should have foreseen the injuries that its unlawful conduct would cause. There must not have been other causes leading to the injury besides the unlawful act itself.[378] Wühler claims that, rather than a principle, causality is a policy used by tribunals to ensure that reparations are awarded on a fair basis.[379] Whether it is a policy or not, de Greiff has claimed that collective reparation programmes cannot follow the traditional legal approach of reparations grounded on a linkage between the claimed violation and the harm as well as holding the direct perpetrator liable for the payment for such harm. Instead they are tools to bring social solidarity civic trust and recognition.[380]

5.6.1 National Reparations Programmes

Significantly, the Peruvian CVR and the Regulations of the PIR's law seem to be in line with de Greiff's reasoning, as they completely omit to refer to causality as a requirement for either the individual or the collective component of the national reparations programme. At most, the CVR referred to the existence of a link between marginalization and the intensity of the violence suffered.[381] The CVR thus suggests that marginalization and poverty were the causes of the violence suffered. Yet the IER maintained that a causal relationship between the injuries asserted and the violations claimed was an important element in the Commission's analysis of the petitions.[382] However, the IER failed to clarify how its use of presumptions (and of analogies in particular) constituted a test of causality.

5.6.2 Mass Claims Reparations

In the context of the UNCC, the standard of factual causation was already established by the UNSC – harms 'directly' caused by the invasion and occupation of Kuwait by Iraq.[383] Consequently, the UNCC decided that in order to establish whether a harm was a direct consequence of the Iraqi invasion, 'considerations of logic, fairness

377 See: Chapter II in the Section on Causality.
378 van Zoelen, *supra* n. 8, p. 39.
379 Wühler, N., "Causation and Directness of Loss as Elements of Compensability before the United Nations Compensation Commission", in R. Lillich (ed.), *The United Nations Compensation Commission* (New York, Transnational Publishers 1995), p. 233.
380 de Greiff, *supra* n. 35, p. 451-452.
381 Laplante, *supra* n. 34, p. 71.
382 IER's Final Report, Vol. 3, p. 61.
383 Wühler, *supra* n. 379, p. 207; Gattini, *supra* n. 6, p. 172.

and equity' were applicable. After studying relevant jurisprudence, it concluded that direct and indirect losses are used as synonyms for proximate and remote losses, respectively. Thus, an adequate test to determine such direct or indirect loss was that of 'proximate cause'.[384] Significantly, Rovine and Hanessian have affirmed that the questions related to the foreseeability of damage were more meaningful than the application a direct test.[385]

The UNCC determined the meaning of direct loss as any loss arising from: i) Iraq's military operations during the period between 2 August 1990 up until 2 March 1991, for which it is liable; ii) departure from or an inability to leave Iraq or Kuwait; iii) actions or omissions by officials, agents, or employees of the government of Iraq or its controlled entities; iv) the breakdown of civil order in Kuwait or Iraq; and v) hostage-taking or other illegal detention.[386] In addition, vi) any direct environmental damage could be compensated.[387] Furthermore, the UNCC clarified that direct loss could also stem from: vii) the military actions of the coalition against Iraq; viii) mental pain and anguish, regardless of the existence of physical injury;[388] and even ix) death as a result of health problems stemming from the lack of availability of medical facilities during the occupation.[389] In addition, regarding businesses, direct loss could include x) losses in future earnings and profits 'where they can be ascertained with reasonable certainty'.[390]

The UNCC also outlined which losses are not to be considered 'direct'. Losses as a consequence of the embargo,[391] the costs of military operations of Kuwait, losses that could have been reasonably prevented.[392] Finally, the UNCC was confronted with certain losses arising simultaneously out of Iraq's liability and out of the UN sanctions imposed during the war (parallel causation). In this light, the UNCC decided that as long as the claim could demonstrate a direct causation stemming from Iraq's liability, it would be compensated.[393]

---

384 See: UNCC, *supra* n. 356, p. 21-22.

385 Rovine, A.W. and Hannesian, G., "Toward a Foreseeability Approach to Causation Questions at the United Nations Compensation Commission", in R. Lillich (ed.), *The United Nations Compensation Commission* (New York, Transnational Publishers 1995), p. 249.

386 UNCC Decision 1, *supra* n. 285, para. 18; UNCC Decision 7, *supra* n. 226, para. 6, 21, and 34.

387 UNCC Decision 7, *supra* n. 226, para. 35.

388 van Zoelen, *supra* n. 8, p. 45.

389 Wühler, *supra* n. 379, p. 223; UNCC Decision 12, *Claims for which Established Filing Deadlines are Extended, Doc.* S/AC.26/1992/12, 25 September 1992.

390 UNCC Decision 9, *supra* n. 326, para. 19.

391 Wühler, *supra* n. 283, p. 259.

392 van Zoelen, *supra* n. 8, p. 45.

393 UNCC Decision 15, *Compensation for Business Losses Resulting from Iraq's Unlawful Invasion and Occupation of Kuwait where the Trade Embargo and Related Measures were also a cause*, Doc. S/AC 26/1992/15, 4 January 1993, para. II.

The EECC upheld a 'sufficiently close causal connection' between the injury and the unlawful conduct as a precondition to be awarded reparations.[394] Hence, it discussed the standard of legal causation at length to find out which test would reveal such a sufficient causality.[395] While the EECC's research into international law confirmed that sufficient legal causation is generally a precondition for awards of compensation, it found that under international law there is no uniform causal test. Instead, various tests are used, including 'reasonable, direct, proximate, foreseeable or certain'.[396] The EECC adopted the test of 'proximate cause'. In applying this test, the EECC gave weight to two elements: whether a given damage was foreseeable by the wrongful actor, and whether a given damage was compensable.[397]

5.7 Implementation of Collective Reparations

In general, the process of implementing reparations for a large number of victims is marked by similar difficulties across cases. These include how to translate recommendations and initiatives into benefits, how to define time frames for the effective implementation of the reparations, how to define the institutions involved, and how to identify and reach out to victims and beneficiaries, among others.[398]

5.7.1 National Reparations Programmes

The CVR's recommendations on reparations were made law in 2005 through the PIR's law and the CMAN was tasked with developing a reparations programme and overseeing its implementation.[399] This Commission was helped with the identification of individual and collective victims by the National Council of Reparations (NCR).[400] The implementation of the reparations was done by different national ministries, in particular those of agriculture, education, women, and social development, as well as regional and local governments.[401] The CMAN was in charge of coordinating these 'executing entities'.[402] At the local level, the Managing Committee (Comité

394 EECC, *Eritrea's Damages Claims*, *supra* n. 146, para. 29, 39; EECC, *Ethiopia's Damages Claims*, *supra* n. 146, para. 29, 39.
395 EECC Decision 7, *Guidance Regarding Jus ad Bellum Liability*, 27 July 2007, para. 7-14.
396 Ibid., para. 7.
397 Ibid., para. 13.
398 Correa, *supra* n. 125, p. 216.
399 The CMAN also issues reports.
400 Articles 51 and 64 of the Regulations of the PIR's law. The NCR is an organ under the Ministry of Justice and Human Rights and is in charge of the legal framework and functioning of the Unique Victims Registry. The members of the Reparations Council hold an *ad honorem* position, and cannot be part of the public administration. See the official website. Available at: <https://www.minjus.gob.pe/consejo-de-reparaciones/>.
401 Articles 28 and 53 of the Regulations of the PIR's law.
402 Articles 54 and 57 of the Regulations of the PIR's law.

de Gestión) supervises the implementation of collective reparations on behalf of the community that elected each committee. Although the CMAN's mandate includes the supervision of PIR compliance, the whole collective reparation process has also been monitored by civil society organizations, namely the ICTJ and APRODEH.[403] These two NGOs have constantly issued reports regarding the status of the implementation as well as providing recommendations to improve such implementation.

The PIR was composed of seven reparations programmes,[404] of which collective reparations constituted four main projects: institutional strengthening, productive capacity and economic infrastructure support, support for the displaced to return, and the strengthening of basic services and cultural heritage.[405] The CMAN unilaterally decided to present a PIR plan that only focused on two forms of collective reparations: productive capacity and economic infrastructure support, and the strengthening of basic services and cultural heritage.[406] The CMAN seemed to have prioritised measures aimed at tackling marginalisation and poverty[407] and, thus, it embraced a transformative approach. This led to some frustration among victims who complained about mostly receiving reparations in the form of public services to which they had been entitled prior to their victimisation.[408]

The CMAN followed the CVR's recommendations and adopted a decentralised approach, moreover establishing a specific amount of money for each community to implement the collective reparations.[409] In addition, the implementation of collective reparations was to be a gradual process in which the collectivities most affected and impoverished were to be prioritised.[410] Through consultations in the affected communities, the CMAN prioritized a number of communities to receive around USD 33,000 for infrastructural projects negotiated between communities and implemented by local councils.[411] The implementation of the projects started in 2007 and by 2011 almost 60% of the approved projects had been implemented.[412] At the beginning, communities chose to build community centres, irrigation projects, and

403 The two organisations follow up on the reparations and issue reports that contains recommendations.

404 These progammes were: civil rights restitution, reparations in education, reparations in health, collective reparations, symbolic reparations and economic reparations. See: CVR's Final Report, Vol. IX, p. 159-202.

405 CVR's Final Report, Vol. IX, p. 196-200; Article 27 of the Regulations of the PIR's law.

406 Roht-Arriaza, N., "Reparations and Economic, Social and Cultural Rights" in D.N. Sharp, (ed.) *Justice and economic violence in transition* (New York, Springer 2014), p. 120; ICTJ and APRODEH, *supra* n. 63, p. 12.

407 Articles 7(e), and 58 of the Regulations of the PIR's law; Guillerot and Carranza, *supra* n. 7, p. 31.

408 Laplante, *supra* n. 69, p. 370; Correa, Guillerot, and Magarrell, *supra* n. 41, p. 411.

409 CVR's Final Report, Vol. IX, p. 195-196; Articles 7(j) and 29 of the Regulations of the PIR's law.

410 Article 29 of the Regulations of the PIR's law.

411 Article 58 of the Regulations of the PIR's law; Roht-Arriaza, *supra* n. 406, p. 120; ICTJ and APRODEH, *supra* n. 63, p. 9; Yet the criteria in prioritizing were not transparent. See: Guillerot and Carranza, *supra* n. 7, p. 31.

412 ICTJ and APRODEH, *supra* n. 63, p. 12.

schools. However, the priorities later changed to water, sanitation, livestock, and management training.[413] The implementation of projects is still ongoing as of 2018, so all collective reparations have not yet been completed.

This implementation was not exempt from problems. According to the ICTJ and APRODEH, the selection of the priority communities was not transparent.[414] Furthermore, delays in the implementation of projects have been evident.[415] Despite the fact that reparations were to be implemented within 6 years, at present there are still a few projects that remain pending in rural communities.[416] And by 2017 very few projects had taken place in urban communities.[417] Although the CMAN established that every approved project should start and end with a ceremony,[418] this practice has helped very few victims to distinguish collective reparations from national policies to eradicate poverty.[419] Hence, the government has failed to link service-based collective reparations with symbolic measures.[420] This is perhaps a consequence of victims having received very little information on the process of reparations. In some communities, less than 21% of the population participated in the selection of the projects.[421] In addition, women were underrepresented to the point of near absence.[422]

This shows that although the design and implementation of the collective reparations was meant to be grounded on victims' participatory approach, this ambition fell short in practice. According to Laplante, victims' participation was affected by the lack of sufficient outreach from the CMAN. In addition, Laplante claims that the CMAN did not demonstrate an availability to meet with victims and to consult victims' organisations.[423] In fact, the ICTJ contends that one of the problems in implementing the collective reparations in Peru is that the projects implemented were not chosen by the victims but by the CMAN, and thus they had no relationship with the damage suffered.[424] Significantly, a 2011 survey conducted on

413 Roht-Arriaza, *supra* n. 406, p. 120-121; ICTJ and APRODEH, *supra* n. 63, p. 12-13.

414 ICTJ and APRODEH, *supra* n. 63, p. 10.

415 Laplante, L.J. and Theidon, K., "Truth with Consequences: Justice in Post-Truth Commission Peru", *Human Rights Quaterly* (2007), p. 231.

416 CVR's Final Report, Vol. IX, p. 203; ; CMAN's Annual Report 2016, p. 53.

417 Namely in three urban areas: Yamana, La Pax y Pocras. See: The financed projects in the CMAN's website: <https://cman.minjus.gob.pe/wp-content/uploads/2017/07/ProyectosFinanciados_COLECTIVAS.pdf> and <http://andina.pe/agencia/noticia-a-mediados-ano-se-iniciaran-reparaciones-colectivas-zona-urbana-anuncia-cman-227546.aspx>; Roht-Arriaza, *supra* n. 406, p. 121.

418 ICTJ and APRODEH, *supra* n. 63, p. 9.

419 Waardt, *supra* n. 153, p. 838-839.

420 ICTJ, *Victims in of Peru's internal conflict still await Reparations* (ICTJ 2013). Available at: <https://www.ictj.org/news/victims-peru-civil-war-still-await-reparations>.

421 ICTJ and APRODEH, *supra* n. 63, p. 12-13.

422 Guillerot and Carranza, *supra* n. 7, p. 32.

423 Laplante, L.J., "Negotiating Reparation Rights: The Participatory and Symbolic Quotients" 19 *Buffalo Human Rights Law Review* (2012), p. 25.

424 ICTJ and APRODEH, *supra* n. 298, p. 29.

communities where collective reparations took place showed that victims considered the projects to be insufficient. Victims based their responses not on the delays, the lack of participation, or the nature of the reparations, but rather on their desire to receive more service-oriented projects.[425] Significantly, in its 2016 report, the CMAN recommended that the participation of victims should be strengthened, either directly or through organizations.[426]

The reparations were supposed to be financed by the government itself. In this light, the CVR proposed the creation of a National Reparations Fund financed by an annual budget allocation and resource grant from the Peruvian national fund set up to recover assets from former state officials who had committed the crime of state embezzlement,[427] known as FEDADOI.[428] The Peruvian government did not create a national reparations fund. Even so, by 2009 more than USD 53 million had been spent on collective reparations. The majority of the money came from the national budget and the FEDADOI. Additionally, several municipalities allocated a part of their budget to extend approved projects. Mining companies also contributed to the implementation of collective reparations.[429] Finally, the Regulations of the PIR's law foresaw the possibility for the CMAN to seek international cooperation in the financing of reparations.[430]

The CVR recommended a system for the prevention of double reparations which was subsequently embraced by the PIR's Regulations. To this end, the reparations would not benefit: persons who had previously received reparations or benefits, or indemnification via a national political, judicial, or administrative procedure, as well as those who had received reparations within the Inter-American System of Human Rights.[431] In addition, victims who had received benefits from reparations programmes would leave civil suits against the State without effect, but would not interrupt or suspend criminal cases against individual perpetrators. If the criminal cases lead to civil claims, then the victims would need to return the benefits or compensation received from the state reparations programmes.[432]

Although the majority of TRCs are called upon to recommend reparations, the Moroccan IER is the only one that has also dealt with the implementation of reparations, albeit partially. The IER implemented a part of the individual reparations ordered and provided immediate health assistance through its in-house medical unit. The collective reparations recommended were nevertheless implemented by other

---

425 ICTJ and APRODEH, *supra* n. 63, p. 38-39.
426 CMAN's Annual Report 2016, p. 53.
427 CVR's Final Report, Vol. IX, p. 204.
428 FEDAOI stands for Fondo Especial de Administración de Dineros Obtenidos Ilícitamente.
429 ICTJ and APRODEH, *supra* n. 63, p. 15; Roht-Arriaza, *supra* n. 406, p. 138-139.
430 Article 58, Regulations of the PIR's law.
431 CVR's Final Report, Vol. IX, p. 153-156; Article 52 of the Regulations of the PIR's law.
432 de Greiff, *supra* n. 127, p. 59; OHCHR, *supra* n. 33, p. 35.

bodies.[433] It is important to recall that among the individual measures ordered by the IER, financial compensation played an important role. The implementation of financial compensation awards followed the approach of the IAC. They were distributed in different forms: pensions, lump sums, and apportionments among family members.[434] During this process, a gender-sensitive method was employed. For instance, the apportioning technique favoured women and tried to overcome the inequalities that Morocco's national Sharia law imposed on women's enjoyment of their rights. More specifically, the IAC determined that widows were to receive 40% of the monetary awards, in contrast to the 8% that widows would usually obtain under local inheritance law.[435]

The collective reparations proposed by the IER were embraced by the King, who tasked the National Council on Human Rights (known by its French acronym CNDH),[436] the successor of the CCDH,[437] with the implementation of those reparations. The CNDH, in its capacity as a policymaking body, was aided by the *Fondation Caisse de Dépot et de Gestion* (FCDG),[438] a non-profit organisation funded by the state *Caisse de Dépot et de Gestion*. The FCDG acted as a project management agency for the CCDH, making calls for project proposals and assisting in the organisation of the approval and implementation of projects.[439] It also played a key role in providing technical, financial, and logistical support.[440] In order to implement the community reparations, the CCDH and the FCDG designed a 6-step plan:[441]

433 Alston and Knuckey, *supra* n. 165, p. 197, Footnote 32.

434 OHCHR, *supra* n. 33, p. 31-32.

435 OHCHR, *supra* n. 33, p. 32; Rubio-Marín, R., "The Gender of Reparations in Transitional Societies" in R. Rubio-Marín (ed.), *The Gender of Reparations: Unsettling Sexual Hierarchies while Redressing Human Rights Violations* (Cambridge, CUP 2009), p. 17.

436 In French: *Conseil National des Droits de l'Homme.*

437 Royal Decree No. 1.11.19 of March 1, 2011 allowed for this. Available at: <http://www.ccdh.org.ma/sites/default/files/documents/CNDH-BO-Fr_1_.pdf>.

438 The FCDG is a non-profit organisation created by the stated-owned financial institution called *Caisse de Dépôt et de Gestion* which is committed to solidarity actions through the support of projects related to social development and social responsibility. See the official website: <http://www.fondationcdg.ma/presentation>.

439 Guillerot and Carranza, *supra* n. 7, p. 27.

440 Ibid., p. 56.

441 IER Follow-up Report, December 2009, p. 63-71.

1) Institutional building by establishing four bodies to implement the CR.[442]
2) Designing local projects aiming to improve the living conditions of communities, with special attention to women and children, to preserve memory, and to reinforce local stakeholders' capacity with the participation of members of the affected communities.
3) The mobilization of partners to support the implementation of communities' reparations.
4) Developing a proposal to convert four former secret detention centres into projects of memory preservation.
5) Capacity building on empowerment, positive conflict management, good governance, gender approach, and project architecture through training sessions.
6) Designing income-generating projects through the involvement of a number of social stakeholders, including the ministries.

In 2007, Morocco started implementing its community reparations programmes. In 2008, the FCDG launched the first call for proposals for community reparations projects to be implemented by local NGOs. The proposals included the following themes: i) building the capacity of local stakeholders in areas of local governance; ii) memorialization; iii) supporting income-generating activities; iv) gender mainstreaming; and v) environmental protection. The budget for the implementation of collective reparations was around USD 6.5 million. This was financed by the national government, as well as by international donors. For instance, the European Commission donated approximately USD 3.7 million (EUR 3 million) as part of a special agreement between the EU and Morocco called the EU European Neighbourhood Policy of 2004.[443] The United Nations Development Programme also financed the said collective reparations.[444] However, individual reparations were mostly financed by the Moroccan government.[445]

In their implementation, CR were characterized by open dialogue with different actors and mediation so that the affected regions might benefit from economic and

---

442 1) National Steering Committee composed of the CCDH, the FCDG, the Ministry of Finance, the Ministry of the Interior, donors, representatives of local coordination bodies, and the Central Management Unit whose mandate was to ensure that the collective reparations are implemented according to recommendations of the IER; 2) The Central Management Unit hosted by the FCDG was responsible for the human, technical, financial and logistical management of the projects; 3) Regional Coordination Bodies: each region has a coordination body that represents a number of local authorities and NGOs, 4) Council Coordination Bodies composed of one representative of each community whose mandate was to facilitate information between them and the steering committee. See: Guillerot and Carranza, *supra* n. 7, p. 56.

443 Guillerot and Carranza, *supra* n. 7, p. 12, 27, 58; ICTJ, *Morocco: Gender and the Transitional Justice Process* (ICTJ 2011), p. 35, 57.

444 Lefranc and Vairel, *supra* n. 216, p. 239.

445 Article 23 of the IER's statute stipulates that the IER was allocated a special budget.

social development programmes and receive justice and reinstatement.[446] The IER created a plan for reparations which would benefit not just specific affected victims but also society as a whole. The plan included the participation of many actors: victims, state actors, human rights organizations, and local development organizations.[447] As in Peru, affirmative action was also applied in the implementation – the most affected communities were prioritised.[448] In addition, women were also given priority. This is perhaps a consequence of the special attention that the IER gave to women during the conduct of the consultations that led to the adoption of its recommendations.[449]

By 2006, the distribution of individual compensation to victims had almost been completed, with USD 85 million distributed to some 9,000 people. The CCDH had signed agreements with ministries and official agencies to provide victims and their families with medical care and vocational training at the state's expense.[450]

By 2011, 5 years after the IER Final report, advances were made in compensating victims and in implementing the community reparations. The implementation of other individual measures, such as medical and social rehabilitation, only began in 2011. The recommendations on institutional and legislative reforms have in large measure yet to be carried out.[451]

5.7.2 Mass Claims Reparations

As already mentioned earlier, individuals and corporations needed to submit their claims to the UNCC through their national governments. Governments were in charge of collecting, consolidating, and submitting claims to the UNCC.[452] In consolidating the claims, each government was expected to verify them to avoid fraud and the excessive submission of claims.[453] To this end, some governments established national programmes to assist claimants.[454] However, no standards for claim verification existed.[455] There were only two uniform rules for claims: i) claims needed to be submitted in an official form provided by the UNCC,[456] and ii) deadlines for filing claims needed to be met, although the UNCC did accept late claims.[457]

446 IER's Final Report, Vol. 3, p. 35.
447 IER'S Final Report, Vol. 5, p. 393.
448 Guillerot and Carranza, *supra* n. 7, p. 27.
449 IER's Final Report, Vol. 1, p. 75-76.
450 ICTJ, *supra* n. 79.
451 ICTJ, *supra* n. 443, p. 8, 9.
452 In special situations, entities such as the UNHCR were allowed to bring the claims on behalf of individuals. See: Petrović, *supra* n. 90, p. 851.
453 van Zoelen, *supra* n. 8, p. 6.
454 Taylor, *supra* n. 97, p. 203.
455 van Zoelen, *supra* n. 8, p. 32.
456 Category 'A' claims needed to be submitted in an electronic form and the rest of categories on paper. See: Article 7, UNCC's Rules.
457 Taylor, *supra* n. 97, p. 201-202.

In addition, governments were allowed to deduct a fee from the awards, depending on the amount requested.[458] Once a claim had been submitted to the UNCC, it was first examined by the Secretariat, which in turn would send it to the Governing Council and later to the panels. A panel needed to complete its report within 120 days for urgent claims and within 180 days for all others.[459] Once the panel submitted its decision and the Governing Council approved it, the decision was final and no appeal mechanism existed.[460] Compensation granted was given to the governments or special agencies to distribute to individual claimants within a fixed time period of 6 months.[461] Once completed, this had to be reported to the UNCC within 3 months with a description of the mechanism employed to distribute the compensation.[462] If the government failed to properly disburse the awards within a 12-month period, it was required to return the undistributed awards to the Commission.[463] Significantly, states were free to create mechanisms to distribute payments 'in a fair, efficient and timely manner'.[464]

The UNCC also established a system to prevent double compensation. Claimants had the obligation to inform the UNCC about any parallel compensation proceedings regarding the same loss. Governments were encouraged to provide the UNCC with information regarding any parallel proceedings pending against Iraq in their jurisdiction or any losses awarded to individuals as a result of Iraq's occupation and invasion.[465] In sum, before the UNCC, states serve as agents for the implementation of compensation measures. The implementation itself was somewhat straightforward, all things considered. It must be stated, however, that in contrast to most post-conflict situations, Iraq had the resources to pay for the UNCC awards, which made it possible for the compensation to take place.

As opposed to the UNCC, the EECC's legal framework lacks a procedure to distribute the awards. Instead, the EECC trusted that the governments would pay the awards promptly and that relief to the individual victims would be afforded.[466] Neither of the two has happened, however, mostly because of a lack of funding, but

---

458 UNCC Decision 18, *Distribution of Payments and Transparency*, Doc. S/AC.26/Dec.18, 24 March 1994, para. 1.

459 Article 39, UNCC's Rules; UNCC Decision 35, *Further Procedures for Review of Claims Under Article 38*, Doc. S/AC.26/Dec.35, 13 December 1995.

460 Article 40 (4), UNCC's Rules.

461 UNCC Decision 18, *supra* n. 458, para. 3.

462 Ibid., para. 4; UNCC Decision 48, *Return of Undistributed Funds*, Doc. S/AC.26/Dec. 48, 3 Feb, 1998, preamble.

463 UNCC Decision 18, *supra* n. 458, para. 4-6; UNCC Decision 48, *Decision Concerning the Return of Undistributed Funds,* Doc. S/AC.26/Dec.48 (1998), 3 February 1998.

464 UNCC Decision 18, *supra* n. 458.

465 UNCC Decision 13, *Further Measures to Avoid Multiple Recovery of Compensation by Claimants*, Doc. S/AC 26/1992/13, 25 September 1992, para. 2.

466 Dybnis, *supra* n. 109, p. 237.

also because of a lack of political will.[467] Both Eritrea and Ethiopia have expressed their dissatisfaction with the EECC's work.[468] Like the UNCC, the EECC aimed to prevent double compensation. In principle, claims would only be accepted if there was no pending litigation for the same harm, unless such litigation had been filed in a different forum prior the Algiers Agreement.[469] However, this requirement was not respected, as the EECC was not able to monitor it.[470] The EECC held hearings and thereafter granted 15 awards[471] in a series of final decisions with no possibilities for an appeal.[472]

The EECC's work was divided into two different phases: a liability phase and a damages phase. The Commission rendered the final decisions of the liability phase in December 2005 and of the damages phase in August 2009.[473] The second phase involved a number of filings of legal pleadings and evidence, as well as a number of hearings.[474] The applicable law included international law and customary international law.[475] In contrast to the workings of the UNCC, the awards were funded by each country.[476] In addition, the EECC's expenses were borne equally by the two states.[477] Furthermore, the EECC allowed for two types of procedures: individual complaints and mass class complaints. The states, however, mainly used the individual procedure and, in doing so, filed government claims.[478] The only exception came with Eritrea's filing of six complaints on behalf of named individuals, of which four were awarded. The EECC awarded the following amounts:[479]

467 Matheson, M.J., "Eritrea-Ethiopia Claims Commission: Damage Awards",13 *ASIL* (2009). Available at: <https://www.asil.org/insights/volume/13/issue/13/eritrea-ethiopia-claims-commission-damage-awards>.
468 Dybnis, *supra* n. 109, p. 274.
469 Article 5 (8), Algiers Agreement.
470 Kidane, *supra* n. 232, p. 40.
471 Ibid., p. 32.
472 Article 5 (17), Algiers Agreement.
473 Kidane, *supra* n. 232, p. 26.
474 EECC, *Eritrea's Damages Claims*, *supra* n. 146, para. 10; EECC, *Ethiopia's Damages Claims*, *supra* n. 146, para. 10.
475 Kidane, *supra* n. 232, p. 30.
476 This is implied in paragraph 17 of Article 5 of the Algiers Agreement which reads as follows: *"Decisions and awards of the Commission shall be final and binding. The parties agree to honour all decisions and to pay any monetary awards rendered against them promptly."*
477 Article 5 (15), Algiers Agreement.
478 Shelton, *supra* n. 33, p. 187.
479 EECC, *Eritrea's Damages Claims*, *supra n.* 146, Award para. 21; EECC, *Ethiopia's Damages Claims*, *supra* n. 146, p. 106, Award para. E.

Government	Compensation awarded	
Eritrea	Four Eritreans[480] 16 findings of liability	USD 2,065,865 USD 161,455,000 USD 163,520,865
Ethiopia	36 findings	USD 174,036,520

It is important to point out that from the amounts awarded, each country owed the other USD 2,000,000 for failing to take sufficient measures to prevent the rapes of known and unknown victims in a number of cities in both countries.[481] When comparing the awards, it is evident that the EECC had decided, in effect, that Eritrea owed almost 11 million dollars to Ethiopia. This sum, however, has not been paid, and thus no compensation has reached victims.[482] Yet one could also infer that the awards demonstrate the resources that would be needed to compensate all victims in Eritrea and Ethiopia. Significantly, the EECC failed to explain how the awarded money would be used to provide redress to victims. Instead, it contemplated the creation of funds for 'relief programmes for categories of victims'.[483] Furthermore, as per 2017, the awards have not been paid.[484] First of all, this failure may be due to the EECC not requiring the governments to identify individual victims, as it considered doing so 'impossible, and certainly inordinately expensive'.[485] Furthermore, a lack of political will from both states to honour the awards was also a decisive element in the failure to provide reparations.[486] In addition, it may be the case that the lack of a dedicated source of funding for the EECC awards has played a role in this. Finally, it was left to each government's discretion to invest their compensation as they saw fit. Yet the EECC advised both governments to use the awards 'to develop and support health programs' for victims, especially for those who had suffered rape.[487]

---

480 Of the six individual claims by Eritrean individual persons, only four were awarded compensation. EECC, *Eritrea's Damages Claims*, *supra* n. 146, para. 20.

481 EECC, *Ethiopia's Damages Claims*, *supra* n. 146, Award para. A (2); EECC, *Eritrea's Damages Claims*, *supra* n. 146, Award para. 6.

482 Giroud and Moss, *supra* n. 44, p. 491; Dybnis, *supra* n. 109, p. 256.

483 EECC Decision 8, *Relief to War Victims*, 27 July 2007, para. 6.

484 Echeverria, G., *The UN Principles and Guidelines on Reparation: is there an Enforceable Right to Reparation for Victims of Human Rights and International Humanitarian Law Violations?*. An unpublished thesis submitted for the Degree of Doctor of Philosophy, University of Essex, 2017, p. 182-183.

485 EECC Decision 8, *supra* n. 483, para. 5.

486 Brilmayer, Giorgetti and Charlton, *supra* n. 331, p. 144.

487 EECC, *Eritrea's Damages Claims*, *supra* n. 146, para. 239; EECC, *Ethiopia's Damages Claims*, *supra* n. 146, para. 110.

5.8 Main Challenges of Implementation

In all of these cases, the design of reparations programmes usually faces similar dilemmas: which measures, which evidence, and for which victims?[488] This is exacerbated by the difficulty in distinguishing between levels of suffering and by the limited resources available. Furthermore, even when these questions have been answered, there are also challenges in the implementation and administration of reparations programmes,[489] such as: for how long? How to operationalize them? Finding a balance between all these aspects may require the incorporation of both symbolic and material measures that deliver goods and services.[490] In this light, victims not only find an answer to their basic needs but also find acknowledgement and truth. It must be stated that material and symbolic measures need to take place in a parallel fashion. Otherwise, the goods and services may be confused with the social services that people are normally supposed to receive as citizens. If victims first receive the symbolic measures, then popular discontent may be well grounded because victims' basic needs did not take priority.[491]

In addition, implementing symbolic and material measures in a parallel fashion allows victims to distinguish between national social services policies and reparations in the form of social services. Peru is an example of the problem inherent in only providing victims with social services as a form of collective reparations. In addition, political will (or the lack thereof) may be one of the biggest obstacles in materialising reparations for large numbers of victims. With this in mind, the CVR strongly emphasised the importance of a strong political will as a precondition for the implementation of reparations.[492] Financing reparations is by far one of the biggest challenges surrounding their implementation. Creative funding solutions should be embraced, such as special taxes for those who benefit from a certain conflict or injustices, the recovery of illegal assets, or debt swaps, such as the Peruvian one.[493] In Peru, the implementation of collective reparations has been affected by budgetary restrictions and a lack of information that have prevented victims from accessing those reparations.[494]

The cases of Peru and Morocco show that collective reparations are to be grounded on a participatory approach where the victims have a say in the design and implementation of their awards. To this end, sufficient outreach to victims is decisive.

488 Roht-Arriaza, *supra* n. 134, p. 179-181.

489 Hayner, *supra* n. 22. p. 180-181.

490 Correa, Guillerot, and Magarrell, *supra* n. 41, p. 407.

491 Guillerot and Carranza, *supra* n. 7, p. 50.

492 CVR's Final Report, Vol. IX, p. 147.

493 OHCHR, *supra* n. 33, p. 132-33.

494 Pérez-León Acevedo, J.P. , "Reparations and Prosecutions after Serious Human Rights Violations: Two Pending Issues in Peru's Transitional Justice Agenda", *Oxford Transitional Justice Working Papers Series* (2010), p. 3. Available at: <https://www.law.ox.ac.uk/sites/files/oxlaw/acevedo1.pdf>.

Regrettably, outreach was a significant problem in both of the aforementioned cases. While in Peru the main problem regarding the outreach to victims was the lack of a strong policy from the CMAN, in Morocco the outreach was attempted through inadequate means. Specifically, the IER published its recommendations on its website. Although the publication had the purpose of enhancing the IER's transparency and legitimacy, publishing the report also carried the potential benefit of motivating victims to demand the implementation of the recommended reparations which they had now been made aware of. However, the high levels of illiteracy and limited internet access among victims made it difficult for them to even know about the IER's work.[495]

The UNCC represents a balance between individual reparations, fairness, and an expedient process to a large number of victims.[496] It is an example of practical justice for the victims of the crime of aggression[497] and has contributed greatly to the process of international claims resolutions.[498] Despite having awarded individual reparations, flexibility in the identification of victims and the evidence required to prove the claims tend to resemble collective reparations.

6 Conclusions

During the last few decades, there has been increasing concern for the need to bring justice to victims of GVHR in societies in transition by providing, among other things, reparations. Increasingly, reparation is recognised as one of the key elements of transitional justice processes.[499] While the legal right to and the necessity of reparations in transitioning societies is often undisputed, repairing all the damage that resulted from past legacies of GVHR while simultaneously rebuilding institutions and affording ESCR to all citizens is often unrealistic. This is especially true in contexts in which the country is confronted with general issues of poverty and a lack of resources. Hence, full reparations are not provided through national reparations programmes.[500] The larger the claims, the more difficult it is to strike a balance between individual justice and fairness.[501]

National reparations programmes usually establish a 'lump sum of money, services and/or a pension for survivors of violations or their family members'.[502]

495 OHCHR, *supra* n. 33, p. 17, Footnote 26.
496 Taylor, *supra* n. 97, p. 213.
497 Caron and Morris, *supra* n. 90, p. 183.
498 Caron and Morris, *supra* n. 90, p. 185.
499 Tomuschat, *supra* n. 2, p. 579-589, 581.
500 Wierda, M. and de Greiff, P. , *Reparations and the International Criminal Court: A Prospective Role for the Trust Fund for Victims,* International Center for Transitional Justice, 2004; Correa, *supra* n. 125, p. 188.
501 Wühler, *supra* n. 283, p. 266.
502 Roht-Arriaza, *supra* n. 137, p. 663.

While scholars have submitted that, in an ideal scenario, reparations under TJ would consist of a combination of individual and collective awards,[503] they have also accepted that collective reparations are a more realistic and inclusive option for the implementing state. First, in the aftermath of an armed conflict or civil war, a State's economy is generally in ruins. The only way that a state could fulfil its obligation to repair the victims of crimes carried out in the course of the conflict would be to adopt collective reparations, meaning through far-reaching payments or social services. Second, Tomuschat states that '[a]ny individualization of the reparation process would have disruptive effects.' This not only applies to the state's general economy and its ability to provide basic social programmes to all of its citizens, but also to victims themselves.[504] In addition, individual reparations and mass reparations programmes carry the risk of disproportionately benefiting the wealthier, more educated, and urban victims at the expense of poor rural victims.

In this light, collective reparations open the door for a better scenario that allows more victims to benefit from the transitional justice process.[505] Within collective reparations, it is claimed that a transformative approach is the most appropriate. Considering that most GVHR are both a cause and a consequence of inequality and marginalisation, reparations should be aimed at transforming those inequalities and marginalisation. Yet it is important to keep in mind the close relationship between collective reparations and development strategies.[506] Reparations, whether individual or collective, potentially have important spill-over effects on long-term development[507] and the prevention of further crimes. Yet reparations carry a symbolic dimension that social policies do not. Thus, while there are definite similarities between the two, they are conceptually distinct, and reparations should not be perceived as a reclassified form of ESCR.[508]

Although reparations in the form of social programmes may be more feasible and attractive for low-income countries, it must be noted that poorer countries will still face significant challenges in providing reparations. Hence, they require the support of the international community.

Mass claims procedures are usually established to address GVHR that amount to grave violations of international humanitarian law and usually restrict their remedies to those of financial compensation. Although these procedures differ from national reparations programmes, it is evident that they also share some similarities,

503 Ibid., p. 696; Roht-Arriaza and Orlovsky, *supra* n. 43, p. 194; Guillerot and Carranza, *supra* n. 7, p. 40.
504 Magarrell, *supra* n. 5, p. 5-7.
505 de Greiff, *supra* n. 127, p. 60.
506 de Greiff, *supra* n. 276, p. 33, 57.
507 Roht-Arriaza and Orlovsky, *supra* n. 43, p. 174, 205.
508 Buckley-Zistel, S., "Connecting Transitional Justice and Development", (paper presented at the 'International Conference on the Contribution of Civil Society and Victim Participation in Transitional Justice Processes', Marburg (2009); Correa, *supra* n. 125, p. 210.

such as: i) a flexible understanding of the requirements to meet the burden of proof;[509] ii) the potential to provide reparations to a large number of victims; and iii) selective beneficiaries. In addition, as the experience of the UNCC, the EECC, and the Peruvian CVR shows, both measures of reparation seek to avoid double compensation. Both claims procedures and national reparations programmes avoid flooding courts with thousands of individual claims or lawsuits by creating reparations outside the courtroom. In their work, they usually apply relevant rules of international law. For instance, national reparations bodies usually refer to international human rights law, while the mass compensation commissions turn to international law or international humanitarian law.[510]

National collective reparations programmes may be preferred by states because they provide goods and services that help states achieve distributive justice and development.[511] Commissions may be preferable when, in addition to awarding reparations to victims, states need to establish the liability of state actors or armed groups under humanitarian law. While no reparation effort will ever be perfect, some approaches have certain benefits over others.[512] In addition, it must be noted that financial compensation may not contribute to achieving reconciliation and peace. Accordingly, measures of non-repetition would be considered more adequate,[513] while socio-economic services and physical and psychological reparations would be necessary to achieve sustainable reconciliation.[514] Collective reparations are likely to remain resonant in the context of grave violations of human rights and humanitarian law.

CRs may benefit victims and perpetrators. In contrast, individual reparations are supposed to only benefit victims.[515] To meet the challenges of insufficient evidence, claims commissions and TRCs have developed novel techniques. The UNNC has adopted a number of techniques, such as relaxing the standard of proof, clustering or grouping categories of claims, altering evidentiary presumptions, employing statistical sampling, and awarding fixed amounts to certain categories of victims or claims.[516] This has responded to the common difficulty that victims face in

---

509 van Haersolte-van Hof, *supra* n. 358, p. 22; Kristjánsdóttir, *supra* n. 50, p. 185.

510 Article 31, UNCC's Rules.

511 P. de Greiff, "Articulating the Links Between Transitional Justice and Development: Justice and Social Integration" in P. de Greiff and R. Duthie (eds.), *Transitional Justice and Development: Making connections* (New York, Social Science Research Council 2009), p. 41.

512 Correa, *supra* n. 125, p. 185; Buckley-Zistel, *supra* n. 508.

513 Tomuschat, *supra* n. 2, p. 587.

514 Hamber, B., "Repairing the Irreparable: Dealing with double-binds of making reparations for crimes of the past", 5 *Ethnicity and Health* (2000), p. 224.

515 Guillerot and Carranza, *supra* n. 7, p. 41.

516 Niebergall, *supra* n. 3, p. 148-149, 151, 161-165; Kristjánsdóttir, *supra* n. 50, p. 189-190.

gathering evidence.[517] Similarly, the EECC relaxed the standard of evidence, adopted evidentiary presumptions and grouped categories of claims. This is illustrative of the many difficulties that such bodies face but also of how they are prepared and competent to solve those difficulties in creative ways.

517 McKay, F., "What Outcome for Victims?", in D. Shelton (ed.), *The Oxford Handbook of International Human Rights Law* (Oxford, Oxford University Press 2013), p. 945.

Chapter VI
Conclusions

Reparation

The action of restoring something to a proper or former state;
spiritual restoration; the action of making amends for a wrong or loss;
compensation for war damage by a defeated state.
What it cost no one is telling.
Can't subtract what might have been.
Can't add up to a sum we understand.
Can't subdivide what once was seen.
Can carve a tombstone for the dead,
memorialise with flowers and crosses,
exhume a body, clear a name,
issue receipts for wrongs and losses.
But can't repair, and can't restore
an uncut arm, unbruised genital,
untroubled sleep, unscarred face,
unweeping mother, children, faith[1]

1 Introduction

The primary aim of this research was to assess the interplay and compatibility of the individual right to receive reparations with the increasing trend to grant collective awards in the context of gross violations of human rights. While the discourse surrounding the right of all victims of crime, including those of GVHR, to receive reparations clearly establishes that victims are entitled to collective measures *in addition* to individual reparations, in practice collective measures are rarely awarded in a supplementary manner. Instead, when addressing the harm caused by gross violations of human rights, judicial and non-judicial bodies tend to award victims *only* collective reparations. In this light, the main research question of this book was:

What are the tensions between the individual right to receive reparations and awarding collective reparations for victims of gross violations of human rights?

1 Loudily, F., "Facing a Bloody Past: Discourses and Practices of Transitional Justice", in C.T. Salmon (ed.) *Communication Yearbook 34* (New York, Routledge 2010), p. 411 citing de Kok, I., *Seasonal fires: Selected and new poems* (New York, Seven Stories 2006), p. 139.

This research analysed the understanding of collective reparations by judicial and non-judicial bodies within three frameworks, namely international human rights law, international criminal law and a selection of transitional justice processes. In conducting such an analysis, as justified in the methodology section of the introductory chapter, the research was limited to studying specific case law from the IACtHR, the ICC and the ECCC. Additionally, the practices of non-judicial mechanisms were examined, specifically those of the Peruvian and Moroccan Truth Commissions and of two mass claims compensation commissions (the UNCC and the EECC). In the course of its inquiry, this research included an examination of the definition, scope and characteristics of collective reparations, as well as their legal foundations and the major challenges faced by their implementation. This final chapter will begin by summarising the general findings of the book based on each chapter's individual conclusions. Subsequently, it will lay a foundation for establishing clear contours regarding the definition of collective reparations with the aim not only of clarifying the content and scope of collective reparations, but also of providing victims of GVHR with realistic expectations regarding the meaning of the right to reparations. Finally, this chapter will address the main challenges that collective reparations present to the three frameworks studied. It is important to note that the analysis conducted in this research neither attempted to empirically assess nor deny the importance and merits of collective reparations when addressing the suffering of victims of GVHR, but rather to employ the lens of human rights to appraise the legal foundations on the basis of which victims of GVHR increasingly receive only collective reparations.

2 The Main Findings of This Research

2.1 Developments Concerning the Right to Reparations

The understanding of victims' reparations within international law has evolved over time. Initially reparations were understood as a state obligation *vis-à-vis* another state, but with the adoption of international human rights instruments, reparations are nowadays considered to be a state obligation in relation to both states and individuals. Reparations under public international law and human rights law share similar characteristics.[2] Yet those characteristics have a different meaning within these fields. For instance, in both fields *restitutio in integrum* has been acknowledged to be a guiding principle when granting reparations. While under international law the ICJ has understood *restitutio in integrum* as measures of restitution aimed to restore the damage caused by the infringement or a violation, the IACtHR has understood it as

2 They should be full, adequate and proportional to the damage incurred, and they should aim for *restitutio in integrum*.

the combination of at least three measures: financial compensation, rehabilitation and satisfaction,[3] especially when addressing GVHR.

Despite the fact that the measures of reparation in the field of international human rights law were understood on the basis of those recognised in public international law (restitution, compensation, and satisfaction), international human rights law also includes measures of rehabilitation and guarantees of non-repetition. Within the field of international human rights law, the research shows a victim-oriented trend in the measures granted by the courts, in particular the IACtHR and the ECtHR. Since the classical understanding of reparations is grounded on tort law and the laws of state responsibility, at first, declaratory judgments and financial compensation played a prominent role in reparations in the field of human rights, especially at the ECtHR. Over the years, however, the IACtHR's remedial approach has contributed to a more holistic and creative understanding of reparations, including both material and non-material (symbolic) measures. With the aim of addressing the particular needs of individual victims as well as preventing further violations, the IACtHR has awarded the five recognised measures of reparation (restitution, compensation, rehabilitation, satisfaction, and guarantees of non-repetition).[4] The IACtHR has not developed a formula that determines an exact combination of appropriate measures; instead it has decided a combination on a case-by-case basis. Yet, the IACtHR usually grants a combination of material and symbolic measures.

Under both public international law and human rights law, reparations can be granted if certain procedural requirements are met (i.e. causality, standard of proof). However, the tests employed by the courts in determining those characteristics vary. International human rights courts usually rely on a flexible approach towards causality, the standard of proof, and the use of presumptions. Although under public international law the state obligation of cessation and assurances and guarantees of non-repetition indirectly protect collective interests, collective reparations do not exist as such. The latter have been developed by the IACtHR with the purpose of providing redress and aiming to transform the lives of victims in cases involving large numbers of victims.[5]

2.2 Collective Reparations at the Inter-American Court of Human Rights

Collective awards belong to the realm of human rights law. In this regard, the IACtHR has been a pioneer by transporting these awards, originally conceived under

3 IACtHR (Judgment) 26 May 2001, *"Street Children" (Villagrán-Morales et al.)* v. *Guatelama*, Separate Opinion of Judge A.A. Cançado Trindade, para. 28, 35 and 37.

4 Principles on Reparations.

5 The ECtHR has ordered states to create national mechanisms that can provide redress to victims in its pilot judgments. While this is not a collective reparation per se, it does provide redress for a large number of victims.

the auspices of transitional justice mechanisms, to a regional human rights court. The court has ordered different collective awards that are related to measures of satisfaction, but that sometimes go beyond satisfaction, such as the reopening of a school and a medical dispensary in a village affected by GVHR;[6] the establishment of a health centre so that victims can obtain medical and psychological care in their own village;[7] the investment of a specific amount of money in works or services in the collective interest;[8] and the creation of specific programmes to provide free psychological and psychiatric treatment at the collective, family and individual level.[9] Yet, the IACtHR has not further defined the concept and content of collective reparations, nor has it identified any difference between collective reparations developed within the transitional justice framework and within human rights law. Neither has it elaborated on how these measures stem from the individual right to reparations as enshrined in Article 63 of the ACHR.

Yet, the findings of Chapter III point out that collective reparations present a better response in cases where the victims share a strong communal sense of identity (i.e. indigenous and tribal peoples) or where individual reparations may have a disruptive effect in the order of a given community. While the Court has also granted collective reparations in cases involving a large number of victims without assessing the existence of strong communal ties, it accompanies them with individual reparations. From the in-depth research conducted, it is possible to conclude that the Court *only* awards collective reparations in cases related to indigenous and tribal people's ancestral lands. The IACtHR has claimed to have seen in collective reparations an opportunity to tackle the poverty and marginalisation in which most victims live. By trying to prevent people from continuing to be victims of such living conditions,[10] the IACtHR has used collective reparations as a tool to repair victims of violations for which a state has been found guilty as well as to improve the marginalised living conditions of indigenous and tribal people.

Although collective reparations may well be a tool to address structural problems such as poverty and marginalisation, the Court has not adopted the approach of granting *only* collective reparations in cases where other victims, such as *peasants,* live in similar conditions of poverty and marginalisation as those experienced by indigenous and tribal people. In this light, Antowiak has questioned whether the Court's approach of granting *only* CR to indigenous and tribal people is discriminatory

6 IACtHR (Judgment) 10 September 1993, *Aloeboetoe et al.* v. *Surinam*, para. 96.
7 IACtHR (Judgment) 19 November 2004, *Plan de Sánchez Massacre* v. *Guatemala*, para. 110, 117.
8 IACtHR (Judgment) 31 August 2001, *Mayagna (Sumo) Awas Tingni* v. *Nicaragua*, para. 167.
9 IACtHR, *Plan de Sánchez Massacre* v. *Guatemala*, *supra* n. 7, para. 93, 106-108, 117.
10 Roht-Arriaza, N., "Reparations in International Law and Practice" in M.C. Bassiouni (ed.), *The pursuit of international criminal justice: a world study on conflicts, victimization and post conflict justice* (Antwerp, Intersentia 2010, Vol.1), p. 657.

not only towards these two groups, but also towards other unprivileged groups.[11] Yet, as is demonstrated by the findings of this Chapter, in most of the cases where the Court has granted CR, the victims' representatives and/or the IACmmHR have explicitly requested such measures. Finally, despite the fact that the IACtHR has not explained how collective reparations coexist with the right to individual reparations, it may be correctly inferred that the Court interprets the right to individual reparations as a collective one when it comes to violations concerning indigenous and tribal peoples' ancestral lands.

2.3 Collective Reparations in International Criminal Law

International criminal law, as specifically developed by both the ECCC and ICC, has followed the IACtHR's jurisprudence in grating collective reparations. The two aforementioned criminal courts differ from the IACtHR in that they both have explicit provisions in their legal frameworks that authorize them to award collective reparations. Nevertheless, both Courts lack concrete guidelines on how to give content to as well as how to guide the implementation of collective reparations. This may be explained because of the lack of prior precedents for reparations under international criminal law. Furthermore, both the ICC and the ECCC afford justice beyond retributive tenets by providing reparations. In addition, both have recognized that individual perpetrators are not only criminally responsible for the crimes they have committed, but also liable for the harm caused to the victims.[12]

To date, collective reparations have become the hallmark of reparations at the ICC and the ECCC. While the ECCC can only award collective reparations, the ICC is empowered to award individual reparations as well. Collective reparations are believed to be adequate given the uncertainty regarding the number of victims, the complexities in identifying victims and the potential problems that may ensue from individual reparations among communities and victims themselves, especially if those communities are still experiencing violence. This form of reparations is also believed to be more feasible as it requires fewer resources and opens the door to a greater number of victims. Ideally, collective reparations should be awarded on a complementary basis rather than as a substitute for individualized reparations,[13] considering that victims of international crimes suffer both individual and collective

11 Antkowiak, T., "Remedial Approaches to Human Rights Violations: The Inter-American Court of Human Rights and Beyond", 46 *Columbia Journal of Transnational Law* (2008), p. 384, 398.

12 Zegveld, L., "Victims's Reparations Claims and International Criminal Courts: Incompatible Values?", 8 *Journal of International Criminal Justice,* (2010), p. 85.

13 Hamber, B., "Repairing the Irreparable: dealing with the double binds of making reparations for crimes of the past", 5 *Ethnicity and Health* (2000), p. 224-225.

harm.[14] A good example of where this can be achieved is the *Katanga* case before the ICC, where symbolic individual measures were granted in addition to collective reparations.[15]

Before the ICC, redress is provided through two different bodies: the ICC and the TFV. Legally, the assistance provided by the TFV qualifies as humanitarian assistance rather than reparations, the latter always being linked to an ICC order.[16] Nevertheless, the assistance provided has a reparative nature; hence it may clearly overlap with the content of a reparation order. For victims, the distinction between reparations and assistance may be irrelevant in terms of the benefits obtained. The main difference is that the TFV's assistance may be perceived as a symbol of solidarity from the international community not only towards victims who have seen their case become part of the ICC's case load but towards the affected community in general. Similar to the ICC's framework, victims before the ECCC may seek redress through the VSS's assistance, comparable to that provided by the TFV, as well as through reparations. However, the VSS has implemented very limited assistance projects; this is perhaps as a result of a much more limited budget allocated to the ECCC.[17] Consequently, there has been no debate on whether this assistance may overlap with reparations.

Similar to the IACtHR, both the ICC and the ECCC require a causal link between the harm caused to victims and the crimes for which the accused was convicted in order to be eligible for reparations. However, the latter courts are stricter with regard to the causality test as well as with other procedural requirements such as the standard of proof and the evidence needed to prove the harm, as well as requirements relating to the identification of victims.

2.4 Collective Reparations and Non-Judicial Bodies

Reparation is one of the key elements of transitional justice processes.[18] However, repairing all the damage that resulted from past legacies of GVHR while

14 Mégret, F., "The case for collective reparations before the International Criminal Court" in J.M. Wemmers (ed.) Reparations for Victims of Crimes against Humanity (Abingdon, Routledge 2014), p. 175-176.

15 The financial awards granted by the ICC in this case are rather symbolic, as they do not intend to cover the material and moral damage suffered. See: ICC, *Katanga*'s Reparations Order, 24 March 2017, para. 306.

16 Kristjánsdóttir, E., "International Mass Claims Processes and the ICC Trust Fund for Victims" in C. Ferstman, M. Goetz and A. Stephens (eds.), *Reparations for Victims of Genocide, War Crimes and Crimes Against Humanity: Systems in Place and Systems in the Making* (Leiden, Martinus Nijhoff 2009), p. 21.

17 Herman, J., "Realities of Victim Participation: The civil party system in practice at the Extraordinary Chambers in the Courts of Cambodia (ECCC)", 4 *Contemporary Justice Review* (2013), p. 471.

18 Tomuschat, C., "Darfur: Compensation for Victims", 3 *Journal of International Criminal Justice* (2005), p. 581.

simultaneously rebuilding institutions and providing social services to all citizens is often unrealistic. While scholars have submitted that, in an ideal scenario, reparations under TJ would consist of a combination of individual and collective awards,[19] they have also accepted that collective reparations are a more realistic and inclusive option for the implementing state. Within collective reparations, it is claimed that a transformative approach is the most appropriate as these reparations aim to address structural problems such as poverty, inequality and marginalization.

In addition to collective reparations, mass claims procedures have also been established to address GVHR. Although these procedures differ from national reparations programmes, it is evident they also share some similarities, such as: i) a flexible understanding of the requirements to meet the burden of proof;[20] ii) the potential to provide reparations to a large number of victims; and iii) selective beneficiaries. Both claims procedures and national reparations programmes avoid flooding courts with thousands of individual claims or lawsuits by designing reparations outside the courtroom. Of the two, national collective reparations programmes may be preferred by states because they provide goods and services that help states to achieve distributive justice and development in the country.[21] Commissions or Mass Claims Reparations programmes (MCRs) may be preferable when, in addition to awarding reparations to victims, states need to establish the liability of state actors or armed groups under humanitarian law.

Although they provide reparations to a large number of victims, both CRs and MCRs usually restrict their benefits to certain groups of victims, as policies regarding crimes to be compensated are established upfront. While political decisions which result in selective criteria for compensable crimes undermine the individual right to reparations for many victims, collective reparations programmes and mass claims allow a large pool of beneficiaries, within the selected group of eligible victims, to enjoy collective benefits. In comparison to MCRs, collective reparations may benefit larger numbers of victims and even perpetrators. In contrast, individual reparations are only supposed to benefit victims.[22] To meet the challenges of insufficient evidence, claims commissions and TRCs have developed novel techniques such as relaxing the

19 Roht-Arriaza, *supra* n. 10, p. 696; Roht-Arriaza, N. and Orlovsky, K., "A Complementary Relationship: Reparations and Development" in P. de Greiff and R. Duthie (eds.), *Transitional Justice and Development: Making connections* (New York, Social Science Research Council 2009), p. 194; Guillerot, J. and Carranza, R., *The Rabat Report: The Concept and Challenges of Collective Reparations* (ICTJ 2009), p. 40.

20 Kristjánsdóttir, *supra* n. 16, p. 185; van Haersolte-van Hof, J., "Innovations to Speed Mass Claims: New Standards of Proof" in Permanent Court of Arbitration (ed.) *Redressing Injustices through Mass Claims Processes: Innovative Responses to Unique Challenges* (Oxford, OUP 2006) p. 22.

21 de Greiff, P. , "Articulating the Links Between Transitional Justice and Development: Justice and Social Integration" in P. de Greiff and R. Duthie (eds.), *Transitional Justice and Development: Making connections* (New York, Social Science Research Council 2009), p. 41.

22 Guillerot and Carranza, *supra* n. 19, p. 41.

standard of proof, clustering or grouping categories of claims, altering evidentiary presumptions, employing statistical sampling, and awarding fixed amounts to certain categories of victims or claims.[23] This has responded to the common difficulty that victims face in gathering evidence.[24]

2.5 Conclusions

Collective reparations can be traced back to the field of transitional justice.[25] Within a legal setting first embraced by the Inter-American Court of Human Rights and subsequently by international criminal tribunals, to date no tribunal has ever explained, both legally and conceptually, how collective reparations meet the requirements of reparations as understood by public international law and international human rights law (i.e. the causality test, the standard of proof, proportionality, adequacy, etc.). Under international human rights law these requirements were constructed in relation to individual reparations. Whilst international human rights instruments are 'living instruments', the IACtHR has omitted to elaborate how those reparations' requirements have evolved in a way that could be met by collective reparations.

Under both international human rights law and transitional justice mechanisms, collective reparations may be awarded for the benefit of all members of a given community. On the contrary, in international criminal law the constellation of beneficiaries of a case must have a link to the crimes for which the accused was convicted.[26] Thus, the causality requirement is higher than that of TJ and international human rights law. It is clear that collective reparations are a balanced option for judicial and non-judicial bodies struggling to ensure reparations for victims of GVHR in a context where material resources are scare as well as when sufficient evidence to prove a claim is very limited.

---

23 Kristjánsdóttir, *supra* n. 16, p. 189-190; Niebergall, H., "Overcoming Evidentiary Weakness in Reparation Claims Programmes" in C. Ferstman, M. Goetz and A. Stephens (eds.), *Reparations for Victims of, War Crimes and Crimes Against Humanity: Systems in Place and Systems in the Making* (Leiden, Martinus Nijhoff 2009), p. 148-149, 151, 161-165.

24 McKay, F., "What Outcome for Victims?", in D. Shelton (ed.), *The Oxford Handbook of International Human Rights Law* (Oxford, OUP 2013), p. 945.

25 Guillerot and Carranza, *supra* n. 19, p. 10. For a discussion on how the collective dimension of human rights violations is better addressed by and, indeed, inherently better suited to the purview of the political process of transitional justice rather than human rights law. See: Parlevliet, M., "Embracing Concurrent Realities: Revisiting the Relationship between Human Rights and Conflict Resolution", PhD thesis, University of Amsterdam, the Netherlands, p. 60-61.

26 Yet, victims who are not victims in a case may receive reparations from the assistance programme.

3 Collective Reparations: A Bitter but Better Approach?

Dispensing justice in terms of reparations for victims of gross violations of human rights is anything but easy. At the international level, three declarations have been adopted with the aim of acknowledging victims' right to reparations and the necessity of offering redress to victims.[27] While the 2005 Principles to Combat Impunity establish the state's obligation to guarantee the right of victims to obtain full reparations through the awarding of individual and collective measures,[28] the 2005 Principles on Reparations recommend both individual and collective measures of reparations to be used simultaneously. Despite their entitlement to reparations, many victims of GVHR around the world do not see their full right to reparations materialized.

Despite the existence of an individual right to reparations, repairing all the harm suffered by victims of GVHR is materially unattainable. An ideal form of justice in the context of GVHR is difficult to attain, if not impossible.[29] However, providing adequate reparations by taking into account the context in which the crimes took place would ideally entail individual and collective measures of reparation. Yet, providing individual reparations can jeopardise the limited financial and natural resources available within a given country, which is required to reconstruct society, provide social services, and implement the various political reforms required to achieve stability. The problem of limited resources is exacerbated in countries that were already economically poor even before a conflict arose or a repressive government seized power.[30] In addition, Roht-Arriaza submits that individual reparations do not adequately deal with the structural problems that often underline a conflict and are therefore inadequate measures that are unlikely to be in line with the needs of societies emerging from a conflict situation. Furthermore, individual reparations may have disruptive effects. Such effects may extend not only to a state's general economy and its ability to provide basic social programmes to all of its citizens, but also to victims themselves.[31] Complex discussions on who is deserving of the victimhood status, in particular in countries with long-term violent conflict where victim-perpetrators' roles change over time, will need to be held and have the potential to continuously

27 The 1985 Victims Declaration, the 2005 Principles on Reparations, and the 2005 Principles to Combat Impunity.

28 Manrique Rueda, G., "Lands, wars and restoring justice for victims" in J.M. Wemmers (ed.) *Reparations for Victims of Crimes against Humanity* (Abingdon, Routledge 2014), p. 190.

29 See: Letschert, R.M. and Pemberton, A, "Justice as the art of muddling through" in C. Brants, & S. Karstedt (eds.), *Transitional Justice and its Public Sphere: Engagement, Legitimacy, Contestation* (Oxford, Hart Publishers 2017).

30 Roht-Arriaza, N., "Reparations Decisions and Dilemmas", 27 *Hastings International and Comparative Law Review* (2004), p. 185-186; Tomuschat, C., "Reparations for Victims of Grave Human Rights Violations", 10 *Tulane Journal of International and Comparative Law* (2002), p. 175.

31 Tomuschat, *supra* n. 18, p. 586; Magarrell, L., "Reparations in Theory and Practice", *ICTJ* (2007), p. 5-7.

disrupt societies. Furthermore, individual reparations require high standards of evidence and are therefore slow, meaning that proceedings could become rather expensive. And the potential burden on victims participating in these cases should not be underestimated.[32] In addition to the often lack of political will to address victims' suffering, all these challenges, especially those posed by limited resources and determining who is entitled to individual awards, tend to prevent states from providing individual reparations.[33] In addition, individual reparations usually require the identification of victims prior to the awarding of reparations. In the aftermath of GVHR, such identification is usually not possible at the early stage of any process of reparations.

Furthermore, the effects of GVHR include collectively experienced trauma and damage,[34] with such damages being addressed mainly by collective reparations.[35] Despite collective reparations' somewhat narrow predominant focus on collective harm, they constitute a more feasible response to the reparatory needs of victims. In this light, collective reparations are more need-oriented than right-oriented. This is because victims have, in principle, the right to receive reparations for all the harm suffered and collective reparations usually focus on addressing the most basic needs of victims. In light of this, collective reparations present a fair compromise between political will, limited resources, and the imminent, and in most cases, basic needs of victims. Such remedies are seen as a better option than the alternative: a lack of reparations. Collective reparations could be viewed as the middle ground between the needs of victims in the present and the needs of society in the future.[36]

3.1 Towards a Concept

Collective reparations have no single accepted legal or conceptual meaning despite widespread use. This research started with the following preliminary definition, as stated in the introductory chapter:

---

32 Roht-Arriaza, *supra* n. 10, p. 663; Roht-Arriaza, *supra* n. 30, p. 179-181, 185.

33 Roht-Arriaza, *supra* n. 30, p. 158.

34 Wemmers, J.A., "Victim's Need for Justice. Individual versus Collective Justice", in R. Letschert et al. (eds.), *Victimological Approaches to International Crimes: Africa* (Cambridge, Intersentia 2011), p. 145.

35 Rosenfeld, F., "Collective Reparations for Victims of Armed Conflicts", 92 *International Review of the Red Cross* (2010), p. 746.

36 Tomuschat, C., "Individual Reparation Claims in Instances of Grave Human Rights Violations: The Position under General International Law", in A. Randerlzhofer and C. Tomuschat, *State Responsibility and the Individual: Reparations in Instances of Grave Violations of Human Rights* (The Hague, Martinus Nijhoff, 1999), p. 20.

Collective reparations are: i) measures or benefits that are indivisible and diverse; ii) which are awarded to collectives or group of people,[37] iii) in order to alleviate the collective harm that has been caused as a consequence of a violation of international law, iv) in the form of either individual or collective rights. These benefits are commonly framed as political projects (social programmes) and have the potential to transform the social conditions of victims as well as to prevent both further victimisation and collective violence or conflict.

The research demonstrates that this definition fits the understanding of collective reparations as applied by the judicial and non-judicial bodies scrutinized in this study. One element, however, deserves to be highlighted – collective reparations measures can take the form of symbolic (or moral) measures as well as of service-based measures (social services). This definition is still fairly general and, to some extent, vague. However, it provides enough room for reparations to be tailored in accordance with a given society, its culture, the background of a conflict,[38] and with specific victims' needs. This may be better than having a uniform set of specific measures that are not possible to realize in all scenarios where GVHR have been committed. In this light it is important to recall that Tomuschat has affirmed that the weakest point of the 2005 Principles on Reparations is that they aim to provide a uniform regime of reparations regardless of the kind of violations suffered.[39]

There are further unanswered questions surrounding collective reparations. For how long are the victims supposed to benefit from them? On which basis is it decided whether collective reparations should take the form of symbolic, service-based or combined measures? Based on the analysis conducted, collective measures of reparation are decided on the basis of geographic terms (community, town, urban or local area) and on themes such as peace building, social services, income-generating activities, measures aimed at memorialisation, infrastructure projects and judicial reforms. Social services, especially health and educational measures, are commonly awarded. This is because mass violations usually impact the general capacities of a state to provide social services and infrastructure, and these are also the areas where many victims often express an urgent need.[40]

The time frame in which collective reparations are offered varies among the three fields under study. The IACtHR has ordered collective reparations to be granted on a permanent basis (the reopening of a school or the establishment of human

37 For the purposes of this research, the terms 'collectives' and 'groups' of people are used synonymously. However, when referring to indigenous peoples, I will explicitly refer to a group of people but not to collectives. The reason for this is that indigenous peoples are specifically recognized as a group of people under international law.

38 Kiza, E., Rathgeber, C. and Rohne, H., *Victims of War: An Empirical Study on War-Victimization and Victims' Attitudes towards Addressing Atrocities* (Hamburg, Hambgurger Edition 2006), p. 122.

39 Tomuschat, *supra* n. 36, p. 20-21.

40 ICTJ, *Transitional Justice and Development*, ICTJ (2009), p. 1-2.

rights training for the police and military) but also based on a specific amount of money to be devoted to them. When the money has been spent on or invested in the collective reparations projects, then the state is considered to have complied with the order.[41] The ICC, on the other hand, has defined some temporal boundaries. As such, collective reparations are available to the victims for a period of between 2 to 4 years.[42] Furthermore, under TJ, national collective reparations when referring to service-based measures are usually ordered permanently. This is because those social services were supposed to be enjoyed by the victims even before their victimisation. In this light, collective reparations become a bridge that allows access to be had to other rights of an economic, social and cultural nature.

3.2 Purposes and Aims

It is the author's view that reparations for GVHR, whenever possible, should seek not only to address suffering, but also to address the structural problems that led to this suffering. In light of this, collective reparations should aim at meeting victims' needs while transforming conditions that may lead to further GVHR. In other words, they should adopt a preventive approach based on transforming structural problems.

Transformative and preventive

Through service-based measures, collective reparations aim to go beyond repairing the harm endured by victims by helping create conditions to prevent further crimes and also trying to encourage reconciliation. Victims of GVHR are usually the poorest, most excluded and most vulnerable members of society even before their victimization, and their living conditions deteriorated even further as a consequence of the victimization. Therefore, tackling issues of poverty and inequality has become one of the aims of collective reparations.

Reparations are especially a concern for impoverished victims.[43] Addressing the poverty in which victims live, i.e. transforming the lives of victims, should then be the first and foremost aim of collective reparations. Transforming victims' living conditions is to be regarded as a way to prevent further victimisation. Prevention itself is a goal that is important to victims.[44] In this light, transformative reparations may

---

41 IACtHR (Judgment) 15 June 2005, *Moiwana Community* v. *Suriname*, para. 218; IACtHR (Compliance Order) 22 November 2010, *Moiwana Community* v. *Suriname*, para. 39.

42 ICC *Lubanga*'s Filing regarding symbolic collective reparations projects, 19 September 2016, para. 65; ICC *Katanga*'s Draft implementation plan, 24 March 2017, para. 116.

43 van der Merwe, H., "Reparations through different lenses: The culture, rights and politics of healing and empowerment after mass atrocities" in J.M. Wemmers (ed.) *Reparations for Victims of Crimes against Humanity* (Abingdon, Routledge 2014), p. 200.

44 Wemmers, *supra* n. 34, p. 151.

also be an instrument for achieving social justice,[45] though this should not be their only goal. Whilst collective reparations 'can and should contribute to improving the quality of life of the victims and their family members, [their] central objective is the repair and recognition of victims as human beings, whose fundamental rights have been violated.'[46] They are not a substitute for the state's duties such as 'provid[ing] basic needs and social services to everyone regardless of their status as victims'.[47] Reparations and development are linked in many ways: social exclusion is central to both and, through access to social services, both can elicit a change in the lives of people.[48] They should complement each other, rather than substitute or duplicate.[49]

Meeting victims' needs

Victims of international crimes often go through demanding mental processes in order to cope with the suffering they have endured. For many victims, both individual healing as well as collective healing are important.[50] Collective reparations may assist in such healing by addressing victims' needs. In addition, victims are not a homogenous group, and their needs may differ depending on personal characteristics and their societal context. In addition, we know from victimological studies that needs may also change over time, posing many challenges in trying to design adequate reparatory measures that try to take into account individual and collective needs. However, victims' needs may be overwhelming and choices need to be made in order to prioritize them. While victims' views should be the guiding factor, some victimological studies point to the importance of taking Maslow's hierarchy of needs[51] into account when establishing priorities. According to Wemmers, this hierarchy is relevant because it shows how individual and collective needs are linked with each other.[52]

---

45 Walker, M., "Transformative Reparations? A Critical Look at a Current Trend in Thinking about Gender-Just Reparations", 10 *International Journal of Transitional Justice* (2016), p. 110.
46 Magarrell, L., Reparations for Massive or Widespread Human Rights Violations: Sorting Out Claims for Reparations and the Struggle for Social Justice, 22 *Windsor Yearbook of Access to Justice* (2003), p. 95, citing the Peruvian TRC's Final Report, Volume IX section 2.2.2.1, p. 148.
47 Guillerot and Carranza, *supra* n. 19, p. 47
48 Roht-Arriaza, N. and Orlovsky, K., "A Complementary Relationship: Reparations and Development", ICJT 2009, p. 1-2.
49 Ibid., p. 3-4.
50 Wemmers, J.M., "The healing role of reparation" in J.M. Wemmers (ed.) *Reparations for Victims of Crimes against Humanity* (Abingdon, Routledge 2014), p. 224.
51 This is a psychology theory of the hierarchy of needs proposed by Abraham Maslow. See: Mathes, E., "Maslow's Hierarchy of Needs as a Guide for Living" 21 *Journal of Humanistic Psychology* (1981).
52 Wemmers, *supra* n. 50, p. 224-227.

4 Collective Reparations: Tensions and Dilemmas

The majority of scholars seem to have followed Roht-Arrianza and Orlovsky, who affirm that collective reparations 'respond to collective harms and harms to social cohesion' while maximizing available resources.[53] This view has also been shared by judicial and non-judicial bodies. Further, judicial bodies have justified collective reparations as a compromise between the need for large-scale reparations and the inadequate evidence available to prove the harm suffered from crimes, resulting from the passage of time and circumstances surrounding those crimes, such as the fact that in some cases people are forced to suddenly leave their homes or property and documents are destroyed. However, the following question needs to be addressed:

What are the tensions between the individual right to receive reparations and awarding collective reparations for victims of gross violations of human rights?

According to Díaz, collective reparations are usually employed as a strategy to deny individual reparations.[54] In addition, she submits that collective reparations should be limited to groups that share a collective identity, such as indigenous and tribal peoples, ethnic minorities (i.e. Afro-Colombians), and some communities with strong communal identities that have suffered damages of a collective nature, such as GVHR. Otherwise, victims may perceive collective reparations as a pragmatic and cheaper substitute for individual reparations, provoking frustration rather than redress.[55]

However, international law's individualistic approach is not a realistic and sometimes not even a desirable approach when dealing with a vast numbers of victims. This tension between what the right to reparations *ought to be* (individual) and what reparations *can be* (collective) in the context of GVHR seems to reach a more appropriate balance when collective reparations are accompanied by individual forms of reparations.[56] While, in principle, international law focuses on the individual and there is no justification for solely collective reparations, both international human rights law, by means of the jurisprudence of the IACtHR, and international criminal law, by means of the legal instruments and jurisprudence of the ICC and the ECCC,

53 Roht-Arriaza and Orlovsky, *supra* n. 48, p. 3.

54 Díaz Gómez, C., "Elementos para un programa administrative de reparaciones colectivas en Colombia" in C. Díaz Gómez (ed.), *Tareas Pendientes: Propuestas para la formulación de políticas públicas de la reparación en Colombia* (Bogotá, ICTJ 2010), p. 272.

55 Ibid., p. 273-280. The IACtHR seems to be in line with Díaz's approach by granting only collective reparations in cases related to indigenous and tribal people's ancestral lands.

56 Correa, C., "Reparations for Victims of Massive Crimes. Making Concrete a Message of Inclusion", in R. Letschert et al. (eds.), *Victimological Approaches to International Crimes: Africa* (Cambridge, Intersentia 2011), p. 202, 209-210.

have contributed to the justification of granting solely collective reparations in certain scenarios. This, however, has not been embraced without challenges and dilemmas.

4.1 Main Tensions

There are two main tensions between the individual right to receive reparations and awarding *only* collective reparations for victims of GVHR. First, under international human rights law, granting CR as standalone awards to victims may be discriminatory. While the IACtHR has used CR as a tool to tackle the poverty and marginalization in which indigenous and tribal peoples live, it has not adopted this approach towards other unprivileged groups. Secondly, under international human rights law, international criminal law and TJ processes, granting *only* CR to victims of GVHR does not seem to fulfill the requirements of the individual right to reparations. In this light, the IACtHR has explicitly stated that CR supplement individual awards as well as are part of the individual right to receive reparations. In addition, the CR ordered by the ICC and the ECCC are difficult to be distinguished from the content of the humanitarian assistance projects provided by the TFV and the VSS to any victim of crimes under these tribunals' jurisdiction. Similarly, national CR programmes seem to have similar objectives than those of development measures, and thus, they are difficult to distinguish from each other. Consequently, CR may be adopted as a way to substitute the state's obligation to provide social services rather than to repair the harm endured by victims.

4.2 Dilemmas: Beneficiaries and Groups

Although victims may not obtain redress for their individual harm, collective reparations allow for a more victim-inclusive approach in terms of the number of beneficiaries. The flexibility of this approach is such that in national collective reparations programmes, not only victims, but also perpetrators may benefit from reparations. The concept of a 'beneficiary' is a very open concept within particular TJ processes, whereas it constitutes a more restricted concept within international human rights law and an even more stringent concept within international criminal law. The latter, also having to consider the rights of the accused, thereby requires that only the victims of the actions for which a perpetrator is found guilty are the ones who can benefit from collective reparations.

In addition, the identification (or the lack thereof) of victims plays a role in determining the content of collective reparations before the ICC. This court has shown that a great deal of flexibility in the identification of victims is afforded in relation to moral or symbolic reparations. In the *Lubanga* case, for instance, the ICC based its decision to grant collective reparations on the limited resources available and the large number of unidentified victims at the time of the judgment. To date, a significant number of victims remain unidentified and, consequently, only symbolic measures of reparations have been approved.

Under transitional justice mechanisms and international human rights law, communities and groups as such may be beneficiaries of reparations, while international criminal law requires that only the members of a given community who have been recognised as victims in a particular case are to be considered as beneficiaries. The former faces challenges in foreseeing the consequences of recognising communities and groups as beneficiaries. Would doing so imply that these groups may also be recognised as entities entitled to other rights beyond the right to reparations? International human rights courts, especially the IACtHR, should clarify a clear set of boundaries on this matter. Since this Court was the pioneer in granting collective reparations, it is desirable that it also contributes to a better understanding of these reparations. Furthermore, recognising only the victims in a case as beneficiaries, as required by the ICC, also brings difficult challenges. The commission of GVHR usually victimises entire communities and providing benefits only to a selected group of people may create tensions among victims.

4.3 Dilemmas: Adequacy and its Content

Courts and non-judicial bodies decide without legal guidelines, and on a case-by-case basis, when only collective reparations or a combination of them with individual reparations are adequate (depending on whether their mandate allows for this). The ideal behind collective reparations programmes is to ensure that a large number of victims benefit from any given programme. Yet, this ideal only becomes meaningful when the victims receive something that they deem to be necessary or important for them. Here, the importance of victims' participation in the design and implementation of the programmes becomes evident. Victim participation, in turn, requires an early identification of the victims by the competent body. However, identifying victims of GVHR is neither easy nor possible in all cases.[57]

Therefore, a key aspect governing the adequacy of collective reparations is the requirement that they should respond to victims' needs and wishes. In this light, judicial and non-judicial bodies need to create mechanisms to ensure the participation of victims. As has been shown in Chapter III, the IACtHR has often taken into account victims' wishes when deciding the adequate reparations in a given case. Victimological studies have pointed out that victims of GVHR often prioritize security, poverty elimination, and their livelihood.[58] Yet, many of them also express

---

57 Contreras-Garduño, D. and Fraser, J., "The Identification of Victims before the Inter-American Court of Human Rights and the International Criminal Court and its Impact on Participation and Reparation: A Domino Effect?" *Inter-American and European Human Rights Journal* (2015), p. 202.

58 McKay, *supra* n. 24, p. 926.

a desire to receive individual reparations.[59] Consequently, courts and non-judicial bodies face the challenge of finding a balance between all the needs and views of the victims when giving content to collective reparations. Ideally, some individual measures, such as an apology or financial compensation, no matter how symbolic they are, should accompany the collective approach.

As has been shown in this study, such a balance is possible to be reached. Not only was this proved by the IACtHR in several of its judgments and the ICC through the *Katanga* case, but also the Peruvian CVR and the Moroccan IER strived for such an approach by recommending both individual and collective reparations. All in all, the content of collective reparations is open to interpretation, with the needs and views of the victims being the guiding factor.

4.4 Dilemmas: Standard of Proof and the Causality Requirement

The principle of *actori incumbit onus probandi* applies to reparations proceedings before both the courts and non-judicial bodies. However, international human rights courts and even the ICJ have shifted the burden of proof to ameliorate the inequalities of the parties in gathering evidence.[60] The reversal of the burden of proof is not possible under international criminal law in relation to all parts of the proceedings, including the reparations stage. Although the type and quantity of evidence (standard of proof) play an important role in reparations, judicial and non-judicial bodies usually tend to avoid determining a strictly required standard of proof. This is evident in the case of the ICJ and regional human rights courts, as well as with MCRs. However, under international criminal law, it has been accepted that the standard of proof of the 'preponderance of probabilities' is the most adequate one in relation to reparations.

Further, under TRCs, the standard of proof is mostly absent, as these bodies usually rely on presumptions to determine the existence of harm. Judicial bodies, especially when determining the moral harm of direct and indirect victims, also use presumptions. Yet, those presumptions are based on proven facts or other evidence such as, for instance, close links to the direct victims. In the case of the IACtHR such presumptions are rebuttable. In this way, a state has the opportunity to challenge them by bringing well-founded objections.

Regarding the causality requirement, all judicial bodies require causality. It seems that judicial bodies share the view of applying a causality test with regard to material damage while applying a presumption regarding moral damage. Consequently,

59 ICC *Lubanga's* Principles on Reparations, 7 August 2012, para. 220, para. 15; ICC *Lubanga's* Victims Observations, 18 April 2012, para. 15; ICC (Observations) *Prosecutor* v. *Thomas Lubanga Dyilo*, Observations du groupe de victimes VO2 concernant la fixation de la peine et des réparations, ICC-01/04-01/06-2869, 18 April 2012, para. 16; ICC *Katanga*'s Report on Reparations Application, 21 January 2015, para. 42, 49.

60 However, the ICC may ask for state assistance in procuring evidence.

a higher causality requirement is applied when seeking a financial award as opposed to a symbolic award. For example, the ICJ in the *Bosnia and Herzegovina against Serbia and Montenegro* case awarded satisfaction when compensation did not meet the causality test.

In comparison to public international law and international human rights law, international criminal law requires a stricter causality test. Under transitional justice mechanisms, the causality requirement is absent before truth commissions, as causality is normally presumed by them. Under MCRs, presumptions are usually applied in conjunction with other mass claims techniques such as the clustering of claims.

Reparations, whether individual or collective, require a standard of proof and causality test to be met. International courts usually affirm the need for flexibility in applying those requirements, especially in cases of GVHR, so as to account for victims' difficulty in compiling evidence. Similar flexibility is evident in mass claims procedures. However, judicial and non-judicial bodies do not define the specific test required and are silent regarding the difference between the tests applied to collective reparations as opposed to those applied to individual reparations. Consequently, victims seeking reparations are presented with uncertainty regarding what is required from them in order to be granted collective reparations.

4.5 Dilemmas: Assessment of Harm

It is commonly accepted that GVHR cause immeasurable individual and collective harm. Nevertheless, for the purposes of awarding reparations, judicial and non-judicial bodies are required to define the harms resulting from the proven violations. In particular, in international criminal law this assessment of harm is especially important, as the convicted person can only be liable for the reparations of the harm resulting from the crimes of which he or she was convicted.[61] Despite its importance, no single method of assessing harm becomes clear within and across judicial and non-judicial bodies. The research has shown that at times experts may be called to help judicial bodies to assess the harm, but that in the majority of cases, a court is the one to conduct an assessment of the harm. Whether the members of a given bench are financial experts in quantifying harms that are multidimensional and multi-layered can be questioned.

Courts have usually relied on the principle of equity when there is a lack of sufficient evidence for a claim to be assessed in financial terms. This is done especially when it comes to moral harm. In this light, it is important to recall that Crawford has stated that the wide discretion in the moral harm assessment conducted by the courts

61 However, this assessment may be delegated. In this light, the ICC has delegated the assessment of harm to the TFV in the *Lubanga* case.

is seen as a reflection of the willingness of human rights bodies in vindicating the violated rights rather than engaging in an accurate economic valuation of losses. In addition, MCR techniques such as sampling and grouping have also been invoked by courts (i.e. the *Katanga* case) as a means to accelerate the reparations process. In addition, monetary calculations conducted by victims have also been taken into account in harm assessment (i.e. the *Katanga* case).

While it is clear that courts may need to have a certain flexibility in assessing harm, it is also clear that courts should aim at creating guidelines in this regard. This will surely increase the legitimacy of their decisions as much as it can help victims to have more certainty as to what they can expected from a reparations process.

4.6 Extraordinary Justice: A Justification

Collective reparations have played an important role in addressing the issue of reparations for victims of gross violations of human rights under three major fields of adjudication: international human rights law, international criminal law and transitional justice. Since the legitimacy of the work of different mechanisms within these fields is supported by reparations, collective reparations are an option to legitimize the awarding mechanisms in cases in which other measures of reparations, such as individual ones, cannot be implemented.

Despite the recognition of victims' right to reparations within the three fields of study, the full, partial, or even symbolic realization of this right in relation to mass crimes is largely influenced by the context in which the right is exercised. Relevant variables include the framework through which reparations may be claimed; the magnitude of the claims for redress and the capacity of the states and institutions to support awards of reparations, the resolution of competing political imperatives such as national security, reconciliation, reconstruction, and development; and the determination of eligibility and responsibility for reparations, particularly where non-state entities are perceived as perpetrators of violations.

Although collective reparations may be perceived as settling for less, they do address both a greater number of victims and the broader consequences of GVHR.[62] Collective reparations aim to address social injustices and to enhance community development. They are not, however, social policies. Collective reparations and development should be mutually reinforcing.[63] However, collective reparations represent a compromise and a middle ground between legal entitlements and pragmatism in exceptional situations. In this light, it is important to recall that although GVHR have been addressed by regional human rights courts such as the IACtHR, these judicial mechanisms have been established to deal with 'common

62 Magarrell, *supra* n. 46, p. 90-91.
63 Ibid., p. 95-98.

crimes' rather than GVHR. Furthermore, the ICC, the ECCC, national reparations programmes, and mass claims are created to provide 'exceptional' justice, which implies significant limitations on the justice that they may dispense. The ICC and the ECCC focus on the prosecution of the perpetrators most directly responsible for the commission of the gravest human rights violations. National reparations programmes and claims commissions focus on repairing a limited number of crimes that are not considered common, but are rather committed under the exceptional circumstances of a conflict or an authoritarian regime. In view of these institutional restrictions, it can be stated that all of these legal mechanisms provide victims with the trilogy of basic justice, described by Boven as truth, justice, and reparations,[64] only in extraordinary circumstances.

Gray has called reparations within transitional justice 'tools for extraordinary justice'.[65] He also affirms that the greater the delay in providing reparations to victims of GVHR, the looser and more complex the issue of reparations becomes. The reason for this is that new generations would find themselves paying for what other generations or individuals had done to persons who are already deceased. In this case, the deceased's heirs or family would receive the reparations: non-perpetrators would say 'I did not commit those GVHR', and 'it was not you' who actually suffered from those GVHR.[66] In these cases, Gray proposes collective funding as the only way to realistically ensure reparations.[67]

Furthermore, Gray affirms that 'ordinary justice' focuses on compensating harm individually,[68] which is neither realistic nor desirable when dealing with crimes of mass scale. GVHR are extraordinary cases that should be dealt with by extraordinary measures and, to some extent, creativity. Collective reparations should complement individual measures when possible.[69]

All in all, making use of the concept of extraordinary and ordinary justice as used by Gray, reparations for extraordinary cases, regardless of whether they are resolved within international human rights or criminal law, or in a transitional justice context, should be approached on an extraordinary basis rather than an ordinary one. Given that collective reparations themselves constitute an extraordinary approach to reparations, it is possible to conclude that *there are indeed tensions between the individual right to receive reparations and awarding collective reparations for victims of gross violations of human rights.* These tensions suggest that awarding

64 van Boven, T., "Victim-Oriented Perspectives" in T. Bonacker and C. Safferling (eds.) *Victims of international Crimes: An Interdisciplinary Discourse,* The Hague: Asser Press, 2013, p. 22.
65 Gray, D.C., "A no-excuse approach to transitional justice: reparations as tools of extraordinary justice", 87 *Washington University Law Review* (2010), p. 1043.
66 Ibid., p. 1045-1047.
67 Ibid., p. 1048.
68 Ibid., p. 1000.
69 de Greiff, P. , "Reparations Programs: Patterns, Tendencies, and Challenges" 50 *Politorbis* (2010), p. 64.

only collective reparations for victims of GVHR does not meet the requirement of the individual right to reparations. However, human rights instruments were originally not created with the idea of addressing extraordinary cases of large-scale human rights abuses in international courts.

While the Principles on Reparations were already 'designed with a fair degree of flexibility' so that reparations for individuals and groups can be tailored on a case-by-case basis, rather than in an uniform manner,[70] there is a need to clarify that in extraordinary cases collective reparations may be the minimum requirement for the right to reparations to be satisfied. Collective reparations may well be a 'better' choice not only for states, but also for courts when addressing gross violations of human rights. This is because justice is accommodated according to present needs but also according to near and long-term future needs,[71] as well as according to the resources available not only to implement reparations but also to meet the requirements to be able to be granted reparations (procedural requirements).

Whether reparations are justified on the grounds of extraordinary justice, the potential they have to enable survival and secure some aspects of the future generations,[72] or because governments prefer them because they are perceived as less expensive,[73] eensuring their compliance should be a priority when granting or adopting these kinds of reparations. It is submitted that Courts and non-judicial bodies need to delineate the boundaries of each aspect of collective reparations in order to ensure their implementation. In addition, this will afford victims some degree of certainty as to what to expect and seek in the proceedings. All in all, the lack of a uniform concept of collective reparations may not be a problem, especially if we accept that the concept of reparations is constantly evolving.[74] However, the lack of a detailed elaboration of the choices in providing collective reparations by courts and non-judicial bodies is indeed a problem.

---

70 van Boven, T., "Victims' Rights to a Remedy and Reparations: The New United Nations Principles and Guidelines", in C. Ferstman, M. Goetz and A. Stephens (eds.), *Reparations for victims of genocide, war crimes and crimes against humanity: systems in place and systems in the making* (Leiden, Martinus Nijhoff 2009), p. 39.

71 Tomuschat, *supra* n. 36, p. 20.

72 Roht-Arriaza, *supra* n. 10, p. 655.

73 Ibid., p. 690.

74 Guillerot and Carranza, *supra* n. 19, p. 41.

Samenvatting

Hoofdstuk 1: Introductie en onderzoeksvraag

Grove schendingen van de mensenrechten, die hardnekkig en bij herhaling worden gepleegd, hebben wereldwijd geleid tot een aanzienlijk aantal slachtoffers. Degenen die niet zijn vermoord, zijn diep geraakt door het vermoorden van hun dierbaren en door ernstige inbreuken op hun rechten als gevolg van misstanden zoals langdurige gevangenschap en marteling, verminking, verkrachting, of de vernietiging van hun bezittingen en hun middelen van bestaan. De fysieke, psychologische en economische gevolgen op individueel en maatschappelijk vlak zijn tot op zekere hoogte onmeetbaar en onherstelbaar. Het merendeel van de grove mensenrechtenschendingen vindt plaats te midden van politieke instabiliteit, in situaties waarin overheidsinstellingen nauwelijks functioneren en de rechtsstaat ontbreekt. Binnen deze context is het bewerkstelligen van gerechtigheid in de nasleep van een conflict een uiterst gecompliceerde zaak. Bovendien worden landen in de overgang naar een meer democratische bestuursvorm geconfronteerd met diverse obstakels bij het aanpakken van gedaan onrecht. Deze obstakels kunnen zowel van politieke en juridische, als van materiële aard zijn. Een aantal factoren kan de zoektocht naar en verkrijging van gerechtigheid door de slachtoffers bemoeilijken, zoals het grote aantal slachtoffers, het probleem om, met name bij langdurige conflicten, te bepalen wie nu het slachtoffer en/of de dader is, en zowel het capaciteitsgebrek als de beperkte middelen van het desbetreffende land. Deze omstandigheden leiden er ook toe, dat landen beperkte mogelijkheden hebben tot het doen van herstelbetalingen, of hiertoe zelfs helemaal niet in staat zijn. Aangezien overheidsorganen vaak direct of indirect betrokken zijn bij het plegen van grove mensenrechtenschendingen, werkt de onmogelijkheid of de onwil om deze organen ter verantwoording te roepen een cultuur van straffeloosheid in de hand.

Lange tijd hebben slachtoffers vertrouwd op de bereidheid en het vermogen van landen om te voorzien in enige vorm van gerechtigheid, omdat zij voor het instellen van hun vorderingen geen beroep konden doen op internationale justitiemechanismen als de nationale wegen naar gerechtigheid niet beschikbaar of ineffectief waren. Hierin is echter geleidelijk verandering gekomen. Vandaag de dag vormt het herstel of het 'rechtzetten' van het door slachtoffers geleden onrecht, vooral in geval van bijzonder ernstige schade, voor landen zowel een morele als een juridische verplichting. Slachtoffers kunnen zich nu wenden tot internationale gerechten die zich bij grove mensenrechtenschendingen, met inbegrip van de schendingen die kunnen worden geclassificeerd als internationale misdrijven, richten op het faciliteren van herstel. De wijdverbreide erkenning van het recht van slachtoffers op rechtsmiddelen en rechtsherstel heeft ook geleid tot het vaststellen van de Basisbeginselen en Richtlijnen over het Recht op Rechtsmiddelen en Rechtsherstel voor Slachtoffers van Grove Schendingen van de Rechten van de Mens en het Internationale Humanitaire Recht.

Conform deze Beginselen kunnen slachtoffers rechtsherstel krijgen in de vorm van restitutie, compensatie, rehabilitatie, genoegdoening of garanties van niet-herhaling. Bij de toekenning van rechtsherstel aan slachtoffers van grove mensenrechtenschendingen valt een trend op, zowel bij de gerechtelijke als de buitengerechtelijke organen: indien sprake is van grote aantallen slachtoffers wijst men voornamelijk collectieve voorzieningen toe, omdat deze vorm van rechtsherstel het meest passend wordt geacht. Voorts neigen niet alleen overheden tot het opzetten van programma's die toegankelijk zijn voor een groot aantal begunstigden, maar hebben ook waarheidscommissies herhaaldelijk aanbevelingen gedaan voor collectief rechtsherstel. Het Inter-Amerikaans Hof voor de Rechten van de Mens (*Inter-American Court of Human Rights*, *IACtHR*), dat van alle organen op het gebied van de mensenrechten de meest vergaande vormen van rechtsherstel kent, heeft ook collectieve herstelbetalingen (CH) toegekend aan slachtoffers van massamisdaden. Het Cambodjatribunaal (*Extraordinary Chambers in the Courts of Cambodia, ECCC*) en het Internationaal Strafhof (*International Criminal Court, ICC*) hebben zich aan deze praktijk gespiegeld. De toegewezen collectieve voorzieningen omvatten programma's op het gebied van huisvesting en gezondheid, evenals programma's voor gemeenschapsontwikkeling. Deze CH worden zelden toegewezen in combinatie met individuele herstelbetalingen.

Ofschoon in het discours over het recht op herstelbetalingen van alle slachtoffers van misdrijven, met inbegrip van grove mensenrechtenschendingen, duidelijk wordt gesteld dat slachtoffers recht hebben op collectieve voorzieningen naast de individuele herstelbetalingen, worden collectieve voorzieningen in de praktijk zelden toegekend als aanvulling. Gerechtelijke en buitengerechtelijke organen zijn bij de behandeling van schade die is veroorzaakt door grove mensenrechtenschendingen juist geneigd tot het toekennen van enkel CH aan slachtoffers. De onderzoeksvraag van dit boek was daarom: *Welk spanningsveld is er tussen het individuele recht op herstelbetalingen en de toewijzing van collectieve herstelbetalingen aan de slachtoffers van grove mensenrechtenschendingen?* Voor het antwoord op deze vraag werd een analyse gemaakt van de opvatting van CH bij gerechtelijke en buitengerechtelijke organen op drie terreinen, te weten het internationaal recht inzake mensenrechten, het internationaal strafrecht en een aantal processen van overgangsrechtspraak. Bij deze analyse lag de onderzoeksfocus op specifieke jurisprudentie van het *IACtHR*, het Internationaal Strafhof en het Cambodjatribunaal. Daarnaast werden buitengerechtelijke mechanismen bestudeerd, in het bijzonder van de Peruaanse en Marokkaanse Waarheidscommissies en van twee commissies voor de vergoeding van massavorderingen (*United Nations Compensation Commission, UNCC* en de *Eritrea-Ethiopia Claims Commission, EECC*).

Hoofdstuk II: Ontwikkelingen met betrekking tot het recht op herstelbetalingen

De opvattingen in het internationaal recht over herstelbetalingen aan slachtoffers hebben zich in de loop der tijd ontwikkeld. Aanvankelijk zag men herstelbetalingen als een verplichting van een land jegens een ander land. De vaststelling van een internationaal mensenrechteninstrumentarium heeft er echter toe geleid, dat men heden ten dage herstelbetalingen ziet als een verplichting van een land zowel jegens landen als individuen. Herstelbetalingen conform het internationaal publiekrecht en het recht inzake mensenrechten vertonen dezelfde kenmerken. Toch wordt op voornoemde terreinen aan deze kenmerken een andere betekenis toegekend. Zo vormt restitutio in integrum op beide terreinen een algemeen erkend en leidend beginsel bij de toekenning van herstelbetalingen. Restitutio in integrum wordt door het Internationaal Gerechtshof volgens internationaal recht geïnterpreteerd als restitutiemaatregelen gericht op het herstel van de schade als gevolg van de inbreuk of een schending, terwijl het *IACtHR* dit beschouwt als een combinatie van tenminste drie maatregelen: financiële compensatie, rehabilitatie en genoegdoening, in het bijzonder bij de behandeling van grove mensenrechtenschendingen.

Ondanks het feit dat de maatregelen voor rechtsherstel op het terrein van het internationale recht inzake mensenrechten werden afgeleid van de in het internationaal publiekrecht erkende maatregelen (restitutie, compensatie en genoegdoening), kent het internationale recht inzake mensenrechten tevens rehabilitatiemaatregelen en garanties van niet-herhaling. Dit onderzoek toont dat er op het terrein van het internationale recht inzake mensenrechten sprake is van een slachtoffergerichte trend bij de door de gerechten, i.h.b. het *IACtHR* en het Europese Hof voor de Rechten van de Mens (EHRM), toegekende maatregelen. Aanvankelijk speelden declaratoire vonnissen en financiële compensatie een belangrijke rol bij de herstelbetalingen op het terrein van de mensenrechten, in het bijzonder bij het EHRM. Dit is te verklaren uit de klassieke opvatting dat herstelbetalingen zijn gebaseerd op het recht inzake de onrechtmatige daad en overheidsaansprakelijkheid. In de loop der tijd heeft de correctieve benadering van het *IACtHR* bijgedragen tot een meer holistische en creatieve opvatting van herstelbetalingen, met inbegrip van zowel materiele als immateriële (symbolische) maatregelen. Ter leniging van de bijzondere behoeften van individuele slachtoffers en ter voorkoming van verdere schendingen heeft het *IACtHR* de vijf erkende maatregelen voor rechtsherstel (restitutie, compensatie, rehabilitatie, genoegdoening en garanties van niet-herhaling) toegekend. Het *IACtHR* heeft geen formule ontwikkeld voor het vaststellen van een juiste combinatie van passende maatregelen, maar heeft van geval tot geval gekozen voor een combinatie.

Het *IACtHR* kent doorgaans een combinatie van materiële en symbolische maatregelen toe.

Volgens het internationaal publiekrecht en het recht inzake mensenrechten kunnen herstelbetalingen worden toegekend, indien is voldaan aan bepaalde procedurele vereisten (bijv. causaliteit, bewijsstandaard). De door de gerechten gehanteerde toetsen ter vaststelling van deze kenmerken verschillen echter. Internationale gerechten inzake mensenrechten hanteren doorgaans een flexibele benadering van causaliteit, de bewijsstandaard en het gebruik van vooronderstellingen. Ofschoon het internationaal publiekrecht op indirecte wijze collectieve belangen beschermt via de verplichting van de overheid tot stopzetting en niet-herhalingsverzekeringen en -garanties, kent dit geen CH als zodanig. Deze laatste zijn ontwikkeld door het *IACtHR* met het oogmerk om genoegdoening te verschaffen en om in zaken waarin het grote aantallen slachtoffers betreft de levens van slachtoffers te transformeren.

Hoofdstuk III: Collectieve herstelbetalingen bij het Inter-Amerikaans Hof voor de Rechten van de Mens

Collectieve vergoedingen behoren tot het domein van het recht inzake mensenrechten. Het *IACtHR* heeft op dit terrein pionierswerk verricht door voornoemde vergoedingen, die oorspronkelijk waren ontwikkeld in het kader van overgangsrechtelijke mechanismen, te transponeren naar een regionaal gerecht voor mensenrechten. Het Hof heeft diverse collectieve vergoedingen toegekend, die verwant zijn aan genoegdoeningsmaatregelen, maar die soms genoegdoening overstijgen, zoals het heropenen van een school en een apotheek in een dorp waar grove mensenrechtenschendingen hebben plaatsgevonden, het oprichten van een gezondheidscentrum zodat slachtoffers in hun eigen dorp medische en psychologische zorg kunnen krijgen, het investeren van een bepaald geldbedrag in werken of diensten in het algemeen belang, en het inrichten van specifieke programma's waarmee kan worden voorzien in gratis psychologische en psychiatrische behandelingen op collectief, gezins- en individueel niveau. Het *IACtHR* heeft echter geen nadere invulling gegeven aan het concept en de inhoud van CH. Evenmin heeft men de verschillen in kaart gebracht tussen CH die zijn ontwikkeld als onderdeel van het overgangsrecht en herstelbetalingen binnen het kader van het recht inzake mensenrechten. Men heeft evenmin nader uitgewerkt hoe deze maatregelen voortkomen uit het individuele recht op herstelbetalingen zoals dit is verankerd in Artikel 63 van de *American Convention on Human Rights*.

De bevindingen in hoofdstuk 3 tonen dat CH een beter antwoord vormen in die gevallen, waarin de slachtoffers een sterk gemeenschappelijk identiteitsgevoel delen (i.e. inheemse en in stamverband levende volkeren), of waarin individuele herstelbetalingen ontwrichtend kunnen zijn voor de orde van een bepaalde gemeenschap. Het Hof heeft weliswaar in zaken met een groot aantal slachtoffers CH toegewezen zonder onderzoek naar de aanwezigheid van sterke gemeenschapsbanden, maar het heeft deze hier gecombineerd met individuele herstelbetalingen. Uit het diepgaand onderzoek kan worden geconcludeerd, dat het Hof enkel CH toekent in zaken die land van de voorouders van inheemse en in stamverband levende volkeren betreffen. Het *IACtHR* heeft betoogd dat het CH ziet als een kans om de armoede en marginalisatie waarin de meeste slachtoffers leven aan te pakken. Het *IACtHR* tracht te voorkomen dat mensen het slachtoffer blijven van dergelijke leefomstandigheden en heeft CH ingezet als middel om slachtoffers van schendingen, ten aanzien waarvan een land schuldig is bevonden, te compenseren, en om de gemarginaliseerde leefomstandigheden van inheemse en in stamverband levende volkeren te verbeteren.

Ofschoon CH een middel kunnen zijn om structurele problemen zoals armoede en marginalisatie aan te pakken, heeft het Hof de strategie om enkel CH toe te wijzen niet gehanteerd in gevallen waarin andere slachtoffers, bijv. boeren, leven onder omstandigheden van armoede en marginalisatie die vergelijkbaar zijn met die van de inheemse en in stamverband levende volkeren. In dit verband heeft Antowiak de vraag opgeworpen of de aanpak van het Hof, d.w.z. dat CH enkel worden toegekend aan inheemse en in stamverband levende volkeren, discriminerend is, niet alleen ten opzichte van deze twee groepen, maar ook ten opzichte van andere kansarme groepen. Zoals echter blijkt uit de bevindingen van dit hoofdstuk, hebben in het merendeel der gevallen waarin het Hof CH toekende, de vertegenwoordigers van de slachtoffers en/of de Inter-Amerikaanse Commissie voor de Rechten van de Mens expliciet dergelijke voorzieningen gevorderd. Tot slot kan men, ondanks het feit dat het *IACtHR* zich niet heeft uitgelaten over de verhouding tussen CH en het recht op individuele herstelbetalingen, concluderen dat het Hof het recht op individuele herstelbetalingen interpreteert als een collectief recht in geval van schendingen met betrekking tot het land van de voorouders van inheemse en in stamverband levende volkeren.

Hoofdstuk IV: Collectieve herstelbetalingen in het internationaal strafrecht

Het internationaal strafrecht, met name zoals dit is ontwikkeld door het Cambodjatribunaal en het Internationaal Strafhof, heeft de jurisprudentie van het *IACtHR* inzake de toekenning van CH gevolgd. Het verschil tussen beide voornoemde strafgerechten en het *IACtHR* bestaat erin, dat de eerdergenoemde gerechten zich kunnen beroepen op expliciete bepalingen in hun juridische stelsels, die hen de bevoegdheid verlenen tot het toekennen van CH. Nochtans beschikken beide gerechten niet over concrete richtlijnen voor de invulling en uitvoering van CH. Dit kan worden verklaard door het ontbreken van precedenten voor herstelbetalingen in het internationaal strafrecht. De door het Internationaal Strafhof en het Cambodjatribunaal toegekende herstelbetalingen realiseren gerechtigheid die verder gaat dan vergelding. Bovendien erkennen beide gerechten dat individuele daders niet alleen strafrechtelijk verantwoordelijk zijn voor de door hen begane misdrijven, maar dat zij ook aansprakelijk zijn voor de aan de slachtoffers toegebrachte schade.

Tegenwoordig kennen het Internationaal Strafhof en het Cambodjatribunaal herstelbetalingen veelal toe in de vorm van CH. Waar het Cambodjatribunaal uitsluitend CH kan toekennen, heeft het Internationaal Strafhof tevens de bevoegdheid tot het toekennen van individuele herstelbetalingen. CH worden geschikt geacht, gezien de onduidelijkheid over het aantal slachtoffers, de ingewikkelde identificatie van slachtoffers en de problemen die tussen gemeenschappen en slachtoffers kunnen ontstaan naar aanleiding van individuele herstelbetalingen, met name als in deze gemeenschappen nog geweld heerst. Deze vorm van herstelbetalingen is ook eenvoudiger uit te voeren, omdat men minder middelen nodig heeft en een groter aantal slachtoffers kan bereiken. CH zouden idealiter moeten worden toegekend naast individuele herstelbetalingen in plaats van ter vervanging ervan, omdat de slachtoffers van internationale misdrijven zowel individuele als collectieve schade lijden. Een goed voorbeeld van het voorgaande is de *Katanga* zaak bij het Internationaal Strafhof, waarin symbolische individuele maatregelen werden toegekend naast CH.

Het Internationaal Strafhof kent twee organen ter verlening van genoegdoening: het Internationaal Strafhof en het Trustfonds voor Slachtoffers (*Trust Fund for Victims, TFV*). Vanuit juridisch oogpunt wordt de door het Trustfonds verleende hulp veeleer gekwalificeerd als humanitaire hulp dan als herstelbetaling, omdat herstelbetalingen altijd zijn gekoppeld aan een beschikking van het Internationaal Strafhof. De verleende hulp beoogt echter ook herstel en kan daarom samenvallen met de inhoud van een beschikking tot rechtsherstel. Zo kunnen slachtoffers bijvoorbeeld toegang krijgen tot voorzieningen in de gezondheidszorg op basis van een hulpmandaat van het Trustfonds en daarnaast toegang krijgen tot voorzieningen in de gezondheidszorg als rehabilitatiemaatregel in het kader van een herstelbeschikking. Gemeten naar het verkregen voordeel is het onderscheid tussen herstelbetalingen en hulp voor de slachtoffers niet relevant. Het belangrijkste verschil is, dat hulp van het Trustfonds kan worden beschouwd als een symbool van solidariteit vanuit de internationale gemeenschap, niet alleen met de slachtoffers, wier zaak gewoon is toegevoegd aan de stapel met zaken van het Internationaal Strafhof, maar ook met de desbetreffende gemeenschap in het algemeen. Evenals bij het Internationaal Strafhof kunnen slachtoffers ten overstaan van het Cambodjatribunaal genoegdoening verkrijgen via de hulp van de *Victims Support Section, VSS,* vergelijkbaar met het Trustfonds, en via herstelbetalingen. De *VSS* heeft echter zeer weinig hulpprojecten geïmplementeerd; dit wordt mogelijkerwijs veroorzaakt doordat aan het Cambodjatribunaal een veel beperkter budget werd toegekend. Een discussie over een mogelijk overlappen van deze hulp en herstelbetalingen ontbreekt daarom.

Om in aanmerking te komen voor herstelbetalingen dient er, evenals bij het *IACtHR*, bij het Internationaal Strafhof en het Cambodjatribunaal sprake te zijn van een causaal verband tussen de door de slachtoffers geleden schade en de misdrijven waarvoor de verdachte is veroordeeld. De laatstgenoemde gerechten hanteren echter strengere maatstaven, zowel ten aanzien van de causaliteitstoets als ten aanzien van andere procedurele vereisten, zoals de bewijsstandaard en het voor het bewijs van de schade vereiste bewijsmateriaal, evenals vereisten met betrekking tot de slachtofferidentificatie.

Hoofdstuk V: Collectieve herstelbetalingen en buitengerechtelijke organen

Rechtsherstel vormt een van de kernonderdelen van overgangsrechtspraak. Het is echter vaak geen haalbare kaart om alle schade als gevolg van in het verleden gepleegde grove mensenrechtenschendingen te herstellen en tegelijkertijd instituties te herbouwen en sociale voorzieningen voor alle burgers te verzorgen. Hoewel herstelbetalingen in het kader van overgangsrechtspraak vanuit wetenschappelijk oogpunt idealiter bestaan uit een combinatie van individuele en collectieve vergoedingen, heeft men ook geaccepteerd dat CH voor het uitvoerende land realistischer en veelomvattender zijn. Gesteld wordt dat bij CH de transformatieve benadering het meest geschikt is, omdat men beoogt via de herstelbetalingen structurele problemen, zoals armoede, ongelijkheid en marginalisatie, aan te pakken.

Voor het aanpakken van grove mensenrechtenschendingen zijn er behalve CH ook procedures voor massavorderingen ingesteld. Ofschoon deze procedures zich onderscheiden van de nationale collectieve herstelbetalingsprogramma's is er duidelijk ook een aantal overeenkomsten, zoals i) flexibiliteit wat betreft de vereisten voor het vaststellen van de bewijslast; ii) de mogelijkheid van herstelbetalingen voor een groot aantal slachtoffers; en iii) selectie van begunstigden. Zowel de massavorderingen als de nationale herstelbetalingsprogramma's voorkomen dat gerechten worden overspoeld met duizenden individuele vorderingen of rechtszaken, door herstelbetalingen buiten de rechtszaal vorm te geven. Landen kunnen een voorkeur hebben voor de tweede optie, de nationale herstelbetalingsprogramma's, omdat deze goederen en diensten leveren, die landen helpen om verdelende gerechtigheid en ontwikkeling in het land te bereiken. Commissies of herstelbetalingsprogramma's op basis van massavorderingen verdienen mogelijkerwijs de voorkeur, als landen naast het toekennen van herstelbetalingen aan slachtoffers, de aansprakelijkheid van overheidsactoren of van gewapende overheidsgroepen conform het humanitaire recht moeten vaststellen.

Ofschoon zowel collectieve herstelbetalingsprogramma's als herstelbetalingsprogramma's op basis van massavorderingen voorzien in herstelbetalingen voor grote aantallen slachtoffers, zijn de voordelen ervan beperkt tot bepaalde groepen slachtoffers, omdat het beleid inzake de te compenseren misdrijven vooraf wordt vastgesteld. Ofschoon politieke beslissingen die resulteren in selectieve criteria ten aanzien van te compenseren misdrijven het individuele recht op herstelbetalingen van veel slachtoffers ondermijnen, laten collectieve herstelbetalingsprogramma's en massavorderingen ruimte voor een grote pool van begunstigden binnen de gekozen groep van in aanmerking komende slachtoffers, die collectieve voordelen geniet. Vergeleken met herstelbetalingsprogramma's op basis van massavorderingen, kunnen CH ten goede komen aan grotere aantallen slachtoffers, en zelfs aan daders. Collectieve herstelbetalingen kunnen echter, in tegenstelling tot massavorderingen en individuele herstelbetalingen, ook de daders ten goede komen (een ziekenhuis bouwen als een collectieve herstelbetalingsmaatregel zal uiteindelijk ten goede komen aan een gehele bevolking zonder onderscheid tussen wie slachtoffer of dader is). Tot slot, een wijdverspreid probleem rond het herstellen van slachtoffers van grove schendingen van mensenrechten is het ontbreken van voldoende bewijs om de geleden schade te bewijzen. Ter oplossing van het probleem van ontoereikend bewijsmateriaal, ontwikkelden de claims commissies en de waarheids- en verzoeningscommissies nieuwe procedés, zoals verlaging van de bewijsstandaard, bundeling of groepering van categorieën van vorderingen, wijziging van bewijsvermoedens, gebruik van statistische steekproeven en toekenning van forfaitaire bedragen aan bepaalde categorieën slachtoffers of vorderingen.

Hoofdstuk VI: Conclusies

Ondanks het bestaan van een individueel recht op herstelbetalingen, is herstel van alle door slachtoffers van grove mensenrechtenschendingen geleden schade in wezen niet haalbaar. Het verstrekken van adequate herstelbetalingen met inachtneming van de context waarin de misdrijven plaatsvonden, zou idealiter individuele en collectieve herstelbetalingsmaatregelen behelzen. Individuele herstelbetalingen kunnen echter de beperkt beschikbare financiële en natuurlijke middelen van een land in gevaar brengen; deze middelen zijn nodig voor de heropbouw van de maatschappij, het aanbieden van sociale voorzieningen en implementeren van diverse, voor het bereiken van stabiliteit vereiste politieke hervormingen. Het probleem van de beperkte middelen wordt verergerd in landen die in economisch opzicht al arm waren, zelfs voordat er een conflict ontstond of een repressieve regering aan de macht kwam.

Roht-Arriaza betoogt bovendien dat individuele herstelbetalingen geen adequate oplossing bieden voor de structurele problemen die vaak aan een conflict ten grondslag liggen, en derhalve inadequate maatregelen zijn die hoogstwaarschijnlijk niet beantwoorden aan de behoeften van gemeenschappen die net uit een conflictsituatie komen. Individuele herstelbetalingen kunnen bovendien een ontwrichtend effect hebben. Dit effect hoeft niet alleen betrekking te hebben op de algemene economie en het vermogen van een land om elementaire sociale voorzieningen voor alle burgers te verzorgen, maar kan zich ook uitstrekken tot de slachtoffers zelf. In het bijzonder in landen met een langlopend gewelddadig conflict waar de rollen van slachtoffer en dader in de loop der tijd zijn gewisseld, moeten er ingewikkelde discussies worden gevoerd over de vraag wie de slachtofferstatus verdient; deze bergen de mogelijkheid in zich van een continue ontwrichting van gemeenschappen. Voor individuele herstelbetalingen geldt voorts een hoge bewijsstandaard, waardoor procedures lang en vrij kostbaar kunnen worden. Ook dient men de mogelijke belasting van slachtoffers in deze zaken niet te onderschatten. Bovendien moeten slachtoffers bij individuele herstelbetalingen gewoonlijk voorafgaand aan de toekenning van de herstelbetalingen worden geïdentificeerd. In de nasleep van grove mensenrechtenschendingen is dit meestal onmogelijk in de vroege fase van enig herstelbetalingsproces.

Grove mensenrechtenschendingen hebben bovendien collectief ervaren trauma's en schade tot gevolg; CH zijn uitermate geschikt voor de aanpak van dergelijke schade. Ondanks het feit dat CH een enigszins beperkte focus hebben en zich vooral richten op collectieve schade, vormen zij een beter antwoord op de behoefte aan herstel bij de slachtoffers. CH zijn meer gericht op behoeften dan op rechten. Dit komt, omdat slachtoffers in beginsel recht hebben op herstelbetalingen voor alle geleden schade, en CH zich doorgaans richten op de meest primaire behoeften van slachtoffers. CH vormen zo een goed compromis tussen politieke wil, beperkte middelen en de imminente, en in veel gevallen, primaire behoeften van slachtoffers. Deze vormen van genoegdoening worden gezien als een betere keuze dan het alternatief: het ontbreken van herstelbetalingen. CH kunnen worden beschouwd als een middenweg tussen de behoeften van de slachtoffers in het heden en de behoeften van de gemeenschap in de toekomst.

Ondanks het feit dat CH veelvuldig worden gehanteerd, ontbreekt een algemeen geaccepteerde juridische of conceptuele definitie. Uit dit onderzoek blijkt echter, dat de volgende definitie overeenkomt met de door de gerechtelijke en buitengerechtelijke organen gehanteerde opvatting van CH. CH zijn: i) maatregelen of vergoedingen die ondeelbaar en divers zijn, ii) die worden toegekend aan collectieven of groepen mensen, iii) ter verlichting van de collectieve schade die is veroorzaakt door een schending van internationaal recht, iv) in de vorm van individuele of collectieve rechten. Deze vergoedingen worden doorgaans verstrekt in de vorm van politieke projecten (sociale programma's) en bergen de mogelijkheid in zich om de sociale condities van slachtoffers te transformeren en om het voortduren van slachtofferschap en collectief geweld of conflict te voorkomen.

Het onderwerp CH roept nog meer onbeantwoorde vragen op. Hoe lang kunnen slachtoffers hierop een beroep doen? Op basis waarvan wordt besloten of CH zullen geschieden in de vorm van symbolische of dienstverlenende maatregelen, of een combinatie hiervan? Uit de uitgevoerde analyse blijkt dat collectieve maatregelen voor rechtsherstel worden toegewezen op basis van geografische criteria (gemeenschap, stad, stedelijk of landelijk gebied) en van thema's, bijv. vredesopbouw, sociale voorzieningen, inkomen genererende activiteiten, herdenkingsmaatregelen, infrastructurele projecten en gerechtelijke hervormingen. Sociale voorzieningen, in het bijzonder maatregelen op het gebied van gezondheid- en onderwijs, worden het meest toegekend. De reden hiervoor is dat massale schendingen doorgaans een weerslag hebben op het algemeen vermogen van een land om sociale voorzieningen en infrastructuur te verzorgen, en dat slachtoffers hieraan juist vaak dringend behoefte hebben.

Binnen de drie onderzochte gebieden – internationaal recht inzake mensenrechten, internationaal strafrecht en overgangsrechtspraak – hanteert men verschillende termijnen voor het aanbieden van CH. Het *IACtHR* heeft CH toegewezen, zowel op een permanente basis (het heropenen van een school of het starten van mensenrechtentrainingen voor de politie en het leger), als op basis van een bepaald geldbedrag. Wanneer het geld is uitgegeven aan of geïnvesteerd in collectieve herstelbetalingsprojecten, wordt het land geacht de beslissing te hebben nageleefd. Het Internationaal Strafhof daarentegen hanteert een aantal termijnen. CH staan gedurende een termijn van 2 tot 4 jaar ter beschikking van de slachtoffers. Op het gebied van de overgangsrechtspraak worden nationale CH die betrekking hebben op dienstverlenende maatregelen gewoonlijk op permanente basis opgelegd. De reden hiervoor is, dat slachtoffers worden geacht deze sociale voorzieningen reeds te hebben ontvangen vóór hun victimisatie. Zo vormen CH een brug die toegang verschaft tot andere, economische, sociale en culturele rechten.

Hoewel het internationale recht zich in beginsel richt op het individu en er geen grond is voor het toekennen van enkel CH, zijn er zowel op het gebied van het internationale recht inzake mensenrechten, via de jurisprudentie van het *IACtHR*, als op het gebied van het internationaal strafrecht, via de juridische instrumenten en de jurisprudentie van het Internationaal Strafhof en het Cambodjatribunaal, bijdragen geleverd ter rechtvaardiging van het toekennen van enkel CH bij bepaalde scenario's. Hierbij is men echter op een aantal problemen gestuit:

a) Vaststelling van de begunstigden: volgens overgangsrechtspraak-mechanismen en het internationale recht inzake mensenrechten, kunnen gemeenschappen en groepen als zodanig begunstigden zijn van herstelbetalingen; volgens het internationaal strafrecht daarentegen kunnen enkel de leden van een bepaalde gemeenschap die in een specifiek geval zijn erkend als slachtoffers worden beschouwd als begunstigden. In het eerste geval ligt het probleem in het voorzien van de gevolgen van de erkenning van gemeenschappen en groepen als begunstigden. Want houdt dit nu in dat deze groepen ook kunnen worden erkend als entiteiten die behalve het recht op herstelbetalingen ook andere rechten hebben? Maar ook indien men uitsluitend de slachtoffers in een zaak erkent als begunstigden zoals het Internationaal Strafhof vereist, stuit men op lastige problemen. Het plegen van grove mensenrechtenschendingen victimiseert doorgaans hele gemeenschappen en het verstrekken van vergoedingen enkel aan een geselecteerde groep mensen kan spanningen creëren.

b) Bepaling van adequaatheid en inhoud: gerechten en buitengerechtelijke organen beslissen zonder juridische of gezaghebbende richtlijnen en van geval tot geval wanneer enkel CH en wanneer een combinatie van deze met individuele herstelbetalingen adequaat is/zijn (al naargelang hun mandaat dit toestaat). Het achterliggende ideaal van collectieve herstelbetalingsprogramma's is om ervoor te zorgen, dat een groot aantal slachtoffers baat heeft bij een bepaald programma. Dit ideaal wordt echter alleen gerealiseerd, indien de slachtoffers iets ontvangen wat voor hen noodzakelijk of belangrijk is. Het is duidelijk dat slachtofferparticipatie bij het ontwerpen en implementeren van de programma's van belang is. Maar participatie van de slachtoffers is op zijn beurt pas mogelijk als deze vroegtijdig zijn geïdentificeerd door een hiertoe bevoegd orgaan. Het identificeren van slachtoffers van grove mensenrechtenschendingen is echter niet in alle gevallen makkelijk of mogelijk.

c) Vervulling van de vereisten van bewijs en causaliteit: Zowel individuele als CH moeten voldoen aan bewijs- en causaliteitsvereisten. Internationale gerechten erkennen doorgaans dat flexibiliteit is vereist bij het toepassen van deze eisen, in het bijzonder in gevallen van grove mensenrechtenschendingen, om de moeilijkheid van bewijsvergaring voor de slachtoffers te verdisconteren. Dezelfde flexibiliteit ziet men ook bij procedures voor massavorderingen. Helaas definiëren de gerechtelijke en buitengerechtelijke organen de vereiste, specifieke toets niet, en laten zij zich evenmin uit over het verschil tussen de toetsen voor collectieve, en die voor individuele herstelbetalingen. Bijgevolg is het voor slachtoffers die herstelbetalingen wensen te verkrijgen onduidelijk, welke vereisten er gelden voor de toekenning van CH aan hen.

d) Vaststelling van de schade: Het is algemeen erkend dat grove mensenrechtenschendingen leiden tot immense individuele en collectieve schade. Voor het toekennen van herstelbetalingen moeten gerechtelijke en buitengerechtelijke organen de schade die het gevolg is van de bewezen schendingen echter definiëren. Dit is in het bijzonder van belang in het internationaal strafrecht, omdat de veroordeelde persoon enkel aansprakelijk kan zijn voor het herstel van de schade die het gevolg is van de misdaden waarvoor hij of zij werd veroordeeld. Ondanks het belang van dit onderwerp komt er noch bij de gerechtelijke, noch bij de buitengerechtelijke organen één enkele methode ter vaststelling van de schade naar voren. Uit het onderzoek is gebleken, dat soms de hulp van deskundigen wordt ingeroepen om gerechtelijke organen te assisteren bij het vaststellen van de schade, maar dat in de meeste de gevallen het gerecht zelf de schade vaststelt. Het is maar de vraag, of de leden van een bepaalde kamer beschikken over voldoende financiële deskundigheid om multidimensionale en veelgelaagde schades te kunnen kwantificeren. Bovendien hebben rechters zich doorgaans beroepen op het billijkheidsbeginsel in de gevallen waarin er onvoldoende bewijs voorhanden was om de financiële omvang van een vordering vast te stellen. Vaak gebeurde dit in gevallen van morele schade.

Ofschoon CH de indruk kunnen wekken dat men met minder genoegen neemt, wordt hierbij wel rekening gehouden met een groter aantal slachtoffers en met de consequenties van grove mensenrechtenschendingen in bredere zin. CH richten zich op de aanpak van sociaal onrecht en op het bevorderen van de ontwikkeling van de gemeenschap; ze vormen echter een compromis en een middenweg tussen juridische rechten en pragmatisme in uitzonderlijke omstandigheden. Het is in dit verband van belang om te memoreren dat, ofschoon regionale gerechten voor de mensenrechten, zoals het *IACtHR,* zich hebben beziggehouden met grove mensenrechtenschendingen, deze gerechtelijke mechanismen werden ingesteld voor de omgang met 'gewone misdrijven' en niet met grove mensenrechtenschendingen. Bovendien werden het Internationaal Strafhof, het Cambodjatribunaal, nationale herstelbetalingsprogramma's en massavorderingen in het leven geroepen om te voorzien in 'buitengewone' gerechtigheid, hetgeen inhoudt dat er belangrijke beperkingen zijn aan de gerechtigheid die zij kunnen realiseren. Het Internationaal Strafhof en het Cambodjatribunaal concentreren zich op de vervolging van de daders die zo direct mogelijk verantwoordelijk zijn voor het begaan van de ernstigste mensenrechtenschendingen. Nationale herstelbetalingsprogramma's en claims commissies concentreren zich op het herstel van een beperkt aantal misdaden, die niet worden beschouwd als gewoon, maar veeleer zijn begaan onder de buitengewone omstandigheden van een conflict of een autoritair regime. Gezien deze institutionele restricties kan worden gesteld, dat al deze rechterlijke en semirechterlijke mechanismen de door Boven beschreven trilogie van elementaire gerechtigheid -waarheid, gerechtigheid en herstel- enkel onder buitengewone omstandigheden aan slachtoffers kunnen bieden. Gray bevestigt dat 'gewone rechtspleging' zich richt op de vergoeding van individuele schade, hetgeen in het geval van op grote schaal gepleegde misdaden niet realistisch noch wenselijk is. Grove mensenrechtenschendingen vormen buitengewone gevallen, die men moet benaderen met buitengewone maatregelen en een zekere creativiteit.

Volgens het concept van buitengewone en gewone rechtspleging, zoals gehanteerd door Gray, moeten herstelbetalingen voor buitengewone gevallen, ongeacht of deze worden berecht conform internationaal recht inzake mensenrechten, internationaal strafrecht of in de context van overgangsrechtspraak, bij voorkeur worden benaderd naar buitengewone en niet naar gewone maatstaven. Aangezien CH zelf een buitengewone vorm van herstelbetalingen zijn, kan worden geconcludeerd dat het individuele recht op herstelbetalingen wel degelijk op gespannen voet staat met de toekenning van CH aan slachtoffers van grove mensenrechtenschendingen. Dit zou betekenen dat met de toekenning van enkel CH aan slachtoffers van grove mensenrechtenschendingen, niet wordt voldaan aan de eis van een individueel recht op herstelbetalingen. Het mensenrechteninstrumentarium is echter oorspronkelijk niet in het leven geroepen ter behandeling van buitengewone zaken met een grootschalige schending van de mensenrechten voor internationale gerechten. Bij de aanpak van grove schendingen van de mensenrechten zouden CH wel eens een 'betere' keuze kunnen zijn, niet alleen voor landen, maar ook voor gerechten. De reden hiervoor is, dat gerechtigheid niet alleen wordt gerealiseerd met inachtneming van huidige behoeften, maar ook met inachtneming van toekomstige behoeften op de kortere en langere termijn, evenals met inachtneming van de beschikbare middelen, niet alleen ter uitvoering van de herstelbetalingen, maar ook ter vervulling van de eisen voor toekenning van herstelbetalingen (procedurele vereisten).

Ongeacht of CH gerechtvaardigd zijn om redenen van buitengewone gerechtigheid, ter vergroting van de overlevingskansen en veiligstelling van enkele aspecten van het bestaansminimum van toekomstige generaties, of omdat overheden hieraan de voorkeur geven vanwege de lagere kosten, dient bij het toekennen of vaststellen van deze vormen van herstelbetalingen de naleving ervan te worden gegarandeerd. Gerechtelijke en buitengerechtelijke organen dienen de grenzen af te bakenen van elk aspect van CH om de implementatie ervan te garanderen. Dit biedt slachtoffers tevens enige zekerheid ten aanzien van hetgeen zij in een procedure kunnen verwachten en vorderen. Het ontbreken van een uniform concept van CH hoeft derhalve geen probleem te zijn, in het bijzonder als wij aanvaarden dat het concept van CH continu in ontwikkeling is. Het ontbreken van een gedetailleerde uitwerking van de keuzes bij de toekenning van CH door gerechtelijke en buitengerechtelijke organen vormt daarentegen wel een probleem.

Resumen

Capítulo I: Introducción y pregunta principal de investigación

La persistencia y la repetición de graves violaciones de los derechos humanos (GVDH) han dado lugar a un enorme número de víctimas en todo el mundo. Los que no han sido asesinados, se han visto afectados por el asesinato de sus seres queridos y por las violaciones de derechos tales como la detención prolongada y la tortura, la mutilación, la violación o la destrucción de sus propiedades, de sus hogares y medios de subsistencia. Las consecuencias físicas, psicológicas y económicas, tanto a nivel individual como social, son en cierta medida inconmensurables e irreparables. También hay que tomar en cuenta que mayoría de las GVDH se producen en plena inestabilidad política, cuando las instituciones estatales apenas funcionan y el Estado de derecho está ausente. Además, los Estados que hacen la transición a una forma de gobierno más democrática se enfrentan a varios obstáculos, consecuencia de los abusos del pasado. Estos obstáculos pueden ser políticos y legales, así como materiales. Asimismo existen varios factores pueden evitar que las víctimas busquen y obtengan justicia. Algunos de ellos son la gran cantidad de víctimas, la dificultad de determinar quién es la víctima y/o el perpetrador, especialmente cuando hablamos de conflictos que han durado mucho tiempo, así como la falta de capacidad y los recursos limitados del Estado en cuestión. Estas circunstancias limitan igualmente la capacidad de los Estados para proporcionar reparaciones. Dado que las autoridades estatales a menudo están directa o indirectamente involucradas en la perpetración de GVDH, una cultura de impunidad comienza a desarrollarse a partir de la incapacidad o falta de voluntad para responsabilizar a dichas autoridades.

Durante muchos años, las víctimas dependieron de la voluntad y la capacidad de los Estados para obtener cualquier tipo de justicia, porque ellas no podían recurrir a mecanismos de justicia internacional para presentar sus reclamos cuando las vías nacionales para la justicia no estaban disponibles o eran ineficaces. Sin embargo, esta situación ha cambiado gradualmente. Reparar o "enmendar" los agravios sufridos por las víctimas, especialmente cuando el daño sufrido es particularmente grave, es hoy en día un imperativo tanto moral como legal para los Estados. Los foros internacionales que tienen como objetivo facilitar la reparación de GVDH, incluidos los que constituyen crímenes internacionales, ahora están disponibles para las víctimas. Además, el reconocimiento generalizado del derecho de una víctima a un remedio y reparación condujo a que la Asamblea General de las Naciones Unidas adoptara de los Principios y directrices básicos sobre el derecho de las víctimas de violaciones manifiestas de las normas internacionales de derechos humanos y de violaciones graves del derecho internacional humanitario a interponer recursos y obtener reparaciones.

De acuerdo con estos Principios, la reparación a las víctimas puede tomar la forma de restitución, compensación, rehabilitación, satisfacción o garantías de no repetición. Sin embargo, se puede identificar una tendencia entre los órganos judiciales y no judiciales respecto de las reparaciones otorgadas a las víctimas de GVDH. Cuando se trata de un gran número de víctimas, dichos órganos tienden a otorgar beneficios predominantemente colectivos, ya que esta forma de reparación se considera la más adecuada. Además, no son solo los gobiernos tienden a crear programas accesibles para un gran número de beneficiarios; las Comisiones de la Verdad también han recomendado repetidamente reparaciones colectivas (RC). Asimismo, la Corte Interamericana de Derechos Humanos (Corte IDH), un tribunal que ha proporcionado las formas más amplias de reparación entre todos los órganos de derechos humanos, también ha otorgado RC a las víctimas de crímenes masivos. Las Cámaras Extraordinarias en los Tribunales de Camboya (CETC) y la Corte Penal Internacional (CPI) han adoptado también esta práctica. Las RC otorgadas incluyen programas de vivienda y salud, así como programas de desarrollo comunitario. Es interesante señalar que dichas RC raramente se conceden junto con reparaciones individuales.

Si bien el discurso que rodea el derecho de todas las víctimas de crímenes, incluidas las de GVDH a recibir reparaciones, establece claramente que tienen derecho a medidas colectivas además de las reparaciones individuales, en la práctica rara vez se otorgan medidas colectivas de manera suplementaria. En cambio, los órganos judiciales y no judiciales tienden a otorgar a las víctimas solamente RC a las víctimas de GVDH, En este sentido, la principal pregunta de investigación de este libro fue: ¿Cuáles son las tensiones entre el derecho individual a recibir reparaciones y la concesión de RC para las víctimas de GVDH? Para responder a esta consulta, esta investigación analizó el entendimiento de las RC por parte de los órganos judiciales y no judiciales en tres marcos a saber, el derecho internacional de los derechos humanos, el derecho penal internacional y una selección de procesos de justicia transicional. Al llevar a cabo dicho análisis, la investigación se limitó a estudiar jurisprudencia específica de la Corte IDH, la CPI y las CETC. Además, se examinaron las prácticas de los mecanismos no judiciales, específicamente las de las Comisiones de la Verdad peruanas y marroquíes y de dos comisiones de indemnización o de reclamaciones masivas (la Comisión de Indemnización de las Naciones Unidas y la Comisión de Reclamaciones de Eritrea y Etiopía).

Capítulo II: Desarrollos relacionados con el derecho a la reparación

El entendimiento de las reparaciones de las víctimas dentro del derecho internacional ha evolucionado con el tiempo. Inicialmente, las reparaciones se entendían como una obligación estatal frente a otro Estado, pero con la adopción de instrumentos internacionales de derechos humanos, las reparaciones se consideran hoy en día una obligación estatal en relación con los Estados y las personas. Las reparaciones bajo el derecho internacional público y de los derechos humanos comparten características similares. Sin embargo, esas características tienen un significado diferente dentro de estas dos áreas del derecho. Por ejemplo, en ambas áreas, *restitutio in integrum* ha sido reconocido como un principio rector al otorgar reparaciones. Mientras que bajo el derecho internacional público, la Corte Internacional de Justicia (CIJ) ha entendido *restitutio in integrum* como aquellas medidas de restitución destinadas a restaurar el daño causado por la infracción o una violación, la Corte IDH lo ha entendido como la combinación de al menos tres medidas: compensación financiera, rehabilitación y satisfacción, especialmente cuando se dirige a GVDH.

A pesar de que las medidas de reparación en el ámbito del derecho internacional de los derechos humanos se construyeron sobre la base de las reconocidas en el derecho internacional público (restitución, indemnización y satisfacción), el derecho internacional de los derechos humanos también incluye medidas de rehabilitación y garantías de no-repetición. Dentro del campo del derecho internacional de los derechos humanos, la investigación muestra una tendencia orientada a favor de las víctimas en las medidas otorgadas por los tribunales, en particular, la Corte IDH y el Tribunal Europeo de Derechos Humanos (TEDH). Dado que la comprensión clásica de las reparaciones se basa en principios relativos al derecho civil de responsabilidad extracontractual y las leyes sobre la responsabilidad del Estado por hechos internacionalmente ilícitos, al principio las sentencias declarativas y la compensación financiera desempeñaron un papel destacado dentro de las reparaciones en el campo de los derechos humanos, especialmente ante el TEDH. Con los años, sin embargo, el enfoque sobre reparaciones de la Corte IDH ha contribuido a un entendimiento más integral y creativo de las reparaciones aportando nuevas perspectivas sobre medidas materiales y no materiales (simbólicas). Con el objetivo de atender las necesidades particulares de las víctimas individuales y prevenir nuevas violaciones, la Corte IDH ha otorgado las cinco medidas reconocidas de reparación (restitución, indemnización, rehabilitación, satisfacción y garantías de no repetición) de una manera creativa. La Corte IDH no ha desarrollado una fórmula general que determine un conjunto de medidas apropiadas; en cambio, decide tomando en consideración las circunstancias especiales del caso. Sin embargo, generalmente otorga una combinación tanto de medidas materiales, como simbólicas.

Según el derecho internacional público y el derecho internacional de los derechos humanos, las reparaciones pueden otorgarse si se cumplen ciertos requisitos de procedimiento (i.e. causalidad, estándar de prueba). Sin embargo, los criterios empleados por los tribunales para determinar si esos requisitos se cumplen, varían. Los tribunales internacionales de derechos humanos por lo general se basan en un enfoque más flexible hacia la causalidad, el estándar de la prueba y el uso de presunciones. Finalmente, aunque en el derecho internacional público la obligación estatal de cesación y las garantías de no repetición protegen indirectamente los intereses colectivos, las RC no existen como tales. Estas últimas han sido desarrolladas por la Corte IDH con el objetivo de proporcionar reparación y con el objetivo de transformar las vidas de las víctimas en casos que involucran a un gran número de víctimas.

Capítulo III: Reparaciones Colectivas en la Corte Interamericana de Derechos Humanos

Las RC pertenecen al ámbito de las leyes de derechos humanos. En este sentido, la Corte IDH ha sido pionera al trasladar estas reparaciones, originalmente concebidos bajo los auspicios de los mecanismos de justicia transicional, a un tribunal regional de derechos humanos. La Corte ha ordenado diferentes RC, que a veces van más allá de la satisfacción, como la reapertura de una escuela y un dispensario médico en un pueblo afectado por GVDH; el establecimiento de un centro de salud para que las víctimas puedan obtener atención médica y psicológica en su propio pueblo; la inversión de una cantidad específica de dinero en servicios de interés comunitario y la creación de programas específicos para proporcionar tratamiento psicológico y psiquiátrico a nivel colectivo, familiar e individual. Sin embargo, la Corte IDH no ha definido el concepto y el contenido de las RC, ni ha identificado ninguna diferencia entre las RC desarrolladas dentro del marco de la justicia transicional y las otorgadas dentro del derecho internacional de los derechos humanos. La Corte tampoco ha explicado cómo estas medidas se derivan del derecho individual a la reparación tal como está consagrado en el Artículo 63 de la Convención Interamericana sobre los Derechos Humanos.

Sin embargo, las conclusiones del Capítulo III muestran que las RC ofrecen una mejor respuesta en casos donde las víctimas comparten un fuerte sentido de identidad común (dos ejemplos son los pueblos indígenas y tribales) o donde las reparaciones individuales pueden ser perjudiciales en el orden de una comunidad. No obstante, la Corte ha otorgado también RC en casos que involucran a un gran número de víctimas aún sin evaluar la existencia de fuertes lazos comunitarios. En estos casos, la Corte ha otorgado reparaciones individuales además de las colectivas. A partir de la investigación exhaustiva realizada, es posible concluir que la Corte otorga solamente RC en casos relativos a las tierras ancestrales de los pueblos indígenas y tribales. En este sentido, la Corte IDH ha sostenido que las RC presentan una oportunidad para abordar la pobreza y la marginación en la que viven la mayoría de las víctimas. Al tratar de evitar que las personas sigan siendo víctimas de tales condiciones de vida, la

Corte IDH ha utilizado las RC como una herramienta para compensar a las víctimas de violaciones perpetradas por el Estado, y para mejorar las condiciones de vida, por lo regular de marginación, de los pueblos indígenas y tribales.

Si bien las RC pueden ser una herramienta para abordar problemas estructurales como la pobreza y la marginación, la Corte no ha otorgado este tipo de medidas en casos en los que las víctimas viven en condiciones similares a las experimentadas por pueblos indígenas y tribales, como es el caso de campesinos. En este contexto, Antowiak cuestionó si el enfoque de la Corte de solo brindar RC a los pueblos indígenas y tribales es discriminatorio no solo para estos dos grupos, sino también para otros grupos no privilegiados. Sin embargo, como lo demuestran los hallazgos de este capítulo, en la mayoría de los casos en que la Corte ha otorgado RC, los representantes de las víctimas y / o la Comisión Interamericana de Derechos Humanos (CIADH) han pedido explícitamente que se les otorguen estas medidas como forma de reparación. En este sentido, la Corte IDH ha otorgado CR en base a las peticiones de las víctimas. Finalmente, aunque la Corte IDH no ha explicado cómo las RC coexisten con el derecho a reparaciones individuales, puede inferirse que la Corte interpreta el derecho a la reparación individual como un derecho colectivo en relación con violaciones a las tierras ancestrales de los pueblos indígenas y tribales.

Capítulo IV: Reparaciones colectivas en derecho penal internacional

El derecho penal internacional desarrollado específicamente por las CETC y la CPI ha seguido el enfoque de la jurisprudencia de la Corte IDH, en cuanto a su modelo de indemnización a través de RC. Sin embargo, los dos tribunales penales mencionados anteriormente se diferencian de la Corte IDH respecto a que sus marcos legales contienen disposiciones explícitas que les permiten otorgar RC. No obstante, éstos dos tribunales carecen de directrices concretas sobre la manera en que deben de darles contenido e implementarlas. Esto puede explicarse por la falta de precedentes sobre reparaciones a víctimas dentro del derecho penal internacional. En este sentido, se debe recordar que, a diferencia de otros tribunales penales internacionales, tanto la CPI como las CETC, brindan justicia más allá de los principios retributivos al proporcionar reparaciones a las víctimas. Estos tribunales han reconocido que los perpetradores individuales no solo son penalmente responsables de los crímenes que han cometido, sino que también son responsables del daño causado a las víctimas.

Hasta la fecha, las RC se han convertido en el sello distintivo de las reparaciones otorgados por la CPI y las CETC. Si bien las CETC solo pueden otorgar RC, la CPI también está facultada para otorgar reparaciones individuales. Cabe recordar, que las RC son consideradas adecuadas dada la incertidumbre con respecto al número de víctimas, las complejidades para identificarlas y los problemas potenciales que pueden surgir de las reparaciones individuales entre las comunidades y las propias víctimas, especialmente si esas comunidades aún están experimentando violencia. También se cree que esta forma de reparación es más factible, ya que requiere menos recursos y abre la puerta a un mayor número de víctimas. Al reconocer que las víctimas de crímenes internacionales sufren daños tanto individuales como colectivos, las RC deberían otorgarse, idealmente, de manera complementaria más que como un sustituto de las reparaciones individualizadas. Un buen ejemplo de dónde se puede lograr esto es el caso *Katanga* ante la CPI, donde se otorgaron medidas individuales simbólicas además de RC.

Dentro de la CPI, las victimas pueden obtener reparaciones a través de dos órganos diferentes: la misma corte (la CPI) y el Fondo Fiduciario en beneficio de las Víctimas (FFV). Sin embargo, hay que tomar en cuenta que, legalmente la asistencia brindada por el FFV es calificada como asistencia humanitaria en lugar de reparaciones. Además, las reparaciones siempre deberán estar vinculadas a una orden de la CPI. No obstante, la asistencia brindada por el FFV tiene un carácter reparador; por lo tanto, su contenido puede coincidir claramente con el contenido de una orden de reparación. Por ejemplo, como parte de la asistencia del FFV, las victimas pueden beneficiarse de acceso a servicios médicos, así como una orden de reparación pueden contener servicios médicos como parte de una medida de rehabilitación. De ahí que, se cuestione la diferencia entre estos beneficios que las victimas pueden obtener de la CPI. Sin embargo, para las víctimas, la distinción entre reparaciones y asistencia puede ser irrelevante en términos de los beneficios obtenidos. La principal diferencia es que las victimas pueden percibir la asistencia del Fondo como un símbolo de solidaridad de la comunidad internacional no solo con las víctimas que han visto su caso convertirse en parte de los casos de la CPI, sino con toda la comunidad afectada en general. Al igual que en el marco del CPI, las víctimas ante las CETC pueden buscar reparación a través de dos vías: la asistencia proporcionada por la Sección de Apoyo a las Víctimas (por su abreviación en inglés VSS), que es comparable a la proporcionada por el FFV, así como a través de reparaciones. Sin embargo, la VSS ha implementado proyectos de asistencia muy limitados; esto es quizás el resultado de que la CETC cuenta con un presupuesto mucho más limitado que aquel asignado a la CPI. En consecuencia, no ha habido debate sobre si la asistencia proporcionada por la VSS puede coincidir con el contenido con las reparaciones otorgadas por las CETC.

Como en el caso de la Corte IDH, tanto la CPI y las CETC requieren un vínculo causal entre el daño causado a las víctimas y los delitos por los cuales el acusado fue condenado para poder recibir reparaciones. Sin embargo, estos tribunales penales son más estrictos respecto al vínculo causal, así como a otras demandas procesales como lo son el estándar de la prueba y la evidencia necesaria para demostrar el daño, y los requisitos para la identificación de víctimas.

Capítulo V: Las reparaciones colectivas y órganos no judiciales

La reparación es uno de los elementos clave de los procesos de justicia transicional (JT). Sin embargo, el esperar que un Estado repare todos daños producto de la perpetración de GVDH mientras que al mismo tiempo reconstruya instituciones y brinde servicios sociales a todos los ciudadanos, es simplemente utópico. Mientras que algunos investigadores académicos han dicho que, en un escenario ideal, las reparaciones bajo JT consistirían en una combinación de reparaciones individuales y colectivas, también han aceptado que las RC son una opción más realista e inclusiva para los Estado. Dentro de las RC, se afirma que un enfoque transformador es el más apropiado ya que estas reparaciones apuntan a abordar problemas estructurales como la pobreza, la desigualdad y la marginación.

Además de las RC, también se han establecido procedimientos de reclamos masivos para abordar GVDH. Aunque estos procedimientos difieren de los programas nacionales de RC, es evidente que también comparten algunas similitudes, tales como: i) una comprensión flexible de los requisitos para cumplir con la carga de la prueba; ii) la posibilidad de proporcionar reparaciones a un gran número de víctimas, y iii) beneficiarios selectivos. Tanto los procedimientos de reclamos masivos, como los programas nacionales de reparaciones, evitan que los tribunales se inunden de miles de reclamos o demandas individuales mediante el diseño de reparaciones que no son de índole judicial, es decir, fuera de los tribunales. Ante estas dos opciones, los Estados pueden preferir los programas nacionales de RC porque proporcionan bienes y servicios que ayudan a los Estados a lograr la justicia distributiva y el desarrollo en el país. Las Comisiones o los Programas de Reparaciones de Reclamaciones Masivas (por su abreviación en inglés MCRs) pueden ser preferibles cuando, además de otorgar reparaciones a las víctimas, los Estados deben establecer la responsabilidad de los actores estatales o grupos armados según el derecho humanitario.

Al mismo tiempo que proporcionan reparaciones a un gran número de víctimas, las RC y los MCRs generalmente limitan sus beneficios a ciertos grupos de víctimas, ya que las políticas para los delitos que se compensarán se establecen de antemano. Si bien las decisiones políticas que dan lugar a criterios selectivos para delitos indemnizables socavan el derecho individual a la reparación de muchas víctimas, las RC y los programas de reparaciones masivas benefician a un amplio grupo de victimas previamente seleccionadas como beneficiarias.. En comparación con los MCRs, las RC pueden beneficiar a un mayor número de víctimas. Sin embargo las CR, a diferencia de las MRCs y las reparaciones individuales también pueden beneficiar a los perpetradores (i.e. el construir un hospital como medida de RC eventualmente va a beneficiar a toda una población sin distinción de quien es víctima o perpetrador). Finalmente, un problema generalizado en torno a reparar víctimas de GVDH es la falta de suficiente evidencia para probar los daños. Para enfrentar los desafíos de evidencia insuficiente, las comisiones de reclamaciones y las Comisiones de la Verdad y la Reconciliación (CVR) han desarrollado técnicas novedosas tales como el flexibilizar el estándar de prueba, la consolidación o agrupación de categorías de reclamaciones, el uso de presunciones probatorias, empleando muestreo estadístico y otorgando montos fijos a ciertas categorías de víctimas o reclamaciones.

Capítulo VI: Conclusiones

A pesar de la existencia de un derecho individual a la reparación, la reparación de todo el daño sufrido por las víctimas de GVDH es materialmente imposible. Proporcionar reparaciones adecuadas mientras se tiene en cuenta el contexto en el que los crímenes ocurrieron, idealmente implicaría el otorgamiento de reparaciones individuales y colectivas. Sin embargo, proporcionar reparaciones individuales puede socavar los limitados recursos financieros y naturales disponibles en un país determinado, mismos que son necesarios para reconstruir la sociedad, proporcionar servicios sociales e implementar las diversas reformas políticas necesarias para lograr la estabilidad. El problema de los recursos limitados se agrava en los países que ya eran económicamente pobres incluso antes de que un conflicto haya ocurrido o de que un gobierno represivo se haga cargo.

Además, Roht-Arriaza sostiene que las reparaciones individuales no abordan adecuadamente los problemas estructurales que a menudo subrayan un conflicto y, por lo tanto, son medidas inadecuadas que es improbable que estén en consonancia con las necesidades de las sociedades que salen de una situación de conflicto. Asimismo, las reparaciones individuales pueden tener efectos perjudiciales. Tales efectos pueden extenderse no solo a la economía general de un Estado y su capacidad de proporcionar programas sociales básicos a todos sus ciudadanos, sino también a las propias víctimas. Sin embargo, esto implica la necesidad de tener discusiones complejas como quién es merecedor de ser reconocido como víctima, discusiones que mientras resultan importantes para adoptar una política de reparaciones, también tienen el potencial de causar perturbaciones dentro de una sociedad, en particular en aquellos países donde los conflictos armados han durado varios años, ya que esto muy probablemente ha permitido que los roles de perpetradores y de víctimas cambien constantemente. Más aún, las reparaciones individuales requieren altos estándares de evidencia y, por lo tanto, son lentas, lo que significa que los procedimientos podrían volverse bastante costosos. La posible carga para las víctimas que participan en estos casos no debe subestimarse. Igualmente, las reparaciones individuales generalmente requieren la identificación de las víctimas antes de otorgar las reparaciones. No obstante, tal identificación generalmente no es posible en la etapa inicial de cualquier proceso de reparación relacionado la comisión de GVDH.

En general, los efectos de GVDH incluyen traumas y daños experimentados colectivamente, y tales daños se pueden abordar mediante RC. A pesar del enfoque predominantemente restringido que señala que RC abordan los daños colectivos, y no individuales, estas reparaciones constituyen una respuesta más factible a las necesidades de reparación de las víctimas. En este sentido, las RC responden más a las principales necesidades de las victimas que al carácter y entendimiento jurídico de lo que son las reparaciones. Esto se debe a que las víctimas tienen, en principio, el derecho a recibir reparaciones por todo el daño sufrido y las RC generalmente se enfocan en atender las necesidades más básicas de las víctimas. A la luz de esto, las RC presentan un compromiso justo entre la voluntad política, los recursos limitados y las inminentes necesidades básicas de las víctimas que se presentan en la mayoría de los casos relacionados a GVDH. Tales remedios son vistos como una mejor opción que la alternativa: la falta de reparaciones. Las RC se pueden considerar como un punto medio entre las necesidades actuales de las víctimas y las necesidades de la sociedad en el futuro.

A pesar de su uso generalizado, las RC no gozan de un significado único y aceptado tanto legal como conceptualmente. Sin embargo, esta investigación demostró que la siguiente definición se ajusta al entendimiento de las RC aplicadas por los órganos judiciales y no judiciales analizados en este estudio. Las RC son: i) medidas o beneficios que son indivisibles y diversos; ii) que se otorgan a colectivos o grupos de personas, iii) para aliviar el daño colectivo que se ha causado como consecuencia de una violación del derecho internacional, iv) ya sea de derechos individuales o colectivos. Estos beneficios comúnmente se enmarcan como proyectos políticos (programas sociales) y tienen el potencial de transformar las condiciones sociales de las víctimas, así como prevenir tanto la victimización adicional como la violencia colectiva o el conflicto.

Hay más preguntas sin respuesta sobre las RC. ¿Por cuánto tiempo se supone que las víctimas se benefician de ellas? ¿Sobre qué base se decide si las RC deben tomar la forma de medidas simbólicas, de servicio o las dos? Con base en el análisis realizado, las medidas colectivas de reparación se deciden sobre la base de términos geográficos (comunidad, ciudad, área urbana o local) y sobre temas como construcción de la paz, como lo son la necesidad de proveer servicios sociales, actividades generadoras de ingresos, medidas destinadas a la conmemoración, proyectos de infraestructura y reformas judiciales, todo esto tomando en cuenta las necesidades urgentes de las víctimas. Los servicios sociales, especialmente las medidas de salud y educación, se otorgan comúnmente. Esto se debe a que las violaciones masivas de derechos humanos suelen afectar las capacidades generales de un Estado para proporcionar servicios sociales e infraestructura, y estas son también las áreas donde muchas víctimas expresan una necesidad urgente.

El marco temporal en el que se ofrecen las RC varía entre las tres ramas en estudio (el derecho internacional de los derechos humanos, el derecho penal internacional y la justicia transicional). La Corte IDH ha ordenado que se otorguen RC de manera permanente (la reapertura de una escuela o el establecimiento de capacitación en derechos humanos para la policía y el ejército), pero también ha ordenado que el tiempo de las RC este basado en una cantidad específica de dinero que se les dedicará. Cuando el dinero se ha gastado o invertido en los proyectos de RC, se considera que el Estado ha cumplido la orden. La CPI, por otro lado, ha definido algunos límites temporales. Como tal, las RC están disponibles para las víctimas por un período de entre 2 a 4 años. Además, bajo los órganos de justicia transicional, las RC nacionales referentes a medidas basadas en servicios sociales, generalmente se ordenan permanentemente. Esto se debe a que dichos servicios sociales debían de ser disfrutados por las víctimas incluso antes de su victimización. En este sentido, las RC se convierten en un puente que permite el acceso a otros derechos de naturaleza económica, social y cultural.

Si bien, en principio, el derecho internacional se centra en el individuo y no hay justificación para RC únicas, tanto el derecho internacional de los derechos humanos, mediante la jurisprudencia de la Corte IDH, y el derecho penal internacional, mediante los instrumentos jurídicos y la jurisprudencia de la CPI y las CETC han contribuido a la justificación de otorgar RC únicamente en ciertos escenarios. Esto, sin embargo, no ha tomado lugar con desafíos:

a) Definición de beneficiarios: bajo los mecanismos de JT y el derecho internacional de los derechos humanos, las comunidades y grupos como tales pueden ser beneficiarios de reparaciones, mientras que el derecho penal internacional requiere que solo los miembros de una comunidad que han sido reconocidos como víctimas en un caso particular sean considerados como beneficiarios. El primer enfoque enfrenta desafíos al prever las consecuencias de reconocer a las comunidades y grupos como beneficiarios. ¿Esto implicaría que estos grupos también pueden ser reconocidos como entidades que tienen derechos más allá del derecho a la reparación? Además, reconocer a las víctimas en un caso como beneficiarios, como exige la CPI, también plantea desafíos. La perpetración de GVDH generalmente victimiza comunidades enteras y proporcionar beneficios solo a un grupo seleccionado de personas puede crear tensiones dentro de una sociedad.

b) Definir su adecuación y contenido: los tribunales y los órganos no judiciales deciden sin pautas legales, y caso por caso, cuando solo las RC o una combinación de reparaciones colectivas e individuales son adecuadas (esto depende de si su el mandato lo permite). El ideal detrás de los programas de RC es garantizar que un gran número de víctimas se beneficie de un programa determinado. Sin embargo, este ideal solo se vuelve significativo cuando las víctimas reciben algo que consideran necesario o importante para ellas. Aquí, la importancia de la participación de las víctimas en el diseño y la implementación de los programas. La participación de las víctimas, a su vez, requiere su identificación temprana por parte del organismo competente. Sin embargo, identificar víctimas de GVDH no es fácil ni posible en todos los casos.

c) Cumplir con los requisitos del estándar de prueba y causalidad: las reparaciones, ya sean individuales o colectivas, requieren un estándar de prueba y de causalidad. Los tribunales internacionales generalmente afirman la necesidad de flexibilidad en la aplicación de estos requisitos, especialmente en casos de GVDH, a fin de dar cuenta de la dificultad de las víctimas en la compilación de pruebas. Una flexibilidad similar es evidente en los procedimientos de reclamos masivos. Sin embargo, los órganos judiciales y no judiciales no definen la prueba específica requerida y guardan silencio sobre la diferencia entre las pruebas aplicadas a las RC y las que se aplican a las reparaciones individuales. En consecuencia, las víctimas que buscan reparación tienen incertidumbre con respecto a lo que se les exige para recibir RC.

d) La evaluación del daño: se acepta comúnmente que la comisión de GVDH causa daños individuales y colectivos inconmensurables. Sin embargo, para efectos de otorgar reparaciones, los órganos judiciales y no judiciales están obligados a definir los daños resultantes de las violaciones comprobadas. En particular, en el derecho penal internacional, esta evaluación del daño es especialmente importante, ya que el condenado solo puede ser responsable de la reparación del daño resultante de los delitos que lo condenaron. A pesar de su importancia, este estudio hace evidente que dentro de los órganos judiciales y extrajudiciales no existe un método único para evaluar los daños. La investigación ha demostrado que a veces expertos pueden ser llamados para ayudar a los órganos judiciales a evaluar el daño, pero que, en la mayoría de los casos, los tribunales son los que realizan la evaluación del daño. Sin embargo, se puede cuestionar la capacidad de los integrantes de una corte para actuar como expertos financieros capaces de conducir la cuantificación de daños que son multidimensionales. Además, los tribunales generalmente se han basado en el principio de equidad cuando no hay pruebas suficientes para que un reclamo de daño se evalúe en términos financieros. Esto se hace especialmente cuando se trata de daño moral.

Aunque las RC pueden ser percibidas como una manera de conformarse con menos, estas incluyen a un mayor número de víctimas, así como las consecuencias más amplias de GVDH. Las RC tienen como objetivo abordar las injusticias sociales y mejorar el desarrollo comunitario. Sin embargo, también representan un compromiso y un término medio entre los derechos legales y el pragmatismo en situaciones excepcionales. Desde este punto de vista, es importante recordar que, aunque las GVDH han sido abordadas por los tribunales regionales de derechos humanos, como la Corte IDH, estos mecanismos judiciales se han establecido para tratar "violaciones comunes de derechos humanos" en lugar de GVDH. Además, la CPI, las CETC, los programas nacionales de reparaciones y las comisiones de reclamaciones masivas se han creado para proporcionar una justicia "excepcional", lo que implica limitaciones significativas en la justicia que pueden proporcionar. La CPI y las CETC se centran en el enjuiciamiento de los perpetradores más directamente responsables de la comisión de graves violaciones de derechos humanos. Los programas nacionales de reparaciones y las comisiones de reclamaciones se centran en reparar un número limitado de delitos que no se consideran comunes, sino que se cometen en las circunstancias excepcionales de un conflicto o un régimen autoritario. A pesar de que los tribunales y órganos no judiciales que proporcionan justicia a las víctimas de GVDH enfrentan restricciones institucionales propias de sus mandatos, se puede afirmar que cumplen con la trilogía de justicia básica aplicable a circunstancias extraordinarias, descrita por van Boven como verdad, justicia y reparación. Además Gray afirma que la "justicia ordinaria" se centra en compensar el daño individualmente, lo cual no es realista ni deseable cuando se trata de crímenes atroces a gran escala. Las GVDH son casos extraordinarios que deben abordarse mediante medidas extraordinarias y, en cierta medida, con creatividad.

En general y haciendo uso del concepto de justicia ordinaria y extraordinaria tal como lo utiliza Gray, las reparaciones para casos extraordinarios, independientemente de si se resuelven dentro del derecho internacional de los derechos humanos o el derecho penal internacional, o en un contexto de justicia transicional, deben abordarse en una base extraordinaria en lugar de una ordinaria. Dado que las RC en sí mismas constituyen un enfoque extraordinario de las reparaciones, es posible concluir que efectivamente existen tensiones entre el derecho individual a recibir reparaciones y el otorgamiento de RC a las víctimas de GVDH. Estas tensiones sugieren que otorgar solamente RC a las víctimas de GVDH no cumple con el requisito del derecho individual a las reparaciones. Sin embargo, los instrumentos de derechos humanos originalmente no se crearon con la idea de abordar casos extraordinarios de abusos contra los derechos humanos a gran escala ante los tribunales internacionales. Las RC pueden ser considerados como una "mejor" opción no solo para los Estados, sino también para los tribunales cuando se abordan GVDH. Esto se debe a que la justicia no solo se adapta de acuerdo con las necesidades actuales sino también de acuerdo con las necesidades futuras a corto y largo plazo, así como según los recursos disponibles no solo para implementar reparaciones sino también para cumplir con los requisitos para poder obtener reparaciones (requisitos de procedimiento).

Las RC pueden ser justificadas por razones de necesidad de justicia extraordinaria, el potencial que tienen para permitir la supervivencia y asegurar algunos aspectos de las generaciones futuras, o porque los gobiernos las prefieren porque las perciben como menos costosas. Cualquiera que sea su justificación, el garantizar su cumplimiento debe ser una prioridad al otorgar o adoptar este tipo de reparaciones. Este estudio señala que los tribunales y órganos no judiciales necesitan delinear los límites de cada aspecto de las RC para garantizar su implementación. Además, esto brindará a las víctimas cierto grado de certeza sobre qué esperar y buscar dentro de un proceso de justicia. En general, la falta de un concepto uniforme de RC puede no ser un problema, especialmente si aceptamos que el concepto de reparación está en constante evolución. Sin embargo, la falta de una explicación detallada por parte de tribunales y órganos no judiciales que justifique el porque se otorgan RC es es realmente un problema.

Résumé

Chapitre I: Introduction et la question principale de cette recherche

La persistance et la récurrence des violations graves des droits de l'homme (VFDH) ont entraîné un nombre important de victimes à travers le monde. Ceux qui n'ont pas été tués, ont été profondément touchés par le meurtre de leurs proches et par de graves violations de leurs droits, tels que des détentions prolongées avec de la torture, des mutilations, des viols, ou la destruction de leurs biens et de leurs moyens de subsistance. Les conséquences physiques, psychologiques et économiques, tant au niveau individuel que sociétal, sont dans une certaine mesure incommensurables et irréparables. La plupart des violations grave des droits de l'homme se produisent en pleine instabilité politique, lorsque les institutions de l'État sont defaillantes et que l'état de droit est absent. Dans ce contexte, assurer la justice au lendemain d'un conflit est une procédure très complexe. En outre, les États en transition vers une forme de gouvernance plus démocratique se heurtent à plusieurs obstacles lorsqu'ils remédient aux abus du passé. Ces obstacles peuvent être de nature politique, juridique et matériel. Un certain nombre de facteurs peuvent empêcher les victimes de demander et d'obtenir justice, comme leur grand nombre, la difficulté de déterminer qui est une victime et/ou perpétrateur, ceci particulierement lorsqu'il s'agit de conflits longs et en l'absence de la capacité et de la limitation des ressources de l'Etat en question. Ces circonstances limitent ou empêchent également les États à offrir des réparations. Les autorites de l'Etat étant souvent directement ou indirectement impliquées dans la perpétration de violations graves des droits de l'homme, une culture de l'impunité commence à se développer dû à l'incapacité ouà la réticence à tenir ces autorités responsables.

Pendant de nombreuses années, les victimes étaient tributaires de la volonté et la capacité des États de rendre justice sous quelque forme que ce soit. En effet les victimes ne pouvaient recourir aux mécanismes internationaux de justice pour faire valoir leurs droits que lorsque les voies de recours nationales s'avéraient indisponibles ou inefficaces. Cependant, cette situation a progressivement changé. Réparer ou 'redresser' les griefs des victimes, notamment lorsque les dommages sont particulièrement graves, constitue aujourd'hui un impératif moral et juridique pour les États. Les voies de recours internationales qui visent à faciliter la réparation des VFDH, y compris celles qui constituent des crimes internationaux, sont maintenant accessibles aux victimes. En outre, la reconnaissance généralisée du droit d'une victime à un recours et à une réparation a conduit à l'adoption des

Principes fondamentaux et directives concernant le droit à un recours et à réparation des victimes de violations flagrantes du droit international des droits de l'homme et de violations graves du droit international humanitaire (Principes sur les réparations).

Selon ces Principes, la réparation pour les victimes peut prendre la forme soit de restitution, d'indemnisation, de réhabilitation, de satisfaction ou de garanties de non-répétition. Cela dit, une tendance a été identifiée parmi les organes judiciaires et non judiciaires concernant les réparations accordées aux victimes de violations flagrantes des droits de l'homme. En effet, lorsqu'il s'agit d'un grand nombre de victimes, des indemnisations essentiellement collectives sont accordées, car cette forme de réparation est jugée la plus appropriée. De plus, ce ne sont pas seulement les gouvernements qui sont enclins à créer des programmes accessibles à un grand nombre de bénéficiaires; les commissions de vérité ont également recommandé à plusieurs reprises des réparations collectives (RC). En outre, la Cour interaméricaine des droits de l'homme (CIDH), qui a accordé les réparations les plus étendues parmi tous les organes des droits de l'homme, a également accordé des RC aux victimes de crimes de masse. Les Chambres extraordinaires au sein des tribunaux cambodgiens (CETC) et la Cour pénale internationale (CPI) ont reflété cette pratique. Les indemnisations collectives accordées comprennent des programmes de logement et de santé, ainsi que des programmes de développement communautaire. Il est à noter que ces RC sont rarement accordées en même temps que des réparations individuelles.

Alors que le discours entourant le droit de toutes les victimes de crimes, y compris celles de VFDH, de recevoir des réparations, établit clairement que les victimes ont droit à des mesures collectives en plus des réparations individuelles. Dans la pratique, les mesures collectives sont rarement accordées de manière complémentaire. Au lieu de cela, lorsqu'ils abordent le préjudice causé par les violations flagrantes des droits de l'homme, les organes judiciaires et non judiciaires ont tendance à n'accorder aux victimes que des RC. Dans ce contexte, la principale question de recherche de ce livre est : *Quelles sont les tensions entre le droit de recevoir des réparations individuelles et l'octroi de réparations collectives aux victimes de violations flagrantes des droits de l'homme ?* Afin de répondre à cette question, cette étude a analysé la compréhension des RC par les organes judiciaires et non judiciaires dans trois cadres, à savoir le droit international des droits de l'homme, le droit pénal international et une sélection de processus de justice transitionnelle. En effectuant une telle analyse, la recherche s'est limitée à l'étude de la jurisprudence spécifique de la CIDH, de la CPI et des CETC. En outre, les pratiques des mécanismes non judiciaires ont été examinées, en particulier celles des commissions de la vérité péruvienne et marocaine et de deux commissions de l'indemnisation et des réclamations de masse (la Commission d'indémnisation des Nations Unies et la Commission des réclamations Érythrée-Éthiopie).

Chapitre II: Les développements concernant le droit à réparation

La compréhension des réparations des victimes dans le droit international a évolué avec le temps. Initialement, les réparations étaient comprises comme une obligation de l'État vis-à-vis d'un autre État. Mais avec l'adoption des instruments internationaux des droits de l'homme, les réparations sont aujourd'hui considérées comme une obligation de l'État vis-à-vis des États et des individus. Les réparations en droit international public et en droit international des droits de l'homme partagent des caractéristiques similaires. Pourtant, ces caractéristiques ont une signification différente dans ces domaines. Par exemple, dans les deux domaines, la *restitutio in integrum* a été reconnue comme un principe directeur lors de l'octroi de réparations. Alors qu'en droit international, la Cour internationale de Justice (CIJ) a compris la *restitutio in integrum* comme des mesures de restitution destinées à réparer les dommages causés par une infraction ou par une violation. Enfin la CIDH l'a compris comme la combinaison d'au moins trois mesures: compensation financière, réhabilitation et satisfaction, et ce plus particulierement aux VFDH.

Malgré le fait que les mesures de réparation dans le domaine du droit international des droits de l'homme ont été comprises sur la base de celles reconnues en droit international public (restitution, indemnisation et satisfaction), le droit international des droits de l'homme comprend également des mesures de réhabilitation et des garanties de non-répétition. Dans le domaine du droit international des droits de l'homme, la recherche montre une tendance axée sur la victime dans les mesures accordées par les tribunaux, en particulier la CIDH et la Cour Européenne des Droits de l'Homme (CEDH). La conception classique des réparations étant fondée sur le droit de la responsabilité civile et le droit de la responsabilité de l'État, les jugements déclaratoires et les compensations financières ont d'abord joué un rôle important dans les réparations dans le domaine des droits de l'homme, particulièrement auprès de la CEDH. Au fil des ans, cependant, l'approche des réparations de la CIDH a contribué à une compréhension plus holistique et créative des réparations, y compris des mesures matérielles et non matérielles (symboliques). Dans le but de répondre aux besoins particuliers des victimes individuelles et de prévenir de nouvelles violations, la CIDH a octroyé les cinq mesures de réparation reconnues (restitution, indemnisation, réadaptation, satisfaction et garanties de non-répétition). La CIDH n'a pas développé de formule qui détermine une combinaison exacte de mesures appropriées; elle a plutôt décidé une combinaison au cas par cas. Pourtant, la CIDH accorde généralement une combinaison de mesures matérielles et symboliques.

En vertu du droit international public et du droit des droits de l'homme, des réparations peuvent être accordées si certaines conditions de procédure sont remplies (c'est-à-dire la causalité et la norme de preuve). Cependant, les tests utilisés par les tribunaux pour déterminer ces caractéristiques varient. Les tribunaux internationaux des droits de l'homme s'appuient généralement sur une approche souple de la causalité, de la norme de preuve et de l'utilisation de présomptions. Bien qu'en vertu du droit international public l'obligation de cessation de l'État et les garanties de non-répétition protègent indirectement les intérêts collectifs, les RC n'existent pas en tant que telles. Ces dernières ont été élaborées par la Cour interaméricaine des droits de l'homme dans le but d'offrir réparation et de viser à transformer la vie des victimes dans les affaires impliquant un grand nombre de victimes.

Chapitre III: Les réparations collectives à la Cour interaméricaine des droits de l'homme

Les RC appartiennent au domaine du droit des droits de l'homme. À cet égard, la CIDH a été une pionnière en transposant ces indemnisations, initialement conçues sous les auspices des mécanismes de justice transitionnelle, à un tribunal régional des droits de l'homme. Le tribunal a ordonné différentes RC liées à des mesures de satisfaction, mais qui vont parfois au-delà de la satisfaction, telles que la réouverture d'une école et d'un dispensaire médical dans un village touché par les VFDH; la création d'un centre de santé permettant aux victimes d'obtenir des soins médicaux et psychologiques dans leur propre village; l'investissement d'une somme d'argent spécifique dans des travaux ou des services d'intérêt collectif; et la création de programmes spécifiques pour fournir un traitement psychologique et psychiatrique gratuit au niveau collectif, familial et individuel. Pourtant, la CIDH ne définit pas davantage le concept et le contenu des RC et n'a pas non plus identifié de différences entre les RC développées dans le cadre de la justice transitionnelle et dans le droit des droits de l'homme. Elle n'a pas non plus précisé comment ces mesures découlent du droit individuel aux réparations tel que consacré par l'article 63 de la Convention Américaine relative aux droits de l'homme (CADH).

Pourtant, les conclusions du chapitre III montrent que les RC offrent une meilleure réponse dans les cas où les victimes partagent un fort sentiment d'identité commune (par exemple les indigènes et peuples tribaux) ou lorsque les réparations individuelles peuvent avoir un effet perturbateur dans l'organisation d'une communauté. Si la CIADH a également accordé des réparations collectives dans les affaires impliquant un grand nombre de victimes sans évaluer l'existence de liens communautaires forts, elle les accompagne de réparations individuelles. De cette recherche approfondie, il est possible de conclure que la Cour n'accorde des RC que dans les cas liés aux terres ancestrales des peuples indigènes et tribaux. La CIADH a affirmé avoir vu dans les RC une opportunité de s'attaquer à la pauvreté et à la marginalisation dans lesquelles vivent la plupart des victimes. En essayant d'empêcher les gens de continuer à être victimes de telles conditions de vie, la Cour interaméricaine des droits de l'homme a utilisé les RC pour réparer les victimes de violations pour lesquelles un État a été reconnu coupable et pour améliorer les conditions de vie marginalisées des peuples indigènes et tribaux.

Bien que les RC puissent être un outil pour résoudre des problèmes structurels tels que la pauvreté et la marginalisation, la Cour n'a pas adopté l'approche consistant à accorder uniquement des RC lorsque d'autres victimes, telles que des paysans vivant dans des conditions similaires de pauvreté et dans la marginalisation, tel que vécu par les indigènes et les peuples tribaux. Dans ce contexte, Antowiak s'est demandé si l'approche de la Cour consistant à accorder uniquement des RC aux peuples indigènes et tribaux est discriminatoire, non seulement à l'égard de ces deux groupes, mais aussi envers d'autres groupes non privilégiés. Pourtant, comme le démontrent les conclusions de ce chapitre, dans la plupart des cas où la Cour a accordé les RC, les représentants des victimes et / ou la Commission interaméricaine des droits de l'homme (CmIADH) ont explicitement demandé de telles mesures. Enfin, bien que la Cour interaméricaine des droits de l'homme n'ait pas expliqué comment les RC coexistent avec le droit à des réparations individuelles, on peut en déduire que la Cour interprète le droit aux réparations individuelles comme un droit collectif en matière de violations concernant les peuples indigènes et tribaux des terres ancestrales.

Chapitre IV: Des réparations collectives en droit pénal international

Le droit pénal international, tel qu'il a été développé spécifiquement par les CETC et la CPI, a suivi la jurisprudence de la Cour internationale de Justice en matière des RC. Les deux tribunaux pénaux susmentionnés se distinguent de la Cour interaméricaine des droits de l'homme en ce qu'ils ont des dispositions explicites dans leurs cadres juridiques qui les autorisent à accorder des RC. Néanmoins, les deux tribunaux manquent de lignes directrices concrètes sur la façon de donner du contenu ainsi que sur la façon de guider la mise en œuvre des RC. Cela peut s'expliquer par l'absence de précédent en matière de réparations en droit pénal international. En outre, contrairement à d'autres tribunaux pénaux internationaux, la CPI que les CETC rendent une justice qui va au-dela des principes en accordant des réparations. En outre, tous les deux ont reconnu que les auteurs individuels sont non seulement responsables pénalement des crimes qu'ils ont commis, mais aussi responsables du préjudice causé aux victimes.

À ce jour, les RC sont devenues le standard des réparations accordées par la CPI et les CETC. Alors que les CETC peuvent seulement accorder des RC, la CPI est également habilitée à accorder des réparations individuelles. Les réparations collectives sont jugées adéquates compte tenu de l'incertitude concernant le nombre de victimes, la complexité de l'identification des victimes et les problèmes potentiels pouvant découler des réparations individuelles au sein des communautés et des victimes elles-mêmes, surtout si ces communautés subissent encore des violences. Cette forme de réparation est également considérée comme plus réalisable car elle nécessite moins de ressources et ouvre la porte à un plus grand nombre de victimes.

Idéalement, les RC devraient être accordées sur une base complémentaire plutôt que comme un substitut aux réparations individualisées, étant donné que les victimes de crimes internationaux souffrent à la fois de dommages individuels et collectifs. Un bon exemple de ce qui peut être réalisé est l'affaire *Katanga* devant la CPI, où des mesures individuelles symboliques ont été accordées en plus des RC.

Devant la CPI, la réparation est assurée par deux organes différents: la CPI et le Fonds au profit des victimes (TFV). Sur le plan juridique, l'assistance fournie par le Fonds est qualifiée d'assistance humanitaire plutôt que de réparation. Les réparations sont toujours liées à une ordonnance de la CPI. Néanmoins, l'assistance fournie a un caractère réparateur; par conséquent, cela peut clairement se chevaucher avec le contenu d'un autre ordre de réparation. Par exemple, les victimes pourraient obtenir l'accès aux services de santé dans le cadre du mandat d'assistance du Fonds et bénéficier d'un accès aux services de santé en tant que mesure de réadaptation dans le cadre d'une ordonnance de réparation. Pour les victimes, la distinction entre les réparations et l'assistance peut être indifférente en termes de bénéfices obtenus. La principale différence est que l'assistance du FPV peut être perçue comme un symbole de solidarité de la part de la communauté internationale, non seulement envers les victimes qui ont vu leur cas faire partie du dossier de la CPI mais envers la communauté touchée en général. À l'instar du cadre de la CPI, les victimes devant les CETC peuvent demander réparation par le biais de l'assistance de la section d'aide aux victimes (connu par son abréviation anglaise VSS), comparable à celle fournie par les Fonds et autre ordre de réparations. Cependant, le VSS a mis en œuvre des projets d'assistance très limités; qui peuvent être dus à un budget beaucoup plus limité alloué aux CETC. Par conséquent, il n'y a pas eu de débat sur la question de savoir si cette assistance peut coincider avec des réparations.

Comme dans le cas de la Cour interaméricaine des droits de l'homme, la CPI et les CETC exigent un lien de causalité entre le préjudice causé aux victimes et les crimes pour lesquels l'accusé a été condamné afin de donner droit à des réparations. Cependant, ces tribunaux pénaux internationauxs sont plus stricts en ce qui concerne le lien de causalité, avec d'autres exigences procédurales telles que la norme de preuve et la preuve nécessaire pour prouver le préjudice, ainsi que les exigences relatives à l'identification des victimes.

Chapitre V: Les réparations collectives et les organes non judiciaires

La réparation est l'un des éléments clés des processus de justice transitionnelle (JT). Cependant, réparer tous les dommages résultant des héritages passés de VFDH tout en reconstruisant simultanément les institutions et en fournissant des services sociaux à tous les citoyens est souvent irréaliste. Alors que certains chercheurs académiques ont soutenu que, dans un scénario idéal, les réparations faites sous justice transitionnelle consisteraient en une combinaison de réparations individuelles et collectives, ils ont également accepté que les RC sont une option plus réaliste et inclusive pour l'État les mettant en œuvre. Au sein des RC, il est affirmé qu'une approche transformative est la plus appropriée car ces réparations visent à résoudre des problèmes structurels tels que la pauvreté, l'inégalité et la marginalisation.

En plus des RC, des procédures de réclamations de masse ont également été établies pour faire face aux VFDH. Bien que ces procédures diffèrent des programmes nationaux des RC, il est évident qu'elles partagent également certaines similitudes, telles que: i) une compréhension flexible des exigences pour répondre à la charge de la preuve; ii) la possibilité de fournir des réparations à un grand nombre de victimes; et iii) les bénéficiaires sélectifs. Les procédures de réclamations et les programmes nationaux de réparations évitent d'inonder les tribunaux de milliers de réclamations individuelles ou des poursuites en concevant des réparations non-judiciaires, c'est-à-dire, en dehors des tribunaux. Des deux, les programmes nationaux des RC peuvent être préférés par les États parce qu'ils fournissent des biens et des services qui aident les États à atteindre la justice distributive et le développement dans le pays. Des Commissions ou des programmes de réclamation de réparations de masse (connu par leurs abréviations anglaise MCRs) peuvent être préférables si, en plus d'accorder des réparations aux victimes, les États doivent établir la responsabilité des acteurs étatiques ou des groupes armés en vertu du droit humanitaire.

Bien qu'elles fournissent des réparations à un grand nombre de victimes, les RC et les MCRs limitent généralement leurs avantages à certains groupes de victimes, car les politiques concernant les crimes à indemniser sont établies à l'avance. Alors que les décisions politiques qui aboutissent à des critères sélectifs pour les crimes indemnisables portent atteinte au droit individuel aux réparations pour de nombreuses victimes, les programmes des RC et les réclamations collectives permettent à un large groupe de bénéficiaires, au sein du groupe sélectionné de victimes éligibles, de profiter de bénéfices collectifs. Cependant, contrairement aux MRC et aux réparations individuelles, les CR peuvent également bénéficier aux auteurs des crimes (par exemple, construire un hôpital en tant que mesure de RC profitera éventuellement à toute une population sans distinction quant à la victime ou l'auteur du crime).

Enfin, un problème répandu autour de la réparation des victimes de GVDH est l'absence de preuves suffisantes pour prouver les dommages. Pour répondre aux défis de preuves insuffisantes, les commissions des réclamations et les Commissions de Vérité et de Réconciliation (CVR) ont développé de nouvelles techniques telles que l'assouplissement de la norme de preuve, le regroupement des catégories de réclamations, l'utilisation des présomptions probatoires, l'échantillonnage statistique et l'attribution de montants fixes à certaines catégories de victimes.

Chapitre VI: Conclusions

Malgré l'existence d'un droit individuel aux réparations, la réparation de tous les dommages subis par les victimes de VFDH est matériellement impossible. Fournir des réparations adéquates tout en tenant compte du context dans lequel les crimes ont eu lieu, impliquerait idealement l'octroi de réparations individuelles et collectives. Pourtant, fournir des réparations individuelles peut compromettre les ressources financières et naturelles, limitées et disponibles dans un pays donné, qui sont nécessaires pour reconstruire la société, fournir des services sociaux et mettre en œuvre les diverses réformes politiques nécessaires pour obtenir la stabilité. Le problème des ressources limitées est exacerbé dans les pays qui étaient déjà économiquement pauvres avant même qu'un conflit ne survienne ou qu'un gouvernement répressif ne prenne le pouvoir.

En outre, Roht-Arriaza soutient que les réparations individuelles ne traitent pas de manière adéquate les problèmes structurels qui sont souvent sous-jacents à un conflit et sont donc des mesures inadéquates en ne correspondant probablement pas aux besoins des sociétés sortant d'une situation de conflit. De plus, les réparations individuelles peuvent avoir des effets perturbateurs. De tels effets peuvent s'étendre non seulement à l'économie générale d'un État et à sa capacité de fournir des programmes sociaux de base à tous ses citoyens, mais aussi aux victimes elles-mêmes. Des discussions complexes telles que qui mérite d'être reconnu comme victime sont non seulement nécessaires mais peuvent aussi causer des perturbations au sein de la société, en particulier dans les pays où des conflits violents ont duré longtemps, où les roles des criminels et des victims changent au file du temps. De surcroit, les réparations individuelles exigent des normes de preuve élevées et sont donc lentes, ce qui signifie que les procédures peuvent etre coûteuses. Le fardeau potentiel pesant sur les victimes participant à ces affaires ne doit pas être sous-estimé. En effet, les réparations individuelles exigent généralement l'identification des victimes avant l'octroi des réparations et au lendemain de VFDH, une telle identification n'est généralement pas possible au tout début d'un processus de réparation.

D'autre-part, les effets des VFDH incluent des traumatismes et des dommages vécus collectivement, ces dommages étant principalement traités par des RC. En dépit du fait que les RC accordent une importance prédominante aux dommages collectifs, elles constituent une réponse plus réaliste aux besoins de réparation des victimes. Dans cette optique, les RC sont plus axées sur les besoins que sur les droits. En effet, les victimes ont, en principe, le droit de recevoir des réparations pour tous les dommages subis et les RC visent généralement à répondre aux besoins les plus élémentaires des victimes. À la lumière de ceci, les réparations collectives présentent un juste compromis entre la volonté politique, les ressources limitées et les besoins imminents, et dans la plupart des cas, aux besoins fondamentaux des victimes. De tels recours sont considérés comme une meilleure option pour éviter un manque de réparations. Les réparations collectives peuvent être considérées comme un compromis entre les besoins des victimes dans le présent et les besoins de la société dans le futur.

Les RC n'ont pas de signification juridique ou conceptuelle acceptée en dépit d'une utilisation répandue. Pourtant, cette étude a prouvé que la définition suivante correspond à la compréhension des RC appliquées par les instances judiciaires et non judiciaires examinées dans cette étude: les réparations collectives sont: i) des mesures ou des avantages indivisibles et divers; ii) qui sont accordées à des collectifs ou à un groupe de personnes, iii) afin d'atténuer le préjudice collectif résultant d'une violation du droit international, iv) soit de droits individuels ou collectifs. Ces avantages sont généralement définis comme des projets politiques (programmes sociaux) et ont le potentiel de transformer les conditions sociales des victimes ainsi que de prévenir à la fois la victimisation et les violences collectives ou les conflits.

Il y a d'autres questions sans réponse concernant les RC: pendant combien de temps les victimes sont-elles supposées en bénéficier? Sur quelle base décide-t-on si les RC doivent prendre la forme de mesures symboliques ou basées sur leur utilité ou les deux? Sur la base de l'analyse menée, les mesures collectives de réparation sont décidées sur la base de termes géographiques (communauté, ville, zone urbaine ou locale) et sur des thèmes tels que la construction de la paix, de services sociaux, d'activités génératrices de revenus, de mesures de commémoration, de projets et des réformes judiciaires. Des services sociaux, en particulier des mesures sanitaires et éducatives, sont généralement attribués. En effet, les violations massives ont généralement un impact sur les capacités générales d'un État à fournir des services sociaux et des infrastructures qui sont aussi des domaines dans lesquels de nombreuses victimes expriment souvent un besoin urgent.

Le délai dans lequel les RC sont offertes varie selon les trois domaines étudiés (le droit international des droits de l'homme, le droit pénal international et la justice transitionnelle). La CIADH a ordonné l'octroi de réparations collectives permanentes (par exemple, la réouverture d'une école ou la mise en place d'une formation aux droits de l'homme pour la police et l'armée), mais a également ordonné que la durée des RC soit fondé sur un budget spécifiquement dédié. Lorsque l'argent a été dépensée ou investi dans les projets de RC, l'État est considéré comme ayant respecté son obligation. D'autre part, la CPI a défini certaines limites temporelles. A ce titre, des RC sont à la disposition des victimes pour une période de 2 à 4 ans. En outre, dans le cadre de JT, les réparations collectives nationales lorsqu'il s'agit de mesures de services sociaux, sont généralement ordonnées de façon permanente. En effet, les victimes auraient dû bénéficier de tels services sociaux avant même leur victimisation. En ce sens, les RC deviennent un pont qui permet l'accès à d'autres droits de nature économiques, socials et culturels.

Bien que, en principe, le droit international se concentre sur l'individu et qu'il n'y ait aucune justification pour qu'il y ait uniquement une CR, aussi bien le droit international des droits de l'homme, à travers la jurisprudence de la Cour interaméricaine, que le droit pénal international, la jurisprudence de la CPI et des CETC, ont contribué à justifier uniquement l'octroi de CRs dans certains scénarios. Ceci, cependant, n'a pas été adopté sans défis:

a) Définir les bénéficiaires: En vertu des mécanismes de justice transitionnelle et du droit international des droits de l'homme, les communautés et les groupes peuvent bénéficier de réparations, alors que le droit pénal international exige que seuls les membres d'une communauté reconnue comme victimes dans un cas particulier peuvent être considérés comme des bénéficiaires. L'approche de la JT et du droit international des droits de l'homme est confrontée à des défis en anticipant les conséquences de la reconnaissance des communautés et des groupes en tant que bénéficiaires. En outre, reconnaître uniquement les victimes dans une affaire en tant que bénéficiaires, comme l'exige la CPI, comporte également des défis. La commission de VFDH victimise généralement des communautés entières et fournir des avantages seulement à un groupe sélectionné de personnes peut créer des tensions dans une société.

b) Définir son adéquation et son contenu: Les tribunaux et les organes non judiciaires décident sans directives légales, et au cas par cas, lorsque seules les réparations collectives ou une combinaison de réparations collectives et individuelles sont adéquates (ceci depend de leur mandat). L'idéal derrière les programmes de RC est de faire en sorte qu'un grand nombre de victimes bénéficient d'un programme donné. Pourtant, cet idéal n'a de sens que lorsque les victimes reçoivent une compensation qu'elles jugent nécessaire ou importante. Dans ce cas, l'importance de la participation des victimes à la conception et à la mise en œuvre des programmes devient priomordiale. Ainsi l'organe competent doit identifier de façon précoce les victimes. Cependant, l'identification des victimes de VFDH n'est ni évidente, ni possible dans tous les cas.

c) Satisfaire aux exigences de norme de preuve et de causalité: Les réparations, qu'elles soient individuelles ou collectives, nécessitent un test de standard de preuve et de causalité. Les tribunaux internationaux affirment généralement la nécessité de faire preuve de souplesse dans l'application de ces exigences, en particulier dans les cas de VFDH, de manière à rendre compte de la difficulté des victimes à rassembler des preuves. Une flexibilité similaire est évidente dans les procédures de réclamations de masse. Toutefois, les organes judiciaires et non judiciaires ne définissent pas le critère spécifique requis et en ne disent rien de la différence entre les critères appliqués aux RC et ceux appliqués aux réparations individuelles. Par conséquent, les victimes en quête de réparation se voient dans l'incertitude quant à ce qui leur est demandé pour obtenir des réparations collectives.

d) Évaluation des dommages: Il est communément admis que la VFDH cause des dommages individuels et collectifs incommensurables. Néanmoins, aux fins de l'octroi des réparations, les organes judiciaires et non judiciaires sont tenus de définir les dommages résultant des violations avérées. En particulier, en droit pénal international, cette évaluation du préjudice est particulièrement importante, étant donné que la personne condamnée peut seulement être tenue responsable des réparations du préjudice résultant des crimes dont elle a été reconnue coupable. Malgré son importance, cette étude montre clairement qu'au sein des instances judiciaires et extrajudiciaires, il n'existe pas de méthode unique pour évaluer les dommages. La recherche a montré que, parfois, des experts peuvent être appelés à aider les organes judiciaires à évaluer le préjudice, mais que dans la majorité des cas, c'est un tribunal qui procède à l'évaluation du préjudice. Cependant, la capacité des membres d'un tribunal à agir en tant qu'experts financiers capables de procéder à la quantification de dommages multidimensionnels peut être remise en question. De plus, les tribunaux ont généralement invoqué le principe de l'équité lorsqu'il n'y a pas suffisamment de preuves pour qu'une réclamation en dommages-intérêts soit évaluée en termes financiers. Cela est particulièrement vrai lorsqu'il s'agit de dommages moraux.

Bien que les réparations collectives puissent être perçues comme un moyen de se contenter de moins, elles incluent un plus grand nombre de victimes ainsi que les conséquences plus larges de VFDH. Les réparations collectives visent à lutter contre les injustices sociales et à renforcer le développement communautaire. Cependant, les RC représentent un compromis entre les droits légaux et le pragmatisme dans des situations exceptionnelles. Dans ce contexte, il est important de rappeler que bien que les tribunaux régionaux des droits de l'homme tels que la Cour Interamericaine de droits de l'Homme se soit penchés sur la VFDH, ces mécanismes judiciaires ont été mis en place pour traiter des 'crimes communs' plutôt que de la VFDH. En outre, la CPI, les CETC, les programmes nationaux de réparation et des recours collectifs sont créés pour assurer une justice 'exceptionnelle', ce qui implique des limitations significatives sur la justice qu'ils peuvent dispenser. La CPI et les CETC se concentrent sur la poursuite des auteurs les plus directement responsables des violations les plus graves des droits de l'homme. Les programmes nationaux de réparations et les commissions des réclamations visent à réparer un nombre limité de crimes qui ne sont pas considérés comme communs mais qui sont plutôt commis dans les circonstances exceptionnelles d'un conflit ou d'un régime autoritaire. Bien que les tribunaux et les organismes non judiciaires qui rendent justice aux victimes de FVDH soient confrontés à des restrictions institutionnelles inhérentes à leurs mandats, on peut dire qu'ils respectent la trilogie de justice fondamentale applicable aux circonstances extraordinaires, décrites par van Boven comme vérité, justice et réparation. Gray affirme que la 'justice ordinaire' est axée sur l'indemnisation individuelle du préjudice, ce qui n'est ni réaliste ni souhaitable lorsqu'il s'agit de crimes de grande échelle. Les VFDH sont des cas extraordinaires qui devraient être traités par des mesures extraordinaires et, dans une certaine mesure, avec créativité.

Dans l'ensemble, en utilisant le concept de justice extraordinaire et ordinaire tel que mentionne par Gray, les réparations pour les cas extraordinaires, qu'elles soient résolues en droit international des droits de l'homme ou en droit penal international, ou dans un contexte de justice transitionnelle, devraient être abordées sur une base extraordinaire plutôt que de façon ordinaire. Étant donné que les réparations collectives elles-mêmes constituent une approche extraordinaire des réparations, il est possible de conclure qu'il existe effectivement des tensions entre le droit individuel de recevoir des réparations et l'octroi des RC aux victimes de violations flagrantes des droits de l'homme. Ces tensions suggèrent que l'octroi des CR uniquement aux victimes de la VFDH ne répond pas à l'exigence du droit individuel à la réparation. Cependant, à l'origine, les instruments relatifs aux droits de l'homme n'avaient pas été créés dans le but de traiter des cas extraordinaires de violations massives des droits de l'homme devant les tribunaux internationaux. Les RC peuvent être considérées comme une option "meilleure" non seulement pour les États, mais aussi pour les tribunaux lorsque des violations graves des droits de l'homme sont traitées. En effet, non seulement la justice est adaptée aux besoins présents mais aussi aux besoins futurs à court et à long terme, ainsi qu'aux ressources disponibles non seulement pour mettre en œuvre les réparations, mais aussi pour satisfaire aux exigences de pouvoir bénéficier de réparations (exigences procédurales).

Les RC peuvent être justifiées par des raisons de justice extraordinaire, le potentiel qu'elles ont pour permettre la survie et la sécurisation de certains aspects des générations futures, ou parce que les gouvernements les préfèrent comme perçues moins dispendieuses. Quelle que soit sa justification, assurer la mise en œuvre des RC doit être une priorité lors de l'octroi ou de l'adoption de ce type de réparations. Cette étude indique que les tribunaux et les organes non judiciaires doivent définir les limites de chaque aspect des RC pour assurer leur mise en œuvre. De plus, cela donnera aux victimes un certain degré de certitude sur à quoi s'attendre et ce qu'elles cherchent dans le processus judiciaire. En général, l'absence d'un concept uniforme des RC ne pose pas de problème, surtout si l'on admet que le concept de réparation évolue constamment. Cependant, l'absence d'explication détaillée qui justifie pourquoi les tribunaux et les organes non judiciaires accordent des RC est réellement un problème.

Bibliography

Books and Books' Chapters

Almeida I., Compensation and Reparation for Gross Violations of Human Rights: Advancing the International Discourse and Action, in C.C. Joyner, ed., Reining in Impunity for International Crimes and Serious Violations of Fundamental Human Rights: Proceedings of the Siracusa Conference, 14-21 September 1998, Erès (1998).

Alston, P. and Knuckey, S., eds., The transformation of human rights fact-finding, OUP (2015).

Ambrus, M., The European Court of Human Rights and Standards of Proof: An Evidentiary Approach towards the Margin of Appreciation, in L. Gruszczynski and W. Werner, eds., Deference in International Courts and Tribunals, OUP (2014).

Babu, R., Remedies Under the WTO Legal System, Martinus Nijhoff (2012).

Bantekas, I. and Oette, L., International Human Rights: Law and Practice, CUP 2016.

Barker, J., The different forms of reparation: compensation, in J. Crawford, A. Pellet and S. Olleson, eds., The Law on International Responsibility, OUP (2010).

Bigi, G., Joint Criminal Enterprise of the Jurisprudence of the International Criminal Tribunal for the Former Yugoslavia and the Prosecution of Senior Political and Military Leaders: The Krajišnik Case, in A. von Bogdandy and R. Wolfrum, eds., Max Planck Yearbook of United Nations Law, Brill (2010).

Bothe, M., The Handbook of International Humanitarian Law, OUP (2013).

Bottigliero, I., Redress for Victims of Crimes under International Law, Martinus Nijhoff (2004).

Brilmayer, L., Giorgetti, C. and Charlton, L., International Claims Commissions: Righting Wrongs after Conflict, Edward Elgar Publishing, 2017.

Brown, C., A Common Law of International Adjudication, OUP (2007).

Burgorgue-Larsen, L., The right to determine reparations, in L. Burgorgue-Larsen and A. Úbeda de Torres, The Inter-American Court of Human Rights: Case Law and Commentary, OUP (2011).

Bydlinski, F., Can the Reparation Awarded to Victims of Violations under the ECHR be Considered a Real 'Just' Satisfaction?, in A. Fenyves, E. Karner and H. Koziol, eds., Tort Law in the Jurisprudence of the European Court of Human Rights, De Gruyter (2011).

Bydlinski, F., Methodological Approaches to the Tort Law of the ECHR, in A. Fenyves, E. Karner and H. Koziol, eds., Tort Law in the Jurisprudence of the European Court of Human Rights, De Gruyter (2011).

Calderón Gamboa, J.F., La reparación integral en la jurisprudencia de la Corte Interamericana de Derechos Humanos: estándares aplicables al nuevo paradigma mexicano (Mexico, CNDD 2013).

Caron, D., International Claims and Compensation Bodies, in C. Romano, K. Alter and Y. Shany, eds., The Oxford Handbook of International Adjudication, OUP (2015).

Cassel, D., The Expanding Scope and Impact of Reparations Awarded by the Inter-American Court of Human Rights, in K. de Feyter et al., eds., Out of the Ashes: Reparations for Gross Violations of Human Rights, Intersentia (2006).

Chynoweth, P., Chapter Three: Legal Research, in A. Knight and L. Ruddock, eds., Advanced Research Methods in the Built Environment, Technology & Engineering, Wiley-Blackwell (2009).

Ciorciari, J.D. and Heindel, A., Hybrid Justice: The Extraordinary Chambers in the Courts of Cambodia, University of Michigan Press (2014).

Citroni, G. and Quintana Osuna, K. I., Reparations for Indigenous Peoples in the Case Law of the Inter-American Court of Human Rights, in F. Lenzerini, ed., Reparations for Indigenous Peoples: International & Comparative Perspectives, OUP (2008).

Contreras-Garduño, D. and Alvarez-Rios, I., A Barren Effort? The Jurisprudence of the Inter-American Court of Human Rights on Jus Cogens?, in Y. Haeck et al., eds., The Realisation of Human Rights: When Theory Meets Practice. Studies in Honour of Leo Zwaak, Intersentia (2013).

Contreras-Garduño, D., The Inter-American System of Human Rights, in A. Mihr and M. Gibney, eds., The SAGE Handbook of Human Rights, SAGE (2014).

Correa, C., Guillerot, J. and Magarrell, L., Reparations and Victim Participation: A Look at the Truth Commission Experience, in C. Ferstman, M. Goetz and A. Stephens, eds., Reparations for Victims of Genocide, War Crimes and Crimes Against Humanity: Systems in Place and Systems in the Making, Martinus Nijhoff (2009).

Correa, C., Reparations for Victims of Massive Crimes. Making Concrete a Message of Inclusion, in R. Letschert et al., eds., Victimological Approaches to International Crimes: Africa, Intersentia (2011).

Crawford, J., State Responsibility: The General Part, CUP (2013).

Crawford, J., The System of International Responsibility, in J. Crawford, A. Pellet and S. Olleson, eds., The Law on International Responsibility, OUP (2010).

Cryer, R. et al., ed., An Introduction to International Criminal Law and Procedure, CUP (2014).

Curry-Sumner, I. et al., Research Skills: Instruction for Lawyers, Ars Aequi Libri (2010).

D'Argent, P., Compliance, Cessation, Reparation and Restitution in the Wall Advisory Opinion, in P.M. Dupuy et al., eds., Common values in International Law, Essays in Honour of Christian Tomuschat, Kehl Engel Verlag (2006).

Danieli, Y., Massive Trauma and the Healing Role of Reparative Justice, in C. Ferstman, M. Goetz and A. Stephens, eds., Reparations for Victims of Genocide, War Crimes and Crimes Against Humanity: Systems in Place and Systems in the Making, Martinus Nijhoff (2009).

De Feyter, K., et al., ed., Out of the Ashes : Reparations for Gross Violations of Human Rights, Intersentia (2006).
De Greiff, P., Articulating the Links Between Transitional Justice and Development: Justice and Social Integration, in P. de Greiff, and R. Duthie, eds., Transitional Justice and Development: Making connections, Social Science Research Council (2009).
De Greiff, P., Justice and Reparations, in P. de Greiff, ed., The Handbook of Reparations, OUP (2006).
Díaz Gómez, C., Elementos para un programa administrativo de reparaciones colectivas en Colombia, in C. Díaz Gómez, ed., Tareas Pendientes: Propuestas para la formulación de políticas públicas de la reparación en Colombia, ICTJ (2010).
Díaz Gómez, C., Introducción, in C. Díaz Gómez, ed., Tareas Pendientes: Propuestas para la formulación de políticas públicas de la reparación en Colombia, ICTJ (2010).
Doak, J., Victims' Rights, Human Rights and Criminal Justice: Reconceiving the Role of Third Parties, Hart Publishing (2008).
Duchêne, A., Ideologies across Nations: The Construction of Linguistic Minorities at the United Nations, De Gruyter Mouton (2008).
Dwertmann, E., The Reparation System of the International Criminal Court, Martinus Nijhoff (2010).
Ebobrah, S., International Human Rights Courts, in C. Romano, K. Alter and Y. Shany, eds., The Oxford Handbook of International Adjudication, OUP (2015).
Echeverria, G., Codifying the Rights of the Victims in International Law: Remedies and Reparation, in Permanent Court of Arbitration, Redressing Injustices through Mass Claims Processes: Innovative Responses to Unique Challenges, OUP (2006).
Elster, J., Land, Justice and Peace, in M. Bergsmo et al., eds., Distributive Justice in Transitions, Torkel Opsahl Academic EPublisher (2010).
Elster, J., Transitional Justice in Historical Perspective, CUP (2004).
Evans, C., The Right to Reparation in International Law for Victims of Armed Conflict, CUP (2012).
Falk, R., Reparations, International Law, and Global Justice: A New Frontier, in P. de Greiff, ed., The Handbook of Reparations, OUP (2006).
Ferrara, A., Assessing the Long-term Impact of Truth Commissions: The Chilean Truth and Reconciliation Commission in Historical Perspective, Routledge (2014).
Ferstman, C. and Goetz, M., Reparations before the International Criminal Court: The Early Jurisprudence on Victim Participation and its Impact on Future Reparations Proceedings, in C. Ferstman, M. Goetz and A. Stephens, eds., Reparations for Victims of Genocide, War Crimes and Crimes Against Humanity: Systems in Place and Systems in the Making, Martinus Nijhoff (2009).
Ferstman, C., Goetz, M. and Stephens, A., eds., Reparations for Victims of Genocide, War Crimes and Crimes Against Humanity: Systems in Place and Systems in the Making, Martinus Nijhoff (2009).
Francioni, F., The Rights of Access to Justice under Customary International Law, in F. Francioni, ed., Access to Justice as a Human Right, OUP (2007).

Freeman, M., Back to the Future: The Historical Dimension of Liberal Justice, in M. du Plessis and S. Peté, eds., Repairing the Past? International Perspectives on Reparations for Human Rights Abuses, Intersentia (2007).
García Ramírez, S., Las Reparaciones en el Sistema Interamericano de Protección de los Derechos Humanos, in El Sistema Interamericano de Protección de los Derechos Humanos en el Umbral del Siglo XXI, Memoria del Seminario, Corte IDH (2003).
Giroud, S. and Moss, S., Mass Claims Processes under Public International Law, in Lein et al., eds., Collective Redress in Europe – Why and How?, British Institute of International and Comparative Law (2015).
Gori, G., Compliance, in D. Shelton, ed., The Oxford Handbook of International Human Rights Law, OUP (2013).
Gray, C., Judicial Remedies in International Law, OUP (1990).
Gray, C., Remedies, in C. Romano, K. Alter and Y. Shany, Y., eds., The Oxford Handbook of International Adjudication, OUP (2015).
Gray, C., The different forms of reparation: restitution, in J. Crawford, A. Pellet and S. Olleson, eds., The Law on International Responsibility, OUP (2010).
Hamber, B., Transforming Societies after Political Violence, Springer (2009).
Hayner, P., Unspeakable Truths: Confronting State terror and atrocity, Routledge (2001).
Hayner, P.B., Reconsidering the Peace-and-Justice Debate: International Justice in Africa and Latin America, in K. Hite and M. Ungar, eds., Sustaining Human Rights in the Twenty-First Century, Woodrow Wilson Center Press (2013).
Heindel, A., Managing Enormous Mass Crimes Indictments: The ECCC Severance Experiment' in S. Meisenberg and I. Stegmiller, The Extraordinary Chambers in the Courts of Cambodia: Assessing their Contribution to International Criminal Law, Asser Press (2016).
Hughes, R. and Elander, M., Justice and the Past: the Khmer Rouge Tribunal, in K. Brickell and S. Springer, eds., The Handbook of Contemporary Cambodia, Routledge (2016).
Hughes, R., Justice processes and discourses of post-conflict reconciliation in Southeast Asia: the experiences of Cambodia and Timor-Leste, in A. McGregor, L. Law and F. Miller, eds., Routledge Handbook of Southeast Asian Development, Routledge (2018).
Huneeus, A., Compliance with Judgments and Decisions, in C. Romano, K. Alter and Y. Shany, eds., The Oxford Handbook of International Adjudication, OUP (2015).
Jorda, C. and De Hemptinne, J., The Status and Role of the Victim, in A. Cassese, P. Gaeta and R.W. Jones, The Rome Statute of the International Crimincal Court: A Commentary, OUP (2002).
Kerbat, Y., Interaction between the forms of reparation, in J. Crawford, A. Pellet and S. Olleson, eds., The Law on International Responsibility, OUP (2010).
Kinsch, P., On the Uncertainties Surrounding the Standard of Proof in Proceedings Before International Courts and Tribunals, in G. Venturini, and S. Bariatti, eds., Diritti Individuali e Giustizia Internationale: Liber Fausto Pocar, Giuffrè (2009).

Kiza, E., Rathgeber, C. and Rohne, H., Victims of War. An Empirical Study on War-Victimization and Victims' Attitudes towards Addressing Atrocities, Hamburger Edition (2006).

Kristjánsdóttir, E., International Mass Claims Processes and the ICC Trust Fund for Victims, in C. Ferstman, M. Goetz and A. Stephens, eds., Reparations for Victims of Genocide, War Crimes and Crimes Against Humanity: Systems in Place and Systems in the Making, Martinus Nijhoff (2009).

Lauterpacht, E. and Nevill, P., The different forms of reparation, in J. Crawford, A. Pellet and S. Olleson, eds., The Law on International Responsibility, OUP (2010).

Law, J., Oxford Dictionary of Law, OUP (2015).

Lee, R.S., ed., The International Criminal Court: The Making of the Rome Statute. Issues, Negotiation, Results, Martinus Nijhoff (1999).

Lee, R.S., The Rome Conference and its Contributions to International Law, in R.S., Lee, ed., The international Criminal Court: The Making of the Rome Statute: Issues, Negotiation and Results, Martinus Nijhoff (1999).

Lefranc, S. and Vairel, F., The emergence of Transitional Justice as a Professional International Practice, in L. Israël and G. Mouralis, Dealing with Wars and Dictatorships: Legal Concepts and Categories in Action, TMC Asser Press -Springer (2014).

Lenzerini, F. and Vrdoljak, A., eds., International Law for Common Goods: Normative Perspectives on Human Rights, Culture and Nature, Hart (2014).

Letschert, R. and Van Boven T., Providing Reparation in Situations of Mass Victimization: Key Challenges Involved, in R. Letschert et al., eds., Victimological Approaches to International Crimes: Africa, Intersentia (2011).

Letschert, R. M. and Pemberton, A., Justice as the art of muddling through in C. Brants and S. Karstedt, eds., Transitional Justice and its Public Sphere: Engagement, Legitimacy, Contestation, Hart Publishers (2017).

Lewis, P. and Friman, H., Reparations to Victims, in R.S. Lee, ed., The International Criminal Court: Elements of Crimes and Rules of Procedure and Evidence, Transnational Publishers, Inc. (2001).

Loudily, F., Facing a Bloody Past: Discourses and Practices of Transitional Justice, in C.T. Salmon, ed., Communication Yearbook 34, Routledge (2010).

Loudiy, F., Transitional Justice and Human Rights in Morocco: Negotiating the Years of Lead, Routledge (2014).

Madrigal-Borloz, V., Damage and Redress in the jurisprudence of the Inter-American Court of Human Rights (1979-2001), in G. Urlich and L. Krabbe Boserup, eds., Human Rights in Development Yearbook 2001: Reparations: redressing past wrongs, Kluwer Law International (2003).

Malarino, E., Activismo Judicial, Punitivización y Nacionalización: Las Tendencias Antidemocráticas y Antiliberales de la CIDH, in Grupo Latinoamericano de Estudios Sobre Derecho Penal Internacional, ed., Sistema Interamericano de Protección de los Derechos Humanos y Derecho Penal Internacional, Konrad Adenauer Stiftung (2011).

Malcolm, E. and Murray, R., eds., The African Charter on Human and Peoples' Rights: The System in Practice 1986-2006, CUP (2008).
Mancini, M., UN Sanctions Targeting Individuals and ICC Proceedings: How to Achieve a Mutually Reinforcing Interaction, in N. Ronzitti, ed., Coercive Diplomacy, Sanctions and International Law, Brill (2016).
Mani, R., Beyond Retribution: Seeking Justice in the Shadows of War, Polity (2002).
Manrique Rueda, G., Lands, wars and restoring justice for victims, in J.M. Wemmers, ed. Reparations for Victims of Crimes against Humanity Routledge (2014).
Marguerítte, T., International Criminal Law and Human Rights, in W. Schabas and N. Bernaz, Routledge Handbook of International Criminal Law, Routledge (2011).
Martinez Ventura, J.E., Análisis del caso Lubanga: El procedimiento de reparaciones, in K. Ambos, E. Malarino and C. Steiner, Análisis de la primera sentencia de la Corte Penal Internacional: El caso Lubanga, Konrad-Aadenauer-Stiftunge and Unión Gráfica Ltda 2014).
McCarthy, C., Reparation for Gross Violations of Human Rights law and International Humanitarian Law at the International Court of Justice, in C. Ferstman, M. Goetz and A. Stephens, eds., Reparations for Victims of Genocide, War Crimes and Crimes Against Humanity: Systems in Place and Systems in the Making, Martinus Nijhoff (2009).
McCarthy, C., Reparations and Victim Support in the International Criminal Court, CUP (2012).
McCarthy, C., The Rome Statute's Regime of Victim Redress Challenges and Prospects, in C. Stahn, ed., The Law and Practice of the International Criminal Court, OUP (2015).
McKay, F., What Outcome for Victims?, in D. Shelton, ed., The Oxford Handbook of International Human Rights Law, OUP (2013).
Medina Quiroga, C., The Battle of Human Rights: Gross, Systematic Violations and the Inter-American System, Martinus Nijhoff (1998).
Mégret, F. The case for collective reparations before the International Criminal Court, in J.M. Wemmers, ed., Reparations for Victims of Crimes against Humanity, Routledge (2014).
Mendelson, M., The International Court of Justice and Sources of International Law, in V. Lowe and M. Fitzmaurice, eds., Fifty Years of the International Court of Justice: Essays in honour of Sir Robert Jennings, CUP (1996).
Mouyal, L., International Investment Law and the Right to Regulate: A Human Rights Perspective, Routledge (2016).
Muttukumaru, C., Reparation to Victims, in R.S. Lee, ed., The International Criminal Court: The Making of the Rome Statute. Issues, Negotiations, Results, Martinus Nijhoff (1999).
Nash Rojas, C., Las Reparaciones ante la Corte Interamericana de Derechos Humanos:1987-2007, Centro de Derechos Humanos/Universidad de Chile (2009).

Nathan, C., Introductory Remarks, in C. Ferstman, M. Goetz and A. Stephens, eds., Reparations for Victims of Genocide, War Crimes and Crimes Against Humanity: Systems in Place and Systems in the Making, Martinus Nijhoff (2009).

Niebergall, H., Overcoming Evidentiary Weakness in Reparation Claims Programmes, in C. Ferstman, M. Goetz and A. Stephens, eds., Reparations for Victims of Genocide, War Crimes and Crimes Against Humanity: Systems in Place and Systems in the Making, Martinus Nijhoff (2009).

O'Shea, A., Reparations under International Criminal Law, in M. du Plessis, and S. Peté, eds., Repairing the Past?: International Perspectives on Reparations for Human Rights Abuses, Intersentia (2007).

Ochoa, J.C., The Rights of Victims in Criminal Justice Proceedings for Serious Human Rights Violations, Martinus Nojhoff (2013).

Odio Benito, E., The International Criminal Court: possible contributions of the Rome Statute to judicial processes in transitional societies, in J. Almqvist and C. Espósito, The Role of Court in Transitional Justice, Routledge (2012).

Oette, L., Bringing Justice to Victims? Responses of Regional and International Human Rights Courts and Treaty Bodies, in C. Ferstman, M. Goetz and A. Stephens, eds., Reparations for Victims of Genocide, War Crimes and Crimes Against Humanity: Systems in Place and Systems in the Making, Martinus Nijhoff (2009).

Oeung, J., Expectations, Challenges and Opportunities of the ECCC, in S.M. Meisenberg and I. Stegmiller, Assessing the History, Establishment, Judicial Independence and Legacy: Assessing Their Contribution to International Criminal Law, T.M.C. Asser Press (2016).

Pasqualucci, J. M., The Practice and Procedure of the Inter-American Court of Human Rights, CUP (2013).

Pellonpää, M., Individual Reparation Claims under the European Convention on Human Rights, in A. Randelzhofer and C. Tomuschat, eds., State Responsibility and the Individual: Reparation in Instances of Grave Violations of Human Rights, Martinus Nijhoff (1999).

Pérez León Acevedo, J.P., Victims' Status at International and Hybrid Criminal Courts: Victims' Status as Witnesses, Victim Participants/Civil Parties and Reparations Claimants, UPÅ (2014).

Peté, S. and Du Plesis, M., Reparations for Gross Violations of Human Rights in Context, in S. Peté and M. du Plesis, M., eds., Repairing the Past? International Perspectives on Reparations for Human Rights Abuses, Intersentia (2007).

Peters, A., Beyond Human Rights: The Legal Status of the Individual in International Law, CUP (2016).

Petrović, D., Other Specific Regimes of Responsibility: The UN Compensation Commission, in J. Crawford, A. Pellet and S. Olleson, eds., The Law on International Responsibility, OUP (2010).

Pisillo-Mazzeschi, R., International Obligation to Provide Reparation Claims?, in A. Randelzhofer and C. Tomuschat, eds., State Responsibility and the Individual: Reparation in Instances of Grave Violations of Human Rights, Martinus Nijhoff (1999).

Ramji-Nogales, J., Bespoke transitional justice at the International Criminal Court, in C. de Vos, S. Kendall and C. Stahn, eds., Contested Justice: The Politics and Practice of International Criminal Court Interventions, CUP (2015).

REDRESS, Reparation: A sourcebook for victims of torture and other violations of human rights and international humanitarian law, The REDRESS Trust (2003).

REDRESS, Torture Survivor's Perceptions of Reparations: Preliminary Survey, The REDRESS Trust (2001).

Reisman, W. M., Compensation for Human Rights Violations: The Practice of the Past Decade in the Americas, in A. Randelzhofer, A and C. Tomuschat, eds., State Responsibility and the Individual: Reparation in Instances of Grave Violations of Human Rights, Martinus Nijhoff (1999).

Riddell, A., Evidence, Fact-Finding, and Experts in C. Romano, K. Alter and Y. Shany, eds., The Oxford Handbook of International Adjudication, OUP (2015).

Rodriguez-Garavito, C., Ethno Reparations: Collective Ethnic Justice and the Reparation of Indigenous Peoples and Black Communities in Colombia in M. Bergsmo et al., Distributive Justice in Transitions, Torkel Opshal Academic EPublisher (2010).

Rodríguez-Pinzón, D., The Inter-American Human Rights System and Transitional Processes, in A. Buyse and M. Hamilton, eds., Transitional Jurisprudence and the ECHR: Justice, Politics and Rights, CUP (2011).

Roht-Arriaza, N. and Mariezcurrena, J., eds., Transitional Justice in the Twenty-First Century: Beyond Truth Versus Justice, CUP (2006).

Roht-Arriaza, N. and Orlovsky, K., A Complementary Relationship: Reparations and Development, in P. de Greiff and R. Duthie, eds., Transitional Justice and Development: Making connections, Social Science Research Council (2009).

Roht-Arriaza, N., Reparations and Economic, Social and Cultural Rights, in D.N. Sharp, ed., Justice and economic violence in transition, Springer (2014).

Roht-Arriaza, N., Reparations in International Law and Practice, in M.C. Bassiouni, ed., The pursuit of international criminal justice: a world study on conflicts, victimization and post conflict justice, Intersentia (2010).

Rombouts, H., Sardaro, P. and Vandeginste S., The Right to Reparations for Victims of Gross and Sytematic Violations of Human Rights, in K. de Feyter et al., ed., Out of the Ashes: Reparations for Gross Violations of Human Rights, Intersentia (2006).

Rovine, A.W. and Hannesian, G., Toward a Foreseeability Approach to Causation Questions at the United Nations Compensation Commission, in R. Lillich, ed., The United Nations Compensation Commission, Transnational Publishers (1995).

Roxin C., Autoria y Dominio del Hecho en Derecho Penal, Marcial Pons (2000).

Rubio-Marin, R., Sandoval, C. and Díaz, C., Repairing Family Members: Gross Human Rights Violations and Communities of Harm, in R. Rubio-Marin, eds., The Gender of Reparations: Unsettling Sexual Hierarchies while Redressing Human Rights Violations, CUP (2009).
Rubio-Marin, R., The Gender of Reparations: Unsettling Sexual Hierarchies while Redressing Human Rights Violations, CUP (2009).
Saffon, M.P. and Uprimny, R., Distributive Justice and the Restitution of Disposed Land in Colombia, in M. Bergsmo et al., Distributive Justice in Transitions, Torkel Opshal Academic EPublisher (2010).
Sandoval Villalba, C., Rehabilitation as a form of reparations under international law, The REDRESS Trust (2009).
Schabas, S.W., International Criminal Courts, in C. Romano, K. Alter and Y. Shany, eds., The Oxford Handbook of International Adjudication, OUP (2015).
Schmid, A.P., Research on Gross Human Rights Violations, COMT (1989).
Schulter, C., Compliance with decisions of the International Court of Justice, OUP (2004).
Scott, S.V., International Law in World Politics, Lynne Rienner Publishers (2004).
Scovazzi, T. and Citroni, G., The Struggle against Enforced Disappearances and the 2007 United Nations Convention, Martinus Nijhoff (2007).
Seibert-Fohr, A., Prosecuting Serious Human Rights Violations, OUP (2009).
Shelton, D., Remedies in International Human Rights Law, OUP (2005).
Shelton, D., Remedies in International Human Rights Law, OUP (2015).
Shelton, D., Reparations for Indigenous Peoples: The Present Value of Past Wrongs, in F. Lenzerini, ed., Reparations for Indigenous Peoples: International and Comparative Perspectives, OUP (2008).
Shelton, D., The UN Principles and Guidelines on Reparations: Context and Contents, in K. de Feyter et al., ed., Out of the Ashes: Reparations for Gross Violations of Human Rights Intersentia (2006).
Singh, R., Raising the Stakes: evidentiary issues in individual claims 61 before the United Nations Compensation Commission, in Permanent Court of Arbitration, Redressing Injustices through Mass Claims Processes: Innovative Responses to Unique Challenges, OUP (2006).
Skaar, E., Malca, C.G. and Eide, T., After Violence: Transitional Justice, Peace and Democracy, Routledge (2015).
Smits, J.M., Redefining Normative Legal Science: Towards an Argumentative Discipline, in F. Coomans, F. Grunfeld and M. Kamminga, eds., Methods of Human Rights Research, Intersentia (2009).
Solis, G.D., The Law of Armed Conflict: International Humanitarian Law in War, CUP (2016).
Sperfeldt, C., The Role of Cambodian Civil Society in the Victim Participation Scheme of the Extraordinary Chambers in the Courts of Cambodia, in T. Bonacker and C. Safferling, Victims of International Crimes: An Interdisciplinary Discourse, Asser Press (2013).

Stern, B., The Obligation to Make Reparation, in J. Crawford, A. Pellet and S. Olleson, eds., The Law on International Responsibility OUP (2010).

Tavani, C., Collective Rights and the Cultural Identity of the Roma: A Case Study of Italy, Martinus Nijhoff (2012).

Taylor, L.A., The United Nations Compensation Commission, in C. Ferstman, M. Goetz and A. Stephens,eds., Reparations for Victims of Genocide, War Crimes and Crimes Against Humanity: Systems in Place and Systems in the Making, Martinus Nijhoff (2009).

Teitel, R., Transitional Justice, OUP (2000).

Tomuschat, C., Human Rights: Between Idealism and Realism, OUP (2008).

Tomuschat, C., Individual Reparation Claims in Instances of Grave Human Rights Violations: The Position under General International Law, in A. Randerlzhofer and C. Tomuschat, State Responsibility and the Individual: Reparations in Instances of Grave Violations of Human Rights, Kluwer Law International (1999).

Tomuschat, C., The Responsibility of Other Entities: Private Individuals, in J. Crawford, A. Pellet and S. Olleson, eds., The Law on International Responsibility, OUP (2010).

Tutu, D., Geen Toekomst zonder Verzoening, De Bezige Bij (1999).

Úbeda de Torres, A., Determination of Victims, in L. Burgorgue-Larsen and A. Úbeda de Torres, The Inter-American Court of Human Rights: Case Law and Commentary, OUP (2001).

Uprimny, R. and Camino Sánchez, N., Propuestas para una restitución de tierras transformadora, in C. Díaz Gómez, ed., Tareas Pendientes: Propuestas para la formulación de políticas publicas de la reparación en Colombia, ICTJ (2010).

Urban Walker, M., Gender and Violence in Focus: A Background for Gender Justice in Reparations, in R. Rubio-Marin, The Gender of Reparations: Unsettling Sexual Hierarchies While Redressing Human Rights Violations, CUP (2009).

Van Boven, T., Reparations: a Requirement of Justice, in IACtHR, ed., Memoria del Seminario: El Sistema Interamericano de Protección de los Derechos Humanos en el Umbral del Siglo, IACtHR (1999).

Van Boven, T., Victim-Oriented Perspectives, in T. Bonacker and C. Safferling, eds., Victims of international Crimes: An Interdisciplinary Discourse, Asser Press (2013).

Van Boven, T., Victims' Rights to a Remedy and Reparation: The New United Nations Principles and Guidelines, in Ferstman, C., Goetz, M. and Stephens, A., eds., Reparations for Victims of Genocide, War Crimes and Crimes Against Humanity: Systems in Place and Systems in the Making, Martinus Nijhoff (2009).

Van der Merwe, H., Reparations through different lenses: The culture, rights and politics of healing and empowerment after mass atrocities, in J.M. Wemmers, ed., Reparations for Victims of Crimes against Humanity, Routledge (2014).

Van Dijk et al., Theory and Practice of the European Convention on Human Rights, Intersentia (2006).

Van Haersolte-van Hof, J., Innovations to Speed Mass Claims: New Standards of Proof, in Permanent Court of Arbitration, ed., Redressing Injustices through Mass Claims Processes: Innovative Responses to Unique Challenges, OUP (2006).

Van Houtte, H., Das, H. and Delmartino, B, The United Nations Compensation Commission, in P. de Greiff, ed., The Handbook of Reparations, OUP (2006).
Villa Arcilla, L., Reparación en y a través de la educación para víctimas de graves violaciones de los derechos humanos, in C. Díaz Gómez, ed., Tareas Pendientes: Propuestas para la formulación de políticas públicas de la reparación en Colombia, ICTJ (2010).
Vos, J.A., The Function of Public International Law, T.M.C. Asser Press (2013).
Watson, J. S., Theory & Reality in the International Protection of Human Rights, Transnational Publishers (1999).
Wellens, K., Negotiations in the Case Law of the International Court of Justice: A Functional Analysis, Routledge (2016).
Wemmers, J.M, Victim's Need for Justice. Individual versus Collective Justice, in R. Letschert et al., eds., Victimological Approaches to International Crimes : Africa, Intersentia (2011).
Wemmers, J.M., The healing role of reparation, in J.M. Wemmers, ed., Reparations for Victims of Crimes against Humanity, Routledge (2014).
Westra, L., Human Rights: The Commons and the Collective, UBC Press (2012).
Wiebelhaus-Brahm, E., Truth Commissions and other Investigative Bodies, in M.C. Bassiouni, ed., The Pursuit of International Criminal Justice: A World Study on Conflicts, Victimization, and Post-Conflict Justice, Intersentia (2010).
Wiebelhaus-Brahm, E., Truth Commissions, in W. Schabas and N. Bernaz, eds., Routledge Handbook of International Criminal Law, Routledge (2011).
Wolfe, S., The Politics of Reparations and Apologies, Springer (2014).
Wühler, N., Causation and Directness of Loss as Elements of Compensability before the United Nations Compensation Commission, in R.B. Lillich, ed., The United Nations Compensation Commission: Thirteenth Sokol Colloquium, Transnational Publishers (1995).
Wyler, E. and Papaux, A., The different forms of reparation: satisfaction, in J. Crawford, A. Pellet and S. Olleson, eds., The Law on International Responsibility, OUP (2010).
Yanev, L., The Theory of Joint Criminal Enterprise at the ECCC: A Difficulty Relationship, in S.M. Meisenberg and I. Stegmiller, The Extraordinary Chambers in the Courts of Cambodia: Assessing their Contribution to International Criminal Law, Asser Press (2016).

Articles and Working Papers

Aldana-Pindell, R., An Emerging Universality of Justiciable Victims' Rights in the Criminal Process to Curtail Impunity for State-Sponsored Crimes, 26 Human Rights Quarterly (2004).
Aldana, R., A Victim-Centered Reflection on Truth Commissions and Prosecutions as a Response to Mass Atrocities, 5 Journal of Human Rights (2006).

Altwicker-Hámori, S., Altwicker T. and Peters, A., Measuring Violations of Human Rights: An Empirical Analysis of Awards in Respect of Non-Pecuniary Damage under the European Convention on Human Rights, 76 Heidelberg Journal of International Law (2016).

Alvarez, I. et al., Conference: Reparations in the Inter-American System: A Comparative Approach, 56 American University Law Review (2007).

Amezcua-Noriega, O. Reparation Principles under International Law and their Possible Application by the International Criminal Court: Some Reflections, Briefing Paper No. 1, Reparations Unit, Essex University, (2011).

Amnesty International, Peru: Truth and Reconciliation Commission – a first step towards a country without injustice (2004).

Antkowiak, T., An Emerging Mandate for International Courts: Victim-Centered Remedies and Restorative Justice, 47 Stanford Journal of International Law (2011).

Antkowiak, T., Remedial Approaches to Human Rights Violations: The Inter-American Court of Human Rights and Beyond, 46 Columbia Journal of Transnational Law (2008).

Aptel, C., Prosecutorial Discretion at the ICC and Victim's Right to Remedy, 10 Journal of International Criminal Justice (2012).

Aubry, S. and Henao-Trip, I.M., Collective Reparations and the International Criminal Court, Briefing Paper No. 2, Reparations Unit, Essex University (2011).

Baillet, C.M., Measuring Compliance with the Inter-American Court of Human Rights: The Ongoing Challenge of Judicial Independence in Latin America, 31 Nordic Journal of Human Rights (2013).

Baluarte, D.C., Strategizing for Compliance: The Evolution of a Compliance Phase of Inter-American Court Litigation and the Strategic Imperative for Victims' Representatives, 27 American University International Law Review (2012).

Basch, F. et al., The Effectiveness of the Inter-American System of Human Rights Protection: A Quantitative Approach to its Functioning and Compliance with its Decision, 7 SUR – International Journal on Human Rights (2010).

Bassiouni, C., International Recognition of Victims' Rights, 6 Human Rights Law Review (2006).

Bassiouni, M. C., International Criminal Law: International Enforcement, 3 Brill (2008).

Birchall, E., Francq E. and Pijnenburg, A., The International Criminal Court and Reparations for Child Victims of Armed Conflict, Briefing Paper No. 4, Reparations Unit, Essex University (2011), p. 25.

Borer, T., A Taxonomy of Victims and Perpetrators: Human Rights and Reconciliation in South Africa, 25 Human Rights Quarterly (2003).

Brodney, M., Implementing Criminal Court-Ordered Collective Reparations: Unpacking Present Debates, 1 Journal of the Oxford Centre for Socio-Legal Studies (2016).

Buckley-Zistel, S., Connecting Transitional Justice and Development, paper presented at International Conference on The Contribution of Civil Society and Victim Participation in Transitional Justice Processes, (2009).

Buti, A., International Law Obligations to Provide Reparations for Human Rights Abuses, 6 Murdoch University Electronic Journal of Law (1999).

Buxbaum, R.M., From Paris to London: The Legal History of European Reparation Claims: 1946-1953, 31 Berkeley Journal of International Law (2013).

Buyse, A., Lost and Regained? Restitution as a Remedy for Human Rights Violations in the Content of International Law, 68 Heidelberg Journal of International Law (2008).

Cançado Trindade, A.A., Compliance with Judgments and Decisions – the Experience of the Inter-American Court of Human Rights: a reassessment, 13 Revista – Instituto Brasileiro de Direitos Humanos (2014).

Capone F. et al., Education and the Law of Reparations in Insecurity and Armed Conflicts, British Institute of International Law (2013).

Carayon, G. and O'Donohue, J., The International Criminal Court's Strategies in Relation to Victims, 15 Journal of International Criminal Justice (2017).

Caron, D. and Morris, B., The UN Compensation Commission: Practical Justice, not Retribution, 13 European Journal of International Law (2002).

Carranza, R., The Right to Reparations in Situations of Poverty, International Center for Transitional Justice Briefing (2009).

Carrillo, A.J. and Palmer, J.S., Transnational Mass Claim Processes (TMCPs) in International Law and Practice, 28 Berkeley Journal of International Law (2010).

Castellanos-Jankiewicz, L., Causation and International State Responsibility, 5 SHARES Research Paper (2012).

Chappell, L., The gender injustice cascade: 'transformative' reparations for victims of sexual and gender-based crimes in the Lubanga case at the International Criminal Court, 21 The International Journal of Human Rights (2017).

CHRAC and REDRESS, Considering Reparations for Victims of the Khmer Rouge Regime: A Discussion Paper (2009).

Ciorciari, J.D. and Heindel, A., Experiments in International Criminal Justice: Lessons from the Khmer Rouge Tribunal, 35 Michigan Journal of International Law (2014).

Clermont, K. and Sherwin, E., A Comparative View of Standards of Proof, 50 American Journal of Comparative Law (2002).

Colandrea, V., On the Power of the European Court of Human Rights to Order Specific Non-Monetary Measures: Some Remarks in Light of the Assanidze, Broniowski and Sejdovic Cases, 7 Human Rights Law Review (2007).

Contreras Garduño, D. and Rombouts, S., Collective Reparations for Indigenous Communities Before the Inter-American Court of Human Rights, 27 Merkourios Utrecht Journal of International and European Law (2011).

Contreras-Garduño, D. and Fraser, J., The Identification of Victims before the Inter-American Court of Human Rights and the International Criminal Court and its Impact on Participation and Reparation: a Domino Effect?, 7 Inter-American and European Human Rights Journal (2015).

Contreras-Garduño, D., Defining Beneficiaries of Collective Reparations: The experience of the IACtHR, 4 Amsterdam Law Forum (2012).

Crawford, J., State Responsibility, Max Planck Encyclopedia of Public International Law (2006).
D'Argent, P., Reparation, Cessation, Assurances and Guarantees of Non-Repetition, 24 SHARES Research Paper (2014).
Dannenbaum, T., The International Criminal Court, Article 79, and Transitional Justice: The case for an Independent Trust Fund for Victims, 28 Wisconsin International Law Journal, (2010).
De Greiff, P., Reparations Programs: Patterns, Tendencies, and Challenges" 50 Politorbis (2010).
Derluyn et al., Victims and/or perpetrators? Towards an interdisciplinary dialogue on child soldiers, 15 BMC International Health and Human Rights (2015).
Donoso, G., Inter-American Court of Human Rights' reparation judgments: Strengths and challenges for a comprehensive approach, 49 Revista IIDH (2009).
Dudai, R., Closing the gap: symbolic reparations and armed groups, 93 International Review of the Red Cross (2011).
Đukić, D., Transitional justice and the International Criminal Court – in the interest of justice?, 89 International Review of the Red Cross (2007).
Dybnis, A., Was the Eritrea-Ethiopia Claims Commission Merely a Zero-Sum Game? Exposing the Limits of Arbitration in Resolving Violent Transitional Conflict, 33 Loyola Los Angeles International and Comparative Law Review (2011).
Echeverria, G., Do victims of torture and other serious human rights violations have an independent and enforceable right to reparations?, 16 The International Journal of Human rights (2012).
Echeverria, G., The UN Principles and Guidelines on Reparation: is there an Enforceable Right to Reparation for Victims of Human Rights and International Humanitarian Law Violations?, An unpublished thesis submitted for the Degree of Doctor of Philosophy, University of Essex (2017).
Expert Seminar on Reparation for Victims of Gross and Systematic Human Rights Violations in the Context of Political Transitions, Catholic University of Leuven (2002).
F. Iliff, F. Maitre-Muhl and A. Sirel, Adverse Consequences of Reparations, Briefing Paper No. 6, Reparations Unit, Essex University (2011).
Ferstman, C., Reparation as Prevention: Considering the Law and Practice of Orders for Cessation and Guarantees of Non-Repetition in Torture Cases, 6 Essex Human Rights Review (2010).
Firchow, P., Must our Communities Bleed to Receive Social Services? Development Projects and Collective Schemes in Colombia, 8 Journal of Peacebuilding and Development (2013).
Firchow, P., The Implementation of the Institutional Programme of Collective Reparations in Colombia, 6 Journal of Human Rights Practice (2014).
Fischer, P., The Victims' Trust Fund of the International Criminal Court – Formation of a Functional Reparations Scheme, 17 Emory International Law Review (2003).

Fox, M. B., Imposing Liability for Losses from Agrresive War: An Economic Analyis of the UN Compensation Commission, 13 European Journal of International Law (2011).
García-Godos, J., Victim Reparations in Transitional Justice: What is at Stake and Why, 26 Nordisk Tidsskrift for Menneskerettigheter (2008).
Garrido, K., Huerta, G., and Valencia, A., Propuestas de reparaciones a las víctimas del conflicto armado interno: ¿qué hacer desde las regiones?: Región Junín, Instituto de Defensa Legal (2012).
Gattini, A., Breach of the Obligation to Prevent and Reparation Thereof in the ICJ's Genocide Judgment, 18 The European Journal of International Law (2007).
Gattini, A., The UN Compensation: Old Rules, New Procedures on War Reparations, 13 European Journal of International Law (2002).
Gillard, E., Reparations for violations of international humanitarian law, 85 International Review of the Red Cross (2003).
Gold, S., International Claims Arising from Iraq's Invasion of Kuwait, 25 The International Lawyer (1991).
Gonzalez-Salzberg, D.A., Do States comply with the compulsory judgments of the Inter-American Court of Human Rights? An empirical study of the compliance with 330 measures of reparations, 13 Revista do Instituto Brasileiro de Direitos Humanos (2014).
Gray, C., A no-excuse approach to transitional justice: reparations as tools of extraordinary justice, 87 Washington University Law Review (2010).
Gray, C., The Choice between Restitution and Compensation, 10 European Journal of International Law (2009).
Gray, C., The Eritrea/Ethiopia Claims Commission Oversteps Its Boundaries: A Partial Award?, 17 The European Journal of International Law (2006).
Groome, D., The Right to Truth: The Evolution of a Right (2015).
Guarnizo-Peralta, D., Guarantees of non-repetition and the right to health: Review of the law and evolving practice of judicial and semi-judicial bodies at the global and regional levels, An unpublished thesis submitted for the Degree of Doctor of Philosophy, University of Essex (2016).
Guha-Roy, S.N., Is the law of responsibilities of states for injuries to aliens a part of a universal international law?, 55 The American Journal of International Law (1961).
Guillerot J. and Magarrell, L., Memorias de un proceso inacabado: reparaciones en la transición peruana, APRODEH & ICTJ (2006).
Guillerot, J. and Carranza, R., The Rabat Report: The Concept and Challenges of Collective Reparations, ICTJ (2009).
Haasdijk, S., The Lack of Uniformity in the Terminology of the International Law of Remedies, 5 Leiden Journal of International Law (1992).
Hamber, B., Repairing the Irreparable: Dealing with double-binds of making reparations for crimes of the past, 5 Ethnicity and Health (2000).

Hawkins D. and Jacoby, W., Partial Compliance: A Comparison of the European and Inter-American Courts for Human Rights, 6 Journal of International Law and International Relations (2010).
Hazan, P., Morocco: Betting on a Truth and Reconciliation Commission,United States Institute of Peace (2006).
Healy, S. and Plaut, M., Ethiopia and Eritrea: Allergic to Persuasion, 7 Briefing Paper Chatham House (2007).
Henselin, M., Heiskanen, V. and Mettraux, G., Reparations to Victims before the International Criminal Court: Lessons from International Mass Claims Processes, 17 Criminal Law Forum (2006).
Henzelin, M, Heiskanen, V. and Mettraux, G., Reparations to Victims before the ICC: Lessons from International Mass Claims Processes, 17 Criminal Law Forum (2016).
Herman, J., Realities of Victim Participation: The civil party system in practice at the Extraordinary Chambers in the Courts of Cambodia (ECCC), 4 Contemporary Justice Review (2013).
Hillebrecht, C., Implementing International Human Rights Law at Home: Domestic Politics and the European Court of Human Rights, 13 Human Rights Review (2012).
Hillebrecht, C., The Domestic Mechanisms of Compliance with International Human Rights Law: Case Studies from the Inter-American Human Rights System, 34 Human Rights Quarterly (2012).
Hillebrecht, C., The power of human rights tribunals: Compliance with the European Court of Human Rights and domestic policy change, 20 European Journal of International Relations (2014).
HRW, Morocco's Truth Commission: Honouring Past Victims during an Uncertain Present, 17 Human Rights Watch (2005).
Huneeus, A., Courts Resisting Courts: Lessons from the Inter-American Court's Struggle to Enforce Human Rights, 44 Cornell International Law Journal (2011).
ICTJ, A Measure of Dignity: The Beginning of Reparations in Post-Revolution Tunisia (2015).
ICTJ , A Practicioner's Perspective on Forms of Justice in Peru and Colombia (2017).
ICTJ, Transitional Justice and Development, ICTJ (2009).
ICTJ, Morocco: Progress report (2005).
ICTJ, Morocco: Gender and the Transitional Justice Process (2011).
ICTJ, Reparaciones en Perú: El largo camino entre las recomendaciones y la implementación, ICTJ (2013).
ICTJ , Transitional Justice in the United Nations Human Rights Council, ICTJ 2011.
ICTJ , Truth and reconciliation in Morocco (2009).
ICTJ, Truth and Reconciliation in Morocco (2009).
ICTJ, Victims in of Peru's internal conflict still await Reparations (2013).
ICTJ , What is Transitional Justice? (2009).
ICTJ and APRODEH, Escuchando las voces de las comunidades: Un estudio sobre la implementación de las Reparaciones Colectivas en el Perú, ICTJ (2010).

ICTJ and APRODEH, Perú ¿Cuánto se ha reparado en nuestras comunidades? Avances, percepciones y recomendaciones sobre reparaciones colectivas en Perú (2007-2011), ICTJ (2011).

Iliff, F., Maitre-Muhl, F. and Sirel, A., "Adverse Consequences of Reparations", Briefing Paper No. 6, Reparations Unit, Essex University (2011).

International Bank for Reconstruction and Development, Colombia: Collective Reparation for Victims through Social Reconstruction Project, (2015).

International Commission of Jurists, The Right to a Remedy and to Reparations for Gross Human Rights Violations, Practitioner's Guide Series 2 (2006).

Jeffery, R., Beyond Repair?: Collective and Moral Reparations at the Khmer Rouge Tribunal, 13 Journal of Human Rights (2014).

Jones, S., Apology Diplomacy: Justice for All?, 122 Netherlands Institute of International Relations 'Clingendael' (2011).

Justice Yaw Appau, Assessment of Damages, Paper Presented at Induction Course for Newly Appointed Circuit Judges at the Judicial Training Institute.

Kalshoven, F., State Responsibility for Warlike Acts of the Armed Forces: From Article 3 of the Hague Convention IV of 1907 to Article 91 of Additional Protocol I of 1977 and beyond, 40 The International and Comparative Law Quarterly (1991).

Kamminga, M., Is the European Convention on Human Rights Sufficiently Equipped to Cope with Gross and Systematic Violations?, 12 Netherlands Quarterly of Human Rights (1994).

Karimova, T., What Amounts to 'a Serious Violation of International Human Rights Law'?, Geneva Academy of International Humanitarian Law and Human Rights, Briefing No. 6 (2014).

Kazazi, M., An Overview of Evidence before the United Nations Compensation Commission, 1 International Law Forum du droit international (1999).

Keller, L.M., Seeking Justice at the International Criminal Court: Victims' Reparations, 29 Thomas Jefferson Law Review (2007).

Kidane, W., Civil Liability for Violations of International Humanitarian Law: The Jurisprudence of the Eritrea-Ethiopia Claims Commission in The Hague, 25 Wisconsin International Law Journal (2007).

Laplante, L.J, The Law of Remedies and the Clean Hand Doctrine: Exclusionary Reparation Policies in Peru's Political Transition, 23 American University International Law Review (2009).

Laplante, L.J. and Theidon, K., Truth with Consequences: Justice and Reparations in Post-Truth Commission Peru, 29 Human Rights Quaterly (2007).

Laplante, L.J., Negotiating Reparation Rights: The Participatory and Symbolic Quotients, 19 Buffalo Human Rights Law Review (2012).

Laplante, L.J., Brining Effective Remedies Home: The Inter-American Human Rights System, Reparations, and the Duty to Prevention, 22 Netherlands Quarterly of Human Rights (2004).

Letschert, R. Inaugural address: Tussen recht en realiteit: Duurzaam herstel na massavictimisatie, Tilburg University Press (2012).

Limón, P. and Von Norman, J., Prioritising Victims to Provide Reparations: Relevant Expertise, Briefing Paper No. 3, Reparations Unit, Essex University (2011).
Liwanga, R.C., The Meaning of "Gross Violation" of Human Rights: A Focus on International Tribunals' Decisions over the DRC Conflicts, 44 Denver Journal of International Law & Policy (2015).
Lopez-Cardenas, C.M., Aproximación a un estándar de reparación integral en procesos colectivos de violación a los Derechos Humanos. Jurisprudencia de la Corte Interamericana de Derechos Humanos" 11 Revista Estudios Socio-Juridicos (2009).
Magarrell, L., Reparations in Theory and Practice, ICTJ (2007).
Magarrell, L., Reparations for Massive or Widespread Human Rights Violations: Sorting Out Claims for Reparations and the Struggle for Social Justice, 22 Windsor Yearbook of Access to Justice (2003).
Manjoo, R., Introduction: Reflections on the concept and implementation of transformative reparations, 21 The International Journal of Human Rights (2017).
Mathes, E., Maslow's Hierarchy of Needs. as a Guide for Living, 21 Journal of Humanistic Psychology (1981).
Matheson, M.J, Eritrea-Ethiopia Claims Commission: Damage Awards,13 ASIL (2009).
Mavroidis, P.C., Remedies in the WTO Legal System: Between a Rock and a Hard Place, 764 EJIL (2000).
Mayeux, B. and Mirabal, J., Collective and Moral Reparations in the Inter-American Court of Human Rights, Human Rights Clinic, The University of Texas School of Law (2009).
McCarthy, C., Reparations under the Rome Statute of the International Criminal Court' and Reparative Justice Theory, 3 The International Journal of Transitional Justice Brill (2009).
McCarthy, C., Victim Redress and International Criminal Justice, 10 Journal of International Criminal Law (2012).
McGovern, F.E., Dispute System Design: The United Nations Compensation Commission, 14 Harvard Negotiation Law Review (2009).
Mégret, F., Justifying Compensation by the International Criminal Courts, 36 Brook Journal of International Law (2010).
Mégret, F., Of Shrines, Memorials and Museums: Using the International Criminal Court's Victim Reparations and Assistance Regime to Promote Transitional Justice, 16 Buffalo Human Rights Law Review (2010).
Mégret, F., The International Criminal Court and the Failure to Mention Symbolic Reparations, 16 International Review of Victimology (2009).
Moffet, L., Elaborating Justice for Victims at the International Criminal Court, 13 Journal of International Criminal Law (2015).
Moffet, L., Reparations for 'Guilty Victims': Navigating Complex Identities of Victim-Perpetrators in Reparation Mechanisms, 10 International Journal of Transitional Justice (2016).

Moffet, L., Reparative complementarity: ensuring an effective remedy for victims in the reparation regime of the International Criminal Court, 21 The International Journal of Human Rights (2012).
Moffett, L., Reparations for victims at the International Criminal Court: a new way forward?, 21 The International Journal of Human Rights (2017).
Murray, R. Serious or Massive Violations under the African Charter on Human and People's Rights: A Comparison with the Inter-American and European Mechanisms, 17 Netherlands Quarterly of Human Rights (1999).
Musila, G.M., The right to an effective remedy under the African Charter on Human and Peoples' Rights, 6 African Human Rights Law Journal (2006).
Neuman, G., Bi-Level Remedies for Human Rights Violations, 55 Harvard International Law Journal (2014).
Neuman, G., Import, Export and Regional Consent in the Inter-American Court of Human Rights, 19 European Journal of International Law (2008).
Nifosi-Sutton, I., The Power of the European Court of Human Rights to Order Specific Non-Monetary Relief: A Critical Appraisal from a Right to Health Perspective, 23 Harvard Human Rights Journal (2010).
Open Society Foundation, The Funding Challenge for Reparations in Cambodia (2013).
Parisi, F. and Fon, V., Causation and Responsibility: The Compensation Principle from Grotius to Calabresi, 64 Maryland Law Review (2005).
Parlevliet, M., Embracing Concurrent Realities: Revisiting the Relationship between Human Rights and Conflict Resolution, A published thesis submitted for the Degree of Doctor of Philosophy, University of Amsterdam (2015).
Pasqualucci, J.M, Victim Reparations in the Inter-American Human Rights System: A Critical Assessment of Current Practice and Procedure, 18 Michigan Journal of International Law (1996).
Path, K. and Kanavaou, A., Converts, not ideologues? The Khmer Rouge practice of thought reform in Cambodia, 1975-1978, 20 Journal of Political Ideologies (2015).
Paúl, A., In search of the standards of proof applied by the Inter-American Court of Human Rights, 55 Revista Instituto Interamericano de Derechos Humanos (2012).
Paúl, A., Sana Crítica: The System for Weighing Evidence Utilized by the Inter-American Court of Human Rights, 18 Buffalo Human Rights Law Review (2012).
Pérez-León Acevedo, J.P., Reparations and Prosecutions after Serious Human Rights Violations: Two Pending Issues in Peru's Transitional Justice Agenda, Oxford Transitional Justice Working Papers Series (2010).
Phan, H.D., Reparation to Victims of Gross Human Rights Violations: The case of Cambodia, 4 East Asia Law Review (2009).
Ramil-Nogales, J. and van Schaak, B., A Collective Response to Mass Violence: Reparations and Healing in Cambodia, in Brining the Khmer Rouge to Justice: Prosecuting Mass Violence before the Cambodian Courts, Santa Clara University School of Law, Legal Studies Research Papers Series, Working Paper (2006).
REDRESS, Moving Reparation forward at the ICC: Recommendations, (2016).

REDRESS, Reaching for Justice: The Right to Reparation in the African Human Rights System, The REDRESS Trust (2013).
REDRESS, Report on the Impact of the Rome Statute System on Victims and Affected Communities, (2010).
Robin Azevedo, V. and Delacroix, D., Categorización étnica, conflicto armado interno y reparaciones simbólicas en el Perú post – Comisión de la Verdad y Reconciliación (CVR), Openedition (2017).
Roht-Arriaza, N., Reparations Decisions and Dilemmas, 27 Hastings International and Comparative Law Review (2004).
Rose, C., An Emerging Norm: The Duty of States to Provide Reparations for Human Rights Violations by Non-State Actors, 33 Hastings International and Comparative Law Review (2010).
Rosenfeld, F., Collective Reparations for Victims of Armed Conflicts, 92 International Review of the Red Cross (2010).
Rousset Siri, A.J., El concepto de reparación integral en la jurisprudencia de la Corte Interamericana de Derechos Humanos, 1 Revista Internacional de Derechos Humanos (2011).
Rubin, E.L., The Practice and Discourse of Legal Scholarship, 86 Michigan Law Review (1988).
Ruiz Chiriboga, O., The Independence of the Inter-American Judge, 11 The Law and Practice of International Courts and Tribunals (2012).
Sandoval Villalba, C., Transitional Justice: Key Concepts, processes and Challenges, Institute for Democracy & Conflict Resolution (2011).
Schabas, W., The International Criminal Court at Ten, 22 Criminal Law Forum (2011).
Schönsteiner, J., Dissuasive Measures and the Society as a Whole: A Working Theory of Reparations in the Inter-American Court of Human Rights, 23 American University International Law Review (2011).
Schwager, E., The Right to Compensation for Victims of an Armed Conflict, 4 Chinese Journal of International Law (2005).
Shelton, D., Righting Wrongs: Reparations in the Articles on State Responsibility, 96 The American Journal of International Law (2002).
Sierra Leone Truth and Reconciliation Report, Witness to Truth: Report of the Sierra Leone Truth and Reconciliation, Vol. II, Chapter 4, (2004).
Sikkink, K. et al., Reparaciones integrales en Colombia: logros y desafíos. Evaluación comparativa y global, Harvard Kennedy School and Carr Center for Human Rights Policy (2014).
Simon Fraser University, Human Security Report 2013: The Decline in Global Violence: Evidence, Explanation and Contestation, Human Security Press (2014).
Slye, R.C., A Limited Amnesty? Insights from Cambodia, Seattle University School of Law Research Paper No. 12-24, (2012).
Sperfeldt, C., Collective Reparations at the Extraordinary Chambers in the Courts of Cambodia, 12 International Criminal Law Review (2012).

Stahn, C., Reparative Justice after the Lubanga Appeal Judgment: New Prospects for Expressivism and Participatory Justice or 'Juridified Victimhood' by Other Means?, 3 Journal of International Criminal Justice (2015).

Starr, S.B., Rethinking 'Effective Remedies': Remedial Deterrence in International Courts, 83 New York University Law Review (2008).

Studzinsky, S., Reparations at the Extraordinary Chambers in Courts of Cambodia (ECCC), in REDRESS, Conference Report: Reparations before the International Criminal Court: Issues and Challenges, The Hague, 12 May 2011 (2011).

Studzinsky, S., "Victim's Participation before the Extraordinary Chambers in the Courts of Cambodia" Zeitschrift für Internationale Strafrechtsdogmatik (2011), p. 887.

Suchova, M., The importance of a Participatory Reparations Process and Its Relationship to the Principles of Reparations, Briefing Paper No. 5, Reparations Unit, Essex University (2011).

Sveaass, N., Gross human rights violations and reparation under international law: approaching rehabilitation as a form of reparation, 4 European Journal of Psychotraumatology (2013).

Tan, M.H., Upholding Human Rights in the Hemisphere: Casting Down Impunity Through the Inter-American Court of Human Rights, 43 Texas International Law Journal (2008).

The REDRESS Trust, Report: Reparations for victims of genocide, crimes against humanity and war crimes: Systems in place and systems in the making, The REDRESS Trust (2007).

Thienel, T., The Burden and Standard of Proof in the European Court of Human Rights, 50 German Yearbook of International Law (2007).

Thomas, T.A., Ubi Jus, Ibi Remedium: The Fundamental Right to a Remedy, 41 San Diego Law Review (2004).

Tomuschat, C., Darfur: Compensation for the Victims, 3 Journal of International Criminal Justice (2005).

Tomuschat, C., Reparations for Victims of Grave Human Rights Violations, 10 Tulane Journal of International and Comparative Law (2002).

United States Institute of Peace, Report of the Chilean National Commission on Truth and Reconciliation, University of Notre Dame Press (1993).

Uprimny-Yepes, R., Transformative Reparations of Massive Gross Human Rights Violations: Between Corrective and Distributive Justice, 27 Netherlands Quarterly of Human Rights (2009).

Uprimny, M.R., Between Corrective and Distributive Justice: Reparations of Gross Human Rights Violations in Times of Transition, 25 Netherlands Quarterly of Human Rights (2009).

Urban Walker, M., Restorative Justice and Reparations, 37 Journal of Social Philosophy (2006).

Van Boven, T. et al., Seminar on the Right to Restitution, Compensation and Rehabilitation for Victims of Gross Violations of Human Rights and Fundamental Freedoms, 12 SIM Special (1992).

Van Boven, T., The need to repair?, 16 The International Journal of Human Rights (2012).
Van den Wyngaert, C., Victims before International Criminal Courts: some views and concerns of an ICC Trial Judge, 44 Case Western Reserve Journal of International Law (2012).
Van Dijck, G., The Ordered Apology, 37 Oxford Journal of Legal Studies (2017).
Van Zoelen, J.E.M. The United Nations Compensation Commission: toward a new law state responsibility?, Doctoraalscriptie Universiteit Utrecht, 1996.
Verdeja, E., A Critical Theory of Reparative Justice, 15 Constellations (2008).
Waardt, M., Are Peruvian Victims Being Mocked?: Politicization of Victimhood and Victims' Motivations for Reparations, 35 Human Rights Quarterly (2013).
Walker, M., Transformative Reparations? A Critical Look at a Current Trend in Thinking about Gender-Just Reparations, 10 International Journal of Transitional Justice (2016).
War Crimes Research Office, The Case-Based Reparations Scheme at the International Criminal Court, Legal Analysis and Edition Project, Washington College of Law (2010).
Wassgren, H., The UN Compensation Commission: Lessons of Legitimacy, State Responsibility and War Reparations, 11 Leiden Journal of International Law (1998).
White, B., Say you're Sorry: Court-Ordered Apologies as a Civil Rights Remedy, 91 Cornell Law Review (2006).
Wierda, M. and de Greiff, P., Reparations and the International Criminal Court: A Prospective Role for the Trust Fund for Victims, ICTJ (2004).
Williams, S., The Severance of Case 002 at the ECCC: A Radical Trial Management Technique or a Step Too Far, 13 Journal of International Criminal Justice (2015).
Wühler, N., The United Nations Compensation Commission: A new contribution to the process of international claims resolutions, 2 Journal of International Economic Law (1999).
Zappalà, S., The Rights of Victims v. the Rights of the Accused, 8 Journal of International Criminal Justice (2010).
Zegveld, L., Remedies for Victims of Violations of International Humanitarian Law, 85 International Review of the Red Cross (2003).
Zegveld, L., Victims's Reparations Claims and International Criminal Courts: Incompatble Values?, 8 Journal of International Criminal Justice (2010).
Zyberi, G., The International Court of Justice and applied forms of reparations for international human rights and humanitarian law violations, 7 Utrecht Law Review (2011).

UN and Selected Documents

ACHPR, Resolution on the Right to a Remedy and Reparation for Women and Girls Victims of Sexual Violence (2007).
CAT, General Comment No. 3 of the Committee against Torture, Implementation of Article 14 by States parties, UN Doc. CAT/C/GC/3 (13 December 2012).

CEDAW, General Recommendation No. 25 on Article 4, paragraph 1 of CEDAW, UN Doc./CEDAW/C/2004/I/WP.1/Rev.1 (2004).
CoE Committee of Ministers, Recommendation on the Re-Examination or Reopening of Certain Cases at Domestic Level Following Judgments of the European Court of Human Rights, Rec No R (2000)/2 (2000).
Comisión Multisectorial de Alto Nivel (CMAN), Annual Report (2013).
Comisión Multisectorial de Alto Nivel (CMAN), Annual Report (2016).
CVR, Final Report, Vol. I (2003).
CVR, Final Report, Vol. II: Actores Armados (2003).
CVR, Final Report, Vol. III: Actores políticos e institucionales (2003).
CVR, Final Report, Volume IX: Recommendations, national compromise to reconciliation (2003).
ECtHR's Practice Directions, Just Satisfaction claims – European Court of Human Rights, 1 January 2016. Available at http://www.echr.coe.int/Documents/PD_satisfaction_claims_ENG.pdf.
Final Act of the Paris Conference on Reparation (1945).
HRC, General Comment No. 29, States of Emergency (Article 4), UN Doc. CCPR/C/21/Rev.1/Add.11 (31 August 2001).
HRC, General Comment No. 31, Nature of the General Legal Obligation Imposed on States Parties to the Covenant, UN Doc. CCPR/C/21/Rev.1/Add.13 (29 March 2004).
IACtHR, Resolution: Supervisión de cumplimiento de sentencias: Aplicabilidad del artículo 65 de la Convención Americana sobre Derechos Humanos (adopted 29 June 2005).
ICC, Resolution Adopted at the 7th plenary meeting by consensus, ICC-ASP/10/Res.3 (2011).
IER, Follow-up Report on the Implementation of Equity and Reconciliation Commission Recommendations: Main Report (2009).
IER, Summary of the Final Report (2006).
IER, Final Report, Volume 1: Truth, Equity and Reconciliation (2009).
IER, Final Report, Volume 2: Establishing Truth and Responsibilities regarding Human Rights Violations (2009).
IER, Final Report, Volume 3: Justice and Reparations for Victims (2009).
IER, Final Report, Volume 4: The Components of Reform and Reconciliation (2009).
IER, Final Report, Volume 5: The Organization of the Work and Activities of the Commission (2009).
ILA, Draft Declaration of International Law Principles on Reparation for Victims of Armed Conflict (Substantive Issues) (2010).
ILC, Commentaries to the Articles on State Responsibility, A/CN.4/SER.A/2001/Add.1 (2001).
ILC, Draft Articles on Responsibility of States for Internationally Wrongful Acts, with commentaries, A/CN.4/SER.A/2001/Add.1 (2001).
ILC, Draft Principles on the Allocation of Loss in the case of Transboundary Harm arising out of Hazardous Activities, UN Doc. A/61/10, (2006).

ILC, Third report of the Special Rapporteur, James Crawford, on State Responsibility, UN Doc. A/CN.4/507 (2000).
Nairobi Declaration on Women's and Girl's Rights to a Remedy and Reparations (2007).
OAS, Access to Justice for Women Victims of Sexual Violence in Mesoamerica, OEA/Ser.L/V/II. Doc. 63 (2011).
OAS, Access to Justice for Women Victims of Violence in the Americas, OEA/Ser. L/V/II. Doc. 6 (2007).
OAS, Principal Guidelines for a Comprehensive Reparations Policy, Doc. No. OEA/Ser/L/V/II.131, 19 February 2008.
Sierra Leone Truth and Reconciliation Commission, Report Vol. 2 (2004).
TFV, Annual Report (2015).
TFV, Programme Progress Report (2009).
TFV, Programme Progress Report, Assistance & Reparations: Achievements, Lessons Learned, and Transitioning (2015).
TFV, Report to the Assembly of States Parties on projects and activities of the Board of Directors of the Trust Fund for Victims for the period 1 July 2015 to 30 June 2016, ICC-ASP/15/14 (2016).
TFV, Strategic Plan 2014-2017, Approved by the TFV Board of Directors (2014).
TFV, Summary of Annual Report (2016).
TFV, Trust Fund for Victims Board of Directors, Lists of Decisions at its 14th Annual Meeting (2016).
UN ECOSOC, Resolution 1235 (XLII), UN Doc. E/4393 (1967).
UN Secretary-General, Report pursuant to paragraph 19 of the UNSC Resolution 687, UN Doc. S/22559 (1991).
UN Report of the Secretary General on the Rule of Law and Transitional Justice in Conflict and Post-Conflict Societies, UN Doc. S/2004/616 (2004).
UN World Conference on Human Rights, Vienna Declaration and Programme of Action, UN Doc. A/CONF.157/23 (1993).
UNCC, Report and Recommendations made by the Panel of Commissioners Concerning the First Instalment of Individual Claims for Damages up to US$ 100,000 (Category "C" Claims), Doc. S/AC.26/1994/3 (1994).
UNCC, Report and Recommendations made by the Panel of Commissioners concerning the First Instalment of Individual Claims for Damages up to US$ 100,000, 21 December 1994.
UNCHR, Annex to Question of the Human Rights of all Persons Subjected to any form of Detention or Imprisonment, UN Doc. E/CN.4/1997/104 (1997).
UNCHR, Comments on Argentina, UN Doc. CCPR/C/79/Add.46 (1995).
UNCHR, Draft Declaration on the Recognition of Gross and Massive Violations of Human Rights Perpetrated on the Orders of Governments or Sanctioned by them as an International Crime, Annex to S. Chernichenko, Recognition of Gross and Massive Violations of Human Rights Perpetrated on the Orders of Governments or Sanctioned by them as an International Crime, Expanded Working Paper, UN Doc. E/CN.4/Sub.2/1997/29 (1997).

UNCHR, Final Report submitted by Mr. Theo van Boven, Special Rapporteur: Proposed Basic Principles and Guidelines, E/CN.4/Sub.2/1993/8 (1993).
UNCHR, Question of the Impunity of Perpetrators of Human Rights Violations (Civil and Political): Revised Final Report Prepared by Mr. Joinet Pursuant to Sub-Commission Decision 1996/119, UN Doc. E/CN.4/Sub.2/1997/20/Rev. 1 (1997).
UNCHR, Report of the independent expert to update the Set of principles to combat impunity, Diane Orentlicher, UN Doc. E/CN.4/2005/102/Add.1 (2005).
UNCHR, Report on the situation of human rights in Kuwait under Iraqi occupation, Walter Kälin, UN Doc. E/CN.4/1992/26 (1992).
UNCHR, Study Concerning the Right to Restitution, Compensation and Rehabilitation for Victims of Gross Violations of Human Rights and Fundamental Freedoms: Final Report, UN Doc. E/CN.4/Sub.2/1993/8 (1993).
UNCHR, Updated Set of Principles for the Protection and Promotion of Human Rights through Action to Combat Impunity, UN Doc. E/CN.4/2005/102/Add.1 (2005).
UNGA, Basic Principles and Guidelines on the Right to a Remedy and Reparation for Victims of Gross Violations of International Human Rights Law and Serious Violations of International Humanitarian Law, UN Doc. A/RES/60/147 (2006).
UNGA, Declaration of Basic Principles of Justice for Victims of Crime and Abuse of Power, UN Doc. A/RES/40/34, (Victims' Declaration) (1985).
UNGA, Human Rights Council: Resolution, UN Doc. A/RES/60/251 (2006).
UNGA, Report of the Special Rapporteur on the Promotion of Truth, Justice, Reparation and Guarantees of Non-recurrence, Pablo de Greiff, UN Doc. A/HRC/21/46 (2012).
UNGA, Report of the Special Rapporteur on the Promotion of Truth, Justice, Reparation and Guarantees of Non-recurrence, Pablo de Greiff, UN Doc. A/HRC/24/42 (2013).
UNGA, Report of the Special Rapporteur on the Promotion of Truth, Justice, Reparation and Guarantees of Non-recurrence, Pablo de Greiff, UN Doc. A/HRC/27/56/Add.1 (2014).
UNGA, Report of the Special Rapporteur on the Promotion of Truth, Justice, Reparation and Guarantees of Non-recurrence, Pablo de Greiff, UN Doc. A/HRC/30/42 (2015).
UNGA, Report of the Special Rapporteur on the Promotion of Truth, Justice, Reparation and Guarantees of Non-recurrence, Pablo de Greiff, UN Doc. A/HRC/34/62/Add.1 (2016).
UNGA, Report of the Special Rapporteur on the promotion of truth, justice, reparation and guarantees of non-recurrence on his global study on transitional justice, Pablo de Greiff, UN Doc. A/HRC/36/50/Add.1 (2017).
UNGA, Towards an Arms Trade Treaty: Establishing Common International Standards for the Import, Export and Transfer of Conventional Arms: Report of the Secretary-General, UN Doc. A/62/278 (2007).
UNHRC, Expanded Working Paper on Recognition of Gross and Massive Violations of Human Rights Perpetrated on the Orders of Governments or Sanctioned by them as an International Crime, Stanislav Chernichenko, UN Doc. E/CN.4/Sub.2/1997/29 (1997).

UNHRC, Final Report of the Special Rapporteur, Theo Van Boven, on the Right to restitution, compensation and rehabilitation for victims of gross violations of human rights and fundamental freedoms to the 45th Session of the United Nations Commission on Human Rights, UN Doc. E/CN.4/Sub.2/1993/8 (1993).

UNHRC, Human Rights in Palestine and Other Occupied Arab Territories: Report of the United Nations Fact Finding Mission on the Gaza Conflict, UN Doc. A/HRC/12/48 (2009).

UNHRC, Report of the Secretary-General: Question of the Realization in All Countries of Economic, Social and Cultural Rights, UN Doc. A/HRC/4/62 (2007).

UNHRC, Report of the Special Rapporteur, Sir Nigel Rodley, on Question of torture and other cruel, inhuman or degrading treatment or punishment, UN Doc. A/55/290 (2000). UNSC, Resolution 171: The Palestine Question, UN Doc. S/RES/171 (1962).

UNHRC, Situation of Human Rights in the Democratic People's Republic of Korea, UN Doc. A/HRC/RES/22/13 (2013).

UNOHCHR, Born Free and Equal: Sexual Orientation and Gender Identity in International Human Rights Law, HR/PUB/12/06 (2012).

UNOHCHR, Human Rights Council Establishes New Mandates on Promoting an Equitable International Order and on Truth, Justice and Reparation (2011).

UNOHCHR, Report by the Special Rapporteur on the promotion of truth, justice, reparation and guarantees of non-recurrence, Pablo de Greiff, UN Doc. A/69/518 (2014).

UNOHCHR, Report of the United Nations High Commissioner for Human Rights and Follow-up to the World Conference on Human Rights, UN Doc. E/CN.4/2003/14 (2003).

UNOHCHR, Rule of Law Tools for Post-Conflict States: Reparations Programmes, HR/PUB/08/1 (2008).

UNOHCHR, Rule of Law Tools for Post-Conflict States: Truth Commissions, HR/PUB/06/1 (2006).

UNOHCHR, Study on the Right to the Truth: Report of the Office of the United Nations High Commissioner for Human Rights, UN Doc. E/CN.4/2006/91 (2006).

UNOHCHR Working Group on Enforced or Involuntary Disappearances, General Comment on Article 19 of the Declaration on the Protection of All Persons from Enforced Disappearance, E/CN.4/1998/43 (1998).

World Bank, World Development's Report: Conflict, Security and Development (2011).

Miscellaneous

Andina (Agencia Peruana de Noticias), A mediados de año se iniciarán reparaciones colectivas en zona urbana, anuncia CMAN, 12 April 2009. Available at: <http://andina.pe/agencia/noticia-a-mediados-ano-se-iniciaran-reparaciones-colectivas-zona-urbana-anuncia-cman-227546.aspx>.

CMAN, Ministerio de Justicia y Derechos Humanos acompaño en Tingo María entrega de restos de 26 víctimas del periodo de violencia, 16 Mart 2018. Available at: <https://cman.minjus.gob.pe/minjusdh-acompano-en-tingo-maria-entrega-de-restos-de-26-victimas-del-periodo-de-violencia/>.

CMAN, Ministerio de Justicia y Derechos Humanos inicia proyectos de Reparaciones Colectivas en 145 comunidades, 18 Mart 2017. Available at: <https://cman.minjus.gob.pe/minjusddhh-inicia-proyectos-de-reparaciones-colectivas-en-145-comunidades-para-generar-desarrollo-sostenible/>.

CMAN, Projects website. Available at: <https://cman.minjus.gob.pe/wp-content/uploads/2017/07/ProyectosFinanciados_COLECTIVAS.pdf>.

Contreras-Garduño, D., "Passing the buck: the ICC Trial Chamber's approach in Lubanga Reparations decision", 15 August 2015, blog post. Available at: <https://armedgroups-internationallaw.org/2012/08/15/guest-post-by-diana-contreras-garduno-passing-the-buck-the-icc-trial-chambers-approach-in-lubanga-reparations-decision/>.

CICC, Latest News on Jean-Pierre Bemba Gombo, 30 July 2008. Available at: <http://iccnow.org/?mod=newsdetail&news=3088>.

Dylan B., "Dignity" (song) in Bob Dylan's Greatest Hits Volume 3 (1994).

ECCC, Office of Administration Statement. Available at: <https://www.eccc.gov.kh/en/articles/results-forum-developments-eccc%E2%80%99s-proceedings-and-reparations-case-00202>.

ECCC, Reparation Program 2013-2017: for the victims of the Khmer Rouge Regime 1975-1979, 14 January 2014, PowerPoint presentation. Available at: <http://vss.eccc.gov.kh/images/stories/2014/Reparation.pdf>.

ECCC, VSS Fundraising Meeting on Case 002/02 Reparations, 3 April 2017. Available at: <http://www.eccc.gov.kh/sites/default/files/media/Media_Alert_Eng_03.%2004.2017%20.pdf>.

FCDG (Caisse de Dépôt et de Gestion) website. Available at: <http://www.fondationcdg.ma/presentation>.

ICC, Press Release, 18 May 2017. Available at: <https://www.icc-cpi.int/legalAidConsultations?name=pr1305>.

Letter dated 12 October 2000 from the President of the International Tribunal for the Former Yugoslavia Addressed to the Secretary-General, UN Doc. S/2000/1063 (2000).

Letter dated 9 November 2000 from the President of the International Criminal Tribunal for Rwanda Addressed to the Secretary-General, UN Doc. S/2000/1198 (2000).

Nachemson, A., Khmer Rouge Tribunal reparations sought for large set of projects, 7 April 2017. Available at: <http://www.phnompenhpost.com/national/khmer-rouge-tribunal-reparations-sought-large-set-projects>.

Peru's Reparations Council website (Consejo de Reparaciones de Perú). Available at: <https://www.minjus.gob.pe/consejo-de-reparaciones/>.

Sense Agency, Karadzic Gets a Bill from Tribunal, 11 October 2012. Available at: <http://www.sense-agency.com/icty/karadzic-gets-a-bill-from-tribunal.29.html?news_id=14255>.

TFV, Background Summary, August 2008. Available at <https://www.icc-cpi.int/NR/rdonlyres/E582AE21-D718-4798-97ED-C6C9F0D9B42D/0/TFV_Background_Summary_Eng.pdf>.

TFV, Press Release, ICC-TFV-20120325-PR891, 26 March 2013. Available at: <https://reliefweb.int/report/central-african-republic/trust-fund-victims-suspends-its-activities-central-african-republic>.

UN WOMEN Press Release, Turning the tide on sexual violence in conflict, new UN guidance on reparations launched, 11 June 2014. Available at: <http://www.unwomen.org/en/news/stories/2014/6/new-un-guidance-on-reparations-launched>.

UNSC, Security Council Letter dated 14 December 2000 from Secretary-General addressed to the President of the Security Council, UN Doc S/2000/1198 (2000).

VSS, Press Release, Wide Ranging Support for Reparation, 17 March 2017. Available at: <https://kh.boell.org/en/2017/03/17/press-release-victims-support-section-wide-ranging-support-reparation>.

Table of Instruments

International

International Human Rights Law

Convention Against Torture and Other Cruel, Inhuman or Degrading Treatment or Punishment (adopted 10 December 1984, entered into force 16 June 1987) 1465 UNTS 85.
Convention on the Elimination of All Forms of Discrimination Against Women (adopted 18 December 1979, entered into force 3 September 1981) 1249 UNTS 13.
Convention on the Rights of Persons with Disabilities (adopted 13 December 2006, entered into force 3 May 2008) 2525 UNTS 3.
Convention on the Rights of the Child (adopted 20 November 1989, entered into force 2 September 1990) 1577 UNTS 3.
International Convention on the Elimination of All Forms of Discrimination Against Women (adopted 18 December 1979, entered into force 3 September 1981) 1249 UNTS 13.
International Convention for the Protection of All Persons from Enforced Disappearance (adopted 20 December 2006, entered into force 23 December 2010) 2716 UNTS 3.
Optional Protocol to the Convention on the Rights of the Child on a Communications Procedure (adopted 19 December 2011 entered into force 14 April 2014) 2983 UNTS.
Universal Declaration of Human Rights (adopted 10 December 1948) UNGA Res 217 A (III).

International Humanitarian Law

Additional Protocol 1 to the Geneva Conventions (adopted 8 June 1977, entered into force 7 December 1978) 1125 UNTS 3.

Public International Law

Charter of the United Nations (adopted 24 October 1945) 1 UNTS XVI.
Statute of the International Court of Justice (adopted 26 June 1945, entered into force 24 October 1945) 33 UNTS 993.
Vienna Convention on the Law of Treaties (adopted 23 May 1969, entered into force 27 January 1980) 1155 UNTS 331.

International Criminal Law

ECCC

ECCC's Internal Rules (adopted 12 June 2007, entered into force 19 June 2007).
ECCC's Internal Rules, Revision 1 (as amended 1 February 2008).
ECCC's Internal Rules, Revision 2 (as amended 5 September 2008).
ECCC's Internal Rules, Revision 3 (as amended 6 March 2009).
ECCC's Internal Rules, Revision 4 (as amended 11 September 2009).
ECCC's Internal Rules, Revision 5 (as amended 9 February 2010).
ECCC's Internal Rules, Revision 6 (as amended 17 September 2010).
ECCC's Internal Rules, Revision 7 (as amended 23 February 2011).
ECCC's Internal Rules, Revision 8 (as amended 3 August 2011).
ECCC's Internal Rules, Revision 9 (as amended 16 January 2015).
Law on the Establishment of the ECCC for the Prosecution of crimes committed during the period of democratic Kampuchea (entered into force 10 August 2001, as amended 27 October 2004).

ICC

Rome Statute of the International Criminal Court (adopted 17 July 1998, entered into force 1 July 2002) 2187 UNTS 3.
Rules of Procedure and Evidence of the International Criminal Court (adopted 9 September 2002, immediately in force) ICC-ASP/1/3.
Regulations of the Trust Fund for Victims (adopted 3 December 2005, immediately in force) ICC-ASP/4/Res.3.
Regulations of the International Criminal Court (adopted 26 May 2004) ICC-BD/01-01-04.

ICTY

Rules of Procedure and Evidence of the International Criminal Tribunal for the former Yugoslavia (adopted 11 February 1994, entered into force 14 March 1994, as amended).

Regional

Africa

African Charter on Human and Peoples' Rights (adopted 27 June 1981, entered into force 21 October 1986) 1520 UNTS 217.
Protocol to the African Charter on Human and Peoples' Rights on the Establishment of the African Court on Human and Peoples' Rights (adopted 10 June 1998, entered into force 25 January 2004) OAU Doc OAU, LEG/EXP/AFCHPR/PROT (III).

Americas

American Convention on Human Rights (adopted 22 November 1969, entered into force 18 July 1978) 1148 UNTS 123.
American Declaration on the Rights and Duties of the Man (adopted 2 May 1948) OAS Doc OEA/Ser.L.V/II.82 doc.6 rev. 1.
Rules of Procedure of the Inter-American Court of Human Rights (approved LXXXV Regular Period of Sessions, 16-28 November 2009).

Europe

European Convention for the Protection of Human Rights and Fundamental Freedoms (adopted 4 November 1950, entered into force 3 September 1953, as amended) 213 UNTS 222.
Rules of Court of the European Court of Human Rights (adopted 18 September 1959, immediately in force).

National

Morocco

Morocco Royal Decree No. 1.11.19 (adopted 1 March 2011).
Statute of the Instance Equité et Réconciliation (adopted 10 April 2004).

Peru

Ley No. 28592 (adopted 20 July 2005, entered into force 28 July 2005).
Peru Supreme Decree No. 015-2006-Jus: Reglamento de la Ley No. 28592 (adopted 6 July 2006).
Peru Supreme Decree, No. 065-2001-PCM (adopted 2 June 2001).

USA

United States Foreign Assistance Act of 1961 (adopted September 4 1961).

Others

Agreement between the Government of the State of Eritrea and the Government of the Federal Democratic Republic of Ethiopia (Algiers Agreement) (adopted 12 December 2000, immediately in force) 2138 UNTS 94.

Table of Cases, Decisions and Filings

Permanent Court of International Justice

Factory at Chorzów (*Germany* v. *Poland*), Judgment, 26 July 1927.
Factory at Chorzów (*Germany* v. *Poland*), Merits, 13 September 1928.
Factory at Chorzów (*Germany v. Poland*), Judgment, 13 September 1928.
Mavrommatis Palestine Concessions (*Greece v. United Kingdom*), Judgment, 30 August 1924.
S.S. "Wimbledon" (*United Kingdom* v. *Japan*), Judgment, 17 August 1923.

International Court of Justice

Ahmadou Sadio Diallo (*Republic of Guinea* v. *Democratic Republic of the Congo*), Judgment, 19 June 2012.
Ahmadou Sadio Diallo (*Republic of Guinea* v. *Democratic Republic of the Congo*), Judgment, 30 November 2010.
Application of the Convention on the Prevention and Punishment of the Crime of Genocide (*Bosnia and Herzegovina* v. *Serbia* and *Montenegro*, Judgment, 26 February 2007.
Armed Activities on the Territory of the Congo (*Democratic Republic of the Congo* v. *Uganda*), Judgment, 19 December 2005.
Arrest Warrant of 11 April 2000 (*Democratic Republic of the Congo* v. *Belgium*), Judgment, 14 February 2002.
Avena and other Mexican nationals (*Mexico* v. *United States of America*), Judgment, 31 March 2004.
Case concerning East Timor (*Portugal* v. *Australia*), Judgment, 30 June 1995.
Certain Activities carried out by Nicaragua in the Border Area (*Costa Rica* v. *Nicaragua*), Judgment, 16 December 2015.
Construction of a Road in Costa Rica along the San Juan River (*Nicaragua* v. *Costa Rica*), Judgment, 16 December 2015.
Corfu Channel (*United Kingdom of Great Britain* and *Northern Ireland* v. *Albania*), Judgment, 9 April 1949.
Corfu Channel (*United Kingdom of Great Britain* and *Northern Ireland* v. *Albania*), Judgment, 15 December 1949.
Gabčíkovo-Nagymaros Project (*Hungary* v. *Slovakia*), Judgment, 25 September 1997.
Haya de la Torre (*Colombia* v. *Peru*), Judgment, 13 June 1951.

Jurisdictional Immunities of the State (*Germany* v. *Italy: Greece intervening*), Judgment, 3 February 2012.
LaGrand (*Germany* v. *United States of America)*, Judgment, 27 June 2001.
LaGrand (*Germany* v. *United States of America*), Memorial of the Federal Republic of Germany,16 September 1999.
Legal Consequences of the Construction of a Wall in the Occupied Palestinian Territory, Advisory Opinion, 9 July 2004.
Nuclear Test (*Australia* v. *France*), Judgment, 20 December 1974.
Pulp Mills on the River (*Argentina* v. *Uruguay)*, Judgment, 20 April 2010.
Reparation for Injuries Suffered in the Service of the United Nations, Advisory Opinion, 11 April 1949.
Reparation for Injuries Suffered in the Service of the United Nations, Advisory Opinion, 11 April 1949.
T*emple of Preah Vihear* (*Cambodia* v. *Thailand*), Judgment, 15 June 1962.
United States Diplomatic and Consular Staff in Tehran (*United States of America* v. *Iran)*, Judgment, 24 May 1980.
Whaling in the Antarctic (*Australia* v. *Japan: New Zealand intervening*), Judgment, 31 March 2014.

Human Rights Committee

Albert Wilson v. *Philippines*, Comm. No. 868/1999, 7 November 2003.
Bautista de Arellana v. *Colombia*, Comm. No. 563/1993, 27 October 1995.
Félix Enrique Chira Vargas-Machuca v. *Peru*, Comm. No. 906/2000, 26 July 2002.
S. Jegatheeswara Sarma v. *Sri Lanka*, Comm. No. 950/2000), 31 July 2003.

African commission of Human and People's Rights

Centre for Minority Rights Development (Kenya) and Minority Rights Group (on behalf of Endorois Welfare Council) v. *Kenya*, Comm. No. 276/03, 25 November 2009.
Human Rights Organization and Centre on Housing Rights and Evictions v. *Sudan*, Comm. No. 279/03-296/05, 27 May 2009.
John D. Ouko v. *Kenya*, Comm. No. 232/99, 6 November 2000.
Malawi African Association et al. v. *Mauritania*, Comm. No. 54/91-61/91-96/93-98/93-164/97-196/97-210/98, 11 May 2000.
Sir Dawda K. Jawara v. *Gambia*, Comm. No. 147/95-149/96, 11 May 2000.
World Organization against Torture, Lawyers' Committee for Human Rights, Jehovah Witnesses, Inter-African Union for Human Rights v. *Zaire*, Comm. No. 25/89, 47/90, 56/91, 100/93, 26 March-4 April 1996.

European Court of Human Rights

Akdeniz v. *Turkey*, Appl. No. 25165/94, 31 May 2005.
Akdivar and Others v. *Turkey*, Appl. No. 99/195/605/693, 1 April 1998.
Akhmadova and Sadulayeva v. *Russia*, Appl. No. 40464/02, 10 May 2007.
Aksoy v. *Turkey*, Appl. No. 21987/93, 18 December 1996.
Al-Jedda v. *the United Kingdom*, Appl. No. 27021/08, 7 July 2011.
Ališić and Others v. *Bosnia and Herzegovina, Croatia, Serbia, Slovenia and* "The Former Yugoslav Republic of Macedonia", Appl. No. 60642/08, 26 July 2014.
Amuur v. *France*, Appl. No. 19776/92, 25 June 1996.
Ananyev and Others v. *Russia*, Appl. Nos. 42525/07 and 60800/08, 10 January 2012.
Anguelova v. *Bulgaria*, Appl. No. 38361/97, 13 June 2002.
Apicella v. *Italy*, Appl. No. 64890/01, 29 March 2006.
Aslakhanova and others v. *Rusia*, Appl. Nos. 2944/06 and 8300/07, 50184/07, 332/08, 42509/10, 18 December 2012.
Assanidze v. *Georgia*, Appl. No. 71503/01, 8 April 2004.
Broniowski v. *Poland*, Appl. No. 31443/96, 22 June 2004.
Brumărescu v. *Romania*, Appl. No. 28342/95, 23 January 2001.
Çakici v. *Turkey*, Appl. No. 23657/94, 8 July 1999.
Christine Goodwin v. *The United Kingdom*, Appl. No. 28957/95, 11 July 2002.
Driza v. *Albania*, Appl. No. 33771/02, 13 November 2007.
E.P. v. *Italy*, Appl. No. 31127/96, 16 November 1999.
Elci and others v. *Turkey*, Appl. Nos. 23145/93 and 25091/94, 13 November 2003.
Fedorov v. *Russia*, Appl. No. 63997/00, 26 February 2009.
Firstov v. Russia, Appl. 42119/04, 07 July 2014.
Gillow v. *United Kingdom*, Appl. No. 9063/80, 14 September 1987.
Gridin v. Russia, Appl. No, 64890/01, 01 June 2006.
Gruais and Bousquet v. *France*, Appl. No. 67881/01, 10 January 2006.
Guiso-Gallisay v. *Italy*, Appl. No. 58858/00, 22 December 2009.
Hutten-Czapska v. *Poland*, Appl. No. 35014/97, 16 June 2006.
Ilaşcu and Others v. *Moldova And Russia*, Appl. No. 48787/99, 8 July 2004.
Ipek v. *Turkey*, Appl. No. 25760/94, 17 February 2004.
Ireland v. *The United Kingdom*, Appl. No. 5310/71, 18 January 1978.
Jalloh v. *Germany*, Appl. No. 54810/00, 11 July 2006.
Kallweit v. *Germany*, Appl. No. 17792/07, 13 April 2011.
Kaya v. *Turkey*, Appl. No. 158/1996/777/978, 19 February 1998.
Kurt v. *Turkey*, Appl. No. 15/1997/799/1002, 25 May 1998.
Labita v. *Italy*, Appl. No. 26772/95, 6 April 2000.
M.C. and Others v. *Italy*, Appl. No. 5376/11, 3 September 2013.
Mahmut Kaya v. *Turkey*, Appl. No. 22535/93, 28 March 2000.
Manushaqe Puto and Others v. *Albania*, Appl. Nos. 604/07, 43628/07, 46684/07 and 34770/09, 31 July 2012.
Marckx v. *Belgium*, Appl. No. 6833/74, 13 June 1979.

Maria Atanasiu and Others v. *Romania*, Appl. Nos. 30767/05 and 33800/06, 12 October 2010.
McCann and others v. *Great Britain*, Appl. No. 18984/91, 5 September 1995.
Neshkov and Others v. *Bulgaria*, Appl. Nos. 36925/10, 21487/12, 72893/12, 73196/12, 77718/12 and 9717/13, 27 January 2015.
Oleksandr Volkov v. *Ukraine*, Appl. No. 21722/11, 9 January 2013.
Papamichalopoulos and Others v. *Greece*, Appl. No.14556/89, 24 June 1993.
Rutkowski and others v. *Poland*, Appl. Nos. 72287/10, 13927/11 and 46187/11, 7 July 2015.
Sauders v. *The United Kingdom*, Appl. No. 19187/91, 17 December 1996.
Scordino v. *Italy* (No. 1), Appl. No. 36813/97, 29 March 2006.
Scozzari and Giunta v. *Italy*, Appl. No. 39221/98 and 41963/98, 13 July 2000.
Selmouni v. *France*, Appl. No. 25803/94, 28 July 1999.
Sevtap Veznedaroğlu v. Turkey, Appl. No. 32357/96, 11 April 2000.
Suljagić v. *Bosnia and Herzegovina*, Appl. No. 27912/02,3 November 2009.
Tahsin Acar v. *Turkey*, Appl. No. 26307/95, 8 April 2004
Tanrikulu v. *Turkey*, Appl. No. 23763/94, 8 July 1999.
Thlimmenos v. *Greece*, Appl. 34369/97, 6 April 2000.
Torreggiani and Others v. *Italy*, Appl. Nos. 43517/09, 46882/09, 55400/09, 8 January 2013.
UrbáRska Obec Trenčlanske Biskupice v. *Slovakia*, Appl. No. 74258/01, 27 November 2007.
Varga and Others v. *Hungary*, Appl. Nos. 14097/12, 45135/12, 73712/12, 34001/13, 44055/13, and 64586/13, 10 March 2015.
Varnava and others v. *Turkey* Appl. Nos. 16064/90, 16065/90, 16066/90, 16068/90, 16069/90, 16070/90, 16071/90, 16072/90 and 16073/90, 18 September 2009.
Varnava and others v. *Turkey*, Appl. Nos. 16064/90, 16065/90, 16066/90, 16068/90, 16069/90, 16070/90, 16071/90, 16072/90 and 16073/90, 18 September 2009.
Verein Gegen Tierfabriken Schweiz (VgT) v. *Switzerland.* Appl. No. 32772/02, 30 June 2009.
X v. *United Kingdom*, Appl. No. 7215/75, 18 October 1982.
Xenides-Arestis v. *Turkey*, Appl. No. 46347/99, 7 December 2006.
Yaşa v. *Turkey*, Appl. No. 63/1997/847/1054, 2 September 1998.

European Commission of Human Rights

Anthony McGoff v. Sweden, Appl. No. 9017/80, 13 July 1983.

Inter-American Court of Human Rights

19 Merchants v. *Colombia* (merits, reparations and costs), 5 July 2004.
Afro-descendant Communities displaced from the Cacarica River Basin (Operation Genesis) v. *Colombia* (preliminary objections, merits, reparations and costs), 20 November 2013.
Almonacid-Arellano et al. v. *Chile* (preliminary objections, merits, reparations and costs), 26 September 2006.
Aloeboetoe et al. v. *Suriname* (reparations and costs), 10 September 1993.
Aloeboetoe et al. v. *Suriname* (merits), 4 December 1991.
Apitz Barbera et al. ("First Court of Administrative Disputes") v. *Venezuela* (preliminary objections, merits, reparations and costs), 5 August 2008.
Artavia Murillo et al. ("in vitro fertilization") v. *Costa Rica* (preliminary objections, merits, reparations and costs), 28 November 2012.
Baena-Ricardo et al. v. *Panama* (competence), 28 November 2003.
Baldeón-García v. *Peru* (merits, reparations and costs), 6 April 2006.
Bámaca Velásquez v. *Guatemala* (reparations and costs), 22 February 2002.
Barrios Altos v. *Peru* (merits)14 March 2001.
Barrios Altos v. *Peru* (reparations and costs), 30 November 2001.
Bulacio v. *Argentina* (merits, reparations and costs), 18 September 2003.
Cabrera García and Montiel Flores v. *Mexico* (preliminary objections, merits, reparations and costs), 26 November 2010.
Cantoral Benavides v. *Peru* (reparations and costs), 3 December 2001.
Cantos v. Argentina (reparations and costs), 28 November 2002.
Caracazo v. *Venezuela* (merits), 11 November 1999.
Caracazo v. *Venezuela* (reparations and costs), 29 August 2002.
Carpio Nicolle et al. v. *Guatemala* (reparations and costs), 22 November 2004.
Castillo Petruzzi et al. v. *Peru* (reparations and costs), 30 May 1999.
Castillo-Páez v. *Peru* (reparations and costs), 27 November 1998.
Cesti-Hurtado v. *Peru* (reparations and costs), 31 May 2001.
Chaparro Álvarez and Lapo Íñiguez v. *Ecuador* (preliminary objections, merits, reparations and costs), 21 November 2007.
Chitay Nech y Otros v. *Guatemala* (preliminary objections, merits, reparations and costs), 25 May 2010.
Chocrón Chocrón v. *Venezuela* (preliminary objections, merits, reparations and costs), 1 July 2011.
Contreras et al. v. *El Salvador* (merits, reparations and costs), 31 August 2011.
Cruz Sánchez et al. v. Peru (preliminary objections, merits, reparations and costs), 17 April 2015.
De la Cruz-Flores v. *Peru* (merits, reparations and costs), 18 November 2004.
El Amparo v. *Venezuela* (reparations and costs), 14 September 1996.
El Amparo v. *Venezuela* (merits), 18 January 1995.
El Amparo v. *Venezuela* (monitoring compliance with judgment), 4 July 2006.

Five Pensioners v. *Peru* (merits, reparations and costs), 28 February 2003.
Gangaram-Panday v. *Suriname* (merits, reparations and costs), 21 January 1994.
García Lucero et al. v. *Chile* (preliminary objections, merits, and reparations), 28 August 2013.
Garífuna Punta Piedra Community and its Members v. *Honduras* (preliminary objections, merits, and reparations), 8 October 2015.
Garífuna Triunfo de la Cruz Community and its Members v. *Honduras* (merits, reparations and costs), 8 October 2015.
Garrido and Baigorria v. *Argentina* (reparations and costs), 27 August 1998.
Girls Yean & Bosico v. *Dominican Republic* (preliminary objections, merits, and reparations), 8 September 2005.
Godínez-Cruz v. *Honduras* (interpretation of the Judgment on reparations and costs), 17 August 1990.
Gomes Lund et al. ("Guerrilha Do Araguaia") v. *Brazil* (preliminary objections, merits, reparations and costs), 24 November 2010.
González et al. ("Cotton Field") v. *Mexico* (preliminary objections, merits, reparations and costs), 16 November 2009.
Gudiel Álvarez et al. (Diario Militar) v. *Guatemal* (merits, reparations and costs), 20 November 2012.
Gutiérrez-Soller v. *Colombia* (merits, reparations and costs), 12 September 2005.
Herrera-Ulloa v. *Costa Rica* (preliminary objections, merits, reparations and costs), 2 July 2004.
Hilaire, Constantine and Benjamin et al. v. *Trinidad and Tobago* (merits, reparations and costs), 21 June 2002.
Huilca-Tecse v. *Peru* (merits, reparations and costs), 3 March 2005.
Ituango Massacres v. *Colombia* (preliminary objections, merits, reparations and costs), 1 July 2006.
Ituango Massacres v. *Colombia* (monitoring compliance with judgment), 21 May 2013.
Ivcher-Bronstein v. *Peru* (merits, reparations and costs), 6 February 2001.
Juan Humberto Sánchez v. *Honduras* (preliminary objections, merits, reparations and costs), 7 June 2003.
Juvenile Reeducation Institute v. *Paraguay* (preliminary objections, merits, reparations and costs), 2 September 2004.
Kuna Indigenous People of Madungandí and the Emberá Indigenous People of Bayano and their Members v. *Panama* (preliminary objections, merits, reparations and costs),14 October 2014.
La Cantuta v. *Peru* (interpretation of the judgment on merits, reparations and costs) 30 November 2007.
La Cantuta v. *Peru* (merits, reparations and costs), 29 November 2006.
La Cantuta v. *Peru* (monitoring compliance with judgment), 20 November 2009.
Las Dos Erres Massacre v. *Guatemala* (preliminary objections, merits, reparations and costs), 24 November 2009.
Las Palmeras v. *Colombia* (reparations and costs), 26 November 2002.

Las Palmeras v. *Colombia* (merits), 6 December 2001.
Loayza Tamayo v. *Peru* (merits), 17 September 1997.
Loayza Tamayo v. *Peru* (reparations and costs), 27 November 1998.
Lopez-Alvarez v. *Honduras* (merits, reparations and costs), 1 February 2006.
Maritza Urrutia v. *Guatemala* (merits, reparations and costs), 27 November 2003.
Mapiripán Masaccre v. *Colombia* (merits, reparations and costs), 15 September 2005.
Mapiripán Masaccre v. *Colombia* (monitoring compliance with judgment), 8 July 2009.
Massacres of El Mozote and nearby places v. *El Salvador* (merits, reparations and costs), 25 October 2012.
Massacres of El Mozote and nearby places v. *El Salvador* (monitoring compliance with judgment), 31 August 2017.
Mayagna (Sumo) Awas Tingni Community v. *Nicaragua* (merits, reparations and costs), 31 August 2001.
Mayagna (Sumo) Awas Tingni Community v. *Nicaragua* (monitoring compliance with judgment), 3 April 2009.
Mayagna (Sumo) Awas Tingni Community v. *Nicaragua* (monitoring compliance with judgment), 7 May 2008.
Mendoza et al. v. *Argentina* (preliminary objections, merits and reparations), 14 May 2013.
Miembros de la Aldea Chichupac y comunidades vecinas del municipio de Rabinal v. *Guatemala* (preliminary objections, merits, reparations and costs), 30 November 2016.
Miguel Castro-Castro Prison v. *Peru* (interpretation of the judgment on merits, reparations and costs), 2 August 2008.
Miguel Castro-Castro Prison v. *Peru* (merits, reparations and costs), 25 November 2006.
Moiwana Community v. *Suriname* (preliminary objections, merits, reparations and costs), 15 June 2005.
Moiwana Community v. *Suriname* (monitoring compliance with judgment), 22 November 2010.
Molina-Theissen v. *Guatemala* (reparations and costs), 3 July 2004.
Montero-Aranguren et al. (Detention Center of Catia) v. *Venezuela* (preliminary objections, merits, reparations and costs), 5 July 2006.
Myrna Mack Chang v. *Guatemala* (merits, reparations and costs), 25 November 2003.
Neira Alegría et al. v. *Peru* (reparations and costs), 19 September 1996.
Norín Catrimán et al. (Leaders, members and activist of the Mapuche Indigenous People) v. *Chile* (merits, reparations and costs), 29 May 2014.
Pacheco Teruel et al. v. *Honduras* (merits, reparations and costs), 27 April 2012.
Palamara Iribarne v. *Chile* (merits, reparations and costs), 22 November 2005.
Peasant Community of Santa Bárbara v. *Peru* (preliminary objections, merits, reparations and costs), 1 September 2015.
Plan de Sánchez Massacre v. *Guatemala* (reparations), 19 November 2004.
Plan de Sánchez Massacre v. *Guatemala* (merits), 29 April 2004.

Plan de Sánchez Massacre v. *Guatemala* (monitoring compliance with judgment), 25 May 2017.

Plan de Sánchez Massacre v. *Guatemala* (monitoring compliance with judgment),1 July 2009.

Plan de Sánchez Massacre v. *Guatemala* (monitoring compliance with judgment), 28 November 2007.

Pueblo Bello Massacre v. *Colombia* (merits, reparations and costs), 31 January 2006.

Pueblo Bello Massacre v. *Colombia* (monitoring compliance with judgment), 9 July 2009.

Reverón Trujillo v. *Venezuela* (preliminary objection, merits, reparations and costs), 30 June 2009.

Río Negro Massacres v. *Guatemala* (preliminary objection, merits, reparations and costs), 4 September 2012.

Río Negro Massacres v. *Guatemala* (monitoring compliance with judgment), 14 March 2018.

Rochela Massacre v. *Colombia* (merits, reparations and costs), 11 May 2007.

R*odríguez Vera et al. (the disappeared from the Palace of Justice)* v. *Colombia* (preliminary objection, merits, reparations and costs), 14 November 2014.

Santo Domingo Massacre v. *Colombia* (preliminary objection, merits and reparations), 30 November 2012.

Saramaka People v. *Suriname* (preliminary objection, merits, reparations and costs), 28 November 2007.

Saramaka People v. *Suriname* (monitoring compliance with judgment), 23 November 2011.

Sawhoyamaxa Indigenous Commmunity v. *Paraguay* (merits, reparations and costs), 29 March 2006.

Sawhoyamaxa Indigenous Commmunity v. *Paraguay* (monitoring compliance with judgment), 2 February 2007.

Yakye Axa, Sawhoyamaxa and Xákmok Kásek Indigenous communities v. *Paraguay* (monitoring ompliance with judgment), 30 August 2017.

Serrano-Cruz Sisters v. *El Salvador* (merits, reparations and costs), 1 March 2005.

Street Children (Villagrán-Morales et al.) v. *Guatelama* (reparations and costs), 26 May 2001.

Street Children (Villagrán-Morales et al.) v. *Guatelama* (merits), 19 November 1999.

Suárez-Rosero v. *Ecuador* (merits), 12 November 1997.

Suárez-Rosero v. *Ecuador* (reparations and costs), 20 January 1999.

The Barrios Family v. *Venezuela* (merits, reparations and costs), 24 November 2011.

The Kaliña and Lokono Peoples v. Suriname (merits, reparations and costs), 25 November 2015.

The Kichwa Indigenous People of Sarayaku v. *Ecuador* (merits and reparations), 27 June 2012.

The Kichwa Indigenous People of Sarayaku v. *Ecuador* (monitoring compliance with judgment), 22 June 2016.

The Last Temptation of Christ (Olmedo-Bustos et al.) v. *Chile* (merits, reparations and costs), 5 February 2001.
The Supreme Court of Justice (Quintana Coello et al.) v. *Ecuador* (preliminary objection, merits, reparations and costs), 23 August 2013.
Tibi v. *Ecuador* (preliminary objection, merits, reparations and costs), 7 September 2004.
Ticona Estrada et al. v. *Bolivia* (merits, reparations and costs), 27 November 2008.
Tiu Tojín v. *Guatemala* (merits, reparations and costs), 26 November 2008.
Trujillo-Oroza v. *Bolivia* (reparations and costs), 27 February 2002.
Valle Jaramillo et al. v. *Colombia* (merits, reparations and costs), 27 November 2008.
Vargas Areco v. *Paraguay* (merits, reparations and costs), 26 September 2006.
Velásquez Rodríguez v. *Honduras* (interpretation of the judgment of Reparations and costs), 17 August 1990.
Velásquez Rodríguez v. *Honduras* (reparations and costs), 21 July 1989.
Velásquez Rodríguez v. *Honduras* (merits), 29 July 1988.
Vera Vera v. *Ecuador* (preliminary objections, merits, reparations and costs), 19 May 2011.
Vereda La Esperanza v. *Colombia* (preliminary objections, merits, reparations and costs), 31 August 2017.
White Van (Paniagua-Morales et al.) v. *Guatemala* (reparations and costs), 25 May 2001.
White Van (Paniagua-Morales et al.) v. *Guatemala* (merits), 8 March 1998.
Xákmok Kásek Indigenous Community v. *Paraguay* (merits, reparations and costs), 24 August 2010.
Ximenes-Lopes v. *Brazil* (merits, reparations and costs), 4 July 2006.
Yakye Axa Indigenous Community v. *Paraguay* (merits, reparations and costs), 17 June 2005.
Yatama v. *Nicaragua* (preliminary objections, merits, reparations and costs), 23 June 2005.
Zambrano Vélez et al. v. *Ecuador* (merits, reparations and costs), 4 July 2007.

Inter-American Commission of Human Rights

Caloto Massacre v. *Colombia*, Report No. 36/00,13 April 2000.
Comadres v. *El Salvador*, Report No. 13/96, 1 March 1996.
Villatina Massacre v. *Colombia*, Report N. 105/05, 27 October 2005.
Garcia Lucero et al. v. *Chile*, Report No. 23/11, 23 March 2011.

International Criminal Court

Prosecutor v. *Ahmad Al Faqi Al Mahdi*, Case, ICC-01/12-01/15.
Prosecutor v. *Ahmad Al Faqi Al Mahdi*, Order, 17 August 2017, *Reparations Order*, ICC-01/12-01/15-236.
Prosecutor v. *Callixte Mbarushimana*, Case, ICC-01/04-01/10.
Prosecutor v. *Callixte Mbarushimana*, Decision, 16 December 2011, *Decision on the Confirmation of Charges*, ICC-01/04-01/10-465-Red.
Prosecutor v. *Germain Katanga*, Case, ICC-01/04-01/07.

Prosecutor v. *Germain Katanga*, Decision, 13 November 2015, *Decision on the review concerning the reduction of the sentence of Mr. Germain Katanga*, ICC-01/04/01/07-3615.

Prosecutor v. *Germain Katanga*, Decision, 23 May 2014, *Decision on Sentence pursuant to article 76 of the Statute*, ICC-01/04-01/07-3484.

Prosecutor v. *Germain Katanga*, Decision, 8 May 2015, *Decision on the "Demande de clarification concernant la mise en œuvre de la Règle 94 du Règlement de procédure et de preuve" and future stages of the proceedings*, ICC-01/04-01/07-3546-tENG.

Prosecutor v. *Germain Katanga*, Filing, 13 May 2016, *Report on the implementation of Decision No. 3546, including the identification of harm suffered by victims as a result of crimes committed by Germain Katanga (article 75(1) of the Statute and regulation 38(1)(f) of the Regulations of the Court)*, ICC-01/04-01/07-3687-tENG.

Prosecutor v. *Germain Katanga*, Filing, 17 May 2017, *Notification pursuant to regulation 56 of the TFV Regulation regarding the Trust Fund Board of Directors Decision Relevant to complement the payments of individual and collective reparations awards*, ICC-01/04-01/07-3740.

Prosecutor v. *Germain Katanga*, Filing, 21 January 2015, *Annex 1 to Registry Report on Applications for Reparations in accordance with Trial Chamber II's Order of 27 August 2014*, ICC-01/04-01/07-3512-Anx1-Red2.

Prosecutor v. *Germain Katanga*, Filing, 21 January 2015, *Registry Report on Applications for Reparations in accordance with Trial Chamber II's Order of 27 August 2014*, ICC-01/04-01/07-3512.

Prosecutor v. *Germain Katanga*, Filing, 25 July 2017, *Draft implementation plan relevant to Trial Chamber II's order for reparations of 24 March 2017 (ICC-01/04-01/07-3728) with Confidential Annex 1: Detailed Overview of beneficiary categories, proposed awards within each category, and estimated values and budget costs thereto, Public Annex 2: Defence correspondence regarding Mr Katanga's potential participation, Confidential, ex parte available to the Registry only Annex 3: Table of harm categorizations on an individual basis of all 297 victims, Confidential, ex parte available to OPCV Legal Representative only Annex 4: Table of harm categorization of victims represented, Confidential, ex parte available to the Legal Representative only Annex 5: Table of harm categorization of victims represented*, ICC-01/04-01/07-3751-Red.

Prosecutor v. *Germain Katanga*, Filing, 25 June 2014, *Annex A to Defence Notice of Discontinuance of Appeal against the 'Jugement rendu en application de l'article 74 du Statut' rendered by Trial Chamber II on 7 April 2014*, ICC-01/04-01/07-3497-AnxA.

Prosecutor v. *Germain Katanga*, Filing, 30 September 2016, *Defence Observations on the Monetary Value of the Alleged Harm*, ICC-01/04-01/07-3711.

Prosecutor v. *Germain Katanga*, Filing, 30 September 2016, *Observations in response to the Trial Chamber's order of 15 July 2016 With Public redacted version of Annex A: Index of annexes, and public annexes 1-5 and 7-14*, ICC-01/04-01/07-3714-Red.

Prosecutor v. *Germain Katanga*, Judgment, 7 March 2014, *Judgment pursuant to Article 74 of the Statute*, ICC-01/04-01/07-3436-tENG.
Prosecutor v. *Germain Katanga*, Order, 24 March 2017, *Ordonnance de réparation en vertu de l'article 75 du Statut*, ICC-01/04-01/07-3728.
Prosecutor v. *Germain Katanga and Mathieu Ngudjolo Chui*, Case, ICC-01/04-01/07.
Prosecutor v. *Germain Katanga and Mathieu Ngudjolo Chui*, Decision, 30 September 2008, *Decision on the confirmation of charges*, ICC-01/04-01/07-717.
Prosecutor v. *Jean-Pierre Bemba Gombo*, Case, ICC-01/05-01/08.
Prosecutor v. *Jean-Pierre Bemba Gombo*, Decision, 12 December 2008, *Fourth Decision on Victims' Participation*, ICC-01/05-01/08-320.
Prosecutor v. *Jean-Pierre Bemba Gombo*, Filing, 26 April 2016, *Public Redacted Version of Submissions on Sentence ICC-01/05-01/08-3376-Conf*, ICC-01/05-01/08-3376-Red.
Prosecutor v. *Jean-Pierre Bemba Gombo*, Order, 17 November 2008, *Order to File in the Record of the Case a Public Redacted Version of a Decision*, ICC-01/05-01/08-251.
Prosecutor v. *Joseph Kony et* al., Case, ICC-02/04-01/05.
Prosecutor v. *Joseph Kony et* al., Judgment, 25 February 2009, *Judgment on the Appeals of the Defence against the decisions entitled 'Decision on victims' applications for participation a/0010/06, a/0064/06, a/0070/06, a/0081/06, a/0082/06, a/0084/06 to a/0089/06, a/0091/06 to a/0097/06, a/0099/06, a/0100/06, a/0102/06 to a/0104/06, a/0111/06, a/0113/06 to a/0117/06, a/120/06, a/021/06 and a/0123/06 to a/0127/06' of the Pre-Trial Chamber II*, ICC-02/04-179.
Prosecutor v. *Thomas Lubanga Dyilo*, Case, ICC-01/04-01/06.
Prosecutor v. *Thomas Lubanga Dyilo*, Decision, 10 February 2006, *Decision on the Prosecutor's Application for a Warrant of Arrest pursuant to Article 58*, ICC-01/04-01/06-2-tEN.
Prosecutor v. *Thomas Lubanga Dyilo*, Decision, 10 July 2012, *Decision on Sentence pursuant to Article 76 of the Statute*, ICC-01/04-01/06-2901.
Prosecutor v. *Thomas Lubanga Dyilo*, Decision, 14 December 2012, *Decision on the admissibility of the appeals against Trial Chamber I's "Decision establishing the principles and procedures to be applied to reparations" and directions on the further conduct of proceedings*, ICC-01/04-01/06-2953.
Prosecutor v. *Thomas Lubanga Dyilo*, Decision, 15 December 2017, *Décision fixant le montant des reparations auxquelles Thomas Lubanga Dyilo est tenu, with two public annexes (Annex I and Annex III) and one confidential annex, ex parte, Registry, Trust Fund for Victims, Legal Representatives of V01 and V02 groups of Victims and Office of Public Counsel for Victims (Annex II) and confidential redacted version of Annex II*, ICC-01/04-01/06-3379-Red.
Prosecutor v. *Thomas Lubanga Dyilo*, Decision, 17 January 2017, *Decision rejecting the application for leave to appeal of the Legal Representatives of the 01 Group of Victims*, ICC-01/04-01/06-3263-tENG.

Prosecutor v. *Thomas Lubanga Dyilo*, Decision, 18 April 2016, *Decision on the request of the Trust Fund for Victims for leave to appeal against the order of 9 February 2016*, ICC-01/04-01/06-3202-tENG.

Prosecutor v. *Thomas Lubanga Dyilo*, Decision, 18 January 2008, *Decision on victims participation*, ICC-01/04-01/06-1119.

Prosecutor v. *Thomas Lubanga Dyilo*, Decision, 22 September 2015, *Decision on the review concerning the reduction of the sentence of Mr. Thomas Lubanga Dyilo*, ICC-01/04-01/06-3173.

Prosecutor v. *Thomas Lubanga Dyilo*, Decision, 29 January 2007, *Decision on the confirmation of charges*, ICC-01/04-01/06-803-tEN.

Prosecutor v. *Thomas Lubanga Dyilo*, Decision, 7 August 2012, *Decision establishing the principles and procedures to be applied to reparations*, ICC-01/04-01/06-2904.

Prosecutor v. *Thomas Lubanga Dyilo*, Filing, 13 February 2017, *Information regarding Collective Reparations with Three public annexes, one confidential annex, and one confidential ex-parte annex available to Trial Chamber II only*, ICC-01/04-01/06-3273.

Prosecutor v. *Thomas Lubanga Dyilo*, Filing, 15 November 2017, *Third progress report on the implementation of collective reparations as per the Trial Chamber II orders of 21 October 2016 and 6 April 2017 with one confidential, ex parte Annex A available to the Registrar only*, ICC-01/04-01/06.

Prosecutor v. *Thomas Lubanga Dyilo*, Filing, 18 April 2012, *Observations on the sentence and reparations by Victims a/0001/06, a/0003/06,a/0007/06, a/00049/06, a/0149/07, a/0155/07, a/0156/07, a/0162/07, a/0149/08, a/0404/08, a/0405/08, a/0406/08, a/0407/08, a/0409/08, a/0523/08, a/0610/08, a/0611/08, a/0053/09, a/0249/09, a/0292/09, a/0398/09 and a/1622/10*, ICC-01/04-01/06-2864-tENG.

Prosecutor v. *Thomas Lubanga Dyilo*, Filing, 18 April 2012, *OPCV Observations on issues concerning reparations*, ICC-01-04/01-06-2863.

Prosecutor v. *Thomas Lubanga Dyilo*, Filing, 19 September 2016, *Public Redacted version of Filing regarding symbolic collective reparations projects with confidential Annex: Draft Request for Proposals, ICC-01/04-01/06-3223-Conf*, ICC-01/04-01/06-3223-Red.

Prosecutor v. *Thomas Lubanga Dyilo*, Filing, 25 April 2012, *Observations on Reparations in Response to the Scheduling Order of 14 March 2012*, ICC-01/04-01/06-2872.

Prosecutor v. *Thomas Lubanga Dyilo*, Filing, 28 October 2016, *Application from the V01 group of victims requesting leave to appeal the "Order relating to the request of the Office of Public Counsel for Victims of 16 September 2016" and the "Order approving the proposed plan of the Trust Fund for Victims in relation to symbolic collective reparations" of 21 October 2016*, ICC-01/04-01/06-3254-tENG.

Prosecutor v. *Thomas Lubanga Dyilo*, Filing, 3 November 2015, *Annex A to Filing on Reparations and Draft Implementation Plan*, ICC-01/04-01/06-3177-AnxA.

Prosecutor v. *Thomas Lubanga Dyilo*, Filing, 3 November 2015, *Filing on Reparations and Draft Implementation Plan*, ICC-01/04-01/06-3177-Red.

Prosecutor v. *Thomas Lubanga Dyilo*, Filing, 31 May 2016, *First submission of victim dossiers with Twelve confidential, ex parte annexes, available to the Registrar, and Legal Representatives of Victims V01 only*, ICC-01/04-01/06-3208.

Prosecutor v. *Thomas Lubanga Dyilo*, Filing, 7 June 2016, *TFV's Additional Programme Information Filing*, ICC-01/04-01/06-3209.

Prosecutor v. *Thomas Lubanga Dyilo*, Filing, 8 April 2013, *Observations of the Trust Fund for Victims on the appeals against Trial Chamber I 's "Decision establishing the principles and procedures to be applied to reparations"*, ICC-01/04-01/06-3009.

Prosecutor v. *Thomas Lubanga Dyilo*, Filing 15 July 2016, *TC II's Request Concerning the Feasibility of Applying Symbolic Collective Reparations*, ICC-01/04-01/06-3219.

Prosecutor v. *Thomas Lubanga Dyilo*, Judgment, 1 December 2014, *Judgment on the appeals of the Prosecutor and Mr. Lubanga Dyilo against the "Decision on Sentence pursuant to Article 76 of the Statute"*, ICC-01/04-01/06-3122.

Prosecutor v. *Thomas Lubanga Dyilo*, Judgment, 11 July 2008, *Judgment on the Appeals of The Prosecutor and the Defence against Trial Chamber I's Decision on Victims' Participation,* ICC-01/04-01/06.

Prosecutor v. *Thomas Lubanga Dyilo*, Judgment, 14 March 2012, *Judgment pursuant to Article 74 of the Statute*, ICC-01/04-01/06-2842.

Prosecutor v. *Thomas Lubanga Dyilo*, Judgment, 3 March 2015, *Annex A to Judgment on the appeals against the "Decision establishing the principles and procedures to be applied to reparations" of 7 August 2012*, ICC-01/04-01/06-3129-AnxA.

Prosecutor v. *Thomas Lubanga Dyilo*, Judgment, 3 March 2015, *Judgment on the appeals against the "Decision establishing the principles and procedures to be applied to reparations" of 7 August 2012*, ICC-01/04-01/06-3129.

Prosecutor v. *Thomas Lubanga Dyilo*, Order, 21 October 2016, *Order approving the proposed plan of the Trust Fund for Victims in relation to symbolic collective reparations*, ICC-01/04-01/06-3251.

Prosecutor v. *Thomas Lubanga Dyilo*, Order, 25 January 2018, *Order Directing Further Information from the Trust Fund for Victims on the Procedure for Determining Victim Status at the Implementation Stage of Reparations*, ICC-01/04-01/06-3391-tENG.

Prosecutor v. *Thomas Lubanga Dyilo*, Order, 6 April 2017, *Order approving the proposed programmatic framework for collective service-based reparations submitted by the Trust Fund for Victims*, ICC-01/04-01/06-3289.

Prosecutor v. *Thomas Lubanga Dyilo*, Order, 6 October 2016, *Order on the conduct of the hearing to be held on 11 and 13 October 2016*, ICC-01/04-01/06.

Prosecutor v. *Thomas Lubanga Dyilo*, Order, 7 November 2017, *Order Instructing the Trust Fund for Victims to Inform the Chamber of the Progress Made in the Implementation of Reparations*, ICC-01/04-1/06-3376-tENG.

Prosecutor v. *Thomas Lubanga Dyilo*, Order, 9 February 2016, *Order instructing the Trust Fund for Victims to supplement the draft implementation plan*, ICC-01/04-01/06-3198-tENG.

Prosecutor v. *Thomas Lubanga Dyilo*, Transcript, 15 December 2017, *Transcript of Delivery of a Reparations Order*, ICC-01/04-01/06-T-369-ENG ET WT 15-12-2017 1-19 NB T.

Prosecutor v. *Thomas Lubanga Dyilo*, Transcript, 21 August 2015, *Sentence Review Session*, ICC-01/04-01/06-T-366-Red-ENG.

Prosecutor v. *William Samoei Ruto and Joshua Arap Sang*, Case, ICC-01/09-01/11.

Prosecutor v. *William Samoei Ruto and Joshua Arap Sang*, Decision, 5 April 2016, *Public redacted version of Decision on Defence Applications for Judgments of Acquittal*, ICC-01/09-01/11-2027 Red-Corr.

Situation in Central Africa, Decision, 23 October 2012, *Decision on the "Notification by the Board of Directors in accordance with Regulation 50 a) of the regulations of the Trust Fund for Victims to undertake activities in the Central African Republic"*, Case ICC-01/05-41.

Situation in Democratic Republic of Congo, Decision, 11 April 2008, *Notification of the Board of Directors of the Trust Fund for Victims in accordance with Regulation 50 of the Regulations of the Trust Fund*, ICC-01/04-492.

Situation in Uganda, Decision, 5 March 2008, *Notification of the Board of Directors of the Trust Fund for Victims in accordance with Regulation 50 of the Regulations of the Trust Fund*, ICC-02/04-120.

Extraordinary Chambers in the Courts of Cambodia

Case of Kaing Guek Eav alias '*Duch*' *(Case 001)*, Decision, *Direction on Proceedings Relevant to Reparations and on the Filing of Final Written Submissions*, 27 August 2009, No. E159.

Case of Kaing Guek Eav alias '*Duch*' *(Case 001)*, Filing, *Civil Parties' Co-Lawyers' Joint Submission on Reparations*, 14 September 2009, No. E159/3.

Case of Kaing Guek Eav alias '*Duch*' *(Case 001)*, Judgment (Appeals), 13 February 2012, No. 001/18-07-2007-ECCC/SC.

Case of Kaing Guek Eav alias '*Duch*' *(Case 001)*, Judgment, 26 July 2010, No. 001/18-07-2007-ECCC/TC.

Case of Nuon Chea and Khieu Samphan (Case 002/01), Judgment (Appeals), 23 November 2016, No. 002/19-09-2007/ECCC/SC.

Case of Nuon Chea and Khieu Samphan (Case 002/01), Judgment, 7 August 2014, No. 002/19-09-2007/ECCC/TC.

Case of Nuon Chea and Khieu Samphan (Case 002/01), Memorandum, *Initial Specification of the Substance of Reparations Awards Sought by the Civil Party Lead Co-Lawyers Pursuant to Internal Rule 23quinquies3*, 23 September 2011, No. E125.

Case of Nuon Chea et al. (Case 002), Decision, *Decision on Reassessment of Accused IENG Thirith's Fitness to Stand Trial following Supreme Court Chamber Decision on 13 December 2011*, 13 September 2012, No. E138/1/10.

Case of Nuon Chea et al. (Case 002), Decision, *Decision on Appeals Against Orders of the Co-investigating Judges on the Admissibility of Civil Party Applications*, 24 June 2011, No. D404/2/4.

Case of Nuon Chea et al. (Case 002), Decision, *Decision on Appeals Against Orders of the Co-investigating Judges on the Admissibility of Civil Party Applications*, 24 June 2011, No. D411/3/6.

Case of Nuon Chea et al. (Case 002), Filing, *Initial specification of the substance of the awards that the Civil Party Lead Co-lawyers intend to seek-Hearing of 19 October 2011*, 12 March 2012, No. E125/2.

Case of Nuon Chea et al. (Case 002), Order, *Order on the Admissibility of Civil Party Applications Related to Request D250/3*, 13 January 2010, No. D250/3/2.

Case of Nuon Chea et al. (Case 002), Order, *Severance order pursuant to internal rule 89ter*, 22 September 2011, No. 002/19-09-2007/ECCC-E124.

International Criminal Tribunal for the former Yugoslavia

Prosecutor v. *Karadžić*, Case No. IT-95-5/18-T, Decision, 11 October 2012.

Prosecutor v. Kvocka, Case No. IT IT-98-30-1-A, Appeals Judgment, 28 February 2005.

Prosecutor v. Tadić, Case No. IT-94-1-A, Appeals Judgment, 15 July 1999.

Ethiopia-Ethiopia Claim Commission

Decision 3, *Remedies*, 15 August 2001.

Decision 7, *Guidance Regarding Jus ad Bellum Liability*, 27 July 2007.

Decision 8, *Relief to War Victims*, 27 July 2007.

Final Award, *Eritrea's Damages Claims*, 17 August 2009.

Final Award, *Ethiopia's Damages Claims*, 17 August 2009.

Partial Award, *Central Front – Eritrea's Claims 2, 4, 6, 7, 8 & 22*, 28 April 2004.

Partial Award, *Prisoners of War – Eritrea's Claim 17*, 28 April 2004.

United Nations Compensation Commissions

Decision 1, Criteria for Expedited Processing of Urgent Claims, 2 August 1991, Doc. S/AC.26/1991/1.

Decision 10, Provisional Rules for Claims Procedure, 26 June 1992, Doc. No. S/AC.26/1992/10.

Decision 11, Eligibility for Compensation of Members of the Allied Coalition Armed Forces, 26 June 1992, Doc. No. S/AC.26/1992/11.

Decision 12, Claims for which Established Filing Deadlines are Extended, 25 September 1992, Doc. S/AC.26/1992/12.

Decision 13, Further Measures to Avoid Multiple Recovery of Compensation by Claimants, 25 September 1992, Doc. S/AC 26/1992/13.
Decision 15, Compensation for Business Losses Resulting from Iraq's Unlawful Invasion and Occupation of Kuwait where the Trade Embargo and Related Measures were also a cause, 4 January 1993, Doc. S/AC 26/1992/15.
Decision 17, Priority of Payment and Payment Mechanism (Guiding Principles), 24 March 1994, UN Doc. S/AC.26/1994/17.
Decision 18, Distribution of Payments and Transparency, 24 March 1994, Doc. S/AC.26/Dec.18.
Decision 3, Personal Injury and Mental Pain and Anguish, 23 October 1991, Doc. S/AC.26/1991/3.
Decision 35, Further Procedures for Review of Claims Under Article 38, 13 December 1995, Doc. S/AC.26/Dec.35.
Decision 46, Explanatory Statements by Claimants in Categories "D", "E" and "F", 3February 1998, Doc. S/AC.26/Dec.46.
Decision 48, Return of Undistributed Funds, 3 February 1998, Doc. S/AC.26/Dec.48.
Decision 7, Criteria for Additional Categories of Claims, 17 March 1992, Doc. S/AC.26/1991/7/Rev.1.
Decision 8, Determination of Ceilings for Compensation for Mental Pain and Anguish, 27 January 1992, Doc. S/AC.26/1992/8.
Decision 9, Propositions and Conclusion on Compensation for Business Losses: Types of Damages and Their Valuation, 6 March 1992, Doc. S/AC.26/1992/9.

United Nation Security Council

Resolution 1483, Doc. S/RES/1483 (2003).
Resolution 171, UN Doc. S/RES/171 (1962).
Resolution 662, Doc. S/RES/662 (1990).
Resolution 674, Doc. S/RES/674 (1990).
Resolution 687, Doc. S/RES/687 (1991).
Resolution 705, Doc. S/RES/705 (1991).

Curriculum Vitae

Diana Odier-Contreras Garduño received her law degree in 2005 from the IUEM University, Mexico graduating *magna cum laude*, and in 2009 she obtained the degree of an LLM degree in International Law of Human Rights and Criminal Justice from Utrecht University graduating *cum laude*. In 2011, she began her PhD at Utrecht University. As part of her research, she was a Visiting Professional at the IACtHR and a visiting scholar at INTERVICT, Tilburg University.

Alongside the completion of her doctoral thesis, Diana has combined other research activities, lecturing and tutoring responsibilities. She has build up, as well as taught, several well-appreciated courses at the Bachelor and Master level for various departments of Utrecht University, namely the Netherlands Institute of Human Rights, the Willem Pompe Institute for Criminal Law and Criminology and department International and European Law, University College Roosevelt, and University College Utrecht. Diana has also been a guest lecturer in various universities across the Netherlands including Leiden University and Erasmus University Rotterdam, and given several workshops at the Netherlands Institute of International Relations Clingendael.

Diana has several publications in international peer-reviewed journals and participated in various *amicus curiae*, consultancy work, workshops for civil society and moot trials related to human rights law and international criminal law. In 2017, Diana coached the UCU Moot Court team, which won the third place in the Trans-European Moot Court Competition in Strasbourg.

Currently, Diana works as a university lecturer, academic tutor and coordinator of two law programmes (Double Degree Programme and Transnational Law Programme) at UCU. She also serves as a chair of the UCU Council.

Human Rights Research Series

The Network of Human Rights Research is a joint effort by human rights researchers in the Netherlands. Its central research theme is the nature and meaning of international standards in the field of human rights, their application and promotion in the national legal order, their interplay with national standards and the international supervision of such application. The Human Rights Research Series only includes English titles that contribute to a better understanding of the different aspects of human rights.

For previous volumes in the series, please visit http://shr.intersentia.com.

Published titles within the Series:

72. Nelleke Koffeman, Morally Sensitive Issues and Cross-Border Movement in the EU ISBN 978-1-78068-349-2
73. Roland Moerland, The Killing of Death ISBN 978-1-78068-351-5
74. Andrea Broderick, The Long and Winding Road to Disability Equality and Inclusion ISBN 978-1-78068-358-4
75. Christina Peristeridou, The Principle of Legality in European Criminal Law ISBN 978-1-78068-357-7
76. Emilie Kuijt, Humanitarian Assistance and State Sovereignty in International Law ISBN 978-1-78068-366-9
77. Lize R. Glas, The Theory, Potential and Practice of Procedural Dialogue in the European Convention on Human Rights System ISBN 978-1-78068-375-1
78. Paulien de Morree, Rights and Wrongs under the ECHR ISBN 978-1-78068- 418-5
79. Malu Beijer, The Limits of Fundamental Rights Protection by the EU ISBN 978- 1-78068-455-0
80. Marie Elske Gispen, Human Rights and Drug Control ISBN 978-1-78068-454- 3
81. Bart van der Sloot, Privacy as Virtue: Moving Beyond the Individual in the Age of Big Data ISBN 978-1-78068-505-2
82. Mohammad Hadi Zakerhossein, Situation Selection Regime at the International Criminal Court ISBN 978-1-78068-618-9
83. Yi Zhang, Advancing the Right to Health Care in China. Towards Accountability 978-1-78068-705-6

www.ingramcontent.com/pod-product-compliance
Ingram Content Group UK Ltd.
Pitfield, Milton Keynes, MK11 3LW, UK
UKHW051919100926
8556IPUK00021B/1253

9 781780 687056